940.54
KEL   Kelly, Paul H.
        Courage in a season

D0345376

DATE DUE

NOV 0 7 2002		
DEC 1 7 2002		

GAYLORD   #3523PI   Printed in US

COURAGE
IN A
SEASON OF
WAR

Latter-day Saints
Experience World War II

COURAGE

IN A

SEASON OF

WAR

Latter-day Saints
Experience World War II

PAUL H. KELLY AND LIN H. JOHNSON
Foreword by Jack Weyland

Copyright © 2002 by Paul H. Kelly and Lin H. Johnson

All rights reserved

Printed in the United States of America

ACKNOWLEDGEMENTS

My Christmas present in 1998 from my wife, Deanne, was a copy of Tom Brokaw's book, *The Greatest Generation*. While reading it, the thought came to me that our LDS men had taken their part in that war, and at the same time participated in the spread of the gospel to the world. I began calling friends I knew who had served in World War II, who then referred me to their friends. One of the first men I met was Lin Johnson. Lin allowed me to record his stories, then we decided to work together. It has been a rewarding association. Lin has read and reread these stories and made many suggestions to improve them. Cyril and Maxine Burt hosted a dinner at their home and invited some of their friends, whom I subsequently interviewed. When I had gathered several stories, I showed them to my friend, Jack Weyland. He was enthusiastic about the project and became my mentor. Jack has been continuously encouraging, as has his wife Sherry.

Bob Freeman and Dennis Wright, co-directors of the "Saints at War" archival project at Brigham Young University, Provo, have been cooperative and encouraging, and we have shared information and stories.

Numerous people have read the manuscript and made valuable suggestions. To Kip Hartvigsen, chair of the English Department at Brigham Young University-Idaho, our heartfelt thanks for introducing us to Anne Hendricks, who teaches professional editing at the university. Her students, in the first editing class offered by the English department, took our book as a project and did a fine job with it. Our gratitude to Desiree Archibald, James D. Boone, Terrah L. Conrad, Joy L. Cortez, Merrilee Feller, Amanda L. Hansen, Nolan A. Hill, Allison C. King, Kaylene Lloyd, Lucas A. Peless, Jenny E. Rock, Marissa P. Schwegler, and Soren P. Swenson. Their enthusiasm for the stories in this book has been rewarding.

Anne Hendricks designed and formatted the manuscript's layout, as well as completed a second editing of the manuscript, perhaps a bigger job than she bargained for. She has been endlessly cheerful, has shown great feeling for the stories, and impeccable taste in her work. A special thanks to Joy Cortez for her superb design of the book's cover. We also extend our appreciation to Richard Peterson for doing the manuscript's final editing, which he fit into an already full schedule, including a calling to the Fifth Quorum of the Seventy.

I'm grateful to my wife Deanne for her patience and her helpful suggestions. Each time she read through a story she proposed refinements that improved the text.

Finally, our thanks to all the men and women who in World War II placed their lives "between their loved homes and the war's desolation." Thank You for your friendship and for sharing your stories.

PAUL H. KELLY

Being invited to co-author this book has been a challenging and rewarding experience. By compiling the personal accounts of this sad and destructive war, we have attempted to give the reader a ringside seat of the foxholes, the bombers, the prison camps, and life in general, as it was in the war zone.

I acknowledge the determination of my friend Paul Kelly in bringing this work to fruition. It has been a pleasure to work alongside him. We have become good friends. My thanks to my wife, Mary, for her patience and understanding of the time spent in preparation of this book, when I neglected to do some of the things she had scheduled for me to do.

LIN H. JOHNSON

DEDICATION

As a boy I watched many men and women come home from World War II to our small Idaho community. Now, while gathering these stories I have renewed my friendship with some of them and made many new friends. This experience has greatly enriched my life. These remarkable people are my heros. All my life I have remembered Royal Meservy's stake conference report in the old Yellowstone Stake Tabernacle. He had just come from a prisoner of war camp in Germany. The story of how the Lord provided him with a small pile of potatoes, which kept him from starving, is very tender. Cyril Burt, who served in North Africa and Italy, was my scoutmaster. They, and many others, have had a powerful influence upon me. Their examples are still vivid. I express gratitude to them for all they have done to "preserve us a nation." I believe their contribution in building the Kingdom of God to be as significant as that of our pioneer forbearers. This book is dedicated to them.

PAUL H. KELLY

CONTENTS

FOREWORD

Paul Kelly and I have a lot in common. He was around when I first started to write. We were both living in Rapid City, South Dakota. I was the home teacher to his family. He likes to tell people he knew Jack Weyland before he was Jack Weyland.

In a similar manner, I was around when Paul first started to write down the stories of Church members who found themselves involved in World War Two. We both now live in southeastern Idaho, and see each other almost every week.

Nearly each week for the past two years Paul has told me a new story he has obtained from a veteran of the War. They have related their histories in their own words, and with each story I am captivated again. Many accounts are personal and spiritual, some are agonizingly brutal. In some cases veterans have never told their stories, or shared them only with close family members. The narratives by co-author Lin Johnson are as achingly tender as any I know. Stories that Paul first told me more than a year ago remain with me, and still fill me with admiration for the valor shown by these men in their season of war. I believe that you, too, will thrill with the matter-of-fact heroism of these veterans and the poignant hopefulness and faith of their wives and families.

We now are engaged in a war against terrorism. At times our hearts may quaver as we undergo the uncertainty of our times. The accounts of these men and women are reminiscent of those recorded in the Book of Mormon, and are a magnificent example for coming generations to emulate.

Come now and hear their stories.

JACK WEYLAND

INTRODUCTION

Describing the events of his day, the Book of Mormon Prophet Omni writes: *"And it came to pass that . . . we had many seasons of serious war and bloodshed"* (Omni 1:3). He might have been describing our day. Certainly the twentieth century was marked with "many serious seasons of war."

World War II engulfed the earth in the most deadly struggle in recorded history. Virtually "every nation, tongue, and people" were involved. For The Church of Jesus Christ of Latter-day Saints, it was essential that the United States and its allies win this war. Had Hitler, Mussolini and Tojo had their way, the spread of the Gospel would have ceased. But in the timetable of the Lord, the Axis Powers had no chance of permanently prevailing. In the Doctrine and Covenants 117:6, the Lord asks rhetorically: "Have I not made the earth? Do I not hold the destinies of all the armies of the nations of the earth?"

The Church made giant strides as young Latter-day Saint men and women left their communities in "the tops of the mountains" and were thrust into the Allied armed forces, or the supporting work force. As is true of every difficulty the Church and its people have endured, the Lord used the trials and hardships of the war as a means of winnowing much grain from the chaff. As these young men were assigned to their units, it was the first time that many of their comrades had the opportunity of meeting a Mormon. I believe that the events of World War II helped the Church come "out of obscurity."

My own recollections of that war are limited. I was four years old when Japan attacked Pearl Harbor, and though I was too young to grasp what had happened that awful Sunday, I remember the shock and concern expressed by my parents. I have a more vivid memory of VE day, 5 May 1945. When word that the war had ended in Europe reached St. Anthony, Idaho, people immediately began driving up and down Bridge Street, honking their car horns and shouting out of their windows in jubilation. I went home, got in Dad's car parked in the street at the side of our home, and honked the horn until the battery went dead.

Other memories of the war include the rationing of food and other strategic commodities and also the many projects in which my mother was involved to preserve food to send to our boys overseas. There were cloth stars displayed in the windows of many homes, indicating that a son or husband was serving from that home—or in so many cases, a different colored star symbolizing a life given in that service. I recall when the boys came home from the war, many needed a job, and Dad was able to hire some of them.

Many came home to anxious sweethearts and were married; many came home and soon found a sweetheart and were married, and some came home to find a sweetheart married to someone else.

My father was a soldier of the home front. People had to be fed, and since he owned a fresh-pack potato business—an endeavor the government decided was critical to the war effort—Dad was therefore exempt from the draft. The labor force was, out of necessity, made up of older men, women and workers from Mexico. I recall Francisco and Franco and the fun I had with them, as I accompanied them to the farm in summertime, or watched as they loaded railroad boxcars with hundred pound sacks of potatoes from Dad's warehouses in the fall and winter.

On 6 December 1941, my parents, Howard and Irene Kelly, were returning from a visit to my grandparents in Provo, Utah. They stopped in Salt Lake City and purchased a new Studebaker automobile. Their timing was fortuitous; they had this car until after the war ended.

Dean Packer was a medical student at the University of Utah when the war broke out. He and a Japanese-American friend were studying together at the Packers' kitchen table when they received word of the attack on Pearl Harbor—a poignant moment for them. Dean Packer became a surgeon and served in a military hospital in North Carolina, and later my father-in-law.

Eighteen years following the war's end, as a second lieutenant in the United States Air Force, I was assigned to Aviano Air Base, Italy. While home on leave prior to departing for Europe, Dad's veterinarian came to work on some livestock. When Dr. Kershaw found out that I was going to Aviano, he told me that, as a fighter pilot during the war, he led an attack on Aviano, which was then being used by the German Luftwaffe. When I got there, I found that some of the buildings in the village of Aviano still bore bullet marks.

Once, while traveling by car on temporary duty in Germany, we passed through a round-about where a policeman was directing traffic. He saluted, then called out to the driver, who translated: "Tell the young officer that I was a private in Hitler's army."

Four years following my assignment to Italy, I was stationed at Clark Air Base, in the Philippines. During my two years there, I frequently traveled the route of the Bataan Death March. Each kilometer is marked by a sign portraying men holding a comrade up and helping him along. On one trip along this route, our Filipino driver told us he had watched American prisoners pass by his home. He remembered seeing the Japanese soldiers patrolling the line on bicycles and seeing townspeople dart into the line, when the guards had their backs turned, to pull some of the soldiers away. He showed us a steel warehouse where the prisoners were forced to stay without food or water for three hot days. Many died there. Camp O'Donnell, the site where most of Corregidor's victims were incarcerated, was only a few miles from where we lived in Angeles City.

Tom Brokaw, of NBC News, author of the book *The Greatest Generation*, writes that the soldiers of World War II came from the communities of our country, out of the depths of the Great Depression and entered military service. After rescuing the world from two ruthless foes, they came home to build this nation to unprecedented economic and material heights. Our LDS boys were part of this effort. They came from similar backgrounds, performed similar tasks, took their part in building up this great nation, *and* participated in spreading the restored gospel of Jesus Christ around the world. Like those about whom Brokaw writes, the LDS men have been modest in speaking of their wartime experiences, feeling that what they did was not of particular note.

Latter-day Saint men fought in every theater of action—Europe, Africa, the Pacific. Some were doctors, some mechanics, pilots, gunners, or infantrymen. There were both officers and enlisted men. They performed acts of great courage. Some became prisoners of war. Many have told me they felt the Lord's hand moving them out of the way of harm. None profess to know why they survived and others did not. Much of what they had to do was mundane: things that had to be done to sustain life and move the nation's efforts forward. As warriors they were required to take lives and destroy property, acts unthinkable under any other circumstance.

To the best of our knowledge, over 100,000 LDS servicemen were in the military at the height of the war. Considering there were only 860,000 Church members at that time, this is an astonishing number: eleven and a half percent of the entire Church population. The examples of these men and women gave the Church an influence for good in the world far out of proportion to its size.

The stories told here are representative of hundreds not recorded. Soon, many of these stories will be lost, since the participants in that great struggle will have passed to the other side. In these stories we see that the Lord is interested in His family, helping them over the hard spots, but not excusing them from serious trial. He preserved most of them to come home to help build His Kingdom. These stories are true and ought to be remembered and retold. The debt we owe these men is greater than I had imagined.

PAUL H. KELLY

[They] were inspired by a better cause, for they were not fighting for monarchy nor power but they were fighting for their homes and their liberties, their wives and their children, and their all, yea, for their rites of worship and their church. And they were doing that which they felt was the duty which they owed to their God; . . . to defend themselves, and their families, and their lands, their country, and their rights, and their religion.

(Alma 43:45–47)

Hitler infused his inhuman mentality and depravity into his SS troops. Boys, from early years in Hitler's *Jugend* youth group, came to believe it was their mission and destiny to brutalize and trample anyone they were told to hate, and by doing so they performed a great service to the cause of humanity.

As an infantryman in that war, and witness to many of its horrors, I have struggled for over fifty years to comprehend how a nation could be seduced away from decency. I don't believe I'll ever be able to grasp it.

In the early stages of the war, Hitler's legions, well-equipped and precision-trained, toppled government after government throughout Europe, until most of the continent was under his brutal grasp. He was then free to cruelly and systematically exterminate millions of helpless and innocent people whom he chose to call *untermenschen* (subhuman). He alone determined who was fit to live, and his twisted, warped mind delighted in the slaughter. History records many ruthless tyrants, but he stands as the worst of them all.

As the Nazi *blitzkriegs* conquered Europe and threatened to destroy civilization, people worldwide despaired that the light of freedom would ever burn again. When the United States became involved in the war, we were fighting at first in desperation, untrained and poorly equipped, to stem the tide of aggression in Europe as well as in the Pacific, which ironically means "peaceful" in Latin.

America's vast industrial might shifted from producing consumer goods to making tanks, planes, artillery and all the hardware it takes to wage war. The course of the war began to change as our troops and armaments were taken to far-flung battle fronts.

It's interesting to me how the Nazi SS troops, with cold precision, systematically decimated the outmoded defenses of those they conquered. But when they faced the Yanks, for the first time, they met a different kind of foe. We were taken from our civilian security, hastily trained, and thrust into battlefields all across the world. Many times we were overmatched by numerically superior forces, but we still won time after time. One difference was Yankee ingenuity. No textbook solutions, just the ability to improvise and solve whatever the situation required. Our ability to adapt, to abandon cherished military procedures when the circumstance dictated, made the difference in many battlefield crises and eventually gained us total victory.

LIN H. JOHNSON

MISSIONARIES IN EUROPE BEFORE THE WAR

Philemon Kelly (far left), president of the Swiss-German Mission, his wife Susan, and their daughter Connie. The missionaries have come to see them off, as they travel to another part of the mission.

The roots of World War II grew out of World War I. On 11 November 1918, the Great War ended with the signing of the Versailles Treaty. There was no real winner—fatigue and despair stopped the fighting. Billed as the war "to end war and make the world safe for democracy," it accomplished neither. Germany, as the primary aggressor, was assessed huge reparation payments, which she was unable to pay. Spiraling inflation, hopelessness, and the dire economic effects of the Great Depression led to uncertainty and unrest among the German people. By promising to restore prosperity, order, and national pride, Adolf Hitler became Chancellor in 1933.

Hitler bullied his way around Europe, snatching up territory, commandeering world headlines, and setting the people of the world on edge with his startling preachments of hatred. In August 1939, Hitler and the Russian dictator, Joseph Stalin, became allies, and on 1 September 1939, they invaded Poland. This prompted England, and at England's urging, France, to fight Hitler's growing power in Europe. However, neither country was prepared, and France soon fell as Hitler's armies occupied the land and took over its government. After the invasion of France, the German Air Force, the Luftwaffe, began its bombardment of England.

Susan and Philemon Kelly in Germany

Missionary work being done by The Church of Jesus Christ of Latter-day Saints continued in Germany until the autumn of 1939. Beginning in June 1935, Philemon M. Kelly presided over the Swiss-German Mission, which encompassed all of Switzerland and the western half of Germany. The following is a letter to his family dated 16 September 1936. Notice the careful language he uses to get the letter past German censorship:

Thursday spent the entire day traveling to Hamburg. Had a real conversation with a college professor in which he gave many current views of religion and political conditions as he now saw them in Germany. The entire distance was a pleasant series of surprises as new landscapes and green verdure were everywhere apparent. These dear people are a wonderfully progressive and industrious folk. They are persistently endeavoring to adjust themselves to a new environment found after the war [WWI]. This they are accomplishing, and one is well able to note their progress in the last year. Many soldiers were seen returning from Nurnberg where they held the Reich's Party *Tag* (day). This is a wonderful get-together of the present directing class and their many followers.

Although they remained committed to teaching the gospel, missionaries also had to cope with the difficult political climate of this time. Alvin J. Schoenhals, a missionary serving in Germany at the time, recorded these challenges:

In the May 1936 issue of the mission newsletter President Kelly warned: "Be careful what you write. Much correspondence is opened. Be loyal to your calling and honor the laws wherever you are called to serve." Sixteen months later I wished I had read that advice more carefully, as I was arrested and held for more than twenty-three days for having written a letter critical of the Nazi government. Had it not been for President Kelly's intervention, I probably would have come to trial, perhaps [been] incarcerated, and also fined. Within days of being notified of my arrest, he visited me in the prison in which I was being held, and urged me to "Take it well, remain optimistic that no lasting punishment would ensue, and have faith." He retained a prominent attorney, whose intervention with the Berlin Foreign Office brought the alternative of banishment rather than trial, which I was glad to accept.

ALBON L. SMITH

*At home or abroad, on the land or the sea—As thy days
may demand, so thy succor shall be.*

("How Firm a Foundation," *Hymns*, no. 85)

Elder Albon L. Smith in
Germany

In the summer of 1939, shortly after completing my second year at Ricks College, I was called to serve in the East German Mission of the Church. We crossed the Atlantic aboard the *SS Manhattan* and arrived five days later at Cobb, Ireland. We were the last group of missionaries to go to Europe before the outbreak of World War II. I had taken a year of German at Ricks, but when I arrived in Berlin only an occasional word of German would drift down to my knowledge level.

I celebrated my 20th birthday in Berlin. My companion during my short stay in Berlin was Ted Cannon. While we were together, the Gestapo came to our apartment from time to time to outline what our duties would be in case of war. Elder Cannon would tell them that if war comes, "We're going to be in airplanes bombing you." The Gestapo frightened me, as I had never seen any group with the kind of power they had.

I was then assigned to Landsberg, in the eastern part of Germany. Shortly before coming to the mission field, I had an appendectomy, and hadn't gotten my strength back. But this didn't slow down my companion,

Fay Johnson, of Richmond, Utah. We tracted constantly, always starting on the fourth floor of the many apartment buildings in Landsberg.

When entering a shop in Landsberg, it was the custom to raise your right hand and say, "Heil Hitler." This stuck in my craw. It was difficult to hail someone I knew to be a fascist dictator and an evil man, and being an American, it was difficult for me to hail anyone. When I told my companion this he said, "I'll tell you how to do it easier. Just say, 'Heil mit Hitler'" (to hell with Hitler). That came a lot easier, although it was dangerous.

As we walked the streets, it was common to see signs reading "No Jews or dogs allowed." Elder Johnson told me that a few days before I arrived in Landsberg, he had watched the Gestapo strip some Jews naked, then run them down the street lashing them with a horsewhip.

Fife and drum corps made up of Hitler Youth marched nearly every evening in the town square or on a parade ground or meadow. Great displays of war machines manned by soldiers, tanks, and weapons carriers with sidecars, practiced in the streets. I also saw Hitler and heard him speak over the radio.

In late August 1939, the streets filled with a procession of trucks filled with soldiers sitting at attention, a rifle upright in front of them. For three days we were unable to do missionary work as troops, convoys of tanks and motorcycles with sidecars, each carrying two soldiers moved through Landsberg. The convoys stopped on the hour for a fifteen-minute break, and it was only during these times that we could cross a street. On 1 September, Germany attacked Poland, and three days later English Prime Minister Neville Chamberlain declared war on Germany. Germany was not a comfortable place to be for an American missionary, and very shortly we were called to Berlin to prepare to leave the country.

I was in a group of ten missionaries who boarded an overnight train bound for Copenhagen, Denmark. We were allowed to take only ten deutschmarks, about $2.00, with us as we left Berlin. German officers moved up and down the corridors of the railcars, questioning us. We were never sure we would get out of Germany without incident. But the Lord was with us. At customs inspections in Copenhagen, the Germans and the Danes made a thorough inspection of our luggage, looking for cigarettes and liquor, or any items of valuable that might be being taken out of Germany.

Copenhagen was a beautiful, picturesque city. The wide main street was filled with people on bicycles for as many blocks as I could see. The Danish girls were really pretty—even a missionary would notice. For about two weeks, 180 missionaries from the East German Mission and 160 from the West German Mission congregated in this city. We were allowed to go sightseeing, to movies, and we played a little softball. Each day the King of Denmark, dressed in his military uniform, rode through the streets of Copenhagen on his white stallion. He often stopped to talk to people on the streets. I saw him several times.

Every day until noon, we met with Elder Joseph Fielding Smith, who was accompanied by his wife, Sister Jesse Evans Smith. He preached to us and answered gospel questions, and his wife sang to us. It was a remarkable spiritual experience, and I learned much from these sessions. After two weeks, Elder Smith set ten of us apart to serve in Norway. I bought my ticket to Oslo, but when I tried to board the ship in Sweden, the Norwegians would not accept any of the missionaries' visas, and we were all turned back.

The day we returned to Copenhagen, we boarded the ship *Scan York* and left for the United States. Because of minefields laid in the North Atlantic by the Nazis, it was necessary to bring a German pilot aboard to guide us through these treacherous areas. Once, in a dense fog in rough seas, a battleship, guns trained on us, circled us for some time. We could hear the telegraph clicking and watched as flags were run up and down the flagpoles of the two ships, flashing messages back and forth. Finally the battleship disappeared back into the fog, and as it left, the British Union Jack was raised on her fantail. Until that moment our concern was high that we might be blasted out of the water. We also had constant worry about attack by German U-boats. What a relief when we finally docked in New York.

I was reassigned to the Northern States Mission where my mission president was Leo J. Muir. For five months of my mission I had the privilege of being a companion to A. Theodore Tuttle. We remained lifelong friends.

Following his mission, Albon Smith served as an officer in the United States Army Air Corp. He was assigned to the 9th Air Force as a company commander. Late in the war he returned to Germany with his Truck

Company, which was responsible to keep supplies and equipment where they were needed.

He married Mary Elizabeth Hansen on 31 May 1946, in a ceremony performed by his father, who was at the time president of the Idaho Falls Temple. They are parents of ten children and have fifty-five grandchildren and seven great-grandchildren. Albon became a Chevrolet car dealer in Idaho Falls. He has served as a bishop and on the high council.

Elders Albon Smith (left) and Ted Tuttle in a missionary choir. Ted Tuttle's wartime experiences can be found on page 426.

Albon Smith's account extracted from his personal history.

LOWELL J. YANCEY

I will be on your right hand and on your left, and my Spirit shall be in your hearts, and mine angels round about you, to bear you up.

(Doctrine & Covenants 84:88)

Lausanne, Switzerland: August 1939 was the start of some unsettling days for the missionaries in Europe. Although we were in a neutral country, we were surrounded by countries subject to the whims of Adolf Hitler. When I was transferred from Belgium to Switzerland, I traveled to Cologne, then down the Rhine to Basel before reaching Lausanne. On the way there seemed to be endless armies of goose-stepping soldiers, officials greeted each other with the mandatory "Heil Hitler," and at every turn credentials were checked. I had been appointed district leader.

About the 28th of August, I awoke with an earnest concern for the sister missionaries in our area. A compelling feeling came to me that they should be sent to the mission home in Paris. Acting on this urging, I took a pair of elders with me, and together we went to the apartments of these sisters and instructed them to pack their belongings. An hour later we put them on a train to Paris.

When that was accomplished I wondered if I had made a mistake. However, just thirty-six hours later all of the Swiss borders were closed and all communication was severed. This meant that no one could board the train to Paris, there was no mail, no telegraph, and no money from home.

With the departure of the sister missionaries, there were fifty of us left in the French- speaking part of Switzerland for whom I was responsible. Without money, our plight quickly became critical, since very few of us had anything hidden in our mattresses.

I had been scheduled to be released from my mission on 1 August but had agreed to stay a few more weeks to conduct a scheduled district conference for members of the seven branches in our area. With the conclusion of my mission close at hand, I had received approval to take a short trip through Italy and France before going home. Having already purchased my ticket, I was able to get a refund. It gradually became clear that our only alternative was to stay put and hope to receive instructions. Although we disliked doing it, we had to rely on some of our members for food. Most of our rent payments were postponed. In that kind of atmosphere it was hard to keep up much enthusiasm for tracting and teaching. By 1 October we were still without evidence that anyone outside Switzerland was aware of our situation.

Toward the end of October, I felt impressed to take a train to Basel, headquarters of the Swiss-German Mission. I had become acquainted with President Thomas E. McKay, brother to President David O. McKay, while serving as president of the branch at La Chaux de Fonds. A branch at Bienne, in the Swiss-German Mission, was only thirty miles from La Chaux de Fonds. He often came to visit us. I don't think he was aware that we rarely saw our own president.

When I arrived at the mission home in Basel, President McKay said that he had no idea there were still fifty missionaries in Switzerland. I told him our circumstances and asked for some money. He gave me what he could spare and said that he would try to contact Church Headquarters in Salt Lake City and let them know of our plight.

He invited me to spend the night. There was no one there except the President and his wife. From my upstairs bedroom I looked out the window, and in the darkness could see the "fireworks show" of shells being lobbed back and forth over the Maginot Line only a few miles away.

Less than a week following my visit we received a telegram from Church Headquarters advising us to be in Le Havre, France, to catch a boat home. The only problem was that the telegram was a week old when we got it, and that ship was already on its way to New York. Over a period of several weeks we received at least three such telegrams. Finally one came that was only a couple of days old. We were instructed to be in Bordeaux to board the *SS Washington* for home. To our amazement tickets also came, but we had only four or five days to get to Bordeaux. Our instructions said we could not leave the train between Lausanne and Bordeaux.

As district leader, I was guardian of Church records, which I felt must be taken to the mission office. I went to the French consulate and requested a visa to travel to Bordeaux via Paris. The consulate in charge said my request was impossible and would allow no change in my itinerary. On my own I made the decision to leave Lausanne before the rest of the group and take a train to Paris. I took one of the other missionaries with me.

When the train stopped at the French border, we held our breath as border and custom officials came aboard. They checked about half of the passengers for passports, visas, and some baggage. All the while we prayed that we would not be checked and tried to remain as inconspicuous as possible. I don't know what the consequences would have been if they had asked for our passports, and am grateful we never found out.

We arrived in Paris after dark and merged ourselves into the masses of people. Paris was under a blackout. There were swarms of *gendarmes* everywhere, stopping people to check their papers. We finally found a cab to take us to the mission home. President Evans was very surprised when he saw us standing in the doorway with all our luggage. We spent several hours filling him in on the events of the previous six weeks.

We spent two days in Paris before leaving for Bordeaux. However, we had no visas, and it was too dangerous to walk around during daylight as the streets were full of military personnel and equipment. Therefore we didn't see much of the city.

We timed our arrival with the other forty-eight missionaries at Bordeaux to go directly from the railway station to the *SS Washington* and immediately board for home. When we inquired about the ship's location, we were told it would sail four days later than planned. Any money we had left we had already spent on souvenirs. So here we were, fifty missionaries with a huge pile of luggage and nowhere to go. We must have presented a curious scene to the French.

As we stood there I prayed for help with our dilemma. The thought came to me to contact the Salvation Army. I knew nothing about the Salvation Army except that I had seen their uniformed workers ringing bells at the donation pot at Christmastime. I found their address and took one of the other missionaries with me to find them. I told one of their administrators about our plight, and without hesitating he said they would help us.

The floor of the room that we were given was covered with about twelve inches of straw, and that is where we slept. All I remember about the food is that it was mostly French bread and cheese. We were mighty glad to get it.

When we finally boarded the ship, we learned it would be carrying a thousand more passengers than normal. There were cots in all the hallways and any other place there was room to sleep. Huge American flags were painted on both sides of the vessel as well as on the deck, and lights illuminated the ship every night. This was a scary time in the Atlantic with German submarines sinking everything they could, but we were glad to be on our way home.

Some of the missionaries had been released, and some went to assignments within the United States. We were all grateful that Heavenly Father loved us enough to look after our needs and answer our prayers. The Statue of Liberty never looked better to me than when it came into view, and we entered this "land that I love."

"A DATE WHICH WILL LIVE IN INFAMY"

The attack on the U.S. fleet at Pearl Harbor

As the crisis evolved in Europe, the United States struggled to remain neutral, but soon became the supplier of material under the Lend-Lease program, pumping aid into Great Britain to help it withstand the German onslaught. By doing so, the United States acquired a vital interest in keeping the Atlantic sea-lanes open against the depredations of German submarines.

In June 1941, Hitler turned on his ally Russia in a massive surprise attack that American military leaders predicted would flatten Russia in a matter of weeks. Whatever Hitler's reasons for this change of direction, it allowed England needed time to prepare.

Much of the world's attention was focused on the dramatic events in Europe. Less concern was accorded Japan. Hitler's attack on the Soviets relieved the Japanese worry of an attack from Siberia, and in pursuit of her conquests, Japan moved into Indo-China and Thailand, then began looking to the Americas, and on a balmy Sunday morning in December, they attacked.

The Japanese strike on American military forces at Pearl Harbor was a cunningly conceived, well-coordinated, surprise attack. It was *the* event that galvanized the American people and plunged the nation into World War II. On 8 December 1941, in an address to Congress, President Franklin D. Roosevelt stated: "Yesterday, December 7, 1941—a date which will live in infamy—the United States of America was suddenly and deliberately attacked by the naval and air forces of the Empire of Japan." Within four hours, Congress voted to declare war on Japan. Three days later Germany and Italy declared war on the United States, and on 11 December, Congress reciprocated, and the United States was at war on two huge fronts. Then began the gargantuan task of inducting men, training and arming them, and organizing them into the armies, navies, and air forces necessary to do battle in so many places simultaneously.

BILL HARTEN

I was nineteen-years old, just a kid fresh out of high school. Because I wanted to get an education, and since my parents had no money to assist me, I enlisted in the Navy in September 1940. *I first attended the Navy School of Music in Washington D.C., graduating 30 April 1941.

Now onboard the *USS West Virginia*, one of the Navy's largest battleships, we had been at sea for three weeks of training. Our ship, together with six other battleships, returned to Pearl Harbor on December 6.

We berthed somewhere in the middle of "Battleship Row," outboard of the battleship *USS Tennessee*. To the best of my knowledge, it was the first time that the majority of the Pacific Fleet had all been in the harbor at the same time. The battleships were arranged in a long row, and in most cases, two abreast.

Sunday Morning, 0755 hours. Aboard the *USS West Virginia*, all portholes and water-tight compartments were open, and the atmosphere was relaxed. Many of the men had been Christmas shopping the day before and were looking forward to mailing presents to their families. All of the enlisted

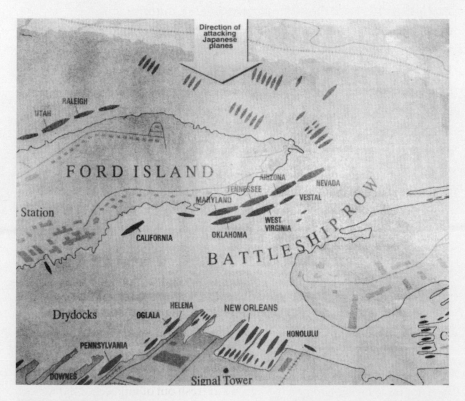

Map indicating U.S. naval ships' locations at Pearl Harbor on 7 December 1941. (*Post Register*, 7 December 1999)

men and most of the officers were aboard ship.

We had just finished eating breakfast when the alarm sounded. The first alarm indicated "fire and rescue." We had practiced this drill many times before—but never on a Sunday—and it occurred to me that this was very unusual. I scurried down the ladder leading to the sick bay. No sooner had I reached the second deck than I heard and felt a terrific explosion. The ship shook and quivered, mess tables fell from their overhead storage racks, china crashed, and paint began chipping off the bulkhead.

Pencil sketch of Bill drawn by his future wife, Jeane Lowe.

Thirty seconds after the first alarm, the signal for "general quarters" (final preparation for battle—all hands at battle stations) was sounded over the ship's intercom. The boatswain's mate yelled the order over and over, at the top of his voice, as the emergency bell clanged. I'd heard the order many times before, but this time it had an especially rousing effect. I ran aft to my battle station, passing Captain Mervin S. Bennion of Salt Lake City, Commander of the *USS West Virginia,* who was hurrying forward to his station. Within minutes he was struck in the stomach by a piece of shrapnel. Although wounded, he continued to lead, and an hour and a half later, just before he died, he gave the order to abandon ship.

Stunned by the force of the explosion, hundreds of men raced down hatchways to take up their battle stations. My battle station was three decks down, approximately twenty feet below the waterline, beneath a thick protective deck of armor plate and close to the base of turret number three. Our responsibilities at our battle station were repair, communications, and first aid.

I began dogging down a door to lock it shut when a second deafening explosion, about two compartments forward, violently wrenched the door from my hands and slammed me against the opposite bulkhead. The lights went out. My head was spinning and my mind went blank. The odor of exploding powder, dust, and nauseating oil fumes, together with shock, made me feel sick and weak.

A flood of oil and water flowed into our compartment, rising around my legs. Men groaned in the blackness. The effects of the concussion left me dizzy, and when I tried to get up, I fell in the slippery, oily water. The ship was listing. It was evident that if this was not soon corrected, she would roll on her side. I knew I had to get out of there fast, but all sense of direction had left me, and the stifling fumes sapped my strength. Groping in the dark for something to pull me toward the escape hatch, my hand found a pipe. The oily water had made everything slippery, but I somehow found the strength to pull myself up, hand over hand, to a door leading to the starboard passageway. The second explosion had knocked out all communications and lights and left no water pressure for fighting fire.

Another terrifying blast jolted the ship!

My hands slipped off the vibrating pipe. I doubled up and fell over onto the coaming [a raised frame around a door to keep water out]. I lay in the darkness, feeling more dead than alive, my mind spinning, my legs weak. It was difficult to breathe. I held on, but doubted I could muster the strength to pull myself up the slanting passageway another time.

The ship's deck was now so steep that men on the upper side were slipping and falling against those below them. After the ship had listed to the point where it seemed it would roll over, it stopped and began to right itself. I heard the sound of splashing feet, and in the dim light of a flashlight saw several dark figures in the passageway. Seeing my shipmates gave me the will to keep going. Everyone seemed to sense that there was little time for escape, but regardless of the danger there was no pushing, crowding, or unnecessary commotion.

By the time it was my turn to go up the ladder, I had to will myself upward—escape now seemed very near. Reaching the second deck I saw an even longer line inching toward an open hatch. The escape hatch had buckled shut, but fortunately the supply hatch was open and I could see daylight. I climbed up a steel beam through the open hatch and out onto the starboard side [right side of the ship looking forward] of the quarter deck.

What I witnessed was heartbreaking. The battleship *Oklahoma* lay on its side. Her screws, like fins of a gruesome dead whale, showed above the surface of the water. Some men clung to her barnacled side; some were swimming for shore. (I learned later that the bowels of that ship entombed almost four hundred of her crew.) I could then see enemy airplanes criss-crossing the sky, and recognized the awful magnitude of what was happening.

By then the *USS West Virginia* was nearly abandoned. With no time to deploy lifeboats, men jumped into water crammed with debris and blanketed in burning oil.

In the fresh air my head cleared and my strength returned. I knew I could make it. All around me were screaming men. The only thing to do was jump into the flames and swim under them to open water. I knew that taking a gulp of burning oil would kill me, but the ship was sinking under me. Jumping feet first to avoid cracking my head on debris in the water, I swam below the surface as far as I could and came up well away from the fire. Then I had to swim around two battleships, about three-quarters of a mile, to reach Ford Island.

Nearing the shore I came across a young sailor, struggling in the water, too exhausted to swim any farther. I rolled him on his back and dragged him the rest of the way. As we struggled out of the surf, two ladies from the Red Cross came to help us. I was covered with oil, but little else. They gave me a pair of pants, a towel, and a bar of soap. Relief and thankfulness washed over me, but I was exhausted. It was then 0850 hours, nearly an hour since the first explosions.

The *USS West Virginia* lost 250 men, one of them the clarinet player from our band. Many died because they were too afraid, injured, or lacked the strength to go up the ladders. Some men locked themselves in airtight compartments and suffocated; others drowned.

On the third day after the attack, a deep-sea diver went down to check the damage to our ship. He was a friend of mine, and I asked him to look for our instruments. He brought up what was left of my trumpet. It was badly scorched, and the brass part had melted away. I still have it, mounted in a case, to remind me that the Lord was with me that day.

As I think of that experience, especially around Pearl Harbor Day, I ponder what might have happened to me. I could easily have been confined in one of those airtight compartments or been burned. Had the wind been slightly different, the bomb that destroyed the *Arizona* might have hit us. We were only fifteen or twenty yards away. I had been a member of the *USS Arizona* band for a time, but was transferred to the *West Virginia* four months prior to the attack. All twenty-one of my former bandmates on the *Arizona* were killed that day. I don't know why I was spared. Perhaps it was because I was meant to come home and marry Jeane and have our family, just like I did.

* * *

After the attack, Jeane Lowe, in Pocatello, Idaho, spent hours waiting for news of her boyfriend, Bill Harten. This is her account:

I was sitting on a little cushion in front of the radio at home as President Roosevelt told the nation of the Japanese attack on Pearl Harbor. Later an announcer said that a Pocatello boy, Bill Harten, went down with the *USS West Virginia,* and was presumed dead. I refused to believe it.

It was Sunday, so none of the stores were open,

Jeane and Bill Harten in 1945. Jeane served as a Navy WAVE during the war.

but I ran and got the man who owned the jewelry store, had him open his store, and bought the most expensive pen and pencil set he had. He engraved Bill's full name on it. I didn't believe he was dead, and I knew that he needed a pen to write me a letter and tell me he was all right. Two weeks later I received my first letter from him, which told how close he had come to death. The letter was signed "Love, Bill." That was the first time he ever signed a letter to me "love."

Taken from the personal records of Bill and Jeane Harten.

PAUL RAY BOREN

There was a cry of war heard throughout the land.

(Alma 16:1)

On 7 December 1941, Paul was a Seaman 2nd Class, on the *USS New Orleans*, at Pearl Harbor. On that fateful morning the *New Orleans* was undergoing routine overhaul, and she was without power, and much of her armament was disassembled. These are Paul's memories of that day.

It was a beautiful Sunday morning, and most of the crew had gone ashore. I had the assignment as the Officer-of-the-Deck's messenger. Standing on the well deck, we heard and then saw planes flying in the clouds high above us. They dived and dropped what we thought were sand bags. We had seen our own planes doing this many times before and didn't think much about it until the "sand bags" started exploding. We stood in dumbfounded amazement as we realized they were using live ammunition.

At the Officer-of-the-Deck's instruction, I raced below decks to the Gunnery Officer's stateroom, saluted, and reported that the OD said planes were bombing Pearl Harbor. "What?" he said. That seemed a silly response as he was watching the same thing we were. I repeated my message. We ran to the well deck and continued watching until a torpedo plane with a round orange insignia on its side flew low across our fantail and launched a torpedo at a battleship. General quarters sounded. The bo's'n, who had the keys to the ammunition lockers, could not be located. Finally someone forced the locks, ammunition was rushed to our guns, and we began returning fire.

I reported to the plotting room down in the center of the ship. We sat in our repair bay as bombs fell along side us. We took a little shrapnel but sustained only minor damage. When I came topside again, I saw the battleships ablaze. Black oil covered the harbor, and acrid smoke hung in the air, stinging our eyes.

To the best of my knowledge, our ship had no casualties, but we had been caught flat-footed.

(Paul's experiences in other areas of the war are continued on page 347)

OPERATION TORCH:
THE INVASION OF
NORTH AFRICA

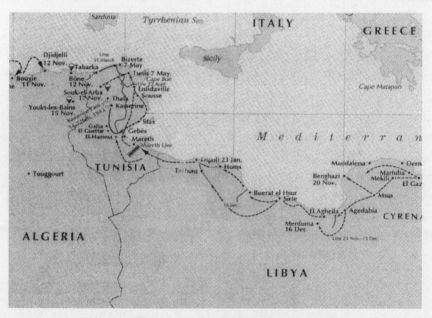

Field of battle for the North Africa Campaign

From September 1940 until May 1943, Axis and Allied forces fought for control of the North African coast. In August 1942 British Lieutenant General Bernard Montgomery took command of the British 8th Army. From 23 October to 4 November, "Monty," as the general was called, stopped the German advance toward Egypt and the Suez at El Alamein, resulting in the first British victory of the war.

British and American leaders only had about sixty days to prepare for "Operation Torch." Never in history had an invasion this large been attempted from so far away, and this became the first "dress rehearsal" for the Normandy Invasion that would take place in June 1944. Because the United States had been at war for less than a year, most of the soldiers sent to invade Africa were green recruits, led by officers who were also learning on the job.

American soldiers first met their Axis counterparts in early November 1942, when troops of the Western Task Force under Major General George S. Patton landed at Casablanca in French Morocco on the Atlantic coast. The Central Task Force, under Major General Lloyd Fredendall, successfully took the Algerian cities Oran and Algiers, along the North African coast of the Mediterranean Sea. When German Field Marshall Erwin Rommel's Afrika Korps were ejected from Africa in May 1943, North Africa became the staging area for what Churchill called the "great soft underbelly of Europe": Sicily, Italy, Greece, and southern France.

A second reason for opening this front was to divert aircraft from Hitler's eastern front in Russia, away from our new ally, the Soviets. Forcing the German High Command to send torpedo-bomber units from Norway to Tunisia greatly improved the survival prospects of American merchant ships in the North Atlantic and the North Sea as they carried vital lend-lease supplies to the beleaguered Russians.

FRANK H. JACOBS

By mid-July 1943 I had completed basic training and been transferred to a replacement depot at Greenville, Pennsylvania. A month later I was at Camp Patrick Henry, from which my unit departed on Saturday, September 4. Five hundred of us were assigned to a hot, small, dark, ship's hold for the trip across the Atlantic. By Sunday afternoon all but a few of us were seasick and vomiting over the sides of the ship. Fortunately I was never sick during the voyage. Every day we had an hour of calisthenics, in which everyone, sick or not, was

Frank H. Jacobs

required to participate. The sick got sicker, and conditions aboard were nauseating. It didn't help that the food was unappetizing and we had just two meals a day. Drinking water was rationed.

We docked at Algiers on Saturday, 26 September, but did not disembark until the next morning. We hadn't been on the wharf twenty minutes before two of our guys were in a "craps game" with some Arabs. New sights and smells assaulted our senses, conditions were primitive, and the flies thick. The constant rain turned the ground into glue-like mud. I had never liked sauerkraut and wieners, but that being our first meal in Algiers, it tasted good.

While sightseeing in the city of Algiers, I observed the customs of the people and browsed through some shops, but it was dirty and there was little to do but go to the Red Cross center.

Friday, 16 October, we waited six hours to board a train to take us to Oran. During that time most of the men got drunk on *vino*. That made it especially unpleasant inside the crowded, stinking cattle cars we were crammed into for our ride through the night. Each time the train stopped we were greeted by Arab kids begging chewing gum, cigarettes, candy, and coffee. Traveling in daylight I discovered the countryside through which we passed was very pretty.

The training schedule at Oran was intensive and demanding, the chow lines long, and the food unappealing. Sometimes we had C-rations three times a day. There was never enough to eat. We had infantry drills, exercise time, hikes along the coast of North Africa, and training in cover and concealment.

Several Sundays while in Oran I got to go to church. There were about forty LDS men who met each week at the Empire Red Cross. I met several fine fellows, including Tom Hamilton, from my hometown. On Thanksgiving day we trained all day in the mud and rain. The dinner we were fed was very disappointing. I got only a cold turkey neck. Before I left Oran I received Grandma's Christmas cake. It didn't last long as I shared it with my eight tentmates. On 6 December we boarded a huge British transport bound for Naples, Italy.

(Frank's other experiences in the war are found on page 44.)

QUENTIN C. MURDOCK

I was a senior at the University of Idaho when war came. In June 1942, I graduated with degrees in agriculture and military science. I had completed my studies in ROTC and was commissioned a second lieutenant, Infantry, United States Army. By August 1942, I had completed training at Ft. Douglas, Utah, and at Camp Robinson, near Little Rock, Arkansas. I then reported to the New York City port of embarkation to ship overseas— destination unknown. I joined a group of other officers aboard the *HMS Queen Elizabeth*. We landed at Greenock, Scotland.

With the invasion of North Africa, I took part in the first of three major amphibious assaults in which I would participate: North Africa, Sicily, and Normandy.

Second Lieutenant Quentin C. Murdock

Upon arriving in England we were designated replacements for North Africa. A ship carried us south through the submarine-infested waters of the Atlantic and into the Mediterranean to Oran, Algeria. Just after I got off the ship, a German plane bombed and sank it. This was my first brush with Lady Luck, but not my last.

At Oran I was assigned to a series of "ones": the 1st Infantry Division, the Big Red 1; the 1st Platoon, Company A, 1st Battalion, 16th Infantry Regiment. The British had been battling General Rommel's German divisions in the deserts of North Africa. In Tunisia we were sent to hit Rommel's rear flank and squeeze the German Army between us and the "Brits." I was assigned to a platoon of forty-two experienced men.

There was a tall, handsome, very likeable Kentuckian in my unit. I met him out in the dark one night. Not having seen him for some time, I asked where he had been. He replied that he had been sent to take care of an enemy machine gun nest. "Did you take it out?" I asked. "You don't hear it any more, do you?" he replied. He was later killed.

We fought all over the country of Tunisia. It was hard and frightening duty, and it took the best we had.

In April 1943, the 1st Division was transported to northern Tunisia and attacked toward Mateur. Here, many of our battles were named for the hill being contested. Hills were numbered according to their height. A battle for Hill 609, which was strategically located, was underway. I led my unit on the attck of nearby Hill 523. This would enable us to bypass and outflank the enemy on 609. Two other units had tried to take Hill 523, but were badly shot up. Our attack on this hill was billed as one of the dirtiest and bloodiest battles of the African campaign. My efforts in that campaign earned me the Silver Star.

Our unit was later presented a Presidential Unit citation for this campaign. The citation describes the action as follows:

> Under the cover of darkness the *1st Battalion, 16th Infantry,* launched an attack against Hill 523, an enemy stronghold and the battalion's objective in the vicinity of Mateur, Tunisia, on 29 April 1943. This strongly fortified enemy position, called the Rock of Chekak, had been successfully held against determined assaults of Allied troops. The battalion's objective was located deep in enemy territory. Crowning 2,000 yards of steady, barren slope affording no cover or concealment was a sheer cliff 50 feet high dominating the surrounding terrain. Digging in was impossible. The enemy occupied the hill with a reinforced company. As the battalion attacked, enemy artillery, aircraft, and machine gun fire was directed on our troops. By dint of extreme courage and great fighting ability the *1st Battalion* drove the enemy from this strategic position. On the following day, 30 April, the enemy, now powerfully reinforced, counter-attacked with ruthless savagery. This battalion . . . fought grimly, tenaciously maintaining its position. . . . Although eventually overpowered by numerically superior enemy forces the *1st Battalion's* heroic stand immobilized sufficient troops to enable the Allied forces in the vicinity to capture nearby Hill 609, thereby insuring a subsequent break-through of enemy lines and the ultimate defeat of the enemy at Bizerte and Tunis.

We next fought in the desert, where being on the offensive left us exposed and very vulnerable. We found that moving at night was safer. At least the Germans could not see the dust, a dead give-away during daylight.

We penetrated into German positions, and by daylight we were over the top on the front side of the hill. I eventually found myself pinned down by a ferocious adversary. Without success I tried to regroup and organize my men to carry on the fight. Falling into a shallow depression in the rock, I saw the Germans setting up machine guns up on a cliff in front of me. I desperately wanted to take out the machine gunners, but my carbine didn't have the necessary range. The Germans raked my position with their machine guns, and there was nowhere to go. During this fight a third of our men died, a third managed to escape, and the rest of us were individually taken prisoner.

Although the Allied forces had the Germans boxed in, just ten days before the defeat of the Nazis in Africa, I became a POW. This made me feel utterly worthless. Never had I considered such a thing—dying, yes; being wounded, yes; but captured, never! I said to myself: "I'm of no value now." As my captors marched me down a hill, a bullet hit between my feet.

The Germans put us to work gathering German and American dead and wounded. As we were carrying the injured, our own artillery saw our movement and began shelling us. This caused additional American casualties before we could move out of range.

At the POW camp in Tunis we had very little to eat. German supply lines had been severed, and they probably had little to give us. We were given dried peas to eat, which we tried to soften by cooking. As we did, weevil crawled out of the peas. After vain attempts to skim these off, hunger took over and we just ate them. I became sick: cold one minute, burning with fever the next. Later, I learned I had malaria. When we arrived in Africa every soldier was given medication to control it, but as prisoners we had none. The malaria recurred many times.

With the Americans pressing the attack, we were marched out of the POW campsite through the city of Tunis. It quickly became apparent who were our friends and who our antagonists. As we paraded through the streets the French stood with their hands pressed to their faces giving the "V" sign, the Arabs kicked and spat on us.

We were put aboard a small freighter. Stuffed down in the hold with prisoners from England, France, and other captives from America, I became even sicker. By this point in the fighting, the United States controlled the Mediterranean Sea. We left Tunis harbor, but two miles out the ship stopped, and there we remained overnight. The next day we were bombed by American planes, but fortunately we sank onto a sandbar far out in the harbor. We did not get very wet. Finally a nearby French fishing boat came alongside, took us on board, and returned us to friendly hands in Tunis. I was hospitalized, and after receiving medication soon felt better. The malaria had not yet been diagnosed. I hated every minute of the ten days I spent as a POW. Being with Americans again was a welcome relief.

I wondered why I was not killed in Africa. There seemed to be no reason. So many times bullets flew past my ears, under my arms, and between my legs. People beside me died. A machine gun, less than fifty yards in front of me fired barrage after barrage directly at me, yet I was not hit. I had survived the experience of being a POW and of my ship sinking. It would be a long time before a satisfactory answer came. It did come, years later.

(Quentin's experience in other areas of the war are found on pages 30 and 77.)

GORDON A. DIXON

I learned about the outbreak of war on 7 December 1941, while my unit was conducting a field problem—the defense of the Douglas Aircraft plant near Los Angeles, California. When word came over the field telephone that "the Japs have bombed Pearl Harbor," we first thought it was part of the field problem. We were told to sit tight and to dispatch our trucks to pick up ammunition. I was commander of a .50 mm–machine gun unit. We moved to provide antiaircraft defense for the Los Angeles Airport and the North American Aviation factory and dug in at the end of the runway at the airport, where we endured the tedium and uncertainty of many early morning alerts raised by the approach of unidentified airplanes.

We eventually shipped to North Africa. We landed near Oran, Algiers, just following the German surrender at Cape Bon. Oran was an important support base for the fighting in southern Europe, and we assisted in forming the antiaircraft defenses for Oran and some smaller nearby ports and airfields. For thirteen months we saw very little action against the enemy. We missed the invasions of Sicily and Italy because our battalion was ordered to send about a quarter of our men back to the United States as guards on a shipload of German POWs.

It was in North Africa that I learned the importance of keeping soldiers busy. To occupy their time we organized an in-depth training program, competitive athletics, and recreational activities.

Soldiers also like fresh meat with their meals. Being so far from our usual source of supply, having fresh meat was uncommon, especially given the fact that it was a low priority on the War Department's list. As an Idaho boy, I had grown up hunting game and knew how to dress an animal. In the countryside near Oran, African gazelles were plentiful. I took five men with me and we went hunting. We shot several gazelles and brought them back to the camp cook, who prepared some excellent meals from them.

Gordon A. Dixon

Our unit was anxious to get into battle, to do our part to finish the war as soon as possible. I became battalion commander and was sent to Italy where I was attached to a mortar battalion—for observation at the front line—my first such experience. I accompanied an infantry battalion commander and watched him direct a frontal assault on a small, well-fortified town at the top of a hill. Two previous attacks had failed. After stiff resistance the town was captured.

My battalion was moved to Italy, reorganized, reequipped, and retrained. We became the 99th Chemical Mortar Battalion and spent eight weeks in training on a peninsula just south of Pisa. We had excellent soldiers and they were in excellent condition. I was pleased with their eagerness and performance. Since we were close to the front lines I sent many of them forward for observation. This proved to be ideal physical and psychological conditioning. Then, to our surprise, we sere sent to Marseille, France to join the 7th Army.

(Gordon Dixon's experiences in the war are continued on page 133.)

OPERATION HUSKY: THE INVASION OF SICLIY

American forces board a Landing Craft Vehicle Personnel (LCVP), popularly known as a Higgins Boat, Sicily, 8 July 1943. They had been mislanded near Gela and had to reboard for transportation to the right sector of the beachhead.

Striking for the first time at the enemy in his own land.

Admiral Sir Alan Cunningham

In January 1943, after completing the North Africa campaign, President Franklin D. Roosevelt and Prime Minister Winston Churchill met at Casablanca to discuss the invasion of Sicily. This largely amphibious invasion, code named Operation Husky, was planned for early July.

10 July 1943, marked the initial assault. 140,000 troops, 3,000 ships, and 3,700 aircraft participated in this campaign. Supervised by U.S. General Eisenhower, General Patton and British General Montgomery led the campaign. Bad weather, which nearly postponed that first assault, provided the Allied forces with protection against sightings by the Italian and German defenders. Although the weather aided sea landings, it caused aircraft to miss their landing zones and lives were lost.

The invasion lasted thirty-eight days, ending on 17 August when U.S. amphibious troops landed along the coast toward Messina. While 100,000 surviving Axis troops were able to escape during the night, 164,000 were lost during this operation.

QUENTIN C. MURDOCK

The 1st Battalion, 16th Infantry was the first to hit the beaches near Gela, Sicily. We were met by fanatic Nazi troops, backed by heavy tanks. We had no weapons powerful enough to stop the tanks that rumbled through our lines. The Germans were attempting to push us back into the sea, but somehow we held and prevented their infantry from following their tanks. A Presidential Unit citation gives a narrative of the fighting:

At H-hour on 10 July 1943, the *1st Battalion, 16th Infantry,* landed in the vicinity of Gela, Sicily, and immediately encountered fierce resistance. Enemy tanks and infantry attempted to thwart the battalion's advance, but it bravely pressed inland despite concerted hostile fire. After reducing several enemy strong points by heavy fighting, the *1st Battalion,* on the morning of 11 July 1943, was firmly lodged in position on the low rolling hills to the north. Despite this initial failure to halt our advance the enemy again charged ruthlessly, endeavoring to drive a deep wedge into our lines. The *1st Battalion* swiftly retaliated with formidable counter-strokes that temporarily repelled the attacking forces. When the enemy once again attacked, with tanks and infantry over-running the battalion's positions, the men stood fast and fought back with one .57–mm gun, grenades, rocket guns, and small arms. Although outnumbered by enemy forces, this battalion courageously hurled back the hostile troops and secured the right flank of the divisions narrow beachhead. During the entire day of 12 July 1943 the *1st Battalion* moved forward over rolling terrain in the face of determined enemy resistance from tanks and infantry, inflicting heavy losses upon the enemy. On the morning of 13 July 1943, when the enemy again counterattacked, the men tenaciously held their ground against tremendous odds and fought back savagely and expertly for thirty hours, repulsing the attacking forces and seizing the town of Niscemi. On 14 July 1943, this organization took up a position east of Niscemi and despite intense enemy shell-fire eliminated all threats to our security . . . casualties included 36 dead, 73 wounded, and 9 missing in action.

During a lull in the action, I used my pick to dig a slit-trench in the hard ground. Another officer sauntered over and struck up a conversation. I expected things to break loose at any time and asked if he had dug a foxhole yet. He said he thought there was plenty of time. After we visited for a moment, he requested to borrow my pick. Tired, I lay down in my hole just as an incoming shell landed next to my hole, where I had been sitting. The concussion knocked me unconscious and covered me with dirt. When I came to, the other lieutenant lay dead, a large shrapnel wound to his head, my pick still clutched in his hand.

For the next twenty-two days we fought our way in a north/north-east direction across the rocky soil of Sicily, under General Omar Bradley.

We joined General Patton's 7th Army near Mt. Etna. It was a rough go as the Germans held the high ground, and we the valleys below.

As the fighting in Sicily ended, the 1st Battalion was withdrawn and shipped back to England. Our battalion was designated to make the initial invasion of Europe.

The sickness with which I suffered when a prisoner in North Africa returned. The doctors finally diagnosed I had malaria and put me on quinine, which controlled the problem. However, I was not finished with Mr. Malaria, and it came again during the fighting at Normandy.

(Quentin's experiences in other areas of the war can be found on pages 22 and 77.)

THE ITALY CAMPAIGN

Scenes from Italy. Many soldiers were affected by seeing the impact of war on women and children in occupied countries.

Photos taken by Claude Burtenshaw during his service in Italy.

With the capture of Sicily by the Allies, the government of Italy, headed by Benito Mussolini, collapsed. Hitler's fellow dictator was shorn of his powers and imprisoned off the island of Ponza. Letting go of their momentum, British and American commanders on Sicily allowed the German armies to escape across the Straits of Messina to the toe of the Italian boot. The British 8th Army followed the Germans into Italy and on 9 September 1943, the U.S. 5th Army, under General Mark Clark, staged a landing at Salerno. It would take until 2 May 1945, before the Axis armies in Italy were defeated. Significantly, the engagement of Nazi forces in Italy prevented the use of these forces against the Allied Invasion of Normandy in June 1944, and subsequently, in any of the battles across France and into Germany.

On 22 January 1944, Allied troops moved up the Italian peninsula and landed at Anzio, a resort city just south of Rome. The general commanding the attack at Anzio conducted a successful landing, but he stopped to regroup and rest his troops and failed to press the enemy. The advantage of surprise was lost. Action that should have taken a matter of days took five difficult months. As Churchill observed: "We sought to throw a raging lion ashore; what we got was a stranded whale."

THOMAS J. HAMILTON

Thomas J. Hamilton, 1942

We departed North Africa and headed for the beachhead at Salerno as part of the invasion force that would retake Italy from the Axis grip. A short time before we were to land, the sergeant barked, "Hamilton, get behind the wheel of that duck." (A "duck" [or DUKW] is a six-by-six amphibious landing craft.) I'm not sure now how many men got into the rig with me. We were briefed that the beach had been cleared of mines. The big front door of our ship let down, and I drove the duck into the water.

DUKWs, better known as ducks, played an important role in amphibious invasions during the war.

I felt the front wheels find land. Was I afraid? There was little time for fear. We hadn't gotten far up the beach when I heard a loud thump. It was a land mine that Ordinance had missed. I do not remember hearing an explosion or feeling anything. About a week later I woke up in a hospital back in Oran. I had no wounds that could be seen on the outside but had suffered internal injuries. I lapsed in and out of consciousness. I did not know until later that I was the only survivor among the men on the landing craft.

We did not have the wonderful communications facilities then that we enjoy now, more than fifty years later. Letters to or from home took weeks to deliver.

Since I was pretty badly broken up and could not write, it was a long time before Marian finally heard that I had been wounded. Eventually she received a telegram telling her of my condition and where I was. Since I had been sent to Italy for the invasion, the military post office was sending my mail to Italy. Then I was evacuated to Africa. It was a time of uncertainty for Marian and me.

My recovery was a long, slow, and painful process. I still deal with some of the effects. My career as a warrior did not last long. It's ironic that my first brush with an enemy mine, which I was trained to disarm, was one that nearly killed me.

CLAUDE J. BURTENSHAW

And their arm shall be my arm.

(Doctrine & Covenants 35:14)

7 December 1941, was my first day home from the hospital, where I had been recovering from an appendectomy. I switched on the radio to hear the 8:00 news and heard the shocking report: "The Japanese have bombed Pearl Harbor!" To one my age the news meant military service.

During my week in the hospital I was visited by a vivacious, attractive young lady whom I'd been dating. We were both school teachers and both returned missionaries. Frances Davis and I were married 27 May 1942, in the Logan Temple. In late August that year I enlisted in the United States Army Air Corps. Frances was expecting our first child.

Following a brief leave at home, I was sent to New York City to await shipment overseas. On 26 February 1943, I was loaded with hundreds of other soldiers aboard a converted British tourist ship and headed across the Atlantic. Two days of seasickness made me feel the sickest I had ever been.

We landed at Casablanca, Morocco, and a few days later we flew to Algiers in North Africa. On 9 June, we were sent to the island of Pantelleria. This Italian island had been taken by U.S. forces just before we landed. This tiny volcanic island was our bivouac area as we supported the invasion of Sicily.

After the Germans were driven out of Naples, our unit was moved there. We lived in a rope factory, home for the winter of 1943–44.

* * *

In a blessing given me as I departed for the service, my stake president counseled me to assume Church leadership roles whenever possible. With no other mandate than this, I found a room in the U.S.O. that could accommodate a fairly large group. I put up signs announcing the time and place of LDS Services and began holding meetings. The first Sunday fifty or sixty people showed up. Because most of the men landing at Naples were being sent forward to fight, there was a different group of men each Sunday. We held a sacrament service, after which a lesson was given. I served as group leader from November 1943 until I left Naples the following June.

It was in Naples that I met Eldin Ricks, an LDS Chaplain. We had known each other years before and were surprised to see each other. Latter-day Saints who were chaplains were supposed to serve Protestants and were advised not to hold denominational services. So he was quite happy that I would do what he felt he could not do, but wanted to.

As the men came to the meetings I took their names and unit numbers and developed a list of LDS men and women serving in Italy. I later began sending a monthly newsletter to them. I met hundreds of LDS servicemen during the winter.

When the Germans were driven from Rome in June 1944, we packed our equipment and, with other units, headed for Rome. We were just entering the city when we were stopped by a messenger vehicle with a letter addressed to the commander of the unit to which I was attached. The letter gave instructions to send me to Foggia, a small town in the south of Italy. I was to transfer from the 6th Air Group to the 12th. It was unheard of for anyone to be transferred like that, especially a corporal. That day I flew back to Foggia to be an assistant to Vernon Cooley, an LDS chaplain who had just arrived in Italy. Since he didn't have an assistant, he asked for me. I was very surprised when this happened. I learned that Eldin Ricks had told Vern about me and was instrumental in getting me assigned to him.

A letter outlining some of our activities, written by my friend, Walden Johnson, to his parents, was printed in the *Church News* of 22 July 1944:

Dear Family,   Italy, Wednesday, June 29, 1944

Since last Sunday I've been away from camp traveling around with Chaplain Vern A. Cooley, Claude Burtenshaw, George I. Cannon (of Salt Lake), Ervin Clark, and Reed Bowen in Chaplain Cooley's Jeep. I was lucky in being able to get time off so I could go with them.

At Naples we stayed with Chaplain Eldin Ricks, who had arranged LDS services at different camps for three successive evenings. We, (Claude, George, Ervin and Reed) attended all of them and assisted where we could. Two of the meetings were conducted out in the open just at dusk and were the most impressive meetings I've been to for a long time.

The most memorable of the two convened under a big pine tree in the middle of a stubble field. It was an old battle ground where the fighting was particularly fierce in the days of the Italian campaign. It's such a peaceful, quiet place now. The growing crops and nature have healed most of the wounds and covered the scars. The stars were out and there was a moon.

It was enjoyable just sitting there partaking of the beauty and quiet. About thirty of us were assembled in testimony meeting. Many of the fellows had recently been in frontline action. They had some remarkable experiences to relate of how their faith had been strengthened and how they had come to have a testimony of the gospel. . . . There was one young fellow there who is not a member of the Church, but he is deeply interested in the gospel and lacked words to express how much he liked the meeting.

One day we went sightseeing to Pompeii and various points of interest. Another day we worked on the card file of all LDS fellows in Italy, getting it up to date. We all went to a transient mess hall (we were the transients, not the mess hall) for dinner. While there we met two other LDS fellows (Lt. Farr and Theron Green, who came to our first meetings in Naples soon after the German evacuation). That made ten of us in all. Just as we were leaving, a pilot (another LDS fellow stationed near where I am) bumped into us. He was on his way to rest camp. That made eleven of us altogether.

We were just climbing into the Jeep when a soldier noticed "Deseret" on Vern's Jeep and stopped to ask if we were Mormons by any chance. He said he was too, so that made twelve of us.

We almost had a meeting right there. It was the most glorious three-and-a-half days that I've spent in Italy just to be with fellows who have the same ideals and with whom I could talk freely. We had some serious

The "Deseret Jeep." Left to right, Walden Johnson, Claude Burtenshaw, and Ervin Clark.

moments; we laughed and had fun; in short it's the closest I've come to being home in a long time.

Much love to each one—Walden

Vernon Cooley was a tremendous fellow. They could not have found a greater man to be a chaplain. The men all wanted to come and spend time with him. Sometimes we would have twenty or thirty LDS men come in to spend the night with us. We let them sleep on the floor, which they always seemed happy to do.

Chaplain Cooley was an unusually humble and patient man. We held Sunday and sometimes mid-week services for four units. I accompanied the hymns on a field organ and often gave the sermons. Eventually there were four LDS chaplains in the area of Foggia and all of them said, "Why don't you do what you were doing in Naples and be our LDS center person?" So I began holding LDS services in Foggia, inviting those in attendance to participate by giving prayers, talks, and teaching assignments.

I also helped with the Protestant services. We traveled about the area, holding services, including meetings for three groups of black service men. In those days blacks were not allowed to mingle with the white units. There was no black chaplain, so I did nearly all the work with them. I went almost every week and preached to them. They were very attentive and appreciative, and they loved to sing the hymns. Working with them was fun and very rewarding.

We also held a Mormon service every Sunday. It was always a big service, and sometimes as many as two-hundred men would show up. In the vicinity of Foggia we had five or six B-24 units and about the same number of B-17 groups. They were flying bombing missions in France, Germany, and Romania, so there were thousands of U.S. servicemen in that area. There was a WAC unit located close by, and we found three of them who were LDS. There were also several nurses who were members of the Church.

During that year we held three Italian Theater conferences for LDS personnel, and had between nine-hundred and a thousand men show up to each of these. Once we held a dance. We gathered up forty or fifty ladies who all had a great time dancing with so many men.

I was associated with many men who didn't make it back or who were killed while flying missions. I wrote at least fifty letters to parents or

Scripture study in Italy. James McQueen (far left) and another serviceman listen as Claude Burtenshaw (far right) and Chaplain Vernon Cooley (2nd from right) lead the discussion.

wives of these men. Many wrote tender letters back, asking questions, some wondering how the Lord could let their son be killed. Some of these folks came to see me after the war. They came because I had been the last person to see their son just a few hours before his last flight.

One young LDS man was killed on the last bombing mission of the war. His plane was badly shot up, and everyone bailed out. His chute caught on a cliff somewhere in the Alps. One of his crew members came to tell me that his body had banged into the rock wall, and he'd died. He'd gotten him out of his chute, but had to leave his body there. Tough things like that happened over and over during the fighting.

During this time at Foggia, I wrote and sent monthly letters to over two thousand LDS servicemen. I became acquainted by name with more people than I did by face. The year at Foggia was as pleasant as war can be.

The newsletters were a combination of encouragement, admonition, and news about the men and the Church in Italy, sent out over the signature of Chaplains Ricks, Cooley, and Irons:

Dear Brethren;   4 July 1944

Though war has made it difficult to commemorate the 24th as we'd like, we have thought it feasible and possible in a small way to recall that day of '47. The plans for a conference-outing are being arranged now. An entire day's activities [are] planned. Religious services, picnic-beach party, and sports will be the inducements. This is no local gathering. We are inviting all LDS men of this theater who can attend. We suggest a three-day pass to the Foggia area for this event.

Three new LDS groups have been organized during June for boys in the areas of Manduria, Hospital Section of Naples, and 91st Division. Were we permanent residents of Italy, we'd suggest the organization of a new stake. It has been quite surprising to a large number of fellows to find LDS men in their area and many times in their [military] organizations. . . . It was one of the sublime spiritual thrills to meet with the men of Manduria. The thrill of LDS men's first meeting in many months has no equal. The three divisions were visited by Chaplains Cooley and Ricks. . . .

In spite of war, our missionary work goes on. Four men of this theater have accepted the gospel and entered in at the gate. To those men we extend a welcoming hand and accept them as brothers in the gospel. Robert Milton Bird, Robert LaVern Fischer, Lee Marion Shelmerdine, and Willy Vogel, may you find the full joy of the gospel which will come by your complete devotion. May you sense, too, your duties and opportunities.

Group organizations are permitting men to advance in the priesthood. We encourage you to be as active as possible and wherever advisable make advancement using the proper procedure. Five men have received advancements during the past month.

This could be the sad part of our letter; however, the following wounded men have been visited and are on the road to recovery. Therefore, we rejoice with them. Glen Sheen–mortar shell wound in the arm; Guy F. Anderson–wounds from flak taken on air raid; Bill Clements–burns (returned to duty); Jesse L. Slater–burns; John Fretwell–wounds from bomb fragments; Robert P. Lambert–perforated ear drums; Merlin Koehn–wound in leg; James F. Brown–injured in plane crash; Dean Gibson–leg broken by machine-gun bullets; John A. Hicks–wrenched knee; Vance Howell–flak wound in leg on raid; Lt. Turner–head injuries from plane crash.

Another newsletter dated 1 November 1944:

Dear Brothers and Sisters:

A return to the basic fundamentals of the gospel was the plea of the General Authorities of the Church at the October conference. There could have been no admonition more timely. It has become the habit of most of us to analyze and justify the many situations brought about by war. . . . In an attempt to be liberal and broad-minded we have sometimes accepted unproven theories and man-made philosophies. It has been this straying and rationalizing that has led many of us to think that we have outgrown or perhaps outlived the simple doctrines of Christ. The prophets of the Lord have spoken in a warning voice. We would do well to listen. . . .

Dear Frances: Thanksgiving Day, 1944
        Today I was grateful for you. . . . Before this day closes I offer my humble prayer for the lovely companion I have. I am grateful too for the little daughter that I do not know, but love and know that someday I shall realize a fuller joy. Being thankful for you includes a love for all the things you are. I love your devotion, except when you forget to write my daily letter. I love your sweetness and thoughtfulness. . . .
        No mail came in at all today, and I wanted some very badly just to give me contact with you on a day that I could use so well with you.
        All my love, Claude

        This monthly newsletter tells how our LDS Servicemen's Groups celebrated Christmas, and of other groups being established.

Dear Brothers and Sisters: 1 January 1945
        In spite of war and our distant wanderings, the holiday brought some joy. All of the groups have specially prepared programs for Sunday preceding Christmas. The Bari Group even found a spirit that they never imagined finding, by the old method of giving to those who are in need. After their well-prepared and rendered program they played Santa to about eighty boys and girls of the area. The men saved their PX rations and prepared a candy treat and other gifts for the children who are members of the Protestant Church where they hold their weekly service.
        This report came from Naples: "Our group here sponsored an Orphanage Christmas program and party for around ninety orphans located in this area. . ."

                                    * * *

        The war in Italy ended 5 May 1945, at which time I was given an additional assignment as the educational representative for our unit. I went to Rome for conferences to plan activities for soldiers awaiting shipment to the Pacific Theater. Chaplain Cooley recommended me for a field commission as a chaplain. But by then I had only one dream—to return home to Frances and our daughter Claudene. For me, military life had lost all its romance.

I suppose that more than anything else during the war that I wanted to give the LDS men I encountered some attachment with the Church. Maybe, had I been any rank other than a lowly corporal, I would have been too occupied with other duties to be of help. I didn't perform miracles; I just did what I felt the servicemen needed.

About 24 July 1945, I boarded a troop carrier at Naples. We enjoyed a wonderful trip across the sometimes stormy Atlantic on waters as smooth as glass. Nothing looked more wonderful to me than the New York skyline and the Statue of Liberty. Within hours of docking we moved to Camp Dix, New Jersey, where I boarded a train headed westward and home.

Claude and Frances Burtenshaw are the parents of six daughters and two sons, grandparents of forty-five grandchildren, and have twenty great-grandchildren—with more on the way.

Claude earned an associate's degree from Ricks College. He obtained his bachelor's, master's, and Doctorate degrees in political science from the University of Utah. He taught political science at Ricks College from 1947 to 1959, and left Ricks College to become president of Carbon College at Price, Utah. In 1970, he became Dean of Students, then Vice President of Utah State University at Logan. In 1980 he retired as Vice President and taught political science courses at USU for another ten years.

Active in politics, Claude ran for the U.S. Senate from Idaho in 1950, 1954, and 1956 on the Democratic ticket. He served in the Idaho House of Representatives from 1952 to 1958, and in the Idaho State Senate from 1958 to 1959. He served on the Logan City Council for twelve years.

Active in the Church throughout their lives, Frances and Claude filled a church-service mission to BYU-Hawaii from 1990 through 1991. Frances passed away in 2001.

Taken from his personal records and oral interview with him by Paul Kelly

FRANK H. JACOBS

On 8 December 1944, we entered the Bay of Naples. Hundreds of capsized boats lay in the water; the docks were in shambles. The harbor was a mass of destruction, testifying to the intensity of the battle that had taken place. This was my first glimpse of war. When we got on shore, poor starving natives approached us, begging for food. They were sleeping in the streets and anywhere else they could find. It was a pitiful sight.

At the replacement depot we slept in pup tents, which did not keep out the pouring rain. I didn't spend a dry hour the whole time I was there. By day we stood in long lines for processing. The chow lines were even longer, but the food was better than the food in Africa had been.

Sunday the 12th I was given a pass to go to church in Naples. Without too much difficulty I found the meeting place and certainly enjoyed the meeting. A friend from Idaho, Claude Burtenshaw, conducted the services, assisted by an LDS chaplain, Eldin Ricks. After church I wandered through the city, seeing the sights and savoring the atmosphere.

I expected to be sent to the front as an infantryman, but I hadn't worried about it and looked at it as another adventure. Tuesday, after dinner, all former coast artillerymen were told to be ready to leave in forty-five minutes. Tired of replacement depots, I was eager to go. Half of the guys were sent directly to the front, and the rest of us were sent to Caserta. I was assigned to 30th Operating Detachment, 35th Anti-Aircraft Brigade, 505th Regiment.

Wednesday morning four of us were told to report to a Major Holt. He picked up my service record and said, "If you guys are good enough, you will be assigned to a nerve center outfit GOR (gun operating room)." He flipped through my service record and asked if I was a Mormon. I said yes. He told the captain who was interviewing us that he knew I'd be OK. At the GOR I was assigned to a crew as a plotter.

The GOR was a communications center. Its function was to gather, evaluate, and disseminate information about enemy air forces as picked up by radio, visual observation posts, Allied Air Corps fighter flights, and ground observers. It was our job to know where and when the enemy aircraft would attack and to destroy as many of them as possible. It was a daunting task. I remained with this unit for the duration of the war, and I came to admire and love the men with whom I served.

Christmas Eve I went with some soldiers to an Italian home. Everyone there was drinking *vino*, so I went back to my quarters to bed. Christmas I worked all day in the GOR, then at a nearby palace I saw a performance of *Madame Butterfly;* what a gorgeous setting for it.

The people around Caserta and Santa Maria were very poor and constantly begged us for food, candy, and cigarettes. There was always a mob of dirty children begging for our leftovers. It would be freezing cold and those poor little souls stood barefooted, with only rags for a covering, waiting for us to eat so they could snatch our scraps. Bedraggled women brought their babies to gain our sympathy. One particular old woman would take food away from the little kids. Our guard was supposed to keep the poor little urchins in the street. Some would scare them with a stick, as though they were pushing animals away from a trough. I didn't like that, and I gave them all the candy I could. To help them, and myself, I hired a woman to do my laundry, and when we had a gravel detail I would pay a couple of Italian men fifteen lira to load our truck for us. Houses of prostitution sprang up and seemed to do a brisk business. I was serious about my ideals and refused to participate in all such so-called thrills.

On 2 February, we arrived at Anzio beachhead to find a precarious situation. As we arrived, we saw evidence of a hurried German retreat.

We moved into quarters on the beach and set up the GOR. I was unloading a truck when the German planes came. This was my first real raid. I hit the ground as shrapnel flew all around me. "Anzio Annie," a huge gun mounted on railroad cars, began shelling us. Shells burst on one side and then the other, then behind and then in front of us. We expected a shell to fall on us any moment. At noon the next day the enemy planes came again. That night "Anzio Annie" shelled us constantly, and German planes filled the sky. Sleep was impossible. Guard duty for four hours nightly was tortuous. Every time I heard a noise, I jumped like a scared rabbit.

On 8 February, several of us were at the beach loading sand bags. I told my buddies to take the load of filled sand bags up to our building while I stayed to fill the few more bags that were needed. After they left, an intense feeling of uneasiness came over me. I thought I heard someone say, *"Go up to the building now."* Did I imagine it? Then the voice came again, with greater urgency—so I headed for shelter. Immediately upon entering the building I went downstairs to wash, just as all hell broke loose. I felt a concussion and heard an explosion. Ceiling plaster fell on me, and I prayed as never before. The men on the floor above screamed, and a couple of them received severe cuts from flying glass. The place where I had been loading sand bags was a bomb crater twenty feet in diameter and fourteen feet deep! I fervently thanked God for preserving my life.

The bombing had such an effect on me that for the next three days, if a pan dropped, I jumped a mile. I wondered how long we could remain on this narrow stretch of land. Our nerves were stretched to the limit. All through this time the GOR remained on the air, continuously passing on the information we gathered. I knew that the Lord had protected me. The captain ordered us into a big tunnel. I had not slept for days.

On 16 February we had raids all night. From 0430 until 0600 hours I sat through a miserable raid at my post in the GOR. From 0600 to 0800 I was assigned to stand guard at the motor pool. For those two hours I lay on my belly, quivering uncontrollably in a damp, cold foxhole, praying as hard as I ever prayed in my life. Artillery shells bombarded our position, the huge shells passing just over my head. At 0700 the German planes strafed and bombed the road ten feet in front of me. When I was relieved, still terrified and cold from lying on the damp ground, I shook so badly I could hardly eat breakfast. Down in the tunnel I lay on a bed the rest of the day, wondering how I would live through this, but the raids continued.

Things remained pretty much the same in this hell-hole through the balance of February and March. Veterans of the fighting in Africa, Sicily, and Salerno said this was the worst they had endured. I know the Lord was with me and that I owed my life to Him.

Monday, 2 April, I left for rest camp at Naples. The hardest part of getting out of Anzio was going to the dock area to wait for the boat to leave. Each minute seemed an hour long. We had to wait two hours with shells exploding around us, before we could depart. We finally arrived in Naples Tuesday afternoon. What a relief not to have continual bombardment, noise, confusion, and concussion.

Naples, with Mt. Vesuvius in the background, is remarkably beautiful. I toured the ancient Roman city of Pompeii, not far away. I went to see the Opera *Carmen* and some other shows. It was very enjoyable, but the time passed too quickly and soon I had to return to Anzio.

I started a laundry business. There was certainly a need for it; it helped pass the time and I made good money. However, the first pair of wool olive drab pants I laundered, I put in a vat of boiling water, and the pants shrank so they wouldn't fit anyone in the outfit.

Toward the end of April the intensity of the raids dropped noticeably. On 12 May the push from Casino commenced. It was a thrill to listen as our artillery pounded the Germans. On 25 May, elements of the 5th Army broke through and on 4 June, Rome fell to the Allies, and our armies pushed north.

On 7 June we left Anzio for Civitavecchia. By the time we got there our soldiers had pushed the Germans ten miles north. Riding along the highway we were cheered by Italian civilians. In the rail yard at Civitavecchea, which was now a bombed-out mass of twisted steel, we discovered "Anzio Annie," the huge gun that had done us so much damage. It was mounted on five railway cars, had a barrel 72-feet long, and had an eleven-inch bore. The base of the barrel was solid steel.

I became the unit's cook. Not because I knew how, but because someone had to do it. We moved to Santa Marinella, a town right on the beach facing the Mediterranean. We lived in two beautiful mansions, and I had a nice kitchen. Duty was light, and I was allowed to visit Rome a couple of times. I saw Irving Berlin's musical *This Is the Army* and got to bathe in the sulphur springs of an ancient Roman ruin.

Our unit was transferred to the 7th Army.

On 1 July the boys of GOR were sent to Naples, the staging area for Southern France. There I had to cook with Brigade. We were feeding 150 men, which meant putting in long, hard hours. I saw several operas and also attended church. The services were wonderful, and it was good to receive the sacrament and to feel again the special spirit of meeting with the Saints.

On 9 August we loaded on a troop transport but stayed in the harbor four days before we pulled anchor. Aboard ship we were briefed about the upcoming operation. Departing the Bay of Naples on the 13th we were visited by Winston Churchill. Aboard a power boat, he moved through that large convoy. Stopping at each ship, he doffed his hat and received our cheers.

15 August 1944: Arrived at St. Maxine, southern France. We stayed aboard the ship and watched as six battleships and several cruisers bombarded

the shore installations for the landing. We were to go in with the 45th Division in the center of the beach. At noon on the 17th we climbed down scramble nets into landing craft and were ashore a half-hour later. Prisoners were already pouring onto the beach, some were old, some very young. The landings were very successful, and we were thankful to the Lord for his help.

The next morning I was up early for a look at France. It was beautiful. I strolled up a road and met a fine looking French lady. She spoke English and told me she had been a dressmaker in Paris. She showed a lot of refinement and culture. She was thrilled to see Americans and told me of the hardships she had been through. Worst of all, she said, were the meager rations and the outrageous black market. I gave her some chocolate bars. She was overjoyed, with this being the first chocolate she had seen since 1939.

* * *

We were at Walburg for my second Christmas away from home. Everyone was drunk the whole day, which I found disgusting. I cleaned and dressed the turkeys and helped serve Christmas dinner. New Year's Eve I baked pies, then cooked and served the New Year's dinner. I'd prepared a good dinner, but everyone was so drunk it was largely unappreciated. That day I was promoted to T5.

March 26th: We crossed the German border, right through the dragon's teeth of the Siegfried Line. You could see pill box after pill box. The roads were full of wrecked vehicles, tanks, and guns that our airmen had knocked out. In the little town of Manshiem we kicked a German family out of their home. They were given an hour to leave. The women were panic stricken and crying. They got carts and tried to get their best stuff moved. On the hour we moved in, and the men went wild over the loot. They destroyed furniture and other things priceless to the people and of no value to them. I was disgusted—this seemed out of harmony with what we were fighting for. Word came down the chain-of-command and looting slowed down. I felt sorry for the people.

Prisoners were coming in, first by the dozens, then hundreds, then by the thousands. I took one standing in the kitchen. He came in with a white flag hollering "Komerad."

On 8 May 1945, Germany surrendered, unconditionally, and war in the European Theatre of Operations officially ended.

Frank Jacobs exploring Paris

May 27th: I got a pass and took a plane to Paris, where I spent two days, then went to Nancy.

I didn't have quite enough points to go home, but several of the men from our unit did, and they left one by one. I was sent to Gosswienstein. While there, I did considerable traveling around Europe, visiting the French Riviera, Luxemburg, Nice, and Czechoslovakia.

I was discharged from the Army at Fort Douglas, Utah. I boarded the train for Idaho and was met at the railroad station by my mother and grandparents, the same people who bade me good-bye as I left for the war.

* * *

In February of 2000, Frank Jacobs reflected further on his wartime experiences: LDS servicemen were not hampered, or pampered, as they served their country. I was in some of the rugged parts of the fighting. I observed that our boys were highly respected—especially as they lived up to the standards of the Church. Reflecting on my assignment as the cook in our outfit, the major used to say: "Jake is a Mormon, has made thousands of gallons of coffee, and has never tasted a drop. He makes the best coffee in the Army."

The First Presidency provided each of us copies of the Book of Mormon and another booklet about our religion. I wore mine out studying them whenever I had some free time. Before that period in my life, I had never had done such an intensive study of the Book of Mormon, a great side effect of the war.

Frank H. Jacobs returned to the University of Idaho where he studied agriculture. There he met Gerry Merrill, from Preston, Idaho. They were married within a year of his discharge. They are parents of three daughters and two sons, and they currently have twenty-nine grandchildren and eight great-grandchildren. Frank was County Agent for Madison County, Idaho, for thirty years before retiring in 1981, after which he became a full-time farmer, working with his two sons and a son-in-law. He has served as a bishop's counselor, bishop, ward executive secretary, ward Sunday School president, home teacher, and temple ordinance worker.

Taken from "The Life of Frank Harris Jacobs and His Pioneer Heritage," a family history.

BYRON CARLYLE PEACOCK

For ye did thrust in the sickle . . . yea, all the day long did ye labor.
(Alma 26:5)

Rather than wait to be drafted, I enlisted in the Army on 10 October 1940. Several of my schoolmates also joined the military.

In September 1942 our division left California and was shipped to the east coast. We embarked from Norfolk, Virginia, 22 October 1942 for an unannounced destination. After the long sea journey and the seasickness that afflicted us, we approached the coast of Africa to the port of Fedala, not far from Casablanca in French Morocco.

Here I was assigned to drive a lieutenant to Rabat, drop him off, return to my unit, and then later in the evening, pick him up. I asked why he didn't have his regular driver chauffeur him to town. He replied, "You don't drink or chase the girls, and I felt I could trust you to take care of this assignment better than any other driver in the company." I took this as a compliment to me, my church, and my parents. Later I was chosen to make a solo drive through strange country to deliver equipment and supplies to one of our outpost units many miles away. Again I was chosen because of my abstinence from drink and for my moral standards.

In April our division went into intensive training for the invasion of Sicily. We had just engaged in the final battles in the defeat of Axis forces in Africa, the first step on the long road to Berlin and final victory. Abandoned and ruined enemy equipment littered the roads in Africa. It was astonishing to see thousands upon thousands of unescorted German troops marching to the rear looking for POW camps. These troops were those the Germans were not able to evacuate from the Cape Bon Peninsula at Bizerte.

Between campaigns a few of us visited Tunis. We visited the native section, the Kasbah. What I saw made me appreciate my home and teachings more than ever. The prostitutes were very bold. They approached us openly on the streets or displayed themselves in windows or doorways. After only a few minutes we beat a hasty retreat. I was convinced that to surrender to temptations here would be worse than to fall on the battlefield.

While in Africa I found an organization of the Church. Some of the fellows in an infantry regiment had been set apart to carry on church activities when possible. It was comforting to again assemble as church members, partake of the sacrament, enjoy the company of members of the Church, and listen to each other's testimonies.

We landed on the beaches of Sicily at Licata on 10 July 1943. The battle for control of Sicily lasted until 17 August at Messina, only three miles from the toe of the boot of Italy.

The invasion of Italy began, and we embarked from Palermo and landed on the beach at Salerno, about thirty miles south of Naples. About this time I received news from home that my dad had been sustained as bishop of the Emery Ward. It filled me with pride and made me more determined than ever to live as I had been taught.

One day, as I returned from driving a load of infantry to Salitto, the lieutenant said, "Corporal Peacock, since you are the only one with any knowledge of the road, I want you to lead a convoy of fifteen trucks up to Salitto." It had been days since I'd had a full night's rest. It had been raining sporadically. I called the other drivers together and told them that it was imperative that we get as far up the road as possible before dark.

We had not gone far when it started to rain. The darkness added to the difficulty of driving, and we had to reduce our speed until we going only five miles per hour. Of necessity we were using black-out or "cat's eyes," which didn't illuminate the road but only served to keep us from bumping someone ahead or being bumped from behind. As we got close to the top of the mountain we had to turn the "cat's eyes" off, lest we be detected. The tenseness kept me alert, but it was very tiring. I relied on the Lord.

Winding up the narrow road in the darkness, I was trying to remember a sharp turn that came just before a bridge. A feeling came over me that I should stop. I slowed down but kept going, then a strong prompting told me to stop, now! I grabbed my flashlight, and covering the lens so only a small beam of light came through, I moved to the front of the truck and discovered the road ended.

A few minutes later we found a way to move ahead. As the night passed I offered up silent prayers, thanking the Lord for his promptings. Had I not heeded it I would have driven over the edge of a deep ravine and all the others would have followed.

Our unit was relieved from the line and sent to the rear for a much needed rest near Naples. During our brief stay I attended church, and it was here that I met Chaplain Eldin Ricks. He set me apart as an LDS group leader for the 3rd Infantry Division. I did not know at the time that I would take an important part in the Church program on the Anzio Beachhead.

Early in the morning of 24 January 1944, our unit took part in the landing at Anzio, Italy. What was to have been a mad dash to Rome turned out to be a long and agonizing stay. For four long months we held on to a piece of real estate ten miles long and ten miles wide. We had no choice. Ahead was a well-dug-in foe, and behind us the Tyrrhenian Sea.

Although we were severely tested while pinned on this beachhead, it was at Anzio that I took part in some of the most spiritual church meetings I have ever attended. One of the first we held was near a grove of trees. We were periodically shelled by our foes and so wore our steel helmets, but when time came for the closing prayer we automatically removed them, although shells were dropping not far away.

It was here that I became acquainted with members of the 442nd Regimental Combat Team, made up of Japanese men. Several of them were Church members. They bore very strong testimonies of the truthfulness of the gospel. Sunday was a day we looked forward to. We enjoyed a bond that no one else did. When we were together there was no military rank, only a spirit of brotherhood. Others had difficulty understanding the feeling of love we shared. Officers would introduce themselves, shake hands with privates, and ask who they were and how they were getting along.

The Graves Registration Section was attached to our unit. I obtained permission to hold graveside services for several of our members, and after this they kept us informed of our members who were killed. One day the major in charge of the Graves Registration Section came up to me in the chow line. He said, "Corporal, you are an official in your church and have authority to hold services at the graves of your fallen members. There are a number in the cemetery you haven't taken care of. We expect you to do it." The commissioned and noncommissioned officers respected my position as group leader and my desire to attend my meetings. Whenever possible they would not assign me or my truck on Sunday so that I could pick up members and drive to services.

There on Anzio beachhead, during the cold days of February and March, we were short of everything, especially hope. For the German troops on the surrounding rugged hills, we were like ducks on a pond. The only thing in our favor was that our foes had to ration their ammo. We were low on ammo as well. Many times I narrowly missed death or serious injury. Our casualties in dead and wounded were high.

One interesting incident at this beachhead shows that the German soldiers were much like us. At night in the vicinity of the Mussolini Canal, the front was separated only by a road between two rows of houses. The Germans moved into these houses at night to be out of the cold. One of our G.I.s played his harmonica at night to help pass the hours of cold and loneliness. As he was playing one night, a German tenor in a nearby house joined in singing with the harmonica. This continued for several nights, to the enjoyment of both camps. Then one night his voice was absent and was never heard again. Perhaps he had been sent on patrol and didn't return. We felt a certain sadness.

In mid-May, U.S. and Allied Forces finally broke out of the Anzio area. Once we had the Germans running, we didn't let them rest. We had been penned up on that beachhead for so long that we enjoyed our new freedom. We chased the Germans until we reached Rome, the eternal city.

It was during the pause near Rome that we had some meaningful experiences. Under the leadership of Chaplain Eldin Ricks, a number of us visited some of the early Christian sites near Naples. One was the place where the Apostle Paul was said to have landed when he came to Rome. We also saw the catacombs where the early Christians hid during the persecution by the Romans. The cathedral of St. Genaris was very interesting, for it had a baptismal font in which, according to our guide, people were baptized by immersion. When we asked him if they now baptized by immersion his answer was, "We felt there was a need for change, so we turned to sprinkling."

They also claimed to have a vial of the blood of Christ, kept from the time of his Crucifixion, and that during a special ceremony it reconstitutes itself. Of course we were never permitted to see it. We also visited the ruins of the ancient city of Pompeii, twelve miles south of Naples.

On the evening of 12 August 1944, a formidable naval convoy left the ports of southern Italy. We landed in southern France. After getting off the beaches, we advanced rapidly, pursuing the retreating Germans. As we liberated French towns we were rewarded with flowers and kisses and saw the joy and happiness on the faces of the people. It made me appreciate that our loved ones were spared the brutal experiences these people had gone through.

Of all the troops in the European Theater of Operations, our division held the record of the longest continuous contact with the enemy. On 15 March 1945, we crossed into Germany.

I was in Salzburg, Austria, when the war ended. I had 125 points, enough to qualify for discharge. I left the Division on 10 May 1945, and boarded the *USS Abraham Lincoln,* bound for the good old USA. Upon entering Chesapeake Bay we heard shore batteries firing at us and could see the shells landing in the water. For a moment this shook us up, until we realized that we were the first soldiers to return from Europe, and this was our welcome.

On 27 June 1945, at Fort Douglas, Utah, I was honorably discharged from the United States Army. I had participated in the following campaigns: Algeria-French Morocco, Tunisia, Sicily, Naples-Foggia, Rome-Arno, Southern France, Rhineland, and Central Europe.

It was good to be home again and have the companionship of family and friends. It was wonderful to go to church regularly, to be away from the sound and smell of war. At times I was uneasy with the peace and quiet of my hometown. Though those five years of military service were often unpleasant I found that I had benefited overall. I knew myself. I had many opportunities to teach about the gospel and be close to my Father in Heaven. I had asked for help and received it freely.

Taken from records furnished by the Brigham Young University's *Saints at War* project.

SAIJI ZAKIMI

And they had fought as if with the strength of God.

(Alma 56:56)

When I saw the Japanese planes attacking Pearl Harbor, I thought, *Those men look just like me.* My ROTC unit was immediately conscripted into the Home Guard and set to work guarding key installations in the area twenty-four hours a day. One month later all those of Japanese ancestry were discharged from their assignment. This decision deeply offended me, for this is my country, too; I was born on American soil, and according to the law of the land, I was a United States citizen. Following the attack on Pearl Harbor there was intense reaction against Americans of Japanese descent. As a group of former ROTC students, we petitioned the powers that be to allow us to serve. We felt that we had to act, to do something to demonstrate our loyalty to the United States of America. We became the Varsity Victory Volunteers and were stationed at Schofield Barracks, where we did Army duty without pay. About a year later we were told, "Okay, we can trust you," and our 4-C classification, (meaning "enemy alien, not fit for service") was changed. We were formed into the 442nd Regimental Combat Team. The shoulder patch for our unit was a coffin with a torch of liberty inside, and our motto was "Go for Broke."

By war's end the 442nd, and its subordinate elements, became the most highly decorated single combat unit of its size in the history of the United States Army: eight Presidential Distinguished Unit Citations and 18,143 individual decorations, including one Medal of Honor; 52 Distinguished Service Crosses; 560 Silver Stars, and 28 Oak Leaf Clusters in lieu of a second Silver Star; 4,000 Bronze Stars and 1,200 Oak Leaf Clusters, representing a second Bronze Star; and at least 9,486 Purple Hearts.

Forming this unit did not end the prejudice against us. Our regiment was sent for training at Camp Shelby, Mississippi. However the blinds on the train were pulled down for the entire journey through the United States. The only place where this was not the case was at Ogden, Utah. Here the light of day was allowed in, and lady volunteers from the Red Cross boarded the train and passed out candy bars and other refreshments to us.

We trained and fought under Caucasian officers. While in those days Mississippi may have been a center of racial intolerance, we were treated well. Other units of soldiers training at Camp Shelby gave us grudging respect—after all, there was a whole regiment of us. Our families back home had been placed in internment camps. This was not a red-letter day in American political history.

After training, we were sent to Italy. We were there to help win the war, and we knew that it might cost us our lives. We quickly moved forward to join the fighting.

It was pitch dark my first night in battle. We exchanged fire with a group of German soldiers who seemed just as surprised to find us as we were to find them. That night one of my best friends was killed. The reality of war sank deeply into our souls and prepared us for the struggles we faced. We wished we were better prepared. *Why didn't we take our training more seriously?* we asked ourselves. We learned quickly to never falter and to never be caught unguarded. I didn't hate the enemy, but I knew I must remain on the offensive or die. Even so, we took heavy casualties; after three months the 442nd was at two-thirds of its original strength.

I didn't worry about dying. I was willing to give my life for my country. But at nineteen years of age, dying is not a thing to be concerned about. We were all young, in our teens or our early twenties. The oldest man in the unit was twenty-six.

The 442nd became renowned for bravery. In the Vosges [Vozh] Mountains of northeastern France, a unit of Texans was trapped by Germans. Another Texas unit had been unable to rescue them, so we were moved to France to attempt the rescue.

I had not yet found The Church of Jesus Christ of Latter-day Saints and knew nothing of the Book of Mormon. I now think of the experience as being like the Stripling Warriors under Helaman in the Book of Mormon. It seems a miracle that none of us was killed, as this fighting was especially bitter and bloody.

It was the first time in history that anyone had penetrated the Vosges Forest against an established enemy force. We understood that the 442nd was considered expendable, and wondered if anyone would be sent to rescue us, should we fail in our objective. We doubted it. One day, waiting for the fighting in the forest to begin, I thought, *The Germans will never give up and we'll never give up*. I came to respect the Germans as fighters. Sometimes during the fighting I wondered if either side would yield, or would we fight until we were annihilated? But if I had to die, I felt that it was worth giving my life for my country.

A wound kept me from being with my unit the day we finally rescued the Texans. A

Saiji Zakimi (left) holding the 442nd Regimental Combat Team's flag, which reads "Bruyeres, France, 21 OCT 44."

German artillery shell had burst in the tops of some trees, and I was hit by a piece of shrapnel. Being wounded surprised me—I had not believed that would happen. That was a prominent feeling among my comrades. One fearless young man would taunt the enemy: "Hey! Here we are, come get us." This fellow was a changed man after he did get hit and returned from convalescence.

The 442nd took more than 800 casualties in reaching the Texans, a unit of about 250 men. We then returned to the bloody fighting in the Po River Valley. I recovered from my shrapnel wound, and it was right back into the fight for me. My notion of being invulnerable was shattered a second time by a second shrapnel wound.

The Germans in Italy surrendered 2 May 1945. I applied for leave to go to Venice and to Switzerland for sight-seeing, but was turned down. I appealed to the commanding general who, while very nice, also vetoed my petitions. The general explained that the Army was responsible to help college students prepare to continue their education and that he was required to see that we attended classes in Florence. Prejudice toward and fear of Asians was still intact.

Our commanding officers were great leaders who wanted us to be the best soldiers possible. We enjoyed their strong respectful leadership, and at war's end we all felt we had fought bravely and unitedly. Our loyalty and love of our country was proven at least to our selves, to our families, and to our friends. None of us ever regretted volunteering to fight for our God and our country, and all that it stood for. There was a sweet sense of accomplishment. I was thankful to God, our leaders, and my fellow soldiers.

PFC Saiji Zakimi returned to Hawaii. In 1950 he was searching for a room in which to stay while working on Maui as a social worker for the state. Struggling financially, he accepted the invitation to room and board at the home of his classmate Edward and his wife, Cheiko Okazaki. His friends warned him, "Don't take that room; they'll convert you to the Mormon Church." He was confident he'd never become a member of another church. The Christlike lives of the Okazakis influenced his interest in The Church of Jesus Christ of Latter-day Saints. He was baptized on 7 May 1950. It was a difficult transition to Mormon Christianity, and Saiji says he used to pray "Lord, please tell me this Church is not true." Back would come the answer "It's true." Saiji embraced it with all his heart.

Zak met Lynn Shiroma on a blind date in March 1949 when he took her to a 442nd anniversary dance. They were married 14 October 1950. They are parents of two sons and two daughters.

Throughout his life, he has served in many positions in the Church: three times as bishop and currently as an ordinance worker and sealer in the Laie, Hawaii, Temple.

CYRIL O. BURT

*My God hath been my support; he hath led me through
mine afflictions in the wilderness; and he hath preserved
me upon the waters of the great deep.*

(2 Nephi 4:20)

I was one of twelve young men from Adams County to board the train at Council, Idaho, headed for Fort Douglas. We stopped to pick up passengers and mail at Pocatello. There I met my brother Gene, who was my best friend. The noise from the engine made it difficult to say what was in our hearts. As we shook hands and bade each other farewell, the lump in my throat felt like a baseball.

After a short time serving in North Africa, we arrived in Italy and moved north on my 21st birthday, 18 February 1944. One of the guys offered me a cigarette, saying, "Today Cyril is a man, or at least is twenty-one years old, so maybe he'll have a smoke." I replied "Sorry, old chap, but I guess I am just not quite man enough for that."

Another time, a group of guys were sitting near my foxhole, talking about wine, women, and song. Ole Chaddock spoke up saying, "The hardest people to try to show a good time are those Mormons! They won't drink, play cards, smoke, dance, or a darned thing. All they want to do is sit around and bat the breeze." About the time he finished this, he noticed some of the guys snickering. His face turned red as he looked at me and said, "Burt, you're a Mormon, aren't you?" I took advantage to tell the boys about our Church and our beliefs. No harm done. They respected me.

On 11 May 1944, the battle for Rome began. The battle was nothing like I expected. I could not see the enemy we were shooting at, and could do nothing to protect myself. Artillery shells were exploding all around us. I had never been so afraid in all my life.

The battle lasted for twenty-four days and nights. It was estimated that the Germans lost 38,000 men. We lost many a good man as well. The ride through Rome as "victors" reminded me of the victory ride of the soldiers of Constantine the Great centuries earlier.

Cyril O. Burt

I wrote home on V-mail:

Dear Mother and all

Just a V-mail tonight to once again inform you that I'm still feeling swell and getting along fine. I'm still hoping you folks aren't worrying about me too much . . . if God's got a purpose for this old fellow on this old earth after the war, there aren't enough Germans on the face of the earth to kill me. . . . They call me corporal now . . . but I'm still a yard bird.

Love Cyril

My first assignment after getting my sergeant stripes was to take a crew of men and my radio truck forward, to high ground, to establish a relay station. By the third day we were out of food and could not get back to Headquarters Battery. I saw a group of infantry unloading K-rations from a truck. I dashed over and asked the sergeant in charge if I could have some for my men. Upon seeing my artilleryman insignia he told me, emphatically, "No!" saying he did not have enough for his own men. It was not unusual to find a little animosity between infantry and artillerymen. However, my men had not eaten since the day before. I went behind some trees, took off my jacket and hung it on a branch. I fell in with the men unloading the truck, and they dropped a case of K-rations on my shoulder. I turned left over the hill, grabbed my jacket, and returned to the radio truck.

Ironically, on 11 November, Armistice Day, we were involved in the most vigorous of any fighting I saw in Italy. Enemy planes were actively strafing and bombing artillery positions and bridges. Counter-battery fire was particularly vicious. On this particular day more than 100 rounds of enemy artillery fire fell in our battalion area.

Once, we were operating a relay station on top of a high mountain, a couple of miles north of where Battalion Headquarters was located. We ran a telephone wire from the radio truck down the mountain so we could speed up communications with our fire direction center. A German shell hit the wire, cutting it, so I volunteered to trace the wire and repair it. Big Ed, our driver said, "You can't go alone, I'm going with you." About half way to HQ Battery we found the break and spliced it, then decided to go on down to headquarters to get some good chow. As we rounded a bend, we saw a dead German lying at the side of the road. About that time the Germans started pouring in 88 mm artillery shells. We dove into the gutter, trying to get low. Big Ed said, "I can't get low enough because I'm lying on this miserable mess kit!" Big Ed weighed over three hundred pounds, and him lying on that mess kit made about as much difference as the average guy lying on a peanut.

An Italian family lived at the top of a mountain where we had our radio truck parked. The family let us sleep in the loft of their barn. Shells constantly overhead, both friendly and enemy, were very nerve racking. The mother of the family died while we were there, from causes that may or may not have been related to war. The family was devastated. Thoughts of my own mother brought tears to my eyes, as they buried this lovely lady in a rocky, shallow grave, in the backyard of their home, in a casket made from C-ration boxes.

The first sergeant had given me three, 10-hour passes to visit Florence in a ten-day period. It was on the last of these, November 25th, that I found out there would be LDS Church services there the following day. When I returned to the battery area, I asked the First Sergeant for another pass, to go to church. He turned me down. Since I had not attended an LDS meeting of any kind during 1944, I was determined to go. I took my case to the battery commander, who gave me permission. I can't express how good it felt to take the sacrament once again.

Our unit fell in love with the beautiful Italian children, who lived in very meager circumstances. Packages from our families made it possible to share Christmas goodies with them. We had planned Christmas for them and were disappointed when our duffel bags were collected on the 10th of December, meaning orders to return to the front would be coming soon.

Christmas Eve the first sergeant informed me that I was Sergeant of the Guard for twenty-four hours. The men were loading up on "Christmas cheer," and it was hard to find enough sober guys to stand guard. The battery commander heard me grumbling and asked "What's the matter Sgt. Burt?" I said, "One squad of Germans could whip this whole damn drunken outfit." Then I noticed he was staggering from a few too many himself. The first sergeant probably put me on guard duty, knowing I would stay sober and keep the troops in line.

On Christmas Day, the cooks served us a hot meal: turkey with all the trimmings. A few Italian civilians who lived nearby were invited to join us for Christmas dinner. Seeing the expressions on their faces brought us more of the Christmas spirit than anything else we could have done.

In the process of relieving the British 1st Division in the Mount Grande area, we parked our radio truck on the west side of a large masonry building. We ran a remote control from the radio truck inside the building so we could have a fire in the basement without the Germans seeing it. Lt. Mitchell and a British officer were in a room on the north side of the building when an enemy 210 mm shell came through the outside wall and stuck in a partition without exploding. The dud actually hit the English officer, knocking both legs out from under him. The concussion knocked Lt. Mitchell to the floor, and dust and debris were everywhere. Had the shell exploded, it may well have killed all of us.

After our commanding officer was killed, a major was sent up to take command. The Ranger corporal, with whom I had been on patrol the night before said, "Sergeant Burt, I have been assigned to show the major our outposts and gun emplacements. You're here to learn what you can about the infantry and we are short of men. Will you go with us as rear guard again?" I had loaned my .45 automatic pistol to a soldier who had to carry supplies forward, so I had no weapon. They handed me an M-1 rifle, and we took off, the corporal in front, the major and a lieutenant next, and me bringing up the rear. We had not gone far when we met the fellow who had borrowed my .45. He said, "You better take your gun. I may never see you again." I strapped on the gunbelt and picked up the M-1.

It was a bright moonlit night as we headed up a long narrow ridge. The corporal stopped us as we approached a long open area without protection of trees: "There is an enemy machine gun nest on the other side of this canyon, and they fire a burst of harassment fire every few minutes. We'll wait until they shoot again, then run like hell!" In a few minutes, the Germans opened up, and dust flew as bullets hit on, above, and below the trail. As soon as the firing stopped we ran. I was carrying two weapons and ammunition and was not in very good running condition; I fell about fifty yards behind.

Suddenly bullets from those German machine guns were flying all around me. I dived behind a small German vehicle that had been knocked out of commission. Bullets slammed into my shelter. When the firing stopped I took off. I felt as if I were sprinting down the barrel of a howitzer. I found the other three guys behind some trees. They thought I had been killed.

Our battalion commander was ordered to do reconnaissance for a new position in the vicinity of Vergato on April 6th. I was assigned to sweep the area for mines. I climbed into the captain's Jeep, and we followed the colonel. The Germans opened fire on us, and we bailed out of the Jeep into a large culvert. There the captain produced a bottle of Scotch whiskey and invited us to settle our nerves. He couldn't understand why I refused.

With the Germans losing the advantage of the high ground and being blasted out of their reinforced concrete pill boxes, we had them on the run. Everywhere we went masses of German soldiers were surrendering.

The Italian people were deliriously happy and treated us like kings. One lady fried eggs for Walt, Hank, and me. We had chicken dinner at one house and supper at another. I even milked a cow for the family. Living conditions were much better for people in the Po Valley. The war's toll was not as terrible on the citizens here, as they seemed to have plenty to eat. We bedded down a half mile from the Po River in an orchard with plenty of nice clean grass, a much different environment than we had been accustomed to.

Coming into the Po Valley, we crossed the Panaro River at Camposanto. It was dark as we reached the Panaro River bridge. We stopped and spoke with an Italian gentleman standing by a pile of rubble. He was weeping as he told us that sixteen members of his family were under that heap. He mumbled that our planes had bombed the building that day. We had no time to comfort him. The old man acknowledged our airplanes had earlier dropped leaflets warning civilians to stay away from the bridge.

Germans across the Po Valley were now surrendering by the thousands.

On 27 April we reached the outskirts of Verona. The next day, Italian partisans found Benito Mussolini and his mistress Clara Petacci; they held a mock trial and executed them.

The Germans were in full retreat. They surrendered 2 May 1945. The fighting ceased at 1400 hours, but we had no official word of capitulation, so our artillery pieces stayed in place to remind the Nazis that we still held the whip-hand. We stood by the road as thousands of German troops marched past, unarmed and looking defeated. No doubt most of them were thankful it was over.

Some of the officers were fairly pompous in their fancy uniforms. Some had smirks on their faces as if to say, "It was not our idea to surrender." One insolent soul swaggered by, and one of our soldiers grabbed the arrogant whelp, jerked off his fancy hat, and kicked his rear-end. I didn't like to see defeated soldiers mistreated, but this one had it coming.

We gathered the surrendering soldiers by the thousands into fields. They had to be organized into units, fed, housed, and cared for. It was a colossal task.

The war in Italy was finally over. This soldier came through without a scratch. My prayers and those of my family and friends all those weeks and months were answered.

Dear Dad, Mom, and all   May 2, 1945

It seems funny to sit here tonight with no noise from big guns pounding away. "All is quiet on the Italian front" as you no doubt have heard. . . . All the Germans in Italy and some in Austria have surrendered unconditionally. . . . When you stop to think of 600,000 to 900,000 soldiers, you realize that it really took a chunk out of what was left of the Nazi army. I can't start to tell you what it feels like to see prisoners of war marching past—men that have been shooting at you and keeping you from going home. It makes you realize what a swell army Uncle Sam must have.

I wish I could describe the way these Italian people have been acting as we have been advancing, pushing the Krauts back. They go hog-wild. They stand along the roads on both sides and wave, shake hands, shout, sing, ring church bells, throw flowers, paper, bread, food, etc. to us. They treat us like kings. Yesterday we were on the march and it was raining to beat heck, and by George those people stood in the rain and cheered and shouted, shook hands with us, and really showed us that they are glad to see us. Naturally it makes us feel swell. . . . I'm so happy about this "war news" that I can't hardly sit still long enough to write this letter.

Your loving son–Cyril

Following the end of fighting there was a payday to remember. Not only did the paymaster pay us up to date, but the war was over! Most everyone had money. In an old masonry building I found eight of my friends lying on the floor, playing five-card stud poker.

Archie said, "Burt, come play my hand while I go to the can." All the guys got strange looks on their faces as I took over, wondering if this Mormon kid from Idaho knew anything about poker. No doubt they thought Archie's money would be gone when he got back.

Little did they realize that my brother Gene and I had spent hours in the old Ace Pool Hall in the little town of Council, Idaho, watching our uncle deal poker. Many were the games Gene and I played to see who would do the chores at night. I pretended ignorance.

Each of us anted up a white chip and received two cards. I had aces wired! "Your bet, Burt." I tossed out a white chip, worth a dollar. Everyone called the bet, until it got around to Halpin, who announced "I'll call, and raise you ten dollars," confidently pitching in two red chips. I called his bet and we received a third card. With a pair of aces in sight and Halpin having a pair of kings, I knew I was high. I stayed with him. Then Halpin raised things considerably. The fourth card dealt gave me a jack and Halpin a seven. Poker-faced, I threw out another white chip. Halpin called and raised. The fifth card was dealt. I knew I had the winning hand, but I still bet just one dollar. Full of certainty, Halpin raised the ante $80.00. Everyone dropped out but the two of us. I slid all Archie's remaining chips to the center. "I'm betting all of Archie's money on this hand."

Was I bluffing, or did I have an ace in the hole? He sat quietly, then finally slid in all his chips.

Aces full beat kings full. I raked in the chips as Halpin cursed. When Archie came back and saw how much I had improved his net worth, his eyes really got big, and I gave him back his seat.

The brass was generous with passes to Venezia (Venice), and a group of us visited that romantic and historic city.

Two days later the first sergeant came to four of us. "Put on your glad rags, you are going back to Venice." A soldier from one of the gun batteries had been accused of raping an Italian girl the day we had been in Venice. The police wanted us to stand in a line-up to see if the girl could identify who did it. I felt the soldier had probably been wrongly accused. At the police station, a frightened little girl, about ten years old, came into the room and looked us over. All of us dressed alike seemed to confuse her, and she was not sure which was perpetrator. I thought to myself, *If that dirty rat raped this little girl, I hope they hang him!* The mother was brought into the room, and she ran screaming to the accused. The police took him away.

I did not have enough points to go home. It required 85 points, and I had just 59. I was sent to Torino, in Italy's northwest.

Luckily, my guardian angel watched over me as closely during the months after the war ended as he did while I was in combat. Letters from home said Maxine was dating other guys. Torino was teeming with beautiful women and excitement. The battalion commander wanted me to drive him to Torino to attend an officer's party. I planned to drop him off, find a date and take in the town. *Why not?* I thought. *Maxine isn't waiting for me any longer.*

As we pulled up to where his party was being held, the captain said, "Wait for me, I'll only be a few minutes." Three hours later I was still waiting, and it was time to take the captain back to camp. I was mad as a hornet.

I finally amassed enough points to go home. I boarded the *USS Johnny Wannamaker,* an unfitted Liberty ship, with a crew of about sixty men and fewer than twenty passengers, on 7 December 1945.

Out in the Atlantic we ran into a powerful storm. The first mate said he had sailed that ocean for thirty years and never witnessed one like it. Riding over the crest of large waves, the ship's propellor would come out of the water, causing the ship to shudder and shake as if it was falling apart. It was slow going. We had anticipated arriving in the United States in just a week.

On 28 December we finally came within sight of land. We could see the buildings of Newport News, Virginia. A signal light began flashing a message. The guys shouted for me to decipher it. Through tears I read: "To the *USS Johnny Wannamaker*—Pilot boarding shortly—tell veterans aboard 'Welcome Home!'"

During the war, Cyril Burt kept a copy of this MIA theme card and scripture with him and read it regularly: "Be strong and of a good courage; be not afraid, neither be thou dismayed: for the Lord thy God is with thee whithersoever thou goest" (Joshua 1:9). M. I. A. Theme, 1942-43
After two years, seven months, and seven days, Cyril Burt returned

to Idaho. He and Maxine Hobbs were soon married in the Idaho Falls Temple. He worked at several jobs, became a farm machinery salesman, and eventually bought a farm machinery dealership in Rexburg.

He has served in a variety of positions in the Church, including an ordinance worker in the Idaho Falls Temple. Cyril also served for six years in the Idaho State Legislature. He and Maxine served a mission together to the San Jose California Mission. They have a raised family of seven children, one of whom died. He and Maxine now have thirty-one grandchildren and eleven great-grandchildren. Cyril served in the bishopric of one of the wards on the Ricks College campus.

Taken from Cyril Burt's personal history.

ASAEL TALL, MD

After my induction, I was assigned to Fort Lewis, Washington, where I took military training, did surgery, and got in shape for overseas duty. We did not know where we were going and most of all, we did not know for how long. My wife, Eva, came to Fort Lewis to be with me, while our children, Marilyn and Bruce, stayed with their grandparents in Idaho. After a time we were placed under secret orders, and all wives had to go home.

On one of the last Sunday nights, I went to hear Elder Hugh B. Brown speak. I remember him saying: "Some of you, I'm sorry to say, will not be coming back. Every one of you men should be living your religion to the fullest. Don't start smoking and drinking. The Lord will bless you."

On Mother's day, 12 May 1943, we were ordered aboard ship at Newport News, Virginia.

I was decidedly nervous about crossing the Atlantic. German submarines had sunk many of our troop ships. Before embarking, I went to a private place, got down on my knees, and with bowed head, pled with my Maker for a safe voyage.

Troops were segregated in those days. About an hour before we were to board ship, our commanding officer asked for ten doctors to volunteer to board a Negro ship. My tentmate volunteered, and the C.O. said "Ace, will you go also?" We boarded a large "dollar line" ship, the *President Roosevelt.* I had beautiful quarters. We ate in a dining room with tablecloths and silverware. It was Army chow, but it was good. It took three weeks to zigzag our way across the Atlantic. The fellows who stayed on the other ship were not so well taken care of. I remembered to thank the Lord for our safe passage and favorable circumstances.

On Thanksgiving day we moved across the Mediterranean to Naples, Italy. We sailed at night in a Red Cross ship with all its lights on. We soon had a new hospital set up on the banks of the Volturno River, about five miles east of Caserta. We were close to the front now. We agreed with someone who said "You could get killed in this war!" We had long wooden buildings for our patients. Our surgery was a nice milk barn, cleaned up and covered inside with white cloth.

Before long I was transferred to the 64th General Hospital at Florence where I was assigned to do surgery in a hospital that was a converted German airplane factory. My nurse and sergeant came with me. I became very busy. My first cases were to dig shrapnel from the backs and legs of soldiers, but I was soon given more serious cases. For one stretch of nineteen days I was at the amputation table. That was tough and sad for me, but it gave me valuable experience. It was while I was with this unit that I was introduced to the newest "wonder drug," penicillin. It was the color of dark vinegar and used mostly to treat gonorrhea, 5cc in each buttocks, on admission. We tried it out on prisoners and found it effective in treating infections.

Early in 1944, I rejoined my own hospital unit. At Bologna we moved the German medical personnel out and took over a private hospital operated by the Bologna City Medical School. This was a fine facility, and we stayed here until the war ended. We were continually busy. We performed surgery every day and many at nights, too. We roomed in a large, lovely Italian home, where we had bathtubs and toilets, but we still slept on cots. Between heavy battles, a few of us at a time would go on trips. One weekend we went to Venice. Lake Como was one of the most beautiful places of all.

On one occasion an Italian civilian was brought into the hospital, his bowels hanging out, which were full of dirt and debris. The hospital commander asked me to do what I could for him. In cleaning him up I noted that his intestines were full of worms. It had been some time since his injury, and despite all we could do, he died.

Wounds were not the only problem suffered by our men in battle. Many of them came in for hernias and appendectomies.

Christmas Eve 1944 was the first time in two years that I was able to take the sacrament. The meeting was held in a room at the USO, with an LDS chaplain conducting. The organist was a WAC, a former Catholic and convert to the Church. It

Dr. Asael Tall, circa 1942

was wonderful to enjoy the company of Latter-day Saints again and to hear their testimonies and prayers.

Due to the intense demands to care for the wounded, my spare time was very limited. I rarely had the opportunity to attend church and didn't know where any groups met. But someone knew that I was there. One day an LDS chaplain came to the hospital. "I understand you have a Mormon doctor here. I want to talk to him." A young man from the chaplain's hometown had stepped on a land mine. The explosion had damaged his liver, and he had been brought to our hospital. My visitor asked me if I were worthy to give a blessing. I said I thought I was. He asked me what priesthood office I held. I replied that I was a seventy.

We went to the young man's room. I noted that his skin was yellowed and he was awfully sick. I anointed and the chaplain sealed the anointing and pronounced a blessing. In the same room with this boy was another soldier who had had surgery. When we finished, the second man asked who we were. I replied that we were Mormons. He said, "Can you pray over me like you did him?" We said we'd be happy to.

I don't know how this non-member soldier found out that I lived in Rigby, Idaho. Years later I received a letter from him in which he reminded me of that night in Bologna when we had "prayed over him." He could not remember the name of our church, so I sent him some pamphlets. He asked to meet with the missionaries. I believe he subsequently joined the Church.

The war in Italy ended 2 May 1945. We had many prisoners to examine and send to German units for medical attention.

I was sent to the beautiful resort city, Bolzano in Northern Italy, as part of the Army of Occupation. We lived in a wonderful hotel with good food and little more to do than hold sick call each morning and afternoon, and to inspect kitchens for both the U.S. troops and German prisoners. Sometime during this period a dinner party was held. There were eighteen doctors there with eighteen English nurses. This made me so uncomfortable that I could not enjoy myself.

In mid-September 1945, my orders came to leave for Livorno. I had plenty of points to go home. After thirty-two months overseas I was going home where I could see my wonderful wife and kids! Marilyn was now thirteen-years old and Bruce eleven. I could hardly wait.

I caught a ship from Livorno to New York. We arrived in New York harbor on 8 October 1945. The Statue of Liberty was a beautiful thing, much bigger than I thought. We were met by Red Cross ladies who inquired if I would like something to drink. I replied, "Do you have a glass of milk?" Boy, did it taste good! That evening we were given a nice steak dinner.

Asael Tall returned to Idaho and opened a medical practice in Rigby with his twin brother Aldin. Asael and his wife, Eva, are parents of three sons and a daughter. They have fourteen grandchildren and thirty-three great-grandchildren.

In the Church Asael served as both ward and stake Sunday School president, high priest group leader, and many times as gospel doctrine teacher.

Asael passed away 30 March 2001.

OPERATION OVERLORD: THE INVASION OF FRANCE, D–DAY, 6 JUNE 1944

While the overall invasion was considered highly successful, the U.S. troops at Omaha Beach suffered many casualties.

Oh, thus be it ever when free men shall stand, between their loved homes and the wars desolation.

("The Star-Spangled Banner," *Hymns*, no. 340)

Leaders of Allied forces hoped the invasion of France could take place as early as November 1942, but we were not ready. Soldiers and Airmen had to be recruited. It takes considerable time and effort to train and equip a civilian to be the solid soldier necessary to destroy a fierce foe.

For two years, men and materiel poured into England. Everything—bandages, bullets, tanks, Jeeps, gas masks, rations, weapons, fuel, airplanes, and Higgins boats—was stockpiled. Then on D-Day, it was all transported across the Channel and onto the beachheads in France. But this took time. German Field Marshall Rommel also continued amassing supplies, erecting steel barriers, planting mines, and pouring concrete into bunkers.

By the time American military men arrived in England, they had been very well trained; nonetheless they were given additional training and instruction to hone their skills so that they could be even more effective as they joined the Allied Expeditionary Force for this climactic battle. Two million men, from England, the United States, France, Poland, and other nations, took part; it was the greatest mass movement of troops in the history of the British and American armies. Troops were transported to the battle zone by navy ships, airplanes, and some aboard plywood (Horsa) gliders. All this was assembled in southern England during the first days of June, but weather delayed departure.

On the morning of June 5th General Erwin Rommel left Normandy for Germany to attend a birthday party for his wife and to consult with Hitler. That night, after receiving a somewhat favorable weather briefing, General Eisenhower polled his senior commanders. They were divided. It was for "Ike" to decide. After some last minute soul-searching, Eisenhower said quietly, but clearly, "OK, let's go." Immediately the execution of this bold yet carefully conceived operation began to unfold.

The objective of the battle plan was to put enough Allied troops on French soil the first day to provide a base to sustain the invasion of Europe. That was essentially achieved, but to say that it went off exactly as planned would be untrue. Changing circumstances on the Cherbourg Peninsula required ingenuity and initiative by individuals on the scene. It was such ingenuity and initiative that carried the day. Things went reasonably well at Utah, Gold, Sword, and Juno beaches, but very badly at Omaha. Early on that first day, nothing went well for the Americans at Omaha Beach. As wave upon wave of infantry landed, most of them seasick and miserable, thousands were slaughtered by gunfire from the heights they'd expected to be subdued by bombs and naval bombardment. Overburdened with equipment, men drowned when they stepped off the landing craft into water over their heads. Accidents happened. Fear paralyzed some. Landing craft could not find assigned landing sites, officers and non-coms were killed, units that had trained together were scattered, and when men got to the beach they were confused, dispirited, and without leadership. Very few got to the beaches with their equipment. They had dumped it to avoid perishing in the surf. Tanks, Jeeps, dozers, and other mobile equipment were lost in the deep water. Men, bunched on the beach, were targets for the enemy. Chaos reigned and blood flowed.

Amidst all this fury, many seized the initiative and struck out on their own to climb the cliffs and attack the entrenched defenders. Officers organized those they found around them. Innumerable gallant and courageous acts were performed.

It was the Navy that finally turned the tide at Omaha Beach. Destroyers began firing at targets on the bluffs, and their five-inch guns silenced most of the ruthless German weapons. This allowed the infantry to get atop the bluffs and come in from behind the German defenders. It was then possible to get our troops inland. In the days that followed, thousands of men and tons of equipment and supplies came ashore across this bloodied ground.

Ernie Pyle, the Pulitzer Prize-winning correspondent of World War II, described the scene at Omaha Beach a few days after the landing:

> The wreckage was vast and startling. The awful waste and destruction of war, even aside from the loss of human life, has always been one of its outstanding features to those who are in it. Anything and everything is expendable. And we did expend on our beachhead in Normandy during those first few hours.

For a mile out from the beach there were scores of tanks and trucks and boats that you could no longer see, for they were at the bottom of the water—swamped by overloading, or hit by shells, or sunk by mines. Most of their crews were lost. . . . On the beach itself, high and dry, were all kinds of wrecked vehicles. . . .

In the water floated empty life rafts and soldiers' packs and ration boxes, and mysterious oranges. On the beach lay snarled rolls of telephone wire and big rolls of steel matting and stacks of broken, rusting rifles. . . .

But there was another and more human litter. It extended in a thin little line, just like a high-water mark, for miles along the beach. This was the strewn personal gear, gear that would never be needed again by those who fought and died to give us our entrance into Europe.

There in a jumbled row for mile on mile were soldiers' packs. There were socks and shoe polish, sewing kits, diaries, Bibles, hand grenades. There were the latest letters from home, with the addresses of each one razored out—one of the security precautions enforced before the boys embarked.

Soldiers carry strange things ashore with them. In every invasion there is at least one soldier at H-hour with a banjo slung over his shoulder. The most ironic piece of equipment marking our beach—this beach first of despair, then of victory—was a tennis racket that some soldier had brought along. It lay lonesomely on the sand, clamped in its press, not a string broken (*Brave Men*, pp. 250–251, Reprinted by permission).

ELWYN A. MEYER

Our ten-man crew had picked up a new B-24G at Topeka, Kansas, and flown to England, arriving 21 April 1944. On what has become known as D-Day we were to fly our fifth mission over Europe. There was profound excitement as we met and the briefing officers uncovered the map of France that pinpointed where we were to lay down our bombs. My job as navigator was to know the exact routes in and out of the target area and to ensure that we arrived and departed on schedule. Our bombing was coordinated with a huge naval bombardment that was to precede the landings. No bombs were to be dropped later than 0545 hours because ground troops would then begin going ashore at Utah, Omaha, Sword, and Juno. We were instructed that we were not to return with any bombs aboard our aircraft.

Elwyn Meyer after 8th combat mission with 44th Bomb Group, 68th Squadron. Shipdam, England. June, 1944.

We departed Shipdam Air Base at 0345 and climbed to 12,000 feet. Weather across the English Channel included intermittent rain and solid cloud cover. We came in in a good, tight formation, although no two aircraft were from the same group, and dropped our bomb load over the beach at 0545. After returning to base, we flew another mission that same day, departing at 1430 hours. It was a very big day for us. By the time we returned that night, the air traffic controllers had to turn on the field lights to show us the way home.

We continued bombing support on the Normandy Peninsula for some time. On D-Day plus three weeks we did a saturation bombing near Caen with 100-pound bombs to allow an advance by troops led by British General Montgomery.

(Elwyn's other experiences in the war are continued on page 232.)

CLINTON V. MURDOCK

Clinton Murdock, Air Corps 2nd
Lieutenant, 1943

The last week of May many paratroopers arrived at our base near Nottingham. On 2 June our unit was put in a compound and kept isolated. We were to have gone on the 4th, but bad weather caused a delay. On 5 June, at 2200 hours, we took off, carrying paratroopers for a drop behind enemy lines. We proceeded south over the Isle of Wight to a point just off the Cherbourg Peninsula, then northeast, over the peninsula. We dropped the paratroopers. As we broke formation, I stayed on the squadron commander's wing. We were in and out of cloud cover and drawing enemy fire. Headed east, we crossed back over the beachhead. From an enemy bunker near the shore line we could see tracers coming at our plane as their gunners attempted to zero in on us. Somehow, I made it back to England without a hole in my plane. Others were not so fortunate. Our operations officer and his crew were shot down and killed. As I was assistant operations officer I became acting Ops officer.

The night of 6 June, we left for our second mission at 1900 hours, towing two gliders. Approaching the beach we met intense antiaircraft fire. We had hoped that our troops had secured this area before we got there, but that was not the case. We were under fire all the way in and back out of our drop zone.

As we passed over the beach on the return flight, one engine started to run away. I tried to feather it, but it would not respond. The oil pressure on that engine was gone. The prop started windmilling, and at this point one engine was not enough to hold us up. We slowly descended toward the Channel. Preparing to ditch, we tried cutting the engine back in to see what would happen. It worked, and we climbed until the prop started going too fast and had to be shut off to keep it from flying apart. Repeating this procedure we gradually gained altitude. Then the prop got to sticking and finally stopped altogether, but we had managed to climb to 1,100 feet. At this altitude one engine kept us airborne until we were across the English Channel, and we landed at an English airfield on the Isle of Wight.

Of the twelve planes that left from our unit earlier that night, only two returned to Welford; two ditched in the ocean and the rest of us landed on the first airfield we could find.

I waited with the plane for two weeks until the engine was replaced. During that time other members of our outfit flew supplies to forward areas of the combat zone in France. I made one trip to France with supplies before I was sent to Italy.

(Clinton's other experiences in the war are continued on page 212.)

QUENTIN C. MURDOCK

Now they never had fought, yet they did not fear death; and they did think more upon the liberty of their fathers than they did upon their lives; yea, they had been taught by their mothers, that if they did not doubt, God would deliver them. And they rehearsed unto me the words of their mothers, saying: We do not doubt our mothers knew it.

(Alma 56:47-48)

When the fighting in Sicily ended, I was returned to England. Our unit was designated to participate in the initial invasion of Europe. This was to be my third major invasion.

Doctors finally diagnosed malaria and put me on quinine, which controlled my recurring sickness.

During the buildup for the D-Day invasion, we had no knowledge of where or when it was to take place. Equipment, personnel, supplies, armaments, and bombs filled warehouses and spilled over, and tanks and various kinds of olive drab military vehicles were parked in the streets, beneath trees. Some thought England would sink under the weight. I was transferred to 1st Battalion Headquarters as the motor officer. My job was to get vehicles loaded for transport to the invasion site, each with the proper supplies. With my invasion experience in Africa and Sicily, I knew some of the things to expect. I also participated in further intensive training. We knew that this would be a vicious fight. Just before the jumping off date, my life was complicated by another recurrence of malaria.

About a week before D-Day, we were called into the staging area for a briefing. Maps detailing the "where" were laid out for us; the "when" we knew was close, but not yet decided. The day before loading, I became violently ill. The regimental surgeon saw me and told me I could not go with the invasion forces. I argued that I was trained, that I had seen the plans, that I must go, they were counting on me. I asked him for some quinine and said that with that I would be all right. I did not, in any way, want to be seen as a sluggard. The doctor reluctantly agreed.

There is no way to adequately describe this invasion experience. In another of the long stretch of firsts, the 16th Infantry Regiment was the first on the beach. Casualties were staggering. I did not go in with the vehicles, but arrived in the second wave, with the battalion commander, minutes behind the first wave.

Already bodies littered the beach; many more were floating in the water. The water washing onto the beach began to have a pink cast. I jumped into chest-deep water and started for shore. Bullets flying past us sounded like a swarm of bees. I dove under the water, wishing I had a snorkel. After about fifty yards I stood on land. Bullets snapped around me and mines detonated. Some of our men were torn apart. Artillery shells landed everywhere. It was a grisly scene.

The citation accompanying our 3rd Presidential Unit award describes the action that day:

On the morning of 6 June 1944, the *16th Infantry Regiment* under the most adverse conditions assaulted the coast of France near Colleville-sur-Mer against a long prepared, determined, and powerfully emplaced enemy. While moving inshore in assault craft, violent seas swamped the regiment's supporting weapons and hurled men and boats into the intricate and almost impenetrable barriers of mine-capped underwater obstacles. From commanding and numerous reinforced concrete pill boxes, machine gun emplacements, and sniper's nests imbedded in cliffsides . . . came a withering hail of artillery and small arms fire that struck down hundreds as they struggled through shoulder-deep water toward the beach.

Within a few hours almost a third of the assault strength were casualties. Men dragged themselves shoreward leaderless and scattered by the loss of key personnel. Blocked from advancing by minefields, pinned down by annihilating fire, wave after wave piled up on a 7-yard wide beachhead until thousands of men lay huddled on the fire-swept shore.

In the face of an apparently hopeless situation, the *16th Infantry Regiment* began its reorganization.

Countless acts of gallantry took place in the face of the superior enemy fire. Men lay in the flat, mine-strewn meadows in plain view of the enemy and returned the direct fire of protected enemy artillery and machine guns with rifle and rocket launcher fire. Leaderless men attached themselves to the forming groups. A breach was blown in the wire and the regiment advanced. Human mine markers lay in the mine fields guiding the passage of the battling troops. With grim determination, suffering terrible casualties, the regiment forced its way forward in a frontal assault on five principle enemy strong points. They engaged the enemy and in a magnificent display of courage and will to win, destroyed them.

The breach opened by the *16th Infantry Regiment* was the main personnel exit for the V Corps for forty-eight hours. Battered to a terrible degree the regiment continued its advance toward its initial objective. They drove back a fanatically resisting enemy and repulsed five separate counterattacks by numerically superior forces until the 1st Division and V Corps beachhead was secured.

We got our vehicles onto Omaha Beachhead. After I thought the area had been cleared, I saw a place where we could move our vehicles to. I walked across an open field and had instructed my unit to bring the vehicles when I signaled. As I was crossing the field a bullet whistled past my ear and struck a tree. I jumped behind the tree. It was quiet and in a few minutes I continued. I gave the signal, but no one appeared. *Where were they?* Agitated, I started back and met them coming. Why had they been so long? I asked. They said they had to stop and capture fifty German soldiers hidden in the trench I had just walked past.

Because of my assignment with the motor vehicles, my platoon was turned over to another officer. During the invasion almost all of my platoon were killed. Of our original group, fewer than five survived. The facts are stark testimony of the terrible battle.

* * *

Quentin Murdock (second from right) with some Army buddies in England, just before the invasion of Normandy. His regiment hit the beaches in the first wave, and three of his friends from this picture died there, as did almost the entire regiment.

After I had been in France for about a month, my malaria recurred. I was sent to a field hospital filled with wounded men. I was sick, but not wounded, and I didn't want to stay there, so I went back to my unit. There I met the regimental surgeon, who wanted to know what I was doing there. "You're sick! You should not be here!" "I'm not going back. I'm okay," I told him. He was a colonel. He ordered me to go back, and I told him I wouldn't. "I'll go to the regimental commander and have him issue a written order sending you to back to the hospital." And that's just what he did.

He may have saved my life. In the hospital I discovered how sick I was. I was flown to a military hospital in Texas. After some time at a hospital there I was given leave to go home. It was so good to see my parents and family. At home I again became violently ill, seriously frightening Mother and Dad. I was transferred to Bushnell Army Hospital at Brigham City, Utah. After I recovered, I was shipped to a troop training center in Texas. There was a need for a decorated soldier to go on a War Bond campaign, and I was selected. I was in Indiana when the war ended.

For many years after the war I struggled with the question as to why I escaped death or injury. I experienced so many narrow escapes. Once, in Africa, I crossed back and forth through a continuing field of machine gun fire that should have ripped me to shreds. Many times bullets killed those close to me. I remember walking through mine fields and seeing associates killed. Somehow I missed stepping on a mine; artillery shells exploded beside me, yet I remained unscathed. The protection was so constant that I was not fully aware of it when it was taking place. Thinking back on my experiences, I wondered, *Why me?* For years the question was never far from my mind.

One night I was awakened from my sleep, and in what is to me a very sacred experience, was given to know that it was my mother's *prayers* that saved me. I still cannot answer what made my mother's prayers so effective in my behalf when other mother's prayers were answered in a different manner, but since that time I have been at peace about that question.

For conspicuous gallantry in action, 1st Lieutenant Quentin C. Murdock was awarded our nation's third highest military decoration, the Silver Star. He also holds two Bronze Stars for gallantry.

Following his discharge, Quentin returned to Idaho. He served as a county agent for a time, then bought sagebrush land west of Rockford, Idaho, where he has farmed since. He considers himself a third generation pioneer in Bingham County, as both his father and grandfather had taken up sagebrush farmland. He helped pioneer deep-well pump irrigation and the use of sprinkler systems. He was among the first to use wastes from the potato processing industry as cattle feed and helped develop improved methods for sand farming on the Ft. Hall Indian Reservation. For his outstanding contributions to agriculture, Quentin was inducted into the Idaho Agricultural Hall of Fame in March 1989. He and his wife, Meiko, are parents to two daughters and two sons. They have been ordinance workers in the Idaho Falls Temple since 1986.

B. JAY RENCHER

I will go before your face. I will be on your right hand and on your left, and my Spirit shall be in your heart, and mine angels round about you.

(Doctrine & Covenants 84:88)

I graduated from Snowflake High School in 1943. At that time the Church was not calling young men on missions because of the war. I got a surveying job that paid pretty good money, so I decided to stay with that until I was drafted.

I was with the first group of eighteen-year olds drafted from Arizona. Because of my surveying experience, the Army put me with the engineers. I went to Fort Leonard Wood, Missouri, and then Fort Belvoir, Virginia, for training. After eight months I was sent to a survey group in England—the 531st Amphibious Battalion. I had no idea what they were, but supposed we would help survey roads and lay out airports, and do all those things that have to be done to support the planes in the military.

After joining the 531st I learned that it had been hand-picked by General Eisenhower to help crack the beachhead of Europe. Previously my unit had made the invasions of Africa, Sicily, and southern Italy and was the most experienced of any amphibious outfit in the world. We went to France on D-Day, 6 June 1944, with the 4th Infantry Division to Utah Beach. The area behind Utah Beach was wine and orchard country, and we didn't have the hedgerows to contend with like those at Omaha Beach.

B. Jay Rencher

We were a specialized outfit. Our job was to ensure the success of the invasion by clearing the way onto the beaches. The planners expected seventy-five percent of the invasion force to be killed the first hour. Therefore, they told us, we are making this unit triple strength in the hope that someone will last long enough to get the job done. Those odds didn't bother me much because I was eighteen-years old and felt I was immortal. If I had to do it now, it would terrify me.

Our battalion was organized into specialty groups, such as mine detection or demolition. During the six months I was in England we practiced mock invasions on British beaches. Generals Eisenhower and Montgomery often came to watch. Many high-ranking officers observed these drills to see how we were handling the job of removing the obstacles and getting the infantry inland and tanks ashore and beyond. We practiced daily until we knew exactly what to do.

Reportedly, General Erwin Rommel said the war would be won between the high and low tide of the beaches of Europe, and he claimed that if he could stop us on the beaches he would win. And he was right. But on D-Day Rommel was killed by a strafing Allied fighter plane while he was returning to Normandy from a birthday party for his wife. His subordinates had not yet learned of his death and would not act without his approval. Had he been there, he would doubtless have brought in his tank divisions to drive us off the beaches.

Our battalion commander insisted, and General Eisenhower agreed, that we be ashore an hour before anybody else landed. H-hour was 0600 hours. We went in at 0500. There was a two-inch stainless steel cable just below the low-tide line to prevent ships from bringing infantrymen ashore. Our first job was to cut that cable. A landing craft brought us up close to the cable and dumped us out into water up to our necks. Our packs were full of specialized equipment: explosives, TNT, composition C, plastic explosives, and mine detectors. We also carried rifles and ammunition.

About midnight on 5 June, the Air Force began dropping specially trained men of the 82nd and 101st Airborne into the area inland of the beach. These two divisions were very effective in preventing the Germans from bringing up reinforcements. The Navy's big ships bombarded the shoreline for an hour before we landed, to knock out as much of the shore defenses from our path as they could. Two companies of us landed to begin clearing the way for infantry and other units, which would follow us. Each company was assigned about a half mile of beach.

The Germans had big steel structures in the water between the high and low tide levels so that any incoming ships would have their bottoms ripped out of them and sink. We removed these by wrapping plastic explosive around the middle of those big spiders, as we named them, and detonating it. We had a name for everything we were blowing up: "dragon's gate," "dragon's teeth," and "spiders." There were also big concrete pillars with knives set in the tops of them, also designed to cut the bottoms out of ships. To remove these we worked in water up to our necks. We had to clear the barricades out of the way so our landing craft could come to shore, discharge their men and tanks, and get back out safely. That's what we had trained for in England.

We were under sporadic artillery fire, some of which landed very close by. However, that first hour we had fewer casualties and less interference than at any other time during that first day.

The Germans apparently didn't realize we were the invasion force. I suppose they could see that big armada of ships out in the ocean, but our Naval bombardment kept them down in their bomb shelters. Occasionally, those in a machine gun nest would blast away at us.

We concentrated on a small area at a time, and as we cleared it, we put up a big square flourescent marker to indicate where it was safe to land. Finally the beach was opened up, ready for the infantry to arrive.

When we had blown up all the metal obstructions, posts, and concrete pillars, we started to clear the minefield behind the dunes, an area about a half-mile wide. If an infantryman or a vehicle tried to cross this field before it was unblocked, they would be blown up.

We worked in groups of three. Our three were Otis Hamm, Dave Shallenberger of Youngstown, Ohio, and me. We were just getting started when a German machine gun crew in a concrete emplacement in back of the beach opened fire on us. We dived under some of the pillars we had toppled. Earlier, I left fifty pounds of TNT at the base of a dune a short distance away. Dave also had fifty pounds. "Keep shooting at that machine gun bunker," I said. "I'll see if I can get my TNT and slip around back of that bunker and blow it up." They gave me covering fire, and I grabbed the two packs of TNT and dragged them up into the dunes.

I set the TNT against the pill box, lit the fuse, and ran. About fifty yards away I lay down, opened my mouth and screamed as hard as I could to equalize the pressure in my eardrums. The explosion blew that pill box half way to the ocean.

The main German force was about a mile-and-a-half inland. When they saw the three of us with a mine detector, they began firing at us with 88 millimeter artillery—which is fairly large, and they were deadly accurate. The 88 was a fantastic weapon; it was their antiaircraft gun, their anti-tank gun and their anti-personnel piece. In this situation you had to work by instinct; there was no time to think.

I was out in front with the detector, and Dave and Otis were about fifty feet behind me. When I found a mine I tied a rope on it. They would find the rope, pull the mine out, and disable it by pinning the detonator.

We were just getting a good start when we heard an artillery shell. I knew from the sound it would miss us, but the next landed right in the middle of us. I didn't feel anything hit me, but I sure wondered how it could have missed.

Otis was moaning, and as I ran back to help him, I saw that Dave was not moving. My first thought was that Dave was overcome with terror. Otis's leg was mangled so badly that the only thing holding his foot on was his shoe lace. He was in serious trouble, and I knew I had to get him to the aid station.

I ran over to Dave and said, "Dave, we've got to get Otis to the aid station." He didn't respond. I shook him and his helmet rolled off his head. A piece of shrapnel had hit him in the temple and he died instantly. I grabbed Otis and began dragging him back the best I could. Then a couple of infantrymen, who had just landed, helped me get him to the aid station.

I said to them, "Come with me, I need your help." We crawled back to the mine field. "Don't stand up. Not for one second, or we'll all get killed. I'll find a mine, tie a rope to it. You pull it out and insert the pin in it, like this," I instructed. "Put it over to the side of the road. Then run this ribbon along the ground so the tank drivers and infantrymen know exactly where the mines are and where they're not," demonstrating all this as I spoke. "We've got to open a road. There are men and vehicles that need to get off this beach. Let's go!" That's all the training those two got.

In about thirty or forty minutes, crawling on our bellies alligator fashion across the sand, we'd gone the other hundred yards, cleared away the remaining mines and marked the boundaries with ribbons. "Don't stand up to walk out of here to tell your buddies what you just did. You *crawl* back to your buddies! Tell them these ribbons are to mark the road and that they must stay between those ribbons or they're dead!" The three of us crawled back to where their unit was.

By then a few tanks were coming. I went to the tank commanders and cautioned them, "That's your only road out of here. Stay between those ribbons and get out of here or the Germans will blow you to smithereens." A couple of other roads had also been cleared. The word had gotten to the others real fast that you couldn't pick your way through a minefield standing up. You clear a minefield lying flat on your belly.

With the mines cleared, the tanks and infantry got off the beach within minutes of their landing. I think this saved a lot of lives because our troops were able to get behind the German gun emplacements and find cover. We had that beachhead established within two hours after we hit the beach. Infantry landing on the beach were a mile inland within three hours of their arrival. By the end of the first day, we even received a hot meal.

When I got time, I went back to the aid station to check on Otis. Doctors had had to amputate both his legs. They told me that when he came out of the anesthesia and saw that his legs were gone, he declared, "I won't be a cripple all my life," and lay back down and died. The doctor said there was no reason he could not have lived, had he had the determination. So both of my buddies died on that beachhead the first day of the invasion. When we built the roads through the dunes and the mine fields, we named them for men who had died; there was one road named Shallenburger and another named Hamm.

It is impossible to express how badly I felt when they were killed. We had worked and trained together until they were like brothers, except for some of their habits and the way they talked were different because they had not been raised LDS. But there was a bond, and it was mighty strong. We had developed the utmost confidence that we would each do exactly what we were supposed to.

***

In the weeks following the invasion, when we thought the Germans weren't coming as often, we started sleeping out on the sand in our pup-tents. I've always been a sound sleeper. One morning I rolled out of my tent, dressed and walked over to the cook truck where I noticed bullet holes in the sand next to my tent. I asked the guys walking with me when that had happened. They told me that it was during the night. "Weren't you in your hole?" "No," I answered. "I was asleep in my tent."

***

After we finished with Normandy, an amphibious battalion was no longer needed, and since there so few of us left, we were sent to a replacement center. I was assigned to General Hodges 14th Armored Division as a combat engineer. Our division had three battalions of tanks, one of infantry, and one of engineers. The job of the engineers was to clear away any obstacle that would stop the tanks. If we had to retreat, we laid land mines; if there was a bridge, we blew it up. If we were advancing, we sometimes had to rebuild the bridges we had blown up and clear away the mines we had sown.

When the Germans pushed through the Ardennes Forest into France in December 1944, we had to pull back several miles to avoid being cut off by their advance. As we did, we blew trees across roads to slow German progress. We also dynamited a two hundred-foot-long bridge over a river. We came to another river where the Germans had blown a bridge and constructed a pontoon bridge to replace it.

Near the village of Hauten, along the so-called Siegfried Line inside Germany, I was wounded. We had a terrible time pushing the Germans out of this area. We got a call from a tank unit to blow some debris that was blocking a road. A couple of squads of us, about twenty men, were sent forward. Each of us carried fifty pounds of TNT on our backs and an M-1 rifle. The information we had was that the Germans had been pushed out of the area where the road block was and that we would encounter little or no resistence. We felt reasonably secure.

The tankers had told us that Hauten was clear of Germans, and it probably was when the tankers went through. But the Germans had returned with reinforcements. We saw them patrolling the streets, and they had established a machine gun emplacement out in a hay field. We found ourselves in the middle of a German offensive. We decided this was no place for a bunch of men with only fifty pounds of TNT on our backs and no support other than our rifles.

Suddenly we came under fire from the machine gun nest. Our lead men dived for cover along the edge of the road, but they could not get their packs below ground level. My buddy, just ahead of me, crawled back to where I was, and I counted three bullet holes in his back pack. Bullets had gone through the TNT he carried. That was one of the reasons we used TNT: it cannot be set off by shooting it; it has to be detonated with a cap.

One of the men in our unit was a red-headed guy from Texas, one of the sorriest excuses of a man living, but absolutely fearless. I watched in amazement as he jumped up, his M-1 in hand, and charged the machine gun, his rifle spitting bullets which made those manning the machine gun duck for cover. When he got to the gun emplacement, an empty clip popped out of his gun. He knew that if he reached back for another clip they would know his rifle was empty and they'd pick him off. He had no chance in the world to reload that gun and stay alive. Still running hard, his rifle aimed at them, he yelled, "Krauts, get out!" They threw their hands in the air and surrendered! He marched those guys back to where we were, wiped the sweat off his brow and exclaimed, "Wow!" Then he took a clip out of his pack, jammed it in his gun and proclaimed, "Now I'm ready for them!"

The Germans had us badly outgunned; there was a whole enemy company in front of us with machine guns and mortars. Dividing into groups of three, we began a retreat. The best route seemed to be along the edge of the houses. As we moved from house to house, one of us would go up to the second floor where we could see the Germans. We took turns providing covering fire while the others ran to the next house. It was my turn to provide cover. As the other two came out of the house, some Germans began firing a mortar at us from a nearby hill. A shell landed behind my buddies just as they took off. Now it was my turn to run.

The minute I came out of that house, a mortar shell dropped about ten feet behind me. I felt something hit my leg, but since I could still move all right, I ran harder. Every thirty yards or so a mortar shell would land behind me, and each time, my speed increased.

When I got to the house with other men of our own company, there was a Jeep and a medic. Blood was running out of my pant leg onto the floor. "I think I need a little attention," I said to the medic. He cut my pant leg open, looked at my leg, and said, "We better get you back to an aid station, but you're not going to bleed to death. We'll put you in the Jeep and try to get you out of here." He and two others who had been wounded got in the Jeep and we got out. I spent a couple of weeks in the hospital, then I rejoined my unit in late April, 1945.

* * *

There was a prisoner of war camp at Moosburg, close to where we now were. An order came down that we were to try to liberate that camp, which we were told held 105,000 American and Allied POWs.

We had ninety miles to go with fourteen tanks. On 29 April, we left well before daylight. A mile ahead of us, our combat command had cleared the road of any German opposition and radioed us to "Go for it!" We punched through their line, and as we moved along, tanks were dropped off to cover our rear in case any German forces came in behind us. I and the other engineers rode in a half-track. As we entered Moosburg, two of the remaining tanks stayed at the edge of town to stop any enemy units that might be coming, while the six remaining tanks encircled the prison camp.

We drove our half-track up to the gate and confronted the guards. A German lieutenant and two noncoms held up their hands. They had laid

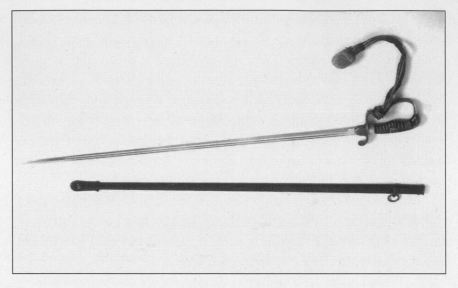

The sword German soldiers surrendered to Jay Rencher at Moosburg POW camp.

their weapons on the ground in front of them. As we collected these, the officer took off his belt, with his sword attached to it, and handed it to me, a lowly PFC.

About that time one of the tank crews hauled down the Nazi flag atop the Moosburg town hall and raised the Stars and Stripes. The town and the encampment was secured by 1400 hours.

The crowd of nearly starved men inside the gate pushed it open with a roar of rejoicing. Through the opened gate thousands of prisoners raced into Moosburg and the surrounding area. Within hours every available pig, chicken and cow had been caught, butchered, and was being cooked.

We'd brought ten days of rations for ourselves and the tank crews in the half-track. It didn't take long until every one of those big boxes had been ripped open and given away. We didn't have anything to eat that night or the next day. But that was all right. The next day trucks brought in plenty of supplies.

***

The Germans never did close the gap our unit made as we raced toward Moosburg. General Patton brought in a whole company of tanks and fortified the road behind us in case the Germans tried to push us back.

But the Germans didn't have any kind of firepower left to pull off any kind of an offensive.

However, we got into a firefight with an SS unit made up of fourteen-, fifteen-, and sixteen-year old kids. They were the fightingest bunch I ever saw. They didn't care if they got killed or wounded—they would not surrender. Everywhere else German Divisions—whole Armies— were surrendering, and we were still fighting like dogs because those kids would not quit.

Finally they withdrew across the Isar River and blew up a bridge. The next day was the 3rd of May, my birthday. We were ordered to go down in that river canyon and build a pontoon bridge. When I looked at that ravine I said to myself: "Rencher, old buddy, you checked in on the 3rd of May and you're going to check out on the 3rd of May. We have no chance in this world." The Germans held all the high ground on the other side. To go down on that river and build a bridge with them shooting down at us was the most preposterous thing I could imagine. It was a suicide mission.

The next morning at 0400 we started for the river, our trucks loaded with pontoons, steel treadway, and everything else needed to build a bridge. We had just started down the dugway to the river and were driving with our blackout lights. Behind us we noticed a guy on a motorbike, his little blackout light also on. When he caught up with the back of the column he asked to speak to the commanding officer. We told him that he was in a Jeep up front.

The column stopped, and the commander walked back along the trucks and told us the news from 7th Army Headquarters, "We feel that the German Army is collapsing. They are surrendering in all areas except this one. There is no need to endanger any more lives—hold the territory you occupy and take no further offensive action. *We think the war is over!*" Boy, when he said that, we pulled out all the flares we always carried and shot them into the air. Machine gun tracer bullets went back and forth in the sky. I'm sure those SS troops on the other side of the river must have wondered what we were doing. These were the last shots we fired in the war. So this eighteen-year old kid from Snowflake, Arizona, fought his way through two of the greatest battles of World War II and made it home. I cannot count the number of times the Lord preserved my life.

After being part of the Army of Occupation in southern Germany, Jay Rencher returned home to Snowflake 23 December 1946. The following is his description of life upon his return: "When I got home I wasn't really interested in getting an education, but when the Congress passed the GI Bill, I decided to go to BYU. That's where I met Louise Burbidge. There was also a feisty little Scotsman, Dean Martin, who insisted that I go to graduate school. He got me a fellowship to attend Rutgers University where I earned a Ph.D. in soil chemistry and plant physiology. I taught at Ricks College for a couple of years, then went to work for the Westinghouse Company at the Idaho Nuclear Energy Laboratory for thirty-five years."

Jay and Louise Rencher are parents of eight children, have thirty-two grandchildren and four great-grandchildren. He has served as Scoutmaster and Explorer leader, stake MIA president, bishop's counselor, and bishop. He and Louise served a mission to the Truk Islands in the Pacific in 1990, and another to Lagos, Nigeria, in 1995. He currently serves as the high priest group leader in his ward in Idaho Falls, Idaho.

Taken from an oral interview with Paul H. Kelly.

NORMAN T. JOHNSON

For the Lord suffereth the righteous to be slain that his justice and judgment may come upon the wicked; therefore ye need not suppose that the righteous are lost because they are slain; but behold, they do enter into the rest of the Lord their God.

(Alma 60:13)

Norman T. Johnson was born almost as World War I ended, 4 November 1918, in Vernal, Utah. He graduated from Uintah High School where he played clarinet in the school band and was active in the Future Farmers of America. He and his brother Duayne worked their father's ranch in the summer. Norman loved the ranch and was a good worker. He attended

Utah State Agricultural College in Logan. From 7 December 1939, to 6 December 1941, he served an LDS mission to the Eastern States. The week he returned from his mission, he volunteered for service in the Army Air Corps and trained as a fighter pilot. He completed basic flying school at Bakersfield, California, and took advanced flight training at Luke Field, Arizona.

Lieutenant Norman T. Johnson, Pursuit Pilot, World War II

While in training Norman and his mother met in San Francisco for a few hours at the home of his aunt. His mother wrote this account.

Toward evening he and I were looking out a large window over the bay—it was nearing sunset. It was a beautiful sight, the sun was sending a soft golden glow over the bay, the bridge, the water, and the shore.

As we looked Norman said, "Mother, I want to tell you something that happened to me over this bay not long ago. I was flying my fighter plane. Our instructor had cautioned us to try never to let these planes go into a spin. Also he instructed us on what we should do in case they did. I was flying quite high, and suddenly my plane went into a spin and began to drop. I worked with all my power and did everything I knew to do. Of course I was praying all the time—but I could not straighten the plane out. I was nearing the water and thought, *Well, this is it* and quit struggling with the controls. At that very instant some other hand than mine had power over the stick and the plane was righted and flew off like a bird."

Norman's first combat assignment after completing his training was in the Aleutian Islands, off the coast of Alaska. Norm said they lost more pilots to the weather there than they did to the Japanese. His mother wrote: "He had some rugged flying experiences there. He missed not being able to attend his church services. Once, while there, he wrote us how he and another elder happened to be together and were able to hold a meeting and partake of the sacrament."

Norman was then transferred to the 492nd Fighter Squadron at Walterboro, South Carolina, for further training in preparation for the invasion of Europe. From South Carolina Norman went to England where he joined the 48th Fighter Group, part of the Ninth Air Force, to train for D-Day. He was now flying the P-47 Thunderbolt.

Norm was with the first wave of airmen to cross the English Channel on that fateful day. On his second mission he was shot down in France. Two days later, on 8 June 1944, he was back in England where he was interviewed by W. W. Chaplin, a war correspondent for NBC Radio. The following is an excerpt of that interview:

CHAPLIN: This is W.W. Chaplin in London. . . . I have here in the studio with me one of the men who has been writing this epic of the skies, writing it in the skies. And he's a rather special case. In the first phase of this invasion literally thousands of our pilots flew to France, did their job there, and then flew back. The pilot who is going to speak to you in just a minute flew to France also, but he didn't fly back. His plane was hit, and he had to make a forced landing right in the battle area. How he got out of that fix I'm going to ask him to tell you himself. . . . This pilot is First Lieutenant Norman T. Johnson of Vernal, Utah, near Salt Lake City. Lieutenant, will you tell us about your experience? Start right at the beginning, if you will. What was your mission yesterday morning?

JOHNSON: Well, I started out pretty early, leading my flight behind our group commander. We were giving close cover to gliders, which were at 1,000 feet. We got over the objective about nine o'clock in the morning, and the gliders were cut loose from the C-47 transports that had been towing them. As soon as we saw the gliders released we turned right to escort the C-47s home. And then my trouble began. My Thunderbolt, "Dangerous Critter," began to sputter, and I began to lose altitude about that time. I got worried and began to look for a landing place.

CHAPLIN: While you were still in the air you must have had a very good view of the ground. What did the part of France where the airborne boys were landed look like on D Plus One?

JOHNSON: I saw the Army engineers moving around clearing the mine fields. I saw one mine explode; the Germans shelling beach positions. The country there looks like New England farm country. On the beaches landing was going on all the time.

CHAPLIN: What you chiefly wanted of course . . . and wanted fast . . . was a place to land. How did you come out on that?

JOHNSON: Well, I skimmed over a long line of trees and made a belly landing in a field, despite poles the Germans had planted there to prevent glider landings. When I got out of the plane I heard some small arms firing pretty close, so I headed into some bushes and kept running for about half a mile. Then I saw some of our paratroopers moving along slowly ahead of me.

CHAPLIN: That must have been a relief. Our own men. Did you head for them on the run?

JOHNSON: No. I jumped into a ditch. I knew they'd never recognize me as an American in my flying suit. They might have fired first and identified me later, so I waved a handkerchief up above the ditch till one of them saw me and beckoned me over. Then ten GI's got around me, every one of them pointing his bayonet at me, and asked me who I was. I said I was American, but that didn't satisfy them.

CHAPLIN: So I suppose you showed them your identification papers.

JOHNSON: That's what they asked for, but we don't carry identification. I showed them my dog tags though, and they accepted that as proof I was okay. They took me back to my plane, but it took us two hours to make that half mile because we were under fire all the way. When I finally examined the plane I found the oil push rod and casing had been broken by a small arms bullet fired from the ground. I brought a piece of that push rod back with me so my crew chief would know he wasn't to blame, that it wasn't engine failure that brought me down. [Note: The Johnson family still has that push rod, which they found in a small army-issue sewing kit returned to them with Norman's belongings.]

CHAPLIN: How did you manage to return to your outfit, Lieutenant?

JOHNSON: Well, the GI's just told me to follow a telephone line they'd been laying out and I'd get to headquarters. It was about six miles, and I got a lift part way in a Jeep with a brigadier general.

CHAPLIN: What chiefly impressed you along the way?

JOHNSON: The German dead. They were everywhere, all along the road. And I saw some of our dead, too, lined up outside a little dispensary.

CHAPLIN: And when you got to the beach . . . have any trouble thumbing a ride back to England?

JOHNSON: I had plenty of trouble finding a ride. I waded out to an LCT, but they weren't leaving, so they put me in an amphibious Jeep that took me to an LST that was loading wounded. But that was anchored and was staying there. So I went to the flagship, and the C.O. put me in a British motor patrol launch that brought me back across the Channel.

CHAPLIN: Have you got a new plane yet?

JOHNSON: Yes, I'm back in business again. I'll be out tomorrow.

CHAPLIN: Thank you very much, Lieutenant. You have just heard Lieutenant Norman T. Johnson. On D-Day he took an active part in the invasion in his Ninth Air Force Thunderbolt "Dangerous Critter," helping to destroy a gun emplacement and a bridge in the zone of operations. And now, despite everything that's happened he's "back in business." That's the kind of fighting men we have.

Eight days later, on 15 June 1944, Lieutenant Norman T. Johnson, in his new P-47, together with his squadron, departed Army Air Force Station 347 in southern England for targets of opportunity over Domfront, France. On this, his 25th mission, he was shot down and killed. It was three months before Norman's family received confirmation of his death. It was a long wait, followed by a painful confirmation:

Dear Mr. Johnson: 29 May 1945

We use this means to express to you our sincere sympathy in the death of your son, Captain Norman T. Johnson, ASN 0-728672, 492nd Fighter Squadron, 48th Fighter Group, who was Killed in Action 15 June 1944.

Captain Johnson (then 1st Lt.) was Flight Commander. He and his flight departed AAF Station 347 in Southern England on 15 June 1944, for targets of opportunity near Domfront, France. He led his flight on a low level bombing run on a marshaling yard at Domfront, France. In the vicinity of the target, light flak came up on both sides. At this time your son was about one hundred (100) feet from the ground. At the completion of the bombing run, he could not be contacted by radio. Neither could his plane be located by his wing man or by the Commander of the cover flight. Later, we learned that his plane crashed and that your son's body was recovered and buried by a French farmer. The body was later removed to an American cemetery by a graves registration company, which effected burial. At this time appropriate religious rites were given by an American chaplain. We are certain that in your son's death there was no lingering suffering.

I knew your son in England, having joined the Group a few months prior to D-Day. There our morale was high for we had a job to do and we were determined to do it well. But the risks of war are great. And many a pilot, in bravely carrying out his mission, has made the supreme sacrifice. Today, this Group honors the name of your son, among others, who have laid down their lives for their brethren.

God, out of His love and wisdom, remembers all of us. He will give you Grace and Comfort, and we know He is close by Norman too.

There is much you will want to cherish in your memory of Norman. The happiness that he brought you will forever remain in your hearts a fond memory. Thank God for that. Look forward with the abiding faith that God does all things well. He has prepared for us a home, a house not built with hands, eternal in the heavens.

> Sincerely yours,
> Doneghey W. Duran
> Chaplain (Capt.), USA.
> Chaplain, 48th Fighter Group

* * *

The following was written by A. Theodore Johnson, Norman's father. This event took place some time between Norman's Aleutian assignment and his duty in England:

When our flying boys first cross the international date line, they have to pay a dollar to each of the other servicemen in the plane they are on, who have already been across. They get each one to sign a dollar bill as evidence that they have become members of a club, the "Short Snorters," they call them.

Momma [Mae T. Johnson] grieved over Norman's death for quite some time. One day she went to town to make some purchases and got some change. When she got home she discovered that one of the bills had written on it, "Short Snorter, N. T. Johnson, 1-28-43, Dutch Harbor, Alaska." It seems like a miracle that that dollar bill would turn up here in Vernal, and that it would be given into Momma's hand. But it is definitely the one Norman had, and we are glad to have it. Later, one of Norman's flying companions came to visit us, and he verified that it was the dollar Norman had signed and sent out. We can't help but think that if the Lord could see that that particular dollar bill found its way to us, He could certainly take care of our boy. We are sure that Norman is now where the Lord wants him to be.

For his meritorious service, Norman T. Johnson was awarded the Air Medal with five Oak Leaf clusters, and posthumously, the Purple Heart. A memorial service was held for Norman on 19 November 1944, in the Vernal 2nd Ward. He is buried in the Maeser Cemetery in Vernal.

Norman's "Short Snorter" dollar: the top of the bill reads: "N.T. Johnson 1-28-43 Dutch Harbor-Alaska." Covering the body of the bill are the crew members' names who were on this particular flight across the international date line.

THE WAR IN FRANCE AND GERMANY

Much of a soldier's life was marching from one battle to another.

The D-Day invasion gave us our toehold in Europe. Then General Dwight Eisenhower had the unenviable position of keeping the war on track. His sometimes bickering generals required the best of Ike's extensive managerial skill. He had to deal simultaneously with the towering ego of the demanding, dithering, British Field Marshall Bernard Law Montgomery, the darling of Winston Churchill, and the equally towering ego of the flamboyant, demanding, but effective General George S. Patton. The campaign throughout Europe became a balancing act: the fluid battlefield situation, public opinion, weather, the needs of soldiers and airmen, and a hostile enemy. Included in that equation were the logistics of supply, the rescue of wounded, the plight of POWs, recovery of the dead, and contingencies of every imaginable kind. However, these tensions were not limited to high level commanders. Mostly, it was the enlisted men who paid the price for fighting this war.

WALTER H. "BEE" PECK

Though deep'ning trials throng your way, Press on, press on, ye Saints of God! Ere long the resurrection day Will spread its life and truth abroad. Though outward ills await us here, The time, at longest, is not long Ere Jesus Christ will reappear, Surrounded by a glorious throng.

("Though Deepening Trials," *Hymns*, no. 122)

Bee, as he was known to his friends, was fun to be with, he had grit and determination and courage without limit. He was born at Moore, Montana, on 14 April 1916, the second of seven children of Margaret Frances Schuster and John Walter Peck, and raised on a ranch at the foot of the Snowy Mountains in central Montana. He loved the ranch, ranching was his life. When the attack on Pearl Harbor came he could have taken an agricultural deferment but felt that he should go and fulfil his duty to his country. He trained at Fort Knox, Kentucky, and in Texas and California as a tank driver.

Being used to thinking and doing things on his own, Bee chafed under army discipline. He came home on furlough and said the hardest thing he ever did in his life was to return to duty.

Bee was assigned to the 4th Armored Tank Division, part of General Patton's 3rd Army. They came ashore at Utah Beach, on the Cherbourg Peninsula, near the town of Carentan. He was a gunner and relief driver. They were immediately on the front lines as the push across France began that June of 1944. One of the first nights there he pitched his pup-tent next to a tank. He wrote some letters, then went to the mail drop. When he returned, he found a bomb crater where his tent had been.

Walter H. "Bee" Peck

At Avranches his unit came under intense German attack. Several tanks were destroyed, and they took many casualties. The tank Bee was in was struck by an armor-piercing shell, which went through the tank, cutting off both his legs below the knees and setting the tank on fire. In the inferno he reached for the open hatch, attempting to get out before the fire found the ammunition they had on board. Providentially, flames seared the stumps of his legs so that he did not bleed to death, but as he was now shorter than he had been only moments before, he struggled to reach the opening. When he did, the metal was so hot that it scorched his left hand and he fell back into the tank. He heard someone say, *"Try again, Peck. You'll make it next time."* He did and managed to pull himself out. He fell off the blistering tank, with his clothes on fire. Landing on the end of one of his stumps broke his leg above the knee. While rolling on the ground in an attempt to extinguish his burning clothes, his clothing became twisted around the bone protruding from the leg. As he raised his head to call for help, a bullet creased his skull.

He remembered being lifted onto a Jeep and a tourniquet being applied to his broken leg. He was so tangled in his clothing, the medics had to cut off his leg at the break with a bayonet to free him. The lurching of the

Jeep, as it was driven to the aid station, brought him to consciousness from time to time. He next remembered being in a large aircraft hangar. He then became aware that he was in a hospital in England and was wrapped in gauze and slathered in petroleum jelly.

The fire had dried up his tear ducts and left him blind. When his sight gradually returned, he was so relieved that it didn't matter to him that he had lost his legs—he could see!

Bee's parents got letters from the Red Cross telling them that his injuries were serious, but not the extent of them. It was awhile before they really knew what had happened. And the prognosis was not promising. What was not known was the depth of Bee's determination—he fought hard to live and to recover. But live he did; however, healing was slow. The following is a letter Bee wrote to his parents, telling them of his injuries:

Dear Folks   August 17, 1944
Just a few lines to let you know that I continue to get along fine. The burns on my hands are fairly well healed. My right hand is nearly as good as new. But I'm not able to write lying flat on my back. So I'm having this written again this week. I've lost both legs and wasn't going to tell you for fear you would worry—but it doesn't seem fair not to let you know exactly how things are. Eventually we would have to face it anyway. They tell me they can make artificial legs that I can get along very well on. It will take some time to learn to use them.

My main problem now is just waiting for things to heal up. I'm in no pain most of the time, and everything is being done for me.

I hope everything is going well at the ranch. I wish I could be there to help you with the fall work.

Give my regards to all—Your Son, Bee

Written at the bottom of the letter was this note by Lucille Pagandok, the Red Cross nurse to whom Bee dictated his letter: "Don't worry about Bee—he looks fine, is getting good care, and is very cheerful!"

Bee's face had been severely burned, and where his whiskers were, infection set in. To treat this the doctors had to remove the skin. Using scalpels, they shaved off as much burned skin every day as he could stand, until the infection cleared up. Fire had damaged his hands so severely that when the bandages were removed he could not bend his fingers. The doctor told him he must exercise his fingers. He did move his fingers, but the pain kept him from bending the joints. One day the doctor asked to see the progress he was making. Bee showed how he could move his fingers but was unable to bend them. The doctor took the hand and bent all the fingers, which split the tender, new skin. His fingers were then bandaged around a dowel so they could heal with room to bend them. It was a painful experience, and he was not happy with the doctor that day, but later he was glad.

What was left of his legs was also severely burned and required a lot of painful skin grafting. The bones had to be modified so that the skin would cover the ends of his legs and he could be prepared for artificial legs. When he was first hospitalized, he was wrapped like a mummy in gauze and petroleum jelly. When the bandages had to be changed, he was laid in a tub of saline solution to soak them off. The odor was sickening, and as the nurse unwrapped him, she sometimes had to leave fast, lose her dinner, then return to continue. To complicate matters even more, some of the donated blood the hospital received was contaminated, and everyone in the ward got hepatitis.

Finally, in October 1944, Bee was healed enough to return to the United States. He was flown back on a "litter plane." It was on this plane that he met NBC correspondent Robert St. John. The following is an excerpt of the broadcast Mr. St. John did featuring Bee—or "Bill" as he called him:

NATIONAL BROADCASTING COMPANY N. Y.
Program: Robert St John Date: October 20, 1944 Time: 10:15–10:30

ROBERT St JOHN—Bill was a farmer before the war, helping his family run one of those wind-swept ranches for which Montana is famous. Bill isn't his real name. I call him that because I don't think he'd like to have me talk about him in a broadcast. And yet, I must, for Bill is an important person in this war. He's a symbol. . . . Bill, to me, is representative of American youth. . . . He told me about himself, as he lay on his litter in a hospital plane, the day before yesterday. The air was a bit bumpy, and Bill had trouble staying put in his litter. His litter was on the top tier. There were three men on litters under him.

Bill wanted to get at a small cardboard box at the foot of his bed. The box held everything Bill owned except of course, a bit of land out in

Montana. When a man's wounded in battle, he loses everything except perhaps for what's in his pockets. But in a cardboard box Bill had an envelope, and in the envelope was something he wanted me to see. And so, as we bounced through the air on the last lap of a four-thousand mile-trip from the Continent to America, Bill struggled to get at that cardboard box. It wasn't easy because Bill doesn't have any legs anymore. He left both of them over in France.

Bill's case is worse than that of most men who lose their legs because his got shot off so high up that I don't see how they'll ever be able to make artificial legs for him. Besides that, Bill's hands are not very pretty to look at. I didn't ask him how it all happened.

What Bill went through out there on one of the battlefields of France must have been worse than anything Dante or Edgar Allen Poe ever dreamed about in their most imaginative nightmares. And yet, Bill never said a word about it. He just kept struggling to get at that small box, at the foot of his bed. And when he finally wiggled himself around so that he could reach it, he quickly dug out an envelope. There were a couple of letters in the envelope. But the letters were not what he wanted me to see. Finally he did find what he was after. His face lighted up beautifully as he pulled it from the envelope.

I must tell you about his face. . . . When I first saw him, I wondered how so old a man, could possible have gotten into the army, especially into a tank outfit. When the nurse on the plane told me that he was still in his twenties, I laughed at her. I refused to believe it until I saw an official paper with his age on it.

I suppose it was his eyes which looked so old. . . . But then they changed, all in an instant. His eyes brightened, and then I knew, even before he showed me what he held in his hands, that his eyes were looking into the future. He didn't hand it to me. He seemed afraid to let it out of his grasp. He just held it so that I could see.

The sky was the blue of heavenly-blue morning glories, for the photograph was all in colors. The barn was the red which all barns ought to be. The chicken houses and the corn cribs and granaries and the dwelling house were a musty, nondescript color. The mountains in the background were tinged with snow. Bill's maimed hands trembled as he explained: "They took it from the hill behind the house. My brother-in-law had some old color film. That's just how it looked the last time I saw it. They tell me it still looks the same. I got the photograph at the hospital over in France the same day the Colonel told me they were sending me back to the States. I guess I bawled that day, for the first time in my life. Maybe it looks like just another ranch in Montana to you, but to me, well, I don't suppose you'd understand. But that place is home to me."

About this time the nurse came through, turning out the lights over the litters, and getting the men off to sleep. Bill had to do some weird wiggling around to get the envelope back into the box. As he put the box under the covers, where his feet should have been, he laughed for the first time like a boy in his twenties and said: "I guess the snow will be on those mountains again, when I get back to Montana."

* * *

After the war, as told by Bee's wife, Tess S. Peck

Bushnell was the closest hospital to Montana, which had facilities for amputees. It was here that I met Bee. One of Bee's friends was seeing a girl with whom I worked, and in order for her to come see him she had to have a chaperone along. The first time we met I was sitting on a couch, when Bee came down the hall in his wheelchair. His friend called to him to stop so that he could introduce us. Bee told him to wait, then moved from his wheelchair and sat beside me, put his arm around me, and said, "Now introduce us." He was so cheerful and had such a gift for "blarney" that I immediately liked him. Marriage was the furthest thing from my mind, but eventually we did marry and moved to Garneill, Montana. He was the kindest, most cheerful man I ever met. Everyone loved him.

We became the parents of two daughters and a son. Bee bought additional land and ran more than 3,000 acres of land, mostly by himself.

Bee joined the Church shortly after we were married. In October 1978, he was called to be bishop of the Lewistown Ward. He threw himself into that calling with the same determination that was his when he recovered from his wounds and learned to walk on wooden legs. The ward members loved him, and because he was retired, he could devote much of his time to their care. After five and one-half years, he was released.

Bee died January 7, 1984, in the Veterans Hospital in Salt Lake City. I still miss him.

LIN H. JOHNSON

And they were exceedingly sorrowful because of their enemies.

(3 Nephi 3:26)

Johnny's Mem-Wars: My father and mother, Oscar and Lucina Johnson, were salt-of-the-earth kind of people. They taught me and my ten brothers and sisters many things; foremost they taught us the gospel of Jesus Christ. I knew the gospel meant everything to them, and they infused this in me, too. I grew up on the west side of the Snake River near Idaho Falls, Idaho. In 1939 I graduated from high school and was attending the University of Idaho at Moscow, when war was declared on Germany and Japan. Drafted into the Army in 1942, I soon found how valuable the gospel was in my life. I was determined to live its precepts.

In the 360th Field Artillery Battalion, 95th Infantry Division, I became known as Johnny. This follows accepted Army nomenclature, since my name is Johnson. Anybody named Petersen becomes Pete, etc. Other name tags came about for various reasons. We had Horsecollar, Pluto, Rabbi, Deacon, Hog Meat, Monster, Tripod, Shorty, Sea Biscuit, Ironhead, and Pappy to name a few. Some were too raunchy to record. We had secret pet names for our least favorite officers. Anybody who didn't have a nickname wondered if he really belonged. General Patton liked his nickname—"Blood and Guts"—and actively promoted it.

It has been a long time since the events of World War II. I should have written them down sooner when the recollection was more vivid, but some of the experiences stir such strong feelings that I couldn't have written objectively. The bitterness would have come through so strongly that the account might have been distorted. The mellowing effect of passing years has made it possible for me to look back as though I had been an observer rather than a participant, and I can write with a little detachment.

My mother, Lucina Weaver Johnson, faithfully copied my letters home, and there is a notebook filled with three years of correspondence. As I read these letters, I'm struck with two thoughts: did I really write some of those things, and how did I ever get those ideas past the vigilance of Army censorship? The home folks weren't supposed to know that we didn't have warm clothes or sleeping bags for the brutal winter campaign and were short of most everything. We did have enough food, though of questionable quality.

I trained at Fort Sill, Oklahoma. The Church had a branch there, and I was able to attend occasionally. I was startled the first time I attended. The opening hymn had the familiar words that hadn't had much meaning before: "We are all enlisted 'til the conflict is o'er, Happy are we, happy are we . . ."

Lin H. Johnson

After basic training I was assigned to the 95th Infantry Division. While serving in the European Theater of Operations in France, Belgium, Holland and Germany, I never encountered another member of the Church.

* * *

In the summer of 1944, my infantry division had just crossed the Channel from England and disembarked on the beaches of the Normandy peninsula in France. This was not long after the D-Day landings, where American units had fought their way ashore and established beachheads for the tide of troops that followed them.

Some American divisions in active combat had lost much of their heavy equipment. Rather than commit our green, untested division to replace them, it was decided to send our heavy equipment to those experienced units to replace what had been lost.

We were bivouacked on the lush green peninsula, awaiting replacement heavy equipment from the U.S. by way of England before we could be considered battle-ready.

The Normandy peninsula is hedgerow country. These formidable fences were formed by planting berry bushes, then tossing rocks and debris

Lin Johnson taking advantage of a quiet moment during the war.

from the fields into the hedge over the years. In some places the hedgerows were higher than a man's head, and several feet thick. They were a formidable obstacle to tanks and invading troops. The hedge's berry bush was similar to our blackberry, and the fruit was starting to ripen. We were enjoying the fruit until a GI was killed when he set off a booby trap left by the retreating enemy. That ended berry picking.

Having a bit of free time one afternoon, two of us Americans were out exploring. The countryside was scarred by shell holes and bomb craters and all the aftermath of pitched battles—wrecked tanks, artillery, trucks—bulldozed into ugly, rusting heaps.

We came unexpectedly upon a green, unscarred knoll with white crosses arranged in geometric precision. It was a sobering and beautiful sight. It was the first American cemetery I had seen. Under each cross was an American soldier killed in D-Day landings and early battles that followed the landings.

As we were looking in the cemetery, we became aware of an older French couple. They were shabbily dressed and carried armloads of flowers. They would stop and say quietly, "*Merci, merci beaucoup!*" then lay a flower on the grave. When they had used all the flowers in their arms, they'd go to the edge of the cemetery and pick another armload of flowers that grew in wild profusion amid the wreckage of battles just fought. Then they'd return and continue their ritual.

On each cross was only a name and serial number; no rank was posted. I came upon a cross that had more flowers than the others. As I stooped to read who was buried there, I recognized his name from the news. It was an American general killed in the invasion.

This gave me pause. We had trained for months to understand "rank has its privileges." Throughout our training there were always separate facilities for officers, always better than those for the enlisted men. Yet here was a general buried among lowly enlisted men. I was surprised there wasn't a separate cemetery for officers, or at least a separate part of the cemetery.

Enemy bullets and shells and bombs did not recognize rank. They killed and wounded without discrimination. In death all men have the same rank. Thus a general and private can lie side by side on a green knoll in France and be equally honored. Each gave all he had.

Intrigued by this older French peasant couple, we stopped to chat with them. With the help of the French phrase book we had been issued and hand gestures, we carried on a ragged conversation. They had a dairy farm close by. The Nazis had butchered and eaten most of their milk cows. Their only son was in the French army when the Nazi juggernaut overran France in the early stages of the war. They had not had a word of him in the intervening four years and presumed him dead.

* * *

Soldiers can be a rough lot. We came from all over the United States and were thrown together to live and learn to fight and hopefully to survive this war and return to our homes. We also learned a lot about each other.

One evening, as we sat together, one of the men who had lived in Nauvoo delivered a bitter attack on the Mormon Church. He boasted that "We killed all the Mormons we could find and chased the rest to Utah." I sat there listening quietly, without comment. When the fellow finished his tirade, another asked my antagonist, "If the Mormons are such a bad lot, why is Johnny here the only one of us who doesn't smoke or drink or chase women?" The critic stormed off into the dark, cursing.

After I left the United States I do not recall having met another member of the Church, nor did I have an opportunity to attend any LDS services. I did however have many discussions about the Church. This letter to my parents tells about some of those conversations.

Dear Folks,   October 30, 1944   Just in France

This is my Sunday in the army. The Sabbath doesn't fall on any particular calendar day, just comes along with a day's lull. Today is just such a day, so I'm doing a bit of reading in the September issue of the *Era*, and reflecting and pondering.

Lots of publicity, unfortunately sketchy, is about the trials of the Fundamentalists in Salt Lake. Much of it is misinterpreted, and fellows with various motives toss the fact at me when they learn I'm a Mormon. Those who are just baiting are best to ignore, but a few of them are honestly misinformed. I've patiently explained the situation that our church brooks no plural marriages, and it was for that very reason the Fundamentalists were excommunicated. Every *Yank* magazine for the last several issues, has at least a brief mention about this matter, and occasionally the *Stars and Stripes,* our daily newspaper, has a back page article. A flurry of inquiries always follows—some jesting, some baiting, some honestly curious. Not one in a dozen ever accepts casually the discovery of my religious affiliation; close and wondering scrutiny usually follows. It seems hard for them to digest the finding that I'm normal and not visibly different from other guys grumbling their way through the war.

At first I thought the publicizing of the trials was adverse, but it's opened many a discussion in which I've straightened out plenty of misconceptions. Spirituality isn't very fitting grist for most G.I. sessions, except when in a tight spot and introspection and identity with something besides earthly things becomes pressing. Most of my closest companions accept my belonging to the mystery religion nominally, but others have lurking suspicions of harems hidden away in Idaho spud fields.

Two interesting experiences while trucking supplies satisfied me a good bit, and I did some explaining.

You recall "Pluto," the Jewish boy from New York who alternated with me as a truck driver. He'd rather have been wolfing some jaded novel or pouring over pin-up cuties. But he was desperate for reading matter and asked if I'd let him read the magazine I'd brought along. It was an issue of the *Improvement Era,* and I warned him that he might not find it interesting. He thumbed along idly, rolling a cigar back and forth across his mouth. Then he came to an article about Palestine. Not a peep came from him while he plunged into the article, following it avidly. After he'd finished, he was speculative and quiet. "What religion did you say you belonged to, Johnny?" I told him, and he gave me a wondering look. "That's a good magazine," he said with his eyes on the French landscape. It surprised him to find our interests ranging so wide.

Another fellow hungry for reading had my *Era* open under the truck tarpaulin, which sheltered us. He looked up when I ducked in from standing guard, and hoped I didn't mind his using my magazine. I told him to stay with it. He did and read it as thoroughly as I did. Maybe more so if I'd care to confess it. One day later on he came to me quietly and said he'd like to learn something about the Mormons if I could spare the time. So one night by a blessed fire in the chill air, he listened while I outlined what we were, what we believed, where we originated. He was doubly curious since his home town is near Palmyra, New York; he'd been on the fringe of something without being acquainted with it. I shot it at him straight from the shoulder. I explained that we were a people as highly spiritual as any he'd ever find. We weren't bigoted or blind, but on the contrary, the most realistic of groups with a definite knowledge of what we wanted and where we were going. He wasn't in the market for any detailed aspects, but I had plenty to dwell on. I explained our Welfare Plan and that we were predominately rural or laboring, prospering mildly but seldom blooming in any sudden wealth. He'd noticed I didn't drink coffee, smoke, or carouse around and wondered what religious superstition was the ground for it. "Superstition be danged!" I said. "Not one thing I refrain from can be proved beneficial by scientific tests. We're not at outs with science on any point."

"I guess it's only logical that you would frown on dancing and amusement, then," he said.

And that's what knocked the pins from under him. I explained our wholehearted support of wholesome entertainment and of our program of dancing and drama and athletics. It was hard for him to link a high moral and spiritual code with enjoyment, but I tossed it at him anyway. He was astonished and told me of his own church and how he thought it was narrow and impractical.

"Whenever I go to service I think what a farce all of this religion business is. People come to be seen in a good place by other people there for the same reason. They give money because it adds stature to the image reflected in other's eyes. Sometimes the pastor sounds phony. He goes at it like a doctor thumping your ribs, or a lawyer lining up a case. Too professional."

I gave him another jolt when I told him we had no paid minister. As far as we are concerned no one is better qualified to do our dealings with God than ourselves.

"Who preaches the sermons, then?"

"Maybe I'd do it, or my neighbor down the road."

By this time he had about all he could digest at once.

"You sound like the most definitely different folks in the world, and maybe you've got something."

By then the fire was out and we went to bed, but I felt satisfied. Don't think I'm converting anyone. That's not the case, nor do I expect it to be. But this much is certain: some fellows are getting used to the idea we're normal and not crazy religious fanatics with a herd of wives, long beards, and going around in physical self-denial to whet our spiritual reception, but it's a slow business.

Love, Lin

* * *

Anytime I work out in the snow and cold my mind draws me back to December and January of 1944–45. I was in the 95th Infantry Division, 360 Field Artillery Battalion.

We had joined Patton's 3rd Army in September of 1944. After some tune-up skirmishes, our first real test came in the mud and rain of Metz, France. Patton's dash across France during the late summer had dangerously stretched supply lines and brought the 3rd Army up against the Maginot Line—that French-built string of fortifications from Switzerland to Belgium. It was built between World Wars I and II. It was captured when the Nazis invaded France.

Metz, France, was the key—a fortified city in the Maginot Line and a road junction through the mountains. It was a historic invasion route through which armies had thundered both east and west in wars past. We were told that Metz had never been taken by frontal assault. Patton said we were going to do it. He liked to do things that hadn't been done before, and we did need the road access to supply our advancing troops. Metz was on high ground, and the city was honey-combed with bunkers and gun emplacements deep under concrete and earth. It was a formidable fortress and a challenge for a green division.

In bloody combat our division dug the Nazis out of their underground bunkers one at a time until the city was under our control, although there remained a few pockets of resistance (these we by-passed and starved out later). We crossed the Moselle River and moved on to "sacred" German soil where we next encountered the enemy at the Siegfried Line. This line of fortifications was a few miles from the Maginot, and parallel to it. It was built by the Germans between the World Wars. It was much like the Maginot Line we had just breached. Every hilltop in this rolling countryside was a concrete underground bunker with artillery emplacements. In between the bunkers were concrete dragon's teeth in a closely spaced pattern so tanks couldn't cross, and everywhere were minefields and barbwire entanglements to stop infantry and patrols. We dashed from the Maginot to the Siegfried in pursuit of the retreating enemy, only to be brought up short by these formidable obstacles.

We had been sleeping outside in the cold and wet. We each had only one blanket and a shelter half. A shelter half is half of a small canvas tent. Two GI's would button these halves together to form a low tent. It was large enough for one, but had to accommodate two. It was a tight fit, and you could only crawl in and out on your belly. A shelter half could only have been designed by someone with half a mind to make a tent.

If we were in a place very long we'd dig underground, creating all sorts of make-shift shelters, both for warmth and for safety from enemy fire. I was resident expert in underground log and dirt shelters. Being from Idaho I knew the rudiments of building spud cellars. Someone had to show the city slickers from New York and Chicago.

The folks back home were told that we all had warm sleeping bags and winter clothes, but we didn't. To survive the cold we used our ingenuity. We made bedrolls of anything we could scrounge from the houses in the towns and villages. I had a window drape, a strip of canvas, a feather tick, and a tablecloth all rolled together. It was bulky and awkward, but cozy.

We didn't have any footgear except leather combat boots. Some genius in quartermaster had decreed that these boots be made with the rough side out, perhaps they thought they'd wear better. It was a goof because the rough fibers outside acted as a wick to suck moisture inside and there was no way to apply waterproofing to the rough exterior.

In the constant rain and mud our feet were never dry, and we began to get trench foot, an ailment I'd read about from World War I. Basically it

A soldier quickly accepted that digging was just part of being a soldier. Here Lin Johnson digs a latrine.

was skin gangrene. Our feet would start showing reddish-purple blotches. Some large tents were set up behind the front lines just out of German artillery rang—about twelve miles. GI's with the worst cases were sent back for a few days to this tent camp. I recall my brief stay. We'd lie in heavenly bliss on canvas cots sheltered from the incessant cold rain. Two rows of GI's would have their bare feet toward a center aisle and hanging over the end of their cots. Medics would come along with a bucket of potassium permanganate and a swab and periodically minister to our extremities. A few days of this treatment usually corrected the problem, and we'd have to go back up to the front lines. A few lucky ones got a stubborn infection that wouldn't clear up readily and were taken farther to the rear to hospital facilities. Unfortunately mine cleared up quickly, and it was back up to the mud and blood.

As I think back I'm amazed at the amount of time we spent in the rain and mud—never dry, constantly cold, and yet we had no respiratory ailments. It was later when we moved into houses that we got sick. GI's, both German and American, would have been content to get comfortable for the winter and wait until spring to resume hostilities. But the generals on both sides had a war on.

Our infantry units would be rousted out of their houses in the morning and told if they wanted a place to sleep that night they'd have to capture the next village. As our units advanced we'd pass the German villagers straggling back through our lines with their pitiful possessions on their backs or pulling a small cart. They were truly pathetic in their rags as they shuffled along in the snow and cold–women, children, and old men. They looked like clotted blood against the snowy expanse. Occasionally their eyes would meet ours, and I've never seen such a look of pure hatred smoldering there. I'm sure a few Nazi spies got through disguised as old women, but we were too cold and weary to search them.

* * *

It didn't take us long to discover that General "Blood and Guts" Patton babied his armored divisions. Infantry divisions like ours were used like meat put through a grinder. Whenever his glamour boys in armored units would hit a tough spot like the Maginot or Siegfried, they'd pull back and the infantry divisions would blast a hole through the fortifications. The glory boys would dash through and chase Krauts and grab headlines until they hit another obstacle, then here would come Patton's hamburger units to take over again. I guess it was good military tactics but didn't endear "Blood and Guts" to the infantry divisions.

During our dash between the Maginot and Siegfried Lines, we stopped a few nights at a mine shelter. It was a grimy wooden barracks with barred windows, which had just recently housed Russian and Polish slave laborers who worked the mine and smelter. Our infantry units just ahead of us had liberated them. We were so cold from sleeping in the snow that a grimy old prison barracks looked like a plush hotel. We unrolled our bedrolls on the cots, fired up the pot-bellied stoves, posted guards, and settled down for what we thought would be our first good night's sleep for several weeks. About midnight the barracks was astir. Everybody was up scratching and cursing. We were crawling with lice and bedbugs and covered with blood where gorged bedbugs had popped. Finally came daylight, and our medic Herbert Petersen (Pete, naturally) went to Battalion Aid Station and returned with a sack of white powder. We all lined up and loosened our belts and shirt collars. A generous portion was dusted in our hair and down our necks as we jigged around, shaking it all the way to our shoes. Like a miracle the lice and bedbugs dropped out of our hair and every other place of refuge. We dusted our bedrolls and cots. The next night we slept in tranquil dusty repose, our first good night's sleep for what seemed ages. This was my introduction to DDT, that great friend of soldiers, which has since been deemed so hazardous.

By late December 1944, we had fought our way across France and crossed the border into Germany. If you've ever watched John Wayne movies, you would get the picture that American soldiers were self-reliant, tough, resourceful men, invincible in all situations. In truth, in the early stages of the war at least, we were mostly a bunch of scared kids. We wondered what we were doing so far from home, killing and being killed in places we couldn't pronounce. Months of combat wrought changes, aging us beyond our years.

By this time we were well into winter. We didn't have winter clothing and had been nursing our frost-bitten bodies and battling the effects of trench foot from endless days in cold and muddy holes and dugouts with our feet never dry. Violence and death were our constant companions.

General Patton had told us when we crossed the border into Germany, that we could move into houses if they were available, to get ourselves out of the snow and cold. After all, he said, they had invited us to their country. My section found an unoccupied house that was surprisingly intact, considering the recent battle in which we had pushed Nazi troops out of the rural village. The German family who owned the house had retreated with the German soldiers.

During this lull in battle we were getting warm for the first time in weeks. We were appreciative of the family for their unintended hospitality.

My three little sisters had sent a package that had mysteriously gotten to the front from Idaho, almost half a world away. In it was a miniature Christmas tree about a foot tall, with some icicles and tinsel. It was nearing Christmas. We set up the little tree on a fireplace mantle and decorated it. The thoughts of each of us went thousands of miles away to our own family circles and what was happening back home.

Then we heard a noise in the barn attached to the house. We had been careless in the flush of victory and had not made a thorough search of the buildings. Snatching our rifles we opened the door into the barn. There was a big pile of straw in one corner. With rifles ready we watched as one of the men approached the straw pile. A young girl emerged, trembling with fear.

We brought her into the house. In rags and cold and hungry, she was crying from fear. She said her name was Anna and that she was from Poland.

One of our group could speak Polish. Anna told us that she had been taken prisoner with all her family. She was sent to be a slave worker on this farm. She'd put in four years with a pitchfork and wheelbarrow, cleaning the barns and tending livestock.

She gratefully wolfed down the meager rations we were able to share with her. We assured her she had nothing to fear from us and gradually she stopped trembling. When she spied the little Christmas tree on the mantle she went over and gazed at it and then started to cry. Hitler's godless Nazism wasn't tolerant of Christian observances or symbols, so she hadn't seen anything like it since her capture.

As she cried, four American soldiers, months in combat, shed tears with her—and we were not ashamed.

We had just exchanged gifts with Anna. We had given her the blessed gift of freedom from slavery. She gave us the gift of her gratitude, and we were grateful that our mothers and sisters had not been brutalized as she had been. For the first time I understood fully why we were involved in this war and why we had to win. After more than half a century, and from half a world away, thanks again, Anna, for your gift that Christmastime. I have had many wonderful Christmases in the intervening years, but I have never received a gift more meaningful.

As New Year's Day approached, I was in an observation post, an old house perched on some high ground looking down on our adversaries below in the snowy wastes of the river valley. The fog lay heavy and close on the rolling hills, and sporadic artillery fire punctuated the white silence.

New Year's Eve: At the stroke of midnight every gun for hundreds of miles, from Switzerland to Holland was fired. I've never seen such pyrotechnics as the quiet was shattered by a deafening and blinding display over the snow-covered earth. I'm sure the Germans joined in with all their weapons. There was no doubt in anyone's mind that 1944 was shot to hell.

* * *

It was bitterly cold and the fog was constant. We heard some disturbing news from north of us. The Nazis had mounted a massive counter attack in Belgium and had broken through our thinly held line there, in the fog and snow of the Ardennes Forest, and were driving for Liege, Belgium, a main supply point for our armies. It became known as the Battle of the

Bulge. It was a brutal and confused battle in the snow and fog. All our planes were grounded, and the Nazis came through with a massed lightning strike with elite units. It was a pivotal battle for the European phase of the war, and it was only through unbelievable heroics that American units stemmed the tide. The break-through didn't occur in 3rd Army lines. Patton's quick action, shifting combat units up from the south blunted the Nazi drive, stalled it, and then we mopped up after the weather cleared so our planes could get in the air. An Airborne division was rushed up to hold Bastogne, Belgium, the main road junction through the mountainous terrain.

Our reconnaissance had indicated a Nazi panzer division was headed down the road toward us. We were pretty jumpy, wondering how much the Germans could muster against our immediate front. Our captain took me and Joe Lowe (a laconic guy from Key West, Florida) out about a mile beyond our position in the village, to a road junction. He told us to use nitro starch to blast out foxholes in the frozen ground. We were left with a bazooka (an anti-tank weapon fired from the shoulder), BAR (Browning Automatic Rifle), grenades, and ammo. Our assignment, in case the Krauts attacked, was to hold them off as long as possible to enable our gun battery to make a strategic withdrawal. Makes a guy feel real good knowing he's expendable, like a round of ammunition when you squeeze off the trigger.

After Joe and I blasted through the frost layer, we dug down a ways and made ourselves somewhat more cozy. Joe allowed as how, if we saw Nazi tanks coming down the road, he could cut across the fields and beat our captain back to France.

Out there in the eerie stillness of the snowbound fog, ears straining for the clanking of approaching Tiger Tanks, you have lots of thoughts. It's easier to be a little braver when there are a hundred men of your unit around you. But when you feel there's only two of you against the whole German Army, it's a bleak, helpless feeling.

Joe and I talked in the stillness. Coming from Key West, he fished for a living. He was about thirty-years old and had hardly a tooth in his mouth. It's bad enough eating Army chow when you have teeth. I don't know how he got by gumming it.

Joe seemed a bit uncomfortable and said he wanted to ask me something.

"Are you a Mormon?"

"Yes."

"Do Mormons believe in God?"

"Yes."

"Do you know how to pray?"

"Yes."

"Will you?"

"Yes, of course."

I had uttered many silent prayers previously, but this was the first time I had done so vocally in front of a member of my unit. Joe squeezed his eyes shut as we knelt side by side in our hole. I groped for words to communicate. As I faltered Joe nudged my ribs, "Be sure to mention we didn't enlist, we were drafted."

I didn't feel it was a very profound prayer, but I stumbled through it somehow.

That afternoon, as the fog lifted a little, we could see an MP a short distance from us. We heard an airplane coming from the enemy lines, flying low and skimming the snowy rolling hills. The engine coughed and died, and the plane made a belly landing in the snow just a short distance from the crossroads where the MP was. The German pilot got out unhurt and reached for his Luger. The MP drilled him clean with a shot from his rifle. He lay dead in the snow—an 18 year-old who had discovered the glory of war.

Just before dark as Joe and I prepared for our night vigil, a Jeep from our outfit came up the road. Shorty Schraudenbach, the driver, told us that the panzer division had turned north. We were to load up our "playthings" and come on back. We'd had orders to move north to flatten the south side of the Bulge in Belgium.

As we were heading back to our unit Joe observed to me, "Maybe we didn't need to pray, being as that Panzer unit decided to change directions."

* * *

The captain summoned me to the command post. "You read maps better than anybody in the battery, Johnson. We're moving north to the Bulge, and you're to go with Lt. Thayer from Battalion, and a scout from each battery to mark our road and find us night bivouac out of the snow and cold, if possible." Highly honored, "Mr. Expendable" prepared to head north.

The next morning five of us set out in a 3/4-ton command car. We had C & K rations, bedrolls, and carbines. At each junction we'd put up signs reading: "360 FA" (field artillery) and an arrow indicating the direction. The high piled snow was festooned with signs from many outfits on the move.

I was let out at a Luxembourg farmstead that looked to be a likely overnight bivouac for my unit. It had a huge barn. I entered and found myself in the midst of a squad of suspicious American infantrymen who had come into the barn to warm themselves. They questioned me about my outfit— hadn't heard of it. Their suspicions grew, and I felt a mite uncomfortable. It wouldn't have been very comforting to be shot or captured by my own troops. I said we were moving up from the south to help flatten the Bulge. They thought I might be a German, because in the initial breakthrough the Germans often dressed in American uniforms, were equipped with American equipment, which they'd captured earlier, and spoke English. It was a confused mess in the snow and fog. Finally one dog face said, "He's got to be one of us or he wouldn't be so ragged and dirty."

After they left, I saw a woman approaching the barn. She entered and began waving her arms, talking in a mixture of French, German, and a bit of English. She wanted me to go to the house and led the way, wringing her hands and jabbering. The house was a small two-story structure. When I entered I could hear moaning from up the narrow stairs. The distraught woman motioned me to follow her up the stairs, and I soon learned the source of the moans. Her daughter was in labor, expecting her first baby any moment. I gathered from their excited talk that they were so relieved I was there because the American soldiers could take care of anything.

I'd had a little experience assisting calves and pigs to arrive, but felt delivering my own species was a little out of my line. I told the woman I had to go out to the road and put up a sign and check for my outfit, but then I'd be back. As I left, the poor girl and her mother both began to wail, thinking I would desert them. I went out to the road and put up the sign with the arrow pointing into the farmyard. I girded my loins to return to the task at the farmhouse. Just then I heard a vehicle approaching, so I waited out of sight behind a snowbank until a Jeep came into view. The bumper markings indicated a medical unit, so I flagged it down. A lieutenant and his driver wore the Red Cross armbands indicating noncombatant medical personnel. I explained the situation, and the lieutenant said he was a doctor. After showing them to the house, I waited while the lieutenant climbed the steep stairs to look at the young girl. Downstairs the grandmother-to-be wrung her hands and tried to talk to me in a mixture of languages. Before long, we heard the wails of a newborn. I gave silent thanks for the baby's deliverance as well as my own. I marveled too at the kindness of the Lord in sending a doctor along that road just at that moment.

After descending the stairs the doctor grinned and said it was a fine baby girl. He said he had trained as an obstetrician but was pressed into service in the medical corps. He said it was nice to deliver a baby after all the patching of bullet and shrapnel wounds he'd been doing. The doctor and his driver then went on their way. I doubt if the girl was married, she looked to be only a teenager, probably a war victim.

Shortly before dark my outfit arrived, blue with cold. They were happy to bed down in that big barn with all the straw, although in the morning they reported being outnumbered by mice and rats.

The battlelines were so confused and fluid, our outfit never did close with the enemy. We groped around in the fog without making any real contact. Finally the fog lifted and we were spectators at an air show. Our fighter planes came out in numbers and flew dozens of sorties, bombing and strafing the Nazis. We watched as the planes would catch a column of tanks and men on the snowy roads. They'd knock out the lead and rear vehicles, then, with the tanks and men penned in the road which was a narrow snowy canyon, would repeatedly bomb and strafe until the whole column was ablaze and the riddled bodies thrown in the air came to rest on the clean white snow, slowly turning it red. We cheered.

It was a no-mercy performance. These German units were Hitler's elite Nazi Storm Troopers, the SS butchers who had shown no mercy to our men at the initial breakthrough, machine-gunning many prisoners. Any of these Nazis who survived the strafing and clawed their way up over the snow banks were shot by GI's before they got very far.

In disarray the SS made a dash back to German lines. They suffered terrific losses and as a consequence were ineffectual in stopping our later advance across the Rhine River. The Battle of the Bulge was Hitler's ill-fated last gasp, and the Nazis were never able to put up very effective resistance after that, due to the loss of their elite units and all the equipment. It was a bold gamble that failed, but it did throw a scare into our forces.

* * *

War is a coarsening and dehumanizing experience. Since life itself has so little value in such circumstances, can anything else be esteemed of much worth?

Sexual conduct was a no-man's-land, with opportunities for dalliance abundant during training or combat. Most soldiers availed themselves of such interludes. After all, they thought, if I am killed, think what I might have missed?

At risk of painting myself with a whited brush, I share this incident:

Our Infantry Division had been pulled out of the frontlines for a brief rest. This was done whenever battle conditions permitted so we could receive replacements for killed and wounded and to allow our filthy bodies the blessing of a hot shower and clean clothing, as well as relieve our combat-stressed minds for a brief time.

We hardly knew ourselves after the muck and turmoil of battle we'd been in for weeks. Three-day passes were issued to part of our unit at alternating times so we wouldn't be loosed on the locals all at once. With two buddies I sampled the strangeness of being out of gun range.

We found a little shop that served what little food was to be had, along with customary liquids. It had long been accepted that I didn't drink alcoholic beverages and that I didn't smoke, or even play poker. All this strangeness was somehow related to my being a Mormon.

As we were in this little shop, three girls came to our table to share the scanty fare and get acquainted. As evening came on we said we'd better be getting along. The girls wanted to pair up and invited us to share their beds for the night. My two buddies readily accepted and were soon out of sight. I told the girl I'd been paired with that I needed to get back to my outfit. She was miffed and coaxed, "You no think I'm pretty enough?"

"You're pretty enough," I lied.

"You come. I make you so happy?"

I lied again, "I'm so happy now I can hardly stand it." This after weeks of combat.

She was really getting out of sorts, and I was mighty uncomfortable. Finally, a light came on in her eyes. "Aha, I think you are one of those kind who likes boys the best!"

I assured her I was normal, but she was disbelieving. "You no act like soldier."

A thought flashed through my mind. I told her to wait right where she was.

Returning the three blocks to our billets, I told a buddy there was a girl waiting at an intersection. He took off on a run.

The next morning he told me I was the dumbest guy alive to pass up a deal like that. "Does it have something to do with being a Mormon?" I assured him it did. "You're an OK sort, Johnny, and I'll fight alongside you anywhere, but you don't know how to enjoy anything. You don't smoke, you don't drink, you don't play poker—and now this. You ought to have a little fun. You might get killed, and think of all you've missed!"

I didn't bother to tell him I had made covenants in a sacred place just prior to leaving for overseas.

* * *

The military used dog tags to positively identify each serviceman. They were never to be taken off unless you were a casualty. Then one tag would be kept by medical attendants or graves registration teams. The other was to remain with the body.

The first dog tags I was issued had my religious preference stamped P, for Protestant. President Heber J. Grant met with military leaders and pointed out we were not Protestant and that our tags should properly be printed LDS. This request was granted, and I was issued new tags. However, they were imprinted DS, the L having been left off in error. I was told there was no time to get that corrected, as we were being shipped overseas to England. Reluctantly, I wore them as issued. My crusty old first sergeant said, "What the hell does it matter? It won't keep you from being killed!"

During the course of the war this led to some interesting conversations. Most of it was good natured banter: "Does DS stand for Damned Sinner?" Thinking the explanation of the printing omission of the L would be an exercise in futility I played along: "No, it doesn't stand for Damned Sinner, but rather Devout Soldier, Divine Soul, or Designated Sacrifice—should I be killed. You take your pick."

The graves registration units had a gruesome assignment to retrieve bodies for burial. Dog tags were the only way to identify bodies. In some instances of GI's trapped in burning vehicles, the aluminum had melted and identification was difficult or near impossible. Graves registration personnel were to identify bodies and remove watches, rings, wallets, and other personal effects to be returned to families.

Most teams did a conscientious job. But I'm ashamed to know there were a few—the lowest of the low—who were worse than the Nazis we were fighting. They took watches and rings from the bodies and kept them. Some of these watches and rings showed up in the Paris black market. How much these wallets and rings would have meant to the grieving families of the dead husbands, sweethearts, fathers, mothers and wives.

One such instance I know first hand. We had been fighting for a little village in Belgium in the bitter cold winter of 1944–1945. The battle see-sawed. First we held the village, then were pushed back and the Nazis re-occupied. We couldn't always retrieve our dead. Many frozen bodies, both ours and the enemy's, were in the contested area.

I have a vivid mental imprint of an Army truck coming back through our position with a load of frozen American GI dead stacked crosswise like cordwood. Sitting atop the load were two graves registration soldiers. On their fingers were many rings and many were the watches on their wrists and arms. It gave me a sick feeling in the pit of my stomach.

One of our men had lost a family member in combat, and that sight triggered something in him. He raised his rifle to shoot the grave robbers from that load of bodies. Someone knocked his gun aside. We were all visibly shaken by this experience.

* * *

Through months of training we were indoctrinated with our purpose in coming across an ocean, thousands of miles from home: destroy tyranny, free enslaved people, crush the enemy armed forces. But it was not until we pushed into Germany and overran the monstrous concentration camps, with their unbelievable atrocities, that I fully understood why we were fighting and why we had to win. For fifty years I've struggled to understand how the German nation could follow a mad man such as Hitler. He determined who was unfit to live and considered it his right to exterminate them.

Words are not adequate to describe the horrors of the camp we overran. It is one thing for armed soldiers to contend with each other in battle, but my mind cannot grasp how the Nazis could sink so low as to herd naked women and children to slaughter by the thousands.

There were several major extermination camps: Buchenwald, Auschwitz, Dachau, Treblinka. There were smaller ones as well—numbering about one hundred—scattered throughout Germany, Poland, Belgium. Our division overran one of the smaller ones.

It was a jarring thing in a beautiful countryside bursting forth with the flowers of spring, to find a slaughter camp nestled in some hills. In their hasty departure, the fleeing Nazis left the grisly evidence: rotting corpses, those barely living, and the incredible stench of death and filth. We went to a nearby German village and asked the frightened villagers about the monstrous evil close by. They feigned innocent surprise and said they were told it was a convalescent hospital. So that they could never more claim they thought it was a "convalescent hospital," we rousted them out of their houses—old men, women and children—and marched them through the camp. Many of them vomited and fainted.

I had a conversation with a Nazi SS prisoner of war who spoke good English. He asked, "Why did you Americans come all those thousands of miles to get involved in a war that was none of your business? If you had stayed out of it we could have cleansed the earth of Jews and all other *untermenschen* (undesirables) and could have had a wonderful world for us noble Aryans." I thought of all the women and children they had slaughtered and thought of my own grandmothers, mother, and sisters and knew why it was my business.

* * *

Finally the hostilities ended, and Germany surrendered. Our unit wound up in Hamburg. It was our job to establish and maintain order in a section of that city. We found a Russian and Polish slave labor camp, which we liberated. Once released, these slaves went on a rampage. We had to lock them up again to establish order. While they were on the loose, the Russians located a distillery. The German who operated it made schnapps, or whiskey. Our captain hit it off well with the brew master who asked that a guard be set at his still. To ingratiate himself to the Americans, this German sent five gallons of his brew over to us each time the guard was changed. Before long, Captain had a drunken unit on his hands.

One evening, as someone was parking a truck by a building, I walked in front of the truck; the drunken driver failed to stop, crushing my leg between the bumper and the wall. The medics placed me on a stretcher and prepared me to go to a hospital. As I was loaded aboard a vehicle, one of my buddies came to say good-bye.

"Johnny, I want you to know I lost money on you."

"Oh, really, I'd be glad to pay you back."

"No" he said. "I'm happy to pay it myself. You see, we watched you. You've never smoked or drank with us, or chased women as we did. I bet you would break down before you left, but you never did."

I ended up in a hospital. My injury, though not overly serious, was enough to get me a trip home on a medical flight. I arrived home with only one dog tag on my neck. I presume the other was left behind in a hospital in France or Germany. I was grateful to be home with that one tag, so I'd know who I was after my long and scary absence.

When my broken bone was knitted up, I was discharged.

Lin H. Johnson returned to his home in Idaho Falls. He finished college, married, and farmed east of Idaho Falls for fifty years. He and his wife, Madge Jensen, have six children, thirty-two grandchildren and five great-grandchildren, with more on the way. Madge died in 1983. Lin and Mary Waddoups were married in 1986, and they live in Lincoln, Idaho.

Lin served as bishop of his ward, on the stake high council and was an ordinance worker in the Idaho Falls Temple for eleven years. For several years he has written a column for the Idaho Falls *Post Register*.

LORIN B. KAUER

Great and terrible was the day that they did come up to battle.

(3 Nephi 4:7)

I entered the armed services in June 1944, a nineteen-year-old kid fresh out of high school from Rexburg, Idaho. After finishing basic training at Camp Hood, Texas, and taking a fifteen-day furlough, I boarded the *SS Acquatainia*. We had arrived in France as the Battle of the Bulge was going on in Belgium. At a small town in Belgium we became part of General Patton's 3rd Army. As soon as we caught our collective breath we were sent in to relieve the 101st Airborne at Bastogne.

Lorin B. Kauer

What I remember most vividly about that battle was the cold and snow. The cold penetrated our clothes and blankets more than I was used to in Idaho winters. Of course we didn't have shelter. We were fortunate to have winter clothing—a big army overcoat and a wool blanket. The wool blanket was a mixed blessing; when it got wet it was hard to dry it out. Many of the men had their hands or feet frozen. I could deal with the cold pretty well because I was used to it, but it was really rough on the soldiers from Southern states.

One problem we had to deal with during the Battle of the Bulge was that a lot of Germans were dressed in American uniforms. You never knew if you were talking to an American or a German. One day I was on patrol, and we came across what we thought were American GI's. After we had moved on I thought, *That's funny, there was only one out of the bunch who talked to me*. The rest of them just hung back. I began to wonder about them and was glad that no one started shooting.

Both the Allies and the Germans suffered heavy casualties during this horrible battle. I remember seeing the dead and frozen bodies loaded on trucks, like so many fence posts. Every day I wondered if I was going to become one of those frozen guys.

Following the Battle of the Bulge our unit was sent to southern France. We were located in a small valley, us on one side, the Germans on the other. At night you could hear the Germans talking as though they were just across the road. We had dug a fox hole and covered it over with six-to nine-inch diameter trees we had cut from the forest around us. The thickness of our roof was a blessing to us. From time to time the Germans would lob mortar shells right on top of us. None of us were killed in these attacks, but one or two were wounded.

Our unit pulled out of southern France and sent to Holland. One of the men in our platoon was my good friend Howard Munns, from Archer, a small community south of Rexburg. A couple of days earlier our lieutenant had been killed. When we got back from patrol one morning we had a brand new lieutenant who asked what we'd seen. After he heard our report he said, "Well, there's Germans out there." He picked out eight men and said, "I'll show you how to patrol." Evidently this new second lieutenant led his patrol right into a machine gun nest. The lieutenant was shot and two of his men were killed. Howard and two others were captured, but the remaining two managed to get back to our lines. When I didn't see Howard, I asked the two what happened. One of them said, "The last we saw, the Germans were marching Howard and the others back to their lines. They were carrying the lieutenant. We were the only two who managed to sneak away."

I wrote my fiancée, Erma Siepert, "Howard is with Etsel Sommers." That's all I said. Etsel had been a prisoner of war for some time, and everyone at home knew it. I knew that if I said that Howard was captured, the censors would have cut it out. Erma phoned Howard's folks and told them, "Lorin wrote and said Howard is with Etsel Sommers, so evidently he was captured." Other than a report that he was missing in action, this was the only news Howard's parents had until the end of the war, so my report gave them hope. Howard survived his POW experience and made it home.

Holland is a beautiful country, especially when spring comes. Tulips burst everywhere, and the canals and windmills add a distinctive quality to the landscape. Where there had been no pitched battles, you wouldn't have known there was a war going on. Except that we'd been so long without bathing that you could smell us five miles away. We and the Germans could smell each other before we could see each other. In a small village we asked some ladies if they would take the soap we gave them and wash our clothes. We bathed, and with clean clothes felt almost human again.

Moving through a small Dutch town near the border of Germany, we maneuvered house-to-house, flushing enemy soldiers from hiding. It was intense, prickly action, and I was wound tight. Frequently we had to throw a hand grenade into houses as we struggled to secure an area. Passing an open door I heard a noise coming from the basement. Snatching a hand grenade, I was about to lob it down the stairs when something made me hesitate. Peering into the dim light I saw a woman, a child in each arm, appear at the bottom of the stairs. Forever since, I have been grateful I did not act faster.

Nights made everybody jumpy. One night, after we had moved into Germany, we were holed up in an old barn. Pack rats running around in the top of the barn set me on edge. One of the guys in another outfit opened up with his rifle. When he stopped firing, I phoned and asked what he shot. He said, "I don't know, but it looked like someone creeping up on me. Wait a minute and I'll crawl out and have a look." Pretty soon he called back and said, sheepishly, "I shot a post."

I hated going out on night patrols. Wandering around in "no-man's land" magnified the night sounds. I questioned the value of these ventures— I think the Germans liked to sleep as much as we did.

We had pushed the Germans up against the Rhine River in the town of Rhineberg. We had another new lieutenant—seems like we went through quite a few second lieutenants. I was with a good buddy from Montpelier, Idaho, Frank Koeven. Pulling the clip out of his Browning Automatic Rifle, he said, "Boy, that was pretty close to us Lorin." There was a hole through

Lorin just returned from guard duty. All of these men are from Idaho. Left to right: Lorin Kauer, Grange Goff, Howard Munns, Ray Torngren, Frank Koeven, [First Name?] McComber.

the clip. The Germans had us held down in a brick factory. The new lieutenant asked me, "What shall we do?" I told him, "I think we better pull back and see if we can get some tanks in here to help us." The lieutenant agreed. Then I told him, "I'll stay and try to hold the Germans down if you'll get these men out." Not very bright on my part. The lieutenant finally got the platoon out, and I was lying there all by myself, shooting at the Germans. One of my buddies was killed right beside me. His death kind of broke me up.

After the lieutenant got everyone out, I managed to get myself out. As we pulled back, we were asked to try again to take the brick factory. The lieutenant asked me, "Do you think you can get back in there and pin them down a little so we can get the tanks positioned so they can start firing?" So I gathered my squad and told him we'd go in. On the way to the factory building, I was hit by German machine gun fire. They hit me in the chin and in the arm. The hit on the chin nearly knocked me out. I dropped my rifle and couldn't pick it up. I wondered what was the matter. When I looked down, blood was squirting out of my arm. I learned later the bullet had cut the cord in the top part of my arm, which held the main muscle to my hand.

Getting hit made me angry, and I stood up and shook my fist at the Germans and told them to come out and fight like men. I suppose I was a bit goofy. The medic who was trying to treat me said, "We are having a heck of a time with you." About this time Frank Koeven ran up beside me and asked if I was all right. I told him I thought so, but by now blood was running down my chin, so I really wasn't sure. Somehow we got over into a ditch. The Germans were still shooting at us, but we finally escaped.

I walked back to an aid station. The doctor there looked at my arm, then my chin, and told me, "I'd better do a little trimming on that, but the wound is so close to your larynx that I don't dare freeze it, or even give you anything to deaden the pain." He got in there with a scalpel and started trimming. Man, I knew he was trimming.

I was awarded the Silver Star for that day, although I didn't feel like I'd done anything special, just what needed to be done at the time.

This ended my action on the frontline. I was taken by ambulance to a hospital at LeMans, France. It was nice to be able to have a shower, clean sheets, and a good bed—things you miss so much being on the front. The doctor sewed up my arm and put it in a cast so that the cord in my arm would heal. I was in the hospital for two months.

35th Infantry Divison—Lorin Kauer's Divison. Lorin's picture is the one circled, in the middle row.

I was under orders to go back to the front when the war in Europe ended 5 May 1945. That evening I was in a Red Cross shelter, and a guy came up and started thumping me on the back, saying "How are you?" I didn't recognize him until he told me his name. Harry Whittaker, another kid from Archer. We sat up all night talking about Rexburg, both a little homesick.

I rejoined my outfit on the banks of the River Elbe. We were on the west bank, and the Russians on the east. The war was over! We stayed on the banks of the Elbe for two months, until they shipped us back to France. We thought we were going to Japan, then the atomic bomb was dropped, and they surrendered. We were a happy bunch of guys and knew we were going home.

On 22 August we sailed out of Le Havre, France, on the *SS Cristobal* bound for Boston. It was a small ship and jumped around on the waves in the Atlantic Ocean. I was seasick most of the way home. We arrived in Boston on 31 August, and I was given a forty-five-day leave.

On 12 September 1945, I married Erma Siepert, my high school sweetheart, in the Salt Lake Temple. Following our honeymoon I was sent to Kentucky for two months. I had been in the Army for only twenty months and didn't have enough regular points on that basis to be discharged. But I had three battle stars, a Purple Heart, and a Silver Star, which gave me the required points, and I was discharged in February 1946. Overall, I felt like being in the Army was a good experience for me. More than anything else, it gave me an appreciation for a good warm bed, a nice meal, and being able to go to bed at night without having to wake up every two hours to relieve

The cost of war: 35th Infantry Division Survivors—Lorin Kauer, middle row, second from right.

someone of guard duty or having to lay in the snow or having water drip down my neck.

I would not want my children to have to go through those experiences, but it was good for me and made me appreciate the things I have.

Lorin and Erma Kauer have seven children, five sons and two daughters. Lorin was a farmer and rancher all his life. In addition he operated an insulation business, which he says helped pay for the farm. "It was a great way to teach our children how to work and take responsibility."

"My time in the hospital in France gave me time to reflect on life. I made a strong commitment to remain active in The Church of Jesus Christ of Latter-day Saints and to serve the Lord throughout my life." Lorin has served in both an elders and seventies quorum presidency, as a member of a stake mission presidency, and on a high council. He has also been a branch president and a bishop.

In 1992–93, he and Erma served a mission in Singapore (three months) and India (fifteen months). In 1996–97 they served another mission in Nauvoo, Illinois.

GORDON A. DIXON

After we trained in North Africa and Italy, we were sent to Marseille, France, to join the 7th Army.

Our convoy stretched over a mile long as we departed the Port of Marseille with our 120 Jeeps with trailers and our large trucks and other equipment. We drove up the Rhone Valley to Epinol, and on 1 December 1944, went into battle on the front line and had five months of intense fighting. We were normally attached to an infantry division to furnish them close fire support. Our 4.2-inch mortar had a range of 3,600 yards with a 25-pound high explosive, or smoke shell, depending upon the requirement. We were in action with the 6th and 12th Army Group, the 7th U.S. Army, the 1st French Army, and with the XI, XXI, and VI Corps. Whenever there was an offensive, we were there. Our supported infantry units liked our shooting. We were used extensively as the Siegfried Line was breeched.

My men came from all parts of the United States and were, for the most part, inductees. They performed gallantly in battle and were highly decorated. The 99th Chemical Mortar Battalion received a Presidential Unit Citation, along with the 3rd Infantry Division, for action in the so-called Colmar Pocket. We managed to keep our casualties to only about ten percent. I attribute this remarkable record to the extensive training we had and to our outstanding staff and company officers.

I was promoted to lieutenant colonel on 1 May 1945. By 8 May, we had completed 150 days in combat, with only four days of rest. The men were tired and had become thin and haggard, yet with the end of the war in sight, they kept going.

I acknowledge the hand of the Lord in preserving my life. One day I had gone forward to check on my men and review the situation at the front. As we were returning to the rear, a voice came into my mind, saying: "Tell your driver to move to the other side of the road." Surprised, I ignored the warning, then it came again, with more intensity: "Tell your driver to move to the left lane!" Accordingly, I instructed my driver. We later learned that stretch of road had not been cleared of mines.

At the end of hostilities we were near Berchtesgaden, Germany, and there we were used to guard captured installations. Some time later we were sent to Camp Lucky Strike, a port on the Mediterranean, from which we returned to the United States, arriving 6 July 1945. We were given a thirty-day leave.

We reassembled at Camp Chaffee, Arkansas, to prepare for the invasion of Japan; however, the dropping of the atomic bomb in August and the subsequent surrender of Japan led to the disbanding of the 99th Battalion. We were relieved not to have to continue fighting. This was the end of my eighteen months of service as commander of a fine battalion of soldiers.

I was invited to remain on active duty but elected to remain with the reserves. I did not feel that the atmosphere around army camps was conducive to raising a family. In 1961 I was promoted to full colonel, and ten years later retired from military service. My career bridged from 1934, when the Army still used leg wrappings as part of the uniform, from seacoast artillery and search lights, to highly sophisticated guided missiles and the "H" bomb.

As I meditate upon this important part of my life, I find that it has helped me in many ways. I learned principles of leadership, how to deal more effectively with people, and became acquainted with the men of other nations. It helped me to be a better teacher, a better father and husband, a better member of the Church, and a better citizen of this great United States. My hope is that the youth of our nation will realize that our freedom is worth the price we must pay for it.

Gordon A. Dixon taught the physical sciences and coached at Ricks College for twenty-seven years. He served in a bishopric in a Rexburg ward. In 1956 he was called as bishop of the first ward organized on the Ricks College Campus. He served in that capacity for seven years. Gordon also served in the stake Sunday School presidency, and later as Patriarch of the Rexburg East Stake. He was president of his Rotary Club and a member of the National Science Association. He and his wife, Elda, were married in 1933. They are the parents of two sons and two daughters. At the time of his death on 29 October 1998, they had nineteen grandchildren and fourteen great-grandchildren.

VERL W. REED

We . . . see the great wickedness one very wicked man can cause to take place among the children of men.

(Alma 46:9)

December 1944. When we docked at Marseilles, France, we saw the remains of many ships in the harbor. The ravages of war could be seen throughout the city and on the docks. Damage was severe no matter where you looked. In the midst of all this, I wondered what would happen to me. Obviously some of us who came off our ship would not return.

While at Marseilles I found several other Mormons, and we gathered for a meeting. There was one fellow who could play a portable organ, which helped to brighten up the meeting. It would be a long time until I could attend another sacrament meeting.

I was in the 42nd Division—known as the Rainbow Division of World War I fame—then commanded by General Douglas MacArthur. Before we left New Jersey our mail was censored, and we were directed to remove the Rainbow Division shoulder patches from our uniforms. Everything was to be secret— to confuse the enemy. It probably confused us more than it did the enemy because when we did go online in France, the Germans had a loudspeaker set up, welcoming the men of the "Rainbow Division," saying they hoped their seasoned troops would not make it too hard on us.

While fighting at Strausbourg, I learned it is a frightening and confusing thing to be in combat. One day Sergeant Fletcher sent us out to patrol behind enemy lines, into the mountains just north of our position. It was quiet in the woods. We watched every opening in the trees, listening intently. The muted sounds of gunfire seemed a long way off. Footprints led up a mountainside, but we saw no one. Openings between the trees permitted us to see enemy-held fields below and tiny villages with their church spires. I wondered whose prayers God would answer.

We found nothing significant and turned back, less tense now, going over ground we had recently covered. One of our men discovered a German land mine in time to prevent us from blundering into it.

On our return we learned that our unit was withdrawing. Walking along in the dark we saw civilian refugees. The refugees pulled carts piled high with their worldly goods. I felt like we had betrayed their trust and wondered how they knew we were withdrawing.

During action against the enemy, communication with E Company was lost. Our platoon was ordered to reestablish contact with them. I was the lead scout. It was

Verl W. Reed

night. Down the road we saw what appeared to be soldiers crossing the road. The captain called to them, and the area ahead erupted in gunfire. We hit the ground. I watched tracers threatening us. Eventually the firing stopped. We were motioned forward, and the firing started again. The driver of one of our M10's (light armored vehicle) was firing his machine guns. There was an explosion and his gun stopped; a shell from a panzerfaust killed him. In a few seconds we were again motioned forward only to encounter more intense firing. We fell back.

In a wooded gully across the road from us, the captain set up a command post. I was positioned on a hilltop where the only protection was a few trees and my imagination. I scooped the snow around me. I knew it wouldn't stop bullets, but somehow it made me feel secure—like what you can't see can't hurt you.

All night enemy shells burst in the trees above us, and limbs or shell fragments fell into our position. A German soldier kept calling "Helfa—Wasser, Americanish." Shortly after dawn there was another artillery barrage. I heard the call to rally with the others. Sergeant Johnston was there with two wounded men, one man's arm dangling loosely. They reported that the captain and two members of my squad were dead. They had been in what I thought was the safest spot.

The wounded were sent back. Sergeant Fletcher took charge and led us to a small village where we took up positions and established a watch. This felt fine to me. We were in a house with no enemy in sight. Looking around the house we found some rye bread and a little jam. A wizened little lady, presumably the owner, came in from somewhere and built a fire in the stove. We heard artillery fire, but it didn't seem to be directed at us.

The smoke from our fire must have attracted the Germans' attention. There was a huge explosion and smoke boiled through the house. Where there had been a brick wall I saw a fifteen-foot hole. A clothes closet to my right was shattered, and a lady's hat fell atop my helmet, giving my buddies a much needed laugh.

After closing the breech in our lines and securing the front, we moved back to a small village for rest and to receive replacements. I lost some good friends that day.

The replacements were as brave as any men and did whatever was assigned them. We spun them good tales of what it was like at the front and watched their faces pale.

After a few weeks we were sent to another area of the front. It was heavily forested and controlled by the Germans. Sometimes we could hear them chopping wood or see smoke from their fires rising above the trees.

It was near midnight and Lonnie, a recent replacement, was standing guard. The other two of us were asleep. I wakened instantly at the snap of a grenade handle being released. Rifle shots rang out and Lonnie yelled, "Come on you! Come on, . . . I'll get yuh." I expected that grenade to explode any second and was relieved when I heard it detonate down the hill. "What is it?" I asked. Lonnie said, "Stay in your sack; I'll take care of them." There was no return fire. I suspected Lonnie, being new, had gotten jumpy. The phone rang, and I heard Lonnie say something about some Krauts in front of us, but that he had taken care of them. By now the other GI was crawling from one end of our fox hole to the other on his hands and knees, shaking like a leaf. I assured him that things were okay, and we laid back down.

There had been no enemy for Lonnie to see. Come dawn, Sergeant. Fletcher took Lonnie away. I never saw him again. One thing for sure—you didn't want someone with you whom you couldn't depend upon.

We picked up rations, ammo, and grenades. The sound of artillery, mortar, and small-arms fire filled the air a few hundred yards in front of us. 1st Battalion had broken through German lines. As we moved forward we passed litter-bearers carrying our wounded. *Were the wounded the lucky ones?* I wondered. They had no more war ahead of them, but we did not know what lay ahead of us.

After a while we moved forward and ran into sniper fire. When the sniping quit we moved up again. A radioman lay face up along the path, red bullet marks stitched across his face.

Suddenly several explosions occurred simultaneously and something zinged off my helmet. Cries of pain came from up and down the line and the terse command of Sergeant Fletcher, "Halt, stand where you are. Don't move, we're in a mine field!" I saw Thornton holding a cloth to his neck. Johnnie looked to be in pain as he grasped the calf of his leg. Our medic and Glader picked their way cautiously to Barton. The medic laid his pouch down to examine Barton's wound. Glader took another step, and there was an explosion and something dropped right on the medic's pouch. We waited for it to blow, but it smoked out. With a hearty sigh of relief, the medic went about his work. We set the wounded at the edge of the road. They were told that there would be someone along shortly to take them to the rear. Then we heard: "Okay, the rest of you, let's go." Warily we started down the road.

"Hold it!" Nelson shouted. "There's a trip wire." Everyone froze. I got down on my elbows and knees and pulled up my sleeves, feeling for a wire. "There's nothing here," Sam said. Grabbing Bob by the arm, the two of them skipped down the road and back. Then Nelson raised up holding a very thin trip wire in his hand. We proceeded with greater caution. The road paralleled a wooded ravine. "There's some Krauts down there," someone barked. Peering into the ravine I saw movement and shouted "Halt!" Two figures started running. Our guns opened up and we heard a cry. Several GI's checked the ravine. They brought up two very young soldiers, one wounded. They were frightened little boys, probably off to see their girlfriends.

We scanned the river for a way to cross. Sergeant Fletcher raised his ammo and rifle high and walked down the bank. Chest deep in the frigid water, he barked, "First Platoon, let's go."

On the other side Fletcher said "Reed, follow up the road." Being lead is the loneliest feeling in the world. *What kind of mortals are we?* I thought. *Going to do battle with tanks?* We had no choice, it had to be done. I moved ahead, eyes alert, listening and wondering where the tanks were. The road wound through a forest. From tracks on the ground we finally concluded that there was just one tank, and it was nowhere to be found.

We walked several miles before we spotted a village. Sergeant Fletcher sent six of us forward. There was no sign of movement—it seemed deserted, we saw no soldiers, no tanks, no army vehicles.

"Reed, go up that knob and see what's on the other side. Take Banks with you." We found nothing significant, but as we started back, Banks called to me. With him was a German soldier who surrendered after I passed by. I guess I looked meaner than Banks.

We walked through town after town, rifles at the ready, one eye watching for cover, the other searching for any point from which we could be shot. Mostly we saw white flags hanging out of windows. The towns were deathly quiet, the civilians all hiding. In a wooded area firing broke out behind me. Then a group of German soldiers came out of a small cave to surrender, their fight gone.

On the other side of some railroad tracks a dirt lane led alongside several small homes. The homes had gardens in front of them, with a picket fence surrounding a small pasture. Someone said he saw GI's across the river. We thought the town had been overrun by our forces, and we became careless. As we started to open a picket gate small arms fire raked the site, pinning seven of us down. The slightest movement brought more fire on our position. We had a light machine gun; the operator set it up and commenced firing. Almost immediately he grabbed his stomach and rolled on his back. We pulled him around us as best we could. As we did a bullet went through his ankle kicking up the dust in front of my face. The man next to me had his rifle shot out of his hands, the bullet barely missing my head. I figured the sniper meant that shot for me. Our situation was suddenly desperate. I felt it was just a matter of time. It all seemed futile. Mentally I gave up. Resting my head down in the dust I thought of my dead buddies. *Joe and Iron, I'll soon be with you and then I'll know what it is all about.* With that thought I felt relief, and whispered a prayer into the dust. I promised the Lord that if I got out of this, I would do what I was supposed to, forever after.

About that time I heard firing behind us and saw Sergeant Johnson pop up from behind the railroad embankment, fire a burst with his grease gun, and duck down. He did it again, and I saw others were firing from down along the tracks. The long barrel of one of our tank destroyer's 90 mm rifle swung toward the enemy and a round screamed over our heads, then another, and another. We became spectators to the battle. At last the firing stopped. Gingerly we stood on wobbly legs, and one by one ran to the cover of the railroad embankment. With every step I expected to feel bullets rip into my back. Safe, we looked at each other, laughing uncontrollably in our relief. The soldiers on the other side of the river, who we thought were ours, were German. This was the third time that day I had been pinned down by enemy fire. Feeling that the war's end was not far away, I wanted to make it, alive.

The next morning we walked into the city of Furth, which was now wholly in our hands. Along the road we saw a trench. There were women and children standing or kneeling beside it, sobbing. As we came near the trench we saw in it the bodies of German soldiers. Some of the women had gotten down and brushed the dirt off the faces of the dead, and looked up at us with eyes full of hate. The bodies of the men in the trenches were probably home guard who had been with their families the day before. I felt like saying "I didn't do it," because indeed I had not, but if they had been firing on us, I surely would have.

Nuremberg had fallen, and we were sent on to Dachau. Earlier the 442nd Regiment had liberated the concentration camp there. Rumor had it that after seeing the butchery done there, some of our soldiers had to be taken off the line for fear of what they would do to the camp guards or the civilians in the area. I felt no desire to go to the death camp, but I had to. The survivors were so thin, their skin so taut over their bones, that they looked like walking corpses. They wanted to give us a gift of something, but they had nothing. Thirty or so carloads of corpses were reported to have been machine gunned shortly before our troops arrived. Other corpses lay in piles—like cordwood.

Rumors were that the German army was about to capitulate. At Augsburg my company was placed on guard duty. We learned that this was where Kesselring and his staff were to turn themselves in. I had never seen so much brass. The German staff in their gray cars, officers sitting upright, stiff, some monocled, passed by me at our check point. We were told we had to salute them, which galled me no end.

When the surrender was complete, we were moved south. We drove past miles of German and Hungarian troops, rifles on their shoulders, marching back to forfeit their arms. It made me a little uneasy, knowing that if they chose to, they could open up on us. We were moved into the Tyrolean Alps to a mountainous valley near the town of Schwatz, about twenty miles north of Innsbruck. We set up checkpoints at strategic areas to apprehend enemy soldiers. Several of these checkpoints were shot up by rogue SS troops carrying concealed weapons. Sometimes a lone GI was found with his throat slit. We were told to be careful: it was not yet all peace and quiet.

I was assigned to Salzburg, Austria, at Regimental Headquarters where I became L Company clerk. I did not have sufficient points to go home, but while in Salzburg, I got to do a lot of sightseeing. On one three-day pass I went to the French city of Nancy. I can't remember much about it except that as I walked down one street many women propositioned me from doorways—maybe I was on the wrong street.

Also during my time at Salzburg, my brother Glen came to visit me. At church services I met several other LDS men. It was good to meet with other Mormons and to partake of the sacrament again. One Sunday the chaplain picked up several of us in his Jeep and drove us to the first LDS post-war conference held in Austria, held near a little town about forty miles from Salzburg. Just prior to our arrival several people had been baptized in a nearby stream. The meeting was conducted in a wooded glen. Some of our group were invited to speak. We tried to join in singing the hymns. I recognized the melodies, but the German words were strange to me.

Being in this spiritual setting among members of the Church was such a contrast to the places I had been and the things I had been doing that it felt strange. It had been only a short time since I had constantly carried a rifle, and without it I felt naked. My eyes kept searching the nearby trees for any threatening movement.

I processed for embarkation at Le Havre, France, along with 500 other GI's, and crossed a stormy Atlantic in January 1946. New York City! I was so happy to be on American soil that I didn't notice there was no brass band to greet us. I traveled by train through the hills of West Virginia, across the grain belt states of Iowa and Kansas, and over the sage covered hills of Wyoming, and on to Salt Lake City. At Fort Douglas I was discharged and given one hundred dollars. After a short visit with my brother Arnold and his wife, Joyce, I boarded the train for Idaho Falls. I called home from the passenger depot and in a short while my youngest brother Lee, now a teenager and much taller than I remembered , picked me up and drove me home.

Verl Reed was born 18 June 1923 in Escalante, Utah. He married Ruth Field in the Idaho Falls Temple. They are parents of a son and three daughters, and have twelve grandchildren. Verl became an accountant. He served several bishops as their ward clerk, one of whom said of Verl, "You couldn't have a better man for that job." Verl passed away on 21 December 1998 in Idaho Falls, Idaho.

IVAN R. MILLER

This freedom that we're fighting for won't seem so
Important by and by, when no one has to die for it.

Maxwell Anderson, *Valley Forge*

In April 1943 I left the South Pacific and returned to the United States to enter Officer's Candidate School at Camp Barkeley, Texas, where I was trained as a medical supply officer. While in the States, I spent several leave times in Idaho, seeing my family and Helen Davenport.

Helen and I were married 8 November 1943, in the Salt Lake Temple. We enjoyed a very short time together before I was on my way to England.

My first assignment was in the medical section of a supply depot located at Wem. Later I was sent to a depot near Oxford to join the 15th Medical Group. I arranged to have the only other LDS man in our unit as my roommate. He was from Manti, Utah.

Prior to leaving for France our commanding officer planned a dance. So that the men would have girls to dance with, the colonel invited the WRENS, the English equivalent of our WACS. I was asked to escort one of the female officers. "I'm can't do that. I'm a married man," I said.

"I'm not asking you to do anything your wife would disapprove of. Just be her escort."

When I refused the officer said, "Do you think your wife is just sitting around home waiting?"

"I wish that's all I had to worry about," I sputtered. "I won't do it!"

So they assigned me to handle the drunk and disorderly and see that they got back to camp.

One of the enlisted men detailed to help me was a wiry,

Lieutenant Ivan R. Miller

tough Cajun from Louisiana. A mouthy corporal was expelled from the dance. As we put him on the truck he yelled, "I'm not staying on this truck!" The young Cajun sat down on the corporal as he said to me, "Don't worry, Lieutenant. He's not getting out of here." And he didn't.

We arrived in France in October 1944, a month after Paris was liberated. We landed at Omaha Beach. The destruction there was plain to see. As we left the beach I saw an old couple sitting on the rubble of what had once been their home. I wanted to stop and help them but could not.

I was stationed at Le Bourget Airfield, where Lindbergh had landed in 1927. One of my first assignments was to escort a convoy of vehicles and supplies to Metz. Nearby there was a forest, and when I found time I went for a walk. I came across a maze of caved-in, eroding trenches from World War I, where I discovered a military cemetery. Wandering among the graves I noticed that the latest dates on the markers were from 1918. The "war to end all wars" had ended only twenty-six years earlier. I puzzled as to why we were back at war so soon. I took off my helmet as a sense of reverence enveloped me. I moved quietly among the graves of those buried there.

In the east I could see the flashes of gunfire reflected on the clouds and hear the rumble of artillery fire. So much for the "war to end all wars."

We were moved to Noirhat, Belgium, and I became depot maintenance officer. One of my extra duties was security officer. It was my job to stop thievery. We employed about a hundred Belgians. They had been overrun by the Germans, then liberated by Americans. These people were desperate for food, clothing, and other necessities. The Belgians had had no opportunity to plant and harvest crops. As a consequence, the civilian populace was living in unimaginable poverty. I was told that a certain man was stealing from us. Picking up a local *gendarme*, I went to confront this man at his home. When we entered the house, the *gendarme*, in perhaps an extra-legal procedure, opened every closet and drawer in the house. In all the home the only food I saw were three small potatoes and a can of lard.

The woman of the house sat quietly crying, and I felt sick about being there. Upstairs the *gendarme* started to pull a bed apart. There was a sheet on the bed with a medical caduceus marking it. Clearly it was ours. It had been washed so many times that the caduceus was barely visible. By this time my embarrassment was acute. I told the *gendarme* that they were not our sheets, which made him furious. I said that there was nothing in the house that I was interested in. As we rode back to the post I wept silently.

On another occasion I was approaching the mess hall. There was an elderly civilian eating from a trash barrel. The closer I got to the man, the faster he grabbed for food and stuffed it in his mouth. I led him into the dining hall and asked the mess sergeant to find something decent for this man to eat. He responded, "We'll take care of him, Lieutenant."

My brother Earl was killed at Aachen, Germany, 16 October 1944. He was a tank commander and had landed in France in the D-Day assault. Earl was hit by a ricocheting mortar shell while refueling his tank. He died that night in a field hospital from internal bleeding. I visited his grave and dedicated it. I felt great sadness, especially as I thought how our parents would mourn his loss. Each time I think of Earl, the sadness returns.

Word came that my friend Grant Humphreys had died in a military plane crash in California. As boys we had been inseparable. He was a clean, upright, honest man. His wife was expecting a baby at the time of his death.

I was working eighteen to twenty hours a day, seven days a week. I suppose my body rebelled. I began to have severe headaches. In March I was sent to the general hospital at Antwerp for treatment. The doctors finally agreed that I had acute, severe spheno-palatine neuralgia. The Antwerp area

Ivan visiting his brother Earl's grave.

was subjected to constant attack by German buzz-bombs and V-2 rockets. Fortunately none of these hit very close to us, but the noise was unnerving. Our antiaircraft guns were credited with knocking down eighty percent of the V-1 buzz bombs, still, some of the rockets got through our defenses. I took photographs of some of the V-1s as they passed over. Occasionally our black-out blinds were blown off the windows, and sometimes I had to brush broken glass off my blankets.

From my journal, 24 March 1945: This may well be a red-letter day in this war. I saw the airborne invasion fleet as it went to help Montgomery in crossing the Rhine. I have never witnessed a more spectacular scene. The planes and gliders and bombers passed overhead for what seemed hours at a time. I do not know how many aircraft took part in the "invasion," but I would hazard a guess of several thousand. C-47's and gliders and B-24's carrying supplies. It is one of the biggest military operations since D-Day.

Germany surrendered 8 May 1945, but we had the war with Japan. I was eager to go home so Helen and I could start our life together.

In June we moved to Foug, France, near Nancy. We had nearly 500 German prisoners assigned to work for us. I became acquainted with some of them and got a good feeling about them. I realized that they were mostly just like us, just on different sides in the war.

In Foug I went to Paris to attend the LDS Servicemen's Conferences. At one of them I saw Dewain Silvester, my good friend from home.

Elder Hugh B. Brown was our visitor for one of the conferences. Before the conference started, Elder Brown and I talked about a meeting three years earlier, prior to my going to the South Pacific. It was good to see him again. A memorable part of being at that conference was to hear a French sister tell how they had met behind closed doors in order to have sacrament meetings during the German occupation. The right to worship was something I had always taken for granted.

In August I got my orders to go home! I went to Marseille to await passage to New York. Priority was given to troops headed for the Far East, and it was thirty days before an opening was available for me. While waiting I thought back over my time in the army. I often sat on a pile of lumber just outside my barracks, and in prayer thanked the Lord for preserving my life. I came through the war without a scratch. I thought of Earl and Grant and so many others and the price they paid.

(Ivan's other experiences in the war can be found on page 365.)

GEORGE EMERY DAVIS

Protect us by thy might, Great God our King!

("My Country, 'Tis of Thee," *Hymns*, no. 339)

Some friends and I tried to enlist in the Air Force, but we ended up serving with the Army Combat Engineers. The Combat Engineers did things such as providing clean drinking water, building pontoon bridges, and clearing minefields so that GI's were not killed or maimed. They were the first units into an area, preparing the way for the progress of the war.

England, Camp Llangadic—When we arrived at this camp, the site was a sea of mud interspersed by rows of tents set on concrete slabs. Our job was to make a suitable living area for a full battalion of men. We first built streets, pushing large rocks into the mud, then smaller and smaller rocks and gravel until the area was level and dry.

The tents were heated by small round stoves lined with bricks, and while the temperature rarely got below freezing, the huts were hard to keep warm. At the center of the camp was a high net-wire enclosure where coal and coke were stored. Each tent was limited to one bucket of coal and coke per day. Uncomfortable with the cold, the troops began stealing fuel. To improve the heating efficiency of the stove, they would knock the brick liners out of them.

Water was piped in from a spring about a mile and a half away. During the whole winter food supplies were chronically short. Marmalade, brussels sprouts, and bread were standard fare. It was not long before the men were trapping rabbits and trading the natives cigarettes and candy bars for food.

George Emery Davis

We were sent to the coast to clear mines that had been set earlier in the war, when fear of a German invasion of England was very real. When the buzzer on our mine detectors sounded, we had to dig up the mine with our bayonets. The mines were then detonated behind a plywood barrier. The detonation of these mines cracked some stained glass windows in a near by church. White tape was used to mark the boundaries of the cleared areas.

One Sunday an officer and some men from another unit came to learn our procedure. I sent two of my men to teach them. Something went wrong, there was a loud explosion, a cloud of smoke, and two dead men. Retrieving their torn bodies was particularly difficult.

As we disembarked from our landing craft onto French soil, evidence of the terrible battle that had taken place was everywhere. Bodies of soldiers who died to take the beachhead were piled up for removal. We first made contact with the Germans near the village of St Lo, which we took after four hours of fierce fighting. When the Germans retreated from St Lo, church bells began ringing as people filled the streets. Many began using the common toilet located alongside the main street, both men and women at the same time. This seemed peculiar to us.

Fighting for the next town was fierce, with the Germans and us taking and retaking the same ground several times. Our Combat Engineers, the 109th Regiment, led the skirmish and lost 110 men that day.

Two of our men, both Polish, one named Pintka and the other Cominski, scouted a small town and located a cache of cider. Cominski got really drunk. The Germans were firing 88 mm cannons at them, one of the shells hit a bloated dead horse nearby, showering Cominski with offal. It sobered him immediately.

Property lines in this farming country were marked by hedgerows. Grain in the fields between the hedgerows had not been harvested and was wasted by the trampling feet of fighting men from both sides. The Germans would retreat across a field, then dig in behind the next hedgerow. This gave them an open field from which to pick off our soldiers as they tried to advance.

We built a battering ram on the front of a tank. With the tank for protection we followed behind, and at the next hedgerow the tank punched a hole with its ram. We then planted explosives in the hole and blew a gap in the hedgerow. Then the Germans would retreat to the next row. And so it went as we painstakingly claimed this region for the Allied Forces.

Our unit was turned toward Paris. After Paris we headed toward Luxemburg, where the citizens were also happy to see us. Female bartenders brought out trays of beer to our soldiers as we passed through.

We were approaching the Saar River, and just beyond that the Seigfried Line, a series of concrete bunkers connected by tunnels just inside Germany. It was heavily fortified. Here General Patton's forces high-jacked the 28th Division's supply convoy, leaving us very short of ammunition, fuel, and other supplies. This caused a wait, allowing the retreating German troops to regroup and entrench themselves in the Siegfried Line. It was a bitter disappointment to me. I thought it caused the loss of time and lives, which could have been avoided had we been able to move more quickly.

We were charged to place explosives into the bunkers of the Siegfried. Under cover of night, charges were fixed at the observation windows of several bunkers. A man was left behind who raced through the connecting tunnels lighting fuses. The Germans, of course, could see the explosions and laid down a heavy artillery barrage on the connecting trenches, knowing about where our man was by watching the fireworks.

On 18 November 1944, we were dug in near Germeter. I was checking for wounded on my outer perimeter when a mortar exploded in some trees above us. Branches and shrapnel fell on my head, and I received a severe concussion.

I was evacuated to Paris. There I saw row after row of wounded GI's awaiting emergency medical procedures. From Paris I was airlifted to Hereford, England, where I remained until March 1945. From Hereford I was sent to Walter Reed Hospital by hospital ship, then to a veteran's hospital at Walla Walla, Washington.

On my birthday, 10 June 1945, I was discharged from the Army.

Following the war, George Emery Davis married Alice Stone. They are parents of five children and have nine grandchildren. George made his living in the sheep and cattle business and was active in the Wool Growers Association. He served two terms as a Commissioner for Fremont County, Idaho. He passed away in 1996.

HARRY J. LEWIES

God bless America, Land that I love. Stand beside her, and guide her, through the night with the light from above. From the mountains, to the prairies, to the oceans white with foam—God bless America, my home sweet home.

Irving Berlin, "God Bless America"

I graduated from high school in St Anthony, Idaho, and entered the ROTC program at the University of Idaho. When the war broke out, I was

Harry J. Lewies

sent to Fort Lewis, Washington. Our enlisted men's uniforms were distinctly different from the dress pinks and sabers of ROTC, but the defining disparity was KP. After four straight days of KP, I was persuaded that I wanted to be an officer. I finished Officer's Candidate School at Fort Benning, Georgia.

So I went to war as a second lieutenant in the U.S. Army Infantry. I served in Patton's 3rd Army. Second lieutenants were required to be at the head of their units in combat, consequently their survival rates were extremely low.

My company had a casualty rate of 150 percent, which meant that I saw nearly every man in my unit wounded or die, replaced, then watched half of the replacements become casualties. In the face of such losses, there is no apparent reason why I survived.

In winter trench foot was a major problem. It was caused from having wet, cold feet. The cold restricted circulation to the skin on the feet. The feet got infected and bled, and the men became unable to walk. Trench foot was especially serious among the men during the Battle of the Bulge. To curb the problem, a directive was received that every man was to change into dry socks; officers were required to guarantee compliance. I was handed enough new socks for every man in my unit. I crawled from foxhole to foxhole in the dark, issued a pair of socks to the men, and waited outside the foxhole while each man changed.

My platoon was made up mostly of kids from the coal mining region of Pennsylvania, with a few equally tough boys from the Ozarks. They were the rejects from the other two platoons in our Company. Some of them were nearly incorrigible, but when we got in the thick of battle I was glad I was on their side. They were fiercely loyal to me, and even now I am glad to see them years later when we have reunions.

We fought mostly in France and Germany. One day I sent Petrowski on an assignment so difficult I doubted it could be done. Surprisingly soon Petrowski was back, having completed the job exactly as I had told him. "Petrowski, you're magnificent. How did you do it?" I exclaimed. "Easy," he said, in his flat eastern accent, "I used my injenoody."

Ours was a scrappy unit. My guys didn't know how to quit. After we got through the Battle of the Bulge, we were the first unit to break through to the German side of the Siegfried Line. The Germans launched a fierce counter attack and pushed us back. As always retreat was difficult. I called in an artillery fusillade right onto our position so that the Germans were held in place while we withdrew.

"Injenoody" was the name of the game. One day we entered a small German village. The people were gone, but there were a few cattle loose in the area. We had been subsisting on K-rations for days, and I assumed K-rations would be our next meal as well. There was still fighting at the edge of the town. Imagine my delight as the mess sergeant handed me a plate of steak and potatoes. I enjoyed this change of diet. When I asked the sergeant where the food came from, he said it was courtesy of the departed villagers.

We entered a village one night and found it deserted. From a house a German couple emerged, staggering drunkenly. *What are we going to do with them?* I wondered. We told them they could walk in front of our convoy. Suddenly they disappeared. "Decoys! A setup by the Germans," I yelled. Then we heard the clanking of a tank as it began to move. I sent my best anti-tank man forward with his bazooka. We heard a whoosh, an explosion, and my man was back. "I nailed 'em." The drunken couple never reappeared.

When our platoon was organized, we were assigned a medic. He was an Italian from the Bronx. On numerous occasions he went forward in the face of withering enemy fire to tend a wounded man. DiCezra and I spent a lot of time together and became close friends. In the Battle of the Bulge the Germans had a deadly weapon we called the "screaming mimi." It fired a barrage of shells simultaneously, which would explode above us— lethal shrapnel decimating whatever was below. As one of these attacks ended, I saw DiCezra just a yard in front of me. He was on his knees, motionless, his back to me, his helmet on the ground. I was about to tell him to get his helmet on when I noticed something peculiar about his head. I rushed to him. Our medic, and my good friend, was dead.

War is not a tidy affair; there is always much confusion. We were clearing out a small town where the fighting was unusually fierce and we were pinned down. I radioed for tank support and was mighty glad to see it arrive. However, when the tank entered the town their guns began firing down a short narrow street. Some of my men were hugging the walls along that street, and when the tank fired, two were killed. In one of the many misfortunes of war, the tank driver could not tell who was there. I got behind the tank and beat on it with my rifle butt until I got the assault stopped. I showed the tank commander the target, and he immediately took care of our problem. It was a hard thing to see casualties come from friendly fire.

After we crossed the Rhine we moved through many towns that had been bombed level. To make a road, some of our tanks were outfitted with a blade like a bulldozer, and the tanks would plow a path through the wreckage. Communications wire was strung from any object above ground level. In seemed incongruous to see a statue in front of a church used to hold up a telephone wire.

Conditions among the civilians were wretched. In one town they were making bread out of sawdust.

When the Germans capitulated, we were moved into Czechoslovakia to keep the peace until the territory could be turned over to the Russians, as agreed to by President Roosevelt at the Yalta Conference. At Prague we paraded through the capital city, our rifles over our shoulders, with just one round of ammunition in the chamber. I never could figure out why just one round. Mostly we saw dignitaries shaking each other's hands, and pretty girls who smiled and waved at us as we passed by.

There was still a lot of animosity among the people there who had been so badly treated by German Czechs, many of whom were Nazi sympathizers. This animosity caused us the most trouble. Out in the countryside a group of civilians were rounding up and hanging those who had been collaborators with the Nazis. I suspect that the Czechs didn't want to wait for justice to move through the court system. It was a challenge to put a stop to this killing, but we eventually succeeded.

After the war, Harry J. Lewies returned to his home in Warm River, Idaho,and married Lillian Glover. They are parents of three daughters and a son. Harry eventually took over his father's business. He developed and operated a ski resort and later a fishing guide business. For a number of years he taught high school; he was an exceptional teacher. He is not a member of the Church, but Lillian is, and Harry has been a great friend to the Church. He and Lillian now live in Billings, Montana.

ELMO J. SEELEY

My word shall . . . all be fulfilled.

(Doctrine & Covenants 1:38)

I grew up in Chester, Idaho, where our family was as poor as the proverbial church mice. I was always small for my age, and I blushed easily, so the girls loved to tease me. Consequently, I entered the Army with an enormous inferiority complex. I prayed constantly for help to overcome my feelings of inadequacy. I promised the Lord that if he would help me overcome this weakness, that I would never refuse to do what he, or one of his servants, asked of me.

While training at Camp Barkley, Texas, I attended the Servicemen's Group sacrament meeting and was asked to speak the following Sunday. Throughout the coming week I worked on my talk every day. But when I arose to speak, every thought left my head, and I couldn't even make sense of my notes. I stumbled around for what seemed forever and finally sat down, devastated.

Most of my service in the war was in France and Germany. I was a tank mechanic with the 12th Armored Division. I always rode in a tank at the rear of the column, so that if anything happened to one of our tanks, I could help repair it.

When our unit arrived in France it had been raining for days. The unit commander said he wanted the oil changed in all the tanks. That meant getting down in the muck all day. For two days I held back while the others rolled around in the mud, but kept a prayer in my heart that the rains would stop. The third morning the clouds parted, and we had sunshine. I finished my work in a matter of hours, work that others had labored at for two full days to accomplish. I made sure to thank my Heavenly Father for the sunshine.

Elmo J. Seeley

Perhaps the most frightened I ever was happened during a retreat. Getting our tanks lined out when retreating was always the most difficult maneuver we had to accomplish. We were in a village and under constant enemy artillery fire. The buildings along the narrow streets were all in flames, which made turning the tanks around slow and difficult. Our position as mechanics was always at the end of the line, so we had to wait until the tanks ahead of us could move out. With flames licking at our armor plate, we were getting mighty hot by the time we got out of that village.

My patriarchal blessing promised that if I would listen to the promptings of the Spirit that I would be kept safe. The subtle work of the Spirit kept me safe more than once. One day a tank began to move up a road when it hit an anti-tank mine. The area on both sides of the road was marshy, and the Germans had sown the road with land mines.

After combat engineers came in and cleared away the mines, our crew was called in to extract the tank, which was beyond repair. We had a sergeant in our unit who may have been the most profane man I have ever known. I drove our maintenance tank up and was about to enter the road where the disabled tank sat. My profane friend said to me, "I don't feel good about your going up that road. I think you can reach it with the winch and cable if you come through that field." I made the approach he suggested and was about to deploy the cable when an officer and his driver passed by in a Jeep and started up the road I had been about to travel. The Jeep hit a mine, and both men were killed.

I had not felt any warning, and I wondered for many years why it was the sergeant who "didn't feel good" about my driving up that road. Finally it came to me that had I said I didn't feel good about walking my tank up that road, this sergeant would have ridiculed my feelings and ordered me to go anyway. Thus it was that the Lord kept his promise.

Another day a column of our tanks was moving along a winding road leading through a narrow cut in a hill. One of the tanks became lodged between the sides of the cut, and both its tracks came off. We decided it would be at least a two-day job to remove and repair the lodged tank. Normally we would be happy for a chance to remain away from the action while making repairs. This time, however, we all felt that we didn't want to remain behind. We asked permission to leave the tank for the Ordnance Company to repair. Permission was granted. Ordnance would take the necessary action.

We waited in another tank on the hillside, just above the disabled tank, until we received word to join the rest of our company. We had gone only fifty yards when an enemy artillery shell hit the spot where we had been waiting, leaving a large crater. Our lives were spared again.

* * *

At one point we were doing a lot of traveling at night. Having been in our tanks continually for three days, we were exhausted by the time the company stopped. My buddy told me to take a nap, saying he would stay awake. I awoke some time later and found every man in the tank asleep. Our company had pulled out and left us behind. We tried to catch up with our unit, but when we came to a fork in the road, it was not clear which way to turn. We apparently took the wrong road. Before long we found ourselves in a beautiful wooded area, which we later learned was behind enemy lines.

We got out of the tank and walked through the trees, our carbines in hand, to look around. Shortly we came upon some German soldiers having breakfast. We pointed our rifles at them, and they raised their hands. They seemed pleased to be captured. Back at the tank there was not room for them inside so we motioned for them to hang onto the top. Surprisingly, they did so, and laughed and joked with each other as we moved back in to our own lines. They seemed relieved to be out of the fighting. I thought they were a lot like the fellows on our side, a bunch of scared kids trying to stay alive.

Finally we had time away from the battle area for rest and recovery. A chow truck was set up to feed us hot meals. This attracted a lot of young German children scavenging for something to eat. Our GI's were hard to please and they groused about the food. I noticed that only the four-to-six-year-old kids were brave enough to retrieve what our soldiers were wasting. Some of these children were angrily booted out of the way by some of our guys, who then threw their uneaten food in the trash cans. I wondered what these kids would remember about Americans.

* * *

One day, while removing track from a tank, my finger got in the way of the sliding hammer and was badly smashed. I didn't think much about it, but after three sleepless nights I went to the medic. He sent me to a field hospital. I didn't feel all that bad. In this case, the treatment was worse than the injury. I spent six weeks recovering from surgery. By the time I was released, my unit had been sent on, and I joined the occupation forces in southern Germany.

For my injury I was offered the Purple Heart. I turned it down. I didn't think I was hurt that bad, and besides medals didn't mean that much to me. Over the years since the war I have discarded the ones I did receive.

Being in the war was a maturing experience for me. Only occasionally was I really frightened. I was also blessed in that I never had bad feelings toward the enemy.

When the fighting stopped I was in southern Germany, near the Swiss border. I hadn't seen another LDS person for many months. I got a pass and found the Church in Basel, Switzerland. Standing at the front door was the mission president, Max Zimmer. He shook my hand, then said he would like me to speak in the sacrament meeting, saying that his daughter would translate for me. I recalled my last attempt to address a group, but also remembered my promise to the Lord. I stood and bore my testimony to those good Saints, and during that few minutes I felt my impairment slip away. It has not returned.

Elmo returned home and was called to serve a mission to the Northern States from 1946–48. After his mission he married Marilyn Brown, from Parker, Idaho. They are the parents of seven children. Elmo served as a bishop for twelve years and on the high council of two stakes. For twenty-five years he was an adult leader with the Boy Scouts. He and Marilyn served a mission to the New Hampshire Manchester Mission.

ELMO C. DAVIS

*I say unto you, the sins of many people have been caused
by the iniquities of their kings; therefore their iniquities
are answered upon the heads of their kings.*

(Mosiah 29:31)

When I arrived in England prior to D-Day, I was stationed at Henley-on-the-Thames, about forty miles from London. Two of my buddies and I took the train to London for some sightseeing. We were downtown when air raid sirens began wailing and people headed for shelter underground. An air raid seemed much more exciting than anything that ever happened on my parents' dairy farm near St. Anthony, Idaho. Having heard about these raids on newscasts, I wanted to watch one. The three of us, feeling the immortality of youth, did not follow the crowd downstairs to the bunkers, but we knew where the shelters were if things got too hot to stay outside.

We watched as German bombers unloaded on the city. Because no bombs fell very close by us, we were in no particular danger. It was spectacular and frightening at the same time, as we observed the search lights slice through the night and play on the Nazi planes, watched bombs fall, felt the ground reverberate as they exploded, and saw parts of London burst into flames. I thought, *I hope this never happens in my country.*

As the raid continued, several American officers ran into the street from a nearby pub, and pulling .45-caliber pistols from their belts, began to fire at the marauding planes. Perhaps they had lost friends in raids over German targets. In any event, they defiantly shook their fists and shot their pistols into the night sky as the enemy bombers headed east toward the Continent. It was wonderful bravado.

My older brother Martin had been anxious to get into the action, so he joined the Canadian Air Force before the United States entered the war. He was stationed in England and flew missions over Europe as a tail gunner on a bomber. He died in May 1943, when his damaged plane crash landed

Elmo C. Davis, 1943

on their home base, as it returned from a bombing mission. I was in basic training at Camp Swift, Texas, when I received word of Martin's death.

I was with the 1st Army, 1501st Engineers, and landed with my unit on Utah Beach just a few days after D-Day. We saw plenty of action. As a combat engineer my specialty was water purification. There were thousands of thirsty men who needed a drink. We had a truck on which a purification unit was mounted, and a 3,000-gallon, portable, canvas water tank. We set it up near a water source, then filtered and chemically treated the water to make it safe to drink. Units on the front would detail men to pick up the water in large cans.

We moved east to northeast with the action. By November 1944 we had crossed the Belgian-German border into the town of Aachen. We wanted a place to stay, out of the cold. We entered a house, and as we began to settle in, an officer told us to move. Just after we left, the house was hit by a German 88 mm artillery shell. We had moved into a deserted barracks close by. Word came to move again. Another 88 mm shell hit the building, again just after we left. Someone must have been watching over me, because orders to move came a third time, and a third shell hit our recently vacated quarters. "Let's get out of here," someone suggested. We pulled out of the town.

In mid-December the Germans attacked with desperate fury, starting the Battle of the Bulge. Allied Forces were caught off guard, and initially the Germans pushed us back in what became one of the largest land battles ever fought. Heavy snow and blizzard conditions prevented our fighter planes from flying during the first two weeks of this battle. In a desperate move, our commanding officers had us dig foxholes in the road over which they thought the German tanks would pass. We were to let the tanks pass over us, then with our rifles fire into the back of each tank in an attempt to hit the engine compartment and disable the tank. I was scared. We saw that we were expendable, like a bullet, or C-rations. I didn't think we had a chance of surviving in the middle of on-coming tanks. Fortunately the weather cleared, and our Air Corps destroyed the German tanks before they got to us.

One morning after we had moved back across the German border, we watched as three German Fulke-Wolf fighters swept in low, past a house in which we were staying. There was a .50-caliber machine gun mounted on our truck. One of our men quickly jumped on the truck and began firing at the planes. He found the range on the last aircraft, and I stared in fascination as over and over bullet holes appeared the full length of the plane. The gunner was walking the bullets forward to the fuselage; the next bullets would have hit the pilot, but at this moment the gun jammed. The plane was so close we could see the pilot looking at us and saw his lips moving as he talked to us. I'm sure what he was saying was not friendly chatter. The planes left the area, but we headed for a foxhole just in case they came back.

When the war ended, our unit was in Weimar, Germany. Nearby was the infamous Buchenwald death camp. There were still inmates there, waiting to find out where they could go. Corpses were stacked in mute testimony of what had gone on in this palace of horror right up to the moment Americans liberated the camp. I noticed the inmates frequently came to the kitchen wanting citrus fruit.

We did a lot of work in Weimar to prepare the area to be turned over to the Russians in exchange for a chunk of the City of Berlin. In a short while I was sent to Frankfurt on the *Maine*. At Frankfurt I received shipping orders to Okinawa. Two days out of Marseille, France, we had news that the atomic bomb had been dropped on Hiroshima and Nagasaki. Japan surrendered. Our ship was diverted to Boston. I was happy to go home.

I didn't meet another LDS serviceman while in England or Europe. I knew of some, but also knew they were not living the way they knew they should. Until I returned home, the last time I partook of the sacrament was at Camp Swift, Texas. I sometimes attended Protestant services.

Elmo married Loa Bagley in the Idaho Falls Temple. They lived in St Anthony, Idaho. In order to earn some extra money he joined the Idaho National Guard. In 1950 North Korea invaded South Korea, and his unit was federalized. He was sent to Korea and got his old job back, this time as the NCO in charge of water purification.

After the Korean war, Elmo worked for the Idaho State Highway department as a construction inspector of roads and bridges. He has served in the Young Men, Sunday School and Aaronic Priesthood. He was ward finance clerk for sixteen years. He and Loa are the parents of two sons.

DEWAIN SILVESTER

Oh, it is wonderful that he should care for me.

("I Stand All Amazed," *Hymns*, no. 193)

After earning a commission as a second lieutenant, United States Army, I was sent to Europe as commander of Battery C, 778th Anti Aircraft Artillery Weapons Battalion, a half-track unit.

I was assigned a Jeep driver named Jack. This man had an uncanny sense of direction; if he had been to a place once, he could always find it again. However, he was night blind, so at night I drove. One night we were on reconnaissance. Jack was in the passenger seat with a submachine gun across his lap. As we drove cautiously through the darkness, we heard an enemy machine gun cock. I grabbed the emergency brake and rolled out and under the Jeep. Jack did the same, with his weapon in his hands. The machine gun began firing. Jack watched as fire came from the muzzle of the enemy gun. Having pinpointed their position, he stood up and shot three enemy soldiers. The only damage to us was seven holes in our windshield. We climbed back in the Jeep and left as fast as we could. The Jeep operated just fine, but in a war zone a windshield is insignificant, and so it was not replaced.

We participated in the Battle of the Bulge. Our unit entered the fight for the Siegfried Line at night. A barrage by the 417th Artillery Regiment, with one hundred battalions (650 men each), fired on enemy fortifications across the river. The night became as light as day. It was a horrendous encounter. There were so many casualties that the next day, as men of the

76th Infantry Division walked across a mine field, many of them stepped on the bodies of their own dead. It was the only safe way to cross.

We crossed the river that night and struggled up the steep slopes of the Saar River canyon. Progress in the dark was hard going. The area was pitch black. To mask our movements from the enemy, we kept our lights off. To move the column forward, I got out of our vehicle and motioned them forward with a blackout light. When I backed into a stone wall the driver, unable to see me, kept moving forward, pinning me against the wall. Thinking he was going over a large rock, he revved the engine until the truck stalled. He backed up, and I fell to the ground, unable to move.

Medics put me on a stretcher and took me to the basement of a monastery, the only building not being shelled. I lay on a litter all night, wondering if I would be able to walk again.

The next morning I was taken to a field hospital, then transferred to a hospital in Luxembourg City. When I awoke the next morning and looked out the window I saw shop windows different from any I had seen elsewhere in Europe. They reminded me of home, and I thought that I was back in the States. *Had I been asleep that long?* From Luxembourg I transferred to a general hospital in Paris. I had no broken bones, but it took six weeks of physical therapy before I could walk again.

When I recovered sufficiently, I was sent to Le Havre, France, and put in charge of a train load of retread soldiers being sent back to the front, none of whom were anxious to return. As we moved through the French countryside, we passed some of the areas where some of my charges had been. At each stop a few more men fled from the train.

The railroads had only recently been returned to French control. We were side tracked, and a trainload of cognac was given priority movement. For some reason the cognac train stopped right by ours. Ever vigilant for something to drink, our GI's got off the waiting train, shot holes in the tank cars and filled their helmets and canteens. They let what liquor they couldn't capture drain on the ground. The troops got pretty rowdy, but by the time our train arrived at its destination, the war was over.

Following the cessation of fighting, I became Battalion Information and Education Officer and was sent to the University of Paris for training.

Shortly after arriving in Paris from my duty post in eastern Germany I learned that LDS services were scheduled at a hotel in the downtown area.

It had been many months since I had attended a sacrament meeting, or for that matter, been with other Church members.

We assembled in a large room, and at the beginning of the meeting we all stood and gave our name and home town. Near the back a man stood and said, "My name is Ivan Miller, from Parker, Idaho." When I said my name and gave my home town as Rexburg, Ivan quickly looked in my direction. Our wives had grown up together in Parker and were close friends. It was wonderful to meet where I could associate with other Mormons, partake of the sacrament, and feel again the Spirit as "two or three are met together" in His name. Following the meeting, Ivan and I had a long visit. I was reluctant to leave these friends and the spirit I felt with these men.

I had just two more assignments after Paris, first as military governor of the town of Neustadt on Dem Orla; and finally at the Army University at Shrivenham, England.

Dewain Silvester married Zola Rudd, and together they raised seven sons. He worked in the broadcasting industry for forty years. He retired as manager of Channel 3 Television when the station was sold. In 1960 Dewain established a travel agency. In the Church he has served on two high councils, in a bishopric and as the advisor to Aaronic Priesthood quorums. For five years he was president of the Ricks College Alumni Association. He and Zola served a mission to the North American Southeast Area of the Church as public affairs directors, and were located in Atlanta, Georgia. He was a sealer in the Idaho Falls Temple up to the time of his death in August 2001.

CANNON C. ANDERSON

Through cloud and sunshine, Lord, abide with me!

("Abide with Me," *Hymns*, no. 166)

I was assigned to the 13th Armored Division, 67th Infantry Battalion, Company A, in Patton's 3rd Army. We landed at Le Havre, France, and I drove a half-track all the way to Braunau, Austria—Adolf Hitler's birthplace. A half-track is a vehicle with truck wheels in front and tank tracks on the rear. It had a steel and wood rack on back and a cab enclosed by one-inch steel to protect the crew. We carried a squad of twelve men, together with two weeks of supplies, ammunition and K-rations, clothes, and our bedding. There was a .50-caliber machine gun mounted just back of the cab, and two .30-caliber machine guns on each side.

My first day in a battle zone is emblazoned in my mind. War was new to me. The only time I had ever been away from our farm was to attend a World Boy Scout Jamboree. I was not ready for the grisly sights we came upon. On the road we passed perhaps thirty dead German soldiers.

The tank sergeant and I set out to reconnoiter. By now we were well into Germany and became targets for German artillery. For cover we entered the courtyard of a small farm. A half-hour later we thought it safe to leave. A meadow bordered the yard, and pipes led from the animal shelters to a cistern, away from the yard. It takes quite a bit of room to turn a half-track around. The sergeant told me to back the half-track into the meadow. I suddenly found myself looking at the sky. The tracks had fallen into the cistern, which left the cab pointing upward. We lost two weeks' supplies in the cistern, and it required one of our 3/4-ton armored tanks to get the half-track horizontal again. We had a disgruntled squad when they found that all their gear was down in that hole.

The enemy was on the run, and our unit moved rapidly across France. We came to a river, and since no crossing was in sight, we proceeded up-stream in search of a bridge. We found a small dam with a road on top. Our sergeant sent two of us forward to investigate. A German unit blocked the way, and the German officer waved a white flag. When we lowered our rifles, the Germans began firing at us. I was angered by their treachery. We called in artillery, and it was not long until they got the message and came forward with their hands over their heads.

Circumstances required us to leave the half-track one day. We came under small arms fire, and I needed a place to get below the surface of the ground, fast. Seeing what I thought was a trench, I dashed for it. It looked like a good place to hide.

Cannon C. Anderson

The abandoned slit trench was filled with human waste, and I immediately vomited, but I had to keep my head down to avoid being shot. It was about the longest half-hour I ever spent. I was in muck up to my knees. As soon as it was safe I plunged into a nearby creek to clean myself, then went to the half-track, changed clothes and threw away everything I had been wearing.

* * *

Late in the war, especially inside Germany, the Nazis used civilians to fight us. Driving our half-track we were second in a long line of similar vehicles. As we passed a house beside the road, the lead vehicle took a hit from the German version of the bazooka, killing three of our men. We immediately surrounded the house, raking it with machine gun fire. When no more firing came from the building, which was now badly shot up, some of us entered the house to search. We found a fifteen-year-old girl, very dead, the weapon laying beside her.

We crossed into Austria about the first of May, 1945. The war ended on May 5th. We entered Braunau and set up camp in a Hitler Youth hostel. It was an excellent facility. It had plenty of clear cold water—good for drinking, but it made for frigid bathing. We located an old tractor with a boiler on it that had been used to thrash grain. We had a tank tow it into camp. We also learned that there was a coal yard some fifty miles away. When we arrived at the coal storage, the burgomaster was unaware the war had ended. "No coal," he announced. He had an immediate change of mind when we trained three .30-caliber machine guns on him. Hot showers were a welcome luxury.

For me, the most painful experience of the war was seeing young children scavenge for food in our garbage. Children also picked up cigarette butts thrown away by GI's, pulled the paper off, and dumped the few shreds of tobacco in cans to take home to their parents, or to use themselves. The most sickening thing I watched was young boys, or girls, soliciting American soldiers to come home for sex with their mothers. War and its convoy of sins is appalling.

Some of our bivouacs lasted a couple of weeks at a time. On these extended stays, I went in search of branches of the Church. These units had not had a priesthood leader in them all during the war. I noted that in some instances they had moved away from standard Church practices in presenting the sacrament.

While in Germany I had the privilege of meeting Elder Ezra Taft Benson while he was on assignment to bring relief to the European Saints.

Barbara Smith and I were married 17 October 1943. When I was drafted she was expecting our first daughter, Linda. Linda was born while I was still in training in the States, but I didn't get to see her until she was nearly a year old.

General Patton had volunteered his 3rd Army to fight in Japan. We were given leave to go home on our way to the Far East. I was at home with my family when the atomic bomb was dropped on Japan and fighting ended. We were relieved and happy. We had been told to expect an 85 percent casualty rate in the invasion of Japan. There is no doubt in my mind that the bomb saved thousands of American and Japanese lives.

After my furlough I reported to Camp Cook, near Lompoc, California, and was shortly thereafter discharged and returned home.

I can now admit that going to war was good for me. I learned a lot about the world. My unit was made up mostly of young men from New York and New Jersey, and I had to live with them. I was very independent. I hated getting up a 0300 hours for KP duty that lasted until 2300 hours that night. More than once I told an officer where to go. I should have kept zippers on my stripes, I lost them so many times. But the discipline came, and I grew under it, in spite of myself. I haven't the slightest urge to repeat the experience, but I wouldn't trade what I learned for anything.

Cannon Anderson entered the furniture and carpet business in Idaho Falls, Idaho. He and Barbara have three daughters and two sons, twelve grandchildren, and four great-grandchildren. Except for his time in the Army,

Cannon has been active in Scouting since 1933. For many years he taught lifesaving and water safety courses. He has served in the bishopric and taught Sunday School "and every other class."

DAVID O. DANCE

And all saints who remember to keep and do these say-ings, walking in obedience to the commandments, shall receive . . . great treasures . . . even hidden treasures.

(Doctrine & Covenants 89:18–19)

I was raised on a farm a few miles west of Blackfoot, Idaho. I was attending Utah State Agricultural College when World War II broke out. I enlisted in the Army Reserve Corp in August 1942. Most of our ROTC group was ordered to report for active duty on 4 April 1943.

After completing Officer Candidate School, I was commissioned a second lieutenant at Camp Davis, North Carolina, in the antiaircraft artillery. By this time we were gaining air superiority in Europe, so I was sent to Fort Benning, Georgia, to be retrained as an infantry officer. I was sent to Camp McCoy, Wisconsin, where I joined with the 76th Infantry Division on 5 August 1944, and became an 81 mm mortar platoon leader.

We arrived at Southhampton, England, on 21 December 1944. All during our training and while traveling to Europe, we were indoctrinated about the need for secrecy about our destination and unit strength. You can imagine our surprise when radios tuned to listen to "Axis Sally" from Berlin, heard her welcome the 76th Infantry Division to England.

A few days later we sailed to Le Havre, France, which still showed the terrible damage inflicted by the fighting. The docks had been destroyed. It was from here we entered the battle zone.

As we moved into battle, I remembered a talk by Elder Hugh B. Brown, who spoke to us while I was at Fort Douglas. He quoted Joshua 1:9, "Be strong and of good courage; be not afraid, neither be thou dismayed: for the Lord thy God is with thee whithersoever thou goest." I memorized it and repeated it to myself frequently, especially when artillery shells were exploding nearby.

Early January 1945 we were in a French field; the snow was deep and it was bitter cold. I recall a night so cold that no one slept. Keeping warm was impossible. We had several fires, some we fueled with lumber torn from a nearby school house. With fifty men around one small fire at the same time, even up close no one kept warm.

We arrived in France just in time to be caught up in Hitler's last gasp. With unmatched fury, the Germans launched a surprise attack through the Ardennes Forest, the

David Oran Dance, shortly after entering the army, 1943.

"Battle of the Bulge." We passed through Bastogne, Belgium, where the Nazis had encircled a unit under the command of General McAuliff. When the Germans demanded their surrender, General McAuliff told them, "Nuts." The trees around Bastogne were denuded and shortened in the bitter fighting. We immediately swung in on the southern shoulder of the now inverted Bulge, in the Grand Duchy of Luxembourg.

We arrived at Echternach in the midst of fierce fighting. The Germans held the high ground and the Sauer River, which had been ingeniously woven into the Siegfried Line defense. The Sauer was at flood stage. Several American units had managed to get across the river, but were pinned down by enemy fire from the hills surrounding the town and were short of both ammunition and food. We were in a difficult position. The Germans fired at every moving object. Attempts to operate at night were frustrated when the enemy dropped flares over our position. Whenever we heard flares pop, we froze as they slowly drifted down. In the bright light any motion was instantaneously picked up, bringing a spurt of shelling.

The combat engineers brought up assault boats about midnight. It was a very dark night. Ten to twelve men were to be loaded into these boats, with ammunition and food for our beleaguered friends on the other side of the Sauer. Knowing where to launch was tricky. If we launched too high or too low from our prescribed route, we would be cut to pieces by enemy fire. As platoon leader I was to be in the first boat.

The German mortar shell would make a soft whistle as it cruised. When it landed, the shell was designed to burst outward and spray shrapnel in all directions. That night I did not hear the characteristic whistle and was standing upright. The explosion lifted me into the air, and the thought flashed through my mind as I thought of the scripture in Joshua: *Where did I go wrong? Why is the Lord letting me down?* My helmet was ripped off; my carbine torn out of my right hand. I felt like I had caught a red hot baseball without a glove.

A medic pulled me to safety and I was taken to a first aid station. I lay in the midst of an assortment of wounded men, in pain, still wondering why I was hurt, what I had done wrong. Then two of my men were brought in to the aid station. They told me that when the assault boat I was to be in reached the middle of the river a shell demolished the boat. There were few survivors. I then understood that the Lord *had* protected me.

At an evacuation hospital two nurses carefully, almost tenderly, removed the grenades and ammunition I had been carrying. In my pain I remember thinking how funny it was to see them be so careful with what we handled so casually every day. On the way to the evacuation hospital I was given a pain shot and received a blood transfusion by the medics. Then the doctors took over and, for several hours, operated on my hand. I was put between white sheets and slept for nearly 72 hours. When I awakened I felt the relief of being away from battle; my fears were gone; I was warm and had hot food to eat. What's more, I had the "million-dollar" wound. I was going home—by way of several hospitals—alive. This experience has become a very sacred thing to me, and I have not often talked about it.

While convalescing at a hospital in England, I found out where 1st Lieutenant Clint Murdock, a close friend from my home ward in Thomas, was stationed. I tried to see him, but we couldn't connect. He was a pilot on a C-47, flying troops and supplies to battle areas across the English Channel. Prior to embarking for France I had a memorable visit with him. He took me to the officer's mess, where we had a fine meal, and sat at tables covered with white clothes. This was a far cry from what I had been accustomed to:

C and K rations eaten from a mess kit, sitting in cold mud. Clint and I had a great visit. It was reassuring to be with someone from home.

After some time I boarded a hospital ship and sailed for home. En route we learned of the German surrender. We landed at Boston on Mother's Day. The first thing I wanted was lots of ice cream. At a Post Exchange I ordered a banana split, a chocolate milkshake, and a strawberry ice cream soda, things I had dreamed about for many months. Much to my dismay, I could eat only a small part of each. They were too rich for my stomach.

During the war, officers received a monthly liquor ration. In the United States we were given a booklet of ration coupons. Having no use for these, I usually gave mine to the enlisted men under my command. After the war, I was sent to Menlo Park, California, for medical attention. Just before getting off the train, I was handed a monthly ration booklet. It was in my shirt pocket, unused and unthought of. That night an Army major came into the officer's club and sat down one stool away from me. He looked at me for a moment, then asked, "Would you happen to have a couple of liquor ration coupons I could borrow? I'm all out. I'll receive my next booklet on Monday and can pay you back then." I slid my booklet over to him.

"You can have the whole book," I told him. He tore out two coupons and handed it back, saying, "No, no. I'll have my ration booklet on Monday and can pay you back."

"That won't be necessary," I said. "You may have it. I don't drink. I really don't want it back." The major thanked me, obviously pleased, and sounding a wee bit incredulous.

When I reported to the doctor assigned to my case, I recognized Doctor Foote as the major to whom I had given my ration booklet, and he recognized me. He examined my hand carefully, then told me that my previous surgeries were well done and that what was needed was time to heal. He asked when I had been home last. I responded, "Oh, about two years ago." He said, "How would you like to have a sixty-day leave to go home?"

"Point me towards the airport," I told him. He made out the necessary papers, and I was soon on my way home.

It was wonderful to be home, to be with my family again, to see old friends and get reacquainted with my younger brother and sisters. When the sixty days were up, I returned to Menlo Park and reported to Dr. Foote. After examining my hand, he asked if I would like another sixty days of leave. This time I re-enrolled at Utah State Agricultural College in Logan. Sixty days was not quite enough to complete the quarter, so I wired the good doctor for a ten-day extension.

Wounds to the hand take a long time to heal. When I again reported back to Major Foote, he again told me that my hand needed more time to heal, and wrote me out a third sixty-day leave. He remarked that if I needed more time, to let him know. I enrolled at USAC for the winter quarter. During this quarter I met a very lovely girl, Jean Richards, who later became my wife. All this drawing full pay as an Army first lieutenant. Adherence to the Word of Wisdom rewarded me handsomely.

David O. Dance married Jean Richards in the Logan Temple. They are parents of six living children and have thirty-one grandchildren. He became a general manager for a major life insurance company. He has served as a bishop, stake president, and regional representative. He and Jean reside in Seattle, Washington. He is a sealer in the Seattle Temple and serves as a patriarch in the Seattle North Stake.

DON RUE HICKMAN

To God's command, soul, heart, and hand, faithful and true we will ever stand.

("True to the Faith," *Hymns*, no. 254)

I was born 16 February 1918, at Torrey, Utah, and in 1927 we moved to Salina, Utah. At age seventeen I was called to serve a mission to the Central States. Upon returning home in 1937 I enrolled at Snow College where I played forward on the basketball team.

It was at Snow College that I met LoRee Terry, a very special girl from Spring City, Sanpete County. On 5 July 1941, as war loomed over the world, I was inducted into the United States Army. On 7 December 1941, I was just completing basic training at Camp Wolters, near Ft. Worth, Texas. My missionary experience and National Guard training were very helpful in preparing me for my military experience. I was selected for Infantry Officers Candidate School at Ft. Benning, Georgia. At graduation, wearing our new, tailored uniforms, we almost forgot the war raging in Europe and the Pacific.

My first duty assignment was to the 3rd Battalion of the 304th Infantry. As it turned out I stayed with that battalion until V-J Day, 1945. Our division trained many men sent as replacements to both the Pacific and European Theaters. During the summer of 1942, we were again tapped for replacements. All leaves and passes had been canceled, and I found myself longing to go to Utah, particularly to see LoRee. One night, as I was deep in thought about my life, about LoRee, and about where the war was leading all of us, I decided to test the rule against leaves with the regimental commander. First I called LoRee, told her I planned to come home, and asked her to marry me. She accepted my proposal. I went to the colonel and said, "Sir, I would like permission to go home to Utah to get married."

He said, "Hickman, you know the general's order—no leaves."

I said, "Yes, sir, but we have not had a break in over three months. We have trained hard. Some of us wish to get married, or at least to say good-bye to our families before we go to war. I think we should have that opportunity." He picked up the phone and called the general, recommended his ban on leaves be lifted, and asked that he be given authority to give me and others leave at once. His request was granted, and I was off to Utah to persuade LoRee's mother to consent to a speedy temple wedding

Waiting for our wedding day, I went to Salt Lake to attend general conference. At the gate I was told I needed a ticket to get in. During the war, attendance was limited to General Authorities and presidents of the 141 stakes. As I turned to leave, I felt a hand on my shoulder and a kind voice say, "Come on, Lieutenant, I can get you in." I turned to see Elder George Albert Smith of the Quorum of the Twelve, who took me by the arm and ushered me into the Tabernacle. During the sessions, David O. McKay, Second Counselor in the First Presidency, said, "Even though we sense the hellish anger of war, even though we feel confident that war will never end war, yet under the existing conditions we find ourselves, as a body, committed to combat this evil thing. With other loyal citizens, we serve our country as bearers of arms, rather than to stand aloof to enjoy a freedom for which others have fought and died." That afternoon President J. Reuben Clark Jr., First Counselor in the First Presidency, read a message by the First Presidency about the war: "Both sides cannot be wholly right. Perhaps neither is without wrong. God will work out in his own due time and in his own sovereign way the justice and right of the conflict, but he will not hold the innocent instrumentalities of the war, our brethren in arms, responsible for the conflict. This is a major crises in the world life of man. God is at the helm." These statements gave me great comfort.

LoRee and I were married on 6 October 1942, in the Manti Temple. After a three-day honeymoon, LoRee accompanied me to the train in Salt Lake City. She taught school at Mt. Pleasant until Christmas break, then joined me in Maryland. We lived in one room of a home where we had kitchen privileges. In the summer of 1943, our division was moved to Camp McCoy, Wisconsin. LoRee and I rented a house in LaCrosse, about fifty miles from the camp.

That summer we learned we would become parents in February. Because I was in the field almost constantly, LoRee decided to return to Utah until the baby came. I was selected to return to Fort Benning, Georgia, to attend advanced infantry officers course. Following the birth of our daughter, DeAnn, LoRee joined me at Fort Benning. After finishing that schooling, we returned to Camp McCoy. In Wisconsin we met another LDS family with whom we held sacrament services each Sunday.

Our unit was alerted for overseas assignment for the war zone in France. Four thousand men boarded the troop ship, the *USS Brazil,* in Boston Harbor, on Thanksgiving day 1944. As the great ship moved slowly away from the dock, I watched the lights of Boston until they grew dim, all the time thinking about LoRee and little DeAnn at home.

We arrived in England and were billeted at Bournmouth. I was now a captain, and commander of Company I of the 3rd Battalion. During the few days we were in England we continued limited training, and we also arranged for our men to visit London. While in London I met with Elder Hugh B. Brown, who was then looking after Church affairs in England and working with LDS Servicemen.

Orders came for us to go to France. Leaving in the middle of the night, with full field equipment, we marched up and down hills and through narrow streets to the train station. It was an arduous hike as we all carried heavy packs. Somehow my supply sergeant, an ex-con, commandeered an automobile. He made several trips to the train station, hauling the stragglers' gear. At the station, I asked the sergeant where he'd gotten the limousine.

"Well," he answered. "I borrowed it."

I said, "Aren't you going to return it?"

He said, "Captain, they told me when I was through with it to leave it right over there." Sometimes it's better not ask too many questions.

At Portsmouth we boarded LSTs (landing ship tanks), which took us to France. It was January 1945 and winter had her icy grip on the land.

We arrived during the final hours of the Battle of the Bulge and belonged to General Patton's Third Army. Within twenty-four hours we were sent to Luxembourg to relieve the 87th Infantry Division along the Sauer and Moselle Rivers in the vicinity of Echternach. Our mission was to cross the river and attack the Siegfried Line.

The Siegfried Line was a series of concrete pillboxes. It was thought that the enemy had evacuated them. I was assigned to verify whether they were empty. I protested that from my observation post I could see enemy soldiers going in and out of the fortifications. "Nevertheless," the officer from Regiment said, "you will send a patrol." This was my company's first action, so I elected to lead the platoon. After advancing a few hundred yards toward the German lines, their firing pinned us down.

The regimental officer who ordered the feint came on the radio and asked, "Are there enemy in the pillboxes?"

"Listen for yourself!" I said, and held the radio open as mortars landed near us.

Later, at the first aid station, the medics stitched a small cut on my face and removed shrapnel from my leg. Several of my men were wounded. This experience was my quick initiation into war.

It was almost like a reprieve when the order came to leave Echternach and attack toward the east. We moved across the Nisses and Saar Rivers into Germany. We engaged in bloody fighting to capture the town of Orenhofen. We lost some good and brave men there.

After returning from reconnaissance one day, I found my company had moved into a draw that seemed to me a likely enemy target. I ordered the platoon leaders to move their men to a new position about three hundred yards away. The men were tired, and there was a lot of grumbling about having to dig new foxholes. Another company from our battalion moved into our previous position. A short time later the enemy began to shell that company. As my men watched, they saw many men blown apart by enemy mortar and artillery fire. Several of my men thanked me for making them move. My position as their commander was solidified.

By early March 1945, it was evident that the German army was crumbling. We moved forward quickly and captured many prisoners. My unit was sent ahead to reconnoiter. We were well ahead of other American forces in the area. We drove several miles into enemy territory, then doubled back toward our troops on an alternate road. Stopping to study a map, we found ourselves in the center of a German platoon. It was almost dark, so we could not be clearly seen. Three German soldiers approached my Jeep. From the backseat my aide opened fire. One German fell. We grabbed another one and pulled him into the Jeep. The firing alerted the Germans nearby, and I could see helmets rising from foxholes all around us. Turning the Jeep around we sped down the road and out of the area. To my surprise and immense relief, the Germans never fired a shot.

Our company continued to push east. Outside the city of Struth we were attacked by twelve German tanks. American tanks moved in to engage them. As we watched the battle, American P-47 fighter aircraft, armed with rockets, arrived overhead. In a very short time our planes knocked out all the German tanks. From that time forward I became a champion of the fighter plane as the best method to counter enemy armor.

We entered Lankensalza, which was a huge Nazi supply area and Luftwaffe fighter base. We found warehouses crammed with high quality food stuffs, army clothing, equipment and supplies of every kind, there was even an aircraft plant.

As we moved on we liberated thousands of American, British, Australian, New Zealand, Canadian, and French prisoners of war. We also captured thousands of enemy soldiers. I interviewed several high-ranking German officers, who said, "You Americans do not know who your real enemy is. It is the Russians. You should let us join you, and we should go against the Russians, now, rather than later." These officers told us how hard they had worked to be captured by Americans rather than Russians.

The most depressing experience I had in World War II was helping to liberate the prisoners held at the Buchenwald concentration camp. I will never forget the skeleton-like men, the gaunt shapeless women, and the children whose expressions reflected, in some small part, what they had seen. As the prisoners looked through the barbed wire, their eyes seemed to say, *I hope you are here to help us*. Walking through the camp I pondered the misery and barbarism that had been inflicted there. I saw the crude barracks. In the basement of the main building I stirred the coals of the furnace and recognized the remains of human bones. A freed prisoner, speaking in a subdued voice, told us that the gas chamber was where the bodies were disposed of. He pointed to hooks on the wall where heel marks showed where victims were hung prior to their deaths. I am a witness that the holocaust did take place.

We dug long trenches to bury the dead. Before removing the living from the compound, someone in high command ordered that German people in the nearby village be marched through the camp to see what their own forces had done. As they walked through the area, many cried. They seemed shocked. One woman cried out, in English, "We didn't know! We didn't know!" I didn't believe her.

At Chemnitz we met Russian soldiers arriving from the east. We heard rumors that Germany had capitulated and waited near a radio for word that the war was over. When the word of victory came, on 5 May 1945, there were victory parties with the Russians. We rested and cleaned up. Meanwhile, men on patrol were still being killed. We learned that Berlin had fallen to the Russians. Why the Russians were allowed to take Berlin, we did not understand. Obviously it was a political decision made by those removed from the battlefield. A million enemy troops in Italy and southern Europe surrendered, unconditionally, to the Allies. A million German troops in northern Germany, Denmark, and Holland, surrendered to British Field Marshal Bernard Montgomery. In Austria, another half million Germans surrendered to the American General, Jacob Devers. In Germany, and in America, people were dancing in the streets. In Spring City, Utah, LoRee and her brothers celebrated and the children beat on pans. The war in Europe was over.

On 8 May 1945, an official from regiment called to tell me that we had a new daughter named Mary, born in Spring City, Utah. "LoRee and baby doing well."

Lt. Colonel Don R. Hickman, 1963

Don Rue Hickman elected to remain in the United States Army. He fought in three major wars–World War II, Korea, and Vietnam. In 1978, after thirty-one years of military service he retired from the Army as a brigadier general, and he and LoRee moved to Provo, Utah.

In the Church he has taught Sunday School, been a home teacher, served as a high counselor, high priest group leader, counselor in the presidency of the BYU Fourth Stake, and has been an example to his associates around the world. In 1992–93 Don and LoRee served a mission in the Florida Jacksonville Mission. Besides battlefield duty, he and his family have lived in Japan, the Canal Zone, Iran, and many places in the United States. He believes that LoRee has always been the consummate military wife. They are parents of four daughters and have twenty-five grandchildren and sixteen great-grandchildren.

THE AIR WAR IN
EUROPE

Foggia Air Base, Italy, 1944-45. Despite having all the controls shot away,
this B-17 successfully landed after a bombing mission. Two men aboard died,
two were wounded.

England's air force had been carrying the war in the skies since 1939. It took considerable time for the United States to build bombers and fighters and train young men, who before the war, hardly knew even what an airport looked like, to fly and maintain these airships. The United States' air force did not become significantly involved until late 1942 and 1943; however, England continued to carry a heavy fighting load until the end of the war.

For the United States, fighting the air war in Europe fell primarily to the 8th Air Force. Bombing on the scale carried out in World War II had never been done before—it was invented almost as it happened. Eventually, some 350,000 men became part of the U.S. 8th Air Force, flying, repairing, and fitting the B-17s, B-24s, and fighter aircraft sent to protect the bombers. When production of fighter planes and bombers reached full capability, the 8th Air Force had sufficient power to mount raids of up to 2,000 bombers and 1,000 fighters at one time. Raids of this size occurred for several months.

The German Luftwaffe was an impressive foe. The Germans had high quality crews and advanced aircraft design, and were well respected by the Allied air crews. The impact of their air superiority was felt by the Allied air forces. According to 8th Air Force records, more than 26,000 airmen were killed during the three-year struggle. Of the 43,000 prisoners of war held by the Germans in May 1945, 28,000 of them were from aircrews. These men paid a fearful price after they were shot down. There was the terror of ejecting from a damaged plane, then the trauma and uncertainty of capture or death as they parachuted into hostile territory.

Losses incurred by the bomber crews in the fall of 1943 and in early 1944 nearly overwhelmed the United States' capacity to replace these men and their equipment. An American-led raid on the ball bearing plants at Schweinfurt and the aircraft factories at Regensburg produced losses of twenty-five percent in one day. Some 600 highly trained crew members were lost on the second Schweinfurt attack. Bomber pilots told of being able to find their way back to base by watching the fires of crashed aircraft.

On a low-level raid over the Plôesti oil fields in Romania, one squadron lost seventeen of its thirty-six bombers to Nazi fighter planes. Despite those losses the raiders knocked out seventy percent of the production of this oil field, which was vital to the Nazis. Given their loss ratios, it is a wonder that the men were willing to make these flights. That they did is remarkable.

With the introduction of sufficient fighter escort planes to protect the bombers, losses dropped dramatically in favor of the Allies.

The last mission against German targets was flown on 20 April 1945.

HUGH RAWLIN ROPER

Behold, it has been made know unto me by an angel, that the spirits of all men, as soon as they are departed from this mortal body, . . . are taken home to that God who gave them life.

(Alma 40:11)

Hugh Rawlin Roper grew up in Oak City, Millard County, Utah. He graduated from Brigham Young University in 1937, with a degree in secondary education. His first teaching job was in a one-room school in the remote village of Gandy, Utah, situated along Utah's western border.

With war seeming imminent, Hugh Roper enlisted in the Army Air Corp. He graduated from flight school as a 2nd lieutenant and received his wings five days after the Japanese attack on Pearl Harbor. Rawlin, as he was known while at Delta High School, where he played football and basketball, was a very likeable young man.

Following flight school he completed advanced training at Reno in heavy bombers. While in Reno, Hugh met Abbie West. They were married there on 11 February 1942. Hugh and Abbie moved to Barkesdale Field, Louisiana, where he was assigned to the 8th Air Force, 93rd Bomb Group, 329th Squadron, under the command of Edward J. "Ted" Timberlake. This unit became known as "Ted's Traveling Circus." From a list of new men, Hugh selected Walter Stewart, of Benjamin, Utah, to be his co-pilot.

When they met, Stewart asked, "How did you know about me and why did you select me?"

"I saw that you were from Utah and I thought there was a pretty good chance that you might be LDS, so I asked for you."

Captain Hugh R. Roper

Stewart replied, "I am LDS and in fact I was serving a mission in Scotland when the war began there." Hugh and Walt became very close friends.

They soon had the rest of their crew and were assigned to fly the B-24D "Liberator," then the largest bomber built. It had a 110-foot wingspan, was seventy feet long, and had four Pratt & Whitney engines, each of which generated 1,200 horsepower.

While at Barkesdale, Hugh and Walt flew several missions over the Gulf of Mexico, some as far south as the Yucatan Peninsula. They were in search of German U-Boats that had been shooting light shipping along the eastern seaboard and in the Gulf.

Hugh was promoted to first lieutenant on 22 June 1942. In August he was stationed at Grenier Field, New Hampshire, for final preparations and training prior to leaving for England. It was here that he was assigned his B-24D. Appropriately, the plane had the letter "H" painted on each of its rudders. Hugh named his plane *Exterminator*.

Finally the time came for the men to leave for England. Hugh recorded in his diary that Abbie came out to the post and they had dinner together. "All the time I had a lump in my throat, as I knew I must tell her that I must leave her that day. I called a cab and stood at the gate with her. While I was waiting I could have cried a thousand times. She was very brave, but when I placed her in the cab, she cried like her sweet heart would break. But it was one of those things and I kissed her good-bye."

Arriving in England, Hugh and his crew were assigned at Alconbury, Huntingdonshire, about seventy-five miles north of London. The perpetual English rain created a quagmire of mud everywhere. The newly arrived American airmen were briefed on the customs of their new English neighbors and settled in for duty.

Being away from Abbie was difficult for Hugh. Almost every day he mentioned in his diary how much he missed her. On 12 September he got his first letter from her, "I got a letter from my darling wife, which made me very lonesome to see her. I dreamed about Abbie that night. I thought I went home to see her and she was not there."

Hugh began flying his required twenty-five missions. The first was an attack of Fives-Lille steel works in Belgium, but his plane was called back and they were put on standby. Their second mission was to bomb the submarine docks at Lorient, France. After takeoff they were called back due to weather over the English Channel.

In late October Hugh and his crew were sent to Holmsley South, near Bournemouth, to work with the 330th Squadron. The commander was Major Cool, and the operations officer, Major Ramsay D. Potts. Hugh was informed that they would be flying antisubmarine patrols over the Bay of Biscay. On 28 October, Hugh set out on his first patrol, southwest of England. Bad weather forced a turnaround. They landed just at dark with only eighty gallons of gas in their tanks from the 2,500 they had left with. Hugh wrote, "I believe it was the closest call I ever had. I thanked God that night that I made it safely."

Belfast, Ireland. 6 December 1942: "This was quite an eventful day. Capt. Ralph McBride, Lt. Wockenfuss, and I were to ferry three movie actresses back to England: Martha Raye, Carol Landis, and Kay Francis. Martha Raye went on my plane. At takeoff the field was overcast, and by the time I was 100 feet off the ground I was on instruments. I finally broke out of the overcast at 2,000 feet. The actress was rather nervous, but was relieved as soon as she could see again. I let her sit in the co-pilot's seat, which she liked very much. She also chased around the plane, talking to the guys. She claimed she was a qualified gunner. When we landed at Alconbury we all had lunch together. I also had my picture taken with Martha Raye." When Martha returned to Hollywood, she wrote to Abbie and told her that she had met Hugh and that he was doing fine. That made Abbie very happy.

While Hugh and other pilots had been in Belfast, most of the 93rd Bomb Group had been sent to North Africa to help the 9th Air Force in their desert offensive. Hugh was preparing for his first Christmas overseas. In a letter to his cousin, Macel Anderson, in Oak City, Hugh wrote: "We have a Christmas tree at our place and it looks good. There is one thing lacking, there is no snow, which kind of detracts from the good old Christmas. I have met a lot of good people and no matter how many I meet, my thoughts are of those at home. I'll tell you there is no one like your own people."

Hugh and the other officers spent Christmas day waiting tables for the enlisted men.

2 February, Hugh wrote, "Today we were briefed to bomb Hamm [Germany]. We took off at 0830 and joined the 44th Group. The formations were poor, and it was very cold—minus 49 degrees at 20,000 feet. We went as far as Belgium but had to turn back because of the cold. About this time, two of my boys got their hands frozen. I took the plane to a lower altitude and Lieutenants Stewart and White took care of them. When we got back I sent them to the hospital where they said they would be all right. I went to see them in the afternoon."

At first, little damage was inflicted on the German war machine by the American bombing, but the problems the Americans had to face taught them valuable strategic and technical lessons.

15 February 1943: "We took off at 2:15 p.m. to bomb a ship that was at Dunkirk. I led the second flight and we joined the 44th. As we got about halfway across the Channel, one of my wingmen turned back. We made a beautiful run on the target; as we were about to drop our bombs, one of the planes ahead of us suddenly nosed straight down. No one could imagine what had happened as we had encountered no flak. We dropped our bombs and headed toward the Channel again when we were jumped by F W 190's. The [British] Spitfires [escorting us] took care of some of them very well, but being in the rear of the formation I was shot at by several of them. I did not know whether I was hit until I was ready to land. One of my engines would not slow down when I pulled back on the throttle. I immediately cut the switch on it. After landing I found my rear turret was pretty well riddled. The gunner was not even scratched. I had other holes in old *Exterminator.* Three ships were lost on this raid, but two of the crews were saved."

By 27 February, *Exterminator* was airworthy again. "This morning we were briefed to make a raid on Brest, France. I had heard how much ack ack [flak] they put up there, so wasn't too well pleased. Five of us took off at 1210 hours, and again met up with the 44th, a group of nine planes. There were also some B-17s. As we made our run on the target, we saw one bunch of flak, but that was all that was very close. My tail-gunner saw six or eight fighters but none of them attacked us. All in all it was an easy raid and everyone got home safely. I also got a letter and a box of candy from Abbie."

Focusing on life at home was common, but couldn't detract from the war. On one flight, Walter Stewart asked Hugh, "Wouldn't you like to go back to Oak City just for a few days and see everyone? Maybe shoot a few baskets with the guys at the town hall—or saddle up your horse and ride up on the Oak City mountain?" Just then a burst of flak hit not far from them and the concussion shook the plane. Hugh said, "Not now, Stu, help me fly this plane." He didn't answer the question and Stu didn't repeat it. Later that evening after they had returned to Cribbage Haven and were taking it easy, Hugh said "You know, I really would love to go home for a few days to see everyone. That would be just great!"

A letter dated 23 May 1943, appeared on the front page of the *Millard County Chronicle*:

> Dear Editor: As of late I have been receiving the *Chronicle* and can say that I get a great deal of enjoyment out of it. I especially like your section on where the servicemen are and what they are doing. It helps me know what a fine effort is being made toward final victory. One thing I notice is that West Millard is doing its part for the Red Cross. That money given is really doing a wonderful work over here and many boys are made happy as a result of it.
>
> I suppose some of my adventures would be interesting, but time, space, and censors don't permit me to say much except that I am trying to do my part as well as I can.
>
> I have traveled quite a lot and have seen some wonderful sights, such as all the squares in London, Big Ben, Buckingham Palace, London Bridge, Ireland, Scotland, Wales, and if I may say so, Germany. However I don't get such a hearty welcome there—should say I am not welcome.
>
> If you know any of the boys who are in England I would be glad to have their full addresses.
>
> Sincerely, Captain Hugh Roper.

* * *

At the end of May, Hugh's unit was transferred into the 201st Provisional Group and began training for a secret mission—a maximum effort, low-level raid on the oil refineries at Plôesti, Romania, the largest oil producer in all Europe. The Allies' decision to attack the refineries had been made by Allied leaders at the Casablanca Conference.

On June 26th, Hugh Roper was assigned to fly two important planners of the Plôesti mission to North Africa. One was Lord Arthur Patrick Hastings, Viscount Forbes, a Royal Air Force wing commander who had been air attaché in the British Embassy in Bucharest, Romania, until the British broke off relations with Romania. Lord Forbes had important knowledge of the refinery complexes and had been advocating attacks on Plôesti since the Germans had taken over. The other was Gerald K. Geerlings, an architect from Connecticut. Geerlings had made a miniature replica of Plôesti, its refineries, and the surrounding terrain. Several days elapsed waiting for everything to be made ready for the trip.

Life on the African coast was, for the most part, a welcome change for the airmen from England. The days were usually filled with sunshine and warmth. In a letter home, Hugh wrote, "It's like pitching your tent halfway between Oak City and Delta, but the Mediterranean is handy for a refreshing swim, and the nights are beautiful."

For his 24th mission, Hugh was selected to lead a mission on Rome, Italy. Because his plane was still in Tunis, he was assigned to fly *Utah Man* with Walter Stewart as co-pilot.

The final entry in Hugh's diary tells of the mission to Rome: "July 19th: This day was one of the biggest days of my life. I was to lead the 93rd Bomb Group on a raid on Rome, Italy. The first time in history it was to be bombed. We left Benghazi [Libya] at 0735 and headed for our target, which was some marshaling yard north of the city, and we arrived at 1319 hours. There was some flak but only a couple of fighters. Our bombs seemed to hit the target well. There were many fires and lots of smoke as we neared the target. It was an all out effort by all the medium and heavy bombers in North Africa. Some of our planes landed at Tunis or Sicily, but none of them were lost."

Following the raid on Rome, all heavy bombardment groups under the 9th Air Force were taken off normal operations, and the airfields they used were quarantined. In preparation for the Plôesti attack, low-level practice flights resumed. A full-scale mock target was erected in the desert and airmen made long, roundabout flights in daily practice bombing of this unnamed target.

The crews were briefed on the target. Most of them had never heard of Plôesti. They were told that they would be making a 2,500 mile round trip—not a total surprise, since special crews had been at work for several days installing extra gas tanks in the planes. Each plane would carry 3,100 gallons of fuel on takeoff. General Brereton

Hugh Roper's flight crew getting ready for a mission. Hugh is in the center, putting his boots on.

told the men that he expected casualties to be as high as fifty percent. He emphasized that if the target were hit well, the war could be shortened by as much as six months. Each of the pilots and navigators were given an oblique drawing of their objectives from low level. Each airman was given a survival kit that included American and British currency and instructions on how to speak phonetically in Romanian, Bulgarian, and Yugoslavian. They were also give a compass that could be disguised as a suspender button.

After the briefing, Col. Addison Baker called the pilots and navigators of the 93rd together and said to them: "We must hit that target tomorrow. I know that if we do not, we will have to go back the very next day to get it."

For several weeks, Hugh, Walter Stewart, and several other men had been regularly holding LDS church services. A meeting had been scheduled for that Saturday evening. Attendance was usually between fifteen and twenty men, but on 31 July 1943, a crowd of ninety men showed up. Walter Stewart conducted this particular meeting. The plan had been to read from the New Testament this time, but shortly after the meeting began, a sergeant in the back stood up and said, "I just want to ask you Mormon boys a question. If I am shot down and killed tomorrow, where will I be after that?" Everyone in the meeting was quiet. Walter took out the Pearl of Great Price and read from it, explaining that we lived before this life, and that we will continue to live afterward, and that we would await the resurrection as provided by Jesus Christ. Stewart explained further aspects of the gospel for some time, all the while the sergeant stood in rapt attention. When Stewart finished, the sergeant thanked him and left. The other men who attended the meeting seemed to take comfort in the things that were said.

Hugh Roper's twenty-fifth mission was the Plôesti raid. Sunday, 1 August 1943, began with a windstorm that raised a gritty fog of sand and dust. One hundred seventy-eight B-24s queued up for takeoff from the several air bases around Benghazi. The planes formed up in their assigned order and headed across the Mediterranean. Several planes experienced mechanical problems and turned back. As the formation approached the Island of Corfu, the lead airplane suddenly spun out of control and crashed into the sea, taking the mission navigator with it. Another plane took the lead, and the group continued.

Reaching the Island of Corfu, the formation turned inland and set a course for Romania, flying over Albania, southern Yugoslavia, and entering Bulgaria at its southwest corner. They flew past Mt. Cherin and the capital city of Sofia. Heavy clouds were encountered over the mountains, and the formation became strung out. Entering Romania, in an attempt to avoid detection by German radar, the bombers dropped from an altitude of 15,000 feet to between fifty and a hundred feet for the remaining 165 miles to Plôesti. At this point, the *Teggie Ann*, carrying the two senior officers—General Uzal G. Ent and Colonel K. K. Compton—assumed navigational duties. In the difficult, low-level navigation, the *Teggie Ann* mistook a landmark and turned into the attack heading twenty miles ahead of the correct point. Then the leader of the 93rd Group saw the refinery on his left and radio silence was broken. The pilots had trained to approach the target from a 127 degree heading, and some were coming in from a 360 degree heading, so their targets were not recognizable. As they approached the outskirts of the city, the Germans were ready for them, and the attackers were met with a terrific anti-aircraft barrage. About this time General Ent broke radio silence and announced, "We have missed our objective. You are cleared to strike targets of opportunity." Despite the ensuing confusion the men acted heroically.

Ramsay Potts, leader of "B" group, and Hugh Roper's plane led his unit on an attack of the Astro Romana Refinery. Russell Longnecker of Broken Bow, Nebraska, was one of Hugh's wingmen. Longnecker described the approach on the target and the anit-aircraft fire. "I noted an 88 [German gun] behind a row of trees at a crossroad. I saw the muzzle flash and caught a glimpse of the projectile as it came toward us. I forced *Thundermug* under this barrage. The shell removed the left aileron, left rudder, and half of the elevator on Captain Roper's ship on my right. I went back into position with him. His plane looked like a junkyard, but he was not wavering a bit. I could see Roper in his cockpit, looking straight ahead, keeping his position."

It was this steadfast courage in the face of extreme danger that won Hugh Roper the Silver Star. Longnecker describes more of the action: "We were going in from the wrong direction, at two hundred forty-five miles per hour, sixty-five miles more than our usual speed, pulling emergency power for so long it was a question how much longer the engines could stand the abuse. . . . Suddenly a huge oil storage tank exploded directly in front of my wingman, Vic Olliffe, raising a solid column of fire and debris two hundred feet, waiting for Olliffe's plane. He couldn't possibly avoid it. The next instant I glanced out and saw Olliffe crossing under Roper and myself, barely clearing us, and then going over a pair of stacks like a hurdler before putting his bombs in a cracking tower. How he missed the explosion, our ships, and the stacks is a mystery and always will be."

Shortly after this, Longnecker became separated from Hugh, but located him again after he had passed the refineries. "We located our indomitable companions, Hugh Roper and Vic Olliffe, and brought our ships together real tight, as before. As I moved back into my old position on Hugh Roper, I could see a display of big holes on his right wing and side, that he had gotten on the target run."

Meanwhile, "A" Force had been severely hit. Five of the six planes in the lead wave had been shot down. The sole surviving plane was Walt Stewart's *Utah Man.*

In the clouds over southwest Bulgaria there was a collision.

Ironically, after surviving Plôesti, Roper and Olliffe, died in a banal cloud collision. *Exterminator* crashed, killing everyone on board. The other plane, *Let 'er Rip*, grazed a mountain top and went into a flat glide. Koen snapped on his chest chute and went out the window amidst falling debris.

Gunners Edgar J. Pearson, Eugene Engdahl and Murray followed him. Pearson's parachute collapsed and he died in the fall. The other three parachutists landed alive, not far from the burning wreckage of their plane.

At the crash site, Bulgarian border police seized the three survivors. The police ordered peasants to gather the bodies of those who had perished in the two planes. The remains of Captain Roper and the others were buried together in a single grave near the crash site.

On 30 December 1943, Hugh Rawlin Roper was awarded the Distinguished Flying Cross, the highest medal given to aviators, and the Silver Star. He was also awarded the Purple Heart. His wife Abbie received these medals on his behalf.

Bulgaria, 1949. U. S. Government workers located the grave where Hugh's remains, along with those of the others who died in the crash, had been buried. The remains were moved to the U.S. Military cemetery in Belgrade, Yugoslavia. In January 1950, Hugh's remains were returned to the United States, and he was buried at the Jefferson Barracks National Cemetery, St Louis, Missouri.

Abbie subsequently remarried.

Taken from Garth Anderson's history Captain Hugh Rawlin Roper.

WALTER STEWART

That the fulness of my gospel might be proclaimed by the weak and the simple unto the ends of the world, and before kings and rulers.

(Doctrine & Covenants 1:23)

In June 1943, Walter Stewart was sent to Benghazi, in the Libyan desert to train for the low-level bombing raid on the Plôesti oil fields in Romania. Previously, he was co-pilot on Hugh Roper's crew. Now he was a command pilot on a B-24 Liberator, and being a graduate of the University of Utah, named his airplane *Utah Man*.

In the following account Walter tells of holding Mutual Improvement (MIA) meetings at night, on the sands near their training base:

We were preparing for a deadly mission. Those chosen to make this raid were a select group—almost all of these men already had impressive combat records. We knew our chances of being alive after a month were slim. When you don't know whether you're going to live or not, things of the Spirit, recorded in the scriptures, become more important to you. I suggested we hold MIA. My crew wondered what MIA was, and I told them it was where I went every Tuesday night while I was growing up. The first Tuesday we met in my tent. After the first night, the boys, nine of them my crew members, decided we'd read the New Testament and talk about it.

We began reading from the Book of Matthew. The boys brought their friends, and my tent quickly became too small, so we decided to meet

The crew of "Utah Man" (back row l to r) Paul E. Johnston, tunnel gunner; Doyle; Walter T. Stewart, pilot; Robert Timmer, co-pilot after 9/43; Loren J. Koon, co-pilot; Unidentified. (kneeling l to r) Richard E. Bartlett, top gunner; Ralph Cummings, bombardier; Caplan, navigator; William Major, waist-gunner; John E. Connolly, crew chief/waist-gunner.

outside. The base at Benghazi had been occupied by the German Luftwaffe, until they were driven out by English armies under Field Marshall Montgomery. We borrowed a portable organ from the chaplain, which I could play, and we sang a hymn and had prayer. When it was dark we poured gasoline over an ant bed and took turns reading the Bible by the light of the fire. We would read a passage, then talk about it. Hugh Roper and I took turns conducting.

The night we came to the account of Christ's baptism, Sergeant Richard E. Bartlett, from Troy, Montana, read:

Then cometh Jesus from Galilee to Jordan unto John, to be baptized of him.

But John forbad him, saying, I have need to be baptized of thee, and comest thou to me?

And Jesus answering said unto him, suffer it to be so now: for thus it becometh us to fulfill all righteousness. Then he suffered him.

And Jesus, when he was baptized, went up straightway out of the water. (Matthew 3: 13-16)

At that moment someone asked Sergeant Bartlett, a devout Catholic, "How could he come up out of the water? How do you do that when you've just been sprinkled on the head? There's something wrong here."

Another said, "Well, that's because you don't baptize the right way. You're supposed to pour water on them." To which Bartlett pointed out, "How could he come up out of the water if John the Baptist poured it on him? That wouldn't be any different."

"Well," said Sergeant Bill Major. "What it was, was the water that came out of his pockets when they went up out of the water. That's a translation problem." Then Bartlett rejoined, "There you have it, men. Here's Sergeant William Major from Southbend, Indiana, telling you about Jesus having pockets. Nobody, not the greatest experts who ever lived know all about how Jesus dressed, or ever talked about him having pockets."

Then Sergeant Bartlett turned to me and said, "Skipper, you tell us what happened." That was the best opening I ever had in my whole life to tell how Jesus was baptized. So I explained, "The word baptize means to 'bury in water.' You see, John baptized, or buried, Jesus in the water, and

Jesus came up out of the water." Bartlett turned to Bill Major and said, "See."

It was all spontaneous. No place in the Bible is there a better description of how baptism is to be done. From then on, the guys would ask me questions about things that puzzled them.

One night the chaplain came to our meeting—he was a great guy, we all liked him. He was from Springfield, Missouri. The men told him, "Oh, look who's come to our meeting. *Padre*, you can ask questions, but don't try to answer them. These Mormons have some real good answers that you may never have heard before."

Our MIA grew to forty-five guys, and I don't think there was ever an absentee.

The British had hired some Sudanese to guard our aircraft. They were big, tall black men with perfect uniforms. They walked at attention, had a feather in their hat, and carried a mean-looking knife at their sides. But they were very friendly with us and they'd smile and salute us.

One day their British officer came to me. "I see you hold meetings at night. Some of my men would like to come."

"Really?" I said. "I didn't know they understand English."

The officer said, "They don't, but they love your singing."

I replied, "Well, they are certainly welcome."

"But," he said, "they won't come unless they can set up your chairs." When it was time for MIA these Sudanese would find me, salute, and say, "You come, you come." They loved to hear us sing. They didn't join in the meeting, but just stood at the edge of the light, waiting for our closing hymn. We could see their teeth shining in the firelight as they laughed and sang.

After holding MIA three times a week for six or seven weeks we were still only to the tenth chapter of Matthew on 31 July 1943, the night before the raid for which we were training. On that afternoon we were told what and where our target was. We now knew we were going to Plôesti, Romania, on Sunday, 1 August. There were to be 178 B-24 bombers. This attack had been in the planning ever since Churchill and Roosevelt met at Casablanca over a year earlier. At the briefing were men who had worked at the seven refineries to tell us anything they could about these plants. Hitler desperately needed that oil to continue the war. That was why we were going. It was a very important mission, the most dangerous of the war.

Just as we were about to leave the briefing, our commanding officer, Colonel Addison E. Baker, got up and said: "They didn't tell you everything." We all sat back down. He declared, "Up in England, when we went for a target and it was clouded over or had other problems, it could be scrubbed. That will not happen tomorrow. This one's different. If we don't hit that target tomorrow, we will go on Monday. This is the most important mission of the war. They will not scrub this mission; there is no question that it's going." We had our orders. Everyone left the meeting subdued.

After the briefing the guys wanted to hold MIA. It was my turn to take charge. It was still daylight. That night there were forty-five guys who always came and at least forty-five more. I played the organ and everyone sang. Then I began: "We're in the 10th chapter of Matthew." As I reached for my Bible, a lieutenant, standing in the back, whom I had never seen before, said, "No, I don't want to read the Bible tonight, I just want to know one thing. If I get shot down where will I be tomorrow night? Or will I be?" And with one voice everyone cried out, "Yes. Tell us." They had questions they had wondered about all their lives. These people were facing death the next day. It was a wonderful setting for teaching.

I reached for my triple combination, but it was too dark to read. "Let me tell you what it says in this book, which is scripture as assuredly as is the Bible." Then I explained the plan of salvation to them. When I finished I said: "Now you know as much about it as I do." That lieutenant had stood, looking at me the whole time. I added, "Tomorrow, if you are shot down, or if you go in the Mediterranean Sea, or if you crash in the mountains, you will be just as alive as you are right now. You will just be changed. Suddenly, you will be amazed at the grand things you're seeing. In the Lord's plan, if you die tomorrow, you'll be just as alive as you are right now."

The lieutenant said, "Thanks, good night. That's what I wanted to know."

I never saw him again. He was shot down the next day.

After making our run on Plôesti, things got rough. Our plane was hit just before we were on the target. We smelled gasoline, we'd been hit in one of the tanks. Expecting we would be out of gas momentarily, we decided that as soon as we got out to some open fields, we would set it down. Accordingly, I made preparations to crash land. The throttles were off, and we were almost at landing speed, when a gunner in the rear of the plane said,

"Do you know we still have two bombs and an incendiary on board?" Talk about the Lord making sure we got home. If we had crashed with that fire bomb in the plane, all our gasoline would instantly have ignited, and our plane have turned into a ball of flame—no one would get out. I shoved the throttles ahead, and that B-24 climbed beautifully.

We decided to go as far as we could in our damaged plane. We went through the hills and never saw a bullet or a fighter plane. We couldn't have taken another bullet and made it. Parts were falling off *Utah Man,* but all four engines were intact and no one was hurt.

I saw Hugh Roper's Liberator. When I got over to where he was, I flew next to him for a minute, but nobody waved at us. In the old days they'd wave me in close, but they just stood there and looked at me. Hugh was my best friend. I remember thinking, *Somebody is hurt or dead on that airplane.*

Because of the damage to my plane they were going way too fast for me. I'd get terrible vibrations at about 150 mph, and they were doing 180. I couldn't keep up. That was the last time I saw Hugh Roper.

We climbed over the Dinaric Alps and came to the Greek coast. I said, "Okay, what have we got?"

Sergeant Connelly said, "Number three tank shows out."

I said, "Well, tell us, how much gas do we have?"

He said, "Let me tell you this way, Skipper. I've never been in a B-24, either in the air, or on the ground, that is so out of gas. Does that answer your question?"

I said, "Okay, you guys, your lives are worth as much to you as mine is to me. We can try to make it. You've heard his message."

Then the navigator said: "What you've got is 450 miles. That's two hours of the best flying you ever did in your life."

All four engines were running, and we had already thrown everything possible overboard, belt buckles, shoes, everything!

"You know the facts. We'll take a vote. Do we crash land here on the beach, or do we go on?"

Then this wonderful voice came over the intercom, "You call that an ocean?" Sergeant Bartlett said, "We've got rivers in Montana wider than that thing. Let's go! Let's go!" So, we went, and the engines kept running.

We let out our trailing antenna, which goes out 300 feet and which we needed to get shortwave radio from the BBC, and we heard an American voice, "Hello, you guys, we've got a good show today." A song began playing, "On a Wing and a Prayer"—exactly our situation. I was praying, and I knew my co-pilot was praying.

Our navigator, Lieutenant Stanley Wertz, did a miraculous job of navigating. He steered us to the right place, all with no radar, no radio beams or landmarks, just the south shore of the Mediterranean Sea.

We went straight in. About half-way down the runway, BANG! Out went the right tire. We skidded to the right, stopped, climbed out of the airplane and kissed the ground. At that moment we thought it was the most beautiful ground in the world! People came running from all over the base, banging on dish pans and waving dish towels. The general picked me up, whirled me around and said, "You brought my airplane back." We were the last ones in.

After the debriefing everybody got real quiet, and Captain Brutus Hamilton told me that Roper was not there. "Oh, he has to be back. I flew by him for ten minutes, but I couldn't keep up. He's back. Did you check at site five or site three?"

"We've checked everywhere. Your name is even on the list as missing in action. Roper's on that list, too."

That was it. Roper collided in heavy clouds with Lieutenant Olliff's aircraft over the mountains of Yugoslavia, on his last required mission. For me, losing my best friend was perhaps the most difficult experience of the war.

After I finished flying thirty-two missions I was retired from flight duty and Lieutenant Larry Coon, my co-pilot became the pilot. On their third mission, over Bremen, Germany, they were shot down on 13 November 1943, and only one bailed out.

I've done the temple work for the twenty men I flew with. I love

Captain Walter Stewart by the wheel of a B-24, November 1944.

those men. At the temple I was asked, "What do you know about these men?"

"I know the minute they died, their names, and where they died."

"That's good enough!" they said.

* * *

After I finished my combat missions, I was assigned to General Timberlake's staff. There were seventeen of us—Jimmy Stewart, the movie actor, and other successful men who were specialists in conducting our assigned operations. My specialty was high-altitude bombing. They were very special people, all very well-trained and good to work with.

Quite often the gentry of Britain would ask to have an American come and give a talk. Kind of cementing relationships, especially with the wives and the farmers who didn't get to know much about the war. One day a lady phoned and asked General Timberlake to send someone to speak on the rural life of American women. The general said to me, "You're the old Mormon preacher. You go talk to those women."

I was thrilled to go because I had been a missionary in Scotland and England four years before this. On my mission, I was never invited *into* places, I was always invited *out*. So to be invited to a meeting of the Women of the Royal Institute—the women's institute of the British world—that was Australia, Canada, everywhere, was an opportunity not to be missed. It was their annual bazaar, like the ones the Relief Society used to have. They had made things to send to their military personnel.

A driver took me to Sandringham, about thirty-five miles from Norwich. When we got there, we found forty to fifty ladies seated in front of the parish hall, and three empty seats. I said to the driver, "I guess they thought that there were three of us." The lady sitting by the empty chairs signaled for us to wait by our car. There was a photographer out in front. Just before picture time, a Rolls Royce automobile pulled up, and to my great surprise, out stepped the Queen of England, with her daughters Princess Elizabeth and Princess Margaret Rose [Princess Elizabeth is now Queen Elizabeth]. These three ladies were directed to the empty chairs.

The lady who had waved at me approached, "Are you Captain Stewart?"

"Yes, Ma'am." I answered.

"Her Majesty wants to meet you." I then asked, "What do I say to her?"

"How do you do, your Highness?" she instructed. "And from then on it's 'Yes, Ma'am' or 'No, Ma'am.' When you're introduced to the princesses, it's 'How do you do, your Royal Highness?' And then it's 'Yes, Ma'am. No, Ma'am' for the rest of the time."

We walked across the street to where the Queen was standing. She put out her hand, took mine, and held on. "You're Captain Stewart, our speaker for today. I'm very happy that you have come," and kept a hold of my hand. She saw the medals on my chest and observed, "You've been very active. I want to know something. Are you married?"

"No, Ma'am."

"Is your mother living?"

"Yes, Ma'am."

"I want you to write her a letter tonight and thank her for sending you over here. We could never win this war without you."

This was refreshing to hear. Many of the British were saying: "Go home Yank! You're in our way. You're loud. You're overpaid," and a lot of other things, but not the Queen. She understood.

Meanwhile all the other ladies were waiting. Of course they weren't standing real close. After she introduced me to several of them, she continued holding onto my hand! I thought, *You'd make a good Relief Society President. You're just so nice!*

The Queen then asked, "How long have you been here?" And I told her about a couple of missions I'd been on, and she knew about them! She knew the Plôesti mission and she knew the medal! They are very conscious about medals in Great Britain.

Then she wanted to know, "What do you know about country women?"

I said, "Well, I have seven sisters, and my mother, and I can talk about them."

"That's what we want to hear. We're very much alike. Did you live on a farm?"

"Yes."

"Do you have electricity on your farms?"

"We got it in 1937."

She said, "That's what I am trying to do over here, is to get electrical power to all the country people. They're right away from everything unless they have electric power. When the war is over, this is what I'll do." And still, she held onto my hand!

I kept glancing out of the corner of my eye at these two pretty girls. Of course one was only thirteen, but the present queen was seventeen at that time and very pretty. A young GI is attracted to pretty girls.

"Oh! You haven't met my daughters!" Now I did feel like I was holding a Relief Society woman's hand.

I said, "Hello, girls, how are you?" I heard the ladies saying, "Did you hear the Yank?" So I said, "Oh, I'm sorry. How do you do your . . ." I acted silly then, and Princess Elizabeth responded, "We just love to meet you guys." They don't say guys. They say blokes. She even said it the American way!

When we were seated, Queen Elizabeth and her daughters sat beside me, and a very beautiful Lady Fermoy asked the lady sitting on the other side of me if she could sit by Captain Stewart. "There are a lot of things here he won't know about. I can tell him because for six months I lived in the United States, while I attended the University of Pittsburgh." I was glad to have a friend. She was wearing very fine clothes and exhibited a fine manner. A very lovely lady.

While we visited, I teased her. "I notice these women have all won prizes for refronting men's shirts or for knitting sweaters and gloves! You didn't get any prizes, what's the matter?"

She explained, "Well, I play a violin."

"Oh," I said, "You could starve to death playing the violin!" She laughed and said "I went to the University of Pittsburgh for six months. My friend Fritz Reiner, conductor of the Pittsburgh Symphony, invited me over as a guest soloist."

And I thought, *Oh brother, she's a real violinist.* Anyway, we had a lot of fun.

Before I got there I'd decided that I was going to tell them I was a Mormon. I had served in the British mission. How often do you get to talk to British ladies, let alone the Queen and other gentry? I told them about rural life where I had grown up, and how my mother had kept hens, chickens, and cows, in order to feed her family. I told them "Nowadays, transportation is a bit different, but when I was a kid it was horse and buggy like it must have been for several of you ladies." They nodded their heads. I told them how the Relief Society holds meetings each month to study world affairs and current events, the scriptures, homemaking, and child care. They were listening with great care and taking notes. Finally I told them "These women of whom I am telling you, this Relief Society, is the women's organization of the Mormon Church. In fact, I'm a Mormon." I finished by telling a little more about the Church, that I had been a missionary in Britain before the war. To this I received a mostly positive response.

Afterward we went around looking at the things the women had done, the knitting and art works. The Queen was my guide, and everyone treated me very well. After a moment the Queen said: "Elizabeth, you show Captain Stewart what you've done." She modeled the sweater she had knitted.

"Now, Margaret Rose, you show him what you've done." She had a skirt made over from one of her mother's old skirts. The Queen said, "My daughters live on the same coupons as any girl in this country. If they get a pair of shoes, it's once a year. They have to make things themselves; they have to take old clothes and make them over." They were so proud showing me their work, and I felt important being treated so graciously by the Queen.

After we finished seeing the exhibits we sat down at a little table, and the ladies brought in tea and crumpets. While I visited with the Queen and two other ladies, the serving lady began pouring tea for the Queen. When she started pouring some for me. I said to her, "Oh, excuse me. I don't drink tea." It was as if I had said I don't breathe. There was a complete, embarrassing silence. The serving lady said "Oh, excuse me, Captain. I had your coffee ready when you first got here."

I blurted, "Oh, please, I don't drink coffee, either."

She looked at me, "Well, what do you drink?"

"Well, I'll tell you what. I'll drink Mormon tea."

"Whatever is that?" Then there was even more of a deadly silence. "What is Mormon tea?"

"Bring me a little hot water. I'll show you." So she brought the hot water. The women in the audience wouldn't look. They're very proper, but their ears stayed tuned.

"You pour some milk in hot water, you put in a little sugar, and you have Mormon tea. It's delicious." Actually it's the worst stuff I ever tasted.

THE AIR WAR IN EUROPE / 199

It would have been okay, but the Queen is not an ordinary person. She is very inquisitive. "Well, Captain, what's wrong with tea?" Here she is, the Queen of England, asking an army captain what's wrong with tea.

I replied, "It's against my religion."

"Oh," she said. "But you're miles from home . . . Well, that's very nice that you keep the rules of your church, but what is wrong with tea?"

"We have a statement in our church that we should not use tea or coffee because they have caffeine in them."

A lady sitting nearby, in an effort to rescue me, said, "You know, ever since I was a young girl, whenever I drink a cup of tea I perspire." That finally took the tea thing away.

Then it was time for the Queen to leave; she turned to me and said again, "You write your mother a letter tonight and thank her, and thank all the American mothers for sending their boys here to help us."

When she was outside she noticed my driver had been invited in for refreshments. She came back in, went to him, and thanked him also for coming to England to help in the war.

She said, "Oh, I'm so glad you've come. My, you're young. Where are you from?"

"Los Angeles."

"Well, you write your mother tonight and tell her . . ." saying the same thing to him as she had to me. *How gracious of her,* I thought. *She didn't have to do that.*

After the Queen left, he began laughing. "My mother is from England. Wait 'til she hears about this—this Mormon spends a day with the Queen. What a miracle—I can't believe all this."

It had been a wonderful day. I had met these very lovely women, the Queen and future Queen of England, Princess Margaret, and Lady Fermoy.

Following the war Walter Stewart returned to Utah where he met and married Ruth Francis in the Salt Lake Temple. He became a seminary teacher. In 1982, he retired as a colonel in the U.S. Air Force Reserve. He has had a lifelong interest in the men of the 93rd Bomb Group. He and Ruth are parents of three sons and two daughters. They now have twenty-seven grandchildren and three great-grandchildren.

His Church service has included construction missions to Norwich England and Flensburg Germany. In 1987 he and Ruth served a mission to Ghana, West Africa, to start a seminary program there. In 1989 they returned for another mission to the West African countries of Liberia and Sierra Leone. They now live in Benjamin, Utah, in the home built by his grandfather, Andrew Jackson Stewart, in which Walt was born. He teaches the high priests group and sometimes directs roadshows in the Benjamin Ward.

SPENCER S. HUNN

And I was led by the Spirit, not knowing beforehand the things which I should do.

(1 Nephi 4:6)

I was born 7 August 1920, in Thistle, a small railroad town in central Utah. Our family moved from Thistle to Provo in 1923, where my parents had a small farm. Following my second year at Brigham Young University, I received a mission call to go to Germany, but with the war going on, my call was changed to the Central States Mission. Upon completion of my mission, I returned to Provo and started school at BYU.

With the war heating up, I volunteered for the Aviation Cadet Training Program and went to Chandler, Arizona, for induction. I started my training at the Cal Aero primary training school at Ontario, California, then went to Chandler for advanced training. One of my classmates was Hal Gunn.

After receiving my commission as a 2nd Lieutenant, I returned to Utah, where Mary Gillespie and I were married. The best thing that ever happened to me was my marriage to Mary. She has every quality that one could want. She is bright; she is beautiful, both physically and spiritually; she is totally unselfish; she is very industrious. All these years later I love her even more than when we married.

Just three months after our wedding I was in England, assigned to the 44th Bomb Group operating out of an airdrome located near Shipdom, East Anglia, flying a B-24 Liberator. I was co-pilot to Charles E. Hughes,

1st Lieutenant Spencer Hunn (kneeling, left) and his flight crew.

from California. He was the best pilot I have ever been around. It was my good fortune to have a man like him to learn from.

After four or five missions flying out of England, the 44th Bomb Group was transferred to Benghazi, Libya, in North Africa. The reason was not told to us, but we started training flying low-level missions over the desert. Intermittently we flew bombing raids, the first ever on Rome, Italy, then on Naples and Sicily.

On 31 July 1943, we reported to the briefing room and were told the reason for our being in Africa was to fly a low-level mission on the Plôesti, Romania, oil refineries.

Takeoff was set for 0800 hours, 1 August, and the route to the target was across the Mediterranean, Greece, Yugoslavia, part of Bulgaria and then Romania. In Romania we flew at just above ground level to avoid enemy radar, and hopefully, to achieve surprise.

Trouble started at takeoff. A B-24 exploded just after its landing gear retracted into the nacelles. We later found out that one of our own soldiers (a traitor) had put hand grenades in the wheel wells.

Our personal trouble became apparent when I checked our fuel consumption and found that we were using fuel much faster than anticipated. Our recourse was to return to base, but because of the importance of this mission we elected to go on to the target; knowing that we would not be able to get home. We didn't tell the crew.

Navigation at low levels is very difficult because of the limited view of the terrain and the inexact details on maps. Consequently, when we arrived in the target area we were confused as to the exact location of each of our targets.

There were five groups of B-24s, one hundred seventy-eight aircraft total, attacking. Each group was assigned a different target. The targets were all located in close proximity to each other, in size a little larger than the Geneva Steel Complex near Provo, Utah.

The bombs we carried were fitted with delay fuses, because at tree-top level an instantaneous fuse would blow up the airplane that dropped it. Fuses of sixty seconds to twenty-four hours were fitted to the bombs.

In the confusion, the general commanding the whole force missed his assigned target and struck ours. Since he was first over, his bombs were exploding by the time we got to the target.

But trouble started before we got right over the target. Our approach was along a railroad track. We were flying at between 60 and 250 feet above the ground. All along the railroad track were antiaircraft gun batteries on railcars. We were so close that I could see the flash from the gun barrels. All of us took some hits—none catastrophic. Ahead we could see our target; it was aflame and great palls of smoke were rising into the sky. Our path was through one of the smoke clouds.

Entering a roiling column, we saw a very tall smoke stack right in front of our six-airplane flight. We climbed up to miss the stack, then dropped down and released our bombs. Ahead I saw a bomb, or bombs, explode— those dropped earlier by the general's plane. I saw three of our planes disappear in the burst. We continued on, dropped our bombs, then tried to evade further explosions and get out of the immediate target area. On the way out I looked *up* at the town clock as we flew by the tower—it was just 1500 hours, seven hours after take off. I also saw a soldier kneel down and fire his rifle at point-blank range.

As we left the immediate target, enemy fighter planes attacked us. There was no semblance of a formation, each pilot was on his own, trying to get away. Several B-24s were shot down by Nazi fighter planes. I also saw a fighter forced into the ground by a B-24. It all happened very quickly.

Of the six bombers in our flight, we were the only one to get through to the target; however we did not escape unscathed. A German shell exploding in the back of our plane injured three of the crew. Additionally, it cut our flight control cables to the rear ailerons and rudders. Only a strand of a multi-wire cable remained. It was just enough. We also had an eight-inch hole in the top of our wing in a gas tank. Fortunately that tank was

Spencer Hunn receiving the Distinguished Flying Cross for the Plôesti Raid. General Johnson, presenting the medal, led this raid.

empty. All this we found out later. We were successful in evading several fighters, and about thirty minutes later we flew into a cloud bank. Not until then could we check the damage we sustained and verify our fuel supply. There was not nearly enough to get us back to Benghazi. We landed in Turkey instead.

Turkey was a non-combatant nation, so our technical status there was that of internees rather than POWs, but we were detained. Turkey did not have prisoner of war camps or stockades; therefore we were incarcerated in a building located outside the city of Ankara. It had large, open rooms that were converted to sleeping quarters. There were toilet and shower facilities, but no kitchen, or any possibility of converting a room into one.

Officers and airmen were kept separated. There were two times each day when we were allowed out of our locked rooms. At 0900 we were allowed an hour to shower and shave, etc. And since there was no means of providing food, we were given parole to walk into Ankara and eat in one of the many restaurants. Parole was limited to three and one-half hours, from 1030 to 1400. We had no money, but the Turks provided what we needed to pay for our meals. The Turkish government also gave us money to purchase clothes.

Parole restrictions were well-defined. We could not leave the city limits of Ankara except to go back and forth to our facility. We could have no means of transportation other than walking, and could not wear any sort of uniform. Control of our parole was accomplished by our signing a form each evening at 5:00 p.m. Each signature was verified at roll call the following morning. It was mandatory that everyone go on parole each day. The system was very effective and made escape nearly impossible.

For the most part our lives were quite comfortable. There was no cruelty by the guards or officials of the government. We were out of the war and physically safe. However, during our flight training we had been taught to do everything possible to escape.

Four of us decided we would leave. While on parole one day we contacted the British Embassy who put us in contact with the Greek underground. Greece was then occupied by the Nazis, but had an effective underground organization.

The problem facing us was to escape without violating our parole. To escape while on parole would have put our government in the awkward position of having to return us to Turkey.

While showering one day, I noticed a trap door in the ceiling that had a built-in ladder.

Four officers, Charles Hughes, Maurice Hause, James Marquis and I, traded places with four airmen. We made certain that our names and faces were not specifically identified when we signed in or out. At roll call we answered to the names of the airmen, and they to ours. This went on for about three weeks. The day for our escape was set for the last Monday of September 1943.

On the morning set for our escape, we instructed the airmen to start a riot in their rooms during the time we were to shower.

The fight started. They broke chairs, windows, and created such a disturbance that all of the guards in the facility went to the airmen's rooms to stop the fight. Before the fight, the four airmen whose identity we had assumed, climbed into the shower room attic, prepared to stay for a minimum of twenty-four hours. After the fight was quieted, roll call for parole was made. That evening the airmen signed their names to the parole sheet. We four did not. Each time the airmen's names were called, we answered. When our names were called, no one answered.

The guards went through the rolls three times, each time making a physical count of those present, and made a search of the facility. No one was found. Four men were missing. After much delay, and with us making as many demands as possible to go eat, the facility commander admitted that four men had escaped, and we were permitted out on parole. As we passed the guard door we answered to the appropriate airman's name. We never learned how long the airmen had to stay up in the attic, or if they were ever found out, but they still have our gratitude for their sacrifice.

We made our way to the railroad station where we met a man, appropriately, with a rose in his lapel. We had only the clothes we were wearing—no luggage, and no knowledge of any plans.

Each of us was handed a train ticket. Mike and I were to go to Istanbul; the other two to Izmir. We were told that another person, also with a rose in his lapel, would be at the respective stations.

We met our contact in Istanbul at 0300 hours and were taken to a safe house where we stayed for two days. We were given a ticket to board an intercostal boat. We passed through the Sea of Marmara, the Dardanelles, and followed the Turkish coast on the Aegean Sea to Izmir.

Reports of our escape had been made public, and the police were searching for us, so we stayed in our cabin during the night and day it took for us to get to Izmir. After most of the passengers had debarked we started for the gangplank. Much to our dismay we saw police on the other end, checking identity papers. We quickly moved away from the line, wondering how we could get off.

We noticed cargo being unloaded from a door in the hold. Most of the cargo was carried off on the shoulders of stevedores, bare to the waist. We took off our shirts, got in line, and picked up some boxes. We put them on our shoulder to hide our faces and followed the line of workers into the warehouse. It was a simple matter to find our way out to the gates.

We met our escort with the rose and were driven across the peninsula to a lone house on a deserted beach on the Mediterranean, still in Turkey. We met Charlie and Jim there. We stayed in that house three days.

Before sunup the fourth day, we were taken to the beach, where a small fishing boat had tied up during the night. We boarded and found there were six Greeks there who were going with us. Twelve days after our escape we reached Cyprus.

From Cyprus we were flown to Tel Aviv, in Palestine, and on to Cairo, where we turned ourselves over to the 9th U.S. Army Air Corps.

Our immediate desire was to return to our organization. The problem was that no one in the 9th knew where it was. Since the commander of the 9th Air Force did not know where the 44th Bomb Group was, he could not give us orders to return.

During the raid on Plôesti our organization was so badly damaged and had lost so many men that they had to be outfitted with new planes and replacement crews. Once they became operational they were sent back to North Africa. In a raid on Livorno, Italy, they once again sustained terrible damage and loss of personnel. At this point no one we could find knew if our outfit was in England or North Africa.

So the 9th Air Force Commander put us on R and R [rest and recovery] leave and told us we could go to Jerusalem.

There we visited all the holy sites; the Mount of Olives, Via de la Rosa, Golgotha, Rachel's tomb, and Bethlehem. When we returned to Cairo, we still had no orders, so we spent two weeks visiting the sites around Cairo. Finally we got general orders to "join your group wherever you can find it."

Jerusalem, Palenstine [now Israel]: Spencer Hunn (3rd from left) and others who had escaped from Turkish prison camp.

With those orders in hand, we hitched rides on military planes, with stops at many cities all across North Africa. We finally found remnants of the 44th Group in Marrakech, Morocco. We were flown from there to England. It had been five months since we had departed for Benghazi.

In June 1944 I was promoted to major and given command of the 66th Squadron. It turned out that Charles Hughes, my best friend, was a member of my unit. When I was made squadron commander he took it well. He said to me, "It is pure hell to have to say *sir* to your co-pilot."

I completed my missions in December 1944 and returned to the States in time to spend Christmas with my wife, Mary, and our thirteen-month-old son, Joseph. I told them that I had been to the site where Joseph had taken Mary to give birth to Jesus. It was a wonderful Christmas.

Following the war, Spencer Hunn returned to school at the University of Utah. A year following his separation from the Air Force he was invited to return to active duty. He did so with the stipulation that he be able to finish his degree while on active duty. The Air Force sent him to Purdue University where he completed a masters degree in jet propulsion and nuclear physics. He was instrumental in the design and building of the Cheyenne Mountain Air Defense Facility near Colorado Springs, Colorado. In 1970 he retired with the rank of brigadier general. Following military service he worked for the Federal Aviation Administration, where he was charged with automating the Air Traffic Control System in the United States. He was later Director of Research and Development for the FAA, his purview included airport planning and design, air traffic control, and aviation safety planning.

He has taught the Gospel Doctrine class in nearly every place he and his family have lived. He served as a counselor in the Ohio District Presidency, twice as bishop—Billerica, Massachusetts, and the BYU 10th Ward; served on high councils in Boston and at BYU. He and Mary have two sons, a daughter, and nine grandchildren. They reside in Orem, Utah.

WAYNE ELDON MURDOCK

Greater love hath no man than this, that a man lay down his life for his friends.

(John 15:13)

Wayne Eldon Murdock was inducted into the Army Air Corps on 20 May 1942. Commissioned a 2nd lieutenant 20 May 1943, at Stockton, California, he completed training as pilot of a B-17 at Camp Kearney, Nebraska, and left for England in November 1943. He was assigned to the 8th Air Force, 91st Bomb Group.

In one of his letters home, Wayne writes:

> This Army is certainly quite a place to meet people and get a pretty good idea as to the attitude generally throughout the United States. No matter where you are, it seems like there is someone from nearly every part of the country. After sitting around, listening to them tell about what they do on their weekends and their ideas of a good time and so on, it certainly makes me appreciate the kind of home you and Mother made for us and the training we all had at home and in the Church. Of course, some of them are probably bragging and stretching their stories, but I know a lot of them aren't. I hear the stuff day after day, and I can't help comparing their standards with the ones I was taught.

Lieutenant Murdock flew several missions over Germany. On 11 January 1944, he took part in a raid on the aircraft industrial complex at Oschersleben, Germany. Fifty-nine bombers were shot down. His was among them. As reported by survivors of his crew, Lieutenant Murdock stayed at the controls of his B-17 while eight of his crew bailed out. These men were taken prisoner. Wayne and his radioman were the last out. Both were killed.

Wayne's parachute failed to open. He fell into the front yard of the home of a German couple living in the village of Ottleben. These people built a coffin and buried him in their garden. Some time later his body was moved to the village cemetery, and a wooden cross erected, upon which was crudely written, "Leo Mordock—Bratfort." "Leo" was Wayne's father's name.

Wayne Eldon Murdock

In an extraordinary chain of events—with the help of The Church of Jesus Christ of Latter-day Saints, in cooperation with the U.S. Army—Wayne's body was finally identified and brought home for burial.

On 19 February 1944, Wayne's family received this telegram: "Report received from the German government through the International Red Cross states your son, 2nd Lieutenant Wayne E. Murdock, who was previously reported missing in action, was killed in action on eleven January in European Area. The Secretary of War extends his deep sympathy."

From the War Department, Commanding General of the Army Air Force, the family received the following:

My Dear Mr Murdock: 6 March 1944

With great regret I have learned that your son, Second Lieutenant Wayne Eldon Murdock, missing in action since 11 Jan 1944, has been reported as having died on that date in the European Area.

He was a dependable officer and strong leader whose agreeable personality and high principles won firm friends for him, and he is greatly missed by his comrades. I hope the knowledge that your son zealously served his Country and made an important contribution to its cause will help to lessen your sorrow. I offer my heartfelt sympathy to you and other members of the family.

Very Sincerely
H.H. Arnold, General U. S. Army
Commanding General, Army Air Forces

Wayne's parents made diligent inquiry through the U S Government as to the disposition of Wayne's body, but little was found in the records. They then turned to the Church. That inquiry brought this answer from the East German mission president:

Dear Brother Murdock   29 September 1948

Brother Victor Billings forwarded to us a letter that you had written to him on 18 April 1948, asking what he could do to locate the grave of your son. . . . We immediately began inquiry in every way available to us. Among other things, we wrote to the city council of the city of Oschersleben, asking if they had any information. Recently we received the two enclosed letters (we have written the translations on the back). As you will note, the letters indicate that no grave has been found of Wayne E. Murdock, but an American flyer was buried in the cemetery of the village of Ottleben, county of Oschersleben. This grave was marked with a wooden cross upon which was written "Leo Mordock."

Upon learning this, we went to the office of the American graves registration command in Berlin to see if they had any more information on this particular grave. According to their files of information gathered from the Germans in the area, the American flyer was buried in the cemetery at Ottleben in July 1944. A woman who said she had prepared the body for burial said that he was young, medium height, rather heavy set, dark hair, a number of gold fillings in his teeth. The grave was marked with a simple wooden cross upon which was crudely written "Leo Mordock—Bratfort."

Last week a British graves registration team exhumed the body and brought it to Berlin and turned it over to the American graves registration command. The Americans found no identification tags or papers of any kind. The body was clad only in the flying coveralls of an Air Force officer. The body is still here in Berlin. As soon as there is room on an airplane, it will be flown to Liege, Belgium, to the permanent cemetery. Then the American graves registration command will make every effort to identify the body. The service and medical records of your son will be sent from Washington. Using this and other information, the Army will try to prove conclusively the identity of the remains. If the body turns out to be that of your son, then you will be notified in due course by the proper Army authorities.

We do not want to build up your hopes to have you disappointed later—but perhaps we should state the possibilities.

Perhaps you will remember that the old style identification tags of the army [which were still in use in 1944] gave the name and number of the soldier, the name of the next of kin, and the address of the next of kin. It is possible that the Germans who buried the body copied on the cross, not the name of your son, but the name of his father "Leo Murdock." An "o" was misread in place of the "u." Further, it is possible that the Germans went on to copy the address, but not being able to read it correctly, they wrote "Bratfort" instead of "Blackfoot."

On the army lists of flyers who were shot down over this area, there is *no name* that is similar to "Leo Mordock," except the name of your son.

One thing is hard to explain, which is that German testimony says that the body was buried in July 1944. Your son was shot down in January. Of course the testimony might be incorrect, or the people might have waited until summer to bury the remains. . . .

We gave a copy of your letter to the graves registration command. If the body is your son's, then you can rest assured that you will be notified and the body will be safely put to rest in a permanent Army cemetery. . . .

We extend to you our sincerest sympathy in your great loss and pray that the Lord will bless and comfort you.

> Sincerely Yours
> Walter Stover,
> Mission President

It was proven that this was indeed the body of Wayne E. Murdock, and it was returned to his hometown for burial. Graveside services were held in the Riverside-Thomas, Idaho, Cemetery, 21 March 1950.

Hearing about his brother's death, 1st Lieutenant Clinton V. Murdock, also a pilot stationed in England, wrote:

> Just received your wire about Wayne. Feel terrible about it. I was so sure he was going to be okay. Guess there isn't a lot to do now. I'll try and get all the information from his intelligence officer, and maybe later I can find some of the details out. Do you have contacts with the rest of his crew's families? If you do, will you let

me know what they have received, if anything? Well, no matter how bad I feel I've still got a job to do over here, and if I didn't do it to the best of my ability, it would sort of be like letting him down. You mentioned in a letter I got today that you were all well, but not happy. I guess it has probably hurt you a lot more than me. I'm sort of getting used to losing my friends, but whether he ever told you or not, Wayne gave his life so that all of you could continue to be happy and get all the joy possible out of life. To not attempt to do so would make his sacrifice in vain. I know this as I feel the same way.

Clint

Compiled from records of the Murdock family.

CLINTON V. MURDOCK

Clinton V. Murdock, Air Corps Cadet, 1942.

I completed a semester at Moscow, Idaho, then enlisted in the Army Air Corps. I already knew the basics of flying when I got to Sequoia Army Air Base at Visalia, California. I had soloed. My final exam was a check ride with "One-ride Lieutenant Porter." He was called that because he gave you just one ride and you were either in or out. He didn't say a word to me the whole time we were flying. When we landed, he just walked off. I went to my commanding officer who asked if I had passed. I told him I didn't know; "One-ride" hadn't said anything. When I asked him if I passed, he growled, "I didn't say you didn't, did I?"

On 6 February 1943, I was commissioned a second lieutenant and assigned to the 75th Troop Carrier Squadron at Valley Army Air Base, Austin, Texas, to transition to C-47s. The C-47 was the military version of the DC-3 airliner, a fine aircraft. But I was sorely disappointed as I had wanted to be a fighter pilot.

In June I was sent to Sedalia, Missouri, Air Force Base. I did a lot of flying, often more than ten hours a day. In July I flew to Idaho and buzzed my folks' farm just west of Blackfoot. In August I trained to tow gliders and to drop paratroopers. By then I had a crew, including a co-pilot, navigator, crew chief and radio operator. We picked up a brand new airplane at Mobile, Alabama. In early October we went to Fort Wayne, Indiana for some final training and for processing to go overseas.

While I was training to fly C-47s, my brother Wayne was training to fly the B-17 Flying Fortress. We were both sent to England. We arranged to meet. That was the last time I saw him. He died during a raid on an aircraft factory in Germany, on 11 January 1944. I had not heard about his death and went to his airbase to see him again the day after he was shot down. Of course, he was not there, and I still did not learn of his death until I received a telegraph from my father. I felt terrible to lose my brother and best friend. But there was little to do but continue the tasks of war.

In January 1944 I was sent to Welford Royal Air Force Base, sixty miles west of London. For one mission, another pilot and I flew to Inverness, Scotland, to pick up some gliders to take back to Welford. We arrived at the Scottish base too late to return that day. The next day the heavy overcast required we fly low throughout the four-hour flight home. As long as it was light and we stayed away from populated areas, we could fly at low altitudes. Because neither of us had a navigator, we had to do our own navigation.

When we neared populated areas, we heard a siren-like sound on our radios. This indicated we were approaching barrage balloons, which the British anchored around every city to catch enemy bombers. There were also dangling cables to ensnare any aircraft that came close. Some of these balloons floated to an elevation of 10,000 feet. Our only recourse was to fly above 10,000 feet, in the clouds and on instruments.

England did not have the navigational aides we were used to. A short time after take-off we were completely unsure of where we were, but proceeded in a southerly direction. The solution provided by the English for planes in such a predicament was to radio the words: "Hello Darky. Hello Darky. Hello Darky" followed by "Give me a steer." In accordance with war-time English protocol, our on-board radio transmitters were limited to a range of five miles. The result was that we flew from Scotland across England repeating "Hello Darky" for what seemed several hours. When someone finally answered, we gave a code name. Mine was "Top Hat, H for How." They would check to see if we were legitimate, then give us a course setting, which we flew until passed off to another voice, who passed us off to another until one told us to begin descending. After two or three course corrections we broke out of the clouds. We were over water, headed east.

We knew that if a plane got lost, it would be picked up by German radio. Controllers, speaking perfect English would direct them to an airport in Belgium or Holland, where the Germans would capture the crew. Having left the base on Scotland's east coast, we were over water, heading east toward land. My co-pilot yelled, "It's a German trap, let's get out of here." I checked the gas gauges. We were flying on empty. I said I would rather be captured than go down in water at night. We proceeded, and landed at Liverpool. We had crossed from one side of Britain to the other.

* * *

By mid-December 1944, I had flown forty or fifty supply missions to forward air strips in France. Later our outfit was moved to France, and I was stationed there for the duration of the war in Europe.

About the time the atomic bomb was dropped on Japan I returned to the United States, and was released from active duty in December 1945.

* * *

Here are some of my feelings about spiritual experiences I had during the war. I have felt in my own case a tendency to make such stories better than they were, so I often feel it pertinent to be silent on such matters. As far as divine intervention in those days—all around me I saw examples of tremendous sacrifice and devotion to the common effort to save humanity. Individual acts of courage and sacrifice were almost routine.

Despite the many mistakes that occurred, the Lord's hand was apparent. The assault on D-Day is a prime example. The most meticulous plans to place paratroopers in strategic places in front of the invasion forces were apparently well-known by the Germans. The drop zones were strewn with poles, ditches cut through them, and other impediments placed to thwart the paratroopers and gliders landings. Enemy troops surrounded our drop zones well before we departed England. What happened? Flying to our designated drop off points we ran into cloud cover, and tightly closed formations of planes, carrying troops and pulling gliders, were scattered. We unloaded soldiers all over the Cherbourg peninsula. Allied intelligence later told us that the Germans thought we had dropped eight divisions, instead of the two that were sent in.

Nick, as he is called by family and friends, returned to his home near Blackfoot, Idaho. He married Joan Packham. They are parents of four sons and three daughters. He purchased a farm near Rockford where he and Joan raised their family. Nick retired from farming and moved to Hurricane, Utah, where he and Joan do aerial photography. They are ordinance workers in the St. George Temple.

Taken from the personal records of Clinton V. Murdock.

HYRUM KERSHAW

My God hath been my support; he hath led me through mine afflictions.

(2 Nephi 4:20)

During February 1943, I was inducted into military service. After completing flight training I was sent to Pocatello Army Air Base, Idaho, for transition instruction to the P-47 Fighter plane. Here I could be with Millie and our new daughter, Launa Lee. Upon completing this training, the wing

Hyrum Kershaw

commander asked me to stay on for two months as an instructor. Looking back, although I was anxious to get to the war zone, it made me a better pilot—the teacher always learns more than the student.

Soon enough I found myself stationed at Tarquinnia Air Base, Italy, a few kilometers north of Rome, attached to the 350th Fighter Group and assigned to the 347th Fighter Squadron. I liked flying the rugged P-47 and felt the Air Corps had trained me well.

My first mission was 1 November 1944. Being the junior pilot in terms of time in the war zone, I drew the aircraft in the poorest mechanical shape. In combat near Milano, my plane lost its electrical power. This shut down the plane's electrical systems, which included the radio; but the engine continued to purr right along, so I headed south. Finding a friendly landing field, but having no communication capability, I had to bluff my way onto the ground. It was an exhilarating initiation!

Although not able to attend any Church services during my combat tour, I acknowledge the Lord's protecting hand on every sortie. Each time I climbed into the cockpit I offered a prayer that I would do my best and return safely.

On Christmas Day 1944, the Germans and Americans agreed to an informal stand down. Our wing commander asked for volunteers to fly patrol over enemy territory to satisfy himself that the enemy was not taking advantage of this truce. Another pilot and I took this assignment. The other pilot was lead. Flying over the Po River Valley, we investigated an area north of Milano where we spotted a suspicious site.

My friend dived onto it, strafing as he went. Immediately the area burst into flames. Flying far enough back as to be in no immediate danger, I saw the concentric concussion rings of a major explosion. We had attacked an immense enemy ammo dump. As we continued the attack with bombs and machine guns, an inferno of flames leaped as high as 6,000 feet. When we landed at Pisa, 250 miles away, we were confident that the ammo dump had been destroyed as smoke from the site was clearly visible in the north.

Some of the pilots in my unit became increasingly timid as they completed more of their missions. My feeling was to do the most I could to shorten the war. On each mission I looked for "targets of opportunity," following the completion of our assigned task. I always used up all 4,000 rounds of ammunition and both 500-pound bombs where they would do the most damage consistent with the war effort.

On a mission over the Po Valley we discovered 200 vehicles under camouflage. I led twelve planes in a circling attack, keeping a constant barrage of fire on the target. The last man out, I was running dangerously low on fuel. Knowing I did not have the fuel needed to get home, I flew west directly above the Po River at tree-top level, to a point I thought safe. Just then, I passed directly into a German machine-gun nest, which opened up on me as their lone target. The Lord preserved me through it. Swinging south, I was shaking uncontrollably and had difficulty flying the plane. On the ground aircraft maintenance counted fifty holes made by .30-caliber bullets.

* * *

During the last week of the war I led a flight into an overcast sky. The whole valley was shrouded in rain clouds, no doubt making the Germans confident to move about. In northeastern Italy I found a hole in the murk. Leaving the other three planes on top, I dropped to ground level where I discovered a large convoy of German trucks, interspersed with the shiny black limousines of the generals, headed north toward Germany. Returning with the other three planes we destroyed every vestige of this convoy, including the fleeing generals. Each P-47 having six .50-caliber machine guns mounted side by side made them capable of devastating a target.

During this same week I led an attack on Aviano Air Base, located at the foot of Mt. Cavallo in the Province of Udine. For this action I received the Silver Star. The citation accompanying this medal tells what happened:

For gallantry in action. On 29 April 1945, Lieutenant Kershaw led a four-plane flight on an armed reconnaissance mission over enemy positions in northern Italy. Upon the approach to the target area, Lieutenant Kershaw sighted an active airdrome near Aviano. Immediately diving through a heavy barrage of anti-aircraft fire, which disabled two guns and heavily damaged his airplane, Lieutenant Kershaw destroyed two enemy planes and probably another. Despite the crippled condition of his aircraft, Lieutenant Kershaw quickly reformed his flight and, in the face of continued strong resistance that further damaged his P-47 and nearly rocked it from control, repeatedly strafed several motor convoys, destroying or damaging a number of vehicles and inflicting casualties upon personnel before exhaustion of ammunition forced him to break off and turn homeward. Determinedly holding his shattered plane airborne to base, Lieutenant Kershaw effected a perfect emergency landing. His gallant devotion to duty and outstanding proficiency in combat reflect highest credit upon himself and the armed forces of the United States.

The destructive power of the weaponry on our planes was always astonishing. I learned that war is no picnic and was greatly relieved when it ended. I flew eighty-six missions in the 180 days before war's end, for which I was awarded the Silver Star, the Distinguished Flying Cross and the Air Medal with four Oak Leaf clusters.

The men of the 350th Fighter Group were informed we were going to the Pacific for combat there. We left Pisa on 1 August 1945, bound for The Philippines. While passing through the Panama Canal we learned atomic bombs had been dropped on Japan and that the Japanese had surrendered. This ended the war. We sailed back through the Canal and up to New York City. During this time we were allowed to open the sealed orders we were carrying. Had we had to continue, these orders stipulated that on 1 November 1945, we were to attack Yokohama harbor. Our fuel capacity would not have allowed us to make the round trip from The Philippines. It would have been a very dangerous situation for pilots. I am grateful to President Truman for having the courage to drop the bomb.

Following active military service Hy reunited with Millie and Launa Lee. He completed a degree in dairy science at the University of Idaho. With his GI Bill benefits, he went on to earn his Doctorate in veterinary medicine at Washington State University in Pullman. He returned to Idaho, and setted in Blackfoot, Idaho, where for thirty-five years he concentrated his practice on large animals. Hyrum served in many Church callings, including the high council. He remained with the inactive Air Force Reserve. He and Millie are parents of seven children, twenty grandchildren and twelve great-grandchildren.

Taken from an oral interview with Paul H. Kelly.

LAWRENCE O. VOLMER

Go your way whithersoever I will, and it shall be given you by the Comforter what you shall do and whither you shall go.

(Doctrine & Covenants 31:11)

Our crew was assigned to the 427th Bombardment Squadron, 303rd Bombardment Group, at Molesworth Air Station, central England, the base that was home until I left England.

Each day presented extraordinary and diverse experiences. With aircraft coming from many different airfields, it would take up to three hours to organize our six hundred bombers into the required groupings for our assigned targets. One of our adversaries on these flights was the cold. It could get as low as sixty degrees below zero inside the plane. We wore special electrically heated suits, gloves, and boots.

I was a radio operator on a B-17 crew and flew thirty combat missions over enemy territory. We returned safely each time. Our safety was not for lack of danger, as evidenced by the following accounts of five of those missions.

Larence O. Volmer

16 December 1943: My first mission, Bremen, Germany. While I was seated at the radio desk taking messages, I heard a voice as real as any I have ever heard say, "Get up! Get up!" Compelled by the urgency in the voice, I immediately jumped to my feet as a piece of flak tore through my table, imbedding itself in the roof of my compartment. Never before or since, have I heard that voice; yet I am sure I would recognize it were I to hear it again. In that moment a sense of calm settled over me, and from that time I did not fear for my safety.

5 January 1944. Target: Kiel, Germany. Our aircraft developed mechanical problems before reaching the target and we had to abort the mission. As we left the formation our navigator picked up a radio compass signal and gave the pilot a routing that was supposed to take us back to England. We were flying at 4,000 feet when we spotted islands off to our left. As we crossed over the islands, the pilot and navigator told us we were seeing the Wash, a landmark on England's east coast. I called back and said this could not be the Wash because we hadn't flown long enough to reach it. Besides, the land lay on our left, not our right. The pilot acknowledged that I was correct and asked if I could establish our true position. By then we were over land, and a battery of 88mm flak guns opened up on us. The first four bursts were close, and as we flew on, the flak got closer and closer. The pilot banked sharply and dropped to ground level. Soon we were over water, the plane barely clearing the waves and the props sometimes slicing through whitecaps. We had been lured into an enemy trap. The Germans, having learned how to bend radio waves, had provided us false information about our location and course. We were lucky to escape. Our tail gunner was hit by some flak, but his helmet saved his life.

After gaining some altitude, the pilot decided we were lost. He asked whether I had located a direction finding station [DF station] for a compass heading. I knew we must get the compass heading. Our navigator had already been deceived once, and this had put us in great danger. It was essential that I determine what signals we could rely upon. The first transmission I received was loud and clear, and the operator gave me a heading. However, that heading did not seem authentic, and given our position, so low over the channel, the signal was too strong to be coming from our DF station in England. I radioed again. Immediately the operator gave me a heading. I had not yet asked for a heading, so I challenged him, requesting that he give me that day's designated code. He answered with the right code numbers. I challenged him again, asking for a different set of numbers. The second time he gave the right numbers and a heading. Still not satisfied, I asked for a third set of numbers. This time they were wrong. It was a German radio operator trying to draw us over Holland, where they could shoot us down.

I continued to search for one of our DF stations. Finally I picked up a very weak signal. I asked the radio operator for authentication. He gave the right numbers, so I knew we were on the proper wave length. Once we had our position and a magnetic heading, it wasn't long before we reached England and returned to our base at Molesworth.

11 January 1944. Target: the Oschersleben aircraft assembly complex. [Note: Volmer's crew flew the same mission on which Lt. Wayne Murdock's plane was shot down and Wayne died. See page 208.] We began this mission as a spare, but another plane had to abort, so we went on the mission even though the engineer's headset was not working. En route to the target I heard a message recalling all aircraft in the 2nd and 3rd Divisions. The weather in England was deteriorating, and landing upon our return would be precarious. I thought it was strange that Division did not also recall us, so I radioed Bomber Command and asked if they also wanted 1st Division to turn around. I received a firm "no!"

The 2nd and 3rd Division planes were not yet out of sight when Luftwaffe fighters rose up through the clouds like a swarm of angry bees, attacking us with snarling ferocity. They continued their brutal assault as they followed us to Oschersleben and most of the way to home base. The bomber just in front of us exploded in flames as it took several direct hits. Our pilot made an emergency dive to avoid the fiery mass in the sky. Through

Lawrence Volmer with his aircraft.

the radio hatch atop the plane I watched in terror as a wing from the disintegrating aircraft barely missed us.

As we commenced our bomb run, a piece of flak cut through one of our oxygen lines, leaving half our crew, including me, without oxygen. We unloaded our bombs. At 28,000 feet, oxygen deprivation occurs quickly. I got down on my knees to hunt for my walk-around oxygen bottle. It had fallen into the supercharger compartment. As I searched the compartment, a bullet ripped through the radio room. It cut the other oxygen line and smashed into our number three engine. Had I not been on my knees, the bullet would have hit me too. I found my oxygen bottle among the loose ammunition. The hose had been smashed between 50 caliber bullets, and was cut in several places, making the bottle useless.

Without oxygen some of our crewmen were passing out, and my eyesight began to fail. In the B-17 the radioman doubled as a gunner. I attempted to take aim at an attacking fighter, but before I could fire my gun my vision faded and I could not see.

Below us was a small formation of crippled B-17s, and we dropped down and joined them. At 17,000 feet we could breathe again, and my eyesight returned. There were a few more fighter attacks, but we could now see to defend ourselves. We finally crossed the Channel to England.

Over England we encountered fog so dense that we could not find Molesworth. My radios were all shot up, so I could not call for directions. Out of the frying pan into the fire—our situation again became critical as we were running out of fuel. The pilot headed back toward the Channel. He told us to put on our parachutes and prepare to bail out. The bomb bay doors were opened. I was disconnecting the mike cord to my heated suit when the navigator recognized an airbase through an opening in the clouds. The pilot said: "Hang on. We're going down." He brought the plane around 180 degrees and set it on the runway. No sooner had the wheels touched ground than our three remaining engines stopped turning. We were completely out of gas and the plane had to be towed off the runway. It would be hard to describe our relief to be back.

D-Day—June 6, 1944. I finished my thirtieth mission on 28 May, over Cologne. I had spent the interim time just kicking around and was still assigned to the 427th Squadron. A pilot came into the barracks and asked if I would be his radio operator, said he wanted to fly down and have a look at the invasion. Off we flew to Normandy in one of the only spare aircraft, a B-17 that had been used to tow targets for fighter pilots to train on. When we arrived it was so cloudy that all we saw was some of the ships firing at the coastline and a few flights of B-17s going in. The pilot turned around and headed back to Molesworth. Later I told a gunner from my squadron about our flight. He had seen us and said he almost opened fire on us. In their briefings they had been instructed to shoot down any aircraft not in a formation or those without up-to-date markings. Of course the tow target plane neither had up-to-date markings nor was it flying in formation. Bomber command was concerned there might be captured B-17s being used by the Germans.

For his meritorious service, Lawrence Volmer was awarded the Distinguished Flying Cross and the Air Medal, with three oak leaf clusters. He returned to the United States where he was assigned to recruiting duty. At the close of the war, he returned to his home in Ammon, Idaho, and married Donna L. Bates, of Rigby.

In 1960 Lawrence was baptized into the Church. He has served as a home teacher, ward financial clerk, secretary to the YMMIA and elders quorum, and assistant to the high priests group leader. He was a farmer for a time, then worked at the Idaho National Engineering Lab near Idaho Falls until he retired. For many years he was president of the Idaho Chapter of the Eighth Air Force Historical Society. He and Donna have one son and four grandchildren.

Taken from personal records of Lawrence O. Volmer.

PAUL W. AHLSTROM

To stand as witnesses of God . . . in all places that ye may be in.

(Mosiah 18:9)

The following excerpts are taken from Paul's journal:

6 April 1944: Today at three o'clock I was working in the depot supply office, Burtonwood, Lancashire, England. The telephone rang. A sergeant answered, listened for a while, then said to me, "Paul, go immediately to your orderly room, pack your bags and be ready to ship tonight." That

LDS Service Group--Paris, France, 1945. Paul Ahlstrom is on the front row, third from left.

was all the notice I had to get my belongings together, and say good-bye to my friends.

When I reached the orderly room I was informed that I would leave for *somewhere,* Saturday morning at ten o'clock. This gave me time to go to Wigan, where I spent a very enjoyable evening with the Wigan MIA. We went swimming, then came back to the chapel where we had a discussion. Then three of us went to a member's home so that I could say good-bye to them. They served us a hot fruit drink and sandwiches.

It was hard for me to leave Wigan because of my Church connections. I was working in the MIA and had a heavy activity program scheduled for the summer months in hopes of getting better attendance at our meetings. We were having success. Attendance had jumped from six to thirty-five. Our soldiers' activities were also going well at camp, with an average attendance of twenty-five each week. My stay in England would have been monotonous had it not been for my Church activity. The Army did not provide activity that interested me as much as it did for those who liked to "cat around."

Dance card and schedule of events for the LDS Forces Conference in Birmingham, England, January 8 and 9, 1944. The LDS servicemen's group held many activities and conferences throughout the war.

7 April: At ten o'clock I reported to the station hospital. The hospital was full of men from many places. None of us knew what was up. We were given a rigid physical examination, which added to the many rumors floating around as to our destination. Of the first ten men, only four of us came up to the standards required. The old doc could not find anything wrong with me.

8 April: This morning Harold Flygare came over to my hut and helped me carry my bags over to the headquarters building. I was being shipped to London and then on to . . . wherever they were sending me. After saying good-bye to Harold, I loaded on a GI truck left Burtonwood. There were plenty of questions in my mind and I was nervous about leaving.

9 April, Easter Sunday, London outskirts: I was awakened by some blowhard with a GI whistle. The branch in London was holding Easter services, but when I asked for a pass I was informed that we were restricted to camp. During the week we amused ourselves playing softball, stood inspections, and were jabbed by the medics.

In front of each tent was a large foxhole. About two a.m. air-raid sirens blew and we were told to get into our hole. This being my first real air raid, it didn't take long for me to slip on some coveralls and dive for cover. When the fright wore off, several of us stuck our heads out to watch the show. The night sky was filled with search lights probing for Jerry raiders. One Nazi bomber caught in the lights twisted and turned seeking safety in the inky dark. Fifteen minutes later, we got the "all clear" signal. The Jerries returned twice that week. Those boys were playing for keeps.

17 April: Last night I was alerted to get my things ready for departure the next morning. Rumor was that we would fly to our destination. It was Sunday. We loaded on a truck, guns, ammunition, and all. Soon we were in the heart of London at a government office. We were ushered into a large waiting room, our baggage weighed, and then to our surprise were told we could spend the day on the town, but to be back by 10:00 p.m.

I was soon out to the LDS Church on Nightingale Lane. I wanted to see the mission president, A.K. Anastasiou. He was out of town; however, Elder Hugh Brown had just arrived to reassume the presidency of the British mission. I met with him for a short time and apprized him that I was going on an undisclosed assignment. President Brown set me apart as an LDS Servicemen's group leader. He also wrote a letter to my wife, saying that we had visited.

24 April: At dark, a group of us were loaded aboard a C-87 airplane. After the motors warmed up we lumbered into the sky. This was my first airplane ride. Soon we saw only white clouds below and stars above us. We learned that our interim destination was Tehran, Iran. Most of us were uncertain where that was, but we did know that Tehran was only half way to our destination.

En route to Teheran, we landed at Casablanca, French Morocco. From the air we saw white stucco and adobe houses. Each little farm was fenced and the livestock—chickens, pigs, goats, donkeys— were inside with the people who lived there.

After the big plane landed and before we could deplane, a medical officer came aboard to give us a briefing. We were instructed to be careful of mosquitoes because of malaria. We were not to let the natives touch us because they all had body lice and VD; we were to drink only the water at Army camps, or that distributed by the Army or Red Cross.

12 May, leaving Tehran: At seven-thirty this morning we boarded a C-87 (a converted B-24) and were soon in the clouds. We passed over the shore of the Caspian Sea and then turned inland at the Russian city of Baku, and proceeded north and west across the rich farmlands of the Ukraine. I was so engrossed in the sights below that I don't think I took my eyes from the window until we landed. From the plane we could see where the Germans and Russians had fought a year earlier. More than half the thatched roof homes had been destroyed, and the entire countryside was a net work of trenches. My first impression of the Russian people was very favorable.

At the Yalta Conference, attended by President Roosevelt, Prime Minister Churchill, and Josef Stalin, arrangements were completed for the United States Air Force to operate three bases in Russia. The purpose was to receive U.S. bombers and fighter planes flying from England to bomb German targets, and to service and rearm those aircraft. On their way to Italy, they bombed the Romanian oil fields. At bases in Italy they were again loaded with fuel and bombs and on the last leg of their journey would bomb targets in occupied France en route back to England.

The Russian bases were at Piryatin, Poltova, and Mirograd in the Ukraine. Headquarters were located at Mirograd—the bomber base. The other two bases were for fighter airplanes. We were sent to Piryatin, with the 385th Bomb Group, 8th Air Force.

21 June 1944: I had wondered what it would be like to be on the receiving end of a bombing raid. I found out.

This afternoon, high in the clear blue sky, we saw the vapor trail and soon a German reconnaissance plane flew over. Our Russian pilots took off, but they were unable to catch the fast German aircraft.

Six hours after the reconnaissance plane left, the air raid siren blared. In less than a minute I was dressed and outside trying to learn the reason for the alarm. We could hear approaching aircraft. A lone plane dropped parachute flares, lighting up the place. Men poured from every tent, searching for a foxhole. Then the sky was filled with planes. The Russians fired every ack-ack gun they had. German planes came in so low that I could see the swastikas on their wings. Russian air defense was weak, and the Germans seemed to be enjoying their game of hide-and-seek with the search lights.

After the planes left we saw bursts of light to the east. The following morning we learned that our headquarters at Mirograd had been heavily hit. Out of seventy-two B-17s, only nine could fly. One American officer was killed. At precisely the same hour as the day before, we spotted another reconnaissance plane. We knew the Jerries would be back tonight. I was placed on guard duty for the night.

When I retired I put my clothes, gas mask, and helmet next to my cot, but couldn't sleep. It didn't matter much, since at midnight we got word that the Jerries were on their way. I dressed in a heartbeat. No need to kid myself, I was scared. As I hit the bottom of my trench, flares began falling, the entire sky above us was full of planes. It was so light I could have read a newspaper. Crouched in the bottom of my foxhole I watched those bombers circle for three hours as they unloaded. Just before they left, one of our fuel dumps was hit. The sky was red with flame.

* * *

The Russians' enthusiasm for singing, especially when marching, was very interesting. The soldiers would sing parts, and a group could be heard from about a mile away. The harmony was wonderful, and there was a strong obligato in most of their marching songs.

At night the people gathered in groups in the village, and the men and women joined in singing their folk songs. There was a marked sadness to their music, probably depicting the sorrows and trials of their life in the

Soviet Union. Some numbers, though, were very joyful and lively, with a loud hurrahs at the end of the phrases. Regardless of the type of music, everyone sang. It seems to be a universal form of recreation.

There were no confections available to the people. Squash seeds were a substitute. One evening in June, I attended a village community concert. There were about three hundred people. Every man and woman had a generous supply of seeds, and the cracking of the seeds and the spitting of the shells continued at a constant pace during the entire evening. Before I was in the area for ten minutes, I was given a share of the seeds and before the evening was over I could spit shells with the best of them.

The weekly camp show had just let out. I wandered over to the dayroom to wait for the ten o'clock news. One of our Russian-speaking GIs was talking to a couple of Russian boys. One twelve-year-old was dressed in rags. There were holes in his trousers everywhere you looked. He had no shirt, and a cape made of course cotton material was his only coat. He had neither shoes or socks, and his feet and legs were calloused. I was wearing a pair of civilian shoes too small for me. I gave them to the boy, and they fit him just right. His expression of appreciation was great.

Through the interpreter he told me that his mother and father had been killed during the German occupation, and he was now living, as best he could, with the village shoemaker. The conversation went from one thing to another, and for some reason I asked him if he ever went to church. "Nyet, nyet. I am a member of the Party, and they won't let us go to church. Maybe when I get older I will be permitted to go." Such was this youngster's plight. No father, no mother, and because of the Party, he was being deprived of what little his country has to offer in the way of religious instruction.

* * *

In Poltova there is an old monastery. About twenty nuns, now peasants of the Ukraine, still lived there. They wished the old religion still existed. Instead, they put up with ridicule and persecution. A member of our detachment, who speaks Russian, was visiting in Poltova. Passing the monastery, he saw an elderly woman herding her goats in the churchyard. He spoke to her. She immediately called him over. She was crying, and expressed her joy that an American soldier could speak to her in her own tongue.

He noticed that her hand was bandaged and inquired about it. She pointed to a group of boys milling in the street. They had just attacked her, one of them striking her across the hand with an iron bar, which cut a deep gash in the back of her hand. He instructed her to go to our medical tent for first aid.

In the conversation she wanted to know if America was going to help Russia religiously, after the war. She said that since the Revolution, the youth of this nation have been taught to abhor anything religious.

As mentioned, Elder Hugh B. Brown set me apart as an LDS Servicemen's group leader before I left England. This authorized me to organize and hold church services wherever I was stationed. For the ten months I was in Russia there were five of us who met together as regularly as our schedules would permit. I suppose these meetings were the first and only Mormon meetings held inside Russia during the war.

One night I stopped at the latrine. I was seated in a corner, when very much to my surprise in walks a Russian lady with a bucket of water and a scrubbing brush. She did not immediately see me and was in the motion of throwing water on the comodes when her eye caught mine. She dropped the bucket, turned and made a hurried exit, laughing at the top of her voice. Is nothing sacred anymore?

7 October: With the advances of our troops into France after D-Day our mission in Russia wound down. Our unit was leaving. Before we boarded a train at Mirgorod, sixty miles east of Piryatin, we were called together by General Henry Walsh, Headquarters Eastern Command. General Permonov, the Russian commandant, spoke to us through an interpreter. After the usual bouquets, he thanked us sincerely for our work and for the opportunity we both had of becoming acquainted. He told us that the Soviet Union was proud to have had us with them, and he wished us a safe journey. He also said that we were being given as fine a train accommodations as they were able to offer.

The train was three hours late, and when it did arrive, it was short three cars. This necessitated our doubling up. Six of us crowded into compartments meant to hold four. We were all so tired that it was not long until a bed was made on the floor and another in the luggage rack and we were all fast asleep.

At Kharkov we stopped for an hour to stretch our legs. There were thousands of people waiting at the station. When another train arrived and those waiting were released to board, they ran for seats. Peasants of all ages, each carrying a bundle on his back or a basket in his hand moved en mass for the train. There seemed to be no respect for age or condition, just the necessity of boarding that train. My thoughts went back in thankfulness for our blessed land.

We crossed the Russian border into Iran on the 13th of October. The next morning we had breakfast and boarded trucks, which bounced over rough roads through some desolate country. Natives crowded the road driving their herds and prodding their heavily laden donkeys. We then traveled on through Palestine and Egypt. From Cairo, we boarded a British ship, took a Mediterranean cruise, and arrived at Portsmouth, England, in late December 1944. From there I was transferred to France and then to Germany. I returned to the United States in January 1946, after thirty-three months of overseas duty.

Prior to World War II, Paul W. Ahlstrom was a missionary in the Central States Mission, following which he and Betty Morley were married in the Salt Lake Temple. After his war-time service, Paul returned to his wife and their son in Idaho Falls. In due time they became parents of four sons and six daughters. They have sixty grandchildren and ten great-grandchildren. He served as a counselor, then stake president for thirteen years; a stake patriarch; and a sealer in the Idaho Falls Temple. He and Betty served a mission at the Chicago Temple in 1992 and 1993.

He established himself in the furniture business. His community involvement included a term as Chairman of the LDS Hospital Board; President of the Idaho Falls Chamber of Commerce; Chairman of the Idaho Falls Downtown Improvement Association; board member of the Teton Peaks Council, Boy Scouts of America; and was instrumental in establishing a Deseret Industries in Idaho Falls. He passed away 26 October 1999.

ELWYN A. MEYER

Experiment upon my words, ...give place for a portion of my words.

(Alma 32:27)

I was born and raised in Granite City, Illinois, just a few miles east of St. Louis, Missouri. Granite City was a steel-making town. It had been settled by Germans. I was brought up in the Evangelical and Reformed Church, but I always had a lot of unanswered questions, and I frequently prayed that the Lord would show me His true church.

By early 1944 I had completed flight and officers training and had been sent to Gowen Field at Boise, Idaho, for transition training. June Gerrard, a little Mormon girl from Taylor, Idaho, worked for the telephone company. One evening I was at a dance when June came in. It was the first time I had seen her. There was something special about her, and when I saw her, I heard a voice say, *That's the one I've picked for you.* One of my friends was just asking June to dance and I moved in front of him and began dancing with her. That was new behavior for me because I was a shy person. We dated nearly every night, as circumstances would allow, for the next two weeks. By the time I was to leave for England we were deeply in love and agreed to write to each other.

Our ten-man crew picked up a new B-24G at Topeka, Kansas, and departed from West Palm Beach, Florida, on 1 April 1944, bound for England. I was the navigator. We flew the southern route via Puerto Rico, then down to Brazil and across the Atlantic to the western coast of Africa. As the compasses aboard the plane were not functioning properly, I was perplexed and concerned. I was not yet a member of the Church, nevertheless I prayed on a regular basis. After leaving Palm Beach, I knelt in the navigator's station to ask the Lord for help. Into my mind came the words, "You've been trained how to navigate—do it." So I did. We arrived safely in England 21 April and immediately began training for D-Day. We were assigned to the 68th Squadron, 44th Bomb Group, 8th Air Force, arriving there 26 May 1944.

The second night we were in England I went to a dance. When the dance was over, I walked a girl home, then returned to the train station and boarded a train. It was about one o'clock in the morning, and when I got off the train nothing looked familiar. I found an MP and asked directions. The MP asked what my duty was. When he learned that I was a navigator he started laughing and loudly told the others on duty that here was a navigator who could not find his way back. I was a long way from home.

Elwyn Meyer in the Navigation School Cadet Program—September, 1943.

Following our support of the Normandy landings, we were assigned a broad range of missions over Germany. On every takeoff I knelt in my station to pray. Although I did not then have a good understanding of the Lord, I always felt that He was there.

For many nights I had a recurring dream. In this dream I saw a hand extended through a cloud and felt the invitation to take hold of it. Being fearful, I would not. Then one night I reached for the hand, but it withdrew just as we touched. The hand reached down and I saw a scar running from inside the wrist to above the elbow, and a voice said, *Today be very careful.*

In a letter to my mother I told her about my dream and the arm with the scar up the inside of the arm. She wrote back to tell me about my grandmother, who had died when I was five years old—she'd had such a scar and had always worn long-sleeved dresses to cover it.

As we boarded our aircraft, I said to our pilot, "Be very careful today."

Our target was an airfield at Chalon sur Marne, which we were to carpet-bomb to deny its use to the enemy. Completing our drop, we lost an engine and had to leave the formation. The pilot turned the aircraft over to the co-pilot and went to assist the engineer, to see if they could restart the failed engine. Noting that we would pass over Paris, then still in enemy

234 / COURAGE IN A SEASON OF WAR

hands, I called a course correction to the co-pilot, which he questioned and refused to take. The two of us got into a shouting match. When the pilot returned, he asked what the problem was. I told him. Upon our successful return to Shipdam I was still fuming. The pilot, co-pilot and I had a long discussion about navigation. After that they always accepted my corrections.

I felt the nearness of my guardian angel many times. One day, en route to Bernberg, Germany, a formation of German JU 88s attacked us. We watched our three lead bombers go down in a flat spin, locked together. Then our wingmen were destroyed. One of them went directly over the top of our aircraft. Our plane had the navigator's windows shot out, but we made it home.

My twenty-ninth mission was to Hamburg, Germany, on 6 August 1944. Our target was an oil refinery. In-flight flak was unusually heavy and our plane was badly damaged. The top half of our left vertical stabilizer was blown off, and a large hole was blasted at the waist gunner's position. We later counted 250 flak holes in the skin of the plane. After we lost two engines, the pilot hit the bail out button. But the plane was still flying. I called the pilot, "It still flies, let's take this thing home." Other crew members agreed.

Our pilot was exceptionally well-acquainted with this aircraft, having been an aircraft manufacturer before becoming a pilot. It is a long way from Hamburg to the coast of England, but the pilot skillfully held the plane in the air—aided I believe—by the Lord. When we landed and rolled to a stop, the two remaining engines quit. Our crew chief met us, then crawled up to measure the fuel left in the tanks—there was none. Looking his new aircraft over and almost in tears he told us the plane would have to be junked. As the pilot walked away, he said, "Danged good airplane! It got us home."

After completing the prescribed number of missions over enemy territory, I was back in the United States in September of 1944. My first call was to June in Boise. I told her "I think you're the one I want to spend my life with. Do you still feel the same way?" She said yes. We were married in my church in Granite City on 21 January 1945.

Elwyn stayed in the service and was stationed at Boca Raton, Florida, and later Yuma, Arizona. After his discharge, Elwyn and June returned to St Louis, where he went back to work in the armament division of Emerson Electric. They were blessed with a daughter and a son. June was active in the Church, but never pressed Elwyn about it, and missionaries were frequent visitors in their home. Finally in 1977, Elwyn announced to June that he wanted to join the Church. He was baptized by his brother-in-law, Sterling Jensen. Prior to his baptism, Elwyn served in the Sunday School and has since been a member of the high council, counselor in a bishopric, and a bishop.

Taken from an oral interview with Paul H. Kelly.

HUGH A. WRIGHT

My Spirit shall be in your hearts, and mine angels round about you, to bear you up.

(Doctrine & Covenants 84:88)

I was in pilot training in central Washington when word was received that the Air Corps was desperately short of gunners. So I went to gunnery school.

After completing gunnery school, while home on leave, I married my sweetheart, Ruth Cherry, in the Logan Temple. After a too brief honeymoon, it was time to leave for England. Fighting a war overpowers the conventions of personal life.

Our crew picked up a brand new B-17G at Lincoln, Nebraska. The "G" model had a plexi-glass window at the waist gunner positions. Previous models had openings there but no covering and were much draftier and colder. We flew the northern route through Bangor, Maine, to Goose Bay, Labrador. An intense storm kept us grounded there ten days. Each day a plane tried to take off, but would crash in the attempt. That seemed pointless to me. I had no desire to be a dead hero.

Arriving in England, our new airplane was given to another crew, and we were assigned to the 731st Bomb Squadron, 452nd Bomb Group.

We began flying our mandatory thirty-five missions.

I was waist gunner. The waist guns were half-way back in the plane. I manned either of two massive machine guns mounted on the right and left sides. Firing these was something like running a jack-hammer.

We always flew in formations. The B-17s were slower-moving than the Luftwaffe fighters, but with our collective on-board guns we could help protect one another in formations. At 25,000 feet the temperature inside our B-17G got as low as 60 degrees below zero. We wore a special suit that had electrical wires woven into it to keep us warm.

Hugh and Ruth Wright

Home base was Deophan Green Air Base near Attelboro, England. We always left early in the morning. Getting out of bed before sunrise is something I always disliked. Being awakened, then having to climb into the pitch blackness of the truck that picked us up, irritated me every time. Most of our missions were over Germany. Top speed for the B-17 was 150 miles per hour. At that rate we were in the air for eight to ten hours.

On 5 December 1944, we flew our third mission, over Berlin, the German capital, then the most heavily defended area in the Reich. The 8th Air Force had last bombed Berlin October 6th. This time we came with 2,400 bombers–B-17s and B-24s–as well as more than 1,300 fighters to provide cover against Luftwaffe fighters. The P 51s and P 47s did a good job of protecting us, but flak fired from guns on the ground was heavy—so heavy, as some have said, that you could almost walk on it. Making this mission even more dangerous was a requirement that we over-fly the target and circle back. This gave enemy gunners a chance to lock on to an individual plane and concentrate fire on it. This was the first of two missions over Berlin in which I participated.

We lost many planes that day. To see one of our planes take a hit, then to watch as they fell and finally to count the men leaving each crippled airship was the most heart-wrenching thing I witnessed. Most planes carried a nine-man crew. Some damaged planes had no parachutes to count. That hurt. Our tears flowed.

I participated in many similar missions, where in the face of heavy enemy opposition we bombed rail yards, ammunition dumps, and industrial sites that were of strategic importance to the Reich.

My thirty-fifth, and last mission took place on 8 April 1945, a strike on a German ordnance depot at Gafenwahr.

I acknowledge the protection of the Lord. It is still tender to me to this day, but each time I climbed aboard our plane to fly a mission, I felt the presence of my mother. She passed away when I was fourteen years old. But she *was* there!

One morning as we took off, our plane would not climb, so another aircraft assumed our position in the formation. That plane was subsequently shot down by an enemy fighter, which swooped past my left window so closely, that were it not for his oxygen mask, I could have seen the expression on the pilot's face. Had we not changed position, our aircraft would have been the one shot down.

Some of the dangers we came through were because of faulty equipment. Once, as we were preparing to land, we discovered our landing gear would not go down. After several attempts to make it work, the pilot instructed me to get down in the wheel well and crank the gear down manually. I had just given the crank a couple of turns when the co-pilot decided to retry the electronic switch. It worked, but now the crank was flailing around inside the wheel well, where I was. On its first turn around, it hit me in the face. I managed to avoid it after the second turn. No serious damage, just surprise and injured pride. We all laughed about it a few days later.

Because I had taken the place of crew members who were sick, I finished my thirty-five missions a few days before the rest of my crew. We were very fortunate; our whole crew came through the war without injury. Recently I have learned that some of these men have passed away. We came from homes all across the United States—Idaho, New Jersey, Illinois, Washington State. I still remember my crewmates, although I have not seen or spoken to any of them since 1945.

These men knew I was LDS. I made it a point to tell them. None of them ever questioned me about the Church, nor did they give me a hard time about it. The members of our crew were good friends, but it was nothing like going home to Ruth.

For his service in the Army Air Corps, Hugh A. Wright was awarded the Air Medal with six oak-leaf clusters. His unit earned a Presidential Citation. He returned to Idaho and in 1950 started an accounting business in St. Anthony. He and Ruth are parents of two sons and a daughter, have nine grandchildren and two great-grandchildren. Hugh has worked extensively with the Aaronic Priesthood young men, was a member of a bishopric, and served

Hugh Wright (front, 2nd from left) and his squad after completing Mission #35, their last mission.

twice as stake clerk, for a total of fifteen years. He is an ordinance worker in the Idaho Falls Temple.

Taken from an oral interview with Paul H. Kelly.

ARDEN HUTCHINGS

. . . willing . . . to stand as witnesses of God at all times and in all things and in all places that ye may be in, even until death.

(Mosiah 18:9)

I was born and raised in Beaver, Utah. At the time of the attack on Pearl Harbor I was serving in the Western States Mission, with headquarters in Denver, Colorado. Prior to my mission I had finished two and one-half years of schooling at Fresno State College in California.

Following my mission I enrolled at the University of Utah. Military recruiters there announced that there would be an exam for entrance into the United States Army Air Corps. Of the five hundred who took the exam, about one hundred passed. We were designated as a CTD (College Training Detachment) and sent as a unit to Sheppard Field, Texas, and shortly thereafter to Stillwater, Oklahoma, to study at Oklahoma A & M University. We were billeted in the university's field house.

Before leaving Utah I was set apart as an LDS group leader. Our first Sunday in Oklahoma, I went to the commanding officer and asked if we could go to church. "What church do you belong to?" he queried. I replied, "I'm a Mormon." He picked up the intercom and directed: "If there are any Mormons in this outfit, I want them to fall out in front of this field house in ten minutes, in class A uniforms." I suppose he thought there might be two or three of us. Ten minutes later there were 120 men, many of whom were returned missionaries and college graduates, standing in formation. The C.O. was dumbfounded! Pleased, I marched the group down Main Street to a beautiful LDS chapel not far from the campus.

The branch president related to me that previously Elder Melvin J. Ballard had stopped in Stillwater. As they were leaving town, Elder Ballard abruptly told Brother Berry, a member who lived in the area, to stop the car. Elder Ballard said, "I see a Mormon chapel on that piece of land, and I see it overflowing with young people." Brother Berry responded, "If the Lord wants a Mormon church on that property, that's what He'll get." He promptly arranged to purchase the land and helped build a chapel on it. It was to this building our group of Mormon soldiers marched our third day in Stillwater. Seeing us come in, the branch president wept with joy as we filled the chapel.

Members of our CTD unit spent a year studying at Oklahoma A & M. The impact and example of our group, with its large contingent of returned missionaries, was overwhelming. There were units from states other than Utah, but our LDS boys pretty much monopolized the CTD and had a significant influence on the atmosphere in the classes and the spirit on campus.

Shortly after our arrival, I was called to be a counselor to the branch president. I had the privilege of performing the marriages of several of the men in the unit. While attending Fresno State College I met Doris Michael.

She had been born and raised in Fresno. We corresponded while I was a missionary. Five months following my release we became engaged and six months later, on 3 July 1943, I performed the wedding of a classmate, after which the branch president performed the wedding for Doris and me.

From Stillwater we were sent to San Antonio for classification as pilots, engineers, or navigators. I qualified for pilot school. I trained at Brook Field, and took further training at Coleman, Sherman, and Pampa, Texas. After flight school I moved to Randolf Field as a flight instructor and test pilot, where I also wrote tech orders for the planes I tested.

Subsequently, I was assigned to fly the B-26, The Martin Marauder, (variously called the "Martin Murderer," the "Widow Maker," or the "Flying Coffin"), with orders to go to France. At transition training in Shreveport, Louisiana, we formed our crews and I became a co-pilot. Soon after arriving in Europe I was made a first pilot.

We arrived in Roy-Ame, France, shortly after the Germans broke through the Ardennes Forest in mid December. We sat in our airplanes day after day, for fifteen days, while blizzards or heavy fog prevented us giving air support to the Battle of the Bulge. All this time reports of mounting U.S. casualties poured in, and the rampaging enemy was reclaiming territory that

Doris and Arden Hutchings

the Allies had conquered, at a frightful cost, only a short time before. Every day our anxiety mounted as flights were scrubbed due to weather. Finally, I believe in answer to prayer, the weather did break, and we could interdict the masses of attacking Germans. We flew what I believe to be the first sortie to reach and give air support to the beleaguered troops at Bastogne.

We were attached to the 354th Bomb Group, nicknamed the "bridge busters." Our aircraft had the very latest equipment, the top secret Norden bomb sights, vector radar, and we had the best navigators available. We bombed from an altitude of between twelve and fourteen thousand feet—above the "cloud of flak" the Germans sent up. Our air strikes had to be made with surgical precision. One assignment was to take out a bridge only 100 yards from the famous Cologne Cathedral—without damaging the cathedral.

We rarely had to go back a second time—with one notable exception—the Ludendorff railway bridge across the Rhine River, at Remagen. Following our third unsuccessful attempt during February, I wrote in my report: "This bridge remains in place only as a result of Divine intervention."

This may have been the case. In early March 1945, a group of U.S. Army soldiers found the Ludendorff bridge, standing and intact. When General Eisenhower learned that this bridge had been captured, he ordered the bridgehead held, but for our troops to stand in place, apparently in deference to British Field Marshall General Montgomery. Montgomery had elaborate plans for crossing the Rhine some distance to the north of Remagan.

About mid-March the flamboyant General George S. Patton arrived at Remagen, saw the situation, and ordered his troops across the Rhine, a day before Montgomery's planned strike. Patton snatched Montgomery's thunder, but in the process saved a lot of lives. Two days later, after combat engineers had two temporary bridges assembled, the Ludendorff bridge fell into the river.

* * *

To gain greater capability as a crew we began training for night flying. Returning to base one night we found the field completely dark, except for a very dim light at either end of the runway. We started our descent. In the blackness it was difficult to know when we neared touchdown. The engineer reported that our wheels were down and locked. Abruptly, I heard metal scraping the ground and felt the plane go out of control as it careened down the runway. For some unknown reason the flight engineer had pulled the wheels back up. When the plane finally came to rest we all hastily exited to watch as the fire-control crew checked the B-26 over. We went to base ops, and the plane went for repairs.

We flew the first relief mission to Eindhoven, Holland, taking in medical and other critical supplies to that newly liberated country. Subsequent missions took us across a wide section of Europe, as we bombed bridges in Austria and Germany.

As a group, my crew often teased me about being a Mormon, but it was all in fun. I knew they liked me and were comfortable flying with me. It was interesting to me that each crew member came to me individually and asked, very seriously, if I were saying my prayers regularly.

The base chaplain dubbed me "The Flying Preacher," and from time to time asked me to substitute for him and give a Sunday sermon. Maybe the congregation was not fully aware that they were hearing Mormon doctrine. One of our planes was inscribed "The Flying Preacher." So it seemed that it was also important to others that I live my religion.

After being with such a large group of LDS men at Stillwater, I realized what an unusual thing it was to be affiliated with so many Church members at one base. When we got to France there was only one other LDS crewman in our bomb group. However, there were enough LDS men in the area to meet for church services and partake of the sacrament each Sunday.

* * *

Following the end of the fighting, I continued flying. I loved to fly, and found it much more enjoyable than waiting for the time to pass. Frequently the base commander asked me to take him to meetings at other bases.

One morning at 0200 hours, I was shaken awake. A fellow pilot, and a very good one at that, was scheduled to return to the United States. He was at Base Operations, very drunk, but refused to board the plane unless "Arden Hutchings is the pilot." The plane was filled with other personnel also going home. The frustrated operations officer called and appealed to me to come pilot this flight to England, so that everyone could get to their respective ports of debarkation on time.

After VE Day we were stationed at Venlo. The city of Venlo is located in a rural area in eastern Holland. It is situated on the Maas River about twenty-five miles west of Dusseldorf, Germany. The imposing Venlo Castle is a major feature of this community. Following the war the U.S. government took over the castle and established a university to provide educational opportunities to the men of the occupation forces. I taught speech classes there.

Later I was sent to Kitsingen, Germany, as the base intelligence officer. Because of my prior experience as a flight instructor, I was assigned to establish a flight school.

From Kitsingen I was assigned to Biarritz American University. This was located in Southern France, near the Spanish border and on the Bay of Biscay. It had been Napoleon's playground. Being on the faculty with men, many of whom had been department heads in a variety of disciplines from major universities all across the United States, was one of the most enjoyable experiences of my military service. I again taught speech classes.

An LDS group leader is an authorized representative of the Church with credentials recognized by United States military officials. I interacted with the chaplaincy who gave me the names of LDS Servicemen assigned to each base. I was responsible to conduct church meetings, and could act in many ways like a branch president. In this calling I learned many valuable lessons about leadership. We usually had from thirty-five to forty Church members in the groups where I served.

One night there was a big party held at the Chateaux Officer's Club. There were to be girls there to dance and mingle with. I was invited, but being uncomfortable with this arrangement, I chose to stay the night alone in my tent on the base. Perhaps it is not the battle zones, terrible as they are, that are the most deadly places in a war. From my observations, it was in the rest and recovery areas where some men became most isolated and vulnerable, that Lucifer worked his hardest. Most of our LDS men remained faithful, but occasionally I found one who struggled in his loneliness; and being away from home, in circumstances where there were few constraints, would stumble. Many times these men had simply fallen in with the wrong crowd. We constantly searched for and reached out to these men.

At Biarritz we had a large group of LDS men awaiting discharge. Their influence and example among their peers and with the faculty was

Arden Hutchings (right) with his brother Donald

powerful. It was a splendid experience to be associated with them. Some became life-long friends.

The blessing I received when being set apart as a group leader—that I would come home safely—was fulfilled to the letter. That blessing was a great comfort to me during some very dangerous times, especially on bombing missions when flak punctured the plane and flew around inside the cockpit, smashing instruments and causing serious damage to our aircraft.

I have always felt good about my service to the United States of America and the service I was privileged to give to the Church during that time.

Arden returned to the United States in May 1946. He and Doris settled in Fresno and Merced, California. Arden became a building contractor, specializing in the construction of church buildings for many denominations. He also put to good use the flight training he received while with the Army Air Corps. Since World War II he has owned and worn out five airplanes.

Arden served as a counselor in the Fresno Stake presidency for seven and a half years, then as the stake president for an additional seven and a half years. He, with Doris, was called to preside over the Florida

South Mission, with headquarters in Ft. Lauderdale. That mission then included southern Florida and all of the Caribbean. He opened the work in the Dominican Republic. He and Doris subsequently served leadership training missions in Zaire, the West Indies, and twice at the MTC in Provo. In 1999 they served a short term mission to the Cody, Wyoming, Visitors' Center. Arden and Doris are parents of nine children. They have thirty-nine grandchildren and ten great-grandchildren. They live in Provo, Utah.

STERLING A. JENSEN

And in the strength of the Lord they did contend against their enemies.

(Words of Mormon 1:14)

My parents had pictorial books of World War I. I remember looking at the carnage, devastation, and desolation involved in war, as portrayed on those pages and wondering if we would ever again be at war and whether I would be involved. These thoughts were of a transitory nature, and I put them at the back of my mind. However, they were brought back to mind when Germany invaded Poland in September 1939. Yet, those events occurred a long way from Idaho Falls and so were of little concern. I graduated from high school in 1941 and enrolled at the University of Idaho, Southern Branch, in Pocatello, to study scientific pharmacy. Things went well, except for a tough English course. I joined a pharmacy fraternity—our initiation took place the night of 6 December 1941. One of the first to awaken Sunday morning, I heard the news of the Japanese invasion at Pearl Harbor—news that changed everyone's life.

I enlisted as an aviation cadet in the U.S. Army Air Corps, in September 1942. Only upon reporting for active duty in February 1943, in Lincoln, Nebraska, did I learn, to my shock, that I was just a private. It was also a surprise that there were insufficient uniforms and shoes, so we drilled in civilian clothes. After a short course at Drury College in Springfield,

Missouri, we were transferred to San Antonio, Texas, for classification and assignment. I had indicated a preference to be a navigator but was told that because of a shortage of pilots I could be either a pilot or a gunner. I opted for pilot training. In rapid succession I took pre-flight training at San Antonio, Texas, primary flight training at Chickasha, Oklahoma, basic flight training at Garden City, Kansas, and advanced flight training at Frederick, Oklahoma. Finally, I graduated and received a commission as a 2nd lieutenant and, most importantly, my set of pilot's wings.

Sterling A. Jensen

Although originally slated to service in the Pacific Theater, our orders were changed. We were loaded on a troop train bound for Camp Kilmer, New Jersey. Ten thousand of us boarded the English liner *Aquatania,* and we landed at Glasgow, Scotland, on Thanksgiving Day 1944.

We arrived at Kimbolton, in the midlands of England on 29 November 1944. Instead of seeing B-24's, for which we had been trained, we saw the single tail fins of the B-17. We had been pulled out of the Pacific because of a shortage of combat crews in Europe. Training began immediately for our transition to the B-17. I found I liked the B-17 better. It was easier to fly, could take more battle damage, continue flying, and, we observed, could fly higher than the B-24.

Out on the flight line we watched planes returning from a bombing mission and wondered why there were red flares coming out of the approaching planes. The briefing officer told us that red flares meant there were wounded on board. The day's target was a synthetic oil refinery at Zeitz, and intense anti-aircraft fire caused an abort on the first bomb run, and the planes had to make another run on the target. Casualties were heavy.

A long spell of bad weather kept us grounded several days, during which time the Battle of the Bulge commenced. Our troops were caught by surprise. They had little winter clothing and ammunition and would not receive supplies until the skies cleared.

Christmas Eve 1944, our first mission. Target: Airdromes in the Frankfurt area. The fog in England was so bad that Jeeps had to lead us to the end of the runway. We set our gyro-compass to the runway heading and took off on instruments, with visibility less than 100 yards. As one plane took off, a radio operator at the end of the runway radioed to send another. We climbed through 400 feet of clouds and broke into the clear. We joined our formation and were on our way. We dropped our bombs from 22,000 feet at 1450 hours. I think we hit a cabbage patch. Weather was still poor when we got back to England. We were diverted from base to base, finally being sent back to Mendelsham, a base we had been diverted from just an hour before. By this time, three groups of thirty planes each were trying to land at this field. It was a mass of dangerous confusion.

Subsequent missions included railroad yards at Euskirchen, Bruhl and Kassel, communications centers at Wittlich and Daun.

On 23 January 1945, there was a tragic accident at the airfield. Our target that day was the Neuss marshaling yards. The morning was cold. All but four of our aircraft had taken off by 0730. Snow flurries whipped by a freezing north wind swept across the base. Personnel who were not flying were returning to bed. Some were just getting ready for duty. A B-17 lifted off. About 25 feet into the air, it tilted to the left and headed for the 525th living quarters, where I lived, a half mile away. It crashed into the orderly room. Its full load of aviation gas exploded, bombs burst, and ammunition fired in all directions. With each explosion more buildings collapsed. The living area was destroyed and nine men died. One young officer from Pocatello, Idaho, who slept in the bed next to mine, had said to me as I was leaving that morning, "Too bad you have to fly while I get to sleep in my nice warm bed." He was among the dead.

26 February, we were to hit the Berlin marshaling yards. At our pre-flight briefing we were told to expect a tail wind going in, so we were loaded with six 1,000-lb. bombs and 2,700 gallons of gas. When we got to elevation the tail wind had turned to a direct head wind, increasing our fuel consumption. After our bomb drop, we separated from our group over the North Sea to take a direct route to the nearest airfield in England. Within sight of the coast two engines ran out of gas. Luckily, an English fighter

base was in sight just as a third engine shut down. We landed on one engine in a stiff cross-wind.

On 19 March 1945, we targeted a chemical plant at Plauen. When the lead plane dropped its bombs it also dropped a smoke marker, signaling to the rest of us to drop our bombs. On this flight my crew spotted two German ME 262 jets under our formation. I was tucked in so close under the lead plane that as they dropped the smoke bomb the chemicals from it coated my windshield so that I could not see through it. I put my goggles on, opened the side window, and flew with one eye until the wind stream cleared the windows. Cold flying duty.

On 28 March 1945, we made a run on a precision tool works plant in Berlin. As we started the bomb run, a battery of anti-aircraft guns picked out our plane. Each burst came closer. My co-pilot insisted I move the plane over, but because we were about to drop our bombs, we had to maintain position. The next burst of AA fire hit in front and above the cockpit and took out part of our plexiglass windscreen. A piece of flak hit my shoulder, but my flak suit protected me. My top turret gunner announced to the crew that I had "had it." In just a moment I assured the crew that I was still very much alive. Due to damage, mine and five other planes didn't get back to our assigned stations. Final tally of aircraft hit and damaged was 24 out of the 37 in our formation. I still have the piece of flak that hit me.

I flew my final mission on 6 April 1945, against Leipzig, carrying six 1,000-lb. bombs. During this flight we had an electrical system malfunction. The oil pressure gauge on #3 engine showed a drop, so I feathered the prop. We couldn't see any oil leak, but due to the electrical malfunction the prop would not unfeather. I kept the plane in formation long enough to drop our bomb load, but when we left the target area, we could not keep up with the formation. We lost all radio contact, and due to the undercast, the navigator could not get a fix on our position. Finally, we broke out of the haze over an English fighter base in France. I lowered the landing gear to indicate that we wanted to land. Just then my navigator gave me a new heading for an American base. I took this heading but there was no field to be found. In the distance I could see the city of Lille. We landed at an old German fighter field on the edge of the city. As we completed our landing roll, my right landing gear dropped into a sand filled, grass covered bomb crater, and as a result, numbers 3 and 4 props were bent. The plane was not repairable. We were flown back to Kimbolton. That was my final flight in a B-17.

Movies such as the recent *Memphis Belle* are typical of Hollywood; the only realism shown was the age of the crew members—gunners were usually between ages seventeen and nineteen—pilots, bombardiers, and navigators from twenty to twenty-one; and the superstition of not changing your routine of preparation. One of my crew members refused to fly one mission when he thought he could not find his lucky cap; luckily, he did. Some worried about being killed on their first mission, then worried about the number thirteen, which we called 12-A, or being killed on their final mission—for very good reasons. If a crew was shot down or was missing, their valuable possessions were sometimes divided up by their "friends." After being delayed because of our forced landing in France, we had to reclaim ours.

Occasionally nerves broke. Returning from a mission, where we had our hydraulic system shot out, I determined to land at an emergency field. One of my officers became violent. We had a three-day pass to go to London, and he thought he would lose it if we didn't land at home. I remembered that our field was muddy, I decided to go there and use the mud to stop us. It worked. The officer immediately disappeared. We finally located him in the mess hall, where the violence started again. I had to take him off my crew. That night we left by train to see London. We later learned that he had attempted to molest two women on a train platform. My bombardier, who was with him, knocked him out and put him on a bus back to the base. But the fellow showed up in London that night. During a V-1 rocket attack that hit close by, he had to be restrained from jumping out the window of our hotel.

After completing my thirty five missions I was sent back to the United States for transition training into the B-29 for duty in the Pacific Theater. I was happy when President Truman ordered the dropping of the atom bomb and Japan surrendered.

The 8th Air Force was the work horse of the air war in Europe. A high percentage of American POWs held by Germany were airmen. Many airmen died. We were engaged in a very dangerous business. We caused substantial damage to the enemy. The 379th Bomb Group, of which I was a part, dropped 25,553 tons of bombs, shot down 315 enemy aircraft confirmed,

99 probables, and damaged 39 more. We lost 149 planes. The entire 8th Air Force lost 4,005 bombers and 2,086 fighters. Over 40,000 men were killed or were taken prisoner. I am grateful to have survived.

For his service as a pilot in the U.S. Army Air Corps, Sterling A. Jensen was awarded six Air Medals and earned three Battle Stars. Returning to Idaho Falls, he met and married Jean Gerrard in May 1946. They are parents of two daughters and have four grandchildren. Sterling became a successful businessman in Idaho Falls. He later worked for the LDS Foundation at Ricks College, where he was an associate of Stephen Moser from Leipzig, Germany. (They have compared their respective experiences, and Steve has thanked Sterling for not bombing him or his family.) Sterling has been a teacher in the Sunday School, Explorer leader, ward clerk, and member of a bishopric. Following his retirement in 1991, he and Jean served a Church Service Mission for the LDS Foundation. They are recipients of the Presidential Service Award from Ricks College. Sterling is presently finance clerk for a Church welfare department farm located near Idaho Falls.

LIFE IN CONTINENTAL EUROPE

The civilians in Europe faced the daunting task of living through not just one, but many armies, Allied and Axis, invading their towns and destroying their homes.

Although World War II invaded the psyche of everyone in America, it may be impossible for U.S. citizens to comprehend the reality of living with combat in our towns and near our homes. War within the continental U.S. has not occurred since the Civil War. And the effects of that war, fought 150 years ago, can still be felt in some parts of the U.S. Imagine then, not just a war between states, but a World War being fought in your homeland.

In Europe, the demands of prosecuting war while under enemy attack brought shortages of every necessity, especially food and medical treatment. At the same time civilians faced danger, sorrow for lost loved ones, and the din of bombing, as well as uncertainty and pandemonium in daily life. Families and whole communities were brutalized as atrocities were committed, often within eyesight of the innocent. Hitler's ruthless actions were doubly disastrous for his own people as Allied airplanes dumped bombs, destroying the social infrastructure and killing and maiming soldiers and citizens. Not only was the "enemy" responsible for havoc among the people of the Axis countries. Hilter added his own terror, as he ordered the murder of millions of Jews, Gypsies, and others he thought were undesireables.

BERND STEPHAN JOST MOSER

I was born 28 April 1938, in Leipzig, Sachsen, Germany, about 110 miles south of Berlin.

When I was between five and seven years old, I remember having to go to the cellar whenever the sirens sounded, signaling approaching bombers. Our house was situated between an important railway line, visible from our window, and an airport to the north. Allied planes were trying to hit those two points, but, often as not, would miss and hit civilian homes.

I recall walking down Bochumer Strasse after one air raid and seeing the charred remains of a human body. The body had been extricated from an air raid shelter that had been hit by a bomb and placed along the sidewalk for removal. I had no idea that fire reduces the size of a human body to such an extent. It is a scene that will always stay with me.

My most vivid recollection of the war is of an air raid that leveled a neighboring duplex. Only my mother and I were at home. The air-raid siren sounded, and we ran to the basement. As was the custom, upon reaching the basement, we turned on the radio to find out the direction from which the attack was coming. Soon the power went off, and all we could hear was the drone of airplanes and bombs dropping. A bomb makes a whistling sound. I have never prayed more fervently than I did that day. I beseeched my Heavenly Father to spare my life.

Suddenly the earth shook. The bomb's impact literally lifted my mother and me off the basement floor. We could see loose bricks in front of the basement floor window. The dividing wall between the duplexes had been toppled by the blast. When the sirens signaled that the attack was over, Mother and I went upstairs. The bomb had missed our house but crashed into the house closest to us, which collapsed like a deck of cards, killing the people huddled in one of the basements. The people in the other basement were trapped. Rescue workers attempted to get them out, but a stove ignited in what was left of the house. Smoke and heat drove the rescuers away.

* * *

When the American army moved into the city, my sister went to the area where they were camped. She spoke English and brought back a Hershey chocolate bar one of the soldiers gave her. It was a real delicacy.

The time immediately after the end of the war was the toughest for us. Food had been rationed for some time, but now there was no food available. I remember my father dividing a loaf of bread into four parts, giving each of us a piece that would have to last for several days. We had the choice of eating it all at once or a bite at a time. The only thing we had to season it was salt. Cooking oil or lard was very hard to obtain. We were able to get some type of fish oil, but it would smell up the house terribly and cause our renters to complain.

Some weeks after the Americans had conquered us, they moved out and the Russians moved in. This was in accordance with an agreement between the Allies, in exchange for portions of Berlin, which had been conquered by the Russians. Since the Americans were the ones who bombed us, we actually welcomed the Russians.

What a mistake that turned out to be.

The Russians quickly imposed communism on East Germany. Communism ruled through fear. You could not confide in anyone other than your parents. If anyone made a derogatory remark about the Russian regime, the Secret Police would appear and the person who spoke the words hauled off, never to be heard of again.

My father and sister escaped to West Germany in 1948. By 1949 it was decided that my mother and I would join them there. I remember sending many packages with personal belongings to West Germany. In those days you could still do that. Then Mother sold our house, telling everyone that we were moving to another part of East Germany.

On a December day in 1949 my mother and I left Leipzig on a train, along with a man we had hired to smuggle us across the border. Our plan was to get off the train at a station a few miles from the border, walk along an abandoned set of railroad tracks, then cut across a field near a guard house while the border patrolmen were changing shifts.

Unfortunately, because of Mother's age (she was 68 at the time), we could not walk fast enough, and when we tried to cross the border near the guard house, the border patrolmen had already returned from their shift. They ran toward us with guns drawn, yelling at us to stop. Naturally we did. They took us and others they had detained to a guard house, keeping us there until morning. It was frustrating to see the lights from a village in West Germany in the distance. How we longed to be there!

The next morning the guards walked us to the nearest town, where we were herded into a gymnasium with a number of others, also picked up the night before. Our passports had been taken from us when we were caught. Someone returned our passports and told us to go back to Leipzig. Since we had sold our home and belongings, there was nothing back in Leipzig for us.

We tried again and headed out on a road leading to a border crossing. After a while we noticed a border patrolman walking toward us. If he had asked us for our passports, we'd have been taken back to the town we just came from.

We sat down by the side of the road to have a sandwich. As the patrolman approached, we gave him a friendly greeting, which he returned, and walked on. As soon as he was out of sight, we left the road and saw the border station in the distance. We then crossed a field and finally crossed the border, which was nothing more than a ditch. We were now in West

Germany, among a group of farmers working in the fields.

We looked back to see a Russian soldier with a German shepherd dog standing at the top of a hill not far from us. Had it not been for those farmers, the Russian would have sent the dog across the border to chase us back into East Germany. Instead we walked to the nearest town and took a bus to Bremerhaven, a port city on the North Sea, where my sister was living.

We immigrated to the United States in 1952, settling near Sheridan, Wyoming.

Steve Moser recently retired from the public relations department at Ricks College, Rexburg, Idaho. He and his wife, Marjean Sommers, are the parents of two sons and a daughter, and have five grandsons. He was baptized a member of the Church in 1964. He has served as a stake executive secretary, counselor in a bishopric, ward clerk, elders quorum president, and Gospel Doctrine teacher.

Taken from the personal history of Stephen Moser.

MARINUS DAVIDSON

You cannot qualify war in harsher terms than I will. War is cruelty, and you cannot refine it.

(William Tecumseh Sherman)

Marinus Davidson was a teenager in Holland when his country was brutally conquered and occupied by Nazi forces during World War II. He was born in 1928 and lived in Sant Poort, Holland, with his parents and his brother Sjaak (Solomon Albertus) in an old duplex apartment. He and Sjaak slept upstairs where they had plenty of air and light, which came through the gaps in the roof tiles.

Early on a morning in May 1940, they heard planes and artillery fire. His parents were not concerned as they believed it to be the Dutch military units on maneuvers. At daylight tanks rumbled through the streets, and Nazis troops took control. Marinus's mother turned on the radio and learned Rotterdam had been bombed and paratroopers dropped. Hitler issued an ultimatum to surrender, which the Dutch military did after five days of futile resistance.

Marinus Davidson

Dutch Jews were in a desperate plight. Knowing what Hitler had done to Jews in Germany, they tried to flee by any means they could—on foot, bicycles—carrying a few pitiful possessions. They were heading for the ocean, trying to find boats to escape to England, but there were not enough boats. As they waded out into the water hoping to find boats, many of them drowned. Those who didn't escape were captured by Nazi soldiers and shipped to the gruesome extermination camps that Hitler had in operation. Many who did not drown later envied those who had. Thus began a five-year occupation of Holland. The Dutch people were not treated as brutally as the Poles and Russians, whom Hitler considered to be less than human, but the occupation was by no means gentle.

Holland has many dairy and truck-garden farms, and the conquerors were in need of all the food to be had. Everything was regulated by military overseers. Many stratagems were used to keep milk cows from being butchered, and elaborate systems were devised to hide food from the Germans.

In their desperate need for slave labor to work in munitions factories and build coastal fortifications, the Nazis would make periodic raids. Unannounced they placed tanks in streets to block an area and make a house-to-house search for men. Marinus was considered too young to be a labor candidate. The parents had the young boys play in the street, so when sudden raids came, they could give a warning.

After four years of occupation, they were heartened to learn of the Normandy invasion, the subsequent liberation of France, and the approach of Allied troops. The Dutch were forbidden to have radios, but they made crude receivers, which they kept carefully hidden and used only when a boy was "playing" outside to warn of approaching soldiers.

The last year of the occupation, 1944–45, was known as the hunger winter. They were without electricity or fuel, huddling in beds to keep warm. The winter was merciless; snow was deep and the waterways frozen solid. People furtively traded what food items they were able to hide from the Nazis.

Marinus's father pushed a cart twenty miles to trade butter and cheese for three sacks of potatoes. This, at the risk of being apprehended and punished. He was ill clad in the bitter cold, but he returned with the precious food.

People huddled in fear, wondering if the Nazis would decide on mass executions as they retreated from the advancing Allied Armies. But as liberating Canadian troops came in, the Nazis were in full retreat.

Marinus's family had desired to come to the United States even before the war but could not obtain the means to do so. They came in 1950 with the help of Lorin Andersen, their sponsor. Marinus was baptized into the Church in 1951. He married Verna Spiers, and they raised a choice family. He worked as a brick mason. Discussing his memories of the war, Marinus stated he was very grateful that the U.S. entered the war. Marinus died in 2001.

Taken from an oral interview with Lin. H. Johnson.

GERARD VAN ZEBEN

Ye are no more strangers and foreigners, but fellowcitizens with the saints.

(Ephesians 2:19)

I was a young boy in the summer of 1940, living with my family in Hilversun, a small town near Amsterdam, Holland. In the spring of that year

Holland had been overrun by the German Army. We were the only Church members in our town. My father was also a member of the Dutch Underground.

Father's responsibility with the Underground was to help get downed British air crews out of our country and back to England. Secreted in a coffee table in our living room was a shortwave radio, used to contact the English as to when these men could be picked up. The radio was cleverly disguised by an artist who had painted a picture on the glass cover so that it looked like a tea service.

As these British fliers were picked up by the Underground, they would be brought to our home. Dad would radio his English contact and ask them to send a plane in to collect these men, giving them the coordinates of a landing site, frequently a meadow near Hilversun. A funeral service would be staged. When the time came for the men to leave, they would get into a coffin, which would be carried to the pickup point. There they would jump out of the coffin, into the waiting airplane. After the plane took off, the funeral procession would move on down the road and the empty coffin buried.

Although we were the only members of the Church in our area, our parents were anxious that we be taught the gospel and practice our religion. When Dad was able to be at home we would gather to partake of the sacrament. Because such meetings were forbidden by the Nazis, we held them in our attic so our neighbors could not hear us.

One Sunday, as we were beginning our meeting, the doorbell rang. Mother went downstairs. Opening the door, she discovered two German soldiers in full battle gear.

"Wie sind Mormonen" ["We're Mormons,"] said one of them.

Mother managed to say, "Sure you are. Sure."

"Yeah," they answered, "we are Mormons. We know you are holding church services." (All my life I have wondered how they knew.)

Mother replied, "No, we can't; it is forbidden."

One of the soldiers answered, "Yeah, yeah, I know, I know."

Mother, in her anxiety and wisdom quietly whispered a quick prayer, then stood aside for them to enter. "Okay, come in. But leave your guns here. We don't take guns into our meeting. You leave them right here."

Two Allied fliers were already in our home, both of whom were attending our sacrament meeting. Imagine their shock! When they saw those two Germans come in they thought they were being betrayed, and of course the German soldiers were equally surprised to see the Englishmen. But after introductions all around, we proceeded with our meeting.

One of the British airmen was a member of the Church. He offered the first sacramental prayer in English, then one of the German soldiers blessed the water in his language. I have never forgotten the overpowering, warm, and comforting Spirit that filled that humble attic, testifying of our Father's love for each of us as we worshiped together, not as enemies, but as fellow Saints.

Gospel ties are powerful, those soldiers never betrayed us, and we never heard from either of them again.

Taken from an oral interview with Robert Freeman for the *Saints at War* archival project. Used by permision.

ELFRIEDE DEININGER PRISON

Ye fearful Saints, fresh courage take; The clouds ye so much dread Are big with mercy and shall break In blessings on your head.

("God Moves in a Mysterious Way," *Hymns*, no. 285)

I was born in Mannheim, Germany, in 1921, the seventh daughter of my parents. My father died seven months before I was born, so my mother had to raise us by herself.

My mom was very religious. She belonged to the Lutheran Church. She read the Bible every morning, prayed, and would think about what she had read throughout the day, but there were so many things she just couldn't understand, so she went to our minister and asked him her questions. He told her not to worry about it; as long as she believed in Jesus Christ, she would be saved. "I was as confused as before," she said. "There were things I didn't understand, and he was no help."

One day in 1928, as she was doing her housework, she heard a voice telling her that today she would have her answers. She looked around, and there was nobody present. Being hard of hearing, she usually didn't hear the doorbell. But that day she heard it. When she opened the door, there stood two missionaries and she invited them in. They took only fifteen minutes to answer every question she had. She wanted to learn more so they gave her a Book of Mormon, and she read it through in two weeks and asked to be baptized.

Before she became a member of the LDS Church, we never had any visits from the minister, but very soon after her conversion he came and talked to her. I'll never forget it. He was so fanatical. Every time he would say something wrong, my mother would reply with something out of the scriptures, and this confused him. Jumping up from his chair and pointing at Mother, he said, "Woman, you are possessed of the devil!" He left in a huff. And he had the nerve to tell his congregation not to have anything to do with Mom, because she was possessed. That was hard on her, but eventually my relatives started to visit us again—they could see that we were not possessed people.

Mom took us with her to Church. But not my oldest sister; she was married and had her own way of thinking. The first time she took me and my sister Helen was on a hot summer day. The balcony door was open, and I could see the linden trees waving in the breeze outside. It was so peaceful I fell asleep. I woke up as they were singing, "Do What Is Right." Mother asked, "How did you like the meeting?" I didn't know what to say, so I said, "These people sure can sing!"

Even now singing fills a big well in my life and where there is song, I am at home. My family sang a lot. We all sang in the branch choir and had a good time with the other choir members. We went to church from then on.

The missionaries often came to our home and Mother always invited them for dinner on Saturday. I remember one young missionary particularly. He received his call just after he got married. His name was John R. Halliday, a music student at Brigham Young University. He came to our home several times a week to practice his clarinet. One day he asked Mother if he could bring his professor who was studying at the music conservatory, to practice with him. His professor was LeRoy Robertson. Brother Robertson played the violin and Elder Halliday the clarinet, and we all enjoyed it very much.

Another memorable visit was from President Philemon Kelly. He was a medical doctor. He asked Mom if he could use our home to do physical exams on the missionaries. She made a nice dinner for President Kelly, and after dinner the missionaries arrived for their checkups. Two of them he had to send home because of physical problems.

* * *

Before Hitler was elected we had the depression, and communism took over. We always feared communism because we saw what happened in Russia with the Revolution. By promising to restore financial stability, Hitler was elected. He made jobs for everybody. He started to build the Autobahn and other really good roads. He provided loans to newlyweds at very low interest so young people were able to buy the furniture they needed to start their households. When a baby came, there was a credit for these loans. We began to have nice things. Hitler decided that every family with three or more children should have a home out of the city. They built homes—whole subdivisions—and every home had a garden, a pig pen and chicken coop.

Hitler admired the Mormon Church. German women were organized according to the pattern of the LDS Relief Society: they held weekly meetings and studied homemaking, child care, current events, and literature. Hitler also borrowed the Boy Scout program, turning it into his famous Hitler Youth movement. He adapted those programs to make himself popular with the people.

I signed up for a government-sponsored program designed to help young people learn an apprenticeship. The one I went to was designed to help farmers in their struggle to supply food. First I attended a camp where the theory of farming was taught and where we worked with professional gardeners. We were issued a thin cotton dress with half sleeves, a windbreaker, knee-hi's, and heavy boots. The stiff boots made blisters on my heels. Our strenuous, regimented schedule was patterned after boot camp for the men.

One night after we had gone to bed, the whistle blew to awaken us. We were ordered to dress in our Sunday best and report to the dining room. The room was decorated with lamps and candles on the tables with streamers attached; it was quite festive. At each place on the table was a cup of hot chocolate and a cookie. A door opened and in came a group of young, uniformed SS men. An accordion player started playing, and the young men invited the girls to dance. It was fun. Two hours later the music stopped and we were ordered back to bed. This went on for several weeks.

After awhile some of the girls were allowed to stay up past the two-hour limit, supposedly to help clean up. Then one day the leaders announced that these girls were to be transferred to a different camp; we were told that they had decided to give the Fuhrer a child, fathered by a young SS man. I had a friend who worked as a nurse on a large estate in the Vienna Forest. She told me that girls came there for that purpose. They were pampered and got the best possible care. As soon as the child was born and weaned, the mothers had to leave. My friend told me that these children were then adopted by wealthy, childless couples.

On another night, I was awakened and told to report to the office. The room was dark, lighted only by a few candles. I am very nearsighted and could see very little in the dim light. The *führerin* of our camp started to question me about my religion. Every German had to carry an identification card. Mine was marked as a god-believer. Catholics and Lutherans had the religion stamped on their card; all the other churches were marked as god-believers. The first question was, "You're a Mormon, right?" *How did they know?* I wondered, and answered, "Yes." Then I was asked about Mormonism and Church history and doctrine. This went on for some time until one of the men turned on the light and asked me to turn around and said to me, "You are very honest." To my wonder, the tables were covered with all kinds of Mormon literature and pictures, especially of the pioneer emigration to Utah. I was then sent back to bed. The next day I was assigned a room to myself and given an alarm clock. I then had the responsibility to wake up the girls in the mornings and make sure we got to the bus on time to go to our work.

* * *

One day Mother received a notice to go to City Hall. I went with her because she couldn't hear very well. It was a very big room filled with tables with people at them. Mom went to a table and cheerfully greeted one of the men, "Good morning!"

"Hiel Hitler!" He screamed back at her. She put her hand to one ear and innocently asked, "What did he say?" The man was so upset that he jumped up, knocking his chair over, and stalked out the door. Another man told her that the next time she came, she should use the back door and come directly to him, that the other man was a fanatic and had gotten a lot of people in trouble. The man told her they found that she was paying tithing to a foreign church. She was told she must not contribute to that "American Church," or they would take away a third of her pension. Her decision was immediate and unfaltering—she would pay her tithing. This made her life more difficult because losing a third of her income made a big difference to her.

Mother was faithful and went to every meeting even though she didn't hear much. When we got home, she would ask what was talked about and make notes. During the week she'd read the scriptures about that particular thing. That way she got a real good education. My! She was further ahead than we were.

In 1939 we held the first LDS youth conference for all of Germany. It was here that I first became aware of Horst Prison. His father was our district president.

Horst worked for a large electrical motor company called B.B.C. As the war started, his company was relocated from near the French border to a place near my hometown. I was at the branch president's home when the doorbell rang. I opened the door and there stood a thoroughly rain-soaked young man. He stepped through the door and introduced himself as Horst Prison. He looked very tired and told us he had ridden his bicycle 150 kilometers from his home to Mannheim. Horst was seated in the living room, and I was asked to keep him company. I didn't know what to say, so I kept silent; then I was called to the kitchen to take his food to him. That was our first meeting. Horst lived with that family for a year while he worked for B.B.C. He came to all our church meetings and participated in all our activities, but I kept my distance. In 1940 Horst was drafted into the army and was stationed at Heidelberg, about 20 km away. Then the branch president's family was evacuated.

Horst continued coming to the meetings but now had nowhere to go after church until his train came in the evening, so Mom invited him to spend his time with us. In the evening Helen and I would walk him to the station, often stopping at the ice cream parlor on the way.

In the spring we had a youth activity. Horst had a day off, so he came along. We went to visit a castle in the Pfalz. It was a beautiful day. Horst picked some forget-me-nots and asked if he could make a hairpiece for me. Later he grabbed my hand and started to run. He stopped and looked at me, and just as he started to speak again a girl stood up between us. There and then I realized he had a crush on me. The next Sunday he asked me for a date.

* * *

In 1938 the missionaries had been removed from Germany because of the danger of war. They were sent to Holland, but they came back in 1939 and were there until shortly before the war started. When they were suddenly removed from Germany a second time, we knew that we were really in trouble.

Prior to their leaving, two missionaries told us the prophet had said that Church members should have a store of food on hand. We laughed, thinking *There's always enough food* and didn't even consider it. I surely remembered those elders when the war started and we had food rationing, and we had less and less to eat. Before the war was over we were on the brink of starvation.

The war started in September 1939, but it was not too bad with the first attack. As a matter of fact, when we had the first air raids, everybody went to see the damage the bombs had done. Little did we know what was ahead of us; it was tough.

We held regular church services. On Sundays, we could hold our meetings as long as we abided by the rules—not to say anything about Zion, Israel, Jehovah—or anything that resembled Judaism. We were not persecuted but had to report to government officials who the speaker was and what the topic was. Once in awhile they would come check on us.

In the beginning, my brother-in-law, an active priesthood holder, was drafted to the local police. We could only take the sacrament when he was there to officiate, But in a short time he was shipped to Russia.

Later, our branch had one other priesthood holder, a traveling elder, the only one in Germany. He was a nice man. He practically kept our branch together. At the beginning, he was excited. "Hitler will lead you to a height you never dreamed about." That brother died before everything got really bad. When the fighting started, all our younger brethren got drafted, and we had only two older brethren, and then they were evacuated. When the air raids started, all our priesthood was gone.

It was a lonely feeling to have no priesthood holders in our midst. But even with our men gone we could still have a prayer. The meetinghouse where we met was bombed out, and houses of other members were also destroyed. Sister Vokt's apartment remained intact, so we met at her place. Sometimes, we finished our meeting just before the bombing began in the evening. We exchanged news about our brethren in the field and had a prayer before going home.

My brother-in-law with the police always prayed that he would never have to be involved in any persecution of the Jews. One day, right after he reported to work, the commander came and told him he could go home. He was given a three-day furlough. At that moment an impression came to him, *Don't go home.* He spent the three days at our meetinghouse, fasting and praying. Upon reporting back to duty, his superior asked, "Where have you been? After you left, we got the order to take the Jews out of their homes. We sent for you, and your wife said she had no idea where you were." He knew that his prayers had been answered. He was not part of that terrible action.

Once in the downtown area I saw a lot of Jews with SS guards. One pretty young Jewess, in the late stages of pregnancy, was thrown to the ground by an SS guard, who jumped on her belly, and . . . ah, . . . it was terrible.

My sister worked for a Jew. She was afraid for his family, but he was okay. He was married to a German woman. The police didn't take him away, but he had to sleep in confinement and do cleanup work after air attacks. I saw him once on the street, but he asked me not to linger by him because of the danger. He survived the war.

* * *

In May 1941, the war with Russia started, and Horst was sent to the East. We wrote to each other, and I kept him informed about our Sunday meetings and the talks that were given. Then Mother passed away. Horst sent greetings. He was fighting in that terrible Russian winter. His feet were frozen, and he had to spend three months in the hospital, after which he was sent home to recuperate. He came to see me and we had a few days together before he went home to his parents. Then he returned to Russia. He was a faithful letter writer. He was wounded again and spent a few weeks in a hospital.

When he thought he would be released he wrote his parents that he would bring a girl home. Well, as it turned out, the doctor decided to keep him hospitalized a little longer. When he came home three months later, he asked me to marry him the next time he could get leave. During this time we began to be bombed heavily. By the end of the war, Mannheim was nearly destroyed.

I was working all day for a company, assembling small electrical motors, and at the same time I was a firefighter. As soon as we heard the alarm we had to change clothes and be ready to go out. We never knew which direction these air raids would come from. We would hear the sound of the falling bombs, then the building would shake and smoke would fill the air. We found whole housing blocks on fire. Some houses would remain standing, so we had to spray the water on the burning places of those houses. The people in the basements, can you imagine? They died when the scalding water came down on them.

As buildings collapsed, people were crushed. It was a law that you had to dig a tunnel to the next house, then fill it up with rocks and leave a pick and shovel beside it, so in an emergency you could open the hole and go to the next house. That's what saved my sister's life. I heard that her

area was being bombed. About 5:00 in the afternoon, we got released from fighting fires. When I got to my sister's house, there was only debris and a lot of smoke where the house once stood I was so afraid that my sister and her three little children were trapped in the rubble. But they had been able to get out through a tunnel. The constant bombing frazzled our nerves, our spirits, and left us exhausted.

Horst received leave, and we were married in January 1944. In preparation for our wedding day my sisters Paula and Helen obtained extra food

Elfriede and Horst Prison on their wedding day.

stamps and were able to cook a nice dinner and make a cake. That evening the sirens went off, and we had to go to a bomb shelter. Luckily the airplanes did not unload their bombs over our city. The next day Horst's parents sent a telegram saying that the mission president would be at their home and that he wanted to perform our marriage and to ordain Horst an elder. We left for Horst's hometown. Due to delays caused by air raids, what should have been a train ride of three hours, took all of one day and a night.

When we finally arrived, all of Horst's extended family were there. The next day was Sunday, and we all went to church. It had been a long time since his aunts and uncles and grandparents had been together. I was glad we were able to take pictures.

Exactly a week after our wedding I got a registered letter informing me that I must report for work the next day or face severe punishment. I was outraged. Horst took the letter to the local party headquarters and they told us not to worry, that they would take care of it. After all, Horst had several decorations for bravery on the front.

After he left again for the Russian front, I returned to work, and I learned I was pregnant. We were very happy about the thought of having a baby. Horst told me he wanted a child so that he would know what he was fighting for. The air raids increased, as did my morning sickness.

A few days after he left, Horst sent a telegram asking me to come visit him in a nearby French town before he left for the front. On the day of my visit I could not shake off my gloom. Horst asked if I thought he would be killed. I said, "No, but I won't see you for a very long time." I also told him that when the war ended, I would try to emigrate to America and he could find me by inquiring at the Church records office in Salt Lake City.

The next day he was shipped out, and I did not see him again for a very long time. Horst wrote a few times, but then the letters stopped coming. In August 1944, I received a letter from the government informing me that Horst was missing in action.

As I went downstairs to receive that letter, my baby was moving and kicking, but that was the last time I felt it. I prayed so hard for Horst and the baby. A week went by and I started to worry about the baby. Finding a doctor was not easy, as most of them were away in military service. Finally I located a woman doctor. She was completely insensitive to my concerns and told me to come back in two weeks.

I was losing weight rapidly and became very weak. I still hoped my baby was okay, but something was different. When I went back to the doctor, she put her stethoscope on my tummy, listened, then told me my baby was dead. "There is no hospital open for you, but there is a midwife nearby who has a private clinic, and in an emergency I will come down, but you will have to pay in advance, for I doubt you will pull through." I was furious. I screamed at her, "If I have to die like an animal, so be it, but you dirty pig, you will not get my money!"

The next day was Sunday and we had air raids all morning. By afternoon the safe signal was sounded. A lady I had worked with saw me and asked if I was carrying a dead baby. She told me about a doctor in Wiesloch who could help me. Paula and Helen went with me, as I was having difficulty walking. We had a terrible time—we had to walk, then catch a train, then walked some more—and finally a bus.

When we arrived at the hospital, a young woman asked if I was in labor. She took me in her arms and carried me to the second floor of the building. She was a doctor. After examining me she told my sisters to come back in the morning but cautioned that I was very low. I don't remember much after that. I woke the next morning in intense pain, and the nurse sitting beside my bed promptly went for the doctor. The delivery was complicated as the baby was in the breech position. It went very slowly. They told me it was a little boy and weighed six and a half pounds. During my recovery it was hard for me to watch the new mothers as they nursed their babies.

I was bitter, and asked the Lord *Why?* A friend from the Church came to visit me. When I told him my bitterness, he said, "Elfriede, that little word 'why' is the biggest tool in the devil's workshop. God loves you and will comfort you if you will let him. He knows 'why' and all about your heartache, but it is best for you. Someday you will understand." His advice helped me accept my plight. I went home as soon as the doctor let me go. I was grateful for all the love and attention I received. My sister Lina came to take me to her apartment in a small town outside Mannheim.

* * *

My brother-in-law, Ludwig, came home on leave, and together we went to Mom's grave. He saluted her and said, "Mother, I am the next one to come." I tried to talk him out of it, but he said he was sure he would follow

Mom in a short time.

Ludwig had been trained as a medic and was serving in France. He told me that one day he had taken two black men prisoners. His commanding officer ordered Ludwig to shoot the two men, as they "were not worth the time and paperwork as POWs." Ludwig refused, saying that these men had rights under the Geneva Convention. His commander got really angry and again ordered Ludwig to shoot them. Again Ludwig refused. The commandant made the men dig a grave, again ordering Ludwig to shoot them, and again Ludwig refused. "I am a soldier, not a murderer!" The officer had Ludwig sent to a death squad in Russia.

On his way there, he spent a night at a field hospital. One of the doctors who had helped train him, recognized him and asked what he was doing there. Ludwig told him.

"You are not going there," the doctor responded, "I need you here. There you will be killed for sure."

The doctor changed Ludwig's orders and kept him at his hospital. As he finished his story he told me, "Oh, Elfriede, I am a sick and old man. I am so tired. Can you imagine how it is when some poor devil is hit and is lying out there crying for his mother? I can't help it. I have to go out there and take him in my arms until he can die. Should I outlive this war I swear I'm leaving this uniform hanging on a nail, and I'm going to church with Lina." He told me several times he knew he would die soon. He left, and was killed two weeks later.

* * *

Horst's grandfather, Peter Prison, was a botanist who gathered all kinds of herbs to supply to pharmacies to make into medicines. Horst often went with his grandfather and learned to recognize many of these plants and their uses. When Horst came home on leave we sometimes walked in the forest, and he would show me many herbs. That knowledge came in handy, for I could use these plants in our hunger years.

One morning we looked out the window and saw a huge dust cloud. As we watched we saw people coming toward our village. We went down to the road to see what was going on. Young boys fourteen to fifteen years old, old men, soldiers with arms in slings and bloody bandages around their heads, some on crutches, all of them looking to be at the end of their strength, struggled past. They were surrounded by guards with rifles and bayonets. When we asked what it was all about, we were told we were prohibited from talking to them. All we were permitted to do was to give these poor souls a drink from the village fountain, then they were driven on like cattle. An hour later a girl from our village rode her bicycle to the next village. When she came back she looked stricken and could hardly speak. She told us that all those who had passed by us now lay in the forest, shot to death.

A short time later we learned that French troops had taken the village next to ours and that girls and women had been raped, some of them murdered. Two days later I saw troops coming. They wore gray-green corduroy coats, a hood, and turbans on their heads. Rifles in hand, they jumped over the garden fences. Lina took a quick look, and we retreated from the windows, too frightened to say anything. We told the children to quietly pray for the Lord's protection.

A Jeep drove around the village announcing that any soldiers hiding in homes must surrender, or within the hour all houses would be burned to the ground and the inhabitants shot. We had no idea there were soldiers hiding in our village, but from every direction they began to show up. The French soldiers directed us to sew white armbands and bring them to the headquarters. Each surrendering soldier got one of these armbands, release papers, and was sent home. The French officers then instructed us to take a piece of white paper and write the name, age, and sex of everyone living in that house. We were ordered to put it on the front door. Some houses were then taken over, and it was announced that for our own safety we should sleep in the attics of designated houses.

The next day I heard little Holger, Lina's five-year-old son, coming up the stairs and shouting "No! No! Don't go up there!" I opened the door, and there was Holger, his arms wrapped around the leg of a huge soldier, trying to prevent the soldier from opening the door. It was a touching picture— that little one trying to protect us. My knees grew weak, and I was shaking with fear. I took Holger inside. The French Moroccan soldier asked if I was scared. Defiant, I told him "No." He grinned at me, handed me a bar of soap and a pair of pants. He spoke no German, and I, no French. He motioned that I was to wash his pants and showed me on his watch the time when he would come back for them. He came back on the minute he had indicated, but the pants were still wet.

He returned two hours later, bringing a big piece of lamb, potatoes, eggs, onions, garlic, and some flour. He gave us to understand that we were his assigned family, responsible to cook for his men and do their laundry. Lina prepared the meal. Right on the dot of noon, Rachau, with four companions arrived. He gestured that we were to sit at the table and eat with them.

With the food on the table, the children all folded their arms and bowed their heads. Rachau wanted to know why. I explained as well as I could that we always prayed before each meal. He nodded, spoke to his men, and they all folded their arms and bowed their heads. I offered the blessing on the food. As these men finished their meals, each burped loudly, which brought giggles from the children. Rachau then got each of them to burp. Then I understood that this was their custom. All five Moroccans laughed, clapped their hands and left. At six o'clock they returned for supper.

It fell my lot to do the laundry. Since we had no washboard, my fingers were soon raw and bleeding from rubbing. When Rachau observed this, he sent two of his men to teach me how to wash clothes. They told me to fill a small washtub with hot soapy water and soak the laundry in it. Then they took off their shoes and socks, stood in the tub and stomped the laundry for almost an hour, singing all the while. All I had to do was rinse it and hang it out to dry. To our amazement, the laundry was clean. From that time on we got the stompers once a week. They also brought us firewood for the cookstove.

One night after dark, there was a knock on the door. There stood Rachau with a lamb on his shoulder. He asked us not to tell anyone, as meat was rationed, but we could share the meat with some other people. The villagers and the soldiers developed a real friendship. Our women were used for work in the fields. One day Rachau was marching his soldiers past a field where several women were working with their men. He halted the soldiers, ordered the women to go home, and the soldiers took the women's places. This sort of thing occurred daily. These Moroccans were very good to us. Without their help we would have starved.

A few weeks later I returned to Mannheim. The city had nearly been destroyed, but I found my sisters alive and well. It took considerable time, but slowly life began to return to normal. Our branch was reorganized and some of our brethren returned, so we had the priesthood in our midst again.

Some of the men had been killed in the war. All those bitter years brought us closer together.

I was called to teach the Gospel Doctrine class. We met at Sister Vokt's apartment because there was no other meeting place available. One Sunday, in the middle of class, the doorbell rang. Sister Vokt opened the door and there stood an American soldier. He was one of the missionaries who had served in our branch prior to the war. What a joy it was to see him. There was not a dry eye in the room. Needless to say, I could not finish my lesson that day. The American told us he had been searching for Church members, but all the places he went had been bombed into ruin. This was the last place he could remember, and he found us. We held a testimony meeting, and there was a strong spirit of love and peace as we testified of the love and mercy and strength we each had received in times of despair and bitter experience. My anger at the Americans for bombing us disappeared in that meeting.

* * *

One day I met a man who had just come back from Russia, after five years as a prisoner of war. He encouraged me to not give up waiting for Horst. He also advised me to be very understanding and patient when he returned. He was sure Horst wouldn't be the same gentle man when he came home that he had been.

I went to live in Saarbrücken, with Horst's parents. Horst's brother, Paul, was very good to me. He always brought a little something for me to eat when I was so weak from hunger and illness.

While our situation had improved somewhat, we still did not have sufficient food to stave off starvation. Nothing is harder than to see children die of starvation. Then we got help from the Church. Elder Ezra Taft Benson visited us at a conference at Karlsruhe. I went there with my father-in-law. We had been promised that one of our General Authorities would be there.

It was cold and raining as we climbed over rubble to our meeting place. Our meetings were nearly over, but no visitors had arrived. We started singing "Come, Come, Ye Saints" just before they arrived. What a joy I cannot tell. We held another meeting and at the end were privileged to shake hands with our Brethren. Shortly after, we received food, blankets, and much needed cloth from the Church. It saved us from starving.

In late December 1949, I went with Horst's mother to the market. As we came home I turned on the radio and heard that Horst was on his way home. We had not heard from him in over two years and didn't know if he was still alive. Next morning at 5:00, we got a telegram telling us we could pick him up at the railroad station in Saarbrücken, that afternoon. His mother, brother, and cousin came along. When the train arrived, two men got off. One left right away, the other stood there. Mother, Alma, and Paul passed right by him. I almost did, but turned and stopped. The man was filthy, had no hair, looked fat, and his teeth were broken and rotted. I was not quite sure until he spoke. He said later that if I too had passed him by, he would have gone away and never returned. The others returned and greeted him. It was a peculiar situation, not like anything I had ever dreamed of. Horst didn't stop talking all the way home, but after we arrived he hardly said anything, except yes or no. For the next few days he was a stranger to me.

After a bath and clean clothes, he looked better. For dinner we had potatoes and spinach. He had a tablespoon of spinach and half of a boiled potato, then turned all white, started perspiring, and almost passed out. That evening, he had only a half slice of bread, with liverwurst. It made him so sick he had to lie down. I went to the doctor for advice. He told me that Horst was in the advanced stages of starvation and could not tolerate food. We put him on a diet of sauerkraut juice and only a spoonful of light food for a time, until his body was strong enough to handle regular food. On this diet he lost all the fluid, which we at first thought was fat.

When we reported his return to the government, they gave him a suit, a coat, and other winter clothing. Horst had all his broken teeth removed and got dentures. I massaged his head with an ointment and slowly his hair returned. When he was strong enough, B.B.C., the company he had worked for before the war, gave him his job back.

It was not an easy adjustment to have Horst back in my life. Horst was very bossy and thought he owned me. I had been alone for so long, having to stand on my own two feet, and now I was told what and how to do everything. And he was very moody. I tried hard to cope with it, but one day, before we had children to consider, I decided to leave. I had had enough. I had saved sufficient money for a ticket home. As Horst slept, I got up and prepared to leave. When I opened the door, he awoke and came after me. He cried, he begged me not to leave him, and promised to change. I felt sorry for him. I realized that he needed time to get over his bitterness. It worked for awhile, but he fell back into his old behavior. Today we could have had counseling that would have helped, but that was unknown then. However, by that time, we had saved enough money to go to America. He told me, "In America I will change so much you won't recognize me anymore." Well, I hoped and believed.

We did come to America and we have a wonderful family. But change for Horst was a long and difficult process. Despite this, in 2001, we will have been married for fifty-seven years, and I love him very much.

Taken from the diary of Elfriede D. Prison.

PRISONERS OF WAR

Pencil sketch drawn by Harold W. Gunn while a prisoner of war. The Air Force silver wings are chained to the Nazi swastika, with a POW camp in the center.

The Geneva Convention, held in 1929, guaranteed "humane treatment, limits to the nature and extent of interrogation, and restrictions on the duties" that prisoners of war could be forced to perform. With the exception of the USSR and Japan, all Allied and Axis forces were signatories of the Convention and generally abided its terms. However, the Germans did not follow the Convention when dealing with Soviet captives. Many Soviets were killed by the Einsatzgruppen, a branch of the Nazi military police referred to as the mobile death squad. Others were sent to slave labor camps, where a high percentage died of overwork, starvation, or brutality. For their part, the Soviets were equally scornful of the rights of POWs, and few German troops survived capture by the Soviets.

In the Pacific, few Japanese troops were taken prisoner as most preferred suicide to surrender. Because the Japanese viewed capture as a "matter of dishonor, they regarded any prisoners they took as having forfeited any right to respect." The Japanese's ill-treatment of POWs became notorious. The horrors of the Bataan Death March, as well as other forms of brutality and forced labor, have come to symbolize life in a Japanese prisoner of war camp. (*Dictionary of World War II*, p. 203)

ROYCE J. FUHRIMAN

Lord God of Hosts, be with us yet, Lest we forget, lest we forget.

("God of Our Fathers, Known of Old," *Hymns*, no. 80)

The Great Depression of the 1930s left most everyone without money. In 1938 I was eighteen years old and had graduated from Preston High School. Preston, Idaho, is located at the north end of Cache Valley, a few miles north of the Utah-Idaho border. I was working in a service station for a dollar a day and could see little in my immediate future to improve my life style.

While attending high school I learned to type, and if I say so myself, I was a very good typist, able to whip out 140 words per minute. Service in the United States Army seemed to offer opportunities. I enlisted and went into the Army as a clerk-typist, my first duty-station—Manila, The Philippines. Life as a clerk in the waterfront Headquarters, Philippine Command in downtown Manila was cushy. I worked five days a week in the Plans and Training Division of the 31st Infantry. There was a houseboy to take care of cleaning my barracks room, plenty to eat, and after work hours, plenty to see on this rather exotic, tropical island of

Sergeant Royce Fuhriman

Luzon. For a young man from southeastern Idaho, it was perfect duty. And the pay? $21.00 a day–one day a month–plus room and board.

1939 turned into 1940. In May 1941, all dependants of U.S. military personnel in the Philippines were sent back to the continental United States. On the morning of 8 December 1941 [because of the international date line], I was shaken awake by my houseboy: "Sergeant, sergeant, wake up, the Japs are bombing Pearl Harbor!" Rubbing the sleep from my eyes, I cussed him for disturbing me, but he assured me it was true. It wasn't long until bombs started falling on us. In a coordinated, simultaneous attack, the Japanese bombed Pearl Harbor in Hawaii and Clark Field, Luzon, about sixty-five miles north of Manila, and then they arrived over Manila. All military aircraft at Clark Field were destroyed or made unusable.

I spent my 21st birthday dodging Japanese bombs. Our unit was moved to Corregidor. Our antiquated weapons were no match for those used by the invaders. From somewhere, our Army Air Forces found some planes to engage the Japanese Zeros. Until we were forced to give up, we fought a delaying action against the highly trained elite of the Imperial Japanese Army. Before we left Corregidor we had eaten all the horses and caribao [water buffalo] on the island, and were starting on the monkeys.

To acknowledge the horror and valor that occurred during the Bataan Death March, kilometer markers indicate the path the prisoners took.

Military personnel on Bataan surrendered on May 6th. A few weeks prior to this, General Douglas MacArthur and his family were evacuated from Corregidor and taken by submarine to Mindanao. There they were picked up by a B-17 and flown to Australia.

The remaining forces on Corregidor were surrendered by General King. We were now cut off from help from sea or by air.

The ninety-kilometer forced march to Camp O'Donnell just north of Clark Field, began within hours of our capture. We helped each other as much as our strength permitted. We were given nothing to eat. I was bone-numbingly tired, shaking with malaria, and each step was anguish. To falter brought stinging rebuke from our guards. The only water I had to drink was from ditches. In the unrelenting tropical heat of early May I became dehydrated. Getting to the brackish water required pushing the bodies of some of my comrades out of the way. Those too sick or too weak to continue were shot, their bloating bodies left to lay in the sun alongside the road, in a last state of disgrace.

Our Japanese captors were brutal and merciless. We could not pack anything with us. To the Japanese warriors, as prisoners of war, we, who "valued life more than honor" were to be treated with less respect than a mongrel dog.

One day I watched as guards encircled a fallen prisoner and jabbed at him with their bayonets for several minutes while he died. We could not rest. Maylon Peterson, my boyhood friend from Franklin County, died along the way.

When I was captured I weighed 155 pounds. A few weeks later I was down to 115. I am uncertain where I found the strength to continue shuffling one foot in front of the other, but I am grateful I could. Occasionally, civilians who watched from the roadside would slip a banana or other food to us. In doing so they took an awful chance. If they were caught, the brutal soldiers would treat them no better than they would one of us. Of the 70,000 American and Filipino soldiers who began the march, only 54,000 arrived at Camp O'Donnell. Within eight weeks of our arrival in camp, another 23,000 died. The Bataan Death March has been called the worst atrocity of the war in the Pacific.

While in Manila I had worked for Colonel James Monihan. I liked him, and he seemed to like me. Shortly after entering Camp O'Donnell, Colonel Monihan found me. "Royce, the senior officers are being shipped out. I don't know what lies ahead. We may be treated better, or they may make it worse on us because we are officers. Either way, as one friend to another, I am giving you the opportunity to come with me, if you like. I am not ordering you to come with me, but each officer is allowed to take one enlisted man as an aide." I decided to take my chances with the officers. As it turned out, it didn't make much difference, the officers were treated as badly as the enlisted men. But it was a good decision.

We were first moved to a camp at Tarlac, farther north of Clark Field, on Luzon. Life in the camps was bleak. If you followed the rules, stayed out of the trouble and did everything right, you could get by. If you didn't bow just right, well . . . Our diet consisted of boiled rice and maybe some squash. We supplemented our diet with whatever we could find. We ate monkeys, snakes, lizards, the Army pack mules, we even ate General Wainwright's polo pony. These animals made the march with us. We never knew if we were going to see another day.

Rank held no privilege in the POW camps. If the colonels and generals wanted their laundry done, they did it themselves. One of the things which kept us busy was digging latrines. Due to the prevalence of dysentery and diarrhea, the latrines were the busiest spots in camp.

On 11 August 1942, we were moved from Tarlac and shipped to Formosa [now Taiwan]. As we marched out of the camp with General Wainwright in the lead, Filipinos lined the streets, gave the "V" sign with their fingers, and whistled "Auld Lange Syne." We were marched to Manila and jammed aboard the Japanese ship, the *Nagara Maru*. Three days later we arrived on Formosa and were sent to Camp Takao.

We fared no better for food or treatment in Takao. A short time later we were moved to a second site, Camp Shirakawa. Food became a major issue for us. A couple of times the person assigned to bring back the thin soup and rice fell and spilled the soup. There was no replacement from the kitchen, but other squads voluntarily made up our loss. Starvation was the means by which we were brought into submission.

We used whatever materials were available to make clothes. Old flour sacks were in high demand. To supplement our food supply, we grew sweet potatoes.

Disposal of human waste was a serious problem. Chinese coolies were brought in to handle this detail. They drove a large cart on which there was a huge barrel. These "honey buckets" were a welcome sight, but the Nips [GI slang for Japanese] bopped the coolies around so much that they were afraid to come into the camp.

With the war going against the Japanese we were transferred again. This time we were stuffed into the hold of the Japanese supply ship *Oryoko Maru*. It was hot, stuffy, and pitch black. The stench of unwashed bodies and urine was overpowering. We were forced to lay shoulder to shoulder in double bunks; there was no room to sit up or roll over. Men were pushed to the limits of their endurance, and some lost the last thread that tied them to sanity. We spent nineteen days in this hellish condition, fourteen of them in Quelung Harbor before we were moved. But our ordeal was not over. We heard the sounds of aircraft overhead—we were being bombed by Americans!

Many years after the war I was visiting with my cousin, Roy Wehrcamp, reminiscing about wartime experiences. I told him about being in the hold of the *Oryoko* on 4 October 1944. Roy stared at me for what seemed several minutes, then said, "I was the bombardier on that plane and was severely reprimanded for being such a lousy shot!" His lousy shot saved the lives of several hundred Americans, including mine.

We finally left the harbor and, after being en route for thirty-five days, arrived at Cheng Chiaton, Manchuria. The cold, in contrast to the heat we were used to, was sharp. Before we could move into our barracks we had to stand in the cold for over two hours while we were harangued by the camp commander and were forced, again, to sign a non-escape pledge. Many developed pneumonia and all of us had severe colds. It must have been twenty degrees below zero.

For two and a half years my mother and dad knew only that I was missing in action. My parents saved this letter. Not wanting to worry them, and to get the letter past Japanese censors, I put a positive spin on these experiences. It came to them eight months after I wrote it.

Dear Folks:

I hope this letter finds you all well and as full of hope as I am as I write this letter. I am now mess sergeant of the camp kitchen. Christmas we killed three pigs, and I stayed up all night helping prepare fifty-one ducks for dinner. We also had plenty of bananas and watermelon. We had a very good program that night. I am looking forward to our release and return home, hoping it will not be too far in the future. This war has taught me to appreciate things as they come and enjoy the present. After some bombings I've been through, I've found that you never know what to expect next, so enjoy things while you can. Well, take care of yourselves until I return. Tell everyone hello for me. Do you think Mike [my pet dog] will still know me?

Love to all, Royce J. Fuhriman

[Mike died six weeks before this letter got home. Mom said it was from a broken heart.]

We were moved one more time—to Cheng Tun, Manchuria, on the edge of the Gobi desert. There we were quartered in an old Russian-built barracks and supply facility. There were two seasons, winter and August. In this last month and until we left, we were being eaten by sand fleas. With the war so nearly over, the Nips put the heat on us so strongly that we sought anything to fill our aching souls. Many of our men lost twenty pounds in the last month of our captivity.

And then one morning in August 1945, we saw an American plane overhead. At 1130 hours six parachutes opened above us. These Americans landed in our midst and were immediately surrounded by armed Japanese guards. They were captured and taken before the camp commander. They told him that Japan had surrendered to the Allies. The Japanese officer refused to believe them, and the six were taken outside and lined up against a wall to be shot. A sudden rain storm caught the guards with their weapons almost ready. The Japanese soldiers detailed to the firing squad refused to go out in the downpour as their guns would get wet and they would have to clean them. The execution was postponed for twenty-four hours. That evening word came through official Japanese channels that World War II had ended with the dropping of the atomic bomb.

Wandering through the mass of wildly cheering prisoners, one of the paratroopers eagerly searched the face of each POW, hoping to recognize someone special. Suddenly, with tears of joy streaming down his cheeks, the young soldier, who had nearly lost his life to the firing squad, raced through the crowd and tenderly embraced his emaciated father. I watched, and wept at this scene, and knew that our trial was finally over.

Four days later huge Russian tanks arrived. These were all driven by women, although the soldiers they carried were men. At 6:30 p.m. on 20 August, 1945, a Russian officer stood in front of us while we were holding a songfest. He announced: "You are free men!" He was nearly mobbed. It was the greatest thrill of my life to that point.

Earlier that day an American cargo plane made some passes overhead and dropped a radio set. The air crew asked if we needed anything, such as penicillin. A doctor in the camp had never heard of the then-new antibiotic. We told him we needed blankets. They had none on board, but the crew took off their flight jackets, eleven of them, and dropped them to us.

It was a powerful experience as our group broke up and left. After spending four years together and sharing the hardships, we had developed a deep bond of friendship with each other that remains to this day. I have participated in survivors groups, and over the years since, whenever I have met one of these men, we have thrown our arms around each other. It has always been good to see them.

I knew both MacArthur and Wainwright in Manila. When I look at pictures of the formal surrender ceremony by the Japanese as it was conducted by General MacArthur aboard the *USS Missouri,* I always look for my friend General Jonathan Wainwright and remember the time at Tarlac when he asked me to scrub his back while we were both in the shower.

We left the Asian mainland at Port Arthur on a troop ship bound for Manila, for repatriation. One morning three buddies asked me to go to breakfast with them. I told them I wanted to shave first. While I shaved and they stood in the chow line, the ship struck a floating mine. My three friends were killed by the explosion. I don't why I didn't go with them. I guess I was supposed to come home to Preston and marry Ilene Brown, so we could have our family of three daughters and a son.

Royce Fuhriman returned to Franklin County in September 1945, after an absence of more than six years. He settled in Preston where he and Ilene raised their four children. In addition to their children, Royce and Ilene have sixteen grandchildren and nine great-grandchildren.

A few years after his return from the war he went into the paint and glass business. He says his favorite calling in the Church was in the Nursery, where he served for seventeen years and "enjoyed every minute of it. I saw lots of lady helpers come and go, but I stayed. I really loved those little kids."

Adapted from his personal records and oral interview with Paul H. Kelly.

HAROLD W. GUNN

I was in prison, and ye came unto me.

(Matthew 25: 36)

I grew up in Salt Lake City where I attended West High School and later the University of Utah. In February 1942, I enlisted as an aviation air cadet. After completing pilot training I was assigned to overseas duty in England, where we began flying missions over continental Europe. Prior to leaving for the war, Geraldine Kluge and I were married in Salt Lake City. In England, I was a co-pilot on a B-17 flying fortress. My unit was the 303rd Bomb Group, Eighth Air Force.

June 22, 1943: Our crew was flying our eleventh mission, bombing in the industrialized Ruhr Valley—our target was Huls, a large synthetic rubber plant. Flying at 27,000 feet we had dropped our bomb load and were headed for England when flak burst into the nose of our plane, killing the navigator

Harold W. Gunn

and exploding the instrument panel in the cockpit. The airplane was out of control and falling in a slow spiraling dive, nose down. The pilot immediately told me to get out. At about 17,000 feet I moved past our navigator, who was lying in a pool of blood. The engineer had opened the escape hatch, but was sitting rigidly, blocking the opening, and unwilling to jump. I dropped into the forward escape passageway and got out of the plane. I fell freely until I could recognize things on the ground, then pulled the rip cord. I had no sensation of falling, but when my parachute billowed above me, my body snapped up straight, and I blacked out for a few moments. When I regained consciousness, my thoughts were about Geraldine. I wondered if we would ever be together again.

I saw German soldiers on bicycles riding to where they thought I would land, but I maneuvered my chute toward the edge of a forest where I anticipated hiding among the trees. With the ground rushing up to meet me I almost came down in a canal, but landed in a cabbage patch just beyond the canal bank.

Shedding my parachute harness, I ran for the cover of the trees. Within a matter of minutes I was greeted by a voice that spoke in thickly accented English "For you, da var is over."

Only three of our crew made it out of the plane. "Happ" Hardacre, one of the waist gunners, survived the crash. The man who jumped just ahead of Happ was caught in an escape hatch that had not fully opened. It slammed shut on him, pinning him in the doorway. With enormous effort Happ forced the door open enough to free the man from the falling plane. It was an act of great courage, but Happ was trapped in the plane himself and rode it to the ground.

I was entering into a whole new realm of my war experience. After capture the Germans put me in solitary confinement for five days at Dulag Luft, near Frankfurt, where they began to interrogate me.

After this introduction to Nazi Germany, we were put aboard an old "square wheeler" train and shipped across Germany. We were so crowded in there that we couldn't straighten our legs. My knees ached, my shoulders ached—in my misery I wanted to cry. I finally crawled up into the luggage rack and felt some relief. I was incarcerated at Stalag Luft III near Sagan, in eastern Germany (then occupied Poland), about ninety miles southeast of Berlin. Now I was a "Kriegie"—GI slang from the German, for POW.

Stalag Luft III was located in a forest. As the trees were cut the stumps were left. Several hastily built wooden barracks housed us. Around the perimeter of the compound was a high barbed-wire fence bisected by strategically placed guard towers. After arriving I was interviewed by a committee of American officers. These officers directed our actions in the compound. In this interview they asked about my training, talents, and interests. Since I had some artistic abilities, these were noted and employed in many interesting ways over the course of the next two years.

Stalag Luft III had an extraordinarily talented contingent of prisoners. Many of the British officers were professional men—lawyers, engineers, architects, chemists, teachers, and doctors, to name a few. The American POWs were equally well-educated and diverse in their capabilities.

The YMCA sent in a few log books. In the cut of a card deck I won one of these. With a brush and water colors I did renderings of scenes of everyday camp life. I also drew portraits of some of the other officers I was especially drawn to. When I did the pictures of these men I asked them to write a short page telling how they came to be "guests" of the Germans.

For all of us there was the misery of sand fleas. We did our utmost to maintain a modicum of cleanliness, and our efforts paid. During the two years I was at Sagan, we never had an outbreak of communicable disease. We also battled to be positive. This was essential to our well-being because the Germans constantly attempted to break our spirits. But when things were going badly, someone would pop a funny. We learned to laugh in the face of adversity. Food furnished by the Germans was inadequate, most often it was watery potato peeling soup. For survival we depended upon the Red Cross parcels that came each week.

Another pervasive problem was the cold. We dressed up to go to bed, putting on extra socks if we could find them, scarves, gloves, and coats. I filled my mattress cover with wood chips and "quilted" it, which helped some to ward off the cold.

United States military doctrine dictated that as prisoners of war it was our duty to attempt escape. We were instructed that even in captivity we were valuable to the Allied war effort and more valuable alive than dead. Thousands of German man-hours were used to recapture escapees and return them to camps, diverting time and effort that could have been used more effectively elsewhere. Escape became more dangerous near the end of the war because German military and civilian police had been given orders to shoot on sight any suspected escapees.

The "X Committee" (escape committee) constantly reviewed different escape proposals. For example, one day someone noticed that when the main gates to the camp were closed there was space enough between the bottom of the gate and the ground for someone to crawl under. In broad daylight,

Sketch of the prison guard tower; one of many sketches from Hal Gunn's log book, which he kept throughout his time at Stalag Luft III.

during a planned diversion caused by prisoners in two adjoining compounds, two men slipped under the gates and disappeared into the forest. Because we were so deep in Germany they were soon recaptured. But escapes such as these were minor compared to the complex scheme formulated by the committee for "The Great Escape." Plans for a major escape effort were just beginning when a new complex, designated the North compound, was opened, and thereafter all American POWs were housed there. By the time I arrived in 1943, some of the British had been there for four years.

Notices signed by Big X were posted, asking for volunteers to play cricket and softball. Most of the prisoners knew what that meant, and five hundred men signed up to dig three long tunnels. These tunnels came to be known as "Tom," "Dick," and "Harry." It was hoped that at least one of these tunnels would not be discovered. Besides the miners, carpenters and engineers were assigned to tunnel. Still others were put to work to design disguises and fashion authentic-looking German uniforms out of old uniforms, blankets, and anything else that could be found. Everyone who worked to carry out the escape plan did an outstanding job. Artists set up shop to forge passports, military orders, and identification. The forgers became so expert that their papers could not be distinguished from an original—even by the gestapo.

A special few who spoke German fluently were assigned to make friends with a guard, to keep him constantly in sight, and to bribe him. Red Cross chocolate and cigarettes were traded for needed, seemingly innocuous items brought in by the bribed guards.

Engineers devised trap doors beneath stoves and drain pipes. These doors were so cleverly designed that they couldn't be detected even by probing guards. Electricians rounded up odd bits of wiring left behind by the camp builders and wired each of the three shafts with electric lights. When the Germans didn't turn on the power during the day, smelly homemade lamps had to be used. These were fabricated from tin cans, with wicks made of pajama cords and used margarine as fuel. An Australian pilot made compasses. These he fashioned by melting phonograph records to make a casing. Shards of broken window glass became lens covers, and sewing needles and razor blades rubbed on a magnet, the pointer.

To prevent discovery we had to keep up a sense of normalcy in the camp. Everyone had to report for roll call morning and night.

"The Great Escape" was planned by POWs in the South compound, which housed British and Norwegian prisoners. When the Germans created the North compound, all of the Americans were moved into it. Removing the Americans from the other two compounds meant that no Americans could escape, even though they had been an important part of planning and working on it. We were still generally aware of the progress as the plans were carried out but could give only moral support to the effort.

Finally the day came for the escape to take place. Map makers had traced many maps and run them off on a makeshift duplicator. The faking of documents was incredibly precise. Whole sheets of simulated typewriting were drawn by hand, complete with strike-overs, imperfect letters and bad shifts. Forgers ripped fine paper from Bibles and linen covers from books to make identification booklets. Letterheads were "embossed" using toothbrush handles. German eagle and swastika stamps were cut from rubber boot heels.

Even the best laid plans can go astray. All sorts of problems occurred, not the least of which was the discovery that the tunnel exit, estimated to reach the woods beyond the camp was ten feet short of the trees and its opening a bare fifteen yards from a sentry tower. But the men were in no mood to be stopped. Waiting for another dark moon and digging another thirty feet of tunnel was risky. The deciding factor was that all the forged papers had been dated and redoing them would take days.

Exiting the tunnel was agonizingly slow. The exit point was collapsing, men with bulky costumes got stuck in the tunnel, there was a power outage due to a blackout—it took over an hour for the first twenty men to make it out. Anxious men waited. Once the line was moving, things went according to plan—until the eighty-first escapee exited the hole and came face to face with a German guard. Sirens blared, there was gunfire, and those still in that compound scrambled to burn papers and destroy equipment and other evidence.

The Americans were fortunate not to have made it out. Within days most of the escapees were recaptured. Upon learning the details of the breakout, Hitler, in a fit of fury, had fifty of the survivors summarily shot. Their remains were cremated and their ashes returned to us in urns. Of the eighty who made it out of the tunnel, only three made it back to England.
[Details of the escape plan are found in the book *Clipped Wings,* by R. W. Kimball, and the movie *The Great Escape* was based on the Allied exploits at Stalag Luft III.]

* * *

Under the terms of the Geneva Convention, a country that took prisoners was required to pay those prisoners an amount equivalent to what a person of equal rank in their military service would receive. In my initial interview with the commander's staff I was asked if I would put that money in a pool for the benefit of the whole group. Of course I agreed; I never expected to see the money anyway. Shortly after my arrival at Stalag Luft III we "purchased" materials from this fund, and under the watchful eyes of our captors, we built a four-hundred-seat theater. This building had a stage and individual seating, complete with arm rests, made from the boxes our Red Cross packages came in.

In this auditorium we put on shows. We did one-act plays and full-scale theatrical productions, some of them original. As in Shakespeare's time, men played female roles. I was the costume designer. When the show was decided upon, the director would tell me what costumes would be needed. I would design them, and the Germans would send to a Berlin costume house for them. We had an enormous pool of talent upon which to draw. We had three or four men who had played in big-name bands, and by listening to the few phonograph records we had, they would duplicate the arrangements of the music. The YMCA sent in a few band instruments, and we had a band known as the "Luftbandsters," a takeoff on what the Germans called us— the Luft Gangsters.

On the opening night of the shows the German officers would attend, dressed in their formal uniforms. They loved our plays, as it was the only cultural diversion they had. The Germans thought that doing these plays would keep us out of trouble. Little did they know that all that time crews were digging in the escape tunnels.

There was a nondenominational church service held in the compound most Sundays. "Padre" McDonald, a Scotsman who had been a paratrooper and had studied for the priesthood, was a mighty preacher. I enjoyed hearing him as he spoke in our theater. He was wonderful, and he really drew a crowd. Some of the other denominations also held services.

I found it interesting that when the Catholics met, they had to wait until the Germans would bring in a priest. I gained an appreciation for the wisdom of the Lord in organizing the priesthood as He has done in our church. We did not depend upon the Germans for the privilege of worshiping.

On 7 November 1943, with permission of Max Zimmer, president of the Swiss Mission, a branch of The Church of Jesus Christ of Latter-day Saints was organized inside Stalag Luft III. We found thirteen LDS POWs, and all of us were present that day. The branch leaders gained permission to announce our meetings at daily roll call. Bill McKell was our presiding elder. I was called to keep a record of our branch.

For a time it was agreed that we would partake of the sacrament only once a month. Initially our lessons were taken from the Book of Mormon. Before leaving the States I was ordained an elder, but it had been some time since we'd had contact with the Church.

The Germans allowed our families to send a limited number of books to us, and over time we amassed a very respectable library. We even had a "singing director" who taught us the hymns. Our meetings were open to all, and sometimes we had as many as nine non-member visitors.

We met in our theater where there was a blackboard. In the winter, heating the hall was a problem. We solved this dilemma by digging the stumps left by the Germans when they cleared the forest when they constructed the camp. We had to dig them out with teaspoons and tin cans, then use a long

"OUTSIDE THE WIRE" WITH BOOKS

Boredom was a great problem at Stalag Luft III. Reading was one way to "escape." In the back of his log, Hal lists over two hundred books he read while there.

pole as a lever to get them out to a point where the taproot could be cut with an ax. The Germans brought in the ax, stood over us with a machine gun while the cut was made, then took the ax away.

Meeting with members of the Church was a great blessing to me. I came to know that even in prison the Lord cares for us. Many times He sent His Spirit to comfort and help me. I gained my testimony in the midst of affliction.

"Woody" was a member of the Tuskegee Airman, an all black fighter pilot group. Woody was a very talented and congenial man. He was assigned to a block where there were a lot of Southerners. The long standing prejudices against blacks in the South was still very strong, and Woody was having almost as much trouble with his fellow prisoners as he was with the Nazis. He was moved to our block, where for a time I watched him as he dealt with a difficult situation. As one of his roommates told me, "I can't overcome a lifetime of training in just a few weeks."

One day a new "kriegie," [prisoner] a Jewish boy from New York was assigned to our room. It was plain to see that Woody was miserable, so I proposed to our group that we bring Woody into our room and asked our Jewish friend if he would mind changing places with Woody. Since several of the other men in the room where Woody was were from New York, the new kriegie readily agreed. About Christmas time, 1944, I approached Woody and asked if he would be willing to change places with our new man, so this new POW could be with his fellow New Yorkers. Woody agreed and the change was made. In view of the criticism that the Church received from many for our perceived prejudice against blacks, I have thought how interesting it is that when many disdained him, two Mormon boys from Utah befriended a black man inside a German prisoner of war camp.

By mid-January 1945 we could hear the sounds of battle as the Russians approached from the east. On 27 January we were given two hours time to prepare to move. I gathered a few things, including my log book, into a backpack I had made for myself out of an old pair of pants and a towel. I had put so much effort into my log book that I felt it would be the last thing I would throw away. After an hour of standing outside the compound in a what was later reported to us as being the worst blizzard in that area in twenty-five years, we set off on a four-day and four-night forced march. Dee, my Mormon friend, Woody, and I set off together.

I had an old blue British RAF long coat, but our clothing was totally inadequate for such miserable conditions. We were marched day and night with only occasional rest stops, none of more than a couple of hours. The straps on my back pack dug into my shoulders making them ache. Frostbite and blisters were also problems. There was no relief from any quarter.

We were near exhaustion when we noticed that Woody was not with us. Thinking perhaps that Woody had moved up in the line, Dee and I trudged ahead, but could not find him. We then worked back down the line, asking the men if they had seen Woody. Someone said they had seen him go off into the forest, saying that he had to get some sleep. We were lucky and found him with his back against a tree, sound asleep. In the ten degree temperature and with the windchill, it would not have been long before he would have died. We got him up, and with his arms around our shoulders we half-carried, half-dragged him along. I did not know until years later that he knew that we had saved his life. It didn't seem a big deal to us; he was our friend.

Only hours later we were moved into a large tile factory. It was heated. I spent the night alongside Woody on a pile of cardboard boxes. The Germans allowed us to rest for a couple of days. They could see that we were at our limit, and I suspect they were also weary of the march and cold.

We traded some of cigarettes to a couple of French prisoners who worked at the tile factory for a simple wooden sled they had made from shipping crates. We piled our belongings on it and took turns—one of us pulling, another pushing, while the other followed along and picked up the things that would fall off the sled. That made things easier.

As we continued on our way, a group of civilian refugees—men, women, and children—fleeing the menacing Russians joined our line. They had wagons pulled by horses. We held onto one of the wagons, which helped pull us along. They reminded me of our pioneers. After several miles this party turned another direction.

As we wallowed through the blizzard I noticed a German woman walking by my side. "Save us from the Russians," she whispered, then slipped something under my arm. It was a loaf of freshly baked black bread. While it was still warm I tore pieces from the loaf and handed them to those closest to me. What a treat it was, but we could do nothing about the Russians.

When we arrived at a railhead we were loaded into cattle cars. There was manure still on the floors. Designed to haul forty men or eight horses,

Hal Gunn's prison file from Stalag Luft III.

the Germans forced sixty or so of us into each car. We spent three miserable days squeezed together, without food or water. Sanitation, unspeakable to begin with, worsened every hour. In my cramped position my knees throbbed, but it was impossible to change positions. The muscles in my legs knotted. I was in terrific pain. I'm sure everyone else was too.

Eventually we reached Moosburg—about thirty kilometers north of Munich—Stalag VII-A. Conditions at Moosburg were beyond comprehension. This camp was built to hold 14,000 men, but eventually more than 100,000 of us were confined there. With the war going badly for them anyway, we overwhelmed the German's capacity and willingness to care for us. But they would not repatriate us.

We spent the last three months of our imprisonment at that camp. Sanitation was nonexistent. The putrid smells of our filth permeated the atmosphere. Our Red Cross packages, upon which we had depended for food, stopped coming. Hunger became so much a part of ours lives that most of our conversations were about food. We talked about our favorite restaurants, the best way to cook a steak, and conjured up recipes for use when we got home.

When Red Cross officials finally came to inspect the camp, they were appalled. Immediately returning to Geneva, Switzerland, they organized a fleet of trucks to bring supplies to us. The Germans allowed these vehicles through their lines. The backs of these were covered with large white canvasses, emblazoned with huge red crosses. We cheered when we saw those trucks pull into the village of Moosburg. "The Great White Fleet" we called them. On that day, for the first time in a very long time, we had food.

On Sunday, 29 April 1945, I wrote the following in my log: Beginning at 10:04:

The time we have all been waiting for has finally come. I am trying to record the events while sitting in rather cramped quarters in our barracks kitchen, the only place with brick walls. Bullets are flying. The chatter of machine gun fire and sporadic rifle reports, punctuated by the heavy explosions of large guns makes a fitting background for our long-awaited liberation. The "Goons" are making a last stand at our gates. Rumors are flying as thick as the bullets. Two men have been victims of stray bullets. The whole camp has been taken in by the rumors. . . . Tanks have been sighted on the hill close by and are believed to be ours. Many "Kriegies" are eating what we hope to be the last "Kriegie" meal behind barbed wires. A heavy explosion just brought down a spray of plaster from the ceiling and walls; [we] Air Force officers are receiving a lasting impression of a ground battle and are feeling very much out of place.

I am now crouched in the street where many "kriegies" have taken shelter. The steady hum of excited conversation reflects the pitch of the moment. We are all nervous, but our morale is very high. There is no sign of panic. Smiles are worn by all and in spite of the apparent danger, we all agree that it is a "good show." A direct hit in Moosburg, the nearest town, sent up a cloud of smoke.

I am now standing in the sunshine at the corner of our block. Many are now outside watching the show. Our camp guards have made us go into the slit trenches. Too many have been injured. Those in the tents are very vulnerable to flying bullets.

The "Goons" are firing from a visible church steeple in Moosburg, a good reason for the damaged buildings, though the diatribe that we read so much about in German propaganda painted a far different picture. We Kriegies have been under the German heel too long to be fooled by their propaganda or feel much sympathy for them at this time. . . .

Until additional excitement arises I will close this erratic account and enjoy the show. . . .

The American flag went up over Moosburg at 12:15 and our camp boasted the same at 13:05—a truly wonderful sight!! At 1:45 two Jeeps and a tank rolled into camp, barely recognizable because of the men clustered upon them. They received a deafening ovation. This account was begun by POW 1613, but is being finished by Lt. Harold W. Gunn, U.S.A.A.F

Following his release, Hal returned to his wife and daughter in Salt Lake City. Five years later he moved his family to Laconia, New Hampshire, where their home became the site of the first meeting of what eventually became the Laconia Ward.

Hal managed a paint and decorating store and was very active in community affairs. He was instrumental in bringing many people into the Church. Hal also served in many positions in their branch, including branch and district president. He and Geraldine headed the MIA in the New England Mission, a responsibility that took them to Maine, New Hampshire, Vermont, and the Maritime Provinces of Canada. He was later called to serve as a counselor in the New Hampshire stake presidency.

After twenty-five years in New Hampshire, he and Geraldine returned to Salt Lake City, where he was called as bishop of his ward in the Millcreek Stake. In 1978, Hal and Geraldine served a mission to Independence, Missouri, where Hal was director of the Visitors Center. They currently reside in Highland, Utah.

Taken from records of Harold and Geraldine Gunn, an oral interview with Paul H. Kelly, and an article by Sheri L Dew for *This People* magazine, Winter 1980.

BLAIR HALE

And we will prove them herewith.

(Abraham 3:25)

A few months after I graduated from the University of Wyoming at Laramie, the Japanese bombed Pearl Harbor, and we were at war. As part of my college curriculum I trained as a pilot and went into cadet training at Hemet, California. I did not qualify as an Army pilot, but did earn a commission as a second lieutenant, and became a bombardier on a B-17 Flying Fortress.

In early December 1942, I was assigned to the 410th Bomb Squadron, 94th Bomb Group (Heavy) for combat crew training at Tucson, Arizona; Pueblo, Colorado; then at Salina (Smokey Hill Air Field), Kansas.

Salina, Kansas, was an overseas processing center. While there the combat crews of our group were delivered new B-17s, and we prepared for the long overseas flight that would take us to join the 8th Air Force in England.

In early May 1943, we began combat flight operations over Germany, and after a couple of weeks, I was selected to receive training at the top-secret British MI-9 intelligence school. The British were very good at this and had been successful in getting large numbers of their military forces out of occupied Europe. The 8th Air Force commander was so impressed with their work that he selected a few U.S. officers for training by the British. No one, except another trainee, knew who we were. Under the so-called "rules of war," operatives caught behind enemy lines and identified as such could be treated as spies and executed.

Because of this training I knew ways to send information through intelligence channels, to make reports on POW camps, and if successful in escape or evasion to pass through the French underground system back to England. I suppose the author of the James Bond stories knew something of this operation.

This super-secret unit was responsible to oversee escape and evasion efforts. It was so covert that the United States Congress and most of the military leadership knew nothing of it. It was named MIS-X, and its headquarters was set up at Camp Hunt, Virginia.

On Sunday, 13 June 1943, all available crews were called out at 0330 to prepare for a high-altitude daylight raid. This was our eighth mission. Our target was the submarine construction facility at Kiel, Germany. With seventy-six B-17s, and an additional 152 heavy bombers, this was a maximum effort by the 8th Air Force. Prior to this date, other strikes on these critical targets had not been very successful. The submarine facilities had been made a priority target because Nazi subs were sinking an alarming tonnage of Allied shipping. Even though it was probable that heavy enemy fighter opposition would be encountered, there were no friendly fighter forces to accompany us.

The German's intelligence system was exceptional. They somehow knew where we were headed before we arrived. About 200 German fighters challenged the formation heading for Kiel. They began their attacks before our main bomber force reached the Danish peninsula. Their force included the yellow-nosed planes of "Goering's Circus," the Luftwaffe's finest. We had seen some of them before, but not in such numbers. We were entering what to this time was the fiercest battle of the air war over Germany.

The viciousness of the attacks resulted in great damage to both sides. From our group of seventy-six bombers, twenty-six were lost; eight from our own 94th Bomb Group. Our crew was flying a substitute aircraft named "Old Tobe." Our two most experienced airmen had been killed when they had flown with another crew a few days before.

"Old Tobe" was hit by flak before we arrived over the target. Within moments we were losing altitude and airspeed. We were also on fire. German fighters came at us from many directions to take advantage of our crippled aircraft. In the nose, the navigator and I were busy firing the three .50-caliber machine guns. Enemy fighters lined up in front and above us and took turns attacking us from every direction. They riddled us with cannon and machine gun fire and silenced our defensive fire.

With the plane's erratic flight and the fact that we had heard nothing from the pilots or other crew members for some time, I signaled the navigator that we should bail out. We buckled on our chest parachutes. As I put mine on I noticed some white silk showing from the pack. By now the plane was out of control, and the navigator seemed unable to open the escape hatch. I pulled him away and unlocked the hatch. As it opened, the strong winds coming through the broken plexiglass nose began to pull the silk out of my parachute and I exited the plane with some of the silk in my arms. I don't recall any feelings of fear or panic.

Relief flooded me as I floated clear of the plane, and I was aware of smoke and fire from the bomb bay. I caught a glimpse of another parachute in the air a few hundred feet above me but could not determine who it was. There was an explosion and what I thought was the wing, with jagged metal edges, floated close by in the air. Then it was deathly quiet until I hit the cold, icy water of the Baltic Sea.

Upon hitting the water, I inflated my "Mae West" life jacket and leaned back to take stock of things. My parachute hung in the air, held by a stiff surface breeze. Instead of releasing the chute I clutched the shroud lines as the wind billowed the canopy and pulled me through the water. Never a very good swimmer I knew I could not withstand the icy temperature for long. In the frigid water I could feel my strength ebbing.

I began to pray. I called upon my Father in Heaven, quietly at first, then aloud. Shortly I saw the top of a ship's smokestack. It drew closer, and I saw a big, black swastika on the funnel. By this time I didn't care whose ship it was, I knew to I had to get out of the water.

As they came alongside me, one of the crew threw me a line and pulled me aboard. Shaking and in pain I could not stand without assistance. They promptly took away my .45-caliber pistol and a cloth sack, containing an escape kit, fastened to my waist, as well as my parachute, Mae West, and wet clothes. I was given dry clothes, a pair of badly worn, oversized shoes, then wrapped in a warm blanket and handed a warm drink. Though they treated me civilly and were friendly, I was not anxious to tell them about me. With my limited German I explained there was someone else in the water. The ship's captain made two big circles, but not finding anyone, resumed course.

Warm, dry, and near exhaustion, I fell asleep. I awakened as we passed between Fehmarn Island and the German mainland, so I was sure of our location when I later saw it on a map in the captain's compartment. The ship's port was Trauvemunde.

My clothes were returned and from the room where I was being held, I could see the contents of my escape kit and pistol laid out on the captain's desk. As the ship's crew was busy getting ready to tie up, I seemed to have been forgotten.

Slipping into the captain's office, I began to tuck the contents of the kit into my clothing. Glancing up, I saw a man in the doorway looking at me. Smiling, I beckoned to him, unpinned the silver wings from my shirt, and handed them to him. Then in the best German I could muster, I said, "*Fur sie kindern.*" [For your children.] "Danke," he replied politely and hurried off.

I left the pistol, ammunition, and a few other things on the desk. I then tucked the French money, a large map of Europe, printed on a silk scarf, a compass, hack-saw blade, and water purification tablets into my flightsuit. The escape kit included high-energy tablets, some morphine and medicine, and bandages, all of which I left.

Two uniformed guards came to take me to a small airbase where I was locked up for the night. The small room was clean and contained a comfortable cot with blankets.

Early the next morning I showed a housemaid, cleaning the hallway near my room, the seat of my wool pants. They were ripped and badly in need of repair. I asked to borrow a needle, thread, and scissors. She brought me a sewing kit, and I hid the contents of my escape kit in my clothing. The hack-saw blade I put behind the zipper of my leather jacket. I undid the lining of the jacket and attached the silk scarf map. A compass, about the size of a quarter, I secured behind the button on the front of my wool pants. I knew the items might be found if I was searched. Shortly after being shot down I sent a message describing the location of ships in the harbor at Trauvemunde

The paper money was soaking wet, so I laid it out on a ledge next to an open barred window. Then I dozed off. In a short time there was a commotion down the hallway. A guard unlocked my cell door and flung it open with such force that it created a breeze on the window ledge above my bed and some of the dried paper money floated down onto the bed. The guard stood rigidly, awaiting the arrival of an officer. Covering the money with a blanket, I stood to greet my visitor. He was a young, smartly dressed medical officer who spoke English well. He bathed and patched up a wound on the back of my head.

Later another visitor came to obtain information about my capture. I gave him only my name, rank, and serial number. Our conversation was civil, but short. While he did not search me, he did want to know about the escape kit and the missing items. I said that I last saw the pistol, ammunition, medicine, and other items on the captain's desk. Perhaps, I suggested, others on the ship had taken what they wanted. He left, and I quickly stuffed the dried-out money into my flight suit.

After the third night, an enlisted soldier with a rifle, accompanied by a young Luftwuffe officer came to take me prisoner. We boarded a passenger train. The entry and exit doors to our compàrtment were locked, but we had access to a lavatory. The clacking of the wheels on the rails was monotonous. I noticed that some times the enlisted guard and the officer were not very alert. There was little or no conversation. The officer was engrossed in a book he was reading, and the guard dozed off now and then.

When I used the lavatory, I noticed a window from which I might escape. The prospect of escape would not leave my mind, and as the miles slipped by I realized that the farther we went into Germany the more difficult it would become to find a way into a friendly country. The intelligence briefings on base, and the escape and evasion instruction I had received, added a sense of urgency. Thinking back, it was probably ill conceived. While I had French money and there were active underground resistance groups from which I might receive assistance, making contact was probably impossible in Northern Germany.

The sun was setting as the train slowed to make a short stop at Luneburg. When the train moved on, I asked permission to go to the lavatory. I shattered the window and swung out into the gathering darkness. Falling to the hard ground of the embankment, I slid into a low fence, almost somersaulting over it, then ran into tall, wet, marsh grass as my guards fired their guns after me. I ran a distance from the railroad track, then rested to think what to do next.

To look less conspicuous, I turned my flight coveralls and leather jacket inside out. I found myself at the edge of town. Turning a corner I came onto a street just across from a beautiful cathedral. Down the center of the street came marching soldiers, counting cadence and singing out in unison as they responded to the commands of their leader. I moved into the shadows, remaining motionless while the troops marched past. Years later I learned that it was in this old Luneberg cathedral, the young Johann Sebastian Bach sang in the choir.

Relieved that the marching troops had not seen me, I moved in the direction I thought would lead me away from the town. At length I came to a wooded area, where I might hide. Then I heard the noise of aircraft engines and suddenly the forest was ablaze with searchlights and anti-aircraft guns firing at British airplanes on a night bombing mission. I hid among some trees and brush, hoping a low-flying friendly aircraft would spot me.

When the excitement subsided I began to hurt. A groin injury made walking painful and the German shoes I had been given on the ship had nearly fallen apart in the rain. The cuts and bruises I had suffered on bailout and escaping from the moving train added to my misery. The harder I tried, the more discouraged I became.

Foraging for something to eat, I looked in barnyards and fields, but without success. I was afraid to approach homes. I reasoned that German civilians would have little sympathy for a downed enemy flyer. It was still springtime and I found some gardens, but there was nothing ready for harvest. I remembered the comfort of the train, and in my confused state didn't know whether to go north to the Baltic Sea ports, or south. The persistent rain made walking exhausting. My leather flight jacket was so soaked it did not shed the rain. I had some matches in a waterproof case, but there was no obscure place to start a fire or source of dry fuel. It was slow going.

Trudging along a small country village road just at daylight, I came to a building with boarded-up windows, which appeared to be abandoned. Through a small, broken gate into a fenced yard I followed the path to a shed. I collapsed onto the floor. Not long afterward I was awakened by a woman who screamed and ran away. I tried to get up but was so sore and tired that I slumped back to the floor and muttered, "Oh, what the hell."

The woman returned with several people, who all tried to converse with me in different languages. Finally someone said in English, "Who are you and where are you going?" I responded, "I'm trying to make my way to the village train station and stopped here to get out of the rain." I noticed that no one had a gun, so I tried to break and run, but it was futile.

About a quarter of a mile down the road was a small village where a civil guard took charge of me. It was a long ride back to the town square of Luneberg. Two young, well-armed officials, talkative and polite, were pleased to take me back into custody. One said in quite good English, "Good try, buddy."

I was jailed, where I was interrogated and given something to eat and my clothes were dried. I was given another pair of old shoes, barely an improvement over the previous pair, which had ruined my feet. When my clothes were given back, the French money was conspicuously missing.

I decided I had better explain who I was. We had been briefed that treatment of a political or civil prisoner was more inhumane than that of a prisoner of war. I described my rescue from the Baltic Sea, my escape from the train, trying to travel the German countryside, and my recapture. Two days later I was returned to military custody.

Two members of the Luftwaffe came for me. I was handcuffed with a special cuff that consisted of flexible chains, with a "T" handle attached. The guard would hold onto the "T" handle, which, when he pulled, would cinch down around my wrists and cut into my skin. Very quickly I became a model prisoner. It was an uncomfortable ride south and west into the interior of Germany and I was never again allowed to go to the lavatory alone.

At Dulag Luft, a central facility for identification and interrogation of Allied air crews near Frankfurt, they took my clothing, leaving me naked. Soon I was shivering and annoyed that all this was taking so long. Finally my clothing was returned to me, and they took me to a small cubicle. I had identified myself as an American flyer whose plane was shot down in the Baltic Sea near Kiel. My interrogation was light compared to others.

All POWs met with members of the Red Cross who examined our wounds and gave us clean bandages and antiseptic. They took down information to be used to notify relatives of our situation. Some weeks later, a notice about my capture appeared in my hometown newspaper, the *Star Valley [Wyoming] Independent.* My family and friends were joyful when they received the news.

I was then sent to Stalag Luft III, near Sagan, Germany (now Poland), which was my home until late January 1945, when we were moved to Moosburg, in southern Germany.

After a few months in camp I learned the names of three kriegies [prisoners] who, because of their home towns and personal behavior, I felt were LDS. I learned that they were in fact members of the Church. We discussed organizing a branch and began a search for other members.

When we talked about having the sacrament I worried about the proper sacramental blessing. Some of the other men had better memories than I, so that problem was resoved. Bread was very scarce, but we saved small scraps of black German bread and pieces of hard Canadian biscuits to use for that sacred purpose. Although we did not then have the LDS scriptures, there were a few Bibles available.

* * *

From its headquarters in the United States, MIS-X sent in products and information to POWs in special packages. For example, maps, compasses, money, radio and camera parts, were secreted in the wooden handles of shaving brushes, shoe brushes, ping pong paddles and checker or chess boards. Some came inside the wrapped core of softballs, or within the laminated layers of playing cards. I came home from the war with a package of Raleigh brand cigarettes. In the lower half of the package was a set of finely detailed tissue-paper maps.

In advance of shipments of parcels, MIS-X would send in a message describing "hot" packages, and to whom they would be addressed. The message would also include instructions about how certain items were obscured, such as "search all wooden handles." Those receiving these

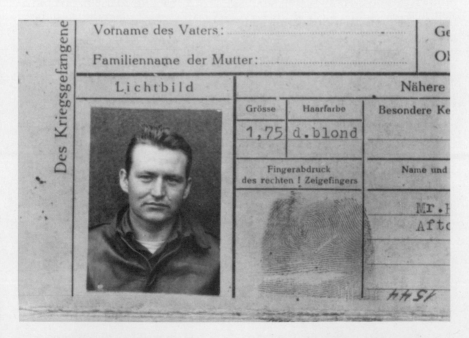

Stalag Luft III prisoner of war identification. Blair Hale, June 1943.

packages knew nothing about their contents, but because of my training, I collected these parcels and recovered the materials.

I have copies of a few of the letters I sent that contained a coded message. I wrote one to my girl friend Ellie, who later became my wife. It contains some peculiar wording that we now discuss with a bit of humor.

One of my first roommates was Lieutenant Anthony Alaimo. Tony was the pilot of one of ten B-26 medium bombers shot down on their first bombing mission over occupied Holland, in May 1943. From New York, he was the son of an Italian immigrant family and spoke Italian fluently. A very likeable, good-natured guy, he became my friend and best buddy.

Tony and I worked out an escape plan, which gained the approval of the escape committee. This plan involved the use of the compass and the silk scarf map, all of which had remained hidden in my clothing, undetected despite several searches by the Germans. We became tunnel-digging companions. For many days we were partners, working on the face of a tunnel that had been started by the British under an abort (a large outside privy). This was the closest building to the perimeter fence facing the forest.

One day when the tunnel was nearing completion, the Germans brought in a horse-drawn, iron-wheeled "honey wagon" to use in pumping out the privy. It was after dark when this chore was completed, and as the wagon was leaving, one of the wheels sank into our tunnel. This caused the guard dogs to fuss. That tunnel, like many others, was found before anyone could escape into the nearby woods. Much to our disappointment, Tony and I had to abandon our plan.

Months later Tony escaped from the Moosburg camp in southeast Germany. With the aid of my silk scarf map and his fluency in Italian, he succeeded in getting into the Italian-speaking area of Switzerland.

[Years later, I learned that Tony had attended law school at the University of Georgia. After a long and distinguished career as an attorney, he was appointed a federal district judge in the State of Georgia. He had that silk map mounted, and it hung in his chambers in Brunswick.

In 1998, when Tony learned that my grandson, David Hancey, was serving a mission in Georgia, he contacted David and his companion. They enjoyed an evening together. Tony treated them to dinner and accepted a copy of the Book of Mormon.]

* * *

In January 1945, units of the Soviet Army were advancing into

This is a composite of Blair's World War II mementos. At top is a German- censored letter sent to Blair's fiancé, containing a coded message from MIS-X. Below, left, is Blair's POW dog tag. The minature flag was smuggled into Stalag Luft III inside a Christmas present. Blair kept it hidden inside the red diary so it would not be confiscated by the Germans. The background is a collection of rice paper maps shipped into POW camps in cigarette packages, like this package of Raleighs. They were meant to help POWs escape and evade German guards.

German Silesia from Poland. On 29 January, the German High Command issued an order to evacuate Stalag Luft III to keep us from falling into the hands of the Russians. Reports were that Hitler wanted to retain the British and Americans to use as hostages.

In a frenzy of activity we began to march into a raging winter storm in snow already several inches deep and still falling. The line stretched for many miles and in the bitter weather, some of our men froze to death. Occasionally we were passed by German soldiers, boys really, moving east in a last-ditch effort to counter the Russian offensive. The march covered about sixty miles. We were allowed only brief rest periods. After about twenty-seven hours we were given a sixteen-hour rest in a large and warm tile factory. It was at this point that I became very ill. I ran a temperature and slept so deeply that I could hardly be awakened. My roommate, Jack Bennett, made a sled and was ready to put me on it when the march continued. Fortunately the weather moderated and I recovered enough to walk.

We reached the railroad junction, where we were crowded sixty, or more, into each boxcar that had recently been used to carry livestock. The train ride was even more appalling than the march. On top of this, we also had to sweat out bombing and strafing by our own aircraft.

Conditions at Moosburg were horrific. Five hundred men were crowded into barracks designed to house only two hundred. The camp itself had been expanded far beyond its capacity. The "honey wagon" could not keep up with the demands, and rats, lice, and bedbugs were epidemic. There was no fuel for heat and only a little scrap wood for cooking.

We continued to record events with a clandestine camera that had been smuggled into the camp. At Stalag Luft III it had been used to make

Cooking German rations on home-made burners at Moosburg Prison, April 1945. Left, Dee Butler, 2nd Lt. of Ogden, UT. Right, Blair Hale, 2nd Lt.

fake passport pictures, and on the winter march to photograph some remarkable scenes. That camera had been kept hidden in the wall of the room I shared with Jack Bennett. The most famous pictures were those Jack took of the arrival of the leading tank when General Patton's 14th Armored Division liberated us near noon on 29 April 1945.

One friend who described what he saw when the Swastika came down and the Stars and Stripes took its place exclaimed: "It was the first time I ever saw 10,000 men all cry." And I was one of them. It had been six hundred eighty-six days since I made my plunge into the icy Baltic Sea. When General Patton arrived with his ivory-handled pistols belted to his waist, we cheered and shouted for joy.

A few days later we marched several miles to a large grassy field where we boarded C-47 transports and were flown to a United States tent camp facility called Camp Lucky Strike, near Le Havre, France. Here we were deloused, took hot showers, got clean clothes, and were given all the food we could eat. We were treated with the greatest respect.

What did I learn from my experience? That is a question many have asked me, and I have asked myself. I like the summary that our remarkable chaplain, *Padre* MacDonald gave: "However absurd it may sound, I actually enjoyed my POW experience." With the most humiliating events forgotten or pushed far into the background, I feel the same way. This experience made me a better person. It taught me how to deal with adversities and disappointments, how to overcome or live with boredom, and how to make the most of what I have been given. It taught me to be accepting and tolerant of other points of view. In a word, I learned patience!

Blair Hale was the sole survivor of his ten-man B-17 crew from the Kiel bombing mission of 13 June 1943. Most of his crew were never found. Blair remained in the United States Air Force after World War II and retired as a lieutenant colonel after twenty-three years of active service.

Returning from Germany he became a personnel officer at Hill Air Force Base, Utah, then went to the Pentagon in Washington D.C. in a General Staff Special Intelligence assignment. Following this he returned to active flying as a combat operation staff officer, specializing in radar, navigation, and bombing, in multi-engine jet aircraft. Successive staff assignments followed, in Intelligence, to Korea and Japan; then back to Hill AFB, as a procurement officer. He finished his career as commander of Air Force ROTC at Utah State University.

After retiring from the military in 1965, Blair served for seventeen years as director of placement and student career counseling at Utah State University. He retired from USU in 1982. Blair served six years as bishop of a married-student ward during the 1970s. He and Ellie served a proselyting mission in Florida in 1983. For six years following their mission, he was director of the twenty-three-stake Family History Center located in the Logan Tabernacle. He and Ellie live in Logan, Utah. They are parents of three children, have twenty grandchildren, and as of May 2001, two great-grandchildren.

ETSEL E. SOMMER

And the walls of the prison were rent.

(Alma 14:27)

I turned eighteen in the January following the bombing of Pearl Harbor and signed up for the draft. By mid-November 1942, I had not been called up, so I joined the Army Air Corps.

I was trained as an engineer and as top turret gunner on the B-17 Flying Fortress. In March 1944, our crew was assigned to fly the first silver B-17G to England. We left Lincoln, Nebraska, and flew to Manchester, New Hampshire, and then out across the Atlantic, making landings at Goose Bay, Labrador; Reykjavik, Iceland; and Glasgow, Scotland. We were then flown to Thedford, England, where we were assigned to the 388th Bomb Group, 8th Air Force, and we settled into a routine of training.

One day I overheard a man say he had been studying for the Methodist ministry. He then began, talking about a group of strange people who lived in Utah and Idaho. He went on to say they have extra wives and don't believe the Bible. By this time the hair on the back of my head started to stand up. My friend John, suspecting where this discussion was leading and knowing I was a Mormon, asked, "And who are these strange people?"

"Oh, they're Mormons, but you'll never meet one in the service as they are conscientious objectors."

"Would you like to meet one?" John inquired. By this time I was on my feet, challenging this know-it-all, and in an instant we were fighting. Between blows I told my

Etsel E. Sommer

antagonist that all eighty of the young men in my high school graduating class were Mormons, and that all eighty of us had volunteered for military service. My Methodist associate finally commented, "Well, if they all fight like you, I'd like to have them around me." Eventually we shook hands. In those days I was a bit feisty. But that Methodist now knew that Mormons are not conscientious objectors.

I did not have any literature about the Church, except an Article of Faith card. John, the other waist gunner on our crew, was a Catholic. We became close friends. I had him read the Articles of Faith, after which he told me he didn't know much about religion. "But" he said, "if you have problems, I'll stand and take the abuse for you."

We flew our first two missions against targets in France and our third to northern Germany. On 9 April, Easter Sunday, we flew with approximately 1,100 other bombers to a target at Pozen, Poland. Our route was up the English Channel, across Denmark, over the North and Baltic Seas, to the mouth of the Oder River, where we turned south toward the target area. We were hit by ack-ack fire and lost our number two engine.

Forced to abandon the group, we turned west, overland. We made it as far as Rotterdam, Holland. There, ack-ack guns shot off ten feet of our left wing, and we had to bail out. Our tail gunner was shot and killed while coming down in his parachute. Seven others, including the pilot and co-pilot were immediately captured when they hit the ground or a roof top.

I landed about a rod from a Lutheran church in the village of Berkel en Rodenrijis. As I floated to the ground, a group of people watched our plane come down. They immediately surrounded me, and a man instructed me, in English, to remove all my clothing. As soon as I landed some women took my parachute, tore it to pieces, and stuffed the pieces into their blouses. In less than five minutes I was in civilian clothes. We walked past the searching German soldiers to a lumberyard where I was fed. I don't know how the soldiers couldn't see the fear in my face. After dark I was taken to a farmhouse where I was united with another member of our crew.

The Dutch people were very kind to John and me, and at great risk to themselves offered every kind of service and comfort. We were housed and fed by these good people for fifteen days. The Germans knew that two men from our downed plane were unaccounted for and put the pressure on the Dutch. Had we and our protectors been caught, there is no doubt that the Nazis would have killed them.

On the fifteenth day the two of us were taken to the Belgian border and told how to crawl through a pasture to reach the Belgian underground on the other side, where, hopefully, we could be smuggled back to England.

We did not see the German guard and his Doberman Pincer. I learned about the dog when, snaking our way through the grass and weeds, the Doberman put his cold nose on the back of my neck. Panic seized me and took my breath away. The guard seemed unconcerned. Maybe he thought we were a couple of kids out after curfew. It occurred to me to grab his rifle, club him with it, and flee. But, not knowing the lay of the land, confused as to the direction to take, and eyeballing the Doberman, I decided against it. In my mind, his having the dog gave him the upper hand. We became prisoners 25 April 1944, at 0115 in the morning.

The SS officer who interrogated us was a handsome man and spoke to us in three different languages, none of which John or I understood. Finally, in flawless English, he said "Do you understand English?" Because we were dressed in civilian clothes he did not know we were military. In my quivering boldness I asked him where he had mastered English. He answered that he had attended the University of Wisconsin, at Madison, and added:

"But we are here to talk about you." I held my dog tags out to him and said, "The only questions I'll answer is the information printed on these." Seeing my dog tags was the first he knew that I was in the U.S. military.

When processing for overseas duty, I insisted that my dog tags be stamped LDS, not Protestant. As the SS officer examined my tags, he asked what LDS meant. "That indicates my religion. I'm a member of The Church of Jesus Christ of Latter-day Saints." Although the interrogation went on for several hours, acting braver than I felt, I gave them only the information required by the Geneva Convention.

Finally our captors put us, along with two guards, on a train to Amsterdam, where John and I spent twenty-one days in solitary confinement, each day being asked if we were ready to talk. Our cell was five by eight feet, the ceiling about six and one-half feet high. There was a cot with a straw mattress, one blanket, and the only other facility was a five-gallon bucket that served as a toilet. We were given only a small loaf of dark brown bread and a glass of warm water each day.

We were grilled daily, but divulged only the information previously mentioned. We were asked how we got to Holland, when the invasion was to take place, and where and how many troops were in England. When the Nazis asked about when the invasion would come, I told them truthfully that I did not know, but I defiantly said when it did come, I hoped our bombs would drop near enough to kill them.

The Germans determined that we were the missing members of the aircrew that had been captured two weeks earlier. About mid-May we were taken from our cells and given a full meal. This nearly killed me. I had lost a lot of weight and my stomach recoiled at the food. We were sent by train to Krems, Austria, to a prisoner of war camp—Stalag XVII-B.

Life in a prison camp was a harsh and painful experience. We nearly starved. All 4,800 of us had some kind of lice, crabs, and other bugs to contend with. Sanitation was poor, and even though the camp was deloused two different times, it didn't help much, since the varmints were still in our beds and in the barracks. Sometimes we were allowed to split Red Cross packages, which gave us a great boost.

We bribed the guards with cigarettes from the Red Cross packages, to give us crystals, wire, and earphones with which we made crude radio receivers. With these we could receive broadcasts by the BBC. The guards

Etsel Sommer's POW photo at Stalag XVII-B.

told us that the U.S. was losing the fight. They would pull raids and take our radio sets, but by the next day we had built other sets, so we knew the progress of the war, despite the misinformation the guards were giving us.

About Thanksgiving 1944, an Air Force sergeant imprisoned with us, found all of the LDS POWs and invited us to a sacrament and testimony meeting. His name was Smith, and he had served a mission in Austria. Of the 4,800 prisoners in our Stalag, thirty of us were Mormons. It was a sweet experience to talk about home and bear our testimonies. It was my privilege to bless and partake of the sacrament. We met again at Christmastime and enjoyed a similar glorious experience. I made a commitment at that time to change my way of life.

Of the thirty LDS men in our compound, twenty-six were from Idaho. Four were from Rexburg, and we had gone to high school together.

I was at Stalag XVII-B about ten months. By April 1945, we knew the war was winding down. The Russians were shelling within two miles of our camp. To move us out of reach of the Russian advance, over a two-week period the Germans marched us up the Danube River, 500 men to a group, to a place in a forest near Hitler's birthplace. About a week later, on 3 May 1945, we were liberated by units of Patton's 3rd Army. This was a great day in my life—to feel *free* again! There our German guards had to give up their guns, and *they* became the POWs.

We were trucked to Regensburg, given physical exams, deloused, and issued new and *clean* clothing, then flown to Camp Lucky Strike at Le Havre, France. On 1 June I boarded the Liberty Ship, the *USS Porpoise*, bound for New Jersey, the United States of America.

As we steamed past the Statue of Liberty and saw the beautiful American flag, I got a lump in my throat and tears flowed down my cheeks.

Not wanting 2,800 former POWs to see me crying, I wiped my eyes with my handkerchief, then turned around and saw that everyone else was doing the same. After debriefing, I was sent home, where I arrived on 20 June 1945.

I do not wish to be perceived as a hero. I only did my job. Those who are buried over there are my heroes—they gave all they had, including their lives, so that we could live in freedom and have the good things of life. Truly, God has blessed America. May he always do so.

After the war, Etsell returned home and married Maxine Scheets. They are parents of five sons and two daughters, have twenty-three grandchildren and three great-grandchildren. He established himself as a masonry contractor. In the Church he was an advisor to Aaronic Priesthood quorums, served as a counselor in two bishoprics, as bishop, and a member of two high councils. He is now a temple ordinance worker.

ROYAL R. MESERVY

In the furnace God may prove thee, Thence to bring thee forth more bright, But can never cease to love thee; Thou art precious in his sight.

("Zion Stands with Hills Surrounded," *Hymns*, no. 43)

Stalag IX-B: I sat on my bunk stripped to the waist, methodically picking the fifty-seven varieties of lice from my shirt and body, squashing each between my fingernails, then dropping it to the floor. It is amazing how many colors lice come in. Until I became a prisoner of war I thought all lice were grayish-black, but they come in red, blue, white, yellow and gray. To complicate things they intermarried, and I found white lice with red spots, yellow spots, blue spots; yellow lice with green spots, black spots, and on and on. I hadn't known that lice could multiply so fast and be so plentiful. But then I had never lived in such filth.

Royal R. Meservy—In the corner of this photo sent home to family, Royal signed it "Same As Always."

One ten-inch hole in the floor served as a toilet for 300 men with weak kidneys and chronic diarrhea. The place stunk like a pig pen, despite the fact that every morning we washed the muck out with water and swept it down with willow brooms. It didn't help much that there was an outdoor latrine for daytime use, an open pit, eight-feet-wide, eight-feet-deep and thirty-feet-long. Its oppressive stench hung over the camp like a shroud.

The lice actually helped pass the time. They itched more than they bit and caused less suffering than the bedbugs, which caused running sores that festered in the sweat and dirt. Fleas were also bothersome, but the lice didn't hide in the daytime, and I could kill them. The twice-daily sessions gave me something to do other than think about home, and it took my mind off the boils under my arms and between my legs. Anything that helped keep a fellow alive and sane was valuable.

When I finished my morning delousing, I put my shirt back on and lay down to rest. I was fatigued. I closed my eyes and saw our farm back home. There were chickens, cows, pigs, and horses. I longed to ride "Old Frank" again. "Old Frank" was over-large for a riding horse, but he was fast. I thought how good it would be to once more race across the wheat stubble in the fall.

I had been at Stalag IX–B for a couple of months. The ability to daydream had become vital. I thought about Mother and Father. I saw them as more kind and sweet, more noble than ever before. There came into my heart the longing to be home. I told myself, *I've got to live, I want to go back home again! I can't be like Smith. Smith just gave up and died—like a horse that gets its back in a furrow, and can't roll over—he wouldn't eat. It would be so easy to die, and it is such a struggle to live. I want to live!*

I went over in my mind the events preceding my capture and how I came to be here. My unit was the 106th Division, known as the "Golden Lions." In early December 1944, we were camped in the bunkers of the Siegfried Line. Then the Germans attacked with astonishing force, and we were ordered to counterattack, to hold at all costs. On the night of 17 December, eight of us lay down in a circle with our knees in each others back to keep warm, and sleep, if we could. A light snow blew across us as we lay on the plowed, frozen ground. That day we had witnessed a 250-man company next to us take nearly 100 percent casualties. We spent most of that day rescuing their wounded.

Two days later nearly thirty of us were surrendered by a medical officer, a major. I probably would have fought to the death had I been in charge. But, strangely, I had a sense of peace come over me on being captured—I sensed that I would be all right.

The thirty of us were marched thirty-eight miles to a railhead. We received no food or water. Our route was littered with the bodies of Americans and other Allied soldiers, and even some Germans, all of which had been stripped of their shoes by hard-pressed civilians in the area. We were loaded onto boxcars, only six meters by two meters, sixty-five of us in each car.

On Christmas Eve some U.S. P-47s strafed our train. The engineer managed to put the train's engine under an overpass to keep the attacking plane from shooting holes in its steam jacket. A bomb fell next to us and blew open the car in front of us and loosened the sliding door on ours. Prisoners poured off the train and scattered into fields along the tracks.

I remained in the car with three others while the guards rounded up the escapees. A very large black man asked if anyone had a Bible. I did. He asked me to read about Jesus. I began in Matthew. In a moment he took the book from me, turned to the 2nd chapter of Luke and read the Christmas story with more fervor and feeling, in a voice more rich than I had ever before, or since, heard. Again a feeling of peace came into my soul. I knew the Lord knew where I was.

The night of 29 January I lay in bed, and concern for my parents, especially my mother, filled my mind. I held a conversation with our Father in Heaven just like I used to talk with my dad. Knowing that by now they would have received word that I was missing in action, I petitioned Him to let my mother know that I had been captured and was okay. A sweet feeling came over me as I was assured that she would know. I picked up my Book of Mormon and wrote the date of this experience in the back of the book.

Some weeks after returning to my home in Idaho, speaking at a sacrament meeting in the St. Anthony Third Ward, I recounted this experience. My mother had come to the meeting with me. On the way home she asked me what the date was that I had spoken of. I told her. She said that on 27 January they received a telegram from the War Department saying that I was missing in action. Father had read my patriarchal blessing and felt only mild concern. Mother had not been able to sleep. On the 29th she went to their bedroom. Locking the door, she lay on the bed, weeping and praying. There came to her the spiritual witness that I was a prisoner of war, that I was all right. She arose and marked the date on the calender. It matched the date in my Book of Mormon.

* * *

In the barracks one morning I rolled on to my side and as I raised myself onto an elbow, a sharp pain pierced my armpit. I had forgotten for a moment how sore that boil was. I took off my shirt to check. Under each arm I had a boil more than two inches across and a light translucent yellow color. The doctor had said that when they got to this condition they could be lanced. I arose carefully. A week before I had stood up too quickly and passed out; the bruise on my head was still tender.

A cold February wind chilled me to the bone. Walking was such a labor. I headed to the hospital barracks, where all the pneumonia patients lay dying. The only warm building in the whole camp was the hospital, and the heat felt good. I had to stand in line, but the doctors, both Americans, worked quickly.

Dr. Burton examined the boils, then said, "Well, these under your arms look ready. Step over here by the window and hold onto the window casing. What are you flinching for? I haven't started yet. How do you think I'm going to drain them if you don't hold still?" he said, not very tenderly.

"But doctor, couldn't you give me something to take the edge off the pain? Those boils are mighty sore."

"Where do you think you are, in the States? We're lucky to have a set of knives and water to boil them in. See that big black fellow there? He's got piles, bad, and I've got to cut them out and sew him up. I have nothing to give him, poor devil. We have no drugs or medicines but our little brown pill."

"You mean the pill you gave me for jaundice?"

"Yes, and for the flu, for diarrhea, for passing out, and for fever. You name it, that's the pill. It's the only thing the Germans have, or at least that they'll give us."

"What kind of pill is it? Aspirin or sulfa?"

"Ha! It's probably bread coated with brown sugar. But if the men think it helps, they're welcome to it. Now, get over here by the window, and hang on as tight as you can. If you want relief from that boil, grab the casing. I haven't got all day."

When finished lancing the boils under my arms, the doctor decided the boils on my legs weren't ready. After being told to come back in about a week, I slowly shuffled back toward my barracks. The sun had come through the clouds and that made me feel better. Down by the kitchen the men from barracks forty lined up for chow. Was that Wes in that line? Wes belonged to barracks 42A, but he kept slipping into others' chow lines. Twice the Germans had caught him and given him the honey bucket detail for a week at a time, but here he was back, trying for an extra meager helping. I didn't blame Wes. He was no different from the rest of us—stealing to help stay alive.

Back at the barracks I got my helmet, which served as my soup bowl. I lined up with the others. As we waited in line the guys discussed food. Even discussions about sex took a backseat to the talk of food. Today was my lucky day. Beside the usual liter of soup, I was given the skull of a horse. There was no meat on it, but my friends and I spent the afternoon grinding the bone to powder between rocks, and eating it. By dark, the only thing left of the skull were the teeth.

* * *

Every evening at dark the Germans locked and shuttered the windows and door. A couple of hours later the lights would go out and we would settle down for the night. One night the lights suddenly came back on, and German non-coms came in. "Rausch! Alle rausch!"

We were led outside and forced to stand in the cold while the Germans counted us. I was shivering, and numb all over. I could not tell how long we had been outside. Returning to the barracks, I took off my shoes and looked at my toes. They were white with cold, and there was no feeling in them. I rubbed them gently and blew on them, and they ached as they warmed.

Three times we were called out into the cold. Men too sick to walk were dragged out or forced out at bayonet point. Before third roll call was over, forty or fifty men had fallen to the ground. I prayed for strength. Somehow I made it. After a speech by the camp commander, we were allowed to return to our barracks. It was twenty minutes before noon. There was no feeling at all in my feet, and their whiteness concerned me. It looked to me that had I tried to manipulate my toes I could have broken one off and not felt it. I learned later that my feet were permanently damaged.

A few minutes after that last roll call, the Protestant chaplain came in. "May I have your attention, please," he called. "I've got the low-down. Last night two Americans were in the kitchen. The night watchman saw the light and opened the door to see what was going on. He was jumped and hit thirteen times with a hatchet. The two men escaped. Before he passed out, the guard made it to the kitchen window and called to the tower guard, 'Amerikans.' The Germans made a quick check and found your barracks and barracks number 23 had the bar removed from the door."

"How come they stood us out under the lights so long?" I asked.

"They were looking for blood. They figure that the man or men who used the ax got some blood on themselves. They're plenty mad."

"What did the Kraut commander say in his speech this morning?" Dick asked.

"He's issued an ultimatum: either we come up with the men who hacked up the guard or there will be no wood, lights, water, or food. He said this will continue until they're found. The guard died in the night."

"We don't get enough wood to even warm this place, and we can do without the lights." observed Kitty.

"That's true," replied the chaplain, "but we can't survive without food or water. We're not getting half enough to eat as it is. We can't afford to go without the little food we get. It'd only weaken us more. But suit yourselves." The chaplain turned and left.

We had a bitter discussion about what to do. Some wanted to turn these two Americans in. Others couldn't imagine such a thing. Finally, we decided to at least search for signs that those two men were from our barracks.

Dick Purl chose Kitty and Charles to help him search. In the seventh bunk they found a pair of bloody overshoes and under it a bloody shirt.

"Okay, Smitty, front and center," Dick demanded. "Tell us about these."

Smitty began to sputter. "I . . . well . . . okay, I did it. But I did it to get bread."

"We can't blame you for that, but you didn't have to kill him."

"I was scared. Besides, what difference does it make? He was just a dirty Kraut!"

"But he was a human being." I said.

"Who helped you, Smitty?" Kitty asked.

"Fred. We were so scared we just didn't think."

"Damn you, Smitty! We promised we wouldn't tell on each other if one of us got caught."

"Sorry, Fred," Smitty replied, "but I'm not taking the rap alone."

"Rap," Fred sneered. "They're not going to turn us in. He was just another stinking Kraut, and not the first one I've killed."

Again a bitter debate ensued. "Okay, guys," Dick called out, "let's have the vote. Raise your hand if you want to turn Smitty and Fred in." Lots of hands went up. "All right, now how many don't want to turn them in?" Only a few hands.

"But," Smitty pleaded, "I only did it 'cause I was hungry."

"Turn us in just because we killed a dirty Kraut! Who started this war?" Fred exploded.

The scene of Nephi holding Laban's sword flashed through my mind. The question seemed the same to me—should these men perish for their deeds, or would all of us?

"All you say is true," I spoke softly, "but if we don't turn you in, they'll come searching and find you anyway. It'll go easier on all of us if we turn you in."

"Can't we just hide the bloody clothes?" pleaded Smitty.

"Where?" Kitty wanted to know. "We can't go outside. The place is crawling with mad Germans."

"We could put them down the latrine."

"They'd only find them when they cleaned the hole out with the honey bucket."

"I'm hungry—in fact, I'm downright starved." It was Charlie. "Let's turn 'em in so we can eat."

"You dirty _____! You've got a yellow streak down your back a mile wide! Scared of a Kraut!" screamed Fred.

"Let's be reasonable. We can't afford to be emotional about this," I declared. "If we don't turn you in, we can't eat, and more of us will die. Just last month three GI's starved to death. We've got to eat."

The bewilderment in the room was absolute. These two men were our buddies. We had been through battles together, and there is a love that grows there, and they would be executed if identified! But they had put the sword at our throats.

Dick stepped outside and returned with the German corporal.

"Sorry, Smitty," Kitty said, "I hate to see you hafta go."

"It's too bad it had to happen," I said quietly. "but. . ." my voice trailed away, stifled by emotion. I thought how hard this was. "It's just too bad you killed him."

The corporal escorted them out. As Fred left he turned, and with a look of hatred in his eyes cursed us roundly.

The Germans shot them.

* * *

The quantity of food we were getting was inadequate to sustain life. I lost a lot of weight and was continually hungry. In the night I prayed for help and promised the Lord that if I could live to have a family, that I would always do what he or his servants asked of me.

I felt a prompting to get out of bed and go outside. To my surprise, the door opened to my touch—somehow the bar was off. I walked to the kitchen. On the ground near the door was a pile of about twenty-five potatoes, each about an inch and a half across. I picked them up, put them inside my shirt and returned to my bed. I rationed them, allowing myself one a day.

I discovered that there were sixteen other LDS men in Stalag IX-B. We began holding meetings and partaking of the sacrament. I acted as group leader. Mike, a fine Protestant man, and I alternately led the men in our barracks in songs and prayer each night.

One day I was approached by the chaplain. He said, "We need a choir. I understand that you can sing. Would you be the director?" I replied that I would be glad to. We had no music of any kind, and nothing to write music on. We had only the music that was in our collective memories. I became the a capella meister. Interestingly, there were a number of very qualified musicians in the camp. The Germans heard us singing and requested that we perform for them. After our first performance, a German officer told me to come by the kitchen every day, and if they had food left, I could have it.

Easter Sunday fell on 1 April in 1945. During our church services I was impressed that we were about to be liberated, but kept the thought to myself. I pondered on my experience as a prisoner of war and thought about the German people. I never hated them. This fight was over principle.

On 2 April we were liberated as tanks from one of Patton's Armored Divisions rolled through the gates of Stalag IX B. I could go *home!*

Royal Meservy returned to his home in Idaho and was shortly called to serve a mission to the Swiss-Austrian Mission. A year into his mission he was transferred to England. Following this mission he went back to Idaho where he met and married Sheila Rachel Koeven. From 1953 to 1955 he left Sheila and their three children to serve in the East German Mission. He received a bachelor of arts degree from Ricks College in 1956, a master's from Utah State, and in 1966, an Ed.D. at the University of California at Los Angeles. Before retiring, Royal had worked as a farmer, a teacher in elementary and secondary schools, and a college professor. He is now retired. He and Sheila are parents of seven children, have forty-six grandchildren, and eleven great-grandchildren.

He currently serves as patriarch in his stake. Besides his missions, Royal has served in numerous church callings, including branch and district president, counselor in the East German Mission presidency, high council, and stake clerk. He also holds the Silver Beaver award from the Boy Scouts of America.

From 1993 to 1995 Royal and Sheila served in the German Dusseldorf Mission. They are currently serving a Church Education System Mission. They reside in Whittier, California.

RALF T. WILSON

*Fear not, I am with thee; Oh, be not dismayed, For I am
thy God and will still give thee aid, I'll strengthen thee,
help thee, and cause thee to stand, Upheld by my righteous,
omnipotent hand.*

("How Firm a Foundation," *Hymns*, no. 85)

When I reported to Fort Lewis, Washington, in March 1941, I found the Infantry units using sticks instead of rifles—it seemed to me that we were ill-prepared for war. As I did not want to be in the infantry I transferred to the Army Air Corps with an assignment to an outfit at Salt Lake City. I liked the idea of being closer to home. I was for about a month, then our outfit was shipped to the island of Mindinao, in the Philippines.

In December, in a coordinated blow, the Japanese High Command struck simultaneously at Pearl Harbor, Clark Field, and Manila. When the Japanese attacked Clark Field, we were ill-prepared. Our unit had almost nothing with which we could defend ourselves. Crates of Enfield rifles, still packed in cosmoline since WWI, were opened, and the rifles were cleaned to make them useable. Ammunition was scarce. The few .45-caliber pistols available were also issued, and we began digging foxholes.

Just before Christmas a Japanese destroyer sailed into the bay at night and shelled the area. We saw the flashes and heard the explosions, but were not threatened. However, the docks at Bugo were destroyed and the pineapple cannery was blown up. We drank a lot of canned pineapple juice.

About the middle of March, three B-17s arrived at our base. General MacArthur and his wife and son had been brought from Corregidor to Bugo on Navy PT Boats. The B-17s came to take the General to Australia.

On 10 May our commanding officer called us together and informed us that he had received orders from General Wainwright to surrender the Island of Mindanao and all the soldiers on it. This was a surprise to us because just two days before we had been alerted to expect planes from Australia to evacuate all Americans on Mindinao, about a thousand men.

No evacuation was attempted. The major told us, "We've got two options. You can either go into prison camp with me, or you can take to the hills. But there are consequences if you go into the hills. If we don't turn in all the men on this island the Japanese will execute 750 men captured on Corregidor. They are being held hostage. Their lives depend on our surrender." What a terrible burden. To a man we agreed to the surrender.

Ralf T. Wilson

The next several hours were unnerving. The savage reputation of the Japanese military was well known to us. We knew of some of the atrocities they had committed in China and in other places they had overrun. I was paralyzed with fear. As our captors had not yet arrived, we began to burn papers that we did not want to fall into their hands. Anxiety stuck in my throat. I needed help beyond myself. Then I remembered my parents' teachings and determined to go off by myself and pray.

In the jungle I came upon an old quarry. It was a beautiful little place. I knelt and opened my heart to the Lord and pleaded for His help. After a time I heard a very clear and distinct voice say, "It's okay, Ralf, you're going to be all right." Immediately a sense of peace washed over me. The sun was shining down through the trees, the birds were singing, and I felt a quiet assurance. The memory of this experience stayed with me from that moment. Through the vicissitudes of the next three and a half years I never doubted that I would go home. I had the Lord's promise. By war's end, of all the American servicemen in The Philippines at the start of hostilities, only about 17 percent were alive. Having assurance from the Lord gave me hope and confidence that others did not know.

After we were taken captive, we were initially held at Camp Casisang. The Japanese immediately got our attention. One evening as we waited for our supper, they tied two Filipino soldiers to posts and nonchalantly shot them. Some of our men were taken away, and we did not see them again until the end of the war. Some we never saw again. I came to hate the Japanese for their barbarity. It took me a long time to overcome this hatred.

During the first three months our treatment was tolerable. The officer in charge had been educated in the United States, and he was somewhat considerate of us. When the war turned against the Japanese, care deteriorated and our rations were cut. Until the Battle of Midway we had radios and some athletic gear in camp. As things got bad for the Japanese, they took these away too. We underwent privation, we were beaten, we were marched, and we were put at forced labor. Not all, but many guards were brutal and took delight in pushing us around and beating us. Some of our men were arbitrarily executed for infractions of rules that seemed to be contrived.

According to the provisions of the Geneva Convention the use of prisoners-of-war as slave laborers is forbidden, but in 1942 our enemy was not paying any attention to those niceties. They had overrun the land and they had themselves and us to feed. We were forced to work in the fields. Planting rice is back-breaking work. Each individual plant has to be inserted into the mud while you stand up to your knees in muck, and leeches attach themselves to your skin.

As we worked in the rice paddies, our conversations inevitably turned to food. Some worked out new ways to cook rice and then others would chime in with a suggestion of something to add to the recipe. After I returned home I was asked if I could still eat rice. I replied that I never got enough of it to get sick of it. The other topic for discussion was how long would we remain prisoners. None of us guessed it would be three and a half years.

After six months at Camp Casisang we were transported to Davao, a city southeast of Mindinao and force-marched to the Davao Penal Colony, a former civilian prison, about twelve miles inland. Surrounded by dense jungle, it was self-supporting, with rice paddies and other fields where we grew camotes—a kind of sweet potato—various fruits, and coffee. Most of the harvest went to the Japanese troops. We slept in barracks on shelves with a thin covering of rice straw as a mattress. We shared the barracks with mosquitos, lice, bedbugs, and fleas. Soon another thousand American POWs were brought in from Luzon. Their presence taxed our already inadequate facilities. Many of these men died within a short time of their arrival.

It is amazing how resourceful and inventive we became while prisoners. Every chance we got, we stole from the Japanese. One man took a 2x4 and fashioned it into a shoe sole, with a leather strap across it. He had hollowed out the inside of his "clompers" and made a small plug for it. Whenever he went to the warehouse he filled each clomper full of rice and marched past the guard. He and several others got away with this for months. One day one of his clompers broke just as he was going through the guard booth. He left a trail of rice, which, of course, the guards saw. He was pretty badly beaten up for that. For a long time after that we could not have clompers. When they did let us wear them again, they had to be very thin.

Another prisoner succeeded in bringing a live chicken past the guard. He caught the chicken while on a work detail. Before coming to the gate he choked it until it was limp, then wrapped his raincoat around it and walked through the gate. They patted him down, but didn't check the raincoat. Luckily the chicken did not start to cluck. The soldier had eggs for a long time until the hen stopped laying, and then he had chicken stew.

One day I spotted a stalk of bananas. On the way back to the compound I broke off the stalk of bananas, then I had to figure out what to do with it. Guards were posted everywhere because someone had escaped. My hunger spurred me on. I took off my raincoat and tied the ends of the sleeves, stripped the bananas from the stalk, and stuffed them into the sleeves. I walked into the camp the same way the fellow took in the chicken. Because the bananas were green when I picked them, I had bananas for some time.

We even devised a way to secure fresh meat. We had water buffalo, or carabao, which we used in working the fields. We mastered two ways of killing them without raising suspicions. First, water buffalos do not drink; they absorb moisture through their skin. We traded off working a carabao without letting it stop to immerse itself in water, until it died of heat exhaustion. We would then call the guards, show them the dead carabao, and ask if we could have the meat. They would send out a butchering detail.

The second method was drowning the animal. In the northern part of the plantation was a river about ten to fifteen feet deep. We found a big stump in the river bottom. When we had to move the buffalo to the other side of the river, we tied a rope to the ring in its nose, threw the rope to the other side and led the animal across. When the guards were not looking someone would dive to the stump and pass the rope under it. While the animal was crossing, it would "drown." We would drag it out, call the guard, and ask for the meat. We worked that one three or four times without being caught.

By June 1944, the American military was beginning to pressure the Japanese on Mindinao. One day our captors blindfolded and hauled us to the docks at Davao, where we were stuffed aboard a ship. When we thought the compartment of the old freighter was filled to capacity, the guards used their rifle butts to shove several dozen more men into the hold. The hold was so crowded there was not room for everyone to sit at the same time. This was the beginning of ninety days of hell as we were transported to Japan. We lived on very thin rations; many had diarrhea. Consequently the ship's hold was filthy and our lives were in constant danger. We stopped in Manila where we were taken to the infamous Bilibid Prison.

On 16 July 1944, we left Manila, bound for Japan. An American submarine sank one of the other prison ships. The guards shot many of the survivors as they struggled to swim to a nearby shore. In an attempt to sink the sub, the Japanese dropped depth charges. To us down in the hold of the old ship, the sound of these explosions was deafening. A few days later we ran into a typhoon. Then one of our boilers sprung a leak. Unable to steer a course or keep up with the convoy, we were abandoned by the other Japanese ships. We finally arrived in Japan in late September.

My unit was sent to work at a copper smelter at Yokkaichi on the island of Honshu. On 7 December 1944, a major earthquake hit Japan. The quaking dropped a major power line nearly on top of where I was working. The electrified wires began whipping back and forth right in our escape route. We ran up an incline, and as we did, the ground opened up; cracks two-and-a-half to three-feet wide appeared directly in front of me. I stared into the openings. I turned around and ran back toward the snapping electrical wires. There was simply no way to get past. Then looking back in the direction of the cracks, I saw them close. We ran quickly into an open field. For me, this was the most frightening experience of the war, but surviving it was another manifestation of the Lord's promise that I would be all right.

The quake caused so much damage that the Japanese had to abandon the facility. We were moved to Toyama on the west coast of Honshu where we remained and worked in a carborundum plant until the end of the war.

All of us learned to understand some basic Japanese commands, but one of our men trained himself to read, speak, and understand the Japanese language. He worked in the officers' mess as an orderly and clerk. The

Japanese had no idea he knew what they were saying. He became our intelligence source, and kept us informed of what he learned. We could not tell what was or wasn't propaganda, but we did know, generally, what the Japanese people were being told by the military. We saw flights of U.S. war planes overflying the Japanese homeland. We watched one of our bombers drop a 500-pound bomb, which landed close to where I was lying on the ground. None of us were hurt.

Three months before the Japanese surrendered we were called together by the camp commander. He was a graduate of Stanford University and spoke excellent English. He said, "You should prepare to die, because the Americans, being foolish, will probably try to invade Japan. The first time an American sets his foot on shore, my orders are to kill every one of you. We will fight to the last man. So why should we die, and you live? So you will die, and then maybe we will die." That was the most frightening news we had heard. There seemed no way out; escape was not an option.

Then one day, many of the guards disappeared. Someone figured out that Japan had surrendered. Some of the guards in some of the camps were captured and beaten to death by prisoners using their fists. That did not occur in our area. I do not believe that the Japanese would have fought to the last man, but we might have been dead before that was determined.

There is no doubt in my mind that use of the atom bomb saved our lives. The bombs dropped on Hiroshima and Nagasaki undoubtedly saved the lives of every then surviving prisoner-of-war in Japan. Even though thousands were killed by these bombs, additional thousands of American and Japanese lives were saved because an invasion was avoided.

News that war had ended left me numb. We had endured so many disappointments that we would not celebrate. We were near starvation, thousands of miles from home, and uncertain of any future different from what we had known for the past three and a half years. When a U.S. Navy fighter began flying repeatedly over our camp, we began to wave and shout. Tears streamed down our faces, and we hugged each other unashamedly.

Later we left our compound for a swim in a nearby river. That was unbelieveably refreshing. It had been more than a year since we had bathed. Soon B-24s began dropping supplies to us, loaded in fifty-gallon drums. These contained everything imaginable. At the same time the Japanese started bringing in supplies. We had all the rice we could eat, and beef and pork. We received uniforms we could put on until we were picked up by the Americans.

I cannot remember being happier than when I saw those big strapping Americans who met us on the shore of Honshu. How young they looked! Their uniforms and equipment were new to us; even their helmets were different than the old WW I wash basin type we had been issued. They carried rifles of a design I had never seen. I had been living in a time warp. Then I understood that I too was different on this 5 September 1945, than I had been when captured three and a half years earlier. Among other things, when I was captured I weighed 170 pounds—I now weighed 117 pounds.

Finally I was aboard the hospital ship *Rescue*. We were instructed to strip to the skin, our hair was cut short, and we were deloused. A hot shower is a luxury I will always appreciate. We had all the hot water and soap we wanted. Then we went to the chow line and enjoyed the food.

The Lord had kept His promise. I was "all right," even through being "all right" does not necessarily include being untroubled. When I have good food, I thank God. Looking back on my experiences I am struck by the sweetness of life with freedom. Perhaps we do not know what a gift it is to be free until we have been deprived of freedom. I am also thankful for the United States. It is the greatest nation on the face of the earth.

When I was processed at Madigan General Hospital at Fort Lewis Washington, it was 2nd Lieutenant Janet Ross, from Seattle, who wrote me a ten-day leave. That was how I met the woman who became my wife. Ten years after we were married, while stationed in Alaska, Jan announced to me that she wanted to join the Church. A counselor in the branch presidency challenged me to get my life in order so that I could baptize her. Just over a year later we were sealed in the Idaho Falls Temple.

Ralf and Jan Wilson are parents of three sons, have five grandchildren and four great grandchildren. After Ralf retired from the Air Force in 1961 they lived in Redmond, Washington, where Ralf served for many years as the senior member of the Seventy and a Stake Missionary. They returned to live in Alta, Wyoming, then moved to Rigby, Idaho. They served a six month mission in Portales, New Mexico. Ralf and Jan are currently ordinance workers in the Idaho Falls Temple.

THE WAR IN THE PACIFIC

U.S. carriers in the Pacific, November 1944. Success in the Pacific
depended largely on the United States' naval superiority.

Perhaps the most striking thing about the Pacific arena is its vastness. The Pacific Ocean extends across many time zones, and from north to south across many climates. Somewhere in the middle is the international date line where today becomes tomorrow–or yesterday–depending on the direction of travel. On one side it is bordered by the American continents, on the other the lands of the Orient, whose people speak other languages and have customs far different from ours.

In 1933, the Japanese, needing raw materials—especially oil and rubber—and coveting room for their increasing population, began moving into China and the South Pacific. Eventually they ruled more than twenty million square miles of land and water. On 27 September 1940, Japan signed a Tripartite Pact with Germany and Italy, an alliance that became known as the "Axis." Japan's attack on the United States Naval fleet at Pearl Harbor was an improbable attempt to extend its domain. Had Japan pressed their attack to the United States' mainland, who knows what conquests they would have made, but they would have been at the end of a very long supply line. Whatever Japan's reasons, 7 December 1941, the sneak attack ensured the United States' entrance into the war. Quickly, most of the nations of the earth joined with us, and the world was at war.

In an attempt to follow the struggle in the Pacific, people in the U.S. pulled out world maps, looking for places such as Corregidor, Bataan, Balikpapan, Halmahera, Saipan, Bougainville, Guadalcanal, Tulagi, Leyte, Tarawa, and numerous other heretofore unknown places—places where their sons and husbands and daughters were being sent.

The toll of the Pacific campaign is mind numbing. Thousands upon thousands of dead and wounded are witness of the cost of this war.

And my soul was rent with anguish, because of the slain of my people. . . . And the day soon cometh that your mortal must put on immortality, and these bodies which are now moldering in corruption must soon become incorruptible bodies; and then ye must stand before the judgment-seat of Christ to be judged according to your works.

(Mormon 6: 16, 21)

MAC S GROESBECK

Thus saith the Lord God unto these bones; Behold, I will cause breath to enter into you, and ye shall live: And I will lay sinews upon you, and will bring up flesh upon you, and cover you with skin, and put breath in you, and ye shall live; and ye shall know that I am the Lord.

(Ezekial 37:5–6)

An article in the newspaper *USA Today*, dated Wednesday, 23 May 2001, is entitled, "Anthropologists Fanning the World as More WWII Sites are Uncovered." It describes the efforts of a team from the U.S. Army's Central Identification Laboratory in Hawaii to recover Americans missing in action from the wars in Vietnam, Korea, and World War II. There are still 78,000 unaccounted for from World War II. However, in 2001, some families received answers about what happened to the crew of one missing plane. On a ridge in the jungle above Milne Bay, Papua, New Guinea, searchers found the site where a B-17 had crashed.

"This B-17 flew into the ridge on the night of October 31, or the wee hours of November 1, 1942. According to military records, the bomber was part of a U. S. Fifth Air Force mission based in Australia dispatched to bomb Japanese shipping. . . . This was a desperate period when the tide was turning against the Japanese. Fresh air crews from the States, young pilots with little more than 300 hours of flying experience, were plunging through darkness over mountainous island terrain with poor topographical maps and lethally unpredictable weather. Seventy percent of U. S. losses in New Guinea were weather related."

Among the bomber's crew members lost was "Sergeant Mac Groesbeck, 26, American Fork, Utah, gunner. Mac, a Mormon raised on a small farm, volunteered to fly on that last mission because the crew was shorthanded." Until the discovery of this wreckage military authorities had no knowledge of the fate of this B-17 or its crew. It was assumed that the men had perished in the sea, somewhere between New Guinea and Australia.

Mac S Groesbeck, 1940

Mac Groesbeck kept a daily diary from Thursday, 13 November 1941, the day he left for duty in the Pacific, until Thursday, 29 October 1942, the day he left on his last flight. For many years this diary was kept by his friend Pete; then about 1980, it was sent to Mac's brother, Byron. The following excerpts from that diary tell the extraordinary story of Mac's experiences.

Thursday, 13 November 1941: At 2:00 p.m. we had roll call and took our last look at the Salt Lake airfield; we were then loaded on a train and shipped to San Francisco. The whole family was at the station to see me off, also Aunt Hazel and Uncle Dick.

Thursday, 20 November 1941: Someone told me that today was Thanksgiving. I had anticipated spending it with Mary, my girlfriend, in Spokane, instead I spent it here on Angel Island, next to Alcatraz. My Thanksgiving dinner consisted to two ham and cheese sandwiches and a tomato salad. In the afternoon I wrote a letter to Mother and one to Mary, received a letter from my brother Byron. Was told that at 3:00 a.m. tomorrow morning we would get up and get ready to sail for "Plum." I wonder where Plum is anyway.

Friday, 21 November 1941: Took a ferry from Angel Island for Pier 7 at San Francisco and boarded the *USS Republic*. About noon ran into Red Miller and asked him where he was bunking. He said he didn't know, but that it was so far down in the ship that he got the bends coming up to the main deck. Our sleeping quarters are plenty crowded.

Friday, 28 November 1941: At 10:30 a.m. sailed into Pearl Harbor. Had a few A-20's do some practice dive bombing on us. Got a pass at 2:00 p.m. until 6:00 p.m. and went in to Honolulu. First thing I did was stop at a curio shop to buy a souvenir to send home. Sent out eight post cards and an airmail letter to Mary, also sent her a bracelet.

Saturday, 29 November 1941: Sailed from Honolulu at 8:00 am this morning. About fifty miles out joined a convoy of seven other ships.

Sunday, 30 November 1941: Here's another Sunday. To me, on Sunday I should go to church, and usually visit with family in the afternoon. Today was just another day at sea.

Sunday, 7 December 1941: At 11:00 a.m. we were all called to our bunks and informed that Japan has declared war on us, and from then on this ship has been in a turmoil. It started with the bombing of Pearl Harbor. We left there just one week ago. Most of the afternoon has been spent hoisting ammunition out of the hold of the ship. My only worry is for Mother at home. I only hope and pray that she won't worry too much.

Tuesday, 9 December 1941: Arose at 4:00 a.m. and stood life boat drill. About 11:00 we changed our course. It was said that our scout plane spotted a Japanese aircraft carrier about 150 miles north of us. Pretty close. Our latest report is that we will sight land tomorrow night—here's hoping.

Saturday, 13 December 1941: About 2:00 p.m. we came to quite a large island on our starboard side, and at 5:00 p.m. dropped anchor at Suva, in the Fiji Islands. Suva is beautiful from the waterfront, much prettier than Honolulu. I think seeing this island is one of the grandest experiences that I have witnessed.

Friday, 19 December 1941: At noon we were called to quarters and told to stand by, ready to abandon ship. It's a funny feeling to be down in the hold waiting for either a bomb to land on the deck, or a torpedo to hit. This ship is loaded with torpedoes and ammunition, so one torpedo could send it down to Davy Jones' locker.

Tuesday, 23 December 1941: We unloaded at Brisbane [Australia] at 2:30 p.m., and marched out to Ascot horse race track and put up in tents. That night they opened the town to us—it didn't cost us anything to ride the trams, see a show, go to a dance, or anything. Spent my time talking with the people and trying to get their money system through my head.

Thursday, 25 December 1941: Today has been, by far, the hottest, dullest Christmas I have ever spent. Was on KP all day. I had plans to spend this Christmas in Spokane, with Mary. I hope she and my folks had a merry Christmas.

Saturday, 3 January 1942: At 12:30 was given a pass until midnight. Three other fellows and I went swimming, then to a movie. After dinner,

Ross and I went to the dance at the Trockadero. The girls outnumber the boys about two-to-one. I met three girls who were exceptionally good dancers and weren't a bit hard to look at either. Spent the evening dancing with them.

Sunday, 4 January 1942: This evening Mike Zundell and Miles Rowe, a couple of kids in the tent went in to town and found a Mormon Church. I wish I had gone along. If I am still in town next Sunday I am going in to church.

Sunday, 11 January 1942: Got up at 5:00 a.m. and spent the whole day in the kitchen. It was a rather easy day on KP. At 7:00 p.m. we held church here. We had a good sermon, but for some reason I don't believe just as the chaplain does.

Sunday, 18 January 1942: Another dull Sunday. How I wish it could have been another Sunday back in Spokane. I hope Mary goes to church this morning. I'll certainly be glad when we can go to church with each other again. This morning I went to services here on the ship. The chaplain gave a good sermon, but there was something lacking. Spent the afternoon reading and playing shuffleboard. [Heading for Brisbane, Australia.] Have been passing islands all day, large ones and small ones. Looks like we are headed for some action. I'm ready for it.

Wednesday, 21 January 1942: We are getting into waters where we can expect almost anything. This morning we rounded the northern tip of Australia at Cape York. There we picked up three Navy ships for escort, a heavy cruiser and two destroyers. The four of us are headed west. We do a lot of zigzagging. Looks to me like we are headed for some place in Java.

Saturday, 24 January 1942: I was just going to dinner as the ship's siren began to blow "abandon ship." At about the same time one of the gun crew began to yell, "Torpedo!" We sighted a periscope about 1,000 yards off our starboard side. It had fired a torpedo that went between us and the *Houston*. There was a lot of confusion on ship for the next fifteen minutes. The sub submerged, and we left a destroyer to take care of it.

Wednesday, 28 January 1942: We sailed in to Soerabaja Harbor [Java] about noon.

Tuesday, 3 February 1942: What a helluva day. I was on KP and at 10:30 we had an air raid alarm. I wasn't excited then, but fifteen minutes later, between twenty and thirty Jap planes began circling over head. Dive bombers began plunging down on our airfield. I crouched down in one corner of the mess hall, plenty scared. The raid lasted half an hour. We didn't lose any men, but we did lose three B-17s, and one hangar was pretty well shot up. This morning we sent up nine bombers. They all reached their target. Seven returned, one made a forced landing and was ok. Major Robinson was shot down in flames.

Friday, 6 February 1942: Found out today that the Japanese reported they destroyed sixty-five B-17s when they raided here last Tuesday. We lost four. We will soon be owing them planes.

Sunday, 8 February 1942: Today has been a very expensive one for us. Sent out nine planes, only seven returned, and most of them were shot up pretty bad. One man was shot. If we only had some help, our bombers can't be a pursuit plane and bomber too. Maybe we will get some soon. Three new planes came in tonight, one cracked up trying to land.

Thursday, 12 February 1942: Lt. LaSalle came to where I was working and asked for two men to go with him on a mission to where the 11th Squadron is. He needed two men to act as gunners. We took off at 9:45 and during the forty minutes flight time we received our instructions. Coming back we followed the coast line but didn't see anything. Personally I would have liked to get in a scrap to see how I would have done.

Thursday, 19 February 1942: If the Japanese only knew how scared they had 80% of this army, they could walk in and take the whole thing. Our planes have been pretty busy today. The Nips have landed on Bali, only an hour's flying time from here. They are also trying to land troops on Java.

Wednesday, 25 February 1942: Had a close shave today. Took off at 10:30 with 5,000 lbs of bombs and a full load of fuel. When we landed with our heavy load, we couldn't stop, burned out our brakes, hit a steam roller with one wing and ran off the end of the runway. In the mud the plane almost nosed over. When we stopped both wheels were afire. At 7:30 tonight I was told to pack my bags. Left by truck for Jakarta.

Friday, 27 February 1942: Put out to sea at 5:30 p.m. headed southeast. Much to my surprise we are going alone, no escort. My bed is a couple of blankets on the hard floor.

Monday, 9 March 1942: This afternoon the fellows who flew down from Java came out to camp. They had some very narrow escapes, more so than we did on the boat. Found out that in the Japanese raid at Broome we lost one B-24 with four men from our squadron. There was only one survivor, and he was in the water for 36 hours before he reached shore. Also heard that Headquarters Squadron and the 9th Squadron were lost on a flight up above Darwin.

Wednesday, 11 March 1942: At 8:00 a.m. our train pulled out of Northam headed for Perth. At 5:30 Fred, Frank and I went to Perth. Perth is a beautiful city with more pretty girls than the law allows, and they sure are crazy to go with an American soldier.

Monday, 20 April 1942: Took off for Port Moresby at 1:35 p.m. We were waved off Moresby three times before we finally landed, refueled, and took off for Rabaul. Had flown for only an hour when our pilot, (not our regular one) got cold feet and turned back. Landed at Cloncurry at 2:45 a.m. The other two aircraft in our flight also turned back. There is to be an investigation about the mission as it should have been completed.

Thursday, 30 April 1942: Today I received twenty-seven letters from the States, twelve of them were from Mary, who in my estimation is the grandest girl I've ever known. It's going to be a happy day when I return home. Was glad to find out that the folks are getting along well.

Monday, 4 May 1942: Ate breakfast and went out to the plane at 1:00 a.m., didn't get off the ground until 3:00 a.m., the last of nine ships to take off. Landed at Horn Island at 6:20, the first to get there. Six planes took off two hours later to complete the mission, but because of oil consumption in one of our engines we could not make the mission. When we took off we blew our tail wheel. This swerved us so badly that just as we were about to get airborne we ran off the end of the runway and over some barrels and posts. Somehow the pilot got the plane off. For a while I thought we were going to crash into the bay. On our way back we sighted a submarine, but had already salvoed our bombs. Lieutenant Lewis made a perfect landing at home base with no tail wheel.

Monday, 11 May 1942: Took off at 6:00 a.m. with eight other planes. At 9:00 a.m. one of the ships turned back, and during the next forty-five minutes four more turned around. Two of them collided, but fortunately neither was rendered helpless. Four of us bombed two enemy ships, sinking one of them, a freighter. Returned to Port Moresby thirty minutes after nineteen Japanese bombers had raided there. Must have dropped 100 bombs. Just landed when the alarm sounded, went up on the hills to one of our machine gun nests.

Friday, 19 June 1942: My birthday. There are nineteen B-17s here at Port Moresby this morning. We got off the ground at 6:00 a.m. After two hours of flying we ran into a terrible storm. We nearly collided with another plane, it was so soupy. We could barely see our own wing tips. We had no deicer boots, and the ice was forming so fast we were forced to drop to 8,000 feet. After a half-hour we decided we could not proceed. Came back through the worst weather I have ever flown in–almost shook the tail off our plane. We landed at Cooktown, Australia.

Wednesday, 24 June 1942: Flew to Port Moresby, landing at 4:30p.m. After supper we were the fourth plane to take off to night-raid Rabaul. Sighted our target about 7:00 p.m., made two passes, dropping our bombs on buildings at the end of the runway. For some reason our incendiary bombs did not go off. Anti-aircraft fire was thick and close and small caliber fire was fanning our tail. Luckily they missed us. We bombed at 6,000 feet. The ship behind us started some bad fires, I could still see their fires from 60 to 80 miles away. Got lost coming back to Moresby, didn't find it until 12:15 a.m. Had lunch, then went back to the plane to try to get a little sleep. At 6:00 a.m. we took off for Cloncurry. Smooth ride all the way, and landed at 11:00. Had a letter from Mother and two from Mary.

Sunday, 28 June 1942: After roll call this morning I went to church. One of the local priests in town comes out every Sunday because we have no chaplain. The services were pretty good, at least they gave you something to think about. Spent this afternoon reading and sleeping.

Tuesday, 14 July 1942: Arrived on Horn Island last night. Awakened at 2:00 a.m. Got off the ground at 3:30. Lucky to get off because of having to take off down-wind, headed for Cloncurry and landed here at 10:00 a.m The crew of the plane coming in behind us told us that only three ships got off Horn Island and that two of them cracked up in the ocean on takeoff. My good friend Pete was in one of them. Three men on Pete's crew were killed— Rice, Houchings, and Lt. Badz. Went to the dance in the evening but it wasn't too good. Everyone felt pretty bad about those crashes.

Wednesday, July 15, 1942: You might expect to get shot down, but when you crack up getting off your own field, that is tough. Rice was about as good a friend as I ever had, used to go to most all the dances with him. I met the plane bringing the survivors back this evening. To my shock Pete wasn't with them. He was the only survivor not returned. He suffered some severe cuts on his legs and head. The boys say Pete was lucky to live as he was swimming around in the water for quite some time and lost a lot of blood. Rice was knocked unconscious and drowned. Houchings was disfigured. They think sharks got him.

Monday, 27 July 1942: Worked on our ship for a couple of hours before we could get it started. Left here [Mareeba] at 7:30 a.m. Reached target at 11:00 a.m., heavy overcast. Couldn't see the target, so left for Horn. Lt Becktold cracked up landing, ran into a parked plane doing 100 mph, demolished both planes, no one hurt. Went over to Thursday Island at 8:30 to see Pete.

Tuesday, 18 August 1942: Returned from week in Sydney last night. Spent the morning getting straightened around. There were three letters from Mary and two from mother. Sent mother a cablegram, a little late for her birthday, but hope it will still carry my sentiments. There is a peculiar "air" around camp. Everyone was called home from their vacations, apparently there is a big push going to start soon. The missions the last couple of weeks have been very rugged. Have lost several planes and quite a few men.

Monday, 31 August 1942: At noon received a very good news broadcast. The Aussies and the Yanks have completely annihilated the Japanese that landed at Fall River. I thought Fall River airport was in their hands, but am happily surprised.

Sunday, 6 September 1942: The rest of the crew came out to the plane at 3:30 a.m. At 4:30 we got off on a search mission. At daylight we dropped down to about 300 feet. Had to fly that low to get under the overcast. We were looking for three enemy ships. At 9:30 received a message of a sighting of three ships 250 miles from us. Tried to get to them but because of weather we turned back. Got another message about five enemy ships, we had missed them by thirty miles. We tried to reach them but didn't have enough gas. Landed at Port Moresby with only ten minutes of fuel. At one point during our mission we were off the water only four or five feet. Traveling at 180 MPH the back wash made a spray of water come up behind the plane. Hone, on plane 435, was shot, also Dunbar and Hartman are both lost, apparently shot down. Captain Kelsey bombed the five ships, crippled one transport.

Wednesday, 16 September 1942: Met a Lieutenant Olsen from Salt Lake. He knew Uncle Roy and almost all my relatives.

Monday, 28 September 1942: Discovered I had three letters from Mary, two from mother, and one from Virgil Jorgenson. I hope this war doesn't last so long that Mary forgets she has an ardent admirer over here. She is by far the grandest person I've ever known. I hope it won't be too long before I see her again.

Monday, 5 October 1942: This morning we flew through fifty minutes of hell. Six of us took off at 2:20 a.m. for Rabaul, six of us reached the target, two got lost in the clouds. The ack-ack barrage was so thick I don't see how we got through it. Then the Zeros hit us and stayed with us for fifty minutes. There were about twenty of them. We knocked down seven or eight. Attacked us at 23,000 feet. Lost about 2,000 feet in the running battle. We had three ships in the formation with feathered engines. Lt. Hageman was shot down. Had two engines on fire. We were going to follow him but stayed in formation to help protect Major Roagt and Captain McKenzie–both had feathered engines. When Lt. Hageman started down, the Zeros swarmed around him like a bunch of bees. I wouldn't be surprised if they were all dead before they hit the water. I watched them fall about 15,000 feet. Then they went into the clouds. Lost a damn good crew. I was so busy I didn't have time to get scared. Froze my fingers throwing out incendiaries over the target. Right after the Zeros left we all got separated. Landed at Moresby at 10:45. We only had twenty-one holes in our ship; we were the only plane in which no one was shot. Left Moresby at 12:05 for Mareeba. Lieutenant Hancock let us fly home. The pilot let me fly the plane alone for one hour. Tonight Bob and I went to the show in Atherton, and stayed at the Baron Valley Hotel.

Friday, 9 October 1942: Found out this morning that there have been several fellows quit combat since the last mission–it was pretty tough– but nothing to quit about. I don't think they were up to getting shot at.

Sunday, 11 October 1942: Right after roll call our crew was told to pack our bags for a two-day stay in Brisbane. We took #403 down to the depot to patch up the holes in it. Took off at 11:00 a.m. Flew about an hour and ran into a bad storm, which lasted all the rest of the way in to Brisbane. Amberly Airdrome was closed. Circled Brisbane at 300 feet until we finally found a field. It too wasn't open, but "any old port in a storm."

Sunday, 18 October 1942: Port Moresby. After flying for three-and-a half hours through pretty bad weather, we arrived at our target, which was Japanese shipping in the Solomons. We flew over the airdrome and they started firing on us. Forty-five minutes later we flew directly over a large boat. I guess they thought we were making a run on them because they started firing at us. That's where they goofed, because that gave away their position. The flareship started dropping flares around this ship. We made a big circle and made a run on him, scoring two very near misses. The ship immediately stopped firing, and moving. It undoubtedly sank as the bombs dropped so close they couldn't help blowing holes in the ship. Then everybody down there cut loose on us. The sky filled with tracers. Looked like a 4th of July celebration. Very nearly ran into one of our ships out in the dark. Returned to Moresby and after eating and refueling took off for Mareeba. I flew one hour and twenty minutes. It's a great thrill to fly it all by yourself.

Thursday, 22 October 1942: Back at Port Moresby. Taxied up to a revetment this morning and spent the day laying around under the wing, then loaded four more 500 pound bombs. At 7:30 p.m. went up to an ack-ack battery to a movie. About fifteen minutes later we heard an enemy plane, and before the alarm sounded we could hear the bombs dropping. Didn't have time to get to a fox-hole, so lay down on the ground. Four bombs landed about fifty yards from me. The next run the Japs missed the field by two miles. Had the search lights on them, but they didn't hit them—too high.

Friday, 23 October 1942: Again we cheated death. Took off from Moresby at 12:00 midnight to hit Rabaul. An hour out we flew into a thunderhead. I was thrown around in the tail like a rubber ball, trying to get my parachute on. Went in to the storm at 15,000 feet. In six seconds we were up to 18,000 feet, then were thrown up and down until we came out of it at 9,000 feet. Were in the storm for six minutes and were blown off course sixty miles. I was upside down as much as I was right side up. At one time we were headed straight down, air speed indicator read 230 MPH, and we were climbing at the rate of 2,000 feet per minute. Logenburger was thrown from the radio compartment to the tail section. I was thrown up to the tail wheel twice. Once I was sitting backwards in the window I sight out of. Took us three hours and fifteen minutes to get back to Moresby. First time I ever kissed the ground when I got out of a plane.

Sunday, 25 October 1942: Met some of the fellows who are coming over here to relieve us. Spent all afternoon going through their B-24s and showing them through our B-17s. They've got a good ship, but I wouldn't trade them. Gave them a few pointers on combat, etc.

Wednesday, 28 October 1942: Stayed down around operations all morning sweating out a trip to Cloncurry. At noon I went down to Gary's tent to listen to some new records he just received from the States. While I was down there the plane to Cloncurry took off without me.

Thursday, 29 October 1942: [Last entry] Spent all morning in my tent. Bob got back from Cloncurry and seems to have had a good time. I guess I missed out on a good time myself.

Taken from the personal diary of Mac S Groesbeck, furnished courtesy of Mac's brothers, Byron, Leslie and Paul.

Mac Groesbeck and crew. Names with x indicate members of crew reported missing in action 31 October 1942. Other members were not along due to illness. Standing (L to R): Botts, gunner; Groesbeck, gunner (x); Longengerger, gunner (x); Robinson, engineer; Burns, bombadier (x); Cipriani, radio (x); McClellan Sitting (L to R): Lt. Kernan, co-pilot; Lt. Hancock, pilot (x); Lt. Carver, navigator (x).

JOHN W. KONING

*I, the Lord, have decreed in mine anger many destructions
upon the waters.*

(D&C 61:5)

After graduating from South High School, I joined the Navy on 3 March 1941. Boot camp was at San Diego. My first choice of duty was in aviation. I really wanted to fly, and worked hard for that. In May of 1941, just seven months before the attack on Pearl Harbor, I was assigned aboard the aircraft carrier *USS Lexington*. Scuttlebutt was that we would be fighting the Japanese. During our drills the talk was always about war with Japan.

The *Lexington* was 888 feet long and had a complement of 100 aircraft. As I walked around on it I thought, *This is a mighty big ship*. It was not big compared to what we have today, because today's carriers are over a thousand feet long and weigh 80,000 tons. The *Lexington* and the *Saratoga* were built originally as battle cruisers and converted to aircraft carriers. The *Lexington* was a great ship, I also enjoyed being surrounded by airplanes.

There were five of us who were LDS who enlisted at the same time I did, but we all went separate ways after boot camp. To the best of my knowledge there were no other LDS servicemen on the *Lexington*. We were required to attend church services, either Catholic or Protestant. When I was at Pearl Harbor I didn't know about any LDS servicemen units or if there were wards in the area.

We did a lot of training aboard ship. In June the *Lexington* was refitted with new air-cooled machine guns, and in August 1941 we were told, "We're getting radar." Few of us had heard of radar. Most other ships had radar installed at that time. In August the ship was painted a dark, wartime gray, more guns were added, and more life rafts put aboard.

We were out to sea for training exercises on Sunday, 7 December, when we got word that Pearl Harbor had been bombed by the Japanese. Even though we had talked a lot about fighting the Japanese, we were surprised at the sneak attack. We underestimated the power of the Japanese, whom we had always considered to be militarily inferior to us. However, we were astonished that they were so far advanced in military technology, especially with their aircraft. The Japanese fighter planes, especially their Zeros, outperformed anything we had. The Zeros were vulnerable. If they were hit in a certain place, they would go down in a burst of flames. Their pilots didn't even carry a parachute, and the crews on some of the Japanese ships we sank refused to be taken prisoner. They considered it a disgrace.

John W. Koning, 17 years old.

After the Pearl Harbor attack, I was assigned to a flying squadron as a rear seat gunner in the Douglas Dauntless Dive bomber. In order to qualify we were given thirty rounds to fire at a target sleeve. Out of the thirty rounds I had about thirteen rounds hit the sleeve and was told, "You're qualified." That was it, followed by on-the-job training. I was put in the rear seat of a dive bomber and sent to war. For the several days following the attack on Pearl Harbor we didn't get much sleep.

Prior to the Battle of the Coral Sea our forces made various strikes on islands in the Pacific. But the Coral Sea was the big turning point. About 1 May 1942, we got word there was a big Japanese task force in our area, so we set out early in the morning to look for them. A scout plane found and reported the Japanese ships' positions, and sure enough, we found four carriers. We managed to sink one of their smaller carriers. We dropped a bomb right on its flight deck, while their planes were down and parked close together. Our fighters strafed them as well. This was the first naval battle ever where the contending ships were out of sight of each other. We and the Japanese flew back and forth, attacking each other.

We headed back and landed on the *Lexington* where we were making the same mistake the Japanese had made. The deck crew was rearming and

Returning to the *U.S.S. Lexington* (shown in upper right corner) after raid during Coral Sea Battle. Front cockpit: Lt. Reynolds; Rear cockpit: John Koning.

refueling the aircraft when the Japanese struck. All hell broke loose; there were bombs exploding and fires breaking out everywhere. This was one time when I was *really* scared!

We attempted to get our aircraft off, but couldn't; the flight deck was too badly damaged. Fires were popping up all over, and huge holes opened onto the deck below. With all the fires and thick black smoke, it was difficult to see or breathe anywhere on the *Lexington*. The bulkhead became cherry red with heat; paint was exploding off the walls. Very quickly a lot of men were killed or seriously injured. Blood flowed on the deck, making walking in some areas exhausting and causing us to slip and slide or fall down. The most grisly thing I saw was three or four guys missing limbs and other parts of their bodies. That really messes up your mind; you wonder if you are you going to be next.

The Japanese attack had not taken long. They were in and out, dumped their bombs and torpedoes and were gone. I don't know how many torpedoes hit us. One torpedo followed another, destroying our armor and doing major damage to the ship.

It took us all day to get the fires under control. Everybody grabbed a fire hose. But when we got the hoses laid out and turned on the water, there was nothing. The water lines were broken somewhere. Now the deck was really hot and burned our feet. About 1700 hours, when we finally had the fires under control, there was a huge explosion. It was probably the ship's magazine, and a lot of debris was thrown up on the deck.

I was up on deck when the explosion occurred. The ship began to roll and reel, and Captain Sherman gave the word to abandon ship, so everybody went over the side. I climbed down a rope thrown over the side. There were thousands of men in the water. Other explosions rocked the ship, and debris landed around us in the water, causing more injuries. It was a terrifying spectacle.

My Mae West kept me afloat until I was picked up by a lifeboat. When I had been in the water about half an hour, an already fully loaded lifeboat came by and someone threw me a line. They pulled me to a nearby destroyer and I was lifted on board, grateful to have survived.

The destroyer took us to Australia. From there I was sent to Hawaii and then to San Francisco, where I was given leave to go home. After my leave I was asked, "What do you want to do and where do you want to go next?" I told them, "I don't want to fly in dive bombers anymore, but I still want to fly." I was sent to advanced gunnery school in Florida. I checked out in the Navy version of the B-24, the PB-4Y1, and was sent to England.

My assignment was as top turret gunner and flight engineer. Our job was to detect German submarines and merchant shipping. We monitored shipping along a certain sector of the Atlantic. Any ships passing through had to give us the code of the day. If they didn't, we attacked.

One day we found a German sub running on the surface in broad daylight. When they surfaced in daylight, we knew it was because they were having mechanical problems. They would normally come up only at night to recharge their batteries but cruised below the surface on their batteries during the day. We fired on the submarine and it broke up and began to sink. Just at that time, three German fighters attacked us. I bagged one, the waist gunner another, and the third decided he'd had enough and left.

As we watched the submarine sink, I remembered my experience on the *Lexington* and asked myself: *What have we done? There are men on that submarine—maybe as many as eighty crew members—their families will soon get word they are missing in action.* In war it is better the enemy than you, but it made me sick inside. I realized that we had just taken somebody's life. It was not a good feeling, even though they were the enemy.

Following the end of fighting in Europe, I was alerted to go to the Pacific to participate in the invasion of the Japanese mainland. The atomic

Final explosion of the *U.S.S. Lexington*

bomb hadn't yet been dropped. Dropping that bomb was the best thing that could have been done. It's too bad it couldn't have been done sooner. It saved thousands of lives. I think it saved almost as many Japanese lives as it did American lives.

Following the war John met Jeannette Jongkees, a Dutch girl, in Los Angeles, who later became his wife. They were married by Bishop Greene, and when John was transferred to Hawaii, they were sealed in the Hawaii Temple. John stayed in the Navy until he retired.

John has served in an elders' quorum presidency, been a ward financial clerk, high priest group leader, Sunday School president, Sunday School teacher, and as a Cub Master for seventeen years. He and Jeannette have two children, a boy and a girl, and five grandchildren—all girls.

PAUL RAY BOREN

My ship, the *USS New Orleans,* a heavy cruiser, participated in seventeen major operations for which battle stars were awarded. Her archives chronicle the breadth of the war in the Pacific: Pearl Harbor, Battle of the Coral Sea, Midway, Guadalcanal, the Solomons, Tassafaronga, Wake Island, Gilbert Islands, Marshall Islands, Truk, Marianas, New Guinea, Saipan, Philippines Sea, Tinian, Guam, Palau Islands, Leyte, Luzon, and Okinawa. I was there for all of it, including Pearl Harbor.

We took part in several sorties following Pearl Harbor, traveling between San Francisco and Brisbane, Australia, but our next big engagement was the battle of the Coral Sea. This battle got under way on 6 May 1942. Our job was to protect the aircraft carriers, which were the focal point of the battle. The carrier *Lexington* took a torpedo, starting a major onboard fire, which they could not control. After they lost power, the *New Orleans* and another cruiser put lines on her in an attempt to tow her to a port where repairs could be made. The sight of the badly listing carrier, heaving in the seas, with battle helmets rolling slowly across the deserted flight deck and tumbling into the safety nets, was a devastating sight.

Because so much damage had been done to the *Lexington,* she eventually had to be abandoned in the dark of night. Lines were thrown over her sides and men went down the lines into the ocean. All of the ships in the area participated in a recovery endeavor that went on all night. The *Lexington* carried a crew of about 3,000. We rescued forty-three officers and 537 enlisted men. Men were thick in the water. We could hear their forlorn calls for help, which from my station aboard ship, reminded me of the sound of bullfrogs in a pond. We may have steamed by many whom we did not see. Some were injured and without strength to respond when help was near. I don't know how many were left in the water because no one could see or hear them. Had this occurred during daylight, I think we would have rescued more of them. This was my first experience with such enormous loss. A vivid impression of that night remains in my mind. It is still painful.

* * *

Paul Ray Boren

The battle for Midway Island is said to have been the turning point in the war in the Pacific. The loss of four Japanese aircraft carriers—ships that had been the backbone of the Japanese Imperial Navy's attack on Pearl Harbor—crippled their ability for further conquest in the Far East. At Midway, the *New Orleans* was assigned to protect the carrier *Enterprise*, which, unfortunately, was sunk.

At midnight of 29 November, we left Espiritu Santos, an island in the New Hebrides chain. We were to sortie with Task Force 67 to intercept one of the so-called "Tokyo Expresses," a convoy of Japanese ships attempting to supply their forces on Guadalcanal. Approximately twenty-four hours later we joined a force of four other cruisers—the *Minneapolis, North Hampton, Pensacola, and Honolulu*—and engaged several Japanese destroyers that were escorting supply vessels. The *Minneapolis* fired a salvo of nine shells, the *Pensacola* and the *New Orleans* also fired salvos. We hit an enemy cruiser, obliterating it. Two other enemy ships were also destroyed.

We were astern the *Minneapolis* when she was struck by a huge Japanese torpedo. She burst into flames, and we had to turn sharply to avoid hitting her. As we were well into our turn, we took the second torpedo (the big fish, as we called it). This torpedo struck our powder magazine and ignited 7,000 gallons of aviation fuel. The blast instantly killed the crews in both turrets one and two. 164 feet of our bow was blown off. The severed bow floated long enough to swing around and collide with our port quarter, denting the plates and crippling the inboard propeller. All engines were stopped, and the ship lay dead in the water.

I was director of fire-control for our antiaircraft guns at my station high above the ship in sky forward. When the torpedo hit I was knocked to the deck unconscious. As I was coming to, I heard one of my companions who was trying to pick me up: "Hey, Boren, come on! We've got to get out of here." I came to enough to climb down a ladder. About this time the ship behind us was hit. Of the five cruisers that we had joined that night, only the *Honolulu* got away.

We were in serious danger of sinking, but miraculously, our water-tight doors in front of turret number two were holding, and we remained afloat. Proceeding very slowly, by morning we were able to reach Tulagi and the harbor on Florida Island, across the strait from Guadalcanal.

Divers cut away the keel and checked the ship's stability. Logs cut from palm trees were lashed to the front of the ship, and in a couple of weeks we were under way to Sydney, Australia, 1,700 miles away, escorted by two battle-damaged destroyers. On Christmas Eve, just at sunset, we steamed into Sydney harbor. The clouds dispersed like the opening of an old-fashioned rolltop desk, displaying the setting sun. It was an extremely emotional moment. Many of us, with no self-consciousness, knelt on the deck and said a heartfelt prayer of thanks.

Ninety days later, with a stub bow, which made us look like a snowplow, we were on our way to the Puget Sound Navy Yard at Bremerton, Washington, to have a new bow installed.

The first Sunday after we arrived at Bremerton, I had the opportunity to go to church. Sunday School was under way. Standing at the pulpit, giving a two and one-half minute talk, was the prettiest girl I had ever seen. I learned that her name was Venola Eddington. The following Sunday was to be conference, in Seattle. I asked Venola if she would go to the conference with me. At the time she was mad at her boyfriend, so she said she would meet me on the ferry the next Sunday morning.

The next Sunday I was on the ferry, watching people come aboard and saw Thayne and Connie, Venola's brother and his wife, followed by Venola. I thought, *Oh you poor old sailor, that beautiful girl will never want to even recognize you*. I slumped down in my seat and pulled a newspaper up in front of me to hide, hoping that she would still see me. She walked all around the ferry before coming up behind me.

We dated the whole time I was in Bremerton. By the time the *New Orleans* was repaired we were in love, and I asked Venola to marry me. The day I gave her the engagement ring was the first time we kissed.

The ship left Bremerton in August, and we participated in the bombardment of Wake Island the 5th and 6th of October 1943.

From our church activity at Bremerton, we knew of seven or eight LDS men aboard the *New Orleans* when we went back to sea duty. We began holding meetings in the chaplain's quarters as often as time and circumstance permitted. We took turns conducting and leading a gospel discussion. On Sundays we administered the sacrament, sang hymns, and studied the scriptures. These meetings were a great strength to me. We activated some men who had drifted from the Church. We had several non-member visitors over the course of time, and we even had a convert baptism. At one point we received from one brother's bishop authorization to confer the Aaronic Priesthood on him. A member of the Reorganized Church and a Lutheran also met with us regularly. The non-members of the Church who met with us told us they liked to associate with us because we acted differently from others on the ship. This made us feel good. It was heartwarming to see men take part in the meetings and to watch the changes that came into their lives as they came into Church activity.

* * *

The war continued to rage. Our ship took part in strikes on Makin Island, Kwajalein, and in the bombardments of Taroa Island and Majuro and Truk. We covered General MacArthur's operations in New Guinea. We delivered bombardment at Tinian, Saipan, Guam, Chichi Jima, Iwo Jima, and several other important operations in the western Pacific, and took part in the Leyte and Luzon operations in the Philippines. Finally we returned to the United States, arriving at Mare Island, California, 11 January 1945.

While at sea, Venola and I wrote often, and our love for each other matured, despite the fact that we were separated by vast stretches of ocean. When we met in Vallejo, we decided to be married right away. We were married in the Mesa Temple 24 January 1945, and honeymooned at Lake Tahoe. I had to return to the war and complete my six years of enlistment.

The *New Orleans* departed San Francisco on 21 March 1945. We arrived at Okinawa on 23 April and began support duties for the occupation of Okinawa. In July our assignment was shifted to Subic Bay, Philippines. We were preparing for operations against mainland Japan when the war ended. With the war over we were dragging for mines in the Yellow Sea.

Venola gave birth to our first child on 6 November 1945. Because there were complications, the Red Cross wired, suggesting that I come home. Venola and I stayed in Bremerton for a time. Then I had to catch a ship to Boston, where I spent the remainder of my enlistment. Venola joined me there.

I have wondered over the years what kind of example for the Church I had been while in the Navy. In 1986 we received an invitation to attend a reunion of the *New Orleans* crew, held at Cypress Gardens, Florida. While there, one of my good friends asked me what I was going to do now that I was retired. I replied that we were going on a mission for the Church. He replied, "You've already done your missionary work. You spent six years in the Navy, and it seemed to me you were teaching the gospel all the time."

The Borens returned to Bremerton where they lived for several years and where Paul worked for Bell Telephone. He and Venola are parents of four children, have eighteen grandchildren and thirteen great-grandchildren. They have been ward and stake dance directors. Paul has served as a bishop's counselor, bishop, and high priests group leader. He passed away 16 March 2002.

Take from the family records of Paul and Venola Boren.

JAMES CLARE REED

There is no other God that can deliver after this sort.

(Daniel 3:29)

In the fall of 1941, I began my senior year at Utah State Agricultural College in Logan, Utah. I will always remember being in the Assembly Hall on December 7th when the attack on Pearl Harbor was announced to a hushed and sad gathering. Not long afterward I learned that my cousin Byron

Mason had been killed aboard the *USS Arizona* on that fateful day. This quickly brought the war home to our family.

On 2 June 1942, I went to Salt Lake City and was sworn in as a Marine recruit and was then told to go home until I could be scheduled into an officer's class. In October I was notified that I was to report to Quantico, Virginia, for Marine Officer's School starting on 1 November.

On 30 October, I boarded a train at Idaho Falls. My family and my fiancée Gwen's family were at the station to see me off. I had never been on a train before. At Quantico, several young bewildered civilians, like me, got off the train. Standing on the platform we were met by a big, tough-looking Marine sergeant who told us to pick up our gear and follow him. Shortly after entering the base we were issued uniforms and told to ship our civilian clothing home. The next morning we stood in line to get our shots, a haircut, and have our pictures taken.

In March 1943 our company was graduated and commissioned second lieutenants. I was ordered to report to Camp Elliot Marine Base near San Diego. I went home to Ririe, Idaho, en route. It was my understanding when I left Quantico that I would be at Camp Elliot for about eight months. With this in mind, Gwen and I decided to get married on May 8th. As soon as I got to California I started looking for an apartment in San Diego, and finally located a one bedroom place with a small kitchen nook. The rent was $80.00 a month, and by then my second lieutenant pay was $120.00.

Camp Elliot was in the desert some fifteen miles east of San Diego. An overseas replacement battalion was being formed, and it was commanded by 1st Lt Curwin Larson, a returned missionary from Snowflake, Arizona. I became his second in command. We were able to arrange it so that one of us could go to church each Sunday in San Diego.

It seemed a long time until May, but it finally came. Gwen and I planned to go to the Arizona Temple. However, no Marines could go out-of-state because many were going AWOL. We contacted Bishop Brazee Hawkins, who said he would perform our ceremony. We thought Gwen's brother would be there, but he could not leave his base. So our landlord and his wife, William and Helen Lainson, went with us to the bishop's home, where we were married. Then the Lainsons treated us to a garden party.

The following Monday when I reported to the base, I was informed that we were going out in the boondocks for a week's maneuvers. After a week of this hot, dirty routine, we received orders for overseas duty. They didn't say which day, just to be ready on an hour's notice. Had it not been for Curwin Larson, I would not have been able to go back to San Diego to see Gwen first. Even then, I had to be where he could get me on the phone at all times. When I left our apartment each morning I didn't know if I would be back that night. Indeed, a few days later when I got to the base, we were loaded on trucks and taken to the docks, where we boarded a French ship, the *Rushambu.* Some honeymoon.

After twenty-one days on the ocean, we arrived at Neumea, New Caledonia. This island had been used by the French as a prison. It is located about 500 miles east of Australia. My assignment was to Headquarters Company, Signal Battalion, 3rd Marine Amphibious Corps. Signal Battalions had the responsibility of maintaining all communications for the entire corps, from the front line in the most bitter fighting, back to division and corps headquarters, and then to Naval headquarters in Pearl Harbor.

When it came time for a coffee break on my first night on duty, my new friends found out I was different. I poured myself a cup of hot water and added canned cream, but no coffee. They all thought this was strange, so I explained why I didn't drink coffee.

After a few weeks, our unit was shipped to Guadalcanal, in the Solomon Islands. Guadalcanal was the site of some of the first and most bitter battles in the South Pacific. Fighting there was still in progress, and Marines had captured Henderson Field on Guadalcanal. We disembarked at Lunga Point and set up our equipment a few miles beyond Henderson Field.

I had been in the South Pacific for two months before I received a letter from Gwen. Somewhere in the 2nd Marine Division was another James C. Reed. One day I got a bundle of Gwen's letters with a note from the other lieutenant Reed, saying, "These are really interesting letters. But I don't think they were for me."

We learned that the 1st Marine Division was not far from us. I located my good friend Curwin Larson, who was in that unit. He knew several LDS men there from Idaho and Utah who had been recruited as a Mormon Battalion. They were no longer a full Battalion because so many of these Mormon Marines had such good leadership qualities that they had been made non-commissioned officers and assigned to other outfits. On Sundays about twenty-five of us would get together in a small clearing in the jungle for sacrament and testimony meetings. This is something I looked forward to each week.

* * *

On 29 September 1943, Captain Anderson, Lieutenant Fox, myself, and sixty enlisted men formed a platoon and boarded a ship at Tassafaronga, Guadalcanal. We didn't know where we were going, but we were combat equipped. On 1 October, we went ashore on the island of Vella Lavella. The jungle was so dense that bull-dozers went ashore ahead of us to open a place to land. Our landing craft let down its front ramp and we waded ashore. No sooner did we get ashore than Japanese planes bombed our ship. A bomb dropped on the landing craft next to ours, killing twenty men.

We surprised the Japanese, so didn't have too much opposition, except through the air. Even though we were outnumbered on land, sea, and in the air, we soon captured the small air strip the Japanese had, and moved inland. This island was one of the most beautiful I saw in the South Pacific. Its dense forest was filled with huge red mahogany trees and coconut groves. The soil was only inches deep, over coral, so we couldn't dig foxholes.

I returned to Guadalcanal in January 1944. Curwin Larson and a Lieutenant Redding were there. They had been in combat at Bougainville and each had a Mormon platoon. Curwin and I had supper together and arranged to have LDS services when we could. Our meetings took place in the jungle clearing where we had met before. We sat on coconut logs and used coconut meat and milk for the sacramental emblems. At these meetings I met several men I knew from home or college. With the Navy and the Marines in the area, there were about 150 members of the Church.

* * *

During the battle of Bougainville our planes would sometimes land at our little air strip if they were having a problem. One day, as I arrived at the air strip in my Jeep, a P-38 fighter plane had just landed. One of its bombs had hung up on its wing while the pilot was over Bougainville. One of his engines was not operating and he was having a problem with his landing gear. As he slid to a stop, the pilot started to climb out of the cockpit just as two Marines ran out to help him. The bomb exploded, killing all three of them. I was grateful I wasn't closer.

When they landed on Guam they got on the beaches all right, but as they moved inland they were blocked by some cliffs, and the Japanese were entrenched above them. Curwin Larson was wounded, got patched up, and went back to the front to be with his men, and was wounded again. He went back the third time and was killed. Victor Longhurst, from Iona, was also killed, as were a large number of our LDS Marines. I also lost a number of friends I had made while in officer's training at Quantico.

Standing on the deck of our ship we watched as Navy warships and Navy and Marine aircraft bombed Peleliu for two hours. This lush tropical island became a smoking white pile of coral rubble. When the barrage stopped, the first wave of our troops hit the beaches. Our group was in the third wave. We soon secured the air strip. Dozers pushed wrecked Japanese planes off the runway, and our Marine Corsairs began to land.

About a mile from the air strip were seven large and steep hills. These rocky ridges were honeycombed with caves where Japanese defenders were dug in. Although we were able to secure most of the island, the enemy forces holed up in the caves caused us severe damage. At night they would wheel their guns into the cave openings and shell us. When we returned their fire, they would pull back into the caves. It took three months of the most exhausting fighting to whip them. Some days it was hard to eat our chow because we could imagine where the fat flies falling in our mess gear had eaten their last meal. There just wasn't enough soil or time to bury all the dead on Peleliu fast enough.

* * *

In early November our captain asked, "Lt. Reed, how would you like to go home for 30 days?" I had no idea this was even possible. I went to the paymaster and withdrew $150.00 and packed a small bag. I left for home aboard a Marine DC-3 and flew to Pearl Harbor. There I located my brother Glenn, who was with the Coast Guard. The next morning, Glenn, and another friend from home came out to the transient camp where we spent most of the day talking. That evening I boarded a flying boat for San Francisco.

It was a real thrill to see the Golden Gate Bridge. I went to eat at the Navy cafeteria, where I loaded my tray with milk shakes, milk, ice cream, steak, ham, eggs, melon, salads—things I hadn't eaten in a year and a half. I could eat only part of it, but it surely tasted good.

Gwen and Clare Reed the day they were sealed in the Salt Lake Temple.

While waiting for transportation, I met Lieutenant Dale Bair, an acquaintance from Idaho Falls. We went sight-seeing in San Francisco. As we walked along a street, two young women stopped us and asked if we had just come from the South Pacific. When we said we had, one of them told us she was the wife of Captain Lilly and asked if we knew him. We answered yes, and she told us she hadn't heard from him for some time. We had to tell her he had been killed on Guam. She had a baby girl he had never seen.

While I was home in Idaho Falls, we purchased a wedding dress for Gwen and then went to Salt Lake City, and on 11 December we were sealed in the Salt Lake Temple.

I got back to Guadalcanal on 12 January 1945. The following journal excerpts give the flavor of what I experienced during that time.

14 March 1945. We left Guadalcanal without knowledge of our destination. At Ulithi we saw a flotilla of ships that stretched as far as the eye could see. There were more than a thousand ships. We passed the aircraft carrier *USS Franklin,* which had been severely damaged by Japanese suicide planes. It looked like a floating junkyard. We are heading for something big.

Okinawa, 1 April 1945. The 3rd Marine Amphibious Corps hit the beaches on Okinawa before sun up. By daylight the Japanese had their suicide planes diving into our fleet and our unit was under intense enemy fire. There was so much anti-aircraft fire in the air that I wondered if a fly could get through it. After we hit the beach and went inland I looked into a deep fox hole and saw my friend Bill Rozeyneck huddled in the bottom of it. Next to him lay his sergeant, dead.

By the end of the first day we moved to the edge of Sobe, near Yonton Airfield. We dug in and set up our communications station. Earlier in the afternoon, Major Wells was killed. Several of us dived into a shell hole where the razor sharp flak from exploding shells rained down on us.

The next morning we turned north. We took numerous casualties. The Japanese had blocked the road, and when we stopped to clear the road they would machine-gun our troops. Along the road were little caves, and as we passed, enemy soldiers from inside emerged and fired on us. To protect ourselves we had to throw grenades into the caves, which was sad, because there were civilians in there too. Night brought air raids, and small Japanese units tried to infiltrate our area, so we had to be constantly on the alert.

Our troops advanced slowly south, but casualties were very high. It was jarring to see the names of good friends on the casualty lists. From our position high on the hillside we could see Kamikazes attack our supply and battleships in the harbor. All night the sky was a network of tracer fire. In a letter from Gwen she said that our friend, Eldon Hebdon, from Rigby, had been killed in the fighting on Sugar Loaf Hill. One night our sentry guard killed a Japanese soldier just a hundred yards from our tent.

6 June 1945. My section was ordered forward this morning. We left at 0800 hours. It had been raining for a week and was still raining. The roads were bottomless mud holes. We plowed along until about noon, passing burned-out tanks and trucks. Towns we passed were just junk heaps, and where artillery positions had been, empty shell casings were piled high.

Finally the sun came out and the rain stopped. We started to relax, but not for long. There was a burst of gunfire and the scream of a dying man calling for a medic. We grabbed our weapons and got up close to a near by embankment in no time at all. The Japanese firing stopped as suddenly as it had started, and a patrol was sent out to locate the Jap guns. At noon, we were fired on again, and that evening, at sunset, the Nips opened up again. That night we slept fully clothed, our weapons close at hand. During the night I awoke with a start. There was someone standing at the foot of my bed. I thought a Japanese soldier had slipped past our outposts. I moved my hand down to my carbine and with my finger on the trigger was about to raise it, when a voice said, "Are the mosquitos eating you up too?" It was Colonel Nelson. What a relief, and what a narrow escape for him. No one was supposed to move about during the night.

Naha, 10 June. I about got mine today. We were real busy with message traffic. I put my helmet on and had everyone take cover except the teletype operator who was receiving a message. Sergeant Carlson was just handing me the phone when a 20 millimeter shell landed in one corner of our tent. The concussion knocked us down, but by some good luck the shrapnel from it missed us. I dove into the gutter and hugged the bottom, praying that no shells would land in there. That evening they opened up on us again.

On 15 June Army general Buckner and some of his staff were up front looking over the lines. They came under fire from Japanese artillery, and General Buckner and several of his staff were killed.

I left Okinawa 14 July. We landed on Guam where we stayed for two days. There I went to the cemetery and found Curwin Larson's and Victor Longhurst's graves. I arrived at Alameda Air Field, California at 0400 hours and by 1900 hours was on the train bound for home.

It was wonderful to be with Gwen and other family members. After spending seventeen wonderful days with them I had to leave for Camp LeJeune, North Carolina. As we traveled we heard reports that the atomic bomb had been dropped and the Japanese had surrendered.

My last night of duty was 30 October, and I left for home on 13 November 1945, where I arrived safely after serving three years and five months in the United States Marine Corps.

Following his release, Clare worked for the Soil Conservation Service, a division of the United States Agriculture Department. This work took him to Texas, Washington, Idaho, Montana, and North Dakota. He retired in 1978, when he and Gwen returned to live in Ririe, Idaho.

Clare served twice as president of the Bismark Branch, was a member of the district presidency, and served on the district council. Following their return to Idaho, Clare and Gwen were called as ordinance workers in the Idaho Falls Temple. Shortly after that he became a sealer. From September 1982 to July 1983, Clare and Gwen served a mission to the Hopi Indians in Arizona.

Gwen and Clare are parents of three sons and two daughters, have twenty-five grandchildren and six great-grandchildren.

Taken from *James Clare Reed, Life Story*, printed in 1993.

The Ririe boys home from the war: Gene Ker (Army), David Ririe (Air Force), Peterson (Navy), and Clare Reed (Marines).

LILLIE J. FITZSIMONS

To . . . comfort those that stand in need of comfort.

(Mosiah 18:9)

After earning my nursing degree at LDS Hospital in Idaho Falls, Idaho, I moved to Provo, Utah, where I worked at the new Utah Valley Hospital. There was a lot of talk about the war, and several of my friends enlisted, or were drafted into the military. The demand for military nurses

Lieutenant Lillie Jacobs

was high, and I decided that I wasn't going to sit on the sidelines. I volunteered as an Army nurse and was immediately commissioned a second lieutenant and sent to San Luis Obispo, California. A few months later I transferred to Palm Springs, California, and from there I was assigned for overseas duty.

In January 1943, we shipped out of San Francisco in a converted cruise ship, bound for Brisbane, Australia. Brisbane was a staging area for medical personnel. From there I was sent to Lae, New Guinea, with about twenty-five other nurses. New Guinea was an active war zone, and Lae had been pried from Japanese control only a short time before we arrived.

The situation in New Guinea was demanding. We worked twelve-hour shifts, sometimes longer, toiling until we completed our tasks. And it was hard work. In addition to nurses there were medical corpsmen and about ten doctors. I can't say enough good about the corpsmen. I don't know how they knew so much, and they worked very hard.

Coming as I did from Sugar City, Idaho, where nearly everyone in our community was LDS, the military environment in New Guinea was new to me. During my eighteen months on New Guinea I went to church only one time. Most of this was due to our heavy work schedule. Somehow the LDS Servicemen found out I was LDS, they contacted me, picked me up at my barracks, and took me to a sacrament meeting. At that meeting there were only three men and myself.

One day I noticed a young soldier reading a Bible. Some of his buddies began to give him a hard time. Because they were all enlisted men and I was an officer, I called them together and suggested that if we all spent more time reading the scriptures, we'd be better off.

I was constantly amazed at the remarkable attitude of the soldiers who were injured as they came into the hospital. I don't know how they held up. The jungles were miserable places, and coming from the continental United States, none of us knew anything about jungles, which were so thick you couldn't see five feet in front of you. A group of Australian soldiers out on a training exercise, fired bullets right through our hospital. They couldn't see us and didn't know we were there.

We rarely saw men who had battle wounds, most of those were treated in field hospitals or in shipboard hospitals. They were then sent back to the States. The most common maladies treated in our hospital were skin problems, followed by mosquito borne diseases, malaria, and dengue fever. We spent most of our effort treating diseases. There were a lot of illnesses not seen in America. We tried one thing, and if that didn't work, we would try another, then another. None of us knew what these diseases were, so we were "practicing" medicine. A lot of good came out of the war. Doctors found out a lot about the body and about tropical diseases. Medicine makes great advances during wartime.

We also had to learn to deal with the tropics, especially the rain. You could hear the rain coming through the jungle a long time before you could see it. The sound of the rain hitting the heavy foliage would come closer and closer to us, and the rivers and creeks would turn into raging torrents and the streams would start changing their courses. The civil engineers had to keep pushing jungle growth away from the hospital.

I really enjoyed the work and the people on New Guinea. It taught me how the human spirit can overcome any disagreeable thing you have to live through, no matter where you are put. If you believe your experiences are miserable, then that's the way it will be. You make the choice in your own mind. The nurses I worked with were from many places. We were kind of a motley group thrown together, but we learned to pull together.

We learned to put up with the snakes and insects that came into our quarters. The quarters we first lived in had a thatched roof. Termites got into it and had a feast. Every morning the top of the mosquito netting around our beds would be covered with saw dust. Mildew got into the leather in our shoes, and they quickly disintegrated. And the food! The food was terrible. We picked weevil out of the bread, which we sliced thinly, so that we could see the dark spots. Nurses are fussy people. The cooks would tell us it was protein, and since the bread was cooked it wouldn't hurt us. All the canned fruit was taken out into the jungle to make "happy juice"–white lightening.

Our mutton and pork came from Australia and was so heavily salted that I couldn't eat it. The butter looked and tasted like yellow axle grease. So whenever we received an invitation for dinner aboard a Navy ship, we always accepted. There we ate like royalty, and we never got enough. The Australians invited us to dinner once, and told us that we would be having fresh corn on the cob. But the cook, never having prepared corn on the cob, deep fried it. It was awful. We didn't go there for dinner any more.

Everywhere we went while in New Guinea, we went under armed guard–even to the latrine at night. If we went out on a date, the officer had to carry a side arm. And there was an armed guard in the hospital at all times.

We were used to doing our nursing in white uniforms and starched hats, but we soon found out how impractical that was. We learned that we could be good nurses in suntan pants and boots. We also became inventive– if we didn't have a piece of equipment we needed, we found a way to improvise.

We had two operating rooms, an x-ray room, a dental clinic, lab facilities, and two hundred and fifty beds in our hospital; but we had only twenty-five nurses. When any of us got sick it put an extra strain on the rest, as there were no replacements. The beds were generally filled all the time.

As medical practitioners we were not immune to infection or disease. I think the first mosquito that bit me following my arrival in New Guinea gave me dengue fever. Dengue fever causes the temperature to spike to 105 degrees for a day, return to normal for a day or two, then shoot up again. When the fever passes you're left feeling weak and depressed. After going back to work I didn't have the strength I previously had. But I had to work or the other, already overloaded, nurses would have to make up the loss.

To prevent our getting malaria we were on Atabrine. Atabrine took the place of quinine, which had been used in the Far East for many years to control malaria. It only controlled the symptoms of the disease, there was no cure. That's what we did for a lot of things, just took care of the symptoms. The Atabrine colored our skin and our eyes, so I looked like I had a wonderful suntan. After I got home it took several months until this was cleared out of my system and my natural coloring returned. We sure could have used penicillin, but that didn't come along until we got to The Philippines.

One night a sergeant walked into the hospital. He said to me, "I need help." He had been stringing electric wires and had been electrocuted.

He was in such a state of shock that he didn't realize he had been burned. We kept him in our hospital for some time, then sent him to a general hospital in the States where there was a burn unit.

* * *

After eighteen months in New Guinea, our unit was sent to The Philippines. We arrived there about the first of August 1944. We were assigned to be part of the invasion force and scheduled to enter Japan five days after the initial landing. There was a desperate need for nurses, and I was immediately put to work in a general hospital located at the University of Santo Tomas. The Japanese had used this facility as a POW camp. When Manila was liberated our forces had freed the internees and made it a hospital.

I fell in love with the Filipino people. They are absolutely wonderful, sweet, and thoughtful people. And they were so happy to see us. A few of us were invited to their homes, and we got to go into their nipa huts, which stood on stilts, and where I watched men carving wood. The Filipinos took care of us, did our laundry, cooked our meals, and helped with the care of patients in the hospital. When I injured my back and became a patient, two small Filipino men who were corpsmen came with a stretcher to carry me down stairs to the X ray unit. I wasn't sure they could get me there, but they did fine.

Manila was a staging area for more than a million personnel brought in to prepare for the invasion of the Japanese homeland. The hospital facility at Santo Tomas was established to treat them. We mostly dealt with the same kinds of sicknesses and skin problems we had seen in New Guinea.

We didn't see any of the Allied prisoners of war who were repatriated–they were all taken care of at Clark Field. We also took care of Japanese captives who were incarcerated at the Bilibid prison in Manila.

Our living conditions in The Philippines were wonderful by comparison to those in New Guinea. For a while we lived in a resort hotel in San Fernando, then in quarters at the University of Santo Tomas.

It was an enormous relief when the atomic bomb was dropped. After the experience of fighting the Japanese armies all through the Pacific Theater we knew that if we had to fight them on their home islands that the war would go on and on. They simply never gave up. They would have to be burned out of their hiding places as we had to do on Iwo Jima and Okinawa.

All my life I had been taught to be kind to other people, to care for them, and the thought of burning them out was terrible. But I hated what was going on around me. The cruelty inflicted by the enemy on our soldiers had to be stopped.

While on New Guinea I toured some of the caves where the Japanese held out. These went back into the mountain for some distance. We heard stories about how our soldiers had been tortured by the enemy. Hearing these things has an affect on you. But you can't dwell on it and you can't allow yourself to be filled with hate because hate doesn't affect those you hate, it only destroys you. Not having to go through the nightmare of fighting through Japan was a great relief; it would have been a blood bath. None of us in the Pacific Theater thought dropping the bomb was a bad idea.

During my tour in The Philippines I did not meet any other Mormons or have the opportunity to attend LDS services. The people I worked with knew what my religion was, and sometimes we got into long conversations about the Church.

Following the Japanese surrender I had the choice to go to Japan with the occupation forces, or to go home. Suddenly I was homesick, and I chose to go home. After leaving The Philippines our ship lost one of its propellers. This slowed our trip dramatically. It took thirty days to get from Manila to San Francisco. All of the female personnel lived in the ship's infirmary. We nurses took care of those who became sick while en route.

I never worried about *my* being in a war zone, never expected anything other than that I would come back. I had a feeling inside that I would return home safely. This feeling stayed with me all the way home.

We skirted a typhoon all the way across the Pacific, and though not in the center of the storm, we felt its wrath. Huge waves fell over the vessel and as it tipped into the swells, our lifeboats hit the water and were torn off the ship. As the storm rolled us into one giant swell we spotted a floating mine atop a wave coming directly at us. Somehow it missed. All this time I felt the calm assurance that we would arrive safely. We did, on 24 December 1945.

During my two and a-half years in the Army, I served in eight different hospital units. My military experience taught me tolerance and that there are good people everywhere. I learned that I could get along with people of different religions and ideals without having to accept their lifestyle or beliefs.

After my discharge from the Army, I was on a train, traveling between Salt Lake City and my home in Sugar City, Idaho. There were a lot of ex-servicemen on this train returning home. One of them approached me and said, "You're Lieutenant Jacobs; you saved my life." It was the man who had walked into the hospital in New Guinea, so severely burned. It was good to see him going home.

Following the war Lillie Jacobs Fitzsimons worked as a nurse in Idaho and California. Three years following the war she married, settled in Sacramento, California, and became the mother of two sons and a daughter. She has five grandchildren and one great-grandchild. Lillie has served in the Primary, Young Women, and the Relief Society. She regularly attends the temple and serves as the genealogical consultant in her ward.

IVAN R. MILLER

It was expedient that he should go up to battle.

(3 Nephi 4:5)

I enlisted in the military in September 1940. At that time you could complete your military service obligation by serving for one year. There was a stir across the country that war could come, so it seemed sensible to enlist. It took the next five years to satisfy this commitment. In those five years I held just three ranks—sergeant, and second and first lieutenant.

I trained as a surgical technician at Letterman General Hospital in San Francisco. I was among those who met the first boatload of casualties following the attack on Pearl Harbor. These were the first battle wounded I had ever seen.

One evening in San Francisco I went out to buy some shoe polish, and I had heard of a little shop that might have the imported English brand I wanted. The owner of the shop was a small Greek fellow. When I tried to pay him, he wouldn't take my money. "But I want to pay you," I protested.

His voice thickened and he got tears in his eyes and said, "That stuff, she's pretty expensive, I get no more. You do your part and helpa dis country. I do my part and helpa you. God bless you, soldier."

On 4 May 1942, our unit landed in the New Hebrides (now called Vanuatu), Island of Efate. En route we received word of General Doolittle's daring air raid on Tokyo. With the news of all the losses we had previously taken, that was a morale booster for America. We landed at Efate during the Battle of the Coral Sea. Because things were so uncertain in that area, we were put ashore without supplies. We had only what we could carry with us. No one knew who would control the island the following day. Someone handed me a Spam sandwich as I went over the side and said, "Be careful with this, it's your supper, and could be your breakfast too." It was three and one-half days before the ship returned, and they pulled out again very quickly, leaving only one five-pound can of Spam and several loaves of bread to feed 150 men.

Efate was a beautiful, green, picturesque, lonely island in the South Pacific. I learned not to like the place over the next year. The island had coconuts with maggots, natives with yaws, flying foxes with screeches, snakes with poison, rats with nerve, scorpions with desires to get into my bed, and giant clams (thirty to thirty-six inches across) stuck in solid coral. It had beautiful moons and lovely nights, daily rain squalls, earthquakes, typhoons, malaria and dysentery, sun to the north of us, and the Southern Cross to the south. The native women wore calico dresses, some with bones stuck through their noses and ears, and Tonkinese people had teeth blackened from chewing beetle nut. There were a few English and French coconut and coffee plantations, not enough letters from home, soldiers with boredom, and lonely, lonesome me.

There were several LDS men on the island, who met together each Sunday. At a meeting in San Francisco, one of our doctors had been set apart as the group leader by Elder Hugh B. Brown. We held our services on the coral beach on Sunday evenings. Our course of study was *Jesus the Christ,* by James E. Talmage. One night during our services, not more than a quarter mile from where we sat, a sub-chaser blew up an enemy submarine that was trying to sneak into our harbor. No one slept through that meeting!

Our group leader was sent back to the States because of an infection in his leg. Before he left he set me apart in that capacity.

One evening the natives came in their outrigger canoes to take a group of us to their island to witness a war dance. Before the ceremony they treated us to a chicken dinner. The old chief and I got into a conversation, with his son acting as interpreter. The chief told me that eleven years prior, they had a couple of missionaries for dinner. I remarked that that was nice. The son said, "You don't understand, Sergeant, the missionaries *were* the dinner." These people had been cannibals. Apparently the next set of missionaries was luckier, as the natives now claimed to be Christians.

Whenever possible LDS servicemen met together to worship. For some there were "formal" meeting places, like this Base Chapel in New Guinea. For others, wherever they could gather would have to do.

We watched as the old chief stood in the middle of their group and shouted some sort of a chant. The rest of the natives, both men and women, shuffled around him in a circle and shouted their responses in unison. The young people danced a wild fandango around the edge of the group. For drums they used two canoes they had turned over. As the ceremony progressed, two warriors jumped into the circle, holding war clubs and spears. They shook their weapons menacingly as they shouted and danced. I could almost picture myself peering over the lip of a big kettle.

I assisted in a surgery, which we carried out in a bunker, under the light of a single light bulb powered by a generator. One of our men had become very sick with a stomach ache. A physician, thinking the man was malingering, prescribed a laxative. By the time one of the other doctors checked him, it was determined that the soldier had a ruptured appendix. I stayed at the man's bedside for nearly thirty-six hours. Unfortunately, he died. Inadequate supplies caused many problems. Nearly all the surgical procedures we used and the implements employed were improvised.

Efate had more flies than I have seen anywhere; they were so numerous they almost blocked out the sun. There was an eight-holer [latrine] back in the jungle. To control flies and other insects, a Navajo soldier from Arizona, was detailed to dump a mixture of oil and gasoline down the holes and toss in a match. Crude, but effective.

One day, the "Indian," as we called him, poured in the prescribed ingredients, but he had forgotten his matches. In a few minutes the camp cook came to answer nature's call. He seated himself comfortably and finished his cigarette. Picking up the seat next to him he dropped the smoldering stub down the hole. The resulting blast instantly raised all the seats in the house and launched "Cookie" off his throne like a shot. Hobbled by the pants at his ankles, he fell flat on his face. After that, "Cookie" always tossed in a match before sitting down.

Ivan earned a degree in Dairy Science at Utah State Agricultural College, Logan, Utah. He worked for many years in the Dairy Industry, eventually becoming general manager of Western General Dairies.

He has been a bishop twice, a high councilman and was a sealer in the Jordan River Temple. Simultaneous to his service as a sealer he was a stake patriarch. He and Helen are parents of three sons and two daughters and have twenty-eight grandchildren.

ANTHONY GARDNER

Jesus, lover of my soul, let me to thy bosom fly.

("Jesus, Lover of My Soul," *Hymns*, no. 102)

I began my military service on 9 September 1940, when seventy-two of us from Fremont County, Idaho, were sworn into the 41st Infantry Division, forming Company G, 116th Medical Regiment. A short time later we were taking basic training at Ft. Lewis, Washington. Following that, I had three months of medical training at Letterman General Hospital in San Francisco, California, and became part of a surgical medical clearing company.

While we were at Ft. Lewis, one of the guys had a guitar, and one night we were singing, when this beautiful baritone voice joined in. We looked around and saw a captain we had never met before. When we finished the song, he introduced himself as Reed Probst and said he had been assigned to serve as our chaplain. He had been a Civilian Conservation Corps chaplain, in Missoula, Montana, and was transferred into the Army. While at Ft. Lewis we attended church in a small branch. There were two or three LDS families living in the Tacoma-Washington area. We met for services in a building belonging to another church.

From Letterman I returned to Fort Lewis the day before the attack on Pearl Harbor. We left from there 20 April 1942, to go to Australia. We were on the water for twenty-two days. In the South Pacific, we had to detour around the Battle of the Coral Sea, which was then taking place. In their quest for more territory, the Japanese were trying to take Australia. They did make a landing up near Darwin in the north, but the Battle of the Coral Sea halted their drive in the South Pacific.

Our unit landed at Melbourne, then moved north to Rockhampton. Because we had no equipment, we had to stay there for several months. Since nearly all newly manufactured war materiel was going to Europe to defeat the Germans, the government didn't have equipment to send us. Our job was to hold the Japanese in place. Although our company had been organized for over a year, we still didn't have the equipment that we were supposed to have when half of our unit was sent to Efate, in the New Hebrides Islands.

Although Chaplain Probst was with us in Melbourne we had not yet been organized into an LDS Servicemen's Group. When we moved to Rockhampton, Chaplain Probst organized an LDS Chorus of about thirty men from our Division. The Chaplain went in to the city of Rockhampton and made himself acquainted with the ministers of some of the other churches. These ministers invited us to sing for their congregations. One Sunday afternoon we were singing for a church service. We were seated in the choir seats, and Chaplain Probst had been invited to speak. When the pastor announced that we were a Mormon choir, an elderly woman in the audience really came alive. We sang a number of familiar hymns. All the time we noticed how fidgety this woman was. We ended our program singing, "Come, Come, Ye Saints," and she began to cry.

The minute the service was over she rushed up to tell Chaplain Probst that she was a member of the Church. She and her husband had lived in Rockhampton for many years without contact with anyone from the Church. Her husband, who had also been a member of the Church, had passed away some time before. This lovely lady was overjoyed at our being there. Although we were getting ready to go to New Guinea, during the remainder of our stay in Rockhampton, those who could, regularly went to her modest home and held a sacrament service. Chaplain Probst was especially good to her.

We shipped out to New Guinea aboard an old Dutch Freighter *The Bonteko*, landing at Oro Bay on the southeast end of the island, then hiked several miles into the jungle. A chain of high mountains, the Owen Stanley Range, extends the length of the island. Down the beach some miles, and on the same side of these mountains were the Japanese. Our objective was to mop-up the Buna Gona area and ensure that the enemy was no longer a threat. There were no roads in this part of New Guinea, and it was two months before any were constructed and we could get a Jeep in to help evacuate our sick and wounded.

The Japanese were not our greatest enemy. We fought instead against malaria, typhus, boredom, bugs, spiders, snakes, and the incessant rain. Typhus was especially difficult to deal with. We did not know its cause and had nothing with which to treat it. Once infected, a person developed a high temperature, was often unable to drink anything, and became comatose. Forty percent of those infected died within a short time. Finally a doctor was sent in and I assisted him in doing two autopsies. We learned that typhus was caused by the bite of a small red mite. Now we could take steps to prevent it.

* * *

We participated in some of the earliest fighting in the Pacific. It was the first time Americans soldiers closed with Japanese soldiers. The Japanese had their best air base at Rabaul, New Britain, from which they bombed and strafed us frequently.

The native people in New Guinea were just wonderful to us and were willing to help us do anything that we asked of them. When the Japanese would overrun their villages they took everything—cleaned out their gardens, killed off their pigs, stole everything they could, and enslaved the natives. Understandably, the Papuans resented that.

We engaged the native people as litter bearers. Rather than use the heavy litters issued by our military, they would take one of our GI blankets, pull some vines down from the trees, sew the edges of the blanket together, and slide two pieces of bamboo through the loops. These simple litters were much lighter and easier to handle, and the patient enjoyed a much gentler ride. The Papuans taught us many things in their willingness to help. They also built us a surgery from bamboo poles and palm leaves and helped build the first roads. In return for their help we provided them with food and medical treatment.

At night the Japanese often tried to infiltrate our position. We set booby traps around our perimeter, which would go off when the enemy was making one of these attempts. One night when this happened, our guard fired in the direction of the action. In the morning we found a badly wounded native instead of an enemy soldier. He was brought in on a litter. His wounds were not the result of good shooting by our guard; in fact his wound was full of maggots, indicating that the wound was quite old. The maggots proved to be a blessing, since we could not treat it. Maggots feed on bad tissue and leave healthy tissue alone. He was in such bad condition that it was three days before he regained consciousness.

One of our supply sergeants, by using a language book, and after many hours of study with the wounded native, finally pieced together what had happened to him.

A Japanese officer had coerced him to be his servant, with a promise to give him tobacco in return. When we invaded the island, and as this Japanese officer was preparing to leave, the native asked the officer for the promised tobacco. The officer pulled his saber and slashed the man's left shoulder, laying it wide open. On the back of his neck, we could see the bones of the vertebrae. With these terrible wounds the native had come to our camp, hoping to get help, and that's when he tripped the alarm.

We couldn't sew the wound up, because in that climate, in a day or two gas gangrene would have set in. Pollution was everywhere.

A few days later we awoke one morning and found the old native gone. Late that night he returned to the hospital with a stick of bananas on his good shoulder, and his wife and two bambinos in tow. After that he was right there wanting to help. He taught us a lot about living in the jungle, and when we had to move our hospital unit, he cried.

Penicillin was just experimental then. We had it in a dry powder that we mixed with sterile saline solution. We had to keep records of how we used it. We could tell that it worked well, especially against infections common to open wounds in the tropics.

Near our camp there was a stream running through a coconut grove that belonged to the Palmolive Company. Our tent hospital was set up by it. We swam in this stream—it was the only luxury we had.

We noticed that the men were getting a lot of ear infections, which were hard to clear up because we could not clean them out. For other infections of the skin we used the same ointments that are used on athlete's foot. We had to evacuate hundreds of men with ear infections because we couldn't do anything to cure it. We finally determined that the cause of this outbreak was the water we were swimming in.

Even the natives had serious rashes, ringworm being the most prominent. The best we could do for them was to swab them with iodine.

In October 1943, our division returned to Australia for rest and recovery and for training in amphibious landings. We returned to New Guinea, in late March 1944. As we landed we met very little resistance from the enemy and were able to secure an air base that the Japanese had recently completed. We then moved to Biak, five hundred miles north of Finchhaven, just off the tip of New Guinea.

One day I was assisting in surgery when Chaplain Probst came in and asked the doctors for me. Chaplain Probst was Regimental Chaplain. Therefore, he was responsible for a lot of troops and had quite a bit of influence.

There were five bodies on the beach that needed immediate temporary burial. The bodies of the dead would break down pretty fast, because of the heat and

Anthony Gardner (r) and Chaplain Reed Probst

humidity. They were wrapped in blankets and needed to be buried until the Graves Registration Officer could evacuate them.

One of the men buried there was LDS. I didn't know him personally but had seen him in our church services. Out there on the beach, Chaplain Probst conducted a short service, and the chaplain and I sang a duet. There were just a handful of people in attendance. It was very touching; I hadn't witnessed anything like this before. We sang "Jesus, Lover of My Soul."

On Easter Sunday 1943, the chaplain had our quartet accompany him to the various Protestant services. He had a Jeep and an assistant who played the portable organ. He was a tall, skinny guy, and a returned missionary. We got into his Jeep, five men and the organ. We held a service at each battalion's location. After three of those, we had an LDS service in the evening. The chaplain was the keynote speaker and sang in the quartet with us. He was so exhausted he could hardly speak when that day was over.

The chaplain was a very conscientious man. On more than one occasion he went out on the battlefield and brought in a wounded man. For his bravery he was awarded the Silver Star, our nation's third-highest medal. He was huskily built with big shoulders, and he also lived right.

The next time I saw him, he was in our hospital. He was in a coma for a week or ten days and had a terrible fever. For months afterward, he continued in pain. I talked to him just after he had awakened from his coma and a few hours before I was evacuated myself in July 1944. It was the last time I saw this good man, who later died from complications.

On his return to Idaho, Anthony married Crystal Josephson at Malad. They were sealed in the Idaho Falls Temple, participating in the first endowment session conducted in that temple, on 5 December 1945. They have five daughters and one son. They now have seventeen grandchildren and nine great-grandchildren, with two more expected very shortly.

Anthony served for many years as a ward financial or membership clerk. He has been a faithful home teacher, and recently has been an assistant to the high priest group leader.

H. GRANT HUMPHREYS

Grant Humphreys was born at Parker, Idaho, 19 May 1919. He completed his college training at the University of Idaho, graduating in 1941. While at the University of Idaho, he was enrolled in the ROTC program and earned a commission as a second lieutenant, Infantry. At Fort Ord, California, he trained with an anti-tank division before transferring to the Army Air Corps. He earned his wings at Luke Field, Arizona, in October 1942.

While in flight training at Santa Anna and Oxnard in southern California, he met Betty Wilson, of Los Angeles. They were married 24 September 1942, in the Arizona Temple at Mesa. Following his training at Luke Field, Grant and Betty moved to northern California, where Grant was stationed at Muroc Field.

As was true of so many men and women at this crucial time, they did not have long to adjust to married life. In January 1943, Grant was transferred to Kiska, in the Aleutian Islands, Alaska. Betty returned to live near her parents in North Hollywood. They would be apart for eleven months.

American forces in the Aleutians fought two foes—the Japanese and the elements of nature. The wind, freezing temperatures, and rain took more Americans out of the fighting than the Japanese did. More than 2,100 casualties were recorded as caused by exposure, exhaustion, and other weather-related causes.

Living conditions in the Aleutians were primitive. The men lived in tents, which were constantly blowing down. The kitchen was in a wall tent that invariably blew down at mealtime, causing the cook to yell for help to put the tent back up and the meal in place. The hospital was also housed in tents, not far from the flight line, so that every time planes took off, the hospital tents were blown down. Hospital patients had to use gas masks to avoid being overcome by fumes from the oil stove. And everyone waded in mud most of the time.

Grant was flying the twin-engined P-38 Lightning, then one of the fastest fighter planes in the U.S. aircraft inventory. Weather was so critical that many times as he and the other fliers returned from missions, the pilots had only a ten- or twelve-minute window of time in which to land, before the "hole" would close and the base be shrouded in dense fog. Failing to get through the "hole" meant ditching in the Bering Sea.

The Aleutian Islands had never been properly mapped. Grant and others still relied upon Rand-McNally road maps, which were all but useless on Kiska. The U.S. government was slow to recognize the strategic importance of the Aleutians. With the outbreak of war on two huge fronts, it was impossible to adequately supply this remote area. As the Alaska Defense Commander, Major General Simon B. Buckner Jr. pointed out, "We're not even the second team up here—we're a sandlot club." Still, General Buckner made strenuous efforts to beef it up every way he could. What he assembled were a few tiny Army garrisons, a scattering of air fields, guarded by a few bombers and fighters, and a Navy fleet of World War I destroyers and wooden "Yippee" boats, which in the words of their commander, the colorful "Squeaky" Anderson, "would sink if they got rammed by a barnacle." They also had a few thousand heroic men—among them, Grant Humphreys, from

Grant Humphreys

Parker, Idaho, and Norman Johnson, of Vernal, Utah.

Not since the War of 1812, had invaders succeeded in taking U.S. territory. The Japanese landed on and occupied Attu and Kiska Islands, 175 miles west of Dutch Harbor. Had they taken Dutch Harbor, they could have isolated most of Alaska, leaving it open for occupation. This would have cut off the United States' best sea lanes to Siberia, which became important when the U.S. sent Lend-Lease materials to the Soviet Union. The Japanese would have also been in a strategic position for bombing Washington State, with its vital ship yards, aircraft factories, and military installations. Put in this context, what this "sandlot club" did with a handful of men was astonishing and essential to the war effort.

While at Kiska, Grant flew a total of fifty missions against enemy targets. He participated in actions against Attu and Amchitka. In April 1943, American aircraft bombed Kiska's nearly completed runway and the North Head gun installations and barracks. It was the heaviest jolt the Japanese received and put the Kiska base out of business. During one attack Grant picked out eight Japanese Zeros, which had been hidden for the previous two weeks. Three were on the beach and five others in well-concealed revetments. Humphreys, with two other P-38s, strafed them. He reported seeing "my tracers go into three of them." Japanese anti-aircraft fire was heavy, and one of the P-38s was lost over the Bering Sea.

On another occasion, the commanding officer wanted to know if the Japanese were still dug-in on Attu. Captain Humphreys took his squadron to find out. Dropping his aircraft to nearly ground level, he flew the length of the enemy runway, drawing fire so that other pilots could pinpoint gun locations and troop strength so his unit could attack them. It worked, and he was decorated for his daring.

It took three weeks to recapture Attu. American casualties were: 500 killed, with 3,330 wounded. The Japanese lost 2,350. The battle's last shots were fired 30 May 1943, two days after the last of approximately seven hundred Japanese staged a desperate attempt to capture Attu. They were driven back by a hastily arranged line of cooks, clerks, and engineers. About five hundred Japanese survivors, without hope of rescue, and cut off from reinforcements, held hand grenades to their chests and committed suicide. Only twenty-nine Japanese soldiers were captured.

* * *

Each Sunday that he was not flying, Grant searched for other LDS men. They administered the sacrament and read from the scriptures. He often commented that this became very important to him during his time in Alaska. His patriarchal blessing admonished him to live so that the Lord could be with him and that he would become a father in Israel. While Grant was in Alaska, Betty gave birth to their first daughter, Carolyn Lee.

It had been a long and hard tour for Grant, and he was grateful to return home with only one injury–a broken collar bone received while playing ball. He returned to California in December 1943, and he and Betty and Carolyn Lee spent the Christmas holidays at his parents' home in Parker, Idaho. After Christmas they returned to Van Nuys, where Grant became an instructor's instructor of pilots.

On 7 August 1944, Grant voluntarily took the place of a pilot scheduled to fly that day, but who was also to be married. Only five minutes into the flight, one of the engines on the P-38 quit. He radioed that he was returning to base. Then the other engine quit. Flying over the city of Van Nuys, Grant elected not to bail out. Seeing an empty school yard, he set his plane down in it. At the far end of the playground was a chain link fence. His plane flipped upside down when it struck the fence. Grant was thrown out of the plane and died from severe head and neck injuries. His heroic actions in steering his plane into that empty school yard, instead of letting it fall into an unsuspecting city, probably saved many lives and was an indication of his great love for his fellow man.

Another daughter, Diane Sue, was born a month after his death. Following military honors at Los Angeles, Grant was buried in the Parker, Idaho Cemetery.

Betty eventually remarried and became the mother of six more children. As promised in his patriarchal blessing, his daughters Carolyn Lee and Diane, grew to maturity, married and have children of their own. Grant is grandfather, and now has great-grandchildren.

Taken from materials written by Alta H. Pierson and Cleo H. Wickham.

J. STEWART DEXTER

For I the Lord am with you, and will stand by you.

(Doctrine & Covenants 68:6)

I enlisted in the Army with a group of about seventy men from Fremont County, Idaho, on 7 September 1940, and received training as an Army combat medic. Our initial training was at Fort Lewis, Washington. When we first arrived there were no uniforms for us, and for the first six weeks we trained in our civilian clothes. We were a good outfit. There was enough trust among us that if we left our pay on our bed we knew it would be there when we got back.

With war imminent, the Church organized to meet the spiritual needs of the servicemen. While at Camp Murrey, near Fort Lewis, I had the privilege of becoming well-acquainted with Elder Hugh B. Brown. On one occasion he came to fill an assignment to speak to us on the evening that he had learned of the death of one of his sons, who was a flyer for the Royal Air Force. I grew to love and admire Elder Brown very much. One thing I do know was that he was very serious about the gospel and what he taught us.

In March 1942 we were shipped to Port Moresby, New Guinea. In New Guinea the Japanese were coming over the Owen-Stanley mountain range, which straddled the island. There were never more than a few of them who got into our camp. At Popendeta the engineers cleared enough land to establish an air strip. Shortly after that we were moved to Popendeta to set up a hospital. I got sick with dengue fever. The Japanese didn't bother us nearly as much as the mosquitos. If it wasn't mosquito bites that made us sick, the men got sick from typhus. Some of our men died of typhus.

The unit we supported participated in the first battle, and victory, of the war with the Japanese. For this we received the Presidential Unit citation. This was very early in the war, when our armies were so green, and we had very little equipment. The Japanese used the equipment they captured in The Philippines against us. Our green troops took on the Japanese soldiers and we defeated them—this was even before the battle of Guadalcanal.

John Stewart Dexter

We had an LDS chaplain with us named Probst. Prior to entering the military I had been invited to receive the Melchezidek Priesthood. It took me some time to get my act together. But we often met with Chaplain Probst, as often as circumstance would allow, and traveled many miles in trucks to attend meetings. Some of the best testimonies and stories I heard in our sacrament meetings came from the non-members who met with us.

Following my service in the Pacific I returned to the United States, where I served as a medic aboard a train, transporting wounded soldiers to hospitals nearest their homes. Some of our patients were repatriated survivors of the Bataan Death March. These men were horribly sick.

I had my own Pullman car, which I was required to keep clean and ready to go. I tended these soldiers. This duty took me all over the United States. Sometimes I discussed the gospel with these men, doing some missionary work. During the Battle of the Bulge I picked up wounded who had fought during that terrible battle. I went to Denver many times, New York, and Atlantic City, New Jersey. I poured a lot of gallons of whiskey down toilets, got in fights with some men who seemed to have to fight. Once I took a blinded man to his home in Denver.

Prior to leaving San Francisco, I married Shirley Davis, from Pioche, Nevada.

Stewart and Shirley Dexter are parents of two sons and three daughters, have nineteen grandchildren and fourteen great-grandchildren. Stewart served a counselor to two bishoprics, on a high council, and as bishop. He has been a Gospel Doctrine teacher and ward mission leader. They live on their farm near Egin, Idaho.

JOSEPH N. BURK

He that is faithful among you shall not perish by the waters.

(Doctrine & Covenants 61:6)

I was born 26 October 1921, in Eagar, Arizona. I grew up in Nutrioso, in an environment that made us close as a family. Nutrioso is a very small town in northeastern Arizona and had a population of less than 150. We learned important lessons about life in this little community. We were quite sheltered: I was fourteen years old before I ever saw a train.

By 1941 news about the war seemed to be all bad. I turned twenty-years-old shortly before the bombing of Pearl Harbor. I expected greetings from the draft board any day. One day my friend Byron Wilkins came to see me. He said several boys from our area were going to enlist in the Navy. He argued that it would be better to take our chances with the Navy, that at least we wouldn't have to sleep in foxholes and would probably get better food.

According to plan, Byron and I and four boys from Eagar and Springerville, caught the bus to Phoenix. We said our good-byes to family and friends. Some told us, "Well, you should be back soon. With all the modern weapons nowadays, the war can't last long."

The enlistment process was a new experience. We were checked by a doctor, got all kinds of tests, and stood in long lines. The induction officer noticed I was tall and asked me, "Do you know what the height limit is to get into the Navy?" He said it was six feet two inches. I told him I was six feet four inches tall. "Oh, well," he said, " the Navy needs good men. Can you stoop a little?" I told him I could. I don't remember meeting anyone in the Navy taller than me.

From boot camp I was picked to go to the Navy electrical school at Moorhead, Kentucky. We were told that if we got good grades we could be promoted to petty officer and pick up a $30.00 per month pay raise. I studied hard and got good grades.

Joseph N. Burk

My next assignment was the Brooklyn Navy Yard. Lots of ships were being built there, and sailors were being assigned to these new ships. One thing that stands out in my mind about this place was seeing coffins being shipped back from the war-zone. That was a dose of reality.

I was assigned aboard a brand-new destroyer, the *USS Black* DD 666. Destroyers are light, fast warships. Their assignment in the war zone is to protect the big ships. We carried a crew of about 280 men. Because the *Black* was a new ship, I was privileged to be aboard when it was commissioned. Our quarters were rather crowded, and I learned, many times, why the regulation height was 6' 2". I bumped my head a lot more than the shorter guys did. My job aboard ship was to care for anything electrical. Most of my work was running down grounds or shorts caused by the salt water, and keeping things running smoothly.

After a shakedown cruise we were attached to the Pacific Fleet. As we entered Pearl Harbor, we steamed past the warships that had been sunk. I especially remember the *Arizona* and the *Utah*. Their top structures were above water, and you could see some of the big guns. As we passed these ships, not a word was spoken. It was a very sobering experience.

We first entered the war zone at Tarawa. Tarawa is about three thousand miles from Hawaii, almost on the equator. When we got there hostilities had ceased. Our Marines had taken the island at great cost in lives. The island had been extensively fortified. Taking a break to go ashore I saw the emptied enemy battlements and watched bulldozers dig trenches in which to bury the defenders' bodies. The strategic importance of this island was its airfield and submarine harbor.

One day we got word to proceed north to one of the Marshall Islands. An American plane had been downed, and the flyers were in the water. Our mission was to rescue them. We usually traveled on a zigzag course to avoid enemy torpedoes. Even though we were alone in hostile waters we ran top speed, straight to our destination, all afternoon and through the night. As daylight broke we came in view of an island. Apprehension over being discovered by the Japanese was intense, but finding our downed airmen concerned us more. Finally, spotting them in the water, we soon had them aboard and were on our way back to Tarawa. Apparently the Japanese didn't spot us, and we met with no resistance. We all felt good about that rescue.

One of my extra duties was to barber. I cut everyone's hair, even the officers. The extra money I made I sent home to my sister Eunice, who put it in the bank for me. After the battle of Tarawa some Japanese prisoners were put on our ship. They badly needed haircuts and the captain asked if I would do it. He said, "They have no money to pay you. Will you just do it for them because they need it?" I told him I would be glad to. As I remember, they were older men, civilians, some women, and a couple of children. I don't know why they were there. The first one was a little hesitant, but after that they trusted me. I tried to give them good haircuts. Although not able to converse with them, I had no hate for them. They were victims of the war, as we all were.

Scuttlebutt was that we were to participate in the invasion of Guam. This proved to be accurate. We arrived there early in the morning as the battle began. The morning of the invasion dawned clear and beautiful. The shelling commenced, and it was devastating. It was an awful carnage, a sad sight. I watched many planes go down that morning. All in all, Guam was a bloody affair.

* * *

One day I noticed one of the boys who had a bunk near mine reading a book. I asked him what he was reading. He said it was the Book of Mormon. He was not LDS, but his girl friend had sent him the book and some tracts. When I told him I was a Mormon we became friends. We spent a lot of time talking about the Church. I believe he was from Ohio. He planned to join the Church when he got home. It was good to share the gospel with someone else and I enjoyed our friendship. I have wondered what happened to him, I hope he followed through and was baptized. To my knowledge I was the only Mormon on the *Black*.

Guam became the staging base for the assault on Leyte Gulf in The Philippines. We were part of an enormous fleet of ships, surely one of the largest and most powerful invasion fleets ever assembled. I remember standing on the deck with a friend and looking out at this mighty armada—my friend remarked, "Can you believe that a nation could come up with an invasion fleet of this size?" I stood there wishing that my family could see it too. We met only token resistence from the Japanese as we neared Leyte Island.

As we approached the Island in the early morning, the troop and supply ships fell back, and the Navy began the attack. The small rocket-firing ships went in close and launched their rockets, and the destroyers bombarded the coastline with their five-inch guns. Planes from our carriers were bombing. The cruisers and battle ships lay farther back and lobbed in huge shells, which sounded like a freight train going over. In a short time all that was left standing were the trunks of palm trees and some brush. It was the greatest display of fireworks I ever saw. The island was pulverized.

While all of this was going on, a bunch of young Filipino boys and girls came alongside, cheering for us as we fired into the island. They were there for some time. They looked great and spoke in English. I thought the girls were very pretty. I wondered what they would be going back to after we finished our job.

After two years the *USS Black* was rotated back to the United States. We arrived in San Francisco about Christmastime. I was given thirty days leave, after which I was transferred to New York City.

One of my memories is a parade through Times Square in the heart of Manhattan. We had drummers and the works. As we marched along, a middle-aged Italian woman yelled to us: "Does anyone know my son Giovanni Martinelli? He is in the Navy. Does anyone know my son?" I thought, *You silly old lady, don't you know there are millions of sailors?* But the sailor next to me and on the outside of our column, took the high ground. "Giovanni Martinelli? Where was he last stationed?" She told him, and he said, "Why sure, I know your boy well. I was there. He is a good sailor, and you can be very proud of him." The woman followed along beside him, thanking him profusely, and when we finally left her she was smiling and looked happy. As we marched on the sailor said, "I didn't know him, but I wanted to make her happy." I wondered to myself *Why I didn't do that*. I thought it was a very nice thing and I have admired that sailor over the years for making that woman so glad.

My next assignment was to Camp Perry, Virginia. I was sent there to receive advanced electrical training. Camp Perry was situated only a few miles from Colonial Williamsburg and not far from Washington D.C.

I found that there was a unit of the Church at Camp Perry and attended meetings on Sunday. One evening a week we got together to read from the Book of Mormon. We had a group of six or seven. One of the instructors at the school joined our study group. He became very interested in the Book of Mormon and studied a lot on his own. Before long he wanted to be baptized, so we planned a weekend to take him to Washington D.C. where one of our group, a returned missionary, performed the baptism.

I was at Camp Perry when Germany surrendered.

The two men who had been leading our LDS Servicemens group were transferred and I was put in charge. The very first Sunday I was to conduct the meeting was difficult for me. There were five or six of us, and things were not going smoothly. Then the door opened, and in walked a couple of chaplains. I welcomed them and asked if they had a message for us. They said, "No, but if you don't mind we would like to sit in and observe your meeting." I told them we were glad to have them, but I was really frustrated. I couldn't think of a worse time for them to come. When the meeting was over they were very nice and congratulated us on a good meeting. I don't know what kind of an impression we made on them. I didn't think we did all that well, but they were nice fellows.

There was a large beautiful LDS chapel in Washington D.C. Because there was a shortage of places to stay in Washington, cots were set up in the cultural hall for service men. We could stay for a nominal fee. I started going to Church there when I got a weekend pass. I met many people from home, including my former music teacher from Round Valley. There were lots of military service women, and girls who worked in civilian jobs. Everyone was friendly, and it was easy to get acquainted. At the time that Japan surrendered I had been dating an LDS girl. She'd had surgery a day or two before V.J. day, and was in the hospital. I had liberty that night and decided to go into town. There was a group of us waiting to catch the bus. A car stopped by me and the driver said they could take four, two guys and two girls, but the girls would have to sit on the guys' laps. Another sailor, two WAVES, and I got in. I had the tall pretty one on my lap, and didn't mind it a bit. They took us downtown where we all got out.

This was Victory over Japan Day, and the crowd was going wild. The men were kissing the women and the women were kissing the men. I was still with the girl who had been on my lap for the ride to town. I said to her, "Well, since everyone is kissing every one, I would like to kiss you."

"That sounds good to me," she said, so I kissed her. Then I kissed the other girl who had been in the car.

"You know," I said, "we could have a good thing going here. If you girls see some guys you would like to kiss, my friend and I will arrange it for you, if you will do the same for us." They seemed glad I had suggested it, so when I saw a girl I thought was pretty I would tell the girl I was with. She would stop the girl and say, "Won't you kiss my sailor? He hasn't had a kiss all night." What a set up! I would kiss the new girl, and there would usually be other girls fall in line to take their turn. Then my girl would see some guy she thought was cute, and I would keep my end of the bargain. The four of us spent the evening cooperating in this fashion. What a night!

Someone began singing, "The Eyes of Texas Are Upon You." A chain formed, everyone with their hands on the waist of the person in front of them, the conga line weaving through the streets. The mood of the crowd was one of joy and relief that the war was finally over. It was quite a celebration.

Shortly after the war ended I was sent to San Pedro, California. I remained there until I was mustered out of the Navy, 10 January 1946.

Joseph N. Burk returned to his home in Arizona. On 22 July 1947, he married Virginia Higgs in the St. George Temple. To them were born three sons and two daughters. Their children have all served missions and have married in the temple, and Joseph has remained active in the Church. He lived in Simi Valley, California, until his death 18 April 2002.

Taken from *This is My Life*, an unpublished autobiography of Joseph N. Burk.

G. ROY MCBRIDE

A Word of Wisdom . . . showing forth the order and will of
God in the temporal salvation of all saints in the last days.

(D & C 89:1–2)

Sweat ran off my forehead and dropped on the gathering pile of chips at my feet. It was hot, the equatorial sun merciless. On each side of me sailors were also engaged in our "favorite" activity, removing rust and paint from the bulkhead, so that a new coat of paint could be applied. We were anchored off an island somewhere in the middle of the Pacific Ocean.

The repetitious, monotonous ping of the hammers was interrupted by: "Seaman First Class McBride, Seaman First Class McBride—report to the quarter-deck in your undress blues." I wondered what kind of trouble I was in.

A few minutes later I presented myself to the officer-of-the-day.

"McBride, you don't drink or smoke do you?"

"No sir," I answered, flabbergasted that with all the men on this ship, that anyone noticed.

"Good," came the reply, "as of now you're the captain's coxswain."

He explained that the previous coxswain had gotten drunk; the captain didn't want that to happen again.

"You're to take him to shore in two minutes."

Really, I thought to myself, *this ought to be interesting.* Born and raised on a farm in Idaho, prior to joining the Navy, I had never been in a boat in my life. I was not even vaguely familiar with the 24-foot whaler I was about to maneuver; I didn't know the bell system to signal the motorman. I don't think I knew there was a motorman.

"Here comes the Captain, let's go!" snapped the officer-of-the-day.

It was about a mile to the dock. Somewhere between the ship and shore I came upon a sandbar and ran the whaler aground. I thought I'd had it. Captain Stephen K. Hall had been on Admiral "Bull" Halsey's staff at Pearl Harbor. But, as I was about to learn, the Captain was a kindly man.

G. Roy McBride

It was obvious that I had just been pressed into service, and he could tell I was nervous. "Sit down in my chair, son. I'll get us off this sand bar and take us in for landing. You pay attention, and while I'm ashore, you take this gig and go practice." I took his seat. He then started ringing the bell, which tells the motorman what to do. By rocking the boat back and forth, he freed it from the grip of the sand, and we were on our way. As we drew up at the dock, two wide-eyed Marine guards snapped to attention. I'm sure they wondered how this seaman first-class rated being brought ashore by a Navy captain.

The motorman and I went to practice. I quickly learned how to operate the whaler. Thus began a wonderful relationship between me and the Captain. He was like a second father to me.

I have thought over the years that no one should ever feel abashed about keeping the Word of Wisdom. My doing so had made a favorable impression upon the officers on my ship.

The USS General C. G. Morton, AP138, was a troop transport, delivering men to the war zone and returning with casualties. The ship's complement included 31 officers and 342 enlisted men. I was with the ship from its commissioning at Richmond, California, 7 July 1944, to the time it was decommissioned on 6 March 1946. We sailed more than 152,000 nautical miles, (or just over six times the circumference of the world.) We crossed the equator twelve times; the Pacific Ocean eleven times; the Atlantic Ocean seven times; passed through the Panama Canal one time, the Suez Canal five times; we traveled over five of the seven seas, touched port on five continents, and carried 49,738 passengers, both military and civilian. Once we circumnavigated the earth. Now, as I examine the itinerary log of our journeys aboard the *General Morton,* it astounds me to think of the places we traveled.

There is an old song about "far away places, with strange sounding names." We went there—Guadalcanal, Tulagi, Pavuvu, Espirito Santo, Noumea, Banika, Cape Cretin, Manus Island, Melbourne, San Diego, Hoogley River, Calcutta, Ulithi, Tinian, Saipan, Hollandia, Leyte, Boston, Manila, Marseilles, Newport News, New York City, Port Said, Suez, Hoboken, Karachi, Ceylon, Singapore, Eniwetok, and San Francisco. We traveled to many of these several times.

* * *

1 March 1945. Departed Calcutta, India, with a group of 20th Air Force antiaircraft gunners bound for Ulithi Atoll in preparation for the invasion of The Philippines. After a five-day layover at Melbourne, Australia, we entered Ulithi's small seaport. The harbor was filled with ships of every kind, awaiting the invasion. Moving slowly, making our way through the congested harbor we encountered a sudden heavy rain squall. The duty officer ordered that we hold our position until the storm cleared. I was posted on the bridge at the time. At that moment there was a huge explosion over by one of the docks; an ammunition ship blew up causing significant damage. Had it not been for the squall, we would have been docking very near that ship as the explosion occurred. There was much talk on board about the hand of Providence saving us. It didn't seem so surprising to me, I felt that it was.

On the morning of the third day at this port we awoke to find the harbor as empty as it had been full the night before. We left shortly. Just over the horizon, the ship's radar picked up a large incoming flight of Japanese aircraft. They were kamikazes—a day too late to bomb our fleet. General quarters was sounded, and we quickly manned our battle stations, where we remained for several tension-filled hours. We maintained radio silence and the Captain decided to fire only if fired upon. Fortunately, the Japanese did not see us. We were far enough over the horizon to be out of their sight. That many kamikazes would have been a serious problem for one lone, unescorted ship. That was the most frightened I was while aboard ship. Our radar men later told us they watched some of these planes drop into the water. Kamikazes had only enough fuel for a one-way flight.

5–11 June 1945. We entered Manila Bay, The Philippines. Manila was badly damaged, the docks still smoldering from fires set during the fighting. Many ships had been sunk in the harbor. The destruction was massive.

Here we configured the ship to return wounded and took on some of the first survivors of Corregidor and the Bataan Death March to be repatriated. These men were in bad shape. Many of them were missing an arm or a leg or an eye, or had other serious problems. They had been treated viciously. This was an especially sad crossing. We had extra doctors and other medical personnel with us for this trip. The *General Morton* could carry 4,000 troops, but when we returned with casualties we could fit only about 800.

26 October 1945. We arrived in New York City where we said good-bye to thirty of our shipmates who had sufficient points for discharge from the Navy. We were hosted at a ship's party and dance at the Ritz Carlton Hotel, where the Horace Heidt Band was playing. During a short intermission, while the dance floor was clear, a drum roll began. Out of the kitchen came a waiter, a quart of milk and a glass balanced on a tray above his head. He crossed the dance floor to the table where I was seated and with a flourish placed the tray in front of me as the drummer finished his roll with a bang. I never did learn who ordered it. I like to think it was the Captain. The fresh milk was a welcomed treat.

Occasionally we carried Red Cross personnel returning to the States; these were often women. When they came aboard, men from the various States were given an assembly point where they could meet the Red Cross representative and catch up on the news from their home state. One of these young ladies was from Idaho Falls. She and I were visiting on the open deck. Shortly, the exec officer, obviously quite drunk, appeared, and ordered me to go below. I didn't like the situation and I refused his order, much to the relief of the young lady. I reported the incident to the officer-of-the-day. Two days later my name appeared on a list to report for a court-martial for refusing to obey an order. I went to Captain Hall for counsel. He advised me to report for the court-martial. He said he would sentence me to two weeks restriction aboard ship. We would not be anywhere near land for more than two weeks!

We were en route from Boston to Marseilles, France, when word came that Japan had surrendered. Jubilation broke out among the ship's crew, along with a surprising number of cigars and bottles of liquor. In the excitement I jammed a cigar in my mouth. Immediately someone grabbed the cigar out of my mouth—"You don't smoke!" he said, up close and in my face.

17–18 January 1946. We passed through the Suez Canal for the last time. On previous trips through the canal, Captain Hall made arrangements for half of the crew to go to Cairo, to see the pyramids, the Nile, and other famous sites in Egypt. On this last trip he allowed the other half of us to make that trip.

We returned to the *"Snortin Morton"* at Port Suez, 18 January, and went on into the Red Sea. I wondered where Moses, through the power of the Lord, had parted the waters.

Our next stop was Karachi, India. We sailed down the coast of India and made our way south, arriving at Colombo, Ceylon, 1 February. On 3 February we crossed the path of an earlier course when we had been en route to Calcutta, India. We had now circumnavigated the world. Somewhere we got into a terrible storm—winds so vicious that when going on deck you had to tie a line to yourself to keep from being swept over board. Huge waves crashed over the ship. Sometimes we were in a deep trough of water, and other times the ship's screw was lifted out of the water, which caused the ship to shudder. Oftimes as the ship crashed through a wave, water splashed over me, high in my post in the "crow's nest." We looked forward to crossing the quieter Pacific.

When the *General Morton* arrived in San Francisco on 6 March I left the ship for the last time, and it was decommissioned. It had been a remarkable experience; nevertheless, I was happy to go home.

Before I left for active duty with the Navy, I was dating Blanche Williams, from Idaho Falls. We had fallen in love, and during a leave at home I had asked her to marry me. She consented. I was discharged in May 1946 and returned home to begin life anew.

Since the Idaho Falls Temple was temporarily closed, we went to Logan to be married. Our parents were with us. We stopped at the Cache County Court House to obtain our marriage license. As we pulled up in front, Dad asked if he should go in with us. I was a veteran of twenty-eight months of Navy service—a world traveler. I told him I thought I could handle it without him.

Inside we found the proper office. When the clerk asked for my birth date, she told me that since I was only twenty years old, I would have to have my father's permission to be married. Blanche, also twenty, was old enough to sign on her own. Red-faced, I went back to the car and asked my father to come give his permission for me to be married. Blanche has kidded me about that ever since. Perhaps we never get too old or too experienced to need our father.

Roy and Blanche McBride are parents of two sons and two daughters, have nineteen grandchildren and five great-grandchildren. Roy served with the Federal Bureau of Investigation for nine years, and as security officer for companies at the Idaho National Engineering Lab. He has been a Scout Master, member of a bishopric, high councilman, counselor in a stake presidency and is currently a sealer and ordinance worker in the Idaho Falls Temple.

ARVIL SHERWOOD JOHNSON

Cry unto him against the power of your enemies.

(Alma 34:22)

I was a Marine sergeant, C. Company, 5th Tank Battalion, 9th Marine Corp, attached to the 28th Battalion Infantry. I landed on Iwo Jima 19 February 1945, thirty-six days before the battle was over. I was commander of a flame-thrower tank. Flame-thrower tanks were a number-one target of the Japanese. When the CB's invented the flame thrower on the MI tanks, they ran the tubing through the barrel of the regular .75-mm gun so the Japanese couldn't tell the difference between it and a regular tank.

Flame thrower tanks were held in reserve for other tanks and infantry to call in to burn out pill boxes, caves and machine gun nests. One day an infantryman knocked on our tank with his rifle. He said there was a Japanese machine gun nest ahead of us, which had all their men pinned down. Would we come burn it out?

Arvil Sherwood Johnson

Besides our flame thrower, our tanks had only .30-caliber machine guns for protection, so a regular .75-mm tank was sent ahead to protect us. The infantryman crawled in the tank. I was acting assistant gunner that day. I gave him my seat so he could look through the periscope and direct us where to go. He buckled himself in. I took a seat on a little X300 radio set in the corner.

The machine gun nest was several hundred yards ahead of our own troops. We proceeded toward our target. That particular day, for some reason, I put on my tank helmet, then put on my tin helmet over that.

The Japanese had planted 1,000-pound aerial bombs in the ground, upside down. When we ran over the top of one of these bombs, they set it off electronically, and it blew up beneath our tank. I flew upward, hitting the roof of the tank. My tin helmet was flattened like an envelope on my head. The explosion blew the treads off and the engine out of our tank. We could not move. I tried to get out of my hatch, but our infantry passenger panicked, pulled me down into the cabin of the tank, and crawled over me to get out.

I crawled under the gun and out the commander's hatch. In doing so, I got all the radio wire wrapped around my legs. When we got off the tank, Lieutenant Kelly was trying to call the other tank. He finally realized he was talking to my leg.

Outside, they pulled my helmet off. I was a little bruised and sore, but none of us was hurt. Another tank took us back to our lines.

Sherwood returned to the United States after war's end. He married Julie McLaughlin. They are parents of three daughters and two sons. Sherwood farmed for awhile and then spent the rest of his life in the excavating business. He has been active in the Church in many callings, including a term as bishop.

RUSSELL HARLAND ROCK

Behold, I have refined thee, but not with silver; I have chosen thee in the furnace of affliction.

(Isaiah 48:10)

My father's first name was Russell, so to avoid confusion, I went by Harland.

I joined the United States Navy in March 1940, thinking the Navy had to be a better way to make a living than doing the hardscabble farm work I was doing for $20.00 per month. The Navy paid $21.00 a month, plus food and clothing. After I completed basic training, I applied to become a Navy medical corpsman. I was the only one of our recruit company to get into the hospital corps, about half the others were assigned aboard the *USS Arizona*. A lot of the guys whose names are inscribed on that memorial at Pearl Harbor were fellows in my recruit company.

I trained for independent field duty at Bethesda Naval Hospital. There I learned to do minor surgery, take x rays, set bones, dispense medicine, and take care of illnesses. At any isolated station I was responsible for sick or injured men until they could be seen by a doctor. I felt I was well-trained.

On 4 December 1941, we left Kodiak, Alaska, aboard an old WW I submarine, bound for Mare Island, California. We were anxious to get there.

Just off the Washington-Oregon coast we were advised of the attack at Pearl Harbor. We did not know what to expect. The U.S. had no coastal defenses to speak of. The Japanese could have sailed up the Columbia River and landed without getting their feet wet. We fully expected to see the Japanese any moment. Considering the task, we were a pitifully thin watch.

Russell Harland Rock

After we had spent some time patrolling the Pacific west of Oregon and Washington, it was determined that the Japanese fleet had pulled back toward their homeland, and we were released to continue to our original destination. We tied up at Mare Island on New Year's Eve. Totally exhausted, our crew had no interest in going into San Francisco for the festivities.

The military buildup was straining Navy facilities, and every billet teemed with enlistees. There was just no place to bunk. I found a set of hammock clews and slung up my hammock on a dock and crawled in. Some time after midnight I felt myself falling. My hammock was slung about five feet off the deck. The fall jarred me to full wakefulness. I saw the Marine sergeant-of-the-guard going into the guard shack. Evidently he didn't like ducking under hammocks so he cut my clews to clear his way.

Naked as a jay-bird, I charged into the guard shack. We had a pretty good fight going when the Shore Patrol arrived and put us both in the brig. At a deck captain's mast the next morning the marine lost a stripe. I thought I would also. However, the commanding officer said, "Well, you like to fight; the Marines are looking for fighters." That night I was on a train bound for the San Diego Marine Corps Depot. Since the Navy furnishes the medical services for the Marine Corps anyway, it seemed a good alternative to losing a hard-earned stripe. So, I became a combat medic, assigned to the 2nd Marine Division at Camp Elliot, California.

I shipped to New Zealand on the Dutch ship *Bloem Fontain*. Her crew was East Indian, but had Dutch officers. It was a dirty old bucket, and the trip was hot and uncomfortable. We landed at Auckland, then went inland about forty miles. At Wurk Worth another medical company was already assigned to the division hospital, so we trained for combat duty. The Marines were very good to us. A medical corpsman is well-respected in the Corps.

While in New Zealand I was sent to a college to study malarial fever and was eventually sent to Guadalcanal. It was here I first saw combat. Guadalcanal is a terrible place. It is mostly jungle, and because it rained constantly, it stunk. We used some British coconut plantations away from the beach for a reserve camp. In the jungles, under the heavy foliage, even at noon it was almost black as night. Fearsome looking giant lizards, ten feet long, weighing 50 to 70 pounds, could put a scare into you.

* * *

When things quieted down I got together with some LDS men from Utah, and we organized and began holding occasional meetings. Some curious non-members came when we started holding regular Sunday meetings. There were several returned missionaries in the group. They consecrated enough oil that all of us could have a vial to carry with us.

The Marine Corps had recruited a lot of Mormons. They called them "The Mormon Battalion." It was a publicity ploy, but when this unit arrived on Guadalcanal, it boosted our membership considerably. We would find our members by whistling "High on a Mountain Top" or "Come, Come, Ye Saints" as we walked down the street. Guys would stick their heads out of tents and ask, "Hey, Mack, where you from?"

We asked permission from the senior chaplain, who happened to be a Catholic, to use the chapel facility for our services. We were denied because "there were Protestant services on Sunday, which we could attend." He wasn't about to let us have our own "peculiar" services. This made us mad. My colonel suggested I go to the division chaplain. The upshot was we got permission to hold services in the chapel.

We held sacrament meeting every Sunday. We sang the hymns of Zion, studied scripture, and bore our testimonies. A returned missionary had a hymn book with him, and we mimeographed the words so everyone could have a copy. Our choir leader was a boy from Iona, Idaho, who had a beautiful

Salt Lake City, Utah, Friday, July 10, 1942

'Mormon Battalion'
Leaves For Training

Newspaper article recognizing the ninty-three members of the Church that formed the first of two platoons of Marines. Known as the "Mormon Batallion," these men served throughout the Pacific.

singing voice. I had known him before we entered military service and was sorry when he was later killed on Guam.

Because of curiosity, or boredom, our services were well attended and often resulted in gospel discussions with members and non-members.

My grandmother sent me a copy of the Book of Mormon. I passed it around to my tentmates and ended up giving it to one of them. This fellow stayed in the Navy for nearly thirty years and about twenty-five years later I received a package in the mail. It was my Book of Mormon. His note said that he had read the book many times and received a great deal of comfort from it. He returned it because my grandmother had written on the fly leaf.

Just prior to our departure for the Marianas, an LDS chaplain came to visit us. He was the Southwest Pacific Senior Chaplain, a full colonel in the Army. He flew to the Solomon Islands to conduct a conference. We put forth a lot of effort to get all the LDS kids there. Company and battalion commanders saw to it that there was transportation. It was held on Guadalcanal. What a rare privilege to be there. It was just like a family reunion; I met a lot of friends. The chaplain encouraged us, told us that by our actions we were doing missionary work.

All of my tentmates were from different religions—one from the Reorganized Church, a shouting Baptist, a Catholic, and me. We often discussed religion. We ganged up on the Catholic boy. He didn't know much about what he believed, so he would go see the Catholic chaplain. Finally the chaplain told him to change his tentmates and not have anything to do with us infidels. But our friend had enough starch to tell the chaplain he wasn't going to give up his buddies.

* * *

After Guadalcanal, I was attached to the 3rd Marine Division. We got orders to go to Bougainville. This was real scary as a large Japanese army was on Bougainville, and their main airbase was just over a mountain at Kahili. We expected very heavy fighting, and we got it.

At Empress Augustus Bay we climbed over the side of the ship into Higgins boats [landing craft]. As soon as we hit the beach, our boats were up-ended in the high surf, making it impossible to return to the ship. It was dirty combat before we secured the beachhead—then the Seabees came in to lay down an airstrip for fighter planes.

We moved inland through dense jungle, stinking swamps, and enemy soldiers. There was no way to get a vehicle through this mess. Some Marine paratroopers were dropped into the jungle ahead of us. Nearly all of them were slaughtered by the enemy. We penetrated about five miles into the jungle, enough to support a fighter strip. U.S. casualties from Japanese artillery, bombers, and fighter planes were heavy. Treating the wounded kept me constantly occupied. We never succeeded in clearing the Japanese from the island, but we isolated them.

I was in charge of surgery. During one attack the Japanese landed on the beach and got right down to the hospital before our men turned them back. During the clash I was wounded slightly, but not seriously enough for a ticket back to the States.

The Seabees dozed trees out of the way and leveled off a sand spit. They then laid steel mats on the sand and made a fighter strip and established control of the area. It was only a five-minute flight over the ridge to an enemy airfield and ground troops.

I contracted malarial fever while on Bougainville, the malignant falciparin type. Finally we were relieved and sent back to Guadalcanal to recuperate. Some army guys had built stills back in the jungle, and were making whiskey. When the Marines heard that whiskey was available they went wild. Being short of containers, the brewers used five-gallon, zinc-lined buckets. The zinc made the whiskey poisonous, and a lot of Marines got sick. I rounded up all the stomach pumps I could find and passed out Ipecac. It was a wild time. The stills were destroyed.

After recovering from malaria, I was transferred to the 3rd Marine Regiment and put in charge of 110 corpsmen. Our division was alerted to be sent to New Ireland at Kavieng. This was the most heavily fortified Japanese base in the Pacific at that time. We were to establish the beachhead at Kavieng. Scuttlebutt was that casualties would be extremely high. Fortunately the Navy neutralized Kavieng and our orders were changed. We were sent to the Marianas—Guam, Rota, Saipan, and Tinian.

At 0400 hours on 21 July 1944, our battleships began lobbing 16-inch shells at Guam from fifteen miles out to sea. As these passed over on their way to the beach, they sounded like a freight train. At dawn we boarded amphibious tanks and headed for the beach. A destroyer escort blanketed the ground ahead of us with a barrage of rockets. We went in on the left flank of the beachhead on Agate Bay, by Adelupe Point. The Japanese were firing artillery and mortars at us. Some of our amphibious tanks were blown out of the water before getting close to land. Closer to the beach we came under withering machine-gun and mortar fire. No sooner did we get on the beach than our LST [landing-ship-tank] was hit and stopped. Several Marines were killed. Somehow I managed to get onto the sand.

We were in hand-to-hand combat from the outset. I was loaded down with medical supplies, my carbine slung over my shoulder, when an enemy soldier came at me with his bayonet extended. He ran past me and a Marine behind me killed him.

We climbed a short distance up a steep hill. Japanese mortar shells fell all over our position. Right away there were a lot of wounded men. I gathered as many as I could into a large shell crater, which appeared a likely spot to establish a first-aid center. I glanced up just as a mortar shell fell on top of us.

Coming to, I saw that others in the shell hole were dead. Then I realized that I had lost my leg—I could see it lying off to the side of me. I knew it was my leg because I had painted my shoe, and there was a painted shoe on that piece of leg. My memory of what happened after that is vague. I do recall giving myself a shot of morphine and putting a tourniquet on what was left of my leg.

In a dream-like state I saw my body lying in the shell hole. I saw other Marines and watched as the battle raged. I floated upward toward a ridge and saw a lot of Marines in my same condition go over that ridge. Intuitively, I knew that if I were to go across that ridge I could not come back; yet it seemed so lovely over there.

My next awareness was of hearing music, but I could not figure out where I was. Slowly regaining consciousness, I recognized I was aboard a ship. The music coming over the ship's loud speakers was Tommy Dorsey's band playing, "I'm Getting Sentimental Over You." My eyes were bandaged. I knew I was hurt; I didn't know how badly.

A doctor came to change the dressing on my leg. He ripped the stiffened dressing from my stump. Screaming in agony I tried to get out of bed and run. The medics grabbed me and held me down. After that, nobody touched my stump. I soaked it with boric acid and removed the bandages myself. The medics gave me morphine so that I could sleep. It doesn't take very long to get addicted to morphine. You crave it to take away the pain.

I was taken to a hospital in Honolulu. It was nice to see nurses again instead of corpsmen, and we had nice clean beds; but I was still hurting.

Dearest Mom & Dad   July 30, 1944

Sunday again, and everything is as well as can be expected. You no doubt have gotten the word that I've been wounded, and you are probably doing a lot of unnecessary worrying. You know me—if anybody was going to get fouled up, I'd be one of the first. But there is no cause to worry as at the present. I'm doing swell and the worst part is over. I was very lucky, and I thank God every day for getting off as easy as I did. I'm getting excellent treatment and care—no red-headed nurse as yet, though! I'll probably be in the States before very long, and I'll get in touch with you as soon as possible then. So 'til then, don't do any worrying on my account. I'll be as good as new in no time. Hope all is well with you. I'll be saying bye for now. I'll be looking for an extra long letter soon. Give my regards to all.

Love, Harland

President Franklin D. Roosevelt came to Hawaii for a conference with Admiral Nimitz and General MacArthur. While there he came to visit us. It was something to see the president in his wheelchair. Like us, he was crippled. He stopped at each bed, shook our hand, and wished us the best.

We were transferred to a hospital at Mare Island, Vallejo, California, near San Francisco. While they were checking us into the hospital, a doctor came into our ward. It was Captain Owens, the medical officer with whom I had worked when I was in surgical training; now the hospital commander. When I got well enough, I became Doctor Owen's patient's assistant. I had the run of the hospital, even got into a little mischief. I became acquainted with Don, another LDS man, from Salt Lake City, and Glen, a devout Baptist from Kansas, who became a good friend.

We learned that Russ Morgan and his orchestra were playing at the Claremont Hotel in San Francisco. Glen and I went over to Berkeley and on what was called "Sorority Row," picked out a likely looking sorority house, went to the door and asked to speak to the house mother. We told her we would like to meet some nice girls to take to dinner and dancing at the Claremont Hotel. Of course we couldn't dance, but we could listen to the orchestra and have dinner. This lady immediately became our friend. She invited us into the parlor and called in all the girls.

"Girls, here are two handsome young heroes just back from the war, and they'd like to take two of you to dinner and dancing at the Claremont Hotel." By this time we were embarrassed. Here we were on crutches. There were about thirty girls. A half-dozen of them had other things to do, or didn't like our looks, or something. But there were lots of pretty girls there. How to choose. We picked a couple and were on our way.

We enjoyed a wonderful meal and the music of the Russ Morgan band. As we came out of the hotel to take the girls home, it was pouring down rain. All the taxis seemed to be tied up by the high-ranking brass.

Standing under the canopy of the hotel, we wondered how we were going to get our dates home by their midnight curfew. Just then a limousine pulled up. The United Nations was being organized in San Francisco, and the Claremont Hotel was the headquarters for King Ibn Saud, of Arabia. When the limousine door opened, Kind Saud got out. We recognized him from pictures in the newspapers. He was a huge man, perhaps six-foot-six. He appeared to have only one eye, and his face bore several noticeable scars. He walked past us with a nod and a smile. He really was *something* to see.

He paused as he entered the hotel and looked back at us. He then turned to one of his aides, who approached us and said the king wished to place his limousine at our disposal. We couldn't believe it. We looked to the king, he nodded affirmatively.

We got into his luxurious car and the chauffeur asked where we wanted to go. We directed him to the Gamma Phi Beta house and pulled up just at midnight. A lot of the other girls were also returning from dates. When they went inside, they peeked out the windows at us and the limousine. We escorted our girls to the door and said goodnight. After that we could date any girl in that sorority house.

When we got back inside the car, the driver asked us where we wanted to go. "Take us back to the bus station, and we'll catch a bus out to Vallejo." He said, "I'll drive you to Vallejo." We told him it was 25 miles away. "That's all right. This limousine is at your disposal, and I am authorized to take you." Glen and I relaxed and enjoyed the ride.

It was still raining heavily when we pulled up to the guard shack at Mare Island. The Marine on duty did a double take. He asked the chauffeur where he wanted to go. "Up to the hospital."

Then the gate guard saw the Chief-of-State insignia on the front of the limousine and asked the driver to please wait. He got on the phone and in about five minutes here came a couple of Marine captains on motorcycles to escort us. They led us over to the Naval hospital in the driving rain. We got out—two enlisted men—went inside and went to bed.

The next morning, my friend Doctor Owens called Glen and me to his office. "All right, just what is going on now?!"

"What do you mean?" we responded.

"What were you doing in that limousine last night?" So we told him the story. "It better be true, because the Navy wants to see you. We have Navy transportation outside to take you to the San Francisco District Headquarters." Glen and I looked at each other in dismay. At headquarters we were taken before a high-ranking officer, who quizzed us about our story. "I sure hope this is true!" Frowning, he picked up the phone and called the Saudi aide at the Claremont. He verified that the king had provided us the use of his limo. When he finished the phone call, he leaned back in his chair and laughed long and heartily. He seemed delighted.

"I've been in this Navy for thirty years and have never seen or heard of the Marines escorting a couple of enlisted men riding in the limousine of a king, through a driving rain storm."

A couple of days later, King Ibn Saud sent Glen and me each a Bulova watch. I still have mine, and it still runs perfectly.

It was nearly Christmas, 1944, and I wanted to go home. Although policy was that we couldn't get leave unless we had a prosthesis, I *really* wanted to be home for Christmas! I went to see my doctor friend at the limb shop, who thought something could be fixed up.

We fashioned a bucket shaped form out of plaster of paris to fit over the stump of my leg, attached a couple of straps to that, and fastened it all to an ankle block and to an artificial foot. I could stand. Walking was another matter! The regulation was when you got a limb, your canes were taken away, and you had to walk on your own. Walking hurt my stump big-time! I have never had such pain—and all the pain medicine I could take didn't help. Anyway, the doctor okayed my leave, and I got to go home for Christmas.

My folks were not expecting me. It was fun to surprise them and wonderful to be with them. It was one of the nicest Christmases I ever had. It even snowed on Christmas Eve.

I was back in Vallejo on 3 January. They started working on my leg. I got so that I could wear that pylon pretty well, and it got so it wasn't hurting as much. One night a group of us went dancing, and I even got right out on the floor with a girl.

I was discharged 5 December 1945. I had purchased a car that summer, so I loaded my stuff in the car and took off for Idaho Falls. A sailor rode with me to Twin Falls. About four o'clock that afternoon, five miles east of Rupert, my car threw a rod. I walked to the nearest house and called my Dad's neighbor, and asked her to ask Dad to come get me. At 0400 the next morning he arrived to tow me home. Where was King Saud when I needed him?

Harland Rock married Embere Ririe in the Idaho Falls Temple in March 1947. They had a daughter, Denys, and adopted another daughter, Mischelle, whom they had sealed to them. Embere passed away in June 1959. Harland later married Doris Villella, who had five children of her own. Together they raised their children. Harland became a tax auditor. He retired in 1981. He served as bishop of the Lincoln Ward and has been an active Church member throughout his life.

Taken from the personal history of Russell Harland Rock.

STERRELL E. DOUGLASS

There were numerous jobs that had to be done to win the war. Some were dangerous; some seemed mundane. All of them were necessary.

A native of Idaho Falls, Sterrell Douglass, following in his father's footsteps, became a machinist. He went to work in the Navy Yard at Bremerton, Washington, in 1940. At that time the Navy Yard at Bremerton employed 3,000 people. By war's end that number had jumped to 30,000. Sterrell spent most of the war building ships. Before he turned 26 years old, he was drafted into the Navy.

Doug, as he was called, became Fireman First Class Douglass aboard an LST [landing ship tank]. His job was making fresh drinking water. The LST's top speed was six knots; even traveling 24 hours a day, it took a long time to get to a destination. On his first voyage, this ship-tank left Panama City, Florida, with a load of telephone poles, crossed the Gulf of Mexico, and passed through the Panama Canal, arriving in Honolulu twenty-

Sterrell E. Douglass

two days later. Doug joked that he never got very far from land, only a mile away—straight down.

Sterrell was the only Church member in the 120 man crew. He doesn't recall meeting another Mormon during the entirety of his military service.

Despite the LST's slow speed, Sterrell traveled long distances. He saw Guam, Tinian, Saipan, Eniwetok and took part in the battle for Okinawa. For the attack on Okinawa they picked up troops at Lingayen Gulf on the east coast of Luzon, The Philippines, and transported them to Okinawa. The landing on Okinawa was the most frightening event in which Sterrell took part.

Approaching the beach they came under intense fire. Bodies of enemy soldiers were floating in the water. Japanese fighter planes were attacking the incoming invaders. The LST commander kept yelling "Make smoke, make smoke!" but the smoke generator would not function. Finally the LST drove up on the beachhead, its big front door dropped open, and one hundred soldiers ran out to join in the battle. The LST immediately reversed itself into the water to begin its four-day trip back to Luzon for another load of soldiers.

When the war ended, Doug was just off the Russell Islands where they were to pick up pontoons and transport them to Japan. They would have been used in landing troops and equipment there, had the U.S. needed to invade Japan.

Following the war, Sterrell Douglass returned to Idaho Falls. He eventually took over his father's machine shop. He married Bonnie Middleton, and they became parents of three daughters and twelve grandchildren. Now retired, he regularly attends the Idaho Falls Temple.

Taken from an oral interview with Paul H. Kelly.

Landing ship tanks (LSTs), large beaching crafts that could disembark troops and supplies directly on shore, were a significant part of the war in the Pacific, as well as amphibious landings in Europe. This particular LST is being loaded for the invasion of France.

EARL E. BAGLEY

At home or abroad, on the land or the sea, As thy days may demand, so thy succor shall be.

("How Firm a Foundation," *Hymns*, no. 85)

I was thirty-two years old when the Japanese bombed Pearl Harbor, married, with three children. One night between shows at a movie theater where I was with my wife, Alice, a commercial was shown about the Navy. They were seeking men who had some background in math and electricity to train as technicians. I did not expect to be drafted into the service, but the idea of getting some training in a new vocation worked its way into my thinking.

Upon taking the required tests for entrance into the Navy, I was offered the rating of third-class petty officer. After much discussion and thinking and talking it over with my wife, our bishop, and several other people, I decided to enlist. With the Navy pay and the allotment I would receive for dependents, I would be making more money than I had ever made before. On Monday, 9 November 1942, at Boise, Idaho, I enlisted in the United States Naval Reserve for the duration of the war.

By the end of March, 1943, I was in Washington D.C. for additional training at the Bliss Electrical School. We lived in the school's dormitory, and I had three roommates, all of whom had names beginning with B. They were all men of high moral standards. One of them had been a minister before joining the Navy. On the first Sunday we were there these fellows invited me to attend a Community Church located near our school. I agreed to go with them, if they would agree to go to church with me the next week.

As promised, the next Sunday they accompanied me to the famous LDS Chapel in Washington D.C. It happened to be Fast Sunday and there were servicemen, politicians, and numerous other people from all across the United States in the congregation. I don't think I ever attended a more inspirational testimony meeting. It was interesting to watch the facial expressions of my fellow sailors when some of the high-ranking men bore humble testimony of the truthfulness of the gospel. I know they were deeply touched, but I could never get them to go another LDS meeting with me. I think they were afraid they would be converted.

I went with my friends to the Community Church. It was an evening meeting much like our firesides. The minister turned the meeting into a question-answer session, and a young lady said she had heard that the Second Coming of Christ would be through the change in the hearts of men, that the attitudes of men would change and that they would become more Christlike. She said this bothered her, that she had always thought that Christ would come personally. The minister said that there were two schools of thought about that, and he could not tell her which was correct. One of my friends raised his hand and told the minister that he was not satisfied with that answer about the Second Coming of Christ. Explaining that he was a Methodist, one of his friends was a Presbyterian, and the other a Mormon, he said we would like a more definitive answer.

As soon as he said his friend was a Mormon, the pastor seemed to forget there was anyone else there. He asked me to come to the pulpit and explain what the Mormons believed about the Second Coming of Christ.

Earl E. Bagley

I began by quoting the 10th Article of Faith: "We believe in the literal gathering of Israel and in the restoration of the Ten Tribes; that Zion will be built upon this, (the American) continent; that Christ will reign personally upon the earth; and that the earth will be renewed and receive its paradisiacal glory." I then enlarged on this for about twenty minutes.

As we were leaving the meeting some elderly men on the back row introduced themselves as the elders of the Community Church and thanked me for the explanation I had given. They seemed to be very much in harmony with what I said.

* * *

Our class graduated from the Bliss School on 18 June 1943. I was assigned to the Radio Materiel School at Treasure Island, California, for additional training in ground and sky search radar. In December 1943, we graduated from the radio technicians school. Next, I reported for duty aboard the CVE [Carrier Vessel Escort] the *USS Gambier Bay,* a newly constructed ship, on 28 December. On the afternoon of 16 January 1944, the *Gambier Bay* cast off from the pier at Astoria, Oregon, and headed down the Columbia River and into the Pacific Ocean on its maiden voyage.

While in port in San Diego, on 21 March 1944, I was set apart as the LDS group leader for the *Gambier Bay,* by Chaplain Boud and Brother Willard Kimball. At that time I knew of only one other LDS man on the ship, Lars Anderson, a returned missionary.

LDS Servicemens Group partaking of the sacrament on the ship's deck.

One day I went to see the ship's chaplain about getting life insurance. The chaplain asked questions about my physical condition and when he had finished said, "You're LDS aren't you?" He told me that he'd had a commanding officer once who was a Mormon, whom he thought highly of, then told me that "If I can do anything for you, I would be glad to do it." I said, "Chaplain, there is one thing I would like, and that is the names of the men who have given their religious preference as LDS in this ship's company." A couple of days later he gave me a list of five men.

We held meetings every Sunday in the library, which was also the Chaplain's office. There were usually four of us in attendance, but we occasionally had visitors. We also attended meetings the Chaplain conducted. Most of the crew did not come to services until we were in battle zones or in other danger. Then there was not room for everyone, and the meetings had to be held out on the deck. It was very revealing to see the fluctuation in the sailors' attitudes when they were in extreme danger and when things were peaceful.

On 12 October we left Manus harbor, heading northwest. It became evident that something was going to happen. Hundreds of ships moved out. As far as the eye could see the ocean was covered with ships. That night Tokyo Rose broadcast that the United States was on its way to invade The Philippines.

When General Douglas MacArthur escaped from The Philippines in 1942, he promised the Filipino people, "I shall return." He kept that promise 20 October 1944, with this huge invasion force. The *Gambier Bay* and seventeen sister ships were there to provide combat air and antisubmarine patrol. During the opening days of the invasion an estimated 100,000 soldiers were landed on Leyte. Though the Japanese seemed to know we were coming, they did not know exactly where the landing would be. At 0430 hours, the morning of 25 October, we were called to general quarters and ordered to launch all of our fighter planes. Two hours later a pilot spotted the eastbound Japanese fleet coming through the San Bernardino Straits, just north of us. We immediately reverted to general quarters. The enemy force had four large battleships, including the *Yamato*, the largest battleship ever built, capable of firing 18-inch projectiles. When the Japanese saw our little group of escort carriers, they assumed we were the United States Third Fleet and reported us as large carriers and battleships as they engaged us in battle. We were definitely outgunned.

Although it was a stormy day and visibility was poor, the Japanese spotted us. The *Yamato* commenced firing from a distance of eighteen-and-a-half miles. Their cruisers and destroyers formed two columns and headed for us. With their ships having a top speed of 30 knots and ours only 17 knots, we were at a distinct disadvantage. We began a zigzag course, moving generally southwest. We had no place to go. Moving into Leyte Gulf would draw the Japanese warships there and trap General MacArthur. All we could do was stay out to sea. We launched as many airplanes as we could before turning to run. We were now going with the wind and could neither launch nor recover aircraft. As the Japanese closed on us they began firing. Our own destroyers and cruisers began laying down a smoke screen, but the wind blew the smoke away from the *Gambier Bay*, leaving us vulnerable.

With the Japanese on our heels, our ships turned to attack them. Though no match for the enemy our destroyer escort made run after run and launched torpedoes, inflicting a great deal of damage on the enemy. Skillfully maneuvering the *Gambier Bay,* our captain dodged hits for over half an hour. I stood on the catwalk off the radar shack and watched as we took a hit on the flight deck that caused some fires fairly close to the bridge. Within a short time fire went through the flight deck onto the hangar deck below, killing several men. Three Japanese cruisers were closing on our port side, and destroyers and a battleship were moving up from starboard. An explosion knocked out our forward engine room, and we began falling behind. A few minutes later our steering was damaged, then our engine room was knocked out and we were dead in the water. The Japanese ships closed on us and held target practice on the *Gambier Bay*. Our destroyers and escorts did a wonderful job of trying to separate a force of twenty-five Japanese ships from us, but eventually the Japanese sank three of them.

When we received the call to return to general quarters at 0645, it was made known to me that this was the end of our ship. I went to my locker and got my white sailor's hat and my shark knife and scabbard. At that moment I had the most peaceful feeling come over me. Although I knew this was the end of the ship, I had no fear and knew that whatever happened, I would be all right. I acknowledge the Lord's protection. The radar shack where I worked was the only compartment that did not take a direct hit until after the ship was abandoned.

About twenty-five minutes later the captain gave the order to abandon ship. We were dumping classified materials. When I went out onto the catwalk there were only two or three sailors still in sight up on the flight deck. By now the ship was listing at least thirty degrees to port and the Japanese ships were still holding target practice on that side. From the catwalk there was a rope extending from the bridge to within six or eight feet of the water. Grabbing it, down I went, hand over hand, and immediately began to swim away from the sinking ship. No one else was anywhere near. After I had moved what I calculated to be one hundred yards from the ship I stopped to look around. Attempting to inflate my life belt I found there was a hole worn in it; there was nothing in sight to hold on to. As I rode up on a wave I could see, about a quarter of a mile down tide, what looked like about a hundred men on rafts. I had to swim back around the ship to reach the other men and some means of security.

Nearing the ship I noticed a raft hugging the hull. A couple of men were trying to push it away. Swimming over, I suggested we slide the raft along the hull and get clear of the fantail. In this manner we were able to free the raft. I think we were only 150 feet from the ship when it rolled over on its side and sank. Ten or fifteen seconds later it suddenly shot up out of the water, stern first, to a height of about forty feet, where it seemed to stall as if deciding whether to go or stay, then disappeared into the sea.

Our position was about sixty miles east of the Philippine Island of Samar and ninety miles north of San Pedro Bay, Leyte, over the Philippine channel, the deepest water in the world.

On the *Gambier Bay*: Captain Goodwin with Lt. William Buderus review their radar "kids." Earl Bagley is the sixth man down on the left.

Our raft had a four-foot aluminum oar in it. By paddling and taking advantage of the tide, we caught up with the other rafts. Many men were wounded—in my raft alone there were four seriously injured men. I do not know how their crewmates got them into the raft. The officers in charge were rearranging the men to keep their wounds out of the water as much as possible. There were about 140 of us. I was asked to leave the raft I was on and get on another. While swimming the fifty or sixty feet to the one to which I was assigned, I noticed we were surrounded by sharks.

During the night my position on the raft was changed from a side to an end seat next to a corner. A large white box, presumably filled with medical supplies was lashed outside the raft near my left arm. About three feet behind my right side was a one-man rubber raft, and in it was a man named Barrett. He had been in the first raft with me. His legs were seriously injured, and he remained unconscious. I was to care for him should he need attention. Barrett's raft began to lose air through its valve late on the second day. I unscrewed the valve core and blew enough air to support Barrett's weight. Barrett was wearing white socks. His feet extended just a little over the end of the raft, and his socks, although out of the water, attracted the sharks. Between the white socks and the white medical supply box, just a few feet apart, I think I had practically all of the sharks in the area following on my corner.

The leaky life belt I was wearing had filled with water, but I was glad I had not taken it off. It had been cumbersome to swim with, but now I was grateful to have it, as I continually had two or three sharks poking their snouts into my back. Without the belt's protection, one of them might have taken a bite of me. The combined weight of the Red Cross box and some of us heavier men kept the raft on a downward slope to my end. I constantly bobbed in and out of the water, so the sharks had easy access to me. The only way I could keep them away was to slap the water beside their heads, then they would back away about a yard. As soon as I stopped slapping, they moved up close and began nudging me in the back again. I had to hold on to the raft with one hand all the time to keep from sliding into the water.

At least two men were killed by sharks the first day. One of them was my friend, Lieutenant Buderus, the officer in charge of the Combat Information Center. His raft was so overloaded that some of the men were hanging around its outside. The Lieutenant thought he should take his turn. A shark bit him across the buttocks and down his legs. The men were able to get him onto the raft, but he died a short while later.

The first day we were on the water, it was mostly cloudy and there was intermittent rain. Using my sailor's hat I caught what water I could and used it to moisten the lips of the sick. Pouring a little in their mouths seemed to revive them some. Someone found a small bottle of malted milk tablets in one of the survival canisters. Each of us were given two of these. The next day we each had a small slice of Spam and some dog biscuits. When I ate the salty Spam my throat constricted because I was so dehydrated, and it took some minutes until I could breathe normally. That was all the food we had for two days. Some of the men took sips of salt water, which caused them to become delirious. In a state of delirium, some of them thought they saw land and began swimming away. That was the last we saw of them. Some died after drinking sea water. Many of the men had hallucinations and had to be given morphine to quiet them.

After the coldness of the night, the second day was bright, sunny, and hot. As they abandoned ship, many men decided they could swim better without their pants and shirts, so were clad only in their underwear. Most of these men received second- and third-degree sunburns on parts of their bodies.

All this time we wondered what had happened to the rescue teams; we had expected to be picked up long before now. During the first day there were Japanese ships moving back and forth near us but none came close to the raft I was on. A friend told me later that one of the Japanese destroyers passed close to his raft, and they saw the Japanese sailors jump up and down, pull their hair, and shake their fists at our men. Another account I heard said that when enemy destroyers passed our men in the water, their crews lined up at attention and saluted the men in the water, but none stopped to pick us up. That turned out to be a good thing.

During the first day we were adrift we watched two different pairs of our planes pass over us without seeing us. Later we were told that ships were sent out to find us, but had been given erroneous directions.

I mentioned earlier the profound sense of security and peace I felt, even before the battle and as I left the sinking ship. During the time we were in the water, and as time began to grow long, and there seemed to be doubts about our being found in time, my thoughts were of the gospel. The words of the hymn, *"How Firm a Foundation"* looped through my mind:

> At home or abroad, on the land or the sea
> As thy days may demand, so thy succor shall be.
> When through the deep waters I call thee to go,
> The rivers of sorrow shall not thee o'erflow,
> For I will be with thee, thy troubles to bless,
> And sanctify to thee thy deepest distress.
> *(Hymns*, no. 85)

I remembered also the last four verses from section 89 of the Doctrine and Covenants:

> And all saints who remember to keep and do these sayings, walking in obedience to the commandments, shall receive health in their navel and marrow to their bones; and shall find wisdom and great treasures of knowledge, even hidden treasures; and shall run and not be weary, and shall walk and not faint. And I, the Lord, give unto them a promise, that the destroying angel shall pass by them, as the children of Israel, and not slay them. Amen. (D&C 89:18–21)

By practicing the law of the fast throughout my life, I knew that I could go without food and water for at least forty-eight hours and be okay. This gave me a confidence that most of my shipmates lacked.

Finally, between 0100 and 0200 hours during the second night, we saw lights in the distance; they were flashing coded messages, but our signalman could not stay alert long enough to send or receive a message. Our exec officer suggested to the captain that we cut our raft loose and paddle toward one of the ships, to find if it was Japanese or American. About 0300 we paddled up to the ship. It was one of our landing ships. They immediately began to take us on board. Men crowded the ladder. One of them flung out his arm; it hit me across the chest and knocked me backward into the drink. My first reflex was to look out for sharks, but there were none. I was the next to last man to board, just ahead of our exec.

After being given a half cup of water we were put into bunks. I immediately dropped off to sleep. For breakfast the next morning we had a cup of split pea soup. I think I have never tasted anything better. We spent all that day and into the night searching for survivors. We found some clinging to planks from our flight deck, and others in very precarious conditions. We did not hear of nearly as many shark attacks as I had thought we would.

About noon a doctor came onboard and began checking all of us. During the time I was in the water I noticed something that looked like mud gathering around spots on my shin. I kept rubbing them off, but soon there were more. Apparently when I went down the rope to get off the ship I got some rope burns on my shin. By the time the doctor got to me, those sores were inflamed and swelling. He painted the sores with iodine and advised me to see another doctor as soon as possible.

My leg became very sore and began to swell. However, I did not see a doctor until I was transferred onto the *USS Tryon,* an auxiliary hospital ship. There was a long line of sick and injured needing medical attention. My leg was now the same size from the ankle to the thigh from the infection. I was treated with sulfa and placed on bed rest.

We arrived at Humboldt Bay, Hollandia, New Guinea, on 1 November 1944. After having been sick it was good to get out on deck. There on the deck I expressed my thankfulness to the Lord then heard an announcement that all mobile *Gambier Bay* patients would board the *S.S. Lurline* for travel to the United States. We first went to Brisbane, Australia, and took on supplies necessary for 15,000 passengers.

On a passenger list I saw the name of my friend Lars Anderson, the only other Melchizedek Priesthood holder aboard the *Gambier Bay.* I had not seen him in the water and was concerned about him. We spent most of our time together. Lars told me that he was alone, clinging to a plank in the ocean for those two days and nights. It is a wonder he was not eaten by sharks or overlooked in the rescue.

On 1 December, I traveled by train from San Francisco to Idaho. It was a relief not to have to worry about the war. It was my third Christmas since joining the Navy and my first at home. Being with Alice and the children for the holidays made them more fun than any I could previously remember. But as all good things come to an end, on 3 January 1945, I caught the train for San Francisco, and three months later was sent back to the Pacific.

On 1 April 1945, I reached Ulithi, in the Marshall Islands where I was assigned aboard the *USS Bedford Victory, AK 231*, an ammunition cargo ship. This ship was about the same size as the *Gambier Bay* but instead of a crew of nearly a thousand, we had only sixty-five. My job was to repair and maintain the torpedo detector and other electronic surveillance gear.

We loaded many tons of ammunition on board and on 25 April sailed for the Ryukyus in support of the invasion of Okinawa. Warships of various types pulled along side us during the night and we passed ammunition to restock them for battle. On 20 May we were directed to Kerama Retto. We moored on the windward side of these small islands, which nullified any benefits of smoke screens, in an area known as Kamikaze Korner. Because we were an ammunition ship we were required to anchor a mile out from other ships. It was rumored that we were the third ammo ship to go into the Okinawa campaign, and that there had been no survivors when the others had been blown up—not an encouraging thought.

The night of 24 May, 150 kamikazes attacked our defending destroyers, warships, and supply ships at Kerama Retto. That day we stood at general quarters for twenty-one consecutive hours. We remained at Kerama Retto until 6 June, during which time many ships came alongside to take on ammunition. Over the TBS radio, I heard pilots pleading with soldiers to hold their fire and let them land, but the gunners did not get the message. Occasionally one of our pilots was shot down by our own soldiers. It was especially hazardous after dark. One night I heard, "Hold your fire! Friendly chick coming home to roost." The response was increased anti-aircraft fire. Running low on fuel and convinced that they were not going to let him through, he said, "To hell with you guys. I'm going around and come in over the Nips. They aren't such good shots as you guys." He did and made it down safely.

There were several times kamikazes could have dived into our ship if something unexpected had not happened. Everybody aboard the *Bedford Victory* was willing to credit God for our being alive after the close calls.

On 6 June the *Bedford Victory* joined a convoy that headed from Saipan to Ulithi, then on to Leyte Gulf. We waited there for the next anticipated invasion, which we thought would be the islands of Japan.

While we waited we pulled light duty. One day a black man, one of the ship's stewards, asked me to read a letter from his wife to him. He was about my age. We had previously been somewhat acquainted, and I knew Ed to be a humble man. I read the letter to him, then asked how he would like to learn to read. He told me that he'd tried before but that he could not learn. I told him that if he was willing to try again I thought I could teach him. "Oh," he said, "I want to learn, I want to learn." For an hour a day I taught him phonics. I taught him the alphabet and how to spell some simple words. He struggled with it, but before I left the ship, Ed had written a letter to his wife in his own handwriting, without help from me. After my discharge I received a letter from her, expressing her gratitude for teaching her husband to read.

On the night of 15 August, we were assembled on the ship's deck watching a movie. About twenty minutes into the movie there was an announcement over the ship's intercom that the Japanese had surrendered. The war was over! Shouting erupted from the group, and everyone else left the area. I had been running the projector. I secured the projection equipment, went to my room, and poured out a mighty prayer of thanksgiving. I learned later that many of the men went to sick bay and got all the denatured alcohol on the ship and drank it. It's a wonder it did not kill them.

I tallied my points; I had far more than needed to go home. On 8 September I packed my gear and was about to leave the *Bedford Victory*. While I was waiting for final inspection of my bags, Ed came out on the deck. We shook hands and tears began to run down his face. He said, "Bagley, you go home and get you a business started, and send for me. I'll work for you. I'd do anything for you. You just send for me." I was touched. I said, "Ed, you'd freeze to death up there in Idaho!"

"No" he said, "I mean it. You send for me. I'll do anything for you."

I was mustered out of the Navy at Puget Sound Navy Yard,

Bremerton, Washington, 25 October 1945, one year to the day after the *Gambier Bay* sank, and just two weeks short of three years from the day I started my Navy career. I arrived home in Idaho Falls on 30 October, genuinely grateful to be with Alice and our children.

Earl and Alice became parents of two more children. He became office manager for a car dealership and worked in accounting and income taxes until he retired at age 70.

Church callings include being a stake missionary, Sunday School superintendent, stake Young Men president, bishop, branch president, and high councilman. At age 72 he was called to be a bishop's councilor and after that, a stake patriarch. He was involved as a leader in Scouting from the time he was 17 and is a recipient of the Silver Beaver Award.

Eventually, the Bagleys relocated to Salt Lake City, via California. In his final years Earl enjoyed singing and playing his harmonica in a fiddlers' band in the Salt Lake Valley. He passed away 1 January 1994, at age 83.

Taken from Earl Bagley's autobiography *When I Was In the U. S. Naval Reserve During World War II.*

HAL R. JOHNSON

Yea, open your mouths and spare not, and you shall be laden with sheaves upon your backs.

(D&C 33:9)

To this day I don't like Spam. I ate my limit while I was at Morotai in the Dutch East Indies during World War II. Spam was served at many meals, and when we went on bombing raids we had Spam sandwiches.

I returned from my Church mission in Brazil, to Idaho Falls, in November 1942. Foreign missions were then thirty months, which allowed us time to learn the language. Since we were at war I felt fortunate to have been able to complete my mission. I immediately volunteered for service in the Army Air Corps and reported for basic training and classification in early February 1943.

While waiting to report for duty I met Virginia Pond at a dance. She had dated the fellow I went to the dance with. Shortly he left to return to his work in the Bremerton Shipyards. As he was leaving he said: "Hal, you take good care of my girl." I did. Thirteen days after our first date, Virginia and I were engaged. We were married on 19 January 1943. There wasn't time for a long courtship; in fact there wasn't even time for much of a honeymoon. Two weeks after our wedding day I was on my way to the service. It was hard to leave my new wife, but marrying Virginia remains the very best decision I have ever made.

After several months of training, I was commissioned a second lieutenant and assigned as a bombardier on a B-24. On 24 September we were assigned to 13th Air Force, the 307th Bomb Group,424th Bomber Squadron on Nadzab Island, New Guinea.

It was from here that I flew my first mission, which took us from Nadzab, New Guinea, to Boiken Plantation, near Wewak. It gave me quite a thrill. I labeled a lot of names on the bombs to make sure the folks back home got in on the war. There was no target visible on the heading we came in on, so we dropped just in from the shore. According to crew members, my bombs positively knocked down three palm trees.

A month later we were permanently stationed on Morotai Island in the Dutch East Indies. Things there were pretty primitive, but for our purposes, it was strategically located. We flew a total of forty-two bombing missions against targets held by the Japanese. Our missions included installations in the Celebes, The Philippines, the Halmaheras, and Borneo.

One night two of us were watching the searchlights play on Japanese planes and the ack-ack batteries sending up their futile barrages against the raiders, when we heard the telltale whistle of a bomb. There were two blurs as we bolted for our foxhole. We felt the ground shake as the bomb burst. Next morning we learned the bomb made a direct hit—on a latrine.

I quickly came to admire the men on our crew. They were fine fellows. We worked well together and genuinely liked each other. When we were not flying at night and it wasn't raining, we spent a lot of time in our tents. The guys all played cards. Cards had never interested me, so while they dealt, I read. But there was not much to do other than fight a war.

We actually held only a little part of a group of islands, and we were continually under threat by 25,000 Japanese Imperial Marines on nearby Halmahera Island. The enemy troops there were reported to be well-equipped and well-fed. Halmahera Island is visible from Morotai. Only our air superiority kept them on their side of the water. However, in early December they threatened invasion, and our planes were flown to the island of Noemfor

Lieutenant Hal Johnson, Summer 1944.

for safekeeping. To top it off, our favorite "radio personality," Tokyo Rose, announced that the entire American garrison on Morotai had been annihilated.

The Japanese increased their nightly air raids. Many of our B-24's, loaded with gas and bombs, prepared for the next day's missions, were destroyed on the ground. But our maintenance personnel worked miracles and somehow every morning we launched our planes. It was widely held that we controlled the strip by day and the Japanese had control by night.

Insects made life unpleasant. The mosquitoes were especially bestial, thriving in the many puddles. Malaria was prevalent and we followed malaria control regulations daily. I was constantly bothered by heat rash. The doctor always said, "You'll be okay when you get back to the States."

A rest leave in Sydney, Australia, was a welcome change from the strain of combat. For nineteen days I did things I had missed, being away from home. My friend and I had a room at the Bernley Officers' Club. We swam at Bondi Beach and ate wonderful food to our hearts' content.

The part of flying that concerned me most was take-off. Because we were so heavily loaded with bombs and fuel, had we crashed during lift-off it would have been all over for us. We were not much concerned about

Eddie Meacham and Hal Johnson (r).

enemy fighters. By this time in the war most of the enemy fighters in our area had been destroyed. But bad weather frequently made things hazardous in this part of the South Pacific.

18 November 1944. Target: Pamoesian oil fields and refinery, Tarakan, Borneo. Our target was the refinery and separation plant on Tarakan Island. Our rendevous went badly, but we did get over the target and how we plastered it! Precision bombing by all squadrons. Huge fires were started and the smoke rose up in a cumulus cloud to at least 12,000 feet. The lead ship in our squadron did not drop his bombs, so we made a second run for his benefit. There was some moderate flak, inaccurate, and our top turret gunner saw a dog-fight between two "zekes" [Japanese fighter planes] and four Thunderbolts. Satisfying mission. Flight time: 10 hours 20 minutes.

3 March 1945. Mission # 31, target: Manado Town, Celebes. We started out this morning to bomb barracks at Tarakan, but two and a half hours out, we lost number three engine and headed back with the prop feathered. We managed to get back to Manado Town, which we bombed through an undercast, and then headed home. With our number three was out, there wasn't enough hydraulic pressure to lock the landing gear in place, but by rocking the plane back and forth the pilot managed to lock the gear. We rigged up two chutes by the waist windows, in case the brakes would not

stop us, but luckily they did and we landed without incident. Bomb load was forty 100-lb napalm bombs. Flight time: 5 hours 25 minutes.

3 April 1945. Mission # 40. Today we went to Puerta Princesa on Palowan Island in The Philippines, from where we were to stage a couple of missions to Kuching in southwestern Borneo. We landed on the strip we used to bomb and that was a rare feeling. Only one strip and no taxi loop, so we had to circle for an hour waiting for our turn to land. We were parked close together—planes from all four squadrons. We were taken over a very dusty road to the transient camp, which was, and I find it hard to believe, the best I have yet seen. Showers for cleaning up, good food, better than the slum-gullion we have at Morotai, and good latrines. Nights were cold enough to use a blanket. Scorpions and centipedes were frequent, but I hung my shoes, A-3 bag, and clothes up every night and was not bothered.

Only occasionally over some targets were our B-24s harassed by enemy fighters. The weather was our most consistent enemy.

My position in the aircraft was up front, just below the cockpit. It was from here that I operated the new Norden bombsight when it was time to drop our bombs. One day as we were returning from a run, the cloud cover made visibility non-existent. We had no radar. The pilot was flying at very low altitude, attempting to find a glimpse of anything that would show him where we were. Sitting at my station in the nose I was doing some humble and urgent praying. Suddenly the clouds ahead opened just in time for the pilot to veer around the cone of a volcano directly ahead of us. My prayer turned to one of thanksgiving. I suppose that the Lord had more for me to accomplish while on this earth.

* * *

Troops on Morotai lived in tents; we even attended church in the chapel tent. There were several installations for different military units on Morotai. I met another LDS man from Idaho Falls who was attached to a neighboring squadron. My friend Eddie and I set about finding all of the LDS men on the Island. No one had been appointed group leader. We just invited all of the Mormons we could find to attend a sacrament meeting each Sunday. We also contacted a Navy chaplain to invite Navy personnel. Our attitude was that it was better to be damned for doing than damned for not doing. Both Eddie Meacham and myself were officers and had access to a

Jeep to drive around the island to invite the Mormons to Church. Between 35 and 40 of us met in the chapel tent. A canteen was the common cup from which we all partook of the sacrament. My missionary experience was very helpful. We enjoyed being together with other LDS servicemen. Eddie and I remained lifelong friends.

It's strange what you remember. My friend Bob had flown sufficient missions to earn a furlough to Australia. When he returned from leave he brought back a wonderful pair of fur-lined flying boots he purchased there. They were especially nice, although he never wore them when he flew. He said he intended to take them home. I expressed my admiration for them, to which he replied whimsically, "Hal, if anything ever happens to me, you can have them." Even though we were in a war zone and flying sorties, none of us thought anything would ever happen to us. It never occurred to me that I wouldn't return to my wife and new son. Whimsy turned to reality for Bob. He and his crew didn't come back from a bombing run over Balik Papan. When his personal effects were packed for shipment home, for some reason that I do not now recall, I did get those boots. I brought them home with me and wore them for years.

After flying my forty-second bombing mission I returned home for rest and recovery. Virginia and I were enjoying being together at Ponds Lodge in Island Park when we got word that the atomic bomb had been dropped on Japan. I will be forever grateful to President Harry Truman for having the courage to use that bomb. Following my leave, I returned to Santa Ana, California, where I was separated from the service. I then went home to be a husband and father and to make my way in the world.

Hal and Virginia are parents of five children, have twenty-five grandchildren and fourteen great-grandchildren. He entered the insurance business in Idaho Falls. His Church callings have included being bishop, counselors in a stake presidency, counselor in the Idaho Falls temple presidency, president of the Brazil North Mission, and president of the Sao Paulo Temple. He is currently patriarch in the Idaho Falls Ammon West Stake.

Taken from an oral interview with Paul H. Kelly and from personal records of Hal Johnson.

LDS group on Morotai. Hal's good friend Eddie Meacham is in front, wearing a white T-shirt.

MERLYN W.V. LOFGREN

Take upon you the name of Christ, and speak the truth in soberness.

(D&C 18:21)

I grew up in North Dakota. When World War II began, I was into my sixteenth year, and many of my friends a year or two older were eagerly enlisting in various branches of military service. Most popular were the Navy and Army Air Corps. With the written consent of my parents I joined the Navy while still seventeen.

After boot camp in San Diego I was sent to the Radar Training Center at Point Loma, California, then to the Small Craft Training Center at San Pedro to await sea duty. I was assigned to the *USS Pine Island,* a seaplane tender, to serve in an air-sea rescue unit attached to Fleet Air Wing 17.

Merlyn Lofgren

Sometime after receiving this assignment, I was directed to report to the commander of Terminal Island for interview by Naval intelligence personnel regarding service in German-occupied Norway. My parents had immigrated from Norway, and I was raised in a household where we spoke Norwegian. Because the war was not going well for Germany, it was concluded that the likelihood for the need of my services would no longer be a factor.

We were sent to Pearl Harbor for gunnery practice, and then to Okinawa where the Japanese Empire was making a last ditch, desperate, and fanatic attempt to win the war.

The kamikazes were in full force, taking a horrible toll on our ships, especially those to the east and those in the Ryukyu chain to the north. The aircraft carriers and their screening destroyers were especially targeted by the suicide planes. My assignment during general quarters was to be on the bridge to plot incoming air attacks. I maintained a small, lucite board with a dull-edged light so the captain could be appraised of enemy aircraft activity after dark.

Radar and radio were, of course, the eyes and ears of the ship, so all communication was centered near my station. We could hear the conversations of the pilots on the shipboard radio and their excitement and fears. Aircraft carriers were particularly vulnerable and dependent on the destroyers and planes for protection.

Our function was to dispatch PBM Mariner planes to pick up the survivors from sunken ships, and other downed pilots, some of whom were B-29 crews flying from Guam to bomb the Japanese mainland.

When we anchored in Buckner Bay, air attacks were a nightly occurrence. When we noted an incoming flight of enemy planes, a motor launch was sent to lay a smoke screen. The full moon was the least desirable calendar event. During those times, it seemed to take forever for the smoke to obscure the ships.

Although our ship took no hits, our sister ship the *USS Curtiss* took a kamikaze hit amid ship, killing several people. After this happened I was transferred to the *Curtiss*. We had to leave port shortly after my transfer to ride out a typhoon. Returning to our position in the bay, we found fragments of suicide planes on a rock outcropping. Poor visibility had apparently caused the pilots to think the rocks were ships. I have wondered what their reaction was when they discovered their mistake as they were about to impact.

I had never been casual where death was concerned. However, as I left the boat that had carried me from the *Curtiss*, to pick up the guard mail from the island, there were bodies of enemy dead lying alongside the road. I found myself detached from that terrible scene and wondering what the business of war had done to cause such a calloused attitude within me. Perhaps it came from thinking of classmates, fighting an enemy in the Pacific and in Europe, dying in lands they did not even know existed a few years previously. Dying because of the greed and malice of a few misdirected leaders.

Following the war, Merlyn Lofgren met Dorothy Dickson in Kalispell, Montana. Merlyn says that his wife "married out of the Church"—something he has warned his children and grandchildren against doing. Merlyn was subsequently baptized, and he and Dorothy were sealed in the Logan Temple. Merlyn earned a degree in pharmacy. They live in Missoula, Montana.

In the Church he has served as a home teacher, bishop's counselor, bishop, counselor in a stake presidency, stake president, and regional representative. From 1996 to 1997, he and Dorothy served a mission to the Turkey, Istanbul Mission. Following that mission they were called to be the Regional Employment Specialists in the Missoula Area. They also served on the Endowment Committee at Ricks College, in Rexburg, Idaho.

Merlyn and Dorothy Lofgren are parents of three daughters and a son, have fifteen grandchildren and four great-grandchildren.

A. THEODORE TUTTLE

Therefore, fear not, little flock; do good; let earth and hell combine against you, for if ye are built upon my rock, they cannot prevail.

(D&C 6:34)

Ted and Marné Tuttle

Marné and Ted Tuttle were married in the Manti Temple 26 July 1943, and only ten days later Ted went to officer training at the Marine Corps Parris Island training ground in South Carolina. Marné joined him in Virginia in November, after Ted completed the officer training course. When Marné arrived Ted's unit was on a training exercise in the field, but before nightfall Marné found an apartment and had a job as a receptionist at a photographer's shop.

Ted was commissioned a second lieutenant, United States Marine Corp on 30 November 1943. After he completed a reserve officer course at Quantico, Virginia, Ted and Marné left for Camp Pendleton, California. In the following, Ted tells some of his experiences in the war:

After a short leave in Utah, we flew to Los Angeles where Mom and Dad Whitaker and many other relatives met us. It was the first time I met Marné's parents. They had been unable to attend our wedding because of gas rationing. We spent a few days there, then on 12 March I left to join the 28th Marines, 2nd Battalion, Fox Company, at Camp Pendleton. I lived in a tent, but it wasn't too bad.

As soon as possible Marné joined me in California. Because apartments were scarce, we went down to San Diego to see Marné's sister

Yvonne and her husband Gordon Hawkins, who lived there. We set up a rickety old bed in their kitchen and sort of moved in with them. We managed to have a good time together. I rode back and forth as often as I could get time off, which wasn't very often. Those hours together with Marné were a little bit of heaven, they were so appreciated.

My training responsibility at this stage was a 60mm mortar section. Later I became liaison officer for my unit, a job I kept all through combat until I became company commander.

During the time I was at Camp Pendleton there were no church services in the tent camp, and getting to the main section of the base was difficult. We also worked on Sundays for several months. I did attend church while visiting Marné in San Diego. But it wasn't until I went overseas that I could actively work in the Church.

We finally sailed aboard the *USS Sea Corporal* on 19 September and arrived in Hilo, Hawaii 26 September 1944.

Living conditions at Camp Tarawa were not bad, but certainly not good either. The training area was dusty, windy, and rocky. But we braved these conditions for the three and a half months we were there. Between training exercises, we got a Jeep and made trips around the Island.

One morning on one of our travels we saw a Mormon chapel. Some of us found our way to the church, and on the back bench I found a paper that had Chaplain Boud's name on it.

We did not have an organized unit of the Church, so I wrote Chaplain Boud, inviting him to come and get us organized. On a Friday afternoon we were notified that the post chapel was reserved for a visit by a Mormon chaplain. We gathered at the appointed hour, but no one came. After we started the meeting, Chaplain Boud walked in and shook our hands. After the meeting he said he had not received my letter, but had the strong impression to come and meet with us. I was set apart as an LDS group leader on 7 October 1944, by Chaplain Boud, with "Stinky" P. Fuller as first counselor and Clarence Larsen as second. We had an active group, each Sunday we held meetings with about a hundred attending.

My Darling Marné,   October 7, 1944—Camp Tarawa, Hawaii
I am divinely happy tonight. I am grateful for the many blessings I have had and now enjoy. Two main reasons for my extraordinary joy: a

letter from you today, and a meeting from which I just returned where Chaplain Boud was present and where I was set apart as group leader in the 5th Marine Division. It is a great honor and the greatest opportunity and responsibility I have ever had in my life. Naturally I am happy, but I also realize the responsibility which is placed on my shoulders—however, I am starting out full of faith and confidence in this movement. God helping and guiding, we surely cannot fail. So you see, my wonderful darling, why I am so thrilled and happy. God grant that I might always be so, because of righteous works and endeavors.

There is drunkenness on all sides of me tonight. It is disgraceful to the highest degree. I'm so thankful for you, my darling, and for the gospel and its teachings and blessings.

All my love to you, my wife – Ted

Dearest Ted   January 18, 1945, 1:00 a.m.—*Really*

Darling–I had to say goodnite once more before turning in. I feel so close to you tonight. I have such a deep longing for you. I have been sitting here holding Davy in my arms after his feeding and was reading a story. I didn't realize how late it was, he had been sleeping soundly for an hour and didn't wake up when I put him down. I love to hold him and cuddle his little head under my chin on my shoulder. He is so sweet.

I hope you are receiving my letters better now. I know how disappointed I am when I don't get one from you. Oh Teddy–darn it all, anyway. 'Tisn't fair!!! We did have a wonderful first year together, didn't we? You are my life and everything dear, sweetheart. Would that you could hurry home faster than fast. But, in the meantime, remember you have a "family" of two who love you so much and are impatiently awaiting your safe return. Goodnite my love. Always, Marné and Boy Bleu

* * *

Finally the day came when we were through with practice. We boarded a ship and headed for Iwo Jima. It seems to me that from the very beginning I have had guidance in situations which made my safety more sure. During the trip from Hawaii to Iwo Jima we held services aboard the ship. This continued until the night before D-day. I had a feeling of expecting something big, and even though this was the first battle with someone shooting at me, I wasn't nervous. There were many tasks that needed doing, and these occupied my mind.

For almost five hours on D-Day we watched the naval bombardment of the island. You couldn't imagine that there would be anything left alive. All I could see was smoke and dust; it looked like all hell had broken loose. Prior to leaving the ship I gathered all the LDS men on the bow of the ship where we had a short prayer.

When we headed for shore, it seemed like a practice problem. Sailing around in the rendevous area we could see the whole drama before us.

There were no bullets coming our way, and it appeared that everything was in our favor. We lifted our fire and it was then, when the enemy came out of their fox holes and entrenchments, that we found that they were alive. Then they rained down death and destruction on us.

I went in the tenth wave, at "H hour" plus 45 minutes. We were told there were no underwater mines and no mortar fire on the beach. As our boat neared the beach, the noise became terrific. The naval and aerial bombardment continued. When our boat reached the shore, a mortar shell landed close by. Another mortar shell landed a few feet from our port side and damaged the track of our amphibious landing craft. We had trouble getting the ramp down and some of us were going over the side when it dropped. I stepped into three feet of water and started for shore just as a huge breaker pulled me and several others under, along with our carbines and mortars.

We were on board ship a long time before going into combat, and in poor physical condition when we hit the beach. I could only run about ten yards before I dropped from exhaustion. But I wasn't the only one. The whole southern end of the island is a heavy sand. You would sink a couple of inches into it wherever you stepped; it was like running through a wheat bin, carrying a fifty-pound pack. When I landed there were already a lot of shell holes in which to fall, and most of them were full of marines when I got there. I struggled ahead under the weight of my pack and other gear. Every now and then the fire would let up and we could get up and run a little ways. By jumping in one shell hole after another, I finally gained a more suitable position. It took me a couple of hours to get three hundred yards to where I was supposed to go.

From then on, it was just a matter of not being where they happened to be shooting. Mortar shells dropped without warning. It was an inexpressible sensation to be in your hole and feel shells land all around you. Often they were so close that sand and rocks were hurled on me. It still seems a miracle to me how any of us got across that beach alive. In fact many did not. We lost fourteen LDS men there.

An hour and a half later I reached the site of the command post. I had initially started out in the wrong direction, since our wave landed too far to the right of the beach. I was sent out to find the captain of F Company and get him on line so we could launch our attack. The rest of the day I assisted in setting up the command post and running messages to the company and regimental command posts.

When darkness came, the Japanese poured heavy mortar fire all over us. Many times these shells hit perilously close. I didn't get much sleep that night. That first night was when our forces were weakest and most vulnerable. When someone is shooting at you, the best way to protect yourself is to get below ground level. It is funny how secure you can feel in a little ol' fox hole. Sometimes, however, I wished it were deeper and smaller. We set up interlocking bands of fire, so anyone trying to infiltrate would be covered, and sent up flares, lighting up the beach like daylight.

The first few nights were really terrors. The days were long, too, but when it is light it does make a difference. We didn't have a lot of distance to go to our objective, since it was to take the hill. But it was rugged. Fortifications were thick as fleas on a dog, and it took a long time to knock all of them out.

I was grave's registration officer and directed the collecting of the dead as well as bringing in the wounded.

Flag Raising on Mt. Suribachi. On D-day plus five [24 February 1945] we took Mt. Suribachi at 1030 hours. Lt. Shrier took a forty-man platoon up the hill. This was Japanese territory, and when we took it we raised the American flag. They found an iron pipe, put a small flag on it, and a picture was taken of those who hoisted it. I experienced a thrill as I saw that flag go up while we watched from below. Our colonel led the men in three hip-hip-hoorays; it was a great event, but it was a small flag and not easily seen.

The colonel turned to me and said, "Tuttle, go down to the ships along the beach and get a large battle flag. It will raise everyone's spirits to see our flag up there." I walked down to the water and boarded LST 779.

While in battle officers don't wear rank insignia. I told the young ensign I wanted a large battle flag. Since I had no insignia showing, he wondered who I was and asked why I wanted it. Pointing to Mt. Suribachi, I said, "If you want to see your flag on top of that mountain, you will bring me one."

While waiting for the flag I went to the galley and filled all the pockets in my dungaree jacket with sandwiches and apples to take back to our men. The officer came back with the flag, and I carried it back to my commanding officer.

"Shall I take it up?" I asked.

"Yes," said Colonel Johnson. I had gone about twenty paces when a radio message came from Lt. Shrier, atop Mt. Suribachi, indicating that they needed fresh batteries for their radio.

The colonel said, "My runner has the batteries; give him the flag." I gave the flag to PFC Rene Gagnon. Gagnon took the flag up the hill, and when he got on top he said, "Come on, guys, let's put it up."

There were six men raising the flag—five marines and one corpsman. As the gentle wind wafted the flag, photographer and newsman Joe Rosenthal turned and took a picture just at that moment. He captured that dramatic action, with Gagnon in that picture. That photograph is now world famous. The Marine Corps statue in Washington DC is replicated from it.

With the larger flag in place it could be seen from all over Iwo Jima and from the support ships at sea.

The ensign who gave me the flag was Alan S. Wood. Wood wrote of this event: "A Marine came on board LST 779, asking for a larger flag, so I gave him our only large flag—which is the one pictured on the first page of *Time* magazine last week [5 March 1945]. The now famous flag was one I ran across one day at Pearl Harbor while I was rummaging around the salvage depot. It was in a duffle bag with some old signal flags—probably from a decommissioned destroyer. It looked brand new and was folded neatly. It seems funny, now that I look back. One might say that that flag was carried from a salvage heap at Pearl Harbor to the bloody heights of Iwo as a symbol of the American fighting spirit to avenge the disaster of Pearl Harbor." (Letter to the Editor, *Time* Magazine, soon after the battle of Iwo Jima)

After finally taking Mt. Suribachi, we had a few days rest; that is, we were not constantly fighting. We thought our mission was over. That was all we had ever practiced for. For the first time we got some better rations. I ate something contaminated and was evacuated to a hospital ship because I had diarrhea and high fever. Several days after being aboard ship I met my buddy George Stoddard. He had been wounded. We could have gone with the ship to Noumea, New Caledonia, for a few weeks recuperation, but instead chose to return to our platoons.

When we returned to the area near Mt. Suribachi, where we thought our battalion was, we found they had been committed to the north end of the island. Upon reaching the battalion command post, George was limping badly and was sent back to the ship, but I stayed on the island and stayed for twenty-four more days, during which we were fighting for our very existence.

Things were hot in the central and northern part of the island. It was really rough, and it never did let up, 'til the last day. And I might add, not even then. That's off the record, of course. The terrain up on that end of Iwo Jima was sandstone. There were caves and little niches dug in every few feet, all of which had to be knocked out individually. The Nips holding them didn't intend to keep open a possible escape route. Once they got in these places they expected to die holding them, and that's what they did. That's what made the campaign so long and drawn out. Some of these caves were big, roomy, and deep. I went down in one, and after some forty yards the tunnel turned and ten yards ahead opened up into a big room, with niches in the wall. It must have taken years to dig them.

It is wearisome to describe the bedlam of the battle field. Our orders were "to put down all organized resistance." The terrain was jagged, with tunnels everywhere, all to the advantage of the enemy, who were on a small camouflaged rise. During those twenty-four days our lives were in constant danger from sniper bullets and enemy infiltration. We slept from sheer exhaustion, and ate when we could. Our artillery fired a barrage which drove the enemy closer to us. We couldn't see them, but had to attack anyway. Most wounds sustained during those times were from the chest up. Men became sick from drinking fruit juices and eating the food we had, and combat fatigue cases increased greatly.

On 2 March 1945, Colonel Chandler Johnson and his runner Corporal Brown, were killed. We had our artillery ashore, and 75 and 105 mm shells were being fired over our heads at the enemy. You get used to shells coming over. They have a certain sound–a familiar "whissshh." Just a short time after they had gone we heard a "short" artillery shell [a shell from our own forces, which doesn't have enough elevation to clear our own troops and lands among them]. It did not make the usual sound.

The phone rang: "A short shell landed on the lines, someone got hit, and we think it's the colonel!" You cannot imagine what it means to lose a commanding officer—there is real physical and psychological shock. The colonel had on his Annapolis ring, and that was all that could be found of him. Brown had been wounded. Stretcher bearers were carrying him down the hill. As I saw them coming I ran to his side. His face was grey with dirt and metal and he was in a state of shock. He didn't recognize me.

I cried "Browny, you'll be okay!" Then I noticed that his leg had been blown off at the knee. He died a short time later.

All this happened on my 26th birthday, 2 March 1945.

* * *

There was a corporal in my platoon who had been in several combat missions prior to Iwo. He was having trouble and couldn't keep up. He told me, "My ticker isn't so good." He saw the doctor and could have gotten a release but didn't want to.

"Well, Lieutenant," he said to me. "I am going on one more mission, and then I will go back to the States and go on limited duty." We had a few more days of intense fighting, and then it was my painful duty as graves registration officer to retrieve his dead body.

Conditions were bad for us all over, we were just about stopped in our attack, but through sheer blood-and-guts determination, drove to final victory. After thirty-six days of bitter fighting, all organized resistance was put down. We were told to "police-up" the area. We lined up and walked down the road, and the Army took over control of the island of Iwo Jima.

When we went back to the southern end of the island we scarcely recognized it, it had changed so much after the SeaBees had restored order to the landscape.

Although my life was almost constantly in danger, I was never injured. I had many close calls, but it seems I was watched over and protected by a power higher than my own.

As a platoon leader I heard some very bad words. Just because I was an officer and they were enlisted men, didn't make me think that I had a right to swear at them. I couldn't swear at my men. My not swearing made me a novelty to them. Even "hell" or "damn" was censored by my men for me, although right next to me they were ripping off profanity as long as your arm. After they found out I was a Mormon I couldn't swear if I had wanted to—and I wanted to!

Before leaving Iwo Jima I took a group of LDS men to the cemetery where I identified and dedicated the graves of all the LDS boys buried there, and we held a memorial service.

We left Iwo Jima on 26 March and arrived at Hawaii on 11 April.

* * *

As LDS group leader, one of Ted's responsibilities was to write the families whose sons were killed in battle. This was not a job he enjoyed, but he faced it with respect. He often received responses from these families, thanking him for his compassion:

Dear Lt. Tuttle,

Received your wonderful letter, also the picture. I shall cherish your letter as it was one of the nicest I have ever received. Thank you very much. We were very proud of our son, he did his job and did it well, although as you say he has tasted death, but he lives, as his spirit is with us at all times, he did not die alone, there were thousands of other wonderful boys who died side by side with him. . . . . My other boy, Bob, is home on a furlough from the European campaign. . . . . God has been very kind to me, he let one boy come back.

My dearest Marné,   Thursday June 19, 1945—Hawaii

Here I am again—still trying to get a letter written to you to say a few of the things in my heart and to tell you some of the things that have happened. . . .One of the fine LDS men came to tell me of a problem he has with his wife. He is only a private. . . . His wife thinks he should have a higher rank. She also commented that he shouldn't spend so much time in church work—also said that she hadn't been to church for a long time and didn't intend to go very often. All in all it wasn't too nice a letter for a good man to receive. He is quite hurt about it, naturally. It surely makes me appreciate you, Marné. Trouble like that has never entered my mind.

Dearest Marné,   July 2, 1945—Hawaii

It is noon, now, very hot, but I want to tell you I love you. I won't have time to write this afternoon. . . . Say, darling, I was talking to one of the LDS fellows here last night. He said he and his wife were both reading the Book of Mormon. They have finished it since the first of the year. Why don't we start doing the same thing, read one chapter of the Book of Mormon and one from the D&C. What do you think of the idea?

July 3, 1945

Cases still come up in company which need punishment. I still have a hard time meting it out, but it has to be done.

Dearest Ted   July 11, 1945—Wapato, Washington

I love you. Hope everything is going ok with you; that you don't have too much meanness to cope with and to mete out punishment for!

Your sweet letter of July 2 got here on the 9th. I have read three chapters from both the Book of Mormon and Doctrine & Covenants.

I received a letter from your mom yesterday in which she tells of the news of Burke Braithwaite's death in The Philippines. It's a tragic thing—after Wilbur came so near being killed. . . . for some undetermined reason his plane failed to gain altitude and crashed before it was far off the ground. Only three survived I believe. It fell into the ocean. Burke's body had not been found. The plane was loaded with bombs and exploded. The survivors were seriously wounded. I am sorry to hear this—what fates were working then? Can we be satisfied by saying he was needed in heaven more than on earth? That kind of rationalizing doesn't satisfy me. Good men and bad are picked off with the same round of ammo—with no discrimination.

Dearest Marné,   July 18, 1945—Hawaii

I've given considerable thought to your query, "Can we be satisfied with the rationalization of saying he was needed more in heaven than on earth?" with respect to Burke's death. That is a difficult question. No one really knows, I guess, but in the light of the gospel we have, it seems more reasonable to suppose that his life's mission was completed and there was more need for him there than here. As to why a good man should be taken we can only conjecture—but this seems to be the best reason: that they are needed to preach the gospel by both example and precept to all these other men who are getting killed. It is, perhaps a moot question, but the real answer lies in the Lord's statement that a man is saved whether he lives or dies if he is living righteously, and a separation from this life a few years sooner really makes little difference. Although it's hard to take.

Dearest Marné   July, 1945

I am alone again tonight. I like to be alone—especially with you. At least when we're alone we're in good company. That's more than I can say when the other officers are in this tent. I get mighty disgusted at times but can't do anything about it. They debase the highest virtues of marriage vows and all things sacred. Sometimes I wonder how I stand it. Guess I'm a pretty calloused codger by now.

* * *

From Ted's Journal: On Friday, 10 August 1945, word came that the proposed surrender of Japan is being considered by the leaders of the Big Four [The United States, France, England, and the USSR]. Rumors are running rampant: "What will the 5th Division do?" "Where are we going?" "What are we going to do if peace is declared?"

But there is the job of putting the peace into effect. I'm truly thankful this day is here. The atomic bomb and Russia's entering into the war were both decisive for us, I believe with the former ranking first. News of acceptance by the Allied nations is eagerly and impatiently awaited. Much hangs on this decision.

13 August 1945: Since yesterday afternoon we have all been speculating as to the outcome of the war since the false news flash declaring the acceptance of surrender terms by Japan. We are constantly hearing bulletins and commentary by noted newsmen who are giving descriptions of what is transpiring in different cities in the U.S. and the world. I am, naturally, happy about this news—yet with all this excitement going on in the world I feel as though I should be more excited. What celebrating I feel is thanksgiving in my heart which will be put into action when I come home and see Marné and all again. For the present I'm thankful for this great news and trust I shall live to appreciate it.

14 August, 1340 hours. The official surrender of Japan has just been announced by President Truman at a news conference. During this

broadcast was the first I was able to thrill to its significance, but it is now a reality, and can be accepted as such. The division band is now parading up and down the street, playing our national anthem and the Marine Corps Hymn. Can't concentrate any longer, will have to write more later.

* * *

My darling,   August 20, 1945

Today I have been busy again; however, I have managed to fill out an application for a test to enter the Foreign Service with the U.S. Department of State. I think I had better enclose a copy of their propaganda rather than try to quote from it. I'm interested in it, however my German is very rusty. . . . But I'd like to try. What do you think of the idea? Would you be willing to go with me to Argentina or Brazil or Germany or elsewhere?

Dearest Marné,   September 1, 1945

Now it can be told!!! I am aboard ship headed for combat or occupational duty (whichever it turns out to be)—I believe it will be peaceful and quiet. From the previous reports of landings, it would seem so. So you can see that I won't be home for some time yet—I still say six months, at least. Scuttlebutt is flying thick and fast, of course. It is much different this time going over. No strain of any kind. No anticipation of being hit and killed. It is much more pleasant. We are on a fairly nice ship, living conditions are good, and all my work is done, at least till we get to our destination.

We landed at Sasebo, Japan, on 22 September 1945—the first Marine division to occupy Japan. (The Marines always have to be first in something.) We stayed here for two weeks unloading ships and doing guard duty, then moved up the coast to Fukuoka. This city is (or was) a large industrial center of approximately 300,000 people. Now the heart is bombed out of it.

It was while in Fukuoka that I had a unique experience. The editor of the Nishi Nippon Newspaper invited me to speak to his club, the "Economic Society of Fukuoka." Its members are editors and businessmen, and, as my interpreter said, "the rich people" of the city.

I spoke of "Democracy in the Reconstruction of Japan." I would read a paragraph, then my host would interpret it. It took about forty-five minutes to deliver. Afterwards they asked me questions for another hour.

With me was a Mormon chaplain and my good friend George Stoddard. George wrote of this experience to Marné in a letter dated 19 April 1987:

When in Fukuoka, Ted and I were asked to speak to members of a civic group. Ted did most of the talking, the topic was 'what would we say to them as leaders in a conquered nation.' He assured them that there would not be massive killings or jailing unless there was active resistance to the occupation. We had been informed that the Japanese people were told 'that to be in the Marine Corps, an individual must have killed either his father or mother, and that to be an officer, one must have killed both parents.' This explained why the local citizens ran from us wherever we went.

Wherever Ted went he left his mark. He was not a neutral person. He never compromised his standards, principles, or actions. His scriptures were always open on a box by his bunk, and did not gather dust. Everyone knew he was a Mormon and that he was in charge—the Division Group Leader.

They knew he was a '70', but did not know what that meant. They called me a '69' and threatened to report me to the '70' if I did not do what they wanted."

* * *

Ted left Sasebo on 9 December 1945, and arrived in San Diego on 24 December. His excitement at being "home" can be seen in his letter to Marné

My precious darling,   December 25, 1945—Camp Pendleton

Gee, but it was a thrill to talk to you this morning. Oh, I'm so thankful for you and for our love and all it means in our lives. And I surely do love you, Marné. Talking to you this morning has made this whole Christmas seem really worthwhile, even tho I'm separated from you. . . I haven't done much celebrating today. Came back to bed after talking to you. At dinner, went out to the tent camp where the men are staying and came back and ate our turkey dinner with milk to drink and ice cream for dessert. I'm thankful to be "home" again and so comfortably situated. Now all I have to await is orders separating me from the Marines.

Within weeks of his release from the military in 1946, A. Theodore Tuttle became a seminary teacher at Midway High School in Menan, Idaho. Following other assignments, he later directed the Reno, Nevada, Institute of Religion. He was then moved into the position as supervisor of seminary and institute teachers for the Church.

At the general conference of the Church on 6 April 1958, Elder Tuttle was called to fill a vacancy in the First Quorum of the Seventy. In that capacity, Elder Tuttle traveled to nearly every nation in the world, and to the islands of the seas. From 1961 to 1976, he served as area supervisor over the following areas: the South American Missions, the Mexico and Central America Missions, the Indian Missions in Western Canada, the West and North Divisions of South America, Australia, New Zealand, and South Pacific, and the Andes South America Area. From 1976 to December 1979, Elder Tuttle served in the presidency of the First Quorum of the Seventy, and from November 1979 to June 1982, as president of the Provo Temple.

Until he passed away on 28 November 1986, Elder Tuttle served as Executive Administrator of Italy/Spain/Portugal and North Central U.S. Area, as a managing director of the Priesthood Department, Advisor to the Young Women; President of the South America South Area; President of North America Northwest Area; a managing director, Priesthood Department and Second Counselor in the Sunday School presidency. In addition to these major assignments, he carried out a continuing weekly assignment to preside at stake conferences throughout the Church.

Elder and Sister Tuttle

Home at last—February 1946. Ted just getting acquainted with his thirteen-month-old son, David.

are parents of four sons and three daughters. In the fall of the year 2000, they had forty-three grandchildren and ten great-grandchildren.

Taken from records and letters furnished by Sister Marné Tuttle.

TOM EGBERT AND WAYNE BOWEN

I saw thousands of them hewn down.

(Mormon 2:15)

Growing up, Wayne Bowen never met Tom Egbert, an Idaho farm boy like himself. In the crucible of war these two Mormon boys ended up in the same Marine platoon. Tom was a replacement to "E" Company, the same unit Wayne was in, and fulfilled the destiny of saving Wayne's life.

Wayne Bowen

Destiny, when it chooses, can write its own script. Such seemed to be the case in 1944.

Wayne was no stranger to combat. He was at Peleliu. On his 20th birthday, 15 September 1944, he saw his first combat. Wayne says of Peleliu: "When we landed I didn't think there was much to worry about because the planes and ships were bombing and shelling the island so much. I didn't think any Japs would be alive. Then we hit the beach, and many other Marines, were killed.

To those of us alive it was a living hell. After seeing so many killed and wounded, I started crying and could not quit. I was sent back to the beach."

Wayne rested in a foxhole, trying to regain his composure. When a Japanese mortar round exploded and a nearby Marine was badly wounded, Wayne decided he was just as well off with his platoon and rejoined them.

"In a few days we were back on board ship. Only eleven of our platoon had not been killed or wounded on Peleliu."

In preparation for the invasion of Japan, the island of Okinawa, located three hundred fifty miles south of Japan, was needed as a staging area for Allied Forces. The 1st Marine Division was part of the assault force assigned to take Okinawa. The battle began 1 April 1945—Easter Sunday.

A heavy naval bombardment from the fleet hammered the island's fortifications, and carrier-based planes dropped tons of bombs. The island was considered softened up when the assault troops were launched shoreward. They met only token resistence, and it was believed that the heavy bombardment had been successful. The Japanese defenders had pulled back from the beaches to caves and tunnels in the rocky ground just in from the beach and waited for the Americans to land. Okinawa had been fortified to an unbelievable extent.

It was the largest invasion since Normandy. An armada of American and Allied ships and a half million men lay offshore. The scene must have been formidable as one Japanese soldier, looking out to sea is reported to have said: "It's seventy percent ships and thirty percent water."

The fighting was bloody and losses severe. In a letter dated 15 April 1945, Wayne writes: "We have really been having some excitement. Almost every night Japanese planes are overhead. . . . Yesterday I killed a chicken with my carbine, and today we boiled it and had a stew. It was pretty good as we have been living on C rations."

Wayne Bowen and Tom Egbert were in the thick of the battle. Several wounded and dying Marines were pinned down. One of their buddies was hit in the chest and gasped: "Now I get to go home." Wayne didn't know if he was talking about going home to South Carolina or to his home in heaven, out of the hell of Okinawa.

Another buddy, Carmen, was lying on his back saying it felt like his leg was blown off. Wayne turned him over—his leg wasn't gone—but there was a big bloody area on his lower back.

All from Idaho but together in the Pacific: (r to l) Wayne Bowen, Tom Egbert, and another friend.

"We were on our hands and knees, crawling. I was a section leader. I stood up to pass on a message and a Jap soldier, just four feet away, pointed his rifle at me and I had mine pointed at him. Then one of our men killed him."

Wayne recounts also, "A short time later we were pinned down. Our lieutenant told me to crawl up a small rise to see if Japanese soldiers were coming in our direction. I inched up the incline, poked my head up, and could see no one coming. Just then a bullet ripped through the left side of my face, breaking my jaw-bone in three places and taking out most of my teeth. I rolled down the hill amongst dead and dying Marines."

In shock, he doesn't recall receiving a shot of morphine, nor does he recall that his good friend and fellow Church member, Tom Egbert, carried him back to the shore for evacuation to a hospital ship. Wayne was sent to a hospital on Saipan, then on to Hawaii, where after several major surgeries and sufficient recovery, he was returned to the United States and discharged.

* * *

Tom Egbert grew up in the community of Ashton, Idaho. He was given two deferments to help on the farm, but in May 1944 found himself at the Marine Corps training facility at Camp Pendleton, California. There he met a number of young men who remained his friends throughout his military service and up to the time of his death many years later.

Tom's unit was sent to Pavuvu, an island in the Russell Islands. War isn't all battle, there are interludes when greater things happen. A fellow Marine wrote: "In the Russell Islands we had nothing to do at night, so we used to sit around and sing a lot. Tom had a beautiful singing voice and would sing "That Wonderful Mother of Mine." You can imagine there were a lot of Marines with tears in their eyes when he sang that."

Tom was real strong and brave. As Wayne describes: We were in the same tent together on Pavuvu. We didn't have any electricity so we would fill a coke bottle with kerosene, put a piece of rope in it for a wick, and that was our light.

We were "E" Company. "F" Company had a great big guy as a heavyweight boxer. He was about six foot seven inches tall and weighed 225 pounds. Tom was one of the bigger men in our company. None of the big guys in our company would box the "F" Company bruiser, but Tom said he would. Tom gave him a real battle so we were right proud of him.

After a time on Pavuvu our outfit was shipped to Okinawa. The fighting was very bad. Our losses were 136%. We were in some bitter fighting, but Tom was always showing courage and was a great inspiration to the rest of us with his great humor, and singing songs, during times that otherwise the morale of the boys would be very low. It would be hard for me to tell all the good qualities that he possessed, but one that impressed me most was his religious convictions, which was what made him such a fine person.

That day on Okinawa, Tom Egbert retrieved Wayne from among the dead and dying Marines and carried him back to the waterfront where Wayne could receive medical help.

Tom was also wounded on Okinawa. One of our guys fired into a Japanese cave that was full of munitions. It blew up half the hill. Tom was hit by shrapnel, a piece of which remained in his shoulder for the rest of his life.

Thomas Russ Egbert, 1945.

* * *

Not very long after Okinawa fell, the atomic bomb was

1st Marine Division Cemetery on Okinawa

dropped on Hiroshima, and the war was over. But the 1st Marine Division had other work to do before heading home. They were sent to China to carry out the provisions of the surrender, and to maintain law and order in the Tientsin, Tangshan, and Chinwangtao areas. Tom spent some time in Peiping, but most of his time in China was spent in Tientsin. He was in China from September 1945 to April 1946, until he finished military service and came home.

Wayne Bowen is the father of one son and two daughters, grandfather of seven and great-grandfather of four. He serves as a home teacher in his Springville, Utah ward.

Tom Egbert and Peggy Wood were married 20 March 1948, at Ashton, Idaho. They were later sealed in the Idaho Falls Temple. They are parents of four sons and five daughters. Tom and Peggy moved to Victor, Idaho, where they were co-founders of "Pierre's Playhouse." Tom was a born mimic, and he was a headliner there for many years. The Playhouse still operates every summer. Tom passed away 25 June 1987.

Take from personal records of Wayne Bowen, and the *History of Thomas Russ Egbert* by his wife Peggy Egbert.

ROSS K. CLEMENTS

They did think more upon the liberty of their fathers than they did upon their lives.

(Alma 56:47)

In the spring of 1942, along with several of my classmates and other young men from Rigby and Sugar City, I was inducted into the Army immediately after high school graduation. Most of us were LDS. For basic training we were sent to Camp Croft, near Spartanburg, South Carolina. The members of the small branch took us under their wings and made our association with the Church very enjoyable. Each Sunday we were invited to someone's home for dinner. I will always be grateful for the kindnesses extended by the good people there.

From South Carolina we were sent to Honolulu, Hawaii, where we awaited further orders. By this time things were changing rapidly in the Pacific Theater. We were in Hawaii for three months. Twice, because of the uncertainty, we were loaded on to ships and were in convoys, and twice returned to port. During our time in Hawaii I was not able to attend church services regularly, but one of the men in my unit, Eldon Hebdon, a returned missionary from Rigby, Idaho, got us together so we could partake of the sacrament and bear our testimonies. Some of the men had not been active in the Church as we grew up, but they came to our meetings. I could tell they were moved by the Spirit and I was thankful for my association with them. We attended services in Honolulu a couple of times and visited the temple at Laie. Our association came to an end when we loaded onto ships the third time and headed for the New Hebrides, islands in the South Pacific near New Zealand.

I learned the gospel in my home. I recall being taught the Articles of Faith by my mother prior to my baptism. While at Schofield Barracks, on Oahu, I recall lying on a cot and reading, for the first time about Helaman and his two thousand stripling warriors, and I had a powerful feeling come to me. These young men knew that their mothers did not doubt the gospel;

Ross K. Clements

and I knew that my mother did not doubt and had faith in the Lord. I was at peace knowing this. Mother wrote nearly every day while I was gone from home. Even on the battlefield we got mail. I was number nine out of a family of twelve, and I knew my family loved me and that they were praying for me. All of my life we had knelt in family prayer every day. The faith I gained as a youth from the teachings of my parents gave me courage.

While I was in grade school, the principal invited Thomas C. Neibaur, the first Mormon to receive the Medal of Honor, to speak to us. Sitting on the floor of the gym I remember seeing that medal hanging on a ribbon around his neck. It aroused great feelings of patriotism in me. As I boarded the ship to leave the United States, I remembered Thomas Neibaur and my two uncles who had served during World War I and hoped I could measure up. I was concerned that I would serve well and finish the task I was sent to do. Arriving at Pearl Harbor, and seeing the wreckage of the Battleship Arizona, inspired in me a sense of awe for the sacrifice made by the men who died there. It was a sacred experience to me.

We arrived in the New Hebrides after nineteen days on the water. There I was assigned to a unit of the New York National Guard. These were very experienced men who had fought at Saipan, Guam, and Christmas Island. After they had been overseas for forty-eight months, the unit could draw one name a month for rotation back to the United States. I was one of two replacements to join them in the South Pacific. They were a pretty "salty" outfit, and I was dubbed the "whipper snapper," because I was so young.

Aboard ship, after leaving the New Hebrides, we were told we were going to participate in the invasion of Okinawa. This would be the last step prior to attacking the Japanese homeland. My assignment was with the anti-tank company of the 65th Regiment of the 27th Infantry. We had big .57 mm guns, designed to disable the bogey wheels of a tank. As it turned out, there were no tanks on Okinawa. Tanks were useless in the rice paddies.

The invasion started on Easter Sunday 1945. Our first job was to unload the ship. This took three days. The fighting had already moved into the island. I was assigned to the infantry. They handed me an M-1 rifle and sent me into the battle. My division was cut up so badly, so quickly, that they were in acute need of replacements.

Our unit fought for six weeks before being relieved by Marines. We suffered 47,000 casualties, of whom 16,000 died. The Japanese lost 60,000; most chose to die rather than surrender. What was most terrible, however, was that over 150,000 Okinawan civilians died in the gruesome fight.

Coming in as a replacement you hear all kinds of stories from the old hands, most of them scary. As we moved up that first night, flares were shot up so that we could see our way. Of course, the enemy could see us as well. We heard a strange bugle call and the Japanese began screaming at us. I was afraid the enemy would make a banzai charge. That was the most frightened I ever was. Our second lieutenant ran for the rear.

Not long after this we were dug in for the night. In our foxholes we took turns keeping watch. The two men in the hole next to us were part of the original New York Guard unit. The man on watch was sitting up and was struck in the head by a piece of shrapnel. He died without making a sound and slumped down into the hole. The other man could not bear the thought of staying the night with a dead body, so got in with us.

One afternoon, as we made an assault on a hill, we were shooting at anything that might be a place of concealment. We got into an exchange of fire, and we all hit the ground. My helmet weighed five pounds, so I didn't want to keep my head up, but I didn't want to be overrun either. I watched. It was then that I felt I earned the respect of the old timers in my unit. I have wondered if they felt the protection of the spirit that flows from the priesthood, but I can't say. I know that when we were withdrawn from battle and were making preparations to invade the Japanese homeland, several of the men said they wanted me to be in their unit.

At the end of the battle, during a mop-up operation, we were coming down a trail, and we ran into a squad of enemy soldiers. We began to fall back. It was raining and conditions were miserable. Just then one of our riflemen got hit by a mortar shell, which mutilated his leg. Our battalion commander had been explaining our situation to the regimental commander over the radio. The CO instructed him to hold on and not to leave the area. Our battalion commander, seeing his man's mangled leg and realizing that he and many others needed immediate care, told his boss, "We're coming down," then reached over and turned the radio off.

We fashioned a stretcher from a poncho and poles cut out of the jungle. The rain made a deep gully out of the trail. The steep sides were treacherously slippery as we slogged our way down the greasy slope. As we waded down the thousand feet of elevation, we used our belts as a tether to keep the back stretcher bearer from falling down. We rotated every few minutes according to our endurance. The injured man moaned continuously as he was jostled and banged around. What was a miserable journey for us must have been a wretched one for him. All the other wounded men of the battalion came down in a similar fashion. It was a very heartwrenching experience for us all; and I was relieved that we had retreated.

* * *

Once I happened to run into a fellow from near my hometown. He was returning from a burial detail. It was raining and he was soaking wet. His teeth were chattering from the cold, so I took my extra sweater from my backpack and gave it to him. He expressed profound gratitude. I never saw him again, but was told that sometime later he was evacuated because of battle fatigue. The story was that two Japanese soldiers happened to come upon him and a group of wounded men waiting for evacuation. This young LDS soldier clubbed them to death with his rifle. He didn't even fire a shot.

Shortly after this I was saddened to learn that Eldon Hebdon, our LDS group leader, had been killed. He was in a different company than I. It was Eldon who had gathered us together, encouraged us, and seen to it that we had the privilege of partaking of the sacrament. I'm anxious to see him again and express my gratitude to him for getting us together and strengthening each of us against the evils surrounding us.

After we returned to Idaho, Lynn Dalling and I went to see Eldon Hebdon's family in Rigby. It was perhaps the most difficult encounter to come out of my wartime experiences. His father was so grief stricken that huge sobs wracked his body. Lynn and I left feeling awful. Forty-five years later I was asked to speak in church about the war. I began thinking about the Hebdons, and the sacrifice that was theirs. I asked myself the question: "What would be harder to do, to give my own life, or the life of my son?" I feel like it would be easier for me to give my own life. And I thought of the Father of us all, who gave the life of His Son as a gift to me.

* * *

On Halloween night I left Okinawa aboard an LST, [landing ship tank] bound for Japan. On the way we were hit by a typhoon, which tossed that little ship around like a matchbox. The storm roared on for several days. Men were sick, and confusion was continual. One of my friends who was aboard another LST told me that the doors on the front of their ship nearly came off in the storm. They had to keep welders working constantly to keep the doors on and the water out. It was good to reach land.

A friend of mine found me and told me that there were Church services being held in Tokyo. I always wanted to go to church. Meeting a Church member was like meeting a family member; we gravitated toward each other, with a feeling of kinship. I was south of Yokohama, and it took about an hour to get to Tokyo by train. Services were held in a hall on a university campus. The group leader was a senior officer.

The second or third time I went to church I noticed about ten Japanese people sitting on the front row. I saw they were taking the sacrament and thought, "This is not right." I didn't know they were members of the Church until the group leader, who was a lieutenant colonel, introduced them. I thought how surprising and remarkable it was that only a few months before, I had been shooting at Japanese soldiers, and now we were partaking of the sacrament together. I was astonished to find out there were Church members in Japan. Still in a state of transition from enemy to brother, I did not make an effort to become acquainted with them. However, I was a witness as they were welcomed back into fellowship with us. It was a tender experience.

One of the things I learned from the war is service. I am as proud of my service in the military as I am of my missionary service. I want to have the flag of the United States of America draped over my casket at my funeral. My observation is that men of a religious persuasion gravitated to the LDS servicemen; they could feel something of our spirit.

The Reestablishment of the LDS Church in Japan

> In 1944 Edward L. Clissold, a member of the Oahu Stake presidency, president of the Hawaii Temple and the Central Pacific Mission, and an active-duty Army officer, . . . was assigned to work in the education and religion section of SCAP (Supreme Commander for the Allied Powers) in Japan.
>
> During his short tour of duty in Japan (only two months), Clissold . . . did what he could to find the remaining Japanese Latter-day Saints from the previous mission era. On 30 October 1945, he placed a small ad in Japanese in a Tokyo newspaper, saying: 'URGENT NOTICE–I would like any member of The Church of Jesus Christ of Near-day Saints (Mormon Church) to contact me as soon as possible. . . . Brother Nara Fujiya, who had shepherded the Japanese Saints from 1924 until 1933, responded to Brother Clissold's notice. As a result, a few other Japanese members were located and integrated into the activities of the LDS servicemen." (R. Lanier Britsch, *From the East, the History of the Latter-Day Saints in Asia, 1851-1996*, pp. 83–85)

Ross Kay Clements returned to Idaho in April of 1946. He attended Ricks College and later served a mission to the North Central States from 1949 to 1951. In 1953 he married Carol Bunnell. They are parents of three sons and three daughters.

Ross completed a bachelor's and master's degree in Agricultural Economics at Utah State University and did postgraduate work at Michigan State University. He was a farmer and high school counselor until his retirement. He served in many positions in the Church, including several high councils, counselor to two bishops, branch president, bishop, stake Sunday School president, and stake missionary. Ross and Carol served in the Perth Australia Mission from 1991 to 1993. They are presently ordinance workers in the Idaho Falls Temple.

Taken from an oral interview with Paul H. Kelly.

CHINA–INDIA–BURMA THEATER

The Burma road was an important strategic position, as the Japanese hoped to cut off mainland China by controlling this location.

China officially entered the war on 9 December 1941, and U.S. general Joseph W. Stillwell was sent, as chief of staff, to advise Chiang Kai-shek. Two significant military objectives in the campaigns in Burma, India and China were to prevent the Japanese from isolating China's ports and transportation centers from the other arenas in the Pacific, as well as provide bases from which the Allied forces could attack Japanese installations. If the invasion of Japan had been carried out, these locations would have been vital for that campaign.

Later seen as an important symbol of the war, the Flying Tigers, led by Claire L. Chennault, fought in Burma and China. This group was manned by American civilian volunteers, who fought in battered planes and continually faced shortages of fuel and supplies. However, because of their daring and unorthodox tactics, the Tigers caused considerable damage to Japanese land and air forces. On 4 July 1942, any Tigers who wished were absorbed into the U.S. 10th Air Force and became an important part of the China Air Task Force. Chennault, still commanding this group, was promoted to brigadier general.

The battles in Burma were particularly fierce, as the Japanese attempted to cut off mainland China and split Burma in two by controlling the Burma Road. British and Indian forces played an important role in maintaining Allied control of the area, but the toll was high. In the battle of Imphal-Kohima, which took place between May and June 1944, British and Indian forces suffered 17,587 casualties. In this same campaign, the Japanese forces faced 30,500 dead (8,400 from disease) and 30,000 wounded.

On 1 May 1945, when Rangoon fell to British Field Marshal William Slim, the capture of Burma was basically complete.

BILL CLARK

Billy Clark was born 2 May 1922, at St. Anthony, Idaho, to William Edward and Lula Brown Clark. Following graduation from high school he entered the National Guard. After war broke out he transferred to the Army

Air Corps, took training in California and Arizona, and received his commission and his wings at Luke Field, Arizona.

Shortly after completing his training, he was assigned to the 14th Air Force, in China. He was a member of the famous Flying Tigers , under the command of Major General Clair L. Chennault, in China and India. He flew forty-eight combat missions. Bill wrote this account of his last mission:

About the 8th of July, 1944, I was on detached service to the 26th Fighter Squadron, based at Henyang, China. The Japanese were making a concentrated drive on the Han-K'ou railroad. They drove us out of Henyang back to Lingling, 210 miles south. We were flying missions in support of Chinese troops.

On the first three missions that day we flew in and out of rainstorms. The canopy of my plane leaked and my parachute got wet. Prior to leaving for the day's fourth mission, I traded chutes with another pilot. We took off about 1600 hours.

I was leading a flight of four P-51s, each loaded with 500 lb. demolition bombs for skip-bombing Japanese river boats carrying supplies. We headed north for about a hundred miles to the Yangtze River. The Yangtze is large and resembles the Hudson River in New York. Upon reaching the river we spotted our target and maneuvered into position to make our pass.

Sending the other three airplanes to bomb from the side, I dove straight in, strafing the small ship to attract the crew's attention while the other P-51s got into position. All three of the other planes' bombs missed our target, and the ship continued on the river. Turning low, I made my run from the side. Skimming the ship's mast I dropped my 500-pounder into the ship. As I cleared its mast, their gun crew fired a three-inch

Bill Clark

gun at me. A bullet hit the underside of my plane, piercing the engine, which made only two or three more revolutions, then stopped dead. My bomb got the supply boat, but the supply boat got me.

Pulling the plane up hard, I managed to gain about four hundred feet of altitude. Heading south, I cleared the river. The country is rough, and the ground rises higher as it gets off the river and away from its banks and is covered with low brush. I kept about four hundred feet of altitude and got ready to bail out. As soon as I thought I had all the ground covered I could at my flying speed, I jettisoned the canopy and rolled the trim tabs forward so the airplane would nose straight down when I let go of the controls. I unsnapped my seat belt, and the wind pulled me out of the plane.

I didn't have much altitude, so I pulled the rip cord right away. The parachute I had borrowed was larger than my own and the harness fit me loosely. It opened abruptly, and I had a slower than usual descent, but the breast strap jerked up and hit my chin, cutting me on the throat and mouth. I bit my tongue and was nearly knocked unconscious, but I revived quickly. As I floated down I could see my plane had gone straight into the ground. It was burning. I also saw a Japanese patrol, about a half mile away.

Undoing my chute harness, I dropped out of it as I hit the ground. I ran for the top of the hill, heading for some dense brush. It was now about 5:30 p.m., not long before dark. Burrowing into the brush, I watched for the enemy patrol. About an hour later it started to rain, and the cloud cover helped make the darkness deeper. After dark I began working myself south toward my base. I had no idea how long it would take.

The hilly country was broken by ravines and covered with a dense growth of brush and trees. In the driving rain I came to a deserted house, where I decided to spend the night. I was cold, my head and throat throbbed, and I could hardly open my mouth.

I must have fallen asleep; but about 0200, a noise woke me. The rain had stopped. I peered through a window, and in the darkness saw Japanese soldiers outside, coming toward the house. I slid through a window and worked my way a short distance into the underbrush. Everything was wet and soggy, so it was pretty easy to move without making noise. After searching the house, the soldiers began working their way in my direction. With fear nearly choking me, I lay as still as I could until they left. As the soldiers passed me I could have touched one's foot with my hand, he was that close.

Finally they moved off and I started south again. I continued until first light, then holed up in thick brush.

As soon as it was dark I moved out. Toward morning I came to another deserted house and decided to spend the day in it. That was a mistake. In late afternoon I saw another Japanese patrol coming. In the middle of the house there was a four by six-foot storage compartment with a high window, which was the only way in or out of it. I covered the opening with some boards, then sat on the floor with my .45 pistol trained on my makeshift cover. I figured this was the end of the line. I had made up my mind not to be taken prisoner. The soldiers searched the house for some time; that they didn't knock the boards out and look into my hiding place still amazes me. I'm sure it was in answer to my prayers, which were fervent and constant. After dark I eased the boards out, and because no one seemed to be around, I got out and walked all the rest of the night.

One day, anxious to be on my way, I started off before dark. As I topped a hill, I came to a little clearing full of people. One of them came forward, and I cautiously tried what little Chinese I knew. To my immense relief this man knew just enough English so that we could communicate. I showed him the flag kept inside my jacket pocket. The Chinese writing on it said I was an American Flying Tiger and asked for help. He indicated that he wanted to take me to the country chief. *Well,* I thought, *what the heck. I might just as well try it.*

We walked to a small settlement where the chief lived. There they gave me the first food I'd had since being shot down. They did a lot of talking among themselves, none of which I could understand. I spoke to the man who knew English and tried to get across my need to get back to my own lines. He said they would see. I told them that the Americans offered a lot of money for a returned pilot, which was true. They said it would take two or three days before they could move me. I wondered if they were checking to see who would offer the most money, the Japanese or the Americans. I told them that whatever the Japanese paid, the Americans would double it, also true.

The next day I was told that two Chinese soldiers and the man who could speak English would go with me. We started two days later. In the meantime, my head was shaved and I was given Chinese clothes to wear over my uniform and a big coolie hat to cover my new haircut.

One of the Chinese soldiers guided and the other scouted ahead in case of Japanese troops. Daily we got reports that a Japanese patrol was following us, which didn't add to my comfort level. A few days later we met some more Chinese soldiers. I thought we were out of enemy territory, but the group's commander told us that the Japanese had us surrounded— we had crossed through their lines without knowing it.

In the morning the Japanese attacked us. It took us three days to fight our way out. We left in the night and

Bill Clark returning to base after being shot down. He is holding a Japanese battle flag.

crawled past Japanese artillery emplacements and sleeping soldiers. As we crept past one gun emplacement, some dogs started barking and carrying on, which scared us half to death. I thought their yapping would wake up the whole Japanese encampment. Somehow we got past without being caught.

We finally got to the railroad, which was just twenty miles north of Lingling, the place from which I had taken off. The Americans had evacuated from there, but I was told there was still a radio there I could use to contact my unit. Our location now was as far as a train could travel without getting into Japanese-held territory. It was also a jumping off place for Chinese troops coming up from the south. I decided we should wait and take the train to Lingling the next morning.

We arrived at the loading platform early in the morning, but the train was not ready to go. About 1000 hours, as we were sitting in front of one of the buildings, sunning ourselves and getting some much needed rest, down the street came a Japanese patrol dressed in Chinese uniforms. We didn't catch on to them until they were a couple of hundred feet away. Abruptly, they threw down their machine guns and started shooting. I rolled through the door and into the building near which I had been sitting and immediately bolted out the back door and up a hill, my three Chinese friends right with me. Shortly a Chinese soldier came to tell us they had killed all the Japanese in the patrol. They told me that this was the same patrol that had been tracking me since I had bailed out up near the Yangtze River.

We boarded the train for Lingling. From the railroad I made my way to the airfield. To my immense relief the radio was still operating. Late in the afternoon a small cargo aircraft took me and my three Chinese friends to Kweilin. It was good to see friendly American faces again. I took my Chinese protectors to the mess hall and told the mess sergeant to give them everything they wanted to eat.

After hearing my report, the Group commander told me that he was going to send me to Kunming for an intelligence debriefing.

Before I left the next morning I saw my Chinese friends paid a goodly sum of American money. They were really tickled. It was hard to say good-bye to them, they had been very good to me and gotten me out of a big jam.

At Kunming I told my story to Intelligence personnel, giving them troop concentrations, gun emplacements, and Japanese troops positions. I was the only pilot to come out of that territory, so the information I had was vital. The Kunming Intelligence staff sent me to Washington DC, to brief the Pentagon staff.

From the time I was shot down until I got to Kunming was twenty-one days. My weight had dropped from 175 to 140 pounds.

It was a very happy day for me when I landed in the United States of America.

As I write this account (in September 1989), I recall all the feelings I had while I was hiding and being hunted. It was as though I had become an animal with an instinct to kill my opponents, to kill if I were trapped. I hope I never have those feelings again.

For his service with Flying Tigers while in China, Billy Clark was awarded the Distinguished Flying Cross. Upon his return to Idaho, he and Margie May Stephenson were married 6 September 1944, in St. Anthony. Their marriage was later solemnized in the opening session of the Idaho Falls Temple, 5 December 1945. They became parents of three sons and two daughters and have twenty-four grandchildren, six great-grandchildren, with four more coming. He was a farmer; built and operated a cattle feed lot; and then opened a truck repair business, which he operated until he retired. Billy died 21 March 1991, in Idaho Falls, Idaho.

RICHARD L. GUNN

And whosoever shall compel thee to go a mile, go with him twain.

(Matthew 5:41)

I was serving an LDS mission in Hawaii when the Japanese gave us a wake-up call at Pearl Harbor. After I finished my mission, having felt first-hand the threat of war I enlisted in the military. There was just enough time prior to my departure for me to complete a quarter of college, and to marry Jeanne Wright in the Salt Lake Temple.

At a farewell assembly at the Joseph Smith Building on the BYU campus concluded for those of us going off to active duty, I exited out the north door with my chemistry professor, Joseph K. Nicholes. At the bottom of the stairs, Professor Nicholes stopped, turned to me, and with his hand on my shoulder looked into my eyes. I have never forgotten that probing look—he seemed to be looking right inside me, and I knew that he had a genuine interest in me.

"Dick," he said, "it's very important, even going to war, to do more than you are asked to do. It's Christ's simple 'second mile' principle. It will truly make a difference."With that, I went off to war.

Arriving at Fort Leonard Wood, Missouri, I was assigned a bunk at the far end of a barracks. While writing a letter home, I saw some soldiers at the other end of the barracks trying to get a head start on learning the parts of a rifle. They were pooling their ignorance. Having had ROTC in high school, I knew the parts of a rifle, so I said to myself, *Okay Brother Nicholes, I'll try your "second mile" advice; let's go to work.*

I found a large sheet of paper on which I drew an "exploded" rifle, and labeled all the parts. Pinning it to the wall, I returned to my letter writing. It just so happened that the base commander was making some spot checks. He saw the chart with the soldiers gathered around it. He asked where the chart had come from. The recruits pointed at me. That evening I received an order to report to the base commander's office the next morning. He asked if I would make a sign for him. Later there were other requests from him that I completed. I was finding out that Brother Nicholes was right.

Half way through basic training, the commander again called me to his office. He had received a request from Washington for six men to receive photogrammetry training (the science of measuring distances on aerial photographs) at Fort Belvoir, Virginia. I was on my way for this highly selective training in map making, which is what I had wanted to do in the first place. Thank you, Brother Nicholes!

I eventually received an assignment to go to India. After arriving in Bombay, we traveled by train all the way across India to Calcutta. About 80 miles out of Calcutta is the village of Khragpur, headquarters of General Curtis LeMay's 20th Bomber Command. Around this base was a ring of satellite airfields used by the massive B-29 Superforts .

Air Transport flew over the "Hump" [the Himalayas] loaded with bombs, fuel, and other supplies, which were later picked up by the B-29s. The B-29s raided north as far as Mukdan, a northern Korea steel mill, and as far south as Singapore. Our unit was designated the 948th Engineers, our assignment, to make navigational maps for each bombing run.

* * *

As far as I know I was the only Mormon at the headquarters base. Most of the men were from the eastern United States and had never heard of Mormonism. Recognizing that I was the only one they had ever known, I felt they would judge the Church by my actions—I took that seriously. Only a few of them went to their church services. Most of my close friends during this time were Jews, and I occasionally attended services with them.

On New Year's Eve our outfit had a party. By this time they all knew my standards, but some of them asked me, as we were getting ready to toast the New Year, if my church would excommunicate me if I had one drink with them. "No, but I have never tasted liquor because of what we call the Word of Wisdom. If I have this one drink I might find it the most wonderful taste in the world, and then for the rest of my life I would have to wrestle with keeping the standards of my church. What do you think I should do?"

"Oh, go get him a bottle of pop!" They never asked me again. I had a definite sense that they respected my stand. I was surprised how often someone would quietly say to me, "I wish I belonged to a church like yours— I wouldn't be hooked on cigarettes and booze."

In November 1944, I became sick and was sent to the hospital. There I found that there were some LDS men at one of the satellite bases. On Sunday, 12 November, I went to that B-29 base. In a letter home I wrote: "There were quite a few LDS men there, and I had a wonderful time mixing with them. It seemed extra good to attend a familiar service, and to speak the same language. I met a captain I knew in the Islands during my mission. Anyway, I enjoyed the meeting very much."

Friday, 17 November. Journal entry—I had just hung up my mess kit from evening chow when I heard some fellows shouting my name. Lt. Taylor, who I had met at the LDS Church services last Sunday, and another fellow introduced as Stone, walked in. They and a couple of other Mormon kids were getting together at Taylor's quarters and wanted to know if I would care to come along. I dropped whatever plans I had. They told me to bring along any photos of my family. We jumped in Taylor's Jeep and went bouncing through the darkness to his quarters.

A radio, a container of fruit juices, cookies, and candy were spread on a table. We talked of home, of church, our activities in the army, our families, and so on. We didn't break up our session until midnight. We had a great time, and I felt more like ground was under my feet.

Right after work the next day, the LDS fellows dropped in again. India had drawn closer to home by a thousand miles. Lt. Taylor gathered all the lost LDS sheep together. There was a fellow named Sorenson, Del Nebeker, and the photographer Rasmussen, who usually has a big smile or a chuckle in progress. I had admired his photographs so much that he gave me one he had taken during a bombing raid.

Sorenson and Nebeker had flown a great number of missions, and they have many stories. Nebeker said he dreamed one night that his plane was shot down, and as the crew huddled together on the ground, their pistols drawn, they watched some Orientals approach them across the fields. They didn't know if they were friendly or a group of the enemy. His dream had a happy ending, the natives were friendly and helped them find their way through Japanese-held territory to their base.

Some time later, Nebeker's bomber was shot down, and Neb parachuted to the ground. As the crew huddled together, some soldiers started to move toward them. They drew their pistols, but Neb said, "Don't shoot, they're friendly." It was exactly as his dream. They were Chinese, and they helped the crew move eight hundred miles through China, to their base.

When we climbed back into the Jeep to return to our bases, it was 0100 hours. The time goes too fast when it is so enjoyed.

The next day was Sunday, and I slipped away from work and hitched a ride to the LDS services. No one there was musically inclined, playing or singing. I became the organist, playing with one finger on a portable Army organ. They had to sing the selections I chose.

Our lesson material was from the Book of Mormon. Next Sunday I am to take the lesson. Again, I must say how much I enjoyed being in this environment.

We organized a branch, although we had no real authority to do so. From this time on we met regularly, generally on a Saturday. We found more LDS men and had an agreeable time together. These simple gatherings of LDS Servicemen, far from home were enormously important to us. It was a powerful testament of the significance of the Church in our lives and of the value we place on LDS companionship. I think we all realized there that we should never take the Church for granted. Its teachings are the heart and core of what is most meaningful in our lives. Our time in India was an anchor to spiritual values.

* * *

After a year and a half in India the war began to wind down and our mapping unit was to be moved to the newly captured island of Okinawa. With the move some of us were given a forty-five-day, Stateside leave. I had a seat on the first plane to leave.

We flew to Karachi, where we boarded a plane for Cairo. Somewhere over Arabia an engine began leaking oil. We made a safe landing on the hard desert sand, and the crew began working on the engine. The area looked like something on a distant planet—nothing was in sight. A strong wind started, and the pilot ordered us back on the plane. He explained that he would rather be in the air with a wounded engine than to remain on the ground while sand ground into all the engines. We were a long way from civilization.

In the air we met the full force of the storm. Everything loose inside the aircraft was flying around us. At times the plane would hit an air pocket and drop for what seemed forever—and when we hit the bottom the wings would bend as we were thrust upward. As I looked around me everyone was praying, an uncommon activity for most of these men. When a hole appeared in the dark swirling clouds, the pilot dropped through it and we landed at Abadan, Iran. Land never felt so good.

A group of Iranians came to meet our unscheduled arrival. Touching our uniforms they told us, "Your President is dead." President Roosevelt had died that day and the Iranians were crying and sorrowful.

We arrived safely in Cairo the next day where we took time to tour the pyramids. But nothing I saw or did was more delightful than arriving in Salt Lake City where I could be with Jeanne and Kaye. By the time my leave was over, the atomic bomb had been dropped and Japan surrendered.

I finished my military service working at an Army engineers office in Kearns—where I had gone to see if they needed any help.

Had it not been for the war I might have missed Joseph K. Nicholes's wonderful advice, which has impacted my life in so many satisfying ways. One of my first excursions as a civilian was to visit with Joseph K. Nicholes and express to him my gratitude for his interest in me.

Richard L. Gunn says that he has never applied for a job in his life, they came to him. He had been a school teacher, curator of the Springville Art Gallery, a member of the faculty at Brigham Young University, and a tour director for BYU Travel Study. Something he continues to do presently. He and Jeanne are parents of six children. Richard served as a member of the Young Men MIA general board for twenty years, as a bishop, high priest group leader, and temple ordinance worker.

MEDAL OF HONOR RECIPIENTS

The design of the Medal of Honor differs slightly from service to service. Both Navy and Army medals consist of an inverted star with clusters of laurels, representing victory, and oak leaves, representing strength, at the points. In the center of the star is the impression of Minerva, the goddess of Wisdom. The thirteen stars in the blue ribbon represent the thirteen colonies.

Preston, Idaho, lies at the northern end of Cache Valley, only a few miles from Idaho's border with Utah. Settled by Mormon pioneers, Preston and its environs seem unremarkable. But the larger community has produced some remarkable people. Two of our latter-day prophets came from this end of Cache Valley. Clifton, a stone's throw to the west, was home to Harold B. Lee, and Ezra Taft Benson was raised in the little community of Whitney, four miles east of Preston, where, among other things, this future Secretary of Agriculture learned to thin sugar beets and milk cows.

In the Preston city cemetery there is a memorial to Leonard C. Brostrom and Nathan Van Noy Jr. Both entered military service at Preston, and both gave their lives with such conspicuous gallantry that they were awarded the Medal of Honor posthumously. Perhaps it should not be surprising that this region, which spawned two of the Lord's prophets, should also give us these noble men.

This region represents many communities throughout the United States that sent men and women who became heroes as they faced war. For some, this valor was recognized by the Medal of Honor, the military's foremost honor. Originally designated to recognize valor in combat, it is given for "conspicuous gallantry and intrepidity at the risk of life, above and beyond the call of duty." Thomas C. Neibaur, the first Latter-day Saint, and first Idahoan, to receive the Medal of Honor, was born at Sharon, not far from the small towns of Paris and Ovid, in nearby Bear Lake County, Idaho, and grew up in Sugar City, Idaho.

THOMAS C. NEIBAUR

The first Church member to receive the Medal of Honor was Thomas C. Neibaur. He was assigned to the famous Rainbow division in France during World War I. Following are excerpts from the story of Private Neibaur as it appeared in the *Improvement Era* of July 1919.

On 16 October we were in a position facing a small round knoll. To the right was a nest of German machine guns shooting down on us, and we could not advance until that nest of machine guns was cleaned out.

The captain called for volunteers to attack the Germans. I volunteered, then my two companions stepped out and said they would go with me.

We crawled to the top of the hill, where we encountered barbed wire entanglements. The distance we had to make was about as far as one of our Salt Lake City blocks. In getting over this wire entanglement I was shot through the thigh of my right leg three times, but no bones were broken. My machine-gun loader and scout were both killed at this wire fence. I dragged myself along the mound of dirt to where I was comparatively safe.

I examined my wounds and concluded they were not extremely serious. When I looked up, I saw about forty-five Germans coming toward me. I quickly turned my automatic rifle on them and fired about fifty shots. The Germans got so close that I could see there was no chance for me to get them all, so I made an attempt to get back over the shell holes to my company.

After I got away from the protection of the pile of dirt, I was in plain view of the fifteen Germans still alive. They kept advancing, shooting as they came. I was hit with a ball in my right hip, which passed into the left hip and there remains to this day. The shot stunned me for a minute, and I fell on my face in the mud. The Germans took my pistol away. I had left my rifle at the wire fence, so I was without anything to defend myself. I expected to be killed or to go back to a German prison.

The Germans continued up the hill, until the boys of my company saw them and fired a volley at them. None of the Germans were killed, but it scared them and they got down out of sight. When they got down, I got up to see if I could stand and walk with my wounds. I found I could, so I crawled back to my pistol which they had not picked up. I got hold of it, then stood up and called to the Germans to hold up their hands. They came out of the shell holes and rushed at me with fixed bayonets. There were seven shots in my pistol. I shot the four Germans in front, and all this time I was calling on them to hold up their hands. When they saw that four out of the fifteen were killed, the other eleven threw up their hands.

I took them back to our lines. When I got there, I was still able to walk, so I told the captain I would take them back to headquarters. A major at First Battalion asked, "Did you take these prisoners?"

I answered, "Yes, sir."

"How did you do it?"

I replied, "They attacked me, and I made a counter-attack." When I gave him the story, he asked for my name and serial number and said, "Son, when you get to the hospital write me a letter. Anything you want you can have. I will get it for you no matter what it costs."

I went to Chaumont to receive the Congressional Medal of Honor and was decorated on the 9th of February by General John J. Pershing, after which I was sent back to the hospital. I was discharged on 19 May 1919, as fully recovered, just two days after my twenty-first birthday.

* * *

In addition to the Medal of Honor, Thomas C. Neibaur was awarded the United Nations Victory Medal; The Order of the Purple Heart; the French Croix de Guerre; the Legion of Honor; the Italian Merit of War; and the Montenegro Silver Medal of War. He was the first private awarded such honors, and among the one-hundred most highly decorated men of the war.

Life following the war was difficult for Tom Neibaur. Plagued by his wounds, it seemed that most every career he tried did not work. After his death in a Boise Veterans Hospital, 23 December 1942, reporter Vardis Fisher wrote the following about his life:

Thomas Niebaur's name perhaps meant nothing to most of those who read of his death. Neibaur, from Sugar City, Idaho, was the only Idahoan to receive the highest honor his country could award.

When I read of Tom's death my . . . memory went back to that day of pomp and glory when Tom Neibaur came back from the war. Of all names in Idaho, his was on most tongues that day. His was the hand everybody wanted to shake; he was the man to whom everybody wanted to give a job. I've no notion how many hands and flags and orators turned out; but I believe the governor and other state dignitaries were here, as well as all the windjammers from eastern Idaho. It was roses, roses all the day under the feet of Tom Neibaur; it was rhetoric with a vengeance from the rostrum; it was sweet flattery and handshaking and a banquet and more speeches.

Robert Browning has a bitter poem to such a hero. "It was roses, roses all the way," but a year later it was oblivion. Well, Tom, rest in peace.

Thomas C Neibaur is buried in the Sugar City Cemetery next to his wife Lois, and three of their sons. His grave is marked with two stones, one provided by the Congress of the United States, giving his name, and reading "Medal Of Honor."

Taken from records provided by Anthony Gardner, a nephew of Tom Neibaur, a medic in the South Pacific during World War II.

LEONARD C. BROSTROM

For I, the Lord, rule in the heavens above, and among the armies of the earth; and in the day when I shall make up my jewels, all men shall know what it is that bespeaketh the power of God.

(Doctrine & Covenants 60:4)

Private, first class, Leonard Brostrom had only eight days of combat experience when, on 28 October 1944, he single handedly knocked out a Japanese pillbox near Dagami, on the Island of Leyte, The Philippines.

A returned missionary, Leonard had just begun his mission in California when the war started. He was allowed to complete it, doing so in Carson City, Nevada. Upon his return home he was drafted without delay .

Leonard's bravery on Leyte is reflected in the citation awarding him the Medal of Honor:

Leonard C. Brostrom was a rifleman with an assault platoon, which ran into powerful resistance near Dagami, Leyte, Philippine Islands, on 28 October 1944. From pillboxes, trenches, and spider holes, so well camouflaged that they could be detected at no more than twenty yards, the enemy poured machine gun and rifle fire, causing severe casualties in the platoon. Realizing that a key pillbox would have to be knocked out if the company were to advance, PFC

Brostrom, without orders and completely ignoring his own safety, ran forward to attack the pillbox with grenades. He immediately became the prime target for all the riflemen in the area, as he rushed to the rear of the pillbox and tossed grenades through the entrance. Six enemy soldiers left a trench in a bayonet charge against the heroic American, but he killed one and drove the others off with rifle fire. As he threw more grenades from his completely exposed position he was wounded several times in the abdomen and knocked to the ground. Although suffering intense pain and rapidly weakening from loss of blood, he slowly rose to his feet and once more hurled his deadly missiles at the pillbox. As he collapsed, the enemy began fleeing from the fortification and were killed by riflemen of his platoon. PFC Brostrom died while being carried from the battlefield, but his intrepidity and unhesitating willingness to sacrifice himself in a one-man attack against overwhelming odds enabled his company to reorganize against attack, and annihilate the entire enemy position.

This award was presented to Carl Brostrom, Leonard's father, by Brigadier General Robert M. Hardaway, representing President Harry S. Truman, at a program held in the Preston 4th Ward Chapel, on 29 November 1945. Speaker for this event was Elder Ezra Taft Benson, of the Quorum of the Twelve Apostles.

Leonard C. Brostrom is buried in the Preston Cemetery. In 1950 the U.S. Army transport ship, *Marine Eagle*, was rechristened the *SS Leonard C. Brostrom*.

Leonard C. Brostrom

NATHAN VAN NOY JR.

And I will punish the world for evil, and the wicked for their iniquity; I will cause the arrogancy of the proud to cease, and will lay down the haughtiness of the terrible.

(2 Nephi 23:11)

Nathan Van Noy Jr., was born at Grace, Idaho, and raised in nearby Preston.

The following account of his heroism was published in *YANK Magazine: The Army Weekly*, dated 31 December 1943, written by Pvt. John McLeod, *YANK* staff correspondent:

NEW GUINEA–The kid was tow-headed, red-cheeked and 19 years old. He joined his outfit as a replacement before it went into its first action.

The fellows in his outfit didn't pay much attention to him. They hardly knew his name, called

Private Nathan Van Noy Jr.

him Whitey or Junior. They called him Junior because he looked even younger than he was, because he didn't have much to say. When he did say something he did so without using the Army's stock phrases of profanity.

"We kind of figured him as a mama's boy," a sergeant in his outfit recalled. "Just goes to show you how wrong you can be."

Junior soon showed that whatever else he was, he was a good soldier.

During his first action he shot down a low-level enemy bomber, which came over Red Beach, near Lae, trying to strafe the beach and barges.

THE ENEMY IS VERY NEAR

Bravery and Death on Scarlet Beach

SEE PAGE 2

Two months after Junior's death *YANK Magazine* published the story of his herosim.

At Scarlet Beach, beyond Finschafen, he didn't have too much luck in his shooting, and he received five shrapnel wounds in his wrist, side and back.

The medics tried to evacuate Junior to a base hospital, but Junior said no. He could get along all right and his outfit was short of good .50–caliber men. It needed him. Again, the medics tried to ship Junior off when he came to them with ulcers in both ears. Junior said no. He went to the aid station for treatment three times a day, but he stayed on his job, digging defense positions, taking his turn by the big Browning machine gun.

The Scarlet Beach defenses needed men.

On the night the Japanese counterattack came, Junior was sound asleep in his hammock, perhaps dreaming that he was no longer a private in the Army, but just plain Nathan Van Noy Jr., playing football with his high school team back at Preston, Idaho, or working in a tow garage after school hours.

Junior was so tired that he slept through all the rain that poured down on his hammock top that night. After the rain stopped shortly before dawn, however, Junior was awakened by whispers in the bush near him.

Sgt. John Fuina of Brooklyn, in charge of the American beach detachment, was restless, and so was T-5 Raymond J. Koch of Wabasha,

Minnesota. They got up together to take a stretch. It was an hour and a half before dawn and still black as midnight.

Gazing out to sea, the two saw three smudges on the skyline. Holding their breaths and clutching each other's arms, they waited. The smudges gradually took more distinct shape as they moved slowly and noiselessly toward shore. They had the decidedly peaked prows of Japanese landing barges.

They were only 300 to 400 hundred yards away.

Sgt. Fuina yelled an alarm and ran toward his .37mm antitank gun to fire an alert. Cpl. Koch ran from hammock to hammock and tent to tent waking the American and Australian gun crews.

Pvt. Van Noy didn't need any waking. At Sgt. Fuina's first yell, he tumbled out of his hammock and dived into his machine-gun pit. His loader, Cpl. Stephen Popa of Detroit, was right after him.

Sgt. Fuina didn't waste any time. He fired one armor-piercing and two HE shells at the nearest barge. An Aussie two-pounder gun joined him. Together they sank the barge, and they could see soldiers clambering out of it, first trying to reach the other barges and then swimming toward the far bank of the Song River.

The other two barges landed right in front of Pvt. Van Noy's .50–caliber position. They beached just fifteen yards away. The barge ramps slowly began to fall. Troops started throwing out grenades by the handful. Pvt. Van Noy held his fire.

When the ramps were all the way down, when the Japanese blew their bugles and began to charge, Pvt. Van Noy pressed his finger on the trigger and cut loose. The first to fall were two Japanese officers trying to scorch Van Noy out of his position with flame throwers.

The remaining troops fell on their faces and continued throwing grenades and firing.

Aussie Bren gunners some yards behind Van Noy's pit began shouting to him to "Get the hell out of there, you bloody fool." Seeing the grenades burst all about the pit, Sgt. Fuina yelled, too, ordering him to get out of his exposed position.

Pvt. Van Noy's loader, Cpl. Popa, crawled from the pit with a shattered leg trailing behind him. He thought Van Noy would follow.

But Pvt. Van Noy changed ammunition belts and kept on firing.

Sgt. Fuina saw a grenade land squarely in the pit. Van Noy's stream of tracers continued to rake up and down the water's edge, where by this time the Japanese were frantically trying to dig into the sand.

Then there were other flashes, and Van Noy's gun ceased firing.

Until dawn the firing crackled around the beached barges. Aussie gunners fired clip after clip from their Bren and Owen guns. Sgt. Fuina loaded his .37 and raked over every square foot of the beach and barges. Pfc. Philip Edwards of Mokane, Missouri, helped out from a far flank with his .50 and knocked out a Japanese .50, which had been firing spasmodically from one of the barges.

When the sun rose out of the Bismark Sea, a skirmish line of infantrymen moved down to the beach to mop up the remnants. There weren't any remnants to mop. Junior's Browning had accounted for at least half of the forty who landed. Aussie gunners and Sgt. Fuina's .37 did the rest. The twenty who swam from the first barge had been disposed of in short order by Australian Owen gunners and a Papuan infantry patrol.

It was a sad lot of victorious soldiers who finally went over to Pvt. Van Noy's weapon pit. Pvt. Van Noy was the only Allied soldier killed in the action. The first grenade in the pit had torn off his left leg. It took a rifle bullet between his eyes to stop him. Even then, the men wondered if he hadn't continued to fire after death. Every bullet in his gun had been fired.

All of his American buddies and the twenty Australians who fought with Junior Van Noy agreed with Sgt. Fuina, when he looked down at the dead soldier's body and said:

"That kid had more guts than all the rest of the Army put together."

That seems to about size it up.

Nathan Van Noy Jr. is buried in the Grace Cemetery, Grace, Idaho. Later the United States rechristened a ship after Nathan.

Monument for Nathan "Junior" Van Noy.

SERVICE IN THE CONTINENTAL U.S.

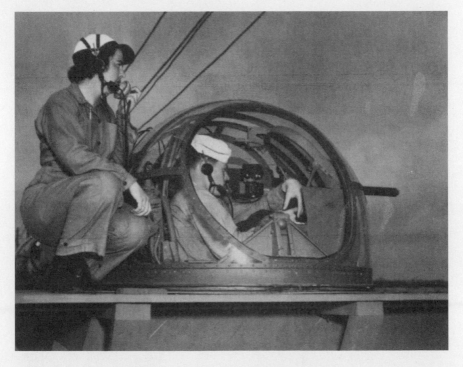

In the United States, women and men provided valuable support services for those serving over seas. Hospitals personnel, shipyard management, flight and weaponry instruction (seen above) were just a few of the critical services provided.

For every man on the front line there were many more in the rear echelons, training those doing the fighting, purchasing supplies, keeping records, nursing the sick and wounded, developing weapons, scheduling transportation, preparing meals, and doing all those things necessary for the execution of the war.

WILMA LAVON ELLIS WILSON

All these things shall give thee experience, and shall be for thy good..

(Doctrine & Covenants 122:7)

I was raised in Honeyville, Utah, so named because of a principal agricultural pursuit—the keeping of honey bees and the production of honey. In my youth I was busily engaged in all the activities of a honey business: the tending of the hives and the extracting and making ready for sale of the honey produced.

I attended the Utah State Agricultural College, then taught school for three years before World War II began. Feeling a patriotic duty to serve and help win the peace, I enlisted in the Women's Army Corp, or WAC. Besides, all the young men were in the Army. I felt that if I could do administrative work I could free up a young man to serve in a capacity more directly related to the prosecution of the war.

My basic training was taken at Ft. Des Moines, Des Moines, Iowa. One other Mormon girl was in basic training when I was. We attended church a few times. On the 24th of July we were at the celebration of that event with the local Saints. There were ball games and food. The main dish was rabbit stew—the first time I had ever tasted it. It was likely the first time for the rabbit as well.

We were issued dog tags the same as the men. Mine was issued to me stamped with a P, for Protestant. I told the first sergeant that I wanted mine stamped LDS.

She asked, "Are you a Catholic?" I said, "No." Then she asked, "Are you a Protestant?" Again I said, "No."

"Well," she said to those around us, "maybe you should have it stamped H, for heathen." We all laughed.

After completing Basic, I was assigned to the 108th WAC Detachment, Ft. McDowell on Angel Island, near San Francisco, California. It is a beautiful place. I spent the entire war there. When we arrived, one of the older girls gave us tips on how to arrange our footlocker to avoid having to rearrange it for inspections.

Wilma Wilson at Golden Gate Park, San Francisco, California.

After I had been there a week, the lieutenant asked for volunteers for a detail. I stepped forward. Despite what I had heard about dirty volunteer details, this one proved to be very interesting. We boarded a truck and rode several miles along the Embarcadero (a road that runs next to all the piers in San Francisco). It was a picturesque ride, and we had a good time. At a large building, a laundry and dry cleaning complex, we loaded packages for our unit. It didn't seem hard to me, as I was used to lifting beehives full of honey, which were much heavier, and it was a good opportunity to get acquainted with the other girls.

Back at the station, I told personnel that I had an interest in photography. There were no openings in that department, and I was given a job in the pay section. I was a good typist and I prepared stencils to print orders and process troops. It was an important job, especially in the discharge section where I worked.

Ft. McDowell had a large complement of buildings: a mess hall, and a big orientation room for meetings, shows, and plays. There was also a hospital, nurses barracks, and a barracks for the WACs. There was a pool hall, bowling alley, chapel, library, and quarters for commissioned officers.

A barracks was designated for "casuals"—those who were transient, either coming or going to an assignment. I'll bet a lot of them didn't know whether they were coming or going. There were also facilities for Japanese, German, and Italian prisoners of war. A Post Exchange, school for dependent children, and a small snack bar rounded out the facilities. It was a very well contained military facility.

Each morning we fell out for reveille and roll call, and marched to breakfast. We did calisthenics, then marched after lunch, stood inspections, and participated in a formal military parade every Friday. Health checks were held regularly, and there were other meetings to attend.

We were encouraged to use our talents. I did oil painting and played on our baseball team. One girl cut hair and gave permanents, and another tailored skirts.

LDS Servicemen's meetings were usually held at night after church. Those of us on Angel Island needed to catch a ferry from San Francisco, which left at a time that made it impossible to attend those meetings.

An outing with the other Wacs. Wilma is in the upper left corner.

Aunt Martha, my father's older sister, lived in Berkeley. Sometimes I stayed with her, and we would go to church together. Three of my boy cousins who were in the Navy sometimes visited us.

When the Protestant chaplain found that I could play the organ, he asked me to play for their Sunday School. This was attended by the children of officers and NCOs who lived on or near the base. The chaplain gave a lesson using a flannel board. I had never seen one used before. He told me where to obtain one in a book store in San Francisco, which I did. They were very valuable to me in later teaching assignments.

I was grateful my parents had taught me to pray. I knew they loved me. In their letters they told me they were praying for me so far from home. This was comforting to a girl, often alone in a strange city. None of the other girls ever gave me a hard time about my religion, or that I went to church.

Probably the most heart wrenching incident that occurred at our base was when two young men, just home from the Pacific, went up into the hills and hung themselves. It was so sad to see their parents as they came to the base to talk with some of the officers about the tragedy.

The highlight of my whole military service was when I was furloughed to go home and marry my sweetheart, Charles Edward Wilson Jr., in the Salt Lake Temple on 5 September 1945. Our honeymoon was unforgettable and over altogether too quickly. We thought Edward might have to go to the Pacific in support of the war with Japan, but with the dropping of the atomic bomb and the subsequent surrender of Japan he was not required to go. He and I were discharged shortly after that.

Wilma and Edward Wilson completed their formal schooling at the Utah State Agricultural College in Logan, then, in 1948, they moved to Lewiston, Utah, where Edward became principal of an elementary school, teaching science, art, and other disciplines. They are parents of three sons and two daughters, have twenty grandchildren and three great-grandchildren. They have been active in the Church all their lives. Wilma taught in all the auxiliaries and in the Relief Society. For many years she served on the Lewiston Library Board and was a 4-H and Cub Scout Leader. She also taught school for

Charles and Wilma Wilson on their wedding day.

fifteen years. Wilma says: "I think I was brave to go into the Army. I am happy I served."

WILLIAM GRANT JARDINE

I have given . . . mine angels charge concerning you.

(Doctrine & Covenants 84:42)

It may seem odd that the Navy would train sailors in Idaho, nevertheless, that was the case. Near the end of my training at Farragut Naval Training Center on Lake Pend Oreille in northern Idaho, many men in our unit were stricken with a fever. Our medical officer prescribed a huge pill to be taken at noon chow. A chief petty officer handed one to each of us as we came through the chow line and made sure we took it.

We had finished our training, and we were scheduled for leave. In addition we were given ten hours liberty to go to nearby Coeur D'Alene. As I got on the bus to ride to town I didn't feel well, and by the time we arrived I was shaking with chills and then fever. I caught the next bus back to Farragut. I went to my barracks, and as I laid down on my bunk, the master at arms noticed I had returned early. I tried to tell him I was sick, but he ordered me to get out of bed and go on guard duty. I picked up my rifle and went out on the line that was my assigned patrol.

The next thing I remember was waking up in sick bay. The man in charge at first thought I was drunk and had passed out. I was lying on a gurney, hardly able to move and burning with fever. I asked the corpsman to please get two elders from the Mormon Church to come administer to me. He had no idea what I was talking about, but said he would try to do as I requested. I told him the names of two men whom I knew held the Melchizedek Priesthood—Jack Hart and Fay Peterson. I managed to struggle off the gurney and into an empty bed.

By this time I was delirious, and I felt sure that Jack and Fay had come a short time earlier and administered to me. I had a feeling of assurance that I would soon be alright. My eyes were swollen shut and my hands puffed out like balloons so that I couldn't close them. A nurse took my temperature and said it was 106 degrees, and that I was being transferred to a hospital. Since I had not been diagnosed, I was put in a ward with men who had scarlet fever.

It was finally determined that I, and several others, were violently allergic to the sulfa drugs we had been given. In a few days the fever dissipated, the swelling went down, and my skin began to peel like an onion. After I recovered somewhat, I was reassigned to another company that was soon due for boot camp leave, so I got a delayed leave. My time at home was enjoyable, but I looked like a scarecrow.

Grant Jardine, 1945

About four months later I chanced to meet Jack Hart in Oakland, and thanked him and Fay for the blessing I felt had saved my life. To my surprise he said neither he nor Fay had come that night, and learned only some time later how very sick I was. To this day I don't know who gave me that blessing, but I felt the power of the priesthood strengthening me. I've had other small miracles in by life, but have been especially grateful for this one. Someday I would like to find and thank those unknown elders who helped bring about my recovery.

* * *

In August 1944, I was a hospital corpsman in a ward in Oak Knoll Naval Hospital in San Leandro, California. The forty patients in our care had kept us very busy in the orthopedic ward. All of them had serious bone injuries—broken legs, arms, shoulders, and backs. A tough Marine master sergeant was having a slow time healing from serious combat wounds. Needing something to do, he assumed unofficial command of the ward. Another Marine, "M," who had seen action in four beach landings in the South Pacific had a serious shoulder wound.

It was the custom in the ward each evening, about 1900 hours, to bring in a large urn of coffee for the men. A new corpsman was responsible for the ward, and due to his inexperience, the coffee did not arrive at the scheduled hour. As I walked into the nurses station, "M," the Marine with the shoulder wound, asked if he could talk to me for a minute. We walked together down to the galley. He opened the door and shoved me in. I spotted the coffee urn there, which should already have been in the ward.

"M" grabbed me with his good arm and spun me around, in a rage. He cursed me, and told me that all hospital corpsmen were a bunch of jerks, and in unprintable Marine language defined what he felt I was. I tried to tell him I didn't know why the coffee was still in the galley, but he felt I was personally responsible.

He grabbed my shoulder. I told him not to do that again. I realized that he was out of control. He threw a gallon jug of milk on the floor, the glass broke, and the milk gushed around the room. Next he pulled a Colt .45 pistol from the cast on his arm and shoulder where it had been concealed. He worked the slide with his good hand, throwing a shell in the chamber and aimed it at me—all the time cursing me and all hospital corpsmen.

I was backed up to the counter and reached behind me into a drawer to get something with which to defend myself. We were facing each other and the gun was still aimed at me. Without warning he turned the gun to the left and fired. The noise was ear shattering. That .45 sounded like a cannon in the small room. The recoil jarred the gun from his hand, and it dropped on the floor. He burst into tears. For the first time I looked down and realized I held a meat cleaver in my hand.

I picked up the gun, ejected the clip, handed him the empty pistol, and told him to get rid of the damn thing quick. We both stood there stunned, our heads ringing from the blast, with milk and glass at our feet. I started to clean up the mess and told the sergeant to take the coffee out to the ward.

During the height of the confrontation, a lieutenant, junior grade, had opened the galley door, seen something violent taking place, and closed it again. I thought she had reported the situation, but she had actually done nothing.

Back in the ward when I passed the marine sergeant's bed he said, "Jardine, what happened in there?" I told him nothing had happened, but I doubted he believed me. He knew gunfire when he heard it.

The next morning the officer in charge of the ward called me into her office and asked if anything had happened that she should know about. I wasn't strictly truthful, but told her that nothing of significance had taken place. Even though she may have had her doubts, she accepted my explanation and didn't press for details or take any action.

When she asked me the question, I realized for the first time what this Marine had been going through. He had been in at least four invasions and experienced more stress than most of us could imagine. Something in his mind had snapped when we were in the galley.

The smell of gunpowder hung in the galley for days. Maybe the cooks got blamed.

About six weeks later, I was on liberty in downtown Oakland and met "M." He was dressed in full uniform, and looked sharp. Without his cast I didn't immediately recognize him and when I did I became apprehensive, wondering what might take place next. He threw his arms around me, hugged me, and fervently thanked me for not reporting what had happened.

I've often wondered if that bullet hole is still in the corner of the wall in Ward 42. I have also been mighty glad that he elected to shoot the wall and not me.

Grant Jardine returned to eastern Idaho where he became a jeweler and watchmaker. For several years he worked at Ricks College in the electronics department. He married Barbara Dansie and together they raised two sons and two daughters. They have seventeen grandchildren and twelve great-grandchildren.

Grant has served in many ward and stake callings, in three bishoprics and as a bishop. He is currently an ordinance worker and sealer in the Idaho Falls Temple.

Barbara passed away in 1997. In July 1998, Grant married Belva Weeks. They reside in Rexburg, Idaho.

LIFE ON THE HOME FRONT

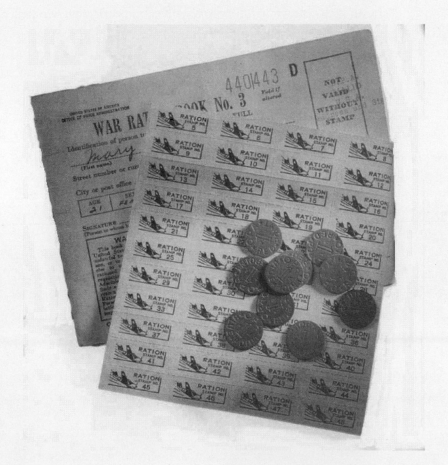

Rationing coupons and stamps were needed for the basic necessities such as food and fuel. However, most people didn't mind doing their part to support the war.

It is not easy to send a loved one off to fight in a war. Typically, young newlyweds were separated for prolonged periods of time. It is hard to imagine the uncertainty of it all. Adding to the uncertainty was the fact that many young men left new wives alone, expecting a baby—would that child ever know its father? Decisions with far reaching consequences were made quickly, and it did not help much that everyone was in a similar situation. These were hard times. Frequently, young wives traveled long distances to be with their husbands, always uncertain if the military would even allow them time together. And when or if they did, there was eventually another painful good-bye. Throughout all this uncertainty, most did very well.

Elder Hugh B. Brown wrote a provocative article to young women of the Church, encouraging them to remember their important role in the war. The following is an excerpt of this article:

To the Girls Behind the Men Behind the Guns

In this world conflict the front lines are often "behind the lines." Civilians are playing a larger part than in any war in history. It is a war against the individual, where truth and error are locked in conflict, right opposed to wrong, good opposed to evil, Christ opposed to anti-Christ. The first and most important duty of every soldier is to "choose whom he will serve." You, young women, also must decide which side you are on and then you will have ample opportunity to prove your quality. . . .

These men want to feel as they go out to fight that there is something in the world that has not gone to pieces. Their thought of home, family, and the verities of life include you, the girl friend, the fiancee. They want to believe that there is still something sweet and clean and pure in the world. To them you symbolize the ideal. . . .

You girls behind the men behind the guns form a line of defense which must not weaken. While that line holds, the front lines will remain impregnable. There must be no compromise, no going over to the enemy, no lowering of standards—no traitors in this line. . . .

Yes, girls, you are called to serve, and when the war is over the heroines will be as numerous and entitled to as great credit as the heroes of the war. Your medal of honor may not be pinned on a uniform, but it will be the highest honor won on life's battlefield—a clean, courageous heart. God himself will reward your valor.

VIRGINIA POND JOHNSON

By the end of World War II it seemed like all I had ever known was war. I met Hal in November 1942, when I was just eighteen. We were engaged thirteen days after our first date and married 19 January 1943, following an engagement of just over one month. He was a returned missionary. We had been married for just two weeks when he left for military service.

While he completed his training, our life together consisted of the weekends when we could get together. I got to spend a month with him while he was stationed at Walla Walla, Washington. Our baby was born two weeks after Hal shipped out from San Francisco.

I loved Hal very much then, and still do all these years later. We had to make important decisions quickly and live with them. But everyone was in the same situation—we were expected to do our part, it was not something I resented. I did learn that "hellos" were easier and more fun than "good-byes."

It would have been nice if Hal could have taken me to the hospital for the birth of our son. This was just one of the things Hal and I missed doing together during the time he was away. But it was a growing experience for me.

For whatever reason I never doubted that Hal would come home. Although his mail was always censored, I looked forward with great anticipation to his letters. I did know where he was, and I listened intently to the news reports and read the newspaper carefully every day. Sometimes

Virginia and Hal Johnson. Photo taken near their first anniversary, January 1944.

news about Hal came from other sources. The following was a letter I received from Lieutenant General George C. Kenney. He informed me that Hal received the air medal for "meritorious achievement while participating as bombardier in aerial flights in the southwest Pacific area from October 26, 1944 to December 2, 1944." The letter read:

Your husband took part in sustained operational flight missions during which hostile contact was probable and expected. These flights included bombing missions against enemy installations, shipping and supply bases, and aided considerably in the recent successes in this theatre.

Almost every hour of every day your husband, and the husbands of other American women, are doing just such things as that here in the southwest Pacific. Theirs is a very real and very tangible contribution to victory and peace.

I would like to tell you how genuinely proud I am to have men such as your husband in my command, and how gratified I am to know that young Americans with such courage and resourcefulness are fighting our country's battle against aggressor nations.

Finally the day came when Hal was home. I was so excited to see him. With our son, Michael, I met Hal in Salt Lake City. It was the first time Hal had seen his son. I was so happy to see him.

As Hal and I were vacationing at

August, 1945, Hal and Virginia with their son Michael. This is the first time Hal had seen his son, who was then about ten months old.

Pond's Lodge in Island Park, Idaho, in August 1945, we heard that the atomic bomb had been dropped on Japan. What a relief to learn that the Japanese had surrendered, and that with the end of the fighting, Hal would not have to go back to the Far East, and we could stay together and plan our lives.

GERALDINE KLUGE GUNN

Because you love me I can bear this weight of loneliness that presses on my heart. We're still together though you are too far away from me to touch or hear or see. Because I know you love me, I am strong, I wait, tho my heart cries, "How long. . .how long!"

(Kathryn Kay)

I am a native of Salt Lake City and graduated from South High School. Harold W. Gunn and I were married in September 1942, while he was in flight training. This was not a "wartime courtship," we had been dating for two-and-a-half years. He became a co-pilot on a B-17 Flying Fortress. I was there, at the exciting time of his graduation and pinned on his wings—a special time for both of us.

Following our wedding, being young and very much in love and wanting to spend as much time with Hal as possible before his anticipated departure for overseas, I joined him and his crew. We moved first to Boise, Idaho, El Paso, Texas, then Rapid City and Pierre, South Dakota then Salina, Kansas, where he completed his training.

At Pierre we lived in a hotel. The people there reached out and embraced those of us in the military. Our daughter, Jerrilyn, could run around the halls of the hotel and do just about what she wanted. The fellows in Hal's crew took Jerrilyn to their hearts and treated her like their own daughter, especially the navigator. He carried Jerrilyn around on his shoulders, like a big brother.

At the time I joined his group, they had been formed into the crew that would operate their assigned aircraft. After they had finished their training for the day, I was their unofficial mascot and went everywhere with them. When they went to the bullfights in El Paso, I went with them. It was fun, and they all treated me with respect and courtesy.

Geraldine Kluge Gunn

Before we were ready for it, the time had come for Hal to go to his assigned overseas duty. He left on 8 February 1943. I returned to Salt Lake City and lived with my parents. Prior to being married I had worked for the *Salt Lake Tribune/Telegram*. They held my job for me. It was a wonderful place to work, especially because Hal had worked there as well. All of the people, including the publisher, were like a very caring family.

I wrote Hal nearly every day. I loved getting his letters, although he could not say much about what he was doing. He did, however, tell me about the raid on which his bombardier was hit by a bullet from an enemy fighter, and the details of how Hal saved this man's life.

I knew when Hal's plane was shot down. I didn't tell my mother that I knew, but I knew. My girlfriend and I met at a small café each morning to have a snack before going to work. The day after I received that impression, I told her "Hal was shot down yesterday." She questioned it, but I told her that I knew it, and that there was no reason to try to tell me anything different.

About a week later, while I was at work, I received a telephone call from Mother. She asked me if I were coming home for supper that evening. I replied that I normally did, then I asked why she called to ask. She said it was because she wanted to fix something I really liked for supper and just wanted to be sure that I would be there.

"Mother, did I get a telegram?" I asked. She tried to evade the question, but I told her she might as well tell me now, as for me to wait until suppertime. Mother read the terse telegram from the Adjutant General. "I regret to inform you that the Commanding General European Area reports your husband, 2nd Lt. Harold W Gunn, missing in action since 22 June. If further details or other information of his status are received, you will be promptly notified." For the first time in my life, I fainted.

When I came to my senses I looked up into the faces of my friends at the *Tribune/Telegram*. Even now when I read the blunt wording of that telegram I relive the emotions of that day.

A couple of weeks after the telegram came, I had a dream. In this dream I was standing on a beach, watching the waves roll in. I saw a lot of B-17s land in the water. The crews from these planes got out of the water and walked up on the beach. As they passed me they turned their heads away from me and continued walking. One of the men however, a member of the Church, whom I knew well from those beautiful days before they all left for England, came directly from his plane and stood in front of me. He spoke, "Gerry, Hal isn't with us, but I want you to know that he is all right. It will be a long hard climb, but he's all right. Don't you worry, he'll be along." I knew I would see Hal again.

A couple of weeks later I received a letter from Hal's best friend, Jack. Jack said that Hal's plane was just in front of his in the formation and that he watched a burst of flak hit Hal's plane, then watched as the plane went out of control, made a slow roll, and lost altitude. He told me that he saw no flames or smoke, and thought Hal could have bailed out, and that I should not worry. This was somewhat reassuring.

Geraldine waiting for letters from her husband, Hal.

On July 30th the following telegram came from the War Department: "Report received through the International Red Cross states that your husband, 2nd Lt Harold W. Gunn is a prisoner of war of the German government. Other information follows." It was a great relief to have verification that he was alive.

Before Hal left to go overseas we worked out a simple

code. We assigned degrees of longitude and latitude to various salutations. If he opened a letter with Dearest Gerry, or Dear Sweetheart, or To my wife, etc—the list was quite long—I could tell about where he was. This worked until he became a prisoner of war. Following that Hal and I had limited correspondence. We were allowed three letters a month. Once I had the opportunity to buy a house, and I wanted to get Hal's approval before going ahead, but by the time we both understood what was going on, it was six months later, and the seller found another buyer. It was frustrating.

I could send him a package every three months, I often included Church books. The Germans furnished a list of acceptable food items that we could mail.

I continued to work for the *Tribune*. I worked at the front desk and took advertising copy. The people there were very supportive. Because I was at the *Tribune,* I probably got more publicity than most other wartime wives.

I kept an extensive scrapbook. On Hal's return I wanted to be able to show him some of the things I felt he would have been interested in. Now, it helps me to recall those events.

A group of us formed a wives'club, which met once a month to go to dinner at the Temple Square Hotel. We exchanged news and kept up with what was going on. Only one other wife had a husband in a prison camp. But it helped to meet together. We had some sad times in our little group when we heard that a husband had been killed.

It was a blow to Jerrilyn when I told her that her friend, Hal's navigator, who had carried her around on his shoulders, had been killed.

When any of the men we knew, who had been POWs, were repatriated, they came to see me, which I really appreciated. From them I got firsthand reports about Hal.

Most of what I did was just keep myself busy, doing ordinary things. I helped keep the newspaper going, kept a stiff upper lip, tried to preserve a sense of humor about things, and waited.

When Hal and the other POWs were moved to Moosburg in January 1945, correspondence between us nearly stopped. When I heard the news that the Moosburg prison camp had been liberated I was so excited I hardly knew what I was doing. I had waited so long for that news that it didn't seem real. I was filled with relief that he was out of German hands, and prayed that he was all right. That day I also received my first letter from him in more than three months and this telegram:

MAY 12TH, 1945: The Secretary of War desires me to express his pleasure that your husband 2/Lt Gunn, Harold W returned to military control date unreported.

When Hal got back to town it was the middle of the night. Returning soldiers were not allowed to let their families know of their arrival. Then, when he was able to call, he couldn't contact any of our family, and so spent several frustrating hours at the Denver & Rio Grande Railway station in downtown Salt Lake.

Because I didn't know exactly when he was coming, I went to visit cousins in Idaho. As I ran to catch the train back to Salt Lake, I fell and hurt my back. So, when Hal met my train he had to carry me off and put me into a wheelchair—not exactly what we had in mind for our reunion. But I was overjoyed to see him and have him there, gently caring for me. At last we were together.

After a few days at home, we went on what they called a "redistribution program," for all the former prisoners of Stalag Luft III and their wives. We spent five weeks at a resort in Santa Monica, California. It was a beautiful place, and the people catered to our every want. We had a wonderful time getting reacquainted.

Five years following WWII, Hal and Gerry Gunn moved to New Hampshire where they purchased a house and 140 acres in Gilford, just outside Laconia. The first meeting of what eventually became the Laconia Ward was held in their home, and the first baptisms in that area were performed in the brook on their property. Branch members tapped their maple trees and processed the syrup to sell for their building fund. She says she held every position available to her in the little Laconia Branch— sometimes a dozen at a time. She was called to preside over the New England Mission Primary by President Truman Madsen. Gerry later served as the mission's Girls Camp Director and was successful in touching the lives of many young women.

She and Hal are parents of one son and five daughters, have thirty grandchildren and thirty-three great- grandchildren. They raised their family in New Hampshire. After living there for twenty-five years they moved back to Utah. They now reside in Highland.

DOTTIE MCKINLAY PACKER

Behold, the field is white already to harvest; therefore whoso desireth to reap let him thrust in his sickle with his might, and reap while the day lasts, that he may treasure up for his soul everlasting salvation in the kingdom of God.

(Doctrine & Covenants 12:3)

In 1943, my husband, Dean, was assigned as a medical officer to the Army Air Corps Overseas Replacement Depot in Greensboro, North Carolina. This was a military base of about fifty thousand personnel who were training to replace airmen overseas.

Our two daughters and I came from Salt Lake City to join him. We rented a house that was comfortable for us and our girls, four-year-old Michaelene, and two-year-old Deanne. In search of a Latter-day Saint church, we asked neighbors, taxi drivers, and the chaplain at the base. We looked in the newspapers and the telephone directory, without success. We assumed there were no other LDS people in Greensboro.

During our first year there, we became friends with other Air Corps couples, but we had to become accustomed to their smoking habits, which at first were quite offensive to us. Eventually, it seemed all right for them to smoke, even in our home. We went with friends to their churches occasionally—mostly at Easter and Christmas. Then one night, I dreamed that I was smoking, and that I liked it. I could even blow smoke rings. When I awakened I was so frightened that I could dream such a thing! In all my young life, smoking had never been a temptation to me. When I told Dean

Dottie McKinlay Packer

about the dream, he was as upset as I. Not that the dream was so bad, but that we had become so used to being without the Church and without Mormon friends. Because the Church was very important to us, we became very anxious about the possibility of losing our testimonies.

We wrote to Church headquarters in Salt Lake City and asked for the address of the nearest ward or branch. We received word back that there was a group that met in Greensboro, but there was no one at the address they gave us. The janitor there told us "the Mormons" had met there previously and gave us the name Ernest Stevens, who was the "pastor" of the Mormons. Then by telephone we found a friendly Sister Stevens who said they were now meeting in a home; she gave us the address.

The next Sunday, Dean was on duty at the base, and I started out alone. I did not take the children because I had to ride the bus and was uncertain about finding the place. When I finally found the right bus, the driver said he would tell me when we came to the address I had given him. I assumed it must be a very nice house if the whole branch was meeting there. When the bus driver stopped in the middle of the poorest neighborhood, with the tiniest houses I had ever seen, I was shocked.

The house I was looking for was the last one at the end of a little, muddy street. I remember thinking as I walked up the street, "I will never come here again." We had been going to Protestant churches occasionally with friends, to big and ornate cathedrals, and for a few moments my pride and indignation were high.

As I walked up the steps to that little house, the door opened and a sweet-faced gray-haired woman smiled and said, "This must be another Latter-day Saint." I threw my arms around her and wept with happiness. I knew I was in the right place and never missed another Sunday.

The woman who greeted me was Sister Stevens. She and her husband were the parents of Ernest, Paul, and Ruth, all of whom were married. These families with their children and grandchildren, together with the couple at whose home we were meeting, were the only active members.

It was not even a branch, just a Sunday School, with Ernest Stevens as superintendent. Ernest's wife, Ruth, was not then a baptized member, but she helped in every way she could. When we started meeting at a place where there was a piano, Ruth played for our meetings, and when we had a party, she helped with the food. The Stevens's daughter Ruth was married to Eugene Gullidge, also a strong member. They were all so devoted and faithful. In my limited vision, I said one day to Ruth Gullidge, "You and Gene should move out west to Utah or Idaho, so you and your children will have companions who are members of the Church." I was surprised and pleased with her answer: "Sister Packer, if we leave here, there will never be a church in Greensboro." Very insightful for such a young woman, I thought.

Dean put up notices of LDS meetings around the base, and soon we had several servicemen, nearly twenty, who attended a Thursday evening meeting at the base chapel. They also came to our Sunday meetings when they could. Colonel Stewart, another member, came a few times to our meetings in that little house. He encouraged us but was often away on assignment.

Eventually, we found a union hall that we could use on Sundays for our now larger group. President Doxey, the mission president, and his wife visited our little group occasionally, and we were lifted and inspired by them.

Some years later, I met Ruth Stevens, Ernest's wife, at general conference in Salt Lake City. I think she was then a Relief Society President in Greensboro. I asked when she had been baptized. She told me that she had become quite ill and had to be hospitalized. She said, "I decided that if I might die, I had better find out what I believed. I had my family bring all my Baptist books to the hospital and I started to study. Before I came home, I had converted myself to Mormonism." I think she was "converted" long before and just didn't know it. She also told me that there were at that time many wards and branches and several stakes in North Carolina. Later, we learned that Eugene Gullidge was a stake president. Good for them all! Good and faithful servants.

Dottie M. Packer has served in the Relief Society, Young Women's and Primary organizations of the Church throughout her life. She and her husband, C. Dean Packer, served missions to England, Spain, and on Temple Square. They were directors of the Church Service Mission for two years. She also served for several years on the Church Writing Committee. They are parents of two daughters and five sons. They have thirty grandchildren, and twenty-six great-grandchildren. Dean passed away 13 April 2000, at their home in Provo, Utah.

MARY TYLER THUESON

If a man marry a wife. . .

(Doctrine & Covenants 132:26)

Have you ever dreamed of a knight in shining armor who came on a white horse and asked you to be his wife? During wartime everything was different. Even proposals of marriage. Love had a way of sneaking in, even if all the knights were dressed in army uniforms.

One evening, when I came home from work, I found a large box on my doorstep. It was from a special young soldier in Louisiana who made my heart flutter and put a sparkle in my eye. It was so securely wrapped and had "insured" stamps all over it, that I thought it must be something very special. I shook it, smelled it, and tried to guess. It was packed so well there wasn't even a rattle. I decided to wait until my roommate cousins, Leah and Rhea, came home before I opened it. I took it in and carefully placed it on the table.

I would just have enough time to wash my hair before they got home. I hurriedly slipped off my skirt and blouse and rushed into the bathroom. I had just finished my task when the girls came in and saw the package. They ran in begging me to open it "right now." It looked so important and exciting! I wrapped a towel around my wet hair, sat down on the bed, and together we opened the mysterious package.

Oh, wow! Right on top of all the packing was a huge Hershey's chocolate bar. What a sweetheart! He knew how much I liked candy, and with wartime rationing it was not easy to get, but why in the world would he insure a candy bar? There must be something else in the box. Together we pulled out packing and more packing. At last we discovered, tucked away in one corner, a little square box. Well, I knew what came in tiny boxes that shape. Sure enough. There was a beautiful diamond ring.

That's how I became engaged, sitting unromantically in my slip, with my wet hair hanging in my eyes and two beaming cousins, at my side.

The year was 1942. I was working as a telephone operator in Idaho Falls, living in an apartment with my cousins, Leah and Rhea Cramer. We had a lot in common. We were all waiting for the war to end and our soldiers to come home so we could get on with our lives.

Being at war was a new experience for all of us, but our country was united and we pulled together. Many things were rationed: gas, tires, sugar, and leather shoes. When we needed toothpaste we had to turn in our old tube before they would sell us a new tube. We bought war bonds to help our nation. Each bond cost $18.75, and when it matured in ten years, it paid us $25.00.

The telephone office had heavy black blinds at the windows to block light from showing through to the outside. We had to give a secret code to get in. Life was not as carefree and happy as it had been before. Every family was affected in some way, and almost every home had a star hanging in its window—sometimes several. There was a star for every member of the family serving in the military. A gold star meant "killed in action." Our hearts quietly ached when we saw a gold star.

This was the beginning of women going to work in non-traditional jobs. Some went to the Coast and worked in munition factories. There was a woman called "Rosie the Riveter" whose picture was in all the papers. She could out-rivet any man in the airplane factory. Many thought this would be the end of "ladylike" women. For how could young women don coveralls, boots, and helmets, work in a factory, and still be a "lady"?

These fears were unfounded. The young women held up their end of the terrible load and when it was all over, they threw away their tools and returned home to marry the young man they had been waiting for. They donned their aprons and ribbons and became ladies again.

We lived for our soldiers' furloughs, which came once or twice a year. There was no gas to go anywhere, but it was fun just walking together, or going to a show once in a while.

Then one day in June of 1944, on his last furlough before going overseas, Walter and I changed our minds. Overnight we made preparations to be married. Who knew when the crazy war would end? We took our mothers on a Greyhound bus with us to Salt Lake City, Utah and I became Mrs. Walter Thueson.

We had a week of furlough left and then my handsome husband left for Camp Polk, Louisiana. I stayed home and waited for him to find a place for us to live. Two weeks later the phone call came for me to come quickly. How exciting! I had hardly been out of the state of Idaho, and now I was going clear across the United States all by myself.

The day was cold for July as I boarded the train, but I was dressed warmly and had my new coat over my arm. I found a seat in the back of the car where I could be by myself. I was not very good at talking to strangers.

As I settled down in my seat, I noticed a lone figure walking down the aisle. She paused at each seat and seemed to be searching for someone. As she came closer, I saw it was my mother. She had come for one last hug and kiss before I left. I was so happy to be going to my new husband. I was all grown up now and would be just fine. Yet, when I looked out the window and saw my mother standing on the platform all alone, so small and sad, suddenly, my heart ached.

Traveling during the war was not easy. In fact, it tested one's endurance and patience. All the newer trains were reserved for our troops, and the old obsolete ones were taken out of mothballs for civilian use. They were slow and uncomfortable. It was even slower because each time we met a troop train we had to pull over on a side track to let it go by. Just outside Denver we sat on a side track for over an hour while a hospital train carefully carried the wounded to the government hospital. We sat silently, with our heads bowed and eyes closed, not wanting to see what the other train carried. Now the war was real.

As we went south it got warmer and warmer. We thought it would be cooler if we opened a window, but the cinders blew in on us. Cinders filled our hair and stuck to our perspiring bodies. The windows were quickly closed and we traveled the rest of the way hot and miserable.

After four hot days and three long nights, we puffed and clanged our way into DeRidder, Louisiana. It was a foreign land as far as I was concerned. I hurried out the door and onto the steps of the train and looked into a sea of khaki and grinning soldiers. They all looked alike and not a familiar face in the crowd. Then I heard someone say, "Are you looking for someone?"

Oh, there he was! Just as handsome and happy as he was what seemed like an eternity ago. My heart skipped a beat and my feet skipped the last two stairs. I was in his strong protective arms again. He didn't seem to notice my limp, disarrayed clothes, or my cinder filled hair.

The local people in DeRidder were very good to make room for the soldiers and their wives. We rented one small room of a four room house. The owners lived in two rooms and rented the fourth room to another soldier and his wife.

The boards on the house were horizontal, and daylight could be seen through the cracks. There was no air conditioning and no refrigeration. Our one-room apartment was shared with dozens of cockroaches, but that was okay. We were together and we were happy.

Each day was a new experience. Fresh vegetables and fruits were brought to our door in a wagon by a gentle black man called Sugar Foot. Several times a week a black woman would come down our street carrying a large block of ice on her head, for the icebox. It seemed just like a chapter out of a storybook.

I went to work in an office on the Army post, and from the information that came across my desk I knew we would soon be separated again. Walt's outfit's equipment was being sent to Horsehead, New York, on its way overseas, but we were not allowed to mention it, even to each other.

One evening Walter came home trying especially hard to be cheerful. He sat there telling me one funny story after another, and I tried to laugh with him. *What is going on? This is not like him at all.* I was beginning to get a little nervous. Then I said, "Well, why don't you take your hat off and stay for awhile?" I reached over and slipped his hat off. Oh, heaven help me! His hair was all gone. He had an army regulation haircut. I burst into tears because I knew that meant he was one step closer to going overseas.

I prayed, "Oh, please, please, let it be over soon. We have only been together for three short months. I will be a good wife and wait patiently, if

C. Walter and Mary Tyler Thueson. Photos taken while they were living in Louisiana.

You'll just bring him home safely. I took the train back to Idaho, this time carrying a wonderful secret, I was expecting a baby.

Soon after arriving home, I received a set of horsehead salt and pepper shakers from my soldier. So, he was in Horsehead, New York. He would be going to the European Theater of war. Next, I received a message telling me that I should gargle with salt water for the next twenty-four hours for my sore throat. Because our letters were censored, this was our pre-arranged code for letting me know he'd be boarding a ship within the next twenty-four hours.

Life in Idaho was not all gloom and doom; we had some happy times, too. My mother and I worked at the Red Cross, folding bandages. We sewed together, visited neighbors, read books, and took walks. We had never had time together as grown-ups, so it was nice.

I often wondered why my mother went to the door and watched when a certain car came down the street. Not until after the war was over did she tell me it was the telegraph operator delivering those dreaded messages. "We regret to inform you..." "Missing" or "Killed in action." Thank heaven he never stopped at our house.

We were so excited at the thoughts of having a baby to love and cuddle. Everything was ready and waiting. Finally, on a beautiful spring morning in May, Mother Nature's alarm rang and we hurried to the hospital.

As I was waking up from the anesthetic I heard the doctor talking to my mother in a quiet voice. Something must be wrong. I hadn't heard my baby cry. What's the matter? Please let me hold my baby. Then I heard my mother say, "Oh, what a pity." The nurse brought my darling little boy over for me to see for just a minute. Such a perfect little body—a miniature copy of his soldier daddy. My mother kissed me on the cheek and told me he had been stillborn. I thought my tears would never end.

With an ache in my heart but determination in my soul, I went to live with my cousins, Rhea and Leah, and to work as a receptionist in a doctor's office. I liked my job and I loved being with my cousins. I almost felt like a human being again. I was even beginning to laugh sometimes.

One night, it seemed we had just gotten comfortable and fallen to sleep, when we heard a young boy out in the street hollering something. We poked each other until we were all awake. Someone said, "Listen! He is saying something about the war." We listened breathlessly and then heard very clearly, "Extra, extra, read all about it. The war has now ended. The surrender has been signed." We all sat straight up in bed, hugged each other, and laughed and cried at the same time.

Thank God it was over and all three of our soldiers made it through safely. There was no more sleep for any of us that night.

Mary Tyler Thueson was born and raised in Ucon, Idaho. In 1946, when her husband returned from service in World War II, they moved to Jerome, Idaho, where they built their own home and raised their family. She is active in the Church and has served as Junior Sunday School coordinator, councilor in the Relief Society presidency, librarian and Primary teacher. She and Walt were active in the Boy Scouts, she as a Den Mother, and he as a Scoutmaster. In 1960 they were chosen as the Scout Family of the Year and honored at the State Capitol in Boise at a luncheon with Governor Robert Smylie. She is a member of the Jerome Ward, where she currently serves as the Family Relations teacher and works in the name extraction program.

LDS SERVICEMEN OF ALLIED AND AXIS FORCES

Horst Prison and other German soldiers standing at Dunkirk, watching the English and American soldiers being shipped back to England after the invasion of France.

The march into Russia—the great challenges were finding enough food and battling the cold.

Missionary work had been going on in England and Europe almost since the establishment of the Church in 1830. While many of the early converts emigrated to the United States, there were goodly numbers of Church members throughout Europe. Prior to World War II, Germany was third highest in Church membership, behind the United States and Canada.

In our twelveth *Article of Faith,* Joseph Smith wrote: "We believe in being subject to kings, presidents, rulers, and magistrates, in obeying, honoring, and sustaining the law." In conformity to this pronouncement, Church members in nations on both sides of the conflict responded to the calls of their respective governments.

THOMAS RICHARD HARRIS

So amid the conflict, whether great or small, Do not be discouraged; God is over all.

("Count Your Blessings," *Hymns,* no.241)

I was born in Edinburgh, Scotland, in 1917, an only child of another Thomas Harris who was a warrant officer in the navy. My father's two brothers were also warrant officers in the navy, so we had a very strong family tradition.

In 1929, we were living in a little village in Wales, when two elders knocked on the door. We were not part of any church organization at the time. The first greeting of the elder was to my father, "I have a message for you." My father, in naval terms, asked him what kind of a message he could possibly have for a man his age, and they began talking about the gospel. They talked into the evening, well into the darkness, then the two elders left on their bicycles with an invitation to return again on Sunday for dinner. Mother prepared dinner for the two elders and ourselves, and just after noon, two more elders arrived, and within the period of an hour, all ten elders of the district arrived, none to be done out of a good meal. By adding a little water to the soup Mother had enough to feed them all. From that Sunday onward, it was customary that all the elders would join us for dinner, and then we would mount our bicycles—a total of thirteen people—and ride to the nearest town of Milford Haven, where we would attend a street meeting. In that way, the gospel was taught to us as a family.

In the latter part of that year, the three of us were baptized in the Atlantic Ocean. I was then twelve years of age, and Father—somewhat in a hasty manner—said, "I think we should all go to Zion." When the pennies were counted, there was not enough money to take everybody to Zion, so he said, "I'll go first and get a job, then I'll send for you." So, six months later he sent for us. We lived in Salt Lake City, and I attended Irving Junior High School, and eventually East High School.

I enjoyed my church activities, and things were, from my point of view, quite uneventful. But, it transpired that my parents, and particularly my father, became disenchanted with the Church. I was shocked one day as we sat around the family table to hear him say to my mother, "This can't be Zion. Let us go back." So, in 1932, we returned to England.

In May of 1935, I joined the British Navy. My first assignment, after the usual boot camp, was to be shore based in Portland, Dorsetshire, and there I was assigned aboard the *HMS Osprey*. Dorsetshire is on the south coast area, not far from the English Channel.

The *Osprey's* responsibility was submarine detection, and we were training a lot of men in that duty. Although it was 1935-36, there was still a feeling that war was going to develop sooner or later. I was there for two years, and then was transferred to the battleship *Royal Sovereign*. This was in the year of the British King's Jubilee.

When I first joined the navy, I didn't meet any other Church members. There were no Church units in Weymouth or in the Osprey areas. In fact, there were only two Latter-day Saints in the whole British Navy. So I had no contact with the Church. I had been ordained a priest in the Aaronic Priesthood and was ordained an Elder when I was in the Plymouth Branch.

After leaving the *Royal Sovereign*, I was assigned to the *HMS Hermes*, an aircraft carrier, where I was to be the secretary to the captain. I was aboard that ship just six weeks with a captain who had just joined the ship a week before, when I had a sudden transfer to Hong Kong, where I was to be the submarine captain's secretary. I went to Hong Kong, and served there for two years.

The *Hermes* was subsequently sent to the Far East where she was sunk. She went down with all hands. So, I was fortunate to have left the *Hermes*, although I didn't know the reason for my transfer at the time.

While in Hong Kong, I enjoyed my twenty-first birthday, and England declared war on Germany. All our submarines were transferred back to the European Theater of war. For a while, I was in Hong Kong with no assignment, I was seemingly forgotten. That lasted nine months, then I was assigned to a very smart-looking cruiser, the *Birmingham*. She only had six-inch guns, but she was a very fast ship.

We arrived back in England, at Portsmouth, where we were re-commissioned, and sent to the northern Atlantic, close to the Arctic Circle. The Germans were laying mines in order to block goods from the United States going to Russia. We intercepted three mine-laying trawlers, took their ships company on board, and locked them up in the cells in the forward part. As we began the intercept of the fourth ship, it endeavored to ram us. Our captain noticed that, and we turned sideways, so all she did was bump up against our side. He then ordered us away five miles; we opened fire and blew her out of the water. The captain dictated that no one was to be rescued.

That was my first experience in war, and it sickened me to see men drowning and be restrained from picking them up. I was upset by the decision, but that's what happened. Those men didn't live long in the waters above the Arctic Circle.

The other POWs were put ashore in Scotland. They had been treated very well; in fact, we had to be careful with comradery because we felt no animosity toward them.

However, my attitude changed when Germany attacked Norway. The British were requested to land troops to assist with Norway's defense. The *Birmingham* transported a load of soldiers there, but it was a disaster from the beginning. The Germans were entrenched. Three weeks later we were sent back to pick up the remnants of the troops we had landed. We spent all night getting men on board, some of them had their hips shot away, their wounds wrapped in newspaper. It was a sad scene.

The biggest shock came when we landed at Aldasnes. In the fjord approaching Aldansnes there appeared to be two sunsets. I couldn't understand it; the sun was setting in the west, and there was this intense red glow in the east. Rounding the last turn in the fjord we found the Germans had firebombed the city and the fires had spread over the region so that there was nowhere for those people to go but into the water. We tried to help, but the fires pushed us out, and the Germans bombed us all the while, restricting our maneuverability, so we couldn't stay there very long. Watching those folks die and seeing the village burn for no apparent reason caused me bitter feelings toward Germany.

A torpedo fired by a German E-boat did some underwater damage to the *Birmingham*, and we put in to the little town of Grimsby, England, a fishing port. I knew very little about Grimsby, and decided to go ashore on a Sunday. It was Mother's Day, and I wondered if I could find a Latter-day Saint meeting hall. On the back of a copy of the *Millennial Star*, which I had, was a list of all the meeting halls in England. It said the Grimsby meeting hall was on Pastor Street. I must have passed it a dozen times!

Eventually, I saw a little light under a door, and when I opened it, I discovered a meeting just getting started. My timing was unbelievable! I sat down by a lady who asked, "Are you a member of the Church?"

"Yes." I answered.

She said, "Would you like to come to my home to dinner?"

"Well, thank you." I said. "I would, very much!"

When the meeting was over, she took me up to the front of the hall to meet the young lady who had conducted the meeting. The young woman was blonde and dressed in a black skirt and red coat. I thought, *What a pretty girl*. The woman introduced us and said, "This is my daughter."

My decision to come ashore was proving to be a good one. We went to their home and had a nice meal. I thought, *This is Sunday; now is when the boyfriend comes in*. But after we had eaten, the young lady said, "Would you like to see Grimsby?"

I said, "Can a duck swim?"

We went out together, and the truth is, we didn't see Grimsby at all!

A few months after that, I was transferred from the *Birmingham*, to the staff of the commander-in-chief of Western Approaches, which was based in Plymouth, England. I married that girl in the black skirt and we made our home in Plymouth, where my parents lived.

Over a period of three days, Plymouth was the target of German bombing attacks. One evening, my new bride and I were taking a walk in the country and saw what appeared to be bright lights in the city. Incendiary bombs! Walking back to the city, we couldn't find an area of more than twenty square feet where an incendiary bomb had not hit.

We had dug an air raid shelter in our garden, which we went into that night while the high explosives were being dropped. We sat in the shelter, hearing bombs explode until about four o'clock in the morning. The Germans were dropping incendiary bombs, followed by high explosives.

Coventry had also been badly pasted. So it was nothing new to the British. The Germans claimed they were aiming at military targets, but if they were, their aim was awfully bad, because the damage was pretty general.

On Saturday morning, we were in the shelter until about four o'clock in the morning before the bombing ceased. The dawn was coming and I said to my wife, "Let's go back in the bedroom and get what sleep we can with what's left of the night." Walking up the garden path to our house, she said, "I think we ought to go back into the air raid shelter."

I said, "We've been there all night."

"I know," she answered, "but I think we ought to go back."

Well, I followed my wife back down the garden path, and we sat in the shelter. We had been there just fifteen minutes, when a solitary aircraft came over. We thought it was one of our fighters returning. But it was a lone German bomber. It dropped a stick of five bombs, and the fifth bomb landed just outside our front door. The front of the house was completely blown in.

When we eventually got up to the bedroom, the glass in the French windows was powdered. We would have been cut to ribbons had we been in that bedroom. So, I have been following my wife down the garden path ever since.

A daughter was born to us. We kept her in a little bassinet in our bedroom. When the air raid siren sounded, it took us just thirty seconds to get her from her bed into the air raid shelter with us.

* * *

The rescue of the remnants of the British and French Armies at Dunkirk was a travesty to Britain. The troops brought back were absolutely unarmed—they left everything on the beaches in France.

The commodore of the naval barracks called us together and said, "Hitler is loading his landing barges and will be over today or tomorrow. He is expected to land paratroopers. We are arming you with a stonickey." A stonickey is a lead pipe of about two feet long with a nail through one end at a 90° angle. We were supposed to attack their paratroopers, knock them down, and hit them over the head with a stonickey. No one said anything about what to do if the paratroopers had a machine gun. Women and children were kept indoors, and we walked the streets all night long, all the next day, waiting for Hitler to arrive. He never came! He stopped his intended invasion of England and turned against Russia, which proved to be a fatal error on his part. Had he landed, our stonickeys would have been useless.

While at Plymouth, President Anastasio of the British Mission, called me to be president of the Plymouth Branch. A lot of American servicemen came over to England and were looking for the Church. We met in a little meeting hall from which we had to sweep the cigarette butts. But, boy, those U.S. servicemen increased the strength of our branch, and they brought in a lot of their friends with them. Many converts came as a result of those boys being there.

Two service boys were my counselors. They were wonderful, just like missionaries, that's the nearest thing to describe them. They wholeheartedly supported me as the branch president and they lived the principles of the gospel. Our branch had most of the programs of the Church, but we didn't have many youth, mostly just older people and the young servicemen.

When the order was issued just prior to D-Day that they were not to leave their barracks, one man was apprehended by the police because he wanted to come bid us farewell. The last I saw of him, he was between two British policemen, being escorted away. We had a fantastic relationship. Oh, we missed them terribly after D-Day.

The air raids continued all the time. One night, during an air raid, it sounded to me as if a bomb hit in our area. I told my wife, "I'm going to see how the Cross family did." When I got up there, the policeman stopped me and said, "You can't go down that street, it's all wiped out."

I said, "I'd like to just walk down and look at one house." He said okay.

So I went down and found the Cross's house. It was absolutely flattened. The rafters were on the ground. They didn't have an air raid shelter. I went home and told my wife, "I'm afraid the Crosses are gone."

Miraculously, I found Brother Cross in a hospital with a broken leg, his wife and daughter were not hurt. "What happened to you?" I asked.

"I can't explain it" he replied. "Because we had no air raid shelter to go to, we were all in our beds upstairs. When the bomb dropped, the concussion had such a cushioning effect that our upstairs just slowly sank down, and we weren't injured, except I had a broken leg. It was a miracle."

It *was* a miracle. I saw that house and there was nothing but a roof on the ground.

On D-Day, I was attached to a naval landing party at Juno, next to Sword and Utah Beaches on Normandy. We secured a building and set up offices for what we called FOBAA, Flat Officer British Assault Area, a British and Canadian assault area. After D-Day, the war seemed to progress rapidly.

When Germany surrendered, I went home to England for five days, then was assigned to the Flag Officer Air-Far East, where planning for the landing on the Japanese mainland was conducted. When we heard that the atom bomb had been dropped, we were grateful that we didn't need to make that landing. Many lives were saved.

Not long after the war ended, Jean and I decided to leave service life and planned that I would start a new career. We contacted an American Serviceman who had told us, "If you ever decide to return to the United States, you can make my home your home." He lived in North Ogden, Utah.

In July 1947, Jean and I and our daughter, Sandra, bid farewell to our families. My parents never did accept the fact that I would forsake a Naval career and break with the family tradition. They discontinued all ties with us, eventually leaving all they possessed to a person whom we had never met.

We reached North Ogden 24 July 1947. We were somewhat surprised at the parades and marching bands. We learned it was not our welcome party, they were observing the centennial celebration of the arrival of the Mormon pioneers to the Salt Lake Valley.

True to his word, our sponsor made his home our home. He and his wife made us welcome until we settled into a home of our own.

For twenty-nine years Thomas R. Harris worked as a hospital administrator, first for the LDS Church and then with Intermountain Health Service system. In the Church he has been an advisor to the priests in the Aaronic Priesthood, branch president, served on three high councils, been a bishop's counselor, bishop, and gospel doctrine teacher. He and Jean served a mission to Ireland. He states "I love this land, these United States. God bless America!"

Two years following their arrival in the United States, their daughter, Sandra, died of leukemia. They also have two sons and eight grandchildren.

KARL HERBERT KLOPFER

*Of a truth I perceive that God is no respecter of persons:
But in every nation he that feareth him, and worketh
righteousness, is accepted with him.*

(Acts 10:34-35)

Karl Herbert Klopfer was born 14 April 1911 at Werdau, a small railroad center and textile town near Zwickau in the German province of Saxony, near the Czechoslovakian border. In 1923 at age twelve, Karl joined the Church with his parents. Following is the account of his life as told by his son, W. Herbert Klopfer:

Karl was an organist and an outstanding student of German, French, and English. In 1928, at the age of seventeen, he planned to immigrate to the United States. The trip had been paid for. But he was called by President Hyrum Valentine to serve a mission in Germany.

While laboring in Beuthen, a coal mining town in the eastern German province of Upper Silesia, immediately west of the Polish border, he and his companion boarded at the home of my mother's parents. My mother, Erna Luise Hein, was then a teenager. A one-sided attraction commenced at that time—Karl for Erna.

Soon after completing his mission, my father was called as foreign language correspondent and interpreter, headquartered in the East German mission home in Berlin. In this capacity he accompanied several of the Twelve, and also toured the mission with President Heber J. Grant in 1935. Karl's command of English was so good, practically without accent, that people oftentimes complimented him on his excellent command of German, assuming that he was a native of an English-speaking country.

After four years of courtship by correspondence, during which time my parents saw each other only three times, they were married on 22 May 1934. They resided in Schoeneberg, a section in the northwest portion of Berlin. I was born 3 February 1936. A month later we moved to the nearby Tiergarten section, then three and one half years later, in September 1939, as Father was called to assume responsibility for all mission affairs, to the mission home on Haendelallee. This home was located in the prestigious and beautiful Hansaviertel suburb, immediately across from the Tiergarten, a large, beautiful, and heavily forested park in the center of Berlin. When we moved to the mission home, my mother's parents joined us. They had been caught in the massive war evacuation movement that started in eastern Germany.

Hitler ordered the attack on Poland 1 September 1939, triggering World War II. The Third Reich regime was at war, initially with the allied nations of Great Britain and France, and later also with the United States and the Soviet Union. All missionaries for the Church were recalled to the United States. Leadership for the Church in all the European countries was put in the hands of faithful local brethren. With the approval of the First Presidency, my father was appointed acting president of the East German Mission by Thomas E. McKay, then president of the Swiss German Mission. He was set apart to this office in December 1939.

In his official capacity, Karl was often summoned to appear before the Nazi officials to explain the teachings and purposes of the Church. As the war advanced, some churches were forbidden to hold meetings, but our Church was not because it followed the twelveth *Article of Faith*, which states "We believe in being subject to kings, presidents, rulers, and magistrates, in obeying, honoring, and sustaining the law."

In February 1940 Father was drafted into German military service. Until 1943 he was stationed in Fuerstenwalde, just east of Berlin. As paymaster in a cavalry unit, and with the rank of a junior officer, he was provided a private room and telephone, enabling him to take care of mission affairs from his military office. He had regular communication with the mission home where his counselors and four native sister missionaries worked. He was permitted to go to and conduct conferences on weekends, sometimes as far away as Danzig on the shores of the Baltic Sea. On those weekends when it was impossible for him to leave his post, either his counselors, or my mother, would travel to and from the post to transact mission business.

The East German mission home was located very near two huge German aircraft defense bunkers, which were camouflaged effectively by the trees and bushes of the Tiergarten. Because of its proximity to monuments, highways, and bunkers, our residential area was in constant danger. This section of Berlin was a priority target for countless enemy air attacks. The first such attack occurred 2 September 1939, day two of the war, by Polish bombers.

In the midst of one of these attacks my appendix ruptured and I was rushed to the hospital. After a six week stay in the hospital, I recovered and my mother took me and my brother on a six-week vacation to Fuerstenwalde, to be with Dad.

Back at the mission home, the air attacks became more frequent. Almost twice each night we had to take cover in our air raid

Back row: Karl Klopfer and his wife Erna; Seated: Karl's sister, Maria, and his parents. Photo taken January 1943.

shelters—the three of us and the four sister missionaries. Two suitcases were always packed. We put on jumpsuits over our pajamas and engaged in fervent prayer for guidance and blessing in our lives before entering the shelter in our basement. Our hearts were filled with prayers and hope that the next bomb would also pass by us. However, danger to our lives and property in Berlin increased to the point of an official evacuation notice. We moved to the home of my father's parents in Werdau, Saxony, a goodly distance south of Berlin, near the Czech border.

While my father was on furlough in Werdau in the fall of 1943, he and mother traveled back to Berlin to care for some mission business and to obtain some personal belongings we had left behind. En route on the train they realized they had forgotten the key to the mission home. They learned that Berlin was scheduled to be bombed again during the coming night. On the 22 November 1943, at about 5:00 P.M., they arrived in an already burning city. The train was unable to proceed to its scheduled destination in the city due to the destruction. Carrying their suitcases, my parents walked through the flaming city. It took them three hours to cover the relatively short distance to the mission home. Arriving there they found that the mission home, and a house on either side, were the only ones still standing. The mission home was locked. Earlier that day, my father's second counselor, Brother Langheinrich, acting upon the promptings of the Spirit, had evacuated the sister missionaries to his home.

My parents could not get in, so began walking to the home of his first counselor, Brother Ranglack. As they proceeded, the first of three more air attacks occurred. As they sought cover in a public air shelter, a pitiful sight of frightened and injured people opened to their eyes. Even though hungry themselves, they passed out what food they had to as many people as possible. Some of the people were without arms or legs, a result of previous bombings. They reached Brother Ranglack's home just before the second air attack. Again they had to go to an air raid shelter.

The next morning they returned to the mission home. To protect their eyes against the smoke from burning buildings, they covered their faces with scarves. During the night the mission home had been destroyed in a raid in which more than 1,000 England-based planes took part. A few minutes after my parents left the home the previous night, it took a direct hit by a 500 pound phosphorus bomb, which fell to the basement, burning the home from the bottom up. Only the walls remained standing. Surely the Lord had protected Mother and Father in allowing them to forget to bring their house key. On that night alone, 100,000 families became homeless in that part of Berlin.

Due to the loss of our home, Father's furlough was extended. Mother and Dad returned to the ruins of the home a week later to see if there was anything salvageable. There wasn't. Their only souvenir was a cooking pot and its lid. As they emerged from the ruins, soldiers outside screamed urgent warnings to leave quickly. An hour later the anticipated explosions of unexploded bombs in the vicinity leveled everything still standing. My parents recognized once more the Lord's hand in preserving their lives.

My parents were miraculously protected yet a third time on this trip. On their return to Werdau their train had just cleared the main depot in Leipzig when a massive air attack on the depot and rail yards brought destruction, and death and injury to many persons. Other trains still in the depot were helplessly caught in this deadly barrage.

We saw our father for the last time while he was on this furlough. On 10 December 1943 he was sent to Denmark, and in March 1944 to the bitterly fought battlefields on the Russian front. For a while we still corresponded successfully. The time came that we learned of his death. Other people saw him many months after we last saw him. Word of such personal contacts with him reached us years later, some of them not until we had immigrated to the United States.

One of the most heartwarming incidents reported to us occurred in Denmark in December 1943. One Sabbath before Christmas, being away from his family my dad felt very lonely. He did not know whether an LDS branch existed in Esbjerg, but felt there might be one. Since he was dressed in full military uniform and did not speak the language, he decided to hum the tune of a favorite hymn as he walked on a city street. He hoped he would attract the attention of someone who could lead him to the Church.

Sure enough, as a little girl passed my father, she asked him in Danish, "Mormon?" and, seeing him nod his head, led him to the branch meetinghouse.

My father took a great risk in surrendering his weapon belt to Erik Thomsen, the branch president, at the back door, and accepting an invitation

Karl Herbert Klopfer

to deliver the Christmas message during sacrament meeting, in English, because German was an enemy tongue.

A young Danish girl who was a member of the branch wrote to my mother about the strange experience of having an enemy soldier in their midst: "Last night I visited the branch. There was a German there, your husband. Even though many Danish people hate Germans, we learned to love this man. He spoke to the congregation in English, and William Orum Pedersen translated. Your husband related how only a month ago, he had lost everything he had, and the mission home had been destroyed. But he was thankful that his wife and children were safe. He then gave testimony of the truthfulness of the Church. It was wonderful to see a man in the uniform we hated speak with so much love for us. He was happy to be among the Saints."

Years later, after my father had died and our family had moved to Salt Lake City in the 1950s, we received another letter—this time from a woman who worked for the Genealogical Society of the Church and whose husband had met my father at the Esbjerg Branch. She had enclosed a letter that my father had written from Russia to the woman's husband in Denmark. It had been censored and displayed a blue diagonal line across its face, but it was intact. We wondered how it had ever reached its destination, having been written in English by a German military officer in Russia, to a man living in Denmark. Dated 17 May 1944, it read:

Dear Brother Olsen,

More than two months ago, I left Denmark. During these weeks I have experienced the dreadful aspect of war, but I have been wonderfully protected from harm and illness. I am thankful to the Lord for His many blessings, and I am looking forward to the time when I will be happy to meet my loved ones at home again. So far, my wife and children have also been protected from the terror of hostile airplanes flying over Germany daily. I am thinking of you and the other dear friends I met while in Esbjerg, and I wish you all the good luck in the world for the future. Give my kindest regards to all I know, will you please?

Sincerely yours, Herbert Klopfer

Correspondence broke down in 1944 when Dad was assigned to the Russian front. We received his last letter on 11 July 1944. He was apparently unaware of the danger he and his unit were in. Six days later, 17 July 1944, Mother had a bad dream. She was afraid that something had happened to Father. In another dream, on July 22 she saw my father as a prisoner. In October 1944, a letter from my father's commanding officer, dated 27 September 1944, was hand-delivered to my mother by a German military officer. The essence of the letter identified 17 July as the date on which father's military division had been trapped by the surrounding Russian army near Brody. Since July 22nd he had been reported missing in action. On that day an offensive breakthrough was planned near Zloczow. Circumstances permitted such offensives only in small units. These units experienced heavy losses and disorganization by the enemy. My father was last seen on 22 July 1944, near Poczorzky.

The war became more bitter and intense, especially on the Russian front. A long period of silence followed—from 1944 to 1948. We did not know what had happened to our father. Nothing ever reached us officially. Then in April 1948, mother had another dream. She saw an injured soldier return from the Russian front who wanted to give her a message, but he did not know where we lived. At last he met a comrade in Berlin who gave him our address. This man came to see Mother and told her of Father's death. Except for this message we would not know what fate he had met. He became a prisoner of war on 22 July 1944. Having been one out of only two or three of a large group of prisoners who had not contracted either typhoid or the flu, he was supposedly still in relatively good physical health. He was transported farther east by his Russian captors and forced into hard labor in a salt mine. With little or no nourishing food, his health deteriorated over the next eight months. He spent his last days in a Russian hospital where six prisoners were forced to lie together on a small, very hard, and uncomfortable wooden board. One by one they died as they lay in comas.

My father died 19 March 1945 of starvation in Puschka, near Kiev, less than two months before the end of this most dreadful of all wars. He died, still acting as wartime president of the East German Mission, deep in Russian territory, having directed the affairs of the mission, to the extent possible, from the battlefield. He was just thirty-three years old.

HORST PETER PRISON

My God hath been my support; he hath led me through mine afflictions.

(2 Nephi 4:20)

[Note: This account came from an oral interview with Horst and Elfriede Prsion. Every effort has been made to maintain the integrity of their words. Only those changes necessary for clarity and sequence were made. As they told their story into my tape recorder, I listened in awe, close to tears. I was struck with how matter-of-factly he recounted his experiences, and the complete lack of rancor and anger in either Horst or Elfriede. PHK]

I was born 26th of April, 1920, at Dudweiler, by Saarbrücken, Germany, about six miles from the French border. My grandfather was the first one in our family who joined the Church. He found a pamphlet in the street and picked it up and brought it home. He set it in the windowsill to dry because it was wet. He read it and found out it was from The Church of Jesus Christ. He wrote to the mission president in Switzerland, and he sent missionaries to him who taught him the gospel. He was a heavy smoker and drinker, and when he joined the Church in 1923, he quit, just like that.

My father used to always tease my grandfather about the Mormons. During World War I one of my father's brothers was killed in Russia. This brother came to my father in a dream, and told him, "Don't tease your father about the Church." He also told him that he should read the books and other things, and join the Church, too. My father became a member in 1924. My mother also joined the Church. I was baptized when I was eight years old. When I was twelve years old I was ordained a deacon and was secretary in the Sunday School.

When I was fourteen years old, I had to find a job. School was out in April and I found a job in June. I worked for a big company and learned to be an electric motor winder. I did that for four years and went to a trade school twice a week at the same time. In 1939 the war started. The company I worked for was moved because they were too close to the French border. I had to go to Mannheim where a sister company was located. I went to my old district president and talked to him about who I could stay with. He said I could stay with his family, so I lived with them and worked for that company. I went to church with him. There was only he and a couple of other brethren, the only priesthood holders left because of the war.

In the middle of January 1940, I got drafted into the army; 12th Company, 321st Regiment,3rd Battalion, 197th Division–Infantry. I went to the area of Kaiserslautern and got my training there. After training, I was sent to Trier, which is very close to the border of Luxembourg. From there, when the French war started, we were moved behind the Maginot Line and

Horst (back row, 2nd from left) and the local branch children

began the invasion of France. Our attack route was, generally, from Luxembourg, then to Rheims, Paris, and to Dunkirk. When we got to Dunkirk, the war was over in France. It lasted only about six weeks.

In Dunkirk up on the coast, the rest of the French Army and the English Army went down and we got the order to not go any farther. So we watched the French and English armies get shipped back to England. It was an order from Hitler not to go in there. Then, from Dunkirk we got transported to Cherbourg. We built there an airport by Cherbourg, and they unloaded bombs there preparing to go on to England. When we had been there about two weeks, we went to Caen on the French coast where we built another airport and unloaded more bombs. We were at Caen and St.Lo until the middle of October. Then we got transported to Holland, as occupation forces.

* * *

There were no other LDS in my unit. And the Church was not too popular with the French. I could not find any LDS Church in Cherbourg or in Caen or Amsterdam. We had coast watch in Holland. I went on a bicycle two hours, so far down the coast, then someone else would come and ride for two hours. We did that every day.

In January, I was sent to a little town called Bayerntal, near to Heidelberg. But Heidelberg didn't have a branch of the Church. The church was in Mannheim about 20 kilometers away.

There were not more than about 30,000 to 35,000 LDS, all over Germany before the war, mostly in the bigger towns. At that time my father was district president, so on Saturdays, I got time off to go to Mannheim. I rode on a streetcar to Mannheim. Then

Horst on guard duty in Holland

Sundays I went to church and had to be back on my base at 10 o'clock at night.

At Heidelberg we got more training. Every Friday evening we went on long hikes; started out going 20 kilometers, then the next Friday he would hike 25, 30, then 48 kilometers one way. We didn't know at that time why we were having the long walks.

Paul: How did your fellow soldiers treat you as a Mormon?

Horst: They knew I was a Mormon, but there was no teasing.

Elfreide: They called him "soda pop club."

* * *

Horst: I was in Heidelberg until June, then the whole division got shipped to the Polish border on the river Bug [Boog]. We didn't know what was going on. The Bug was the border with Russia. Then on 22 June when the war started with Russia, we went over the Bug and we fought the Russians just about every day. I found out why we had those long walks by Heidelberg, because in Russia, the roads just never ended. And it was hot, too.

We had a big fight at Bialystok, then we chased after the Russians again until we got into Minsk. When we got there we saw the Russians had built a big asphalt road going into Moscow. It was the only asphalt road I saw in Russia. The Russians built that road in 1938-39. Before that time from Bug up to Minsk, was only gravel roads and dirt roads and small towns. The countryside was flat and there were thick forests.

Only the big cities had stone houses; in the small towns there were only log houses with straw roofs. The houses weren't too big, some had just two rooms. This is where we stayed.

It was 23 August 1941 when Hitler said, "This is our winter line. We're going to stay here over winter. Some of the generals went to Hitler and told him, "The Russians are running now, why don't we go after them?" But Hitler said, "No, we're going to stay here." So we stayed there.

In the middle of September, the Russians came with five tanks. Me and another guy were in a hole with a machine gun. We shot at a tank, but it was just as good as throwing a handful of gravel at it. The tank came, but we couldn't get our machine gun down the hole, so the tank went over the machine gun and caved the sand in over us. After the tanks left, nothing was poking out of the dirt except my hand. I got myself clear again, then helped the other guy. The tanks were gone, we were still alive, and no injuries. The guy who was with me that day was killed in the summer of 1943, somehow I made it.

From Minsk, we went to Smolensk and fought there. We marched to Vyaz'ma. They told us that there were about a million and a half Russian soldiers in front of us.

It was about the 8th of October. We started out at a little town. About a quarter of a mile ahead the Russians were in a big forest. We got in a big battle with them. Within half an hour we lost all of our officers and twenty-nine other men. In the midst of the fighting I went down on the ground as flat as I could, then I took my spade out and went down in the ground, just like a badger. The bullets were going in right and left and all around me—I heard 'em go in the ground. Then we went into the forest. It took about three or four hours for the shooting to stop.

By now we were beyond the forest. We went on the road for a few miles to a little town, about twenty-five homes. Beyond this town was another big valley. I and another guy had the watch just before daylight. We had a heavy machine gun set up on a little hill. Some other German soldiers had a small machine gun. All of a sudden, in the distance, we saw some trucks coming. So we shot about five or six trucks with our machine guns. Then we saw what must have been 250 trucks coming against us, loaded with Russian soldiers. We started shooting our machine guns. I don't know how many we killed that day. After a while they got too close, so we went back into the town, and our artillery and mortars started firing. We stayed in the town to hold the Russians off. We waited about three days til we got help from our tanks. We went behind our tanks and had another big battle. I was scared all the time when they were shooting.

There were thousands, maybe 650,000 Russian soldiers captured. Some escaped through our lines, maybe a few thousand. When they told us a million and a half Russians attacked we figured 600,000–700,000 of them died there. You couldn't take a step without stepping on a dead Russian soldier. Oh, it was terrible! For miles ahead, and as far as you could see to the left and the right there were dead soldiers. We had to find some of our own wounded soldiers and take them to hospitals.

From there we went toward Moscow. At the end of October it started to rain, every day and every night until about the middle of November. We couldn't make any mileage any more. Before the rains we made 20-30 miles a day, but in the mud, only five to six miles a day. The mud was running in our boot tops. The horses went down to their bellies in the mud. The infantry used horses and wagons. Wagons sunk down to the axles in the mud. We had to help pull them out. We had been chasing after the Russians and took lots of prisoners. We sent them back to Poland, and to the bigger cities like Smolensk and Minsk. Later on they took most of them to Germany.

We continued on towards Moscow. We got into a town called Chast. From Chast we went to Moschicks. Then it got cold, started snowing. Everything froze. Our tanks couldn't go, the wagons couldn't go, the trucks couldn't go. We got up into a forest, fought there. At the end of the forest was a big meadow a quarter of a mile wide and some haystacks. We dug into those haystacks and put our machine guns in front of them. We knew there were Russians on the other side of the meadow because we had some infantry scouts. The next morning the Russians came. All we had to do was shoot. This went on for a few days. The next day those who came didn't have guns, so they picked up the guns from the dead. The slaughter was horrible. These men had no choice. Go fight the Germans, or be shot coming back; either they get killed by the Germans, or killed by their own officers if they retreated. Their only hope to live was to be captured by the Germans and put in a prison camp.

One evening we counted our ammunition. I had only fifty bullets and two hand grenades left. If the Russians had come that morning, it would have been the end of us. But, for some reason they didn't come. So we sent some men to check the other side of the meadow. There was no one there so we got orders to go after the Russians

Horst's division marching into Russia

again. It was cold and snowing. It got to fifty below zero, centigrade. We only had summer coats because in the rainy season the trucks got stuck in the mud and our winter clothing was in those trucks.

* * *

The closest I got to Moscow during the fighting was 17 December 1941, the town of Istra, about five miles before Moscow. That's where I froze my feet and had to go to a field hospital. Others I saw had their noses or their hands frozen, some froze up their feet completely. From there I was transferred to Poland where I stayed in the hospital for seven months. My feet were almost black. The doctor wanted to amputate. I told him to wait a day or two. I prayed to my Heavenly Father. The doctor came in the next morning and saw that my feet were getting just a little color. So my feet didn't get amputated.

After my feet were healed, I had to go to my unit in France. I got two-weeks leave. I went back to my parents home, and Elfriede and I got engaged. After two weeks, I had to go back to France. When enough soldiers were well enough to come out of the hospital—200 to 250 men—we were shipped to Russia again. That was in about August 1942. We didn't fight too much, but had machine guns, artillery and were in trenches. We were there a year, until August 1943, then I got three weeks leave.

Leave started as soon as you crossed the German border. After my leave, I joined my old unit in Russia. It took us ten days to find them because the Russians had started an offensive and we had retreated.

We got orders to go after the Russians again, but then they attacked us. I dug myself a hole again. Three feet from me a shell hit. I knew that there was one-in-a-thousand chance that another would land in that very same place, but I felt prompted to get in that shell hole. After a few seconds a shell hit in the hole I had just vacated. Prompted again, I went back to that hole. Only a few seconds later, another one hit to my left. All I had to do was take my spade, connect the three holes and I was safe.

I lay there for several hours until I got the order to go back to our old line. The Russians were pushing hard. I was talking to my company chief, an officer, when all of a sudden I heard two mortar shells coming. One hit within three feet of me and the other two feet to the right of me, which should have blown me to pieces. A piece of shrapnel hit my right leg. I was sent to the hospital again. That was October 25th, and I was there 'til the first week in January. I got three-weeks leave and I went to my home-town.

Horst (seated, left) and his fellow patients in Polish hospital, recovering from frostbite.

I called Elfriede and told her I wanted to get married. I went to my unit and filled out marriage papers.

My father was the district president and branch president at the same time. He called the Mission President who came to my hometown. I was ordained an elder and we were married on the 20th of January 1944. Then I was given six more weeks of leave. We went to Mannheim for a week, during which there was a big air raid there. It was worse than in Russia, so we went back to my hometown where there had been no air raids. After my leave, I had to go back to my unit in Russia.

When I got back to Russia, my unit was in a different place. In 1941, when we first went to Russia, our battalion was twelve companies. But, by 1944, when I got out there again, our battalion wasn't twelve companies anymore. The casualties were so great, it was only four, and our line was very, very thin.

One morning I was in an outpost about eight miles from our lines to the enemy. We had one of the big telescopes there and we watched the enemy down in the valley.

The next morning the Russians shot their big guns. I counted 200 shells the first day, which fell all around us. The next morning I was there again. I was one of the old soldiers, we had a lot of new recruits who had no battle experience, so I was there when times were critical. The Russians started shooting again. I received another prompting to go back to our old lines. I went back there, but still, it didn't feel right, so I went back to the forest and got into one of the bunkers. After the artillery barrage was over, we counted over 400 shell holes from those big 15.2 centimeters (7 inch) shells. Our line was all shot up. I went back to the outpost where the big binocular had been, and it wasn't there anymore. So, we had to dig ourselves another bunker.

We'd been there for a few days. That's when the Russians started their big offensive, the 22nd of June. It started early in the morning, still dark. They shot everything they had: big artillery, light artillery, twelve inchers, and mortars pounded us for four hours. I was worried. This was serious, this could be the end. I was in a big wheat field with six men in a little bunker. After four hours of this we thought this was the end of the world. We came out of our bunker, the wheat field wasn't there anymore. It was just like it had been plowed.

When they quit shooting, the Russians came by the thousands, with tanks. All we had to do was take our machine gun and just do a sweep. Our position was about nine miles ahead of the main force. The Russians closed those ten miles in back of us and killed about 35,000 Germans.

Hitler wanted us to make it to Moscow, but it was too late. From the 23rd – 28th of June we went from one end of our position to the other, trying to escape, but we couldn't make it. Finally, we got into a little town. A Russian Lieutenant and two men came with a white flag. We let them come; he spoke fluent German. He told us we were surrounded. There was no way out. We didn't hear any more of our artillery shooting because—I don't know how many miles back they were—they were just gone. So, we surrendered. He told us to put our weapons in a pile. I took my identity papers with me.

With us was one general and a few officers. The others were just soldiers, a few non-commissioned officers. I was a sergeant. We went into a prison camp. We walked three days without food, and we had been without food four or five days already. We went to Witebsk, which was a big city, to a prison camp; there they put us in railroad cars.

In three days we got to Moscow; it must have been Red Square. It was 3 October 1944. They told us they held 700,000 captured German soldiers. We got very good food there—wieners, soups, good bread. But we all got diarrhea from eating this agreeable food, after days without food.

German POWs being marched through the streets of Moscow. Horst: "I'm in there somewhere."

Then they put us all together, and we had to march through Moscow, the Russian soldiers lined both sides of the streets. The main street was about a hundred feet wide. The people were angry with us and threw rocks at us, but the soldiers protected us. Later, they divided us in groups of 1,500. We got to the railroad where they put us into cattle cars and they shipped us south to Stalino. It was cold. We left Moscow 5 October 1944 and we arrived in Stalino on 22 October, Elfriede's birthday.

When we got into Stalino all 1,500 men were quarantined for six weeks. They didn't let us do anything, just lay around. The food was bad. Three times a day we got watery soup and a little bread, about 200 grams. Russian bread is heavy and dark. The soup was cabbage soup with once in awhile a small cabbage leaf. After six weeks we had to go to work. I had to walk every morning four kilometers to work in a coal mine, then every evening we walked back. On the way home, some of the guys had water in their legs which were all puffed out, because they were so malnourished. We had to carry them.

Down in the mine we had to work with a pick and shovel. We put the coal into coalcarts, which we had to push to the front of the mine, about a ton of coal, and then they took it out. I worked in the mine til about October, then I got sick. I am 5 foot 4 inches tall, and at that time I weighed about 110 lbs, so being sick was serious. They put us in—you couldn't call it a hospital—just a building where the sick ones were. Food was about the same, the only thing was I didn't have to go to work in the morning. Every evening we had to go outside and stand in lines. The Russians would count how many were sick and try to determine how many had died each day. Sometimes there were five to eight in a day. We stood there sometimes two or three hours, waiting while they counted. There were so many dead and sick they couldn't make their counts tally. Those able had to go to work at 5:00 o'clock every morning, then come home at six o'clock in the evening, get something to eat—soup and a piece of bread—and then get maybe three or four hours sleep.

About the 15th of November, they took all the sick ones away. There were about 500 still alive, 1,000 had died from starvation. On the train they took us about 500 kilometers south to Ammavin to a big camp. On the way down, the food was bad, and it was cold. It was the 15th of December. Many more died on the way. By the time we got down there we had about 200 more dead. We didn't have to work. We got a little bit of bread and could shower. We were issued used clothing.

* * *

In the beginning of April 1945, they looked for about 250 men to go work on the big government farms. I figured it couldn't be any worse than staying there. I was well enough to go, so I was one of the first ones out. They hauled us on trucks.

We planted potatoes, corn, sunflowers, watermelons . . . mostly sunflowers. Then I got into the machine shop. We repaired machinery and discs on the plows. Then we cut hay, using scythes.

After we cut and stacked the hay, we weeded the watermelons and thinned sunflowers where they were too thick. The fields were a mile long and a half mile wide. The corn fields were a mile wide and two miles long. When the corn was ripe, we had to harvest it by hand. The food was a little better on the collective farm. We helped ourselves to corn, watermelon, and potatoes. When the winter came, I worked in one of the fabrication plants. We made those big scales that they have on the road. To mark the weigh beam they gave me a hacksaw to notch where to hang the weights.

The winter of 1946 was over, the war was over, but we weren't allowed to go home. Our captors looked for 80 men to build a new railroad near the town of Ormavisk. We started out with pick and shovel to level out the road bed. Then they brought in the railroad ties. We laid them out and put on the tracks. We nailed them by hand. Then we screwed the rails down, all by hand. At the end of October we went back to town, and I worked at the airfield, shoveling snow and doing odds and ends.

In the springtime of 1947 they needed men for another job. They didn't tell us what it was. They put 240 of us on a railroad and hauled us several hundred miles down to the Caucasus Mountains. There they put us on a ship and took us farther south on the Black Sea to Sochi, a resort city on the coast for the rich Russians.

They took us 200 kilometers into the mountains, to a little town where we had to build a big camp. There was only one big barrack there. We had to build all the other buildings. After six weeks some other prisoners came, all together about 2,500 in that camp. Here, food was good. Then we got divided. I went with twenty-four men into the mountains, cutting timber. We had 7-foot and 12-foot crosscut saws, and each man had an ax. We had to chop the tree out from one side, then had two other men cutting from the other side. We had six man crews cutting timber. They had a tractor to haul the timber out. We cut the trees in eight, ten and twelve foot lengths. They came in with big trucks, each hauling different lengths out into the valley to a sawmill.

The sawmill was two sawhorses, one guy up on top and one guy in the pit, and a big crosscut saw, cutting up and down to make boards. There were about twelve sets of men cutting boards for concrete forms. We German soldier-prisoners were taken there to build a dam, by hand. That was what the boards were for. It was on a river about the size of the Bear River, [in northern Utah] only it ran wilder. We worked there for two years to make the dam.

There was a monastery in the mountains behind our camp. One reason I survived was because during the revolution Stalin killed all the monks who had lived there. On the mountainsides on both sides of the valley there were chestnut trees. And in the valley going up into the mountain there were thousands of cherry trees, pear trees, apple trees, and walnut trees. So, when the cherries were ripe, we ate cherries, and when the pears were ripe, we ate pears.

My grandfather was a botanist. When I was young he had taught me what was good to eat. My grandfather collected herbs for the pharmacists and often took me with him. So I knew a lot of stuff we could eat, and that helped us survive.

There was a forester who took care of the forest. His horse broke a leg, so he had to shoot him. He gave us the carcass, which we cut up into pieces and hauled up to a glacier on the mountainside to bury it in the ice. Every evening someone went up there and brought a piece of horse meat to the camp. We had a grinder. We ground horse meat every night for our twenty-four men, until it was gone. In September the nuts came on. When we had worked eight hours cutting timber, we would go gather chestnuts. Besides that, we had potato soup, cabbage soup, barley soup, even corn—ground up corn—three times a day.

In my unit there were twenty-four men. None of them died, except for five we lost in a river crossing accident. A bridge collapsed, and they drowned. But none died of starvation. All of us got home except those five.

We came to the camp in the Caucasus in 1947. In 1948 they took sixty men out and shipped them home. Then in 1949, they took all those who came from Austria and another 50 or 60 men who were not strong enough to work, and sent them home.

After two years in the slave labor camps, we were allowed to write twenty-five words to our family, once a month. First, the address, then, "I'm still alive." I did that for two years and then didn't write any more. I quit it because I thought I was never going to get home. Only 500 survived from our original unit of 2,500 that had been assembled at Moscow.

Finally, on the 17 December 1949, they told us that they'd let us go home. So, we were hauled down to the coast again, on the Black Sea. There we were loaded into cattle cars, about forty-five men in each one, and they hauled us to the Polish border. We could have been home for Christmas, but the Polish didn't let us go through. We waited there for three days in a forest, and then they let us go.

At Frankfurt we got divided: one group going to southern Germany, one to northern Germany, one staying in East Germany and one that went farther west. I was born near the French border, so I was put on the one going to the French Zone. There was the English Zone, the American Zone, and the French Zone.

When we got to Stuttgart, we were released by the French. That's when I arrived home, 1949, the 29th of December. It had been so long. They announced on the radio that we would be released and also sent telegrams at the same time.

The army changed me. All that fighting and all those dead. You see, men got killed to my right, to my left, behind me, and to the front of me. From the beginning of the war until 1944, I had been with the same guy. He was wounded twice and I was wounded twice. I was with that guy and a couple others from the beginning of the war until the end—now they were all dead.

There were many miracles that preserved my life. Once I got mad at one of the head guys in my company who was my superior in rank, so the company chief, the oberlieutenant, transferred me to another outfit, because I told him something . . . I won't say it here. I was transferred, and I found out that my old outfit was completely destroyed. If I hadn't said that bad word to my superior, I would have been in that unit and been killed. One lieutenant said to me, "When I walk behind you, I feel this peace." He was killed, too.

It took a few weeks to get my life straightened around. I was home three weeks and then went back to work at my company. There was a law that I could get my old job back.

After a while my wife said, "How about going to the United States?" I knew a woman who had been in our branch and was now living in the United States. We wrote her a letter and asked her if she could help us. She said she would help us find a sponsor from America. Our sponsor was a former missionary in Germany before the war, John Holladay, who taught music at the Brigham Young University.

(Elfriede's experiences in the war can be found on page 259.)

Horst and Elfriede and their daughter immigrated to the United States in August 1952. They lived in Provo, Utah, then moved to Kalispell, Montana, and later to Lewistown, Montana. He was employed as an electric motor rewinder and a janitor. Horst served as a ward clerk, high councilor, stake clerk, and stake missionary. Ironically, Horst Peter Prison, a former German soldier, lived in Bishop "Bee" Peck's ward and served as his Executive Secretary. Bishop Peck was a U.S. soldier who lost his legs when a German armor piercing shell went through the tank he was driving, near Avranches, France, a few days after D-Day 1944. (See page 100.)

The Prisons later moved to Leeds, Utah, and Horst and Elfriede were ordinance workers in the St. George Temple. He served as high priests group leader in their ward. In 1990–91 they served in the Germany, Munich Mission. They are parents of three sons and three daughters. They have seventeen grandchildren and eleven great-grandchildren. They currently live in Alberton, Montana.

HUGH B. BROWN
LDS SERVICEMEN'S COORDINATOR

Hugh B. Brown speaking to an LDS Serviceman's group at the Paris Conference, 22 July 1945.

There is perhaps no man who had a greater influence for good among the LDS Servicemen of World War II, was more widely recognized and beloved, or more widely traveled than Hugh B. Brown.

Elder Brown returned from England in February 1940, after presiding over the British Mission. With the beginning of war evident, Church leaders recognized the need to organize LDS Servicemen and encourage their faithful activity in the Church. On 28 April 1941, the *Deseret News* announced the appointment of Hugh B. Brown as LDS Servicemen's Coordinator. Speaking of his new calling, Elder Brown wrote in his journal: "I am to visit the various camps and try to take to the men some spiritual help. Also to advise the men in the camps and the local Church officers in wards and branches near the camps that each is anxious to help keep the spirit of the gospel alive during the emergency."

For the next three years Brother Brown tirelessly traveled the country where there were numbers of Mormon military personnel. Arriving at a military base he would call on the commanding officer and the chaplains, encouraging them to provide facilities and cooperation to LDS men and women. He also sought the appointment of LDS chaplains. As he worked with military leaders, as well as enlisted troops, Elder Brown drew heavily upon his experiences in World War I, where he rose to the rank of major in the Canadian Army, as well as his missionary experiences, to encourage and sustain the men and women he served. There was great need for this support, as seen in Elder Brown's journal entry after the attack on Pearl Harbor:

> When we got word of this day, . . . we knew that war would be declared immediately. . . . There was a strong feeling of despair. Many of the men were despondent because they knew we were not prepared to enter into a war with Japan and Germany. . . . My mission at this time was to bring hope and encouragement and faith to the men, most of them very young, who were serving in our forces. This I am glad to say was done to some extent, and whatever the extent, I give credit where credit is due, for I was inspired beyond myself as I talked to the men and related to them many incidents in my own life that had strengthened and inspired me.

* * *

During his wide travels, his family was a constant concern. His son, Hugh C. Brown, joined the Royal Air Force in England. Elder Brown's concern for his family can be seen in a letter he wrote to his daughter Mary:

We have had another letter from Hugh, and he seems to be in the thick of it now. Almost every day, we think of him and pray that he might be protected. He says that his only regret is that he didn't get there sooner. I feel that he wouldn't have been happy if he had not gone, but really I wish I were there instead of him. If I were running a war, I would take all the old men and keep the young ones at home. When the old men are killed in battle, it just means that the natural processes are being helped along a little, but to see men go whose life is hardly started, seems all wrong.

Part of Elder Brown's empathy toward the servicemen and women he served came from his own experiences as a parent, fearing for the safety of his own soldier-son. When Elder Brown, who had been visiting camps in Montana, returned to Salt Lake City, he learned from his son, Charles and his daughter Zola, that Hugh was missing in action. The details of this are seen in the communique from Hugh C.'s squadron leader to the Browns:

I would like to express my deepest sympathy with you and your family on your son being reported missing. Your son has been with the Squadron since October 1941, and since that time has shown the utmost keenness, both in the air and on the ground. He was an extremely popular member of the squadron, and it is a great loss. On the morning of the 16th, he was detailed for a low patrol over the North Sea with another of this unit. Some seven miles after crossing the coast, conditions became extremely hazy, and your son's aircraft was lost in the haze at low altitude. Another pilot called to your son repeatedly but could get no reply, and so he returned and reported the matter and the position where your son's aircraft was last seen. An intensive search was carried out both from the air and the sea but revealed nothing. It is presumed that in the hazy conditions your son's aircraft struck the sea and disappeared. I feel that there is very little hope of your son being alive and feel that it is best that you should know the true facts which I have given. His loss is very greatly felt by us all. The whole squadron and myself offer our profound sympathy to you and your family.

Yours sincerely,

E. H. Thomas, Squadron Leader.

The sorrowing father returned to Los Angeles to the sorrowing mother. But the work had to move on, and he pursued it faithfully.

* * *

The support Elder Brown gave LDS Servicemen can be seen in the many talks and articles he presented both in the United States and throughout Europe and the Pacific. Each time, he spoke to the specific challenges facing his audience.

Young servicemen faced not only the pressures of battle but the boredom of "down time" and the freedom of being far away from home, where the positive influence of family, friends, and Church leaders encouraged these men to be faithful to gospel teachings. Elder Brown addressed these concerns in the following talk addressed to the young men of the Church and especially to those in uniform:

Thoughts for the Service Men's Quiet Hour

He who does wrong knowingly, intentionally, is a traitor to himself and to the cause he represents. It is unthinkable that any United States service man would deliberately give the advantage to the enemy by surrendering his arms or carelessly walking into a booby trap. . . .

So in life there is a cunning, wily enemy whose whole business is to prepare booby traps and lure men into them. He not only teaches the fool to say in his heart, "There is no God," but he beguiles him into thinking that evil is desirable and inevitable. Sin is the devil's booby trap, and no amount of bravado will change the sinner's status. He who deliberately walks into a booby trap is a booby.

Do not allow either desire for the bait, nor curiosity to know the mechanism, to lure you into any of his deadly traps, which often are cunningly camouflaged to deceive the unwary. And do not be deceived if what you have been taught to recognize as such a trap does not seem to spring at the first contact. Many of them are time bombs, but there are no duds in the armory of sin.

Some men are led to think that because the punishment is not immediate, the danger of sin has been exaggerated or avoided. We may be sure that all the devil's booby traps will explode eventually with deadly and undiscriminating effect.

On 6 June 1943, Hugh Brown was invited to deliver the Baccalaureate Address at the University of Utah. Here he reminds his audience that this war is supported by Providence, and that, as citizens in this country, they have a responsibility to preserve this inheritance for others.

Disciplined Freedom

You must be informed if you are to appreciate the value of your heritage, and have the power to preserve it. . . . He who receives a life estate has definite obligations to those who are to take it after him. You must not allow it to fall into the hands of strangers or to be sold to the highest bidder, or be risked on chance with gamblers. Just now we are defending it from attack by alien enemies who would destroy it utterly. In its defense millions of our fellow citizens are offering their lives. This emphasizes what it costs to make and preserve a great inheritance. . . .

The blight of war is trying men's souls today in every land. . . . We must have a firm belief that an overruling Providence is directing the affairs of nations. And though at times the truth seems to be upon the scaffold and wrong upon the throne, we must never doubt that behind that scaffold God still keeps watch upon His own.

* * *

On 4 March 1944, Hugh B. Brown was appointed president of the British Mission for a second time and asked to act in the dual roll as Servicemen's Coordinator for the European theater of the war. Obtaining any kind of ocean going transportation for civilians was almost impossible. His travel across the Atlantic was aboard the Greek freighter, the *Hellas*.

For seventeen days he was paired with the only other passenger, a cigar-smoking Dutch major. However, his sense of humor about these challenges is evident in his description of this trip:

> When we came aboard on a Coast Guard boat we had to climb the Jacob's ladder over the side and both of us nearly got a dunking, as the Coast Guard boat decided to back away just as we were reaching for the ladder. I dangled from the end of the swinging ladder, and my room mate was a few rungs up from me. I was grateful for the very good grip which I still have in my hands, acquired when I was a boy milking cows.
>
> The following day we sailed out into the ocean, and I sought relief on the deck, which proved to be exactly twelve paces long and three feet wide. We ran immediately into a heavy sea, and I got relief OK, but it was of the more strenuous kind—in reverse—so I came docilely back to the room and took my upper bunk.

Elder Brown landed on 29 March, at Milford Haven, Wales, and was met the next day by President Andre K. Anastasiou and taken to the mission headquarters in southwest London.

One of the officers then stationed in London was J. Allan Jensen. He had served under President Brown in the British Mission before the war. Lt. Jensen remained in London until war's end and helped President Brown untangle the military bureaucracy. Lt. Jensen could also take Elder Brown to dinner in the officer's club for meals that were better fare than British wartime rationing allowed.

In London, Elder Brown immediately began meeting with the LDS servicemen. From a letter to the *Church News,* 17 June 1944, he comments about how much these servicemen needed to meet as members of the Church:

> The really enthusiastic [Church] meetings are where all participate in the good old-fashioned testimony meeting. . . .
>
> There is a quality, a fervor, a soul-melting earnestness about these boys who yesterday have looked into the face of death and who know that tomorrow they must again brave the flak and the enemy fighters, the soupy weather, and the Channel below. When

they say, "I thank God for my blessings," you know they are not just repeating an expected phrase. When they relate powerful experiences of special danger and gratefully acknowledge the protecting power of Providence, the hearty "Amen" of their comrades bespeaks the understanding of fellow pilgrims.

***

Planning a visit to a camp near Liverpool, Elder Brown sent a telegram to the base chaplain saying that he would arrive the following morning at ten o'clock, and that he would like to meet with all the Mormons in the camp. Elder Brown was happily greeted by seventy-five men, all pleased to see someone who represented home.

The chaplain introduced himself and said: "I want to congratulate you on the fact that, though I did not receive your telegram until this morning, all but one of the Mormons serving in this camp are here. What method do you use to accomplish such unusual results?" President Brown invited him to the meeting to see for himself.

The amazed chaplain watched as Elder Brown asked the men how many had served Church missions—half raised their hands. He designated six of those to prepare and administer the sacrament and six to be ready to speak. The chaplain's amazement multiplied as he saw young men called out of a military unit, at random, transformed suddenly into ministers of the gospel. The group suggested they sing for the opening hymn "Come, Come, Ye Saints." There were several who could lead the singing and play the portable organ—even without a hymn book. As the young men sang the last stanza, "And should we die before our journey's through, Happy day, all is well," the chaplain wept.

The young man designated to offer the sacramental prayer on the bread began, "O God, the Eternal Father" then he paused for a full minute before continuing. After the meeting Elder Brown found the young man and asked, "Son, is something troubling you?"

"Why, sir?"

"You seemed to have trouble giving the blessing on the bread. Why did you pause so long?"

The young pilot answered, "Well sir, a few hours ago I was over France and Germany on a bombing mission. We made our run, delivered our

Hugh B. Brown (in the white shirt) and the LDS Serviceman Group. European Theater Conference, Paris, France, 1945.

calling cards, . . . and we had gained altitude and were ready to turn back across the Channel to England when we ran into heavy flak. My tail assembly was almost shot away, one of my engines was out, several of my crew were wounded, and we were high in the air. I could not see any possibility of getting back to England or doing anything other than ditching in the Channel, or landing behind enemy lines.

"Brother Brown, I remembered at that moment what my mother had told me and what I had been taught in Primary, in Sunday School, in seminary and in other institutions of the Church; that is, that 'if you're ever in trouble where men can't help you, call on God, and He will help you.' Now this looked like an impossible situation, and up there above the clouds I cried out, 'Oh, God, if possible sustain this ship until we can get to a landing spot in England.' Brother Brown, He did just that, and when we landed out here and I heard about this meeting, I ran all the way to get here—I didn't even stop to change my battle dress. When I knelt at the sacrament table and named the name of God again, I was smitten with the thought that I hadn't said 'Thank you.' So I paused and under my breath I expressed my gratitude to God for hearing my prayer and bringing us back in safety."

After a two-hour testimony meeting, President Brown suggested that they should end the meeting or miss their dinner. They replied that they "could eat army chow any time" and for another two hours continued their meeting.

When everyone had borne testimony and the meeting was closed, the chaplain said to President Brown, "Sir, I have been a minister of the gospel for twenty-one years, but this has been the most unusual and inspiring event in my ministry. I have never witnessed anything like this in my life."

* * *

Elder Brown's writings also reflect his experiences in a land under constant attack from German bombing:

> I again witnessed the rather eerie scene of flying bombs at night and with the terrible roar of the engine what seems to be a flying ball of fire strikes terror to one's heart as it seems to be headed directly toward the observer. . . . One woman who cringed as one went over her said, "Blimey, I'm glad he wound that one up a bit more." A sense of humor is really a saving grace in these circumstances. Perhaps such a sense was responsible for my starting to hum one of our hymns as I lay flat on my tummy waiting for a bomb to miss me. The first lines of one of the verses are "When the earth begins to tremble, bid our fearful thoughts be still."
>
> There is no way of judging where they will light, as some of them dive immediately when their engines cut out and others glide for some distance before diving. . . . One wonders what he should wish or pray for. If he asks that it go over him he is suggesting that someone else be on the receiving end. In other words, is it a Christian prayer to say "Let it miss me, Lord, and hit my neighbor"? I am advising all of our people to evacuate if possible and at least to send their womenfolk and children out of the city until it is over. That seems to me to be the practical thing to do rather than to doggedly "stick it," as the people here say, and ask God to save us. Sometimes it is a good thing to get out of danger even while you pray.
>
> Now that I have said that I suppose some will wonder at my staying here in the mission home. . . . Well, just for the record, I feel

that for me to go while there are Saints here who cannot go would be to let them down just when they need the faith that as long as I am in this building it will not be destroyed. Others say that this building, having been dedicated, will never be hit. For me to leave would, I fear, test the faith of some of them and cause them to question my faith. Also, there is considerable Church property here which should be protected. . . . I am not a bit brave but I do feel the responsibility and like the captain of a ship feel that I should be the last to leave. . . . I have really never felt that I am in danger of losing my life and therefore have not felt any fear. If I do think one is going to hit me I'll be scared as anyone.

I think the main reason a man of my age, with his future largely behind him, does not wish to die is that he thinks there is still someone who needs him and for whom he is responsible. When one is no longer needed he should die or get some work by which he can pass on something worthwhile to those who come after him. I have looked upon several dead people today who yesterday at this time were as unmindful of their fate as we are tonight and have thought after all that is not such a bad way to go. . . .

We sent one thousand bombers over Berlin last night and dropped thousands of tons of bombs on that city. What must the Master think of CHRISTIANS who are so completely dominated by Satan that they use the inventions which have given them so much power to cause death and misery to one another? Hate is mounting everywhere and one wonders what kind of peace can follow in the wake of so much savagery. About the only Christian principle we seem to follow while bombing is the one which says "it is better to give than to receive."

* * *

So much travel and separation from home was difficult for Elder Brown. During his service in England, he was often lonely for his family. "Guess I'm too old to be away from my mama," he wrote in a letter to Mary. However, letters and as much contact with family helped. His son Charles had been recently married to Grace Bowns. Based in New York, Charles, a civilian pilot occasionally flew into Scotland on Air Transport Command

Elder Brown giving advice to LDS chaplains during the Paris Conference, Summer 1945.

missions and telephoned his father the news from home. Zina wrote often of family activities, children, and assured him of her love. Elder Brown's sense of humor proved to be a help as well. In a letter to Mary he reported on his health:

> My skin is clear and my hair is curly and I walk two hours per day regularly and sleep like a baby, so when you see Mother tell her to stop worrying about my reduced waist line as that is the best thing which has happened, and many a man and woman, who could take a shower bath without getting their knees wet would envy me my streamlined torso.

To his busy schedule was added an additional trial. He developed a painful tick that as he described, felt as though all the "nerves of the side of the head and face seem to be fully charged with electric wires which can be turned on one at a time or all together according to the whim of the head imp" inflicting this pain. "And now for three weeks I've had to wait for a hospital bed and one more week to go and then out comes the nerve and we live happily ever after."

The First Presidency advised him to come home for treatment. He was able to secure air transportation from Scotland to Utah. His family welcomed him, and "it was a great reunion." Following surgery he returned home where, "I had the loving attention of my wife and family and I recovered rapidly." Once healed, Elder Brown was anxious to return to England. Many asked why he wasn't healed and so be allowed to remain at his post. His response was:

> I think always we should pray with the feeling that we do not know really what is best for us; that He does know, and that we should express the desire that He do for us what is best. . . . There is no question in my mind but what I could have been healed, but I am convinced the Lord had a purpose in the program which, it seemed, inevitably had to be followed. I make this explanatory statement that none of you may feel that you, or any of us, lacked faith, or that the Lord was not willing to hear our prayers. He certainly did hear, and has answered in His own way, and His way, as always, has proved to be right.

With the surrender of Germany, Hugh returned to Europe. He flew from New York to Ireland, and then on to England. His reflections on Europe after the war can be seen in the following expert written 22 May 1945.

> It is really wonderful to feel the difference of good cheer and the kind of happiness which is known only to those who have suffered much and lived in fear, who have known dread and sleepless apprehension and are then released, freed, liberated, and made to feel that all is well.
>
> It was raining yesterday and the clouds were heavy, but today the sun is out, the skies are clear, the birds are singing and all seems well with the world. The traditional reserve of the British is still in evidence but there is a quiet "shining through" of the spirit which betrays a wealth of emotion, a depth of gladness the restraint

of which is almost tragic. I think it would do the whole nation good if the people would just break through the restraining dykes which have held back the flood through the centuries and allow the parched social fields to be flooded and refreshed.

The death of President Heber J. Grant deeply saddened him, and Hugh missed his wife and family. Of Zina he wrote, "I have been thinking of her a lot this month which is our month of roses and of memories. Hope we will not spend another June apart."

Hugh flew to Paris on 20 July and stayed at the Hotel Terras, where "American food with the flavor which only French cooks could give was served." A ballet at the Paris Opera and a servicemen's field day in the Bois de Boulogne were followed by a conference at the Hotel Louvois. Three hundred and fifty persons attended the public meeting, the largest LDS meeting that had ever been held in the French capital. Accompanied by Max Zimmer, President of the Swiss Mission, President Brown visited the Saints in Basel, Lausanne, Geneva, Bern, Lucerne, and Zurich.

A series of meetings in the Marseilles area on August 5th may be unique in the annals of U.S. Armed Forces. President Brown addressed five audiences in thirteen hours, traveling by Jeep from one location to another with a small entourage of LDS chaplains and MIA group leaders. Three of the gatherings were interdenominational and two were LDS sacrament and testimony meetings, described as "very enthusiastic."

Waiting for Hugh in London were Zina, Margaret, and Carol. They had arrived by air the day before his return. He describes his emotions at being with his family again:

My own joy upon their arrival can be assumed by the fact that for nearly eight years we have been separated more than we have been together. We now hopefully look forward to an era of teamwork, with Mother, as usual, in the furrow. (To those who were not raised on a farm as I was I should explain that the 'furrow horse' is the one which walks in the furrow when plowing, and the one which keeps the rest of the team, two or many, true to the course marked out by the Gardener.)

Elder Brown had great concern for servicemen as they dealt with the problems of adjustment from military to civilian life. Drawing from his own experience as a returning soldier following World War I, he encouraged these servicemen to "to devote ourselves to the work of reconstruction and that with self-imposed discipline we would strive to be worthy of the country and the freedom for which we fought." Later, still speaking to the returning veterans and their families, he wrote this editorial in the July 1945 issue of *The Millennial Star*:

An Old Veteran Speaks

They [returning veterans] want a little of the earth's surface which they may call their own, upon which they may stamp the imprint of a coat-of-arms which they themselves have fashioned, a little home to which they may retire for the enjoyment of family life, a few good books, some music, and a radio. A place where they may shut out or bring in the outside world at will and where at night they may draw the curtains and invite the Prince of Peace to bring his benediction to a Christian family in a Christian country in a world where the principles of the Prince of Peace have replaced the mad attempts of would-be dictators to rule the world!

And thus do old men dream dreams while they pray the young men may see visions.

Following his release as president of the British Mission, Hugh B. Brown taught at Brigham Young University. In the October 1953 Conference of the Church he was called as an Assistant to the Twelve and in April 1958 was called into the Quorum of the Twelve. From 1961 to 1970 he served as a counselor in the First Presidency of The Church of Jesus Christ of Latter-day Saints. President Brown passed away 2 December 1975.

EPILOGUE

On 2 September 1945, General Douglas MacArthur, supreme commander of the Allied Forces in the Pacific, stood on the quarterdeck of the USS Missouri, anchored in Tokyo Bay, and conducted the proceedings of the surrender of the Japanese Imperial Forces. In a radio broadcast later that day, MacArthur told the American people: "If we do not now devise some greater and more equitable system [to preserve the peace] Armageddon will be at our door. The problem basically is theological and involves a spiritual recrudescence and improvement of human character."

As we look back on past years since the close of World War II, we see the profound impact that the Latter-day Saint servicemen have had in spreading the gospel throughout the world. They and their posterity have since provided a wonderful service to the Church. Some of the men whose stories are recorded here were not members of the Church before the war. Who can tell the extent to which the combined efforts of all who served in that war have had during their lives and in the work of the gospel? Their example and strength has helped moved the Church toward its prophesied destiny.

When Deanne and I arrived in Italy in 1963, we witnessed the blessing that Italy's liberation from Hitler's influence has been. Shortly after WW II, freedom of religion was written into the Italian constitution. Elder Ezra Taft Benson, then president of the European Mission, came to Italy in November 1964, and obtained permission from the Italian government for missionaries to enter Italy. The first group arrived 27 February 1965. Today there are wards and stakes in that land.

On the other side of the world, along the Pacific Rim, and on the Islands of the Pacific, missionaries began their teaching shortly following the cessation of fighting. Missionary work began in The Philippines in 1961, in Manila and other areas of Luzon. Seven years later, as a young district president, I stood on the beach at Lingayen Gulf, near the monument commemorating MacArthur's return to Luzon, and watched our missionaries baptize several Filipino people. The "spiritual recrudescence and improvement of human character" of which General MacArthur so eloquently spoke, is quietly and surely occurring through the efforts of The Church of Jesus Christ of Latter-day Saints across the world. Daniel prophesied it would be so centuries ago. Witness the remarkable strides as President Gordon B. Hinckley goes about the world, urging us forward. None of this could have happened had not the Axis Powers been halted and the soldiers, sailors, and airmen of World War II offered up their sacrifices.

I have not known the terrible terror of war, or the panic of combat, nor have I experienced the horror of seeing a comrade blown to pieces. I have seen the suffering of the wounded and helped carry the caskets of soldiers and airmen. From my office on the flight line at Clark Air Base in the late 1960s, I watched the nightly return of the AirEvac flight from Vietnam, with its cargo of combat wounded. From the bowels of these planes, young men swathed in huge bandages were carefully transferred to waiting ambulances. Some had lost limbs, some had their heads wrapped. Surely they still carry the scars of war.

War is an enormous waste of lives and national resources. This is not to say that war is never necessary. We must fight if others attempt to enslave or slay us. Alma records the viciousness of the warring Lamanites, who "did smite [the Nephites] in their fierce anger." About the defending Nephites he states: "Nevertheless, the Nephites were inspired by a better cause, for they were not fighting for monarchy nor power, but they were fighting for their homes and their liberties, their wives and their children, and their all, yea, for their rites of worship and their church. ...the Lord has said that: ye shall defend your families even unto bloodshed." It is our right and responsibility to protect... "[our] families, [our] lands, [our] country, [our] rights, and [our] religion. (See Alma 43:45-47).

I believe it is proper to reverently remember those who have borne the brunt of battle. Unfortunately, we have not concluded with having "wars and rumors of war." Dreadful battles will yet occur. However, the Lord is in control. "For the day of the Lord of hosts shall be upon everyone that is proud and lofty, and upon everyone that is lifted up; and he shall be brought low: and the Lord alone shall be exalted in that day" (Isaiah 2:12,17). That day he will invite "all to come unto him and partake of his goodness" (2

Nephi 26:33). Peace will envelop the earth as the waters cover the seas, and the righteous will find rest in Him. Then will He avenge the blood of the saints, for He will not suffer their cries any longer (see Mormon 8:41). Christ will reign in our midst, and "he shall judge among the nations, and shall rebuke many people: and they shall beat their swords into plowshares, and their spears into pruning hooks—nation shall not lift up sword against nation, neither shall they learn war any more" (2 Nephi 12:4). It is for that blessed day we yearn.

Paul H. Kelly

They that wait upon the LORD shall renew their strength; they shall mount up with wings as eagles; they shall run, and not be weary; and they shall walk, and not faint.

(Isaiah 40:31)

BIBLIOGRAPHY

All stories used by permission, gathered from oral and written interviews, as well as personal histories and journals and other personal papers. Unless otherwise indicated below, all photographs came from the personal archives of those whose stories are included in this book.

Ambrose, Stephen E. *D-Day, June 6, 1944: The Climactic Battle of World War II*. New York: A Touchstone Book, Simon & Schuster, 1994.

Anderson, Garth L. *Captain Hugh Rawlin Roper*, 1993.

Bagley, Earl E. *When I was In the U. S. Naval Reserves During World War II*. Bound manuscript 1992.

Barker, A. J., Lt Col. *Okinawa*. Bison Books Limited, London, 1981.

Bartlett, John. *Familiar Quotations*. 14th Edition: Boston, 1968.

Bradley, James with Ron Powers. *Flags of our Fathers*. New York: Bantam Books, May 2000.

Brown, Cecil. *Suez to Singapore*. New York: Random House, 1942.

Brokaw, Tom. *The Greatest Generation*. New York: Random House, 1998.

Burk, Joseph N. *This Is My Life, An Autobiography*. Bound manuscript, 1998

Burt, Cyril O. *Two Years, Seven Months and Seven Days*. Typed unpublished manuscript, 1998

Campbell, Eugene E. and Poll, Richard D. *Hugh B. Brown, His Life and Thought*. Pgs. 141-187. Salt Lake City: Bookcraft, Inc., 1975. Used by permission of Deseret Book Company, Salt Lake City, Utah.

Churchill, Winston S. *The Second World War: The Gathering Storm*. Houghton Mifflin Co. 1948.

___. *The Second World War: Their Finest Hour*. Houghton Mifflin Co. 1949.

Current, Richard N., Williams, T. Harry, and Freidel, Frank. *American History, A Survey*. New York: Alfred A. Knopf, 1961.

Deighton, Len. *Blood, Tears and Folly, An Objective Look at World War II*. New Jersey: Castle Books, 1999.

Dew, Sherry L. "Harold W. Gunn, WWII Pilot in the *Real* 'Great Escape.' " *This People Magazine* (Winter, 1980).

Egbert, Peggy. *History of Thomas Russ Egbert*. Unpublished manuscript.

The Eighth Air Force–Start Engines. . .Plus 50 Years. [Video] 8th Air Force Historical Society.

Garfield, Brian. *The Thousand Mile War, World War II in Alaska and the Aleutians*. New York: Bantam Book, 1981.

Farago, Ladislas. *Patton: Ordeal and Triumph*. New York, Dell Publishing Company, 1963.

Gilbert, Martin. *The Second World War, A Complete History*. Revised Ed. New York: Henry Holt and Company, 1991.

Groesbeck, Mac S, *Personal diary*. Unpublished manuscript.

Hale, Blair. *A German POW Tells His Story*. Unpublished personal journal, 2001.

Hickman, Don Rue. *Personal History*. A bound manuscript. Provo, Utah.

Hogg, Ian Vernon, Hutchinson. *Dictionary of World War II*. London: Brockhampton Press, 1994.

Hoyt, Edwin P. *The Men of the* Gambier Bay. Vermont: Paul S. Eriksson, Publisher, 1979.

Hunn, Spencer S. *Unpublished Personal History*. 1996.

Huston, John, *Report From The Aleutians*. World War II Documentary [Video] 1943.

Hymns of The Church of Jesus Christ Of Latter-day Saints. Salt Lake City, Utah, 1985.

Immel, Myra, ed. "Map of the Invasion of Normandy." *World War II*. San Diego: Greenhaven Press, Inc., 2001.

___. "Map of the Invasion of Sicily." *World War II*. San Diego: Greenhaven Press, Inc. 2001.

Jacobs, Frank H. *The Life of Frank H. Jacobs and His Pioneer Heritage, A Family History*.

Johnson, Lin H. *Johnny's Mem-Wars*. Typed manuscript. Idaho Falls, Idaho.

Jordan, Killian, ed. "Women at War" [Photo]. *Our Finest Hour: The Triumphant Spirit of America's World War II Generation*. TimeInc. Home Entertainment, 2000.

Kauer, Lorin B. Typed manuscript

Kehr, William Hale. "Stalag Luft III Branch. *The Ensign* (July 1982): 35–38.

Kelly, Ralph S. and Swan, Connie Kelly, Philemon Merrill Kelly, M.D. *A Collection of Memories*. Bound manuscript, 1991.

Lewis, Jon E., *Eye-Witness D-Day. The Story of the Battle by Those Who Were There*. London: Robinson Publishing Ltd., 1994.

MacArthur, Douglas. *General of the Army, Reminiscences*. New York, McGraw-Hill, 1964.

"Map of Naval ships' locations at Pearl Harbor." *Post Register* (December 7, 1999).

McMillan, George. *The Old Breed, A History of the First Marine Division in World War II*. Washington: Infantry Journal Press, Inc. 1949.

Messenger, Charles. *The Illustrated Book of World War II*. San Diego, 1999.

Miller, Nathan. *War at Sea, A Naval History of World War II*. New York: A Lisa Drew Book. 1995.

National Geographic, Official Journal of the National Geographic Society (December, 1991): 50-77.

Peacock, Byron Carlyle. Courtesy of "Saints at War" Archival Project. Brigaham Young University, JSB 275B, Provo, Utah 84602

Pollak, David, Consolmagno; Joseph, Bennett, Janet R. *The Longest Mission. The Association of Former Prisoners of Stalag Luft III*. 1995.

Prange, Gordon W. *Miracle At Midway*. New York: McGraw Hill Book Company, 1982.

Prison, Elfriede Deininger. *Unpublished diary*.

Pyle, Ernie. *Brave Men*. New York: Henry Holt and Company, Inc., 1944. Used by permission of The Scripps Howard Foundation.

"Radar Kids of *Gambier Bay*." [Photo]. www.ussgambierbay-vc10.com. Robert Potochniak, webmaster. Tony Potochniak, Historian.

Reed, James Clare. *Life Story*. Bound manuscript, printed 1993.

Reed, Verl W. *Life History of Verl W. Reed*. Typed manuscript.

Ryan, Cornelius. *A Bridge Too Far*. New York: Popular Library Edition, published by arrangement with Simon & Schuster, Inc., 1974.

Rudel, Hans Ulrich. *Stuka Pilot*. New York: Ballantine Books, 1966.

Sorge, Martin. "Leonard Brostrom." [Photo]. *Lest We Forget: The Story of the Men and Women from Franklin County, Idaho, who served in the Second World War*. Preston, Idaho: 1995.

Thueson, Mary Tyler, *Footprints In Idaho Soil*. A personal history, 1997.

Van Zeben, Gerard. Courtesy of "Saints at War" Archival Project. Brigham Young University, JSB 275B, Provo, Utah, 84602.